I0902331

VENINI: LIGHT 1921-1985

VENINI
LIGHT 1921-1985

edited by
Marino Barovier and Carla Sonego

LE STANZE DEL VETRO

fondazione
GIORGIO CINI

SKIRA

LE STANZE DEL VETRO

A joint initiative of
Fondazione Giorgio Cini
and Pentagram Stiftung

Scientific Committee
Luca Massimo Barbero, *Chairman*
Marino Barovier
Rosa Barovier Mentasti
David Landau
Jean-Luc Olivié
Valerio Terraroli
Giorgio Vigna

Coordination Management
Fondazione Giorgio Cini
and Pentagram Stiftung
Maria Novella Benzoni

Exhibition Space Design
Selldorf Architects
F. Cattaruzza and F. Millosevich
Architetti Associati

Lighting Design
Alessandro Diaz de Santillana
Fontana Arte

Fondazione Giorgio Cini

Chairman
Giovanni Bazoli

Secretary General
Renata Codello

Department of Facilities
Management, Events Coordination
and Relations with Sponsors
Maria Novella Benzoni

Technical Department
Massimo Altieri
Gloria Pasqualetto
Francesca Salatin

Cultural Development and
Communication
Chiara Casarin
Giovanna Pesaro

Management
Riccardo Savio
Michele Ballarin

Institute of Art History

Director
Luca Massimo Barbero

Coordination Management
Simone Guerriero

Glass Study Centre

Marzia Scalon
Sabina Tutone

Press Office

CASADOROFUNGHER
Comunicazione

Pentagram Stiftung

Chairman
Marie-Rose Kahane

Head of Cultural Projects
Francesca Nisii

VENINI: LIGHT 1921–1985

Exhibition organised by
LE STANZE DEL VETRO

Island of San Giorgio Maggiore
Venice

Exhibition curated by
Marino Barovier

Exhibition Project
Marino Barovier

Head of Conservation
Luisa Mensi

Registrar
Laura Corazzol

Graphic Design of Communication
bruno - Andrea Codolo
and Giacomo Covacich

Communication
CASADOROFUNGHER
Comunicazione

Social Media
Silvia Casalini Martinelli

Organisational Coordinator
Fiammetta Calzavara

Touring Exhibitions Coordinator
Manuela Divari

Education
Artsystem
Anna Fornezza
Chiara Brescacin

Exhibition Set-up and Lighting
OTT ART prodotti per l'arte
Giacomo Andrea Doria
Andrea Riato

Shipping
Apice - Venezia
Alice Zanon

Insurance
Assicurazioni Generali
Marine & Aviation JLT -
Divisione Fine-Art
Alberto Magni

Reception
Artsystem
Valentina Stella *and*
Lara Eva Stasi

Bookshop
Nicoletta Zanetti
Omar Viel

Security
Iniziative Venete

Technical Sponsor
Artsystem

Catalogue edited by
Marino Barovier *and* Carla Sonego

Scientific Research and Coordination
Carla Sonego
Simona Larghi

Catalogue Graphic Project
Tapiro Camplani+Pescolderung

Coordination of Editorial Design and Layout
Enrico Fiorese
Francesca Tiengo

Photographs
Enrico Fiorese

Texts revision
Filomena Moscatelli

Translations from Italian into English
Scarlet Sweetman
Mícheál Ua Nunáin

Translation from Spanish to English of the text by Alberto Campo Baeza
Oona Smyth for *Scriptum*, Rome

All rights reserved under international copyright conventions. No part of this book may be reproduced or utilized in any form or by any means, electronic or mechanical, including photocopying, recording, or any information storage and retrieval system, without permission in writing from the publisher.

© 2022 Servizi Fondazione Pentagram srl
© 2022 The authors of the texts
© 2022 Skira editore, Milano

First printed in Italy in 2022 by Skira editore S.p.A. Palazzo Casati Stampa
Via Torino 61
20123 Milano Italy www.skira.net
Printed and bound in Italy. First edition

ISBN: 978-88-572-4903-2

Distributed in USA, Canada, Central & South America by ARTBOOK | D.A.P.
75, Broad Street, Suite 630,
New York, NY 10004, USA.
Distributed elsewhere in the world by Thames and Hudson Ltd.,
181A High Holborn, London
WC1V 7QX, United Kingdom.

Photo credits:
Courtesy Cambi Casa d'aste, pp. 306, 503
Courtesy Il Ponte Casa d'aste, p. 491
© PIERRE GAUTIER-DELAYE, by SIAE 2022, p. 373

Servizi Fondazione Pentagram is at the disposal of any entitled parties as regards all unidentified iconographic sources

We would like to thank the museums, foundations, public and private archives, collectors, scholars and all those who have contributed to this project:

Giulio Alessandri
Bandar AlTalh
Massimo Altieri
Guido Antonello
Marco Arosio
Capucine Aulanier
Riccardo Avanzi
Luca Massimo Barbero
Gaia Barbieri
Mauro Baronchelli
Marina Barovier
Rosa Barovier Mentasti
Alberto Barzaghi
Gabriella Belli
Maria Novella Benzoni
Maurizio Bianchini
Giancarlo Bisazza
Christina and Bruno Bischofberger
Sara Blumberg
Michele Borrelli
Angelo Boscolo
Chiara Brescacin
Carla Zahra Buda
Renzo Busetto
Guillaume Buttet
Gianluigi Calderone
Giampaolo Caliari
Oliver Patrick Caliari
Fiammetta Calzavara
Alberto Campo Baeza
Leonardo Carrer
Elena Casadoro
Silvia Casalini Martinelli
Chiara Casarin
Micaela Cascella
Michela Cattai
Fabrizio Cattaruzza
Fabrizio Caudana
Emma Cavazzini
Alejandro Cervilla
Rosa Chiesa
Elena Chiesi
Giancarlo Chimento
Silvia Cicognani
Renata Codello
Andrea Codolo
Enrico Coletti
Laura Corazzol
Giacomo Covacich
Maria Rosaria Cozzuto
Aud Cuniberti
Natascia Danieli
Giada Daolio
Pietro De Albertis
Herat De Nicola
Alice Diaz de Santillana
Claudia De Zordo
Franco Deboni
Alessandro Degnoni
Tommy Francesco Demartis
Sigifredo di Canossa
Mara Di Vizia
Leon Diaz de Santillana
Manuela Divari
Duccio Dogheria
Riccardo Domenichini
Giacomo Andrea Doria
Rita Fancsaly
Rossella Fantinato
Francesca Ferrara
Gerardo Figliola
Luigi Fiore
Enrico Fiorese
Anna Fornezza
Francesca Fungher
Cristiana Galante
Erica Galvan
Fabrice Gardin
Emanuele Gatto
Mauro Gerardo
Roberta Giacoi
Nicola Grandesso
Giorgio Grassi Damiani
Guido Grassi Damiani
Silvia Grassi Damiani
Simone Guerriero
Marc Heiremans
Frederick Iseman
Martin Kline
Simona Larghi
Maria Rosa Laria
Jacopo Leone
Howard Lockwood
Anna Lombardi
Dietmar Loretz
Ursula and Rainer Losch
Carlo Lungagnani
Francesco Lurago
Davide Magnani
Cosimo Manicone
Mattia Martinelli
Luisa Mensi
Francesco Millosevich
Bruno Miotto
Leonora Mistretta
Sergio Montefusco
Luigi Monti
Marcello Moretti
Filomena Moscatelli
Tantra Mosconi
Francesca Nisii
Ezio Nodari
Davide Novello
Victoria Ogley
Jim Oliveira
Jean-Luc Olivié
Nancy Olnick
Angela Parente
Gloria Pasqualetto
Mariaconcetta Patti
Jessica Pennisi
Luigi Pescolderung
Paola Pettenella
Antonio Pintus
Camilla Poli
Stefano Poli
Marco Prete
Matteo Primiterra
Renzo Quintavalle
Askan Quittenbaum
Bruno Racine
Domenico Raimondo
Sofia Rinaldi
Giovanni Salmistrari
Teresita Scalco
Marzia Scalon
Andrea Schito
Annabelle Selldorf
Leonardo Serranti
Susie J. Silbert
Sara Simonetti
Anna Somers-Cocks
Anita Sonego
Giorgio Spanu
Rossella Spolaore
Chiara Squarcina
Lara Eva Stasi
Michele Stavagna
Valentina Stella
Christoph Stibor
Matteo Stocco
Caroline Strawson
Scarlet Sweetman
Roberta Tagliavini
Chiara Talamona
Valerio Terraroli
Christoph Thein
Christoph Thun-Hohenstein
Francesca Tiengo
Claudia Timossi
Francesco Toniatti Giacometti
Maurizio Torcellan
Antonia Treccagnoli
Giuliana Tucci
Sabina Tutone
Mícheál Ua Nunáin
Mark Van Wynsberge
Paola Vescovi
Flavio Vido
Pierfrancesco Vido
Omar Viel
Giorgio Vigna
Marco Visentini
Massimo Vitta Zelman
Anna Wagner
Karol Wight
Nicoletta Zanetti
Fabian Zannini
Matteo Zannoni
Alice Zanon
Francesco Zanon
Paolo Zanon
Alma Zevi
Carla Zhara Buda
Mara Zoggia
Taddeo Zuccheri

Fondazione Giorgio Cini, Venice
Fondazione Il Vittoriale degli Italiani, Gardone Riviera
Fondazione Musei Civici di Venezia:
Ca' Pesaro Galleria Internazionale d'Arte Moderna, Venice
Regione Autonoma Friuli Venezia Giulia:
Palazzo del Consiglio Regionale, Trieste

Auditorium Rai Arturo Toscanini di Torino, Turin
Schlosstheater Fulda, Fulda
Teatro dell'Opera di Roma, Rome
Theater der Stadt Schweinfurt, Schweinfurt
Théâtre Royal des Galeries, Brussels

Archivio Centro Studi del Vetro, Fondazione Giorgio Cini onlus, Venice
Archivio del '900, Mart Rovereto, Rovereto
Archivio Patrimonio Artistico, Intesa Sanpaolo
Archivio Storico, Comune di Castrocaro
Archivio Storico Intesa Sanpaolo
Archivio Storico Luce, Rome
Archivio Storico Venini, Murano
Centro Archivi Fondazione MAXXI, Rome
MAMC+ / Musée d'art moderne et contemporain de Saint-Étienne Métropole
Soprintendenza Archeologia, Belle Arti e Paesaggio per l'area metropolitana di Venezia e le province di Belluno, Padova e Treviso
Università Ca' Foscari Venezia, Venice
Università degli Studi di Padova, Padua
Università Iuav di Venezia, Archivio Progetti, Venice

Archivio Marco Arosio, Milan
Archivio Marino Barovier, Venice
Archivio Jan Jacopo Bianchetti
Archivio Marc Heiremans, Brussels
Archivio Giacomo Leone, Catania
Archivio Howard Lockwood, Fort Lee (NJ – USA)

Auctioneers:
Aste Boetto
Della Rocca
Il Ponte
Phillips
Wannenes
Wright

We would also like to thank all those who prefer to remain anonymous

Many thanks also to Venini spa for the great kindness shown in allowing the consultation of their archive materials in preparation for the catalogue and the exhibition

Marino Barovier *also wishes to express his thanks to the authors of the essays in the catalogue. He is particularly grateful to* Marie-Rose Kahane, David Landau *and* Renata Codello

MODERN LIGHT LUMINOUS SCULPTURES

Renata Codello

The splendid documentation contained in this catalogue, of drawings, objects, photographs, settings and architectural structures all lit by the chandeliers and magnificent lighting fixtures produced by the Venini firm, is truly impressive. The decades of Venini output from 1921 to 1985 reflect the historical, political and economic events that our country experienced and demonstrate its fertile relationships with many countries both in Europe and across the ocean.
That the Venini furnace, from its establishment, should have dedicated great attention to the development of chandeliers for illustrious residences, giving concrete shape to the desire for innovation in the lighting of reception areas and the search for new models which departed somewhat from the Venetian tradition, is in some respects not surprising. The partnership between Giacomo Cappellin and Paolo Venini was oriented from its foundation towards being able to anticipate the future by uniting conceptual power with the ability to experiment with all the potentialities of this marvellous material. Carlo Scarpa could not have worked with them for fifteen years if he had not found there a continuing uninterrupted 'tension' where any result considered achieved would then have to be outdone by other lighting products.
It is clear that these extraordinary objects, conventionally referred to as chandeliers, changed scale from the 1930s and became enormous luminous sculptures delineating public areas. From first being installed in theatres, hotels and national and international exhibitions, their presence developed to give a 'typical' character to the architecture of functional buildings for public use: the post office buildings of various Italian towns designed by Angiolo Mazzoni, the most important railway stations of the country, the premises of banking institutions, including those of the Banca d'Italia, up to the prestigious Palazzo della Farnesina – headquarters of the Ministry of Foreign Affairs – of the architect Enrico Del Debbio of 1959. And again, for private customers: chambers of commerce, insurance institutions, office buildings, transatlantic liners, up to the World Trade Center of New York. The exhibition develops themes of exceptional interest and opens up hitherto unexplored research possibilities: the primary function of lighting the areas becomes a substantial element in their modernity, is an element in the representative nature of the institutional buildings, marks the progress of the country through the glass production of a team of creators and a furnace capable of giving expression to visionary projects for the future.
Together with the President Giovanni Bazoli and the Executive Committee of the Fondazione Giorgio I would like to express our gratitude to Pentagram Stiftung which, together with all the collaborators, has made this extraordinary exhibition possible.

Renata Codello
Secretary-General of the Fondazione Giorgio Cini
Venice, July 2022

CONTENTS

Spherical lamp in ribbed glass. Period photograph, 1930s

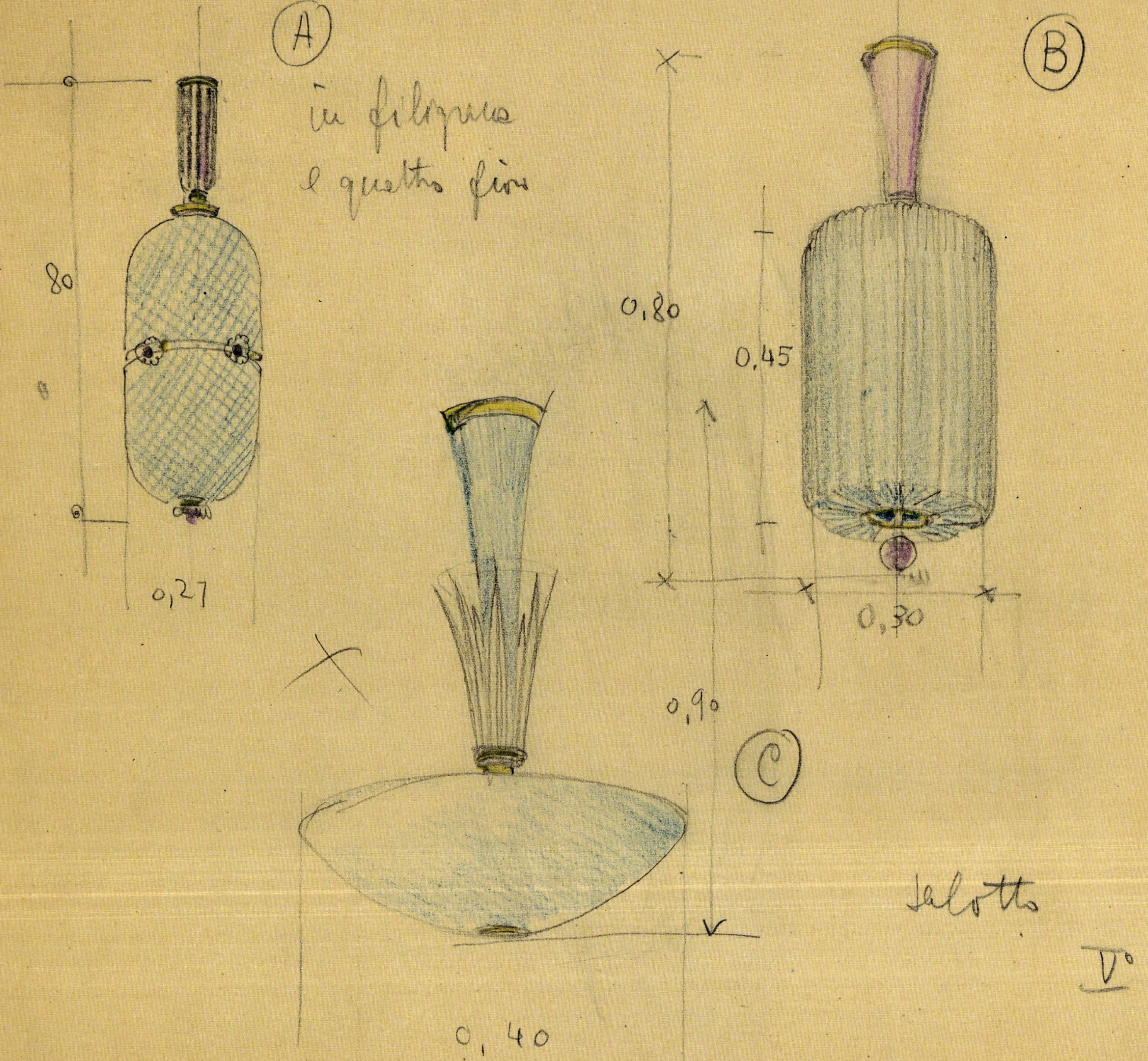
A
in filigrana
e questo fiore
80
0,27
B
0,80
0,45
0,30
0,90
C
0,40
salotto
V°

PREFACE

Marino Barovier

Lighting, whether for domestic use or for the grander areas of public or private spaces of ministerial buildings or post offices, of theatres or hotels, represents an important constituent of Murano glass production.

The Venini firm distinguished itself with significant results in this sector, particularly because of its constant ability to modernise and its characteristic openness to the world of design, aspects which made it a reference point for the foremost national and international architects.

In a period of time like that being reviewed, extending from 1921 to 1985, i.e. from the foundation of V.S.M. Cappellin Venini & C. up to the last year of presence of the Venini family in the glassworks, the firm was able to offer lighting models and solutions of a highly modern kind, always capable of keeping up with the times and reconfirming its leadership in the panorama of Murano glass also in the 'light' sector. Starting with the elegant reinterpretation of the traditional chandelier with arms produced in monochrome transparent glass, solutions were found through research leading to the definition of new types of glass (*pulegoso*, with canes, opaline, patterned etc.) on the one hand and, on the other, the new types of fixtures, such as those with modular elements, a theme developed particularly in the 1930s and from the end of the 1950s.

Contributing to this were various artists, designers and architects who established relationships of cooperation with the glassworks (from Vittorio Zecchin, to Carlo Scarpa, to Massimo Vignelli and beyond) or who made use in an episodic way of the furnace, this being always available with its technical office for the study of new projects thanks also to the availability of Paolo Venini (up to 1959) and later of Ludovico Diaz de Santillana. The wealth of this production is demonstrated both by the various catalogues, among which the Blue Catalogue, the Red Catalogue and the different booklets for the 1960s-70s, and by the extraordinary quantity and quality of the lighting projects produced by the Venini company in Italy and abroad in over sixty years.

For this reason a careful selection of works has been made for the exhibition, recounting through the decades the transformation of Venini lamps, their form and their material. Side-by-side with them, to represent the large installations produced by the glassworks, we wanted to restage and reconstruct two great works: the first, the famous velarium of Palazzo Grassi of 1951 and the second, the monumental 'chandelier' with polyhedrons designed by Carlo Scarpa in 1961 for the Veneto pavilion in Italia 61 in Turin. In the present volume, however, we preferred to give ample space to the numerous projects for which documentation has been traced in the archives of the furnace, so as to illustrate in a comprehensive way an important and exceptional area of Venini production, hitherto neglected (or unknown to most). This work is based on long and careful research on the basis mostly of materials, many of which are unpublished (photographs, drawings, catalogues etc.) coming from the Venini Historical Archive. Cross-checking was then carried out with bibliographical and other sources, and in the case of the works, a comparison was made with the real objects made available by museums, public and private institutions and Italian and foreign collectors.

<<
Drawing for ceiling lamps in three variants (A, B and C), 1930s

VENINI: GLASS AND LIGHT

Marino Barovier

'There is perhaps nothing in interior design which represents the taste, style and custom of a period so well as the chandelier [...] whether in the pensile or ceiling form it seems to be the fruit of new demands, whether those of convenience or of splendour'.[1]

So began Giovanni Mariacher, in 1957, in a small volume on the history of the ancient Venetian glass chandeliers, *Antichi lampadari vitrei veneziani*, where concluding a brief digression on the theme, described how: '(around 1920-25) there was a research movement aimed at new forms in all branches of the art of glass and therefore also in the branch concerning us here, a movement which went side by side with the more conservative activities over which it finally prevailed. This is shown by the models produced by the furnace of Cappellin-Venini, and then Venini & C., of which Vittorio Zecchin was the artistic director in those years'.[2] 'With regard to chandeliers', continued Mariacher, 'it was logical moreover that the change in the means of lighting – especially after the invention of the electric light – should favour a transformation for which a stylistic need was also felt. The trend of the research, often praiseworthy in its efforts and results, was directed towards finding new ways of artistic expression to satisfy new demands, refusing the option of slavish repetition of old forms; and so it has been and will continue to be possible to obtain ever better results by favouring the cooperation between technicians and artists'.[3]

These words not only sum up the characteristics of the Venini firm in this area during the 1920s but also, in a more general way, express the approach which allowed the glassworks to distinguish itself in the lighting sector in the course of its activity and particularly up to the time the family left the company, around the mid1980s.

Historically the aforesaid sector was always of significant importance in the life and organisation of the Murano furnaces, which often owed a good part of their business to lighting commissions whether at the national or international levels.

It is no surprise therefore that from its constitution (1921) the firm V.S.M. Cappellin Venini & C., born out of the partnership between Giacomo Cappellin and Paolo Venini, should have paid particular attention to this area of production, by including in the catalogue various models of chandeliers with arms (pendant lamps and sconces), after the design of Vittorio Zecchin, which as early as the following year began to appear in sector magazines and decorative arts exhibitions, where, as is well known, the furnace participated assiduously.[4] These were lamps of different dimensions (from three

[1] Polyhedrons, detail. Period photograph, 1960s

[2] Chandelier with thirty-six lights, after a design by Vittorio Zecchin, exhibited at the Exposition Universelle of Paris. Period photograph, 1925

[3] Lamps by Napoleone Martinuzzi at the Exposición Internacional of Barcelona. Period photograph, 1929

[4] Luminous installation and sconce, after a design by Napoleone Martinuzzi, in the Post Office building of Ferrara. Period photograph, 1930

to twelve lights, but also from eighteen to thirty) designed both for haut-bourgeois domestic residential settings, and for their reception areas, but also for buildings intended for public use (theatres, hotels, ministries etc.). [2]

Like the bases and bowls of the Cappellin Venini catalogue, they were artefacts in a very minimalist style – easily distinguishable from the production of the time – produced in monochrome transparent glass in muted colours. They were characterised by lines inspired by ancient models such as the classical oil lamp but, above all, the18th-19th century Venetian chandelier which, stripped of the various decorative elements (flowers, leaves etc.), was revisited with extraordinary elegance and sobriety. In most cases the light source, positioned at the extremity of each arm, replacing the candles, was not screened, but there were also fixtures, such as those exhibited in the entrance hall and in Room 19 at the 1st Biennale of Monza in 1923, where the light source was placed in a bell-shaped diffuser body directed upwards. There were, at least until 1925, few models with the cups directed downwards which, exploiting the possibilities of electric light, represented an initial effort to break free from the traditional structure. Particularly notable in this sense was the grandiose chandelier in smoked glass and finishings in green glass produced for the Paris exhibition of 1925 and characterised by the many arms with bell-shaped cups opening out from below upwards and completed at the top by a repetition of curls in green glass.

After the separation between Cappellin and Venini, which occurred in the course of the aforesaid exhibition, and was followed by the subsequent founding of V.S.M. Venini & C. with the arrival of new partners, among whom the Murano sculptor, Napoleone Martinuzzi, who became the artistic director of the firm from 1925 to 1931. While continuing with certain ideas of his predecessor, the artist was able to give a personal touch also in the lighting field by designing various lamps (from cesendello lamps to chandeliers with arms) in transparent glass, often ribbed, in which the plastic quality of the individual elements and of the luminous unit as a whole was accentuated.[5] More original again is his work from 1928 onwards, when having perfected the technique of *pulegoso* glass, Martinuzzi used this semi-opaque material, featuring the inclusion of tiny bubbles (*puleghe*), not only for decorative objects but also for table lamps and pendant and wall fixtures with a body formed by the superimposing of bell-shaped elements, with preference given to the version in *pulegoso cristallo* (white) glass. Similar examples were seen, in particular, at the International Exhibition of Barcelona in 1929 and at the 4th Triennale of Monza in 1930. [3]

Lamps after a design by Napoleone Martinuzzi in *pulegoso* glass, but also in coloured *incamiciato* glass, this too having come into recent use, could be appreciated in certain buildings designed by the architect-engineer Angiolo Mazzoni, who was employed at Office 5 of the Ministry of Communications, an Office for which the furnace worked from 1930 to 1936.

Due to the personal relationship between Mazzoni and Martinuzzi, the latter was called upon by the architect not only as a sculptor, in the creation of works to be placed inside or outside the buildings, but also in the capacity of artistic director of V.S.M. Venini & C.. in projects such as the railway workers free-time building of Rome, officially opened in 1930, the post office building of Ferrara, opened to the public in the same year, and that of Bergamo in 1932, where, among other things, Martinuzzi also created lighting installations (of the cactus kind). [4] In Bergamo, the Venini firm furthermore produced lamps with modular elements in glass with semi-frosted canes and/or in undulating glass, patented by the furnace in April 1931, which Mazzoni would use repeatedly in the railway stations and post office buildings constructed in the course of the 1930s, renewing his collaboration with the glassworks even after Martinuzzi left the company (January 1932).

The new technical lighting solutions aroused the interest of various architects who, as the long list of works carried out by the furnace in those years shows, adopted the Venini modular systems in their projects, particularly with regard to public buildings. Among these must be mentioned Giovanni Greppi, Marcello Piacentini, Paolo Mezzanotte, Brenno Del Giudice etc.

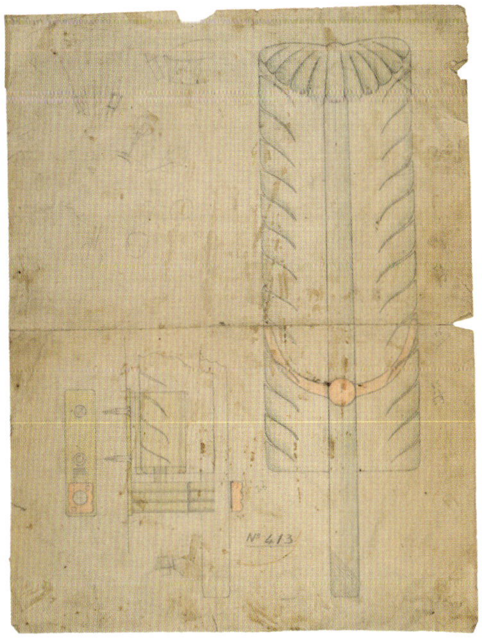

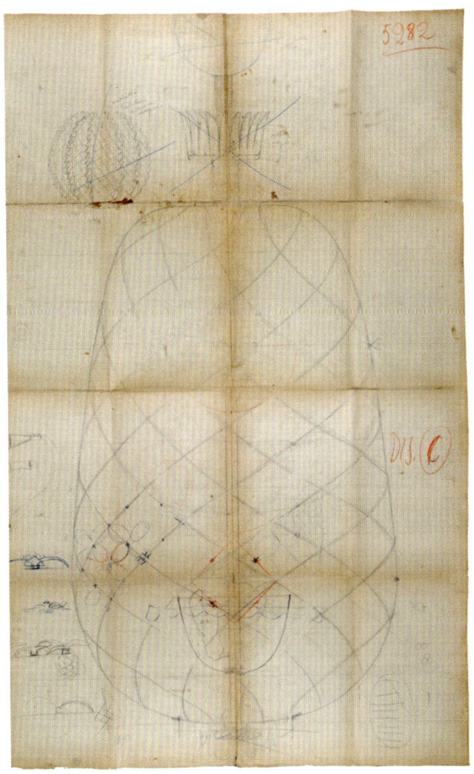

Fixtures with modular elements were also exhibited at the 5th Triennale of Milan in 1933, where in the entrance vestibule a large luminous ceiling cornice in undulating glass was positioned, with a design, particularly appreciated by the critics, of two opposing U's (24 x 2 m). At this exhibition the Venini firm (from 1932, Venini S.A.) distinguished itself, in particular in the 'Crystals, Metals, Lighting' Gallery with the elegant decorative glass pieces designed by the Lombard architect Tomaso Buzzi who, at the request of Paolo Venini, collaborated with the furnace between 1932 and 1933.[6] Buzzi was also the author of some of the fixtures exhibited in the said gallery, such as the sconce in the shape of a feather [5] and the 'oval lamp in "laguna" glass with golden leaves' published in the pages of *Domus* together with other models proposed by the technical office of the glassworks, where the architects Filippo Speciale and Carlo Scarpa at that time worked as designers and planners, the latter being with the Venini firm from c. 1932 to 1947.[7]

At the next Triennale, in 1936, a further variety of lamps were displayed in the room devoted to Venini works, among which, as the catalogue indicates, works carried out with 'the principal collaboration of Carletto Scarpa'[8] to whom Paolo Venini, effectively the director of the furnace, had progressively accorded greater responsibility and independence.

Among the lamps, for example, there was one with modular elements in ribbed glass, fruit of the research which in 1934 and 1935 had led to two patents. Overall, these were pendant and wall lamps produced particularly with vitreous pastes used in the new series of vases and bowls (e.g. corroded glass, *murrine romane* glass). [7] In addition to these there were also original fixtures with diffuser screens composed of elements (flowers, paterae, plates etc.) which were fixed on a metal skeleton, visible through the transparency of the glass.

The same system was also used for the lighting in the elegant banquet hall of the Principi di Piemonte hotel in Turin, which was opened on 23 December 1937. This luxuring building was designed by the engineer Vittorio Bonadè Bottino, while the interior design was the responsibility of the architect Giovanni Chevalley, who to decorate the hall and adjacent passageways availed himself of the work of the Gruppo Arti Decorative, a Venice company of which Paolo Venini was vice-chairman and which brought together the most important entrepreneurs in the decorative arts sector.[9]

Much of the work on the project was carried out by the Venini firm, which in the main foyer placed twelve extremely elegant chandeliers of a spherical-oval shape, with a metal frame and screen with flowers and paterae in *cristallo* glass and finishings in aquamarine and amethyst. [6] On this occasion the glassworks were responsible not only for the lighting but also for the mosaic decoration of the walls of the hall and passageways with grey tesserae and golden inserts. The nine niches made along the perimeter of the hall were embellished with glass decorations depicting flora (plants and flowers) and fauna (fish, a monkey and birds) standing out on a background of golden tesserae. As documented by preparatory drawings kept in the archive of the glassworks, these compositions were studied by the technical office of the furnace and in them can be seen in particular the hand of Carlo Scarpa who, also in the following years, intervened repeatedly both in the establishing of new lighting commissions (e.g. the Casino of the Lido di Venezia, 1938, the Fiat Offices in Turin, 1939-40 etc.) and in the design of new models, such as those exhibited at the 7th Triennale of Milan (1940).

In the 1950s the catalogue was enriched with new contributions due, in some cases, to episodic projects such as that of Gio Ponti, and in others, to designers who established strong relationships with Paolo Venini and his furnace, such as Fulvio Bianconi and Massimo Vignelli.[10]

While to the first we owe the famous chandelier in transparent polychrome glass with a significant chromatic impact, an original revisiting of the traditional-type chandelier with arms (1946-48), Bianconi used the research he had carried out on colours for decorative glass pieces also for new models of floor lamps, notable for their vivid hues (1951). Called upon in 1953 to deal specifically with lighting, around the middle of the decade the young Vignelli designed a great number of serial lamps (pendant, table and wall) inspired by Nordic design, which he reinterpreted using the techniques and colours of Murano.

[5] Drawing for a sconce in the shape of a feather (model no. 413) after a design by Tomaso Buzzi exhibited at the 5th Triennale of Milan, 1933

[6] Proposal for a chandelier with a metal frame and screen with flowers and paterae for the Hotel Principi di Piemonte of Turin, 1937

[7] Lamp with 'tesserae' (model no. 528) after a design by Carlo Scarpa exhibited at the 6th Triennale of Milan. Period photograph, 1936

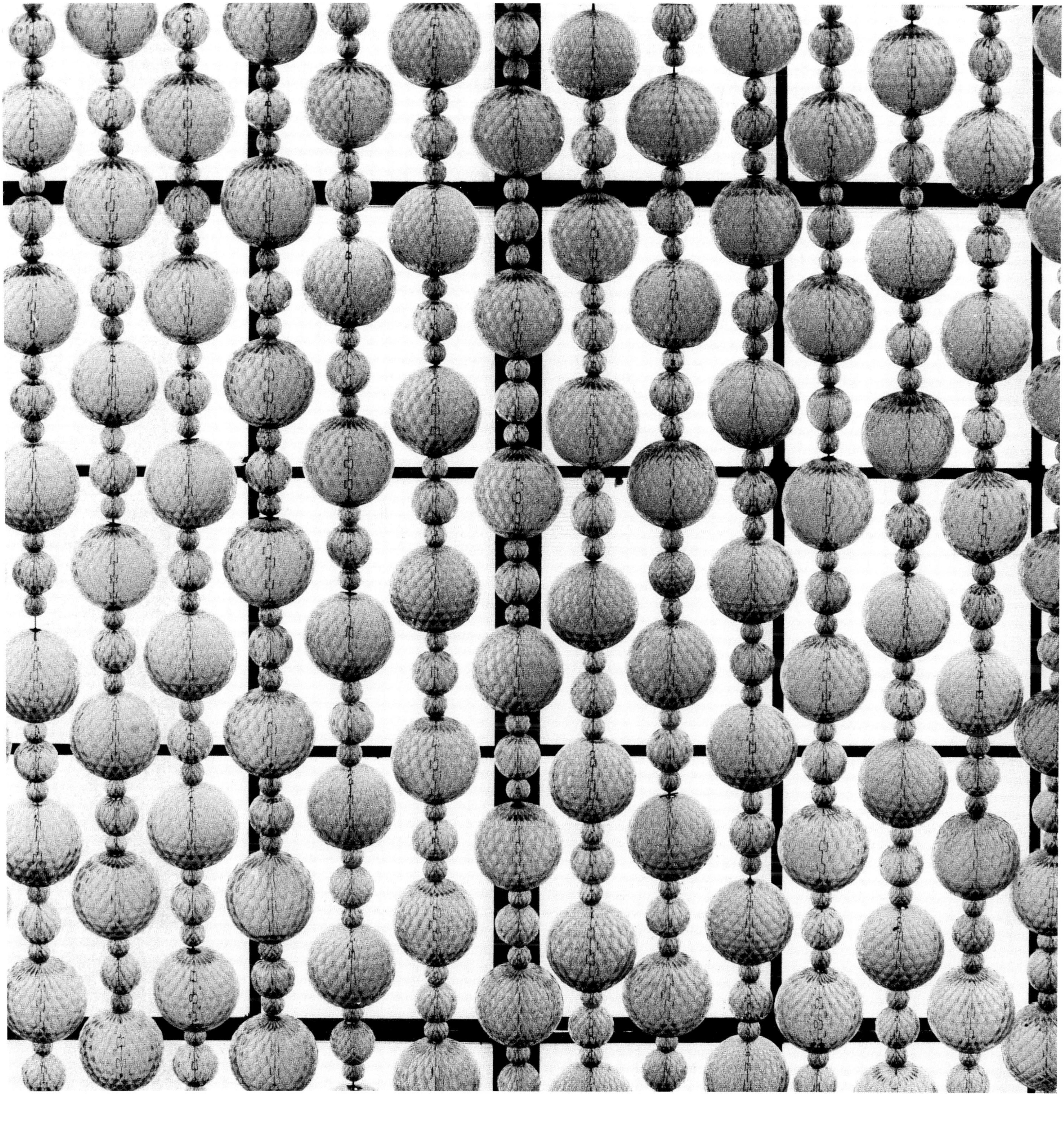

[8] Velarium of Palazzo Grassi with balloton spheres, detail. Period photograph, 1951

[9] Sconce and chandeliers with *poliedri*, Palazzo della Farnesina in Rome. Period photograph, c. 1960

Produced in monochrome *opalino* glass with *fasce di colore* and vertical bands, or in *tessuto* glass with thin bichrome canes, the Vignelli models were repeatedly illustrated in sector magazines and exhibited at different events, such as the Biennale of Venice in 1956 and 1958, receiving considerable appreciation as shown by the awarding of the *Compasso d'Oro* prize for two of them (nos. 4039-40) in 1956. Among the projects of this decade, the velarium of Palazzo Grassi in Venice is particularly worthy of note: this was executed in 1951 on the occasion of the renovation of the building, which had become the headquarters of the recently constituted Centro Internazionale delle Arti e del Costume.[11] It was an installation (13 x 16 m) designed as a screen for the skylight of the courtyard which was created so that this space could be exploited during events promoted by the Centre. This solution, devised by the architects in charge of the reorganisation of the Palazzo, took concrete shape thanks to the exchange with Paolo Venini and with the technical office of the glassworks. To filter the light coming from above, a series of 'festoons' was positioned, formed of steel cables and spheres in *cristallo balloton* glass in three sizes, in a pre-established sequence. [8] The festoons at the top were attached to a rectangular plate of prism glass and, falling downwards as far as the cornice of the last floor, gave concrete shape to the concept of four curved semi-transparent walls. The courtyard was thus transformed into a 'luminous hall with a ceiling of glass globes'.[12]

Further research on the use of modular elements, promoted by Paolo Venini himself, led towards the end of the 1950s to the invention of a module, the *poliedro* [polyhedron] [1], which proved to be fundamental for the continued strength and success of the glassworks in the lighting field in the following decades. The project was studied with a view to the Exposition Universelle in Brussels in April 1958 where the Venini firm had to produce, which it duly did, a great chandelier to be placed in the hall of the reception building of the Italian pavilion. The initial idea was to have an element which would be 'stackable' so as to obtain simply executed structured screens. The outcome of this research, developed with the involvement of Ignazio Gardella — one of the designers of the pavilion — Paolo Venini and Massimo Vignelli, was a polyhedron with a hexagonal cross-section, blown into moulds in transparent glass, of a very versatile composition. Equipped with a little metal hook at the top, to the definition of which Tobia Scarpa, present in the furnace from 1957-58, also made a contribution, the elements could be united to form a vitreous consistency that hid the light source and the supporting metal structure, which was equipped with radiating rods (*reste*).

The *poliedri* were proposed in different dimensions, both for the smaller-sized lamps, such as those seen at the Biennale of 1958, and for the monumental chandeliers, such as that exhibited in Brussels. This latter item, which boasted a diameter of 2.70 metres and a height of 4.60 metres, was executed with 1,500 *poliedri* of 19 cm in height.

The success of the new modular system was immediate, so much so that it was used almost at once by architects such as Enrico Del Debbio, who used it to give shape to the many lamps designed between 1958 and 1959 for the Palazzo della Farnesina, the headquarters of the Ministry of Foreign Affairs in Rome.

Numerous commissions followed one another from Italy and abroad and the *poliedri* were repeatedly adapted for the lighting of various public buildings such as theatres, hotels, institutional premises, but also banks, shops and ships, to the extent that they became almost a 'stylistic hallmark' for the glassworks, which also included them in catalogues for lamps for domestic use. Generally proposed in two colour variants with delicate hues, these elements were used to enliven fixtures often of a cylindrical form or with bodies with variously combined cylindrical volumes, with a symmetrical or sloping structure. [9]

In 1961, Carlo Scarpa chose to use the *poliedri* for the large chandelier of the Veneto pavilion, prepared by the architect for the Turin event, Italia 61, organised to celebrate the centenary of the Unity of Italy. [10] This was a genuine installation (base 5 x 5 m and maximum height 4.5 m) which thanks to Scarpa's extraordinary design demonstrated the further possibilities of these modular elements.

[10] Installation with *poliedri* after a design by Carlo Scarpa, Veneto pavilion, Italia 61. Period photograph, 1961

[11] Side view of the luminous ceiling with trefoil canes, Schlosstheater in Fulda. Period photograph, 1978

Positioned in the centre of the square area, over a similarly shaped pool of water, the fixture was composed of a structured volume in the shape of an upside-down pyramid extending downwards. Described as an 'enormous stalactite',[13] the installation was made out of approximately 3,000 polychrome *poliedri* in muted hues which made it like a 'streaming cascade of tender vibrations of light and colour which animates the space and enhances the pool under it, filling it with myriads of reflections'.[14] The project, which as a columnist noted a few days after the inauguration 'demanded months of work from the glassmakers of Murano',[15] was overseen by the new director of the furnace, the thirty-year-old architect Ludovico Diaz de Santillana who had replaced his father-in-law Paolo Venini, following the latter's premature death in July 1959. De Santillana in his new role, on the one hand maintained the organisation and direction given by the Lawyer (as Venini was called in the glassworks) and on the other was able to give a new impetus by developing certain areas, such as that of lighting, to which because of his training he devoted himself assiduously, favouring in particular the modular elements sector. Starting with experiments made towards the end of the 1950s with hollow cylindrical canes to produce fixtures and large installations, new types of modules began to be used in addition to the *poliedri*: from solid canes with a square cross-section (*canne quadre*) employed in the Opera Hall of Florence (1961) and in the Olivetti store in Dusseldorf by Ignazio Gardella (1960-61), to the *gocce* used by Stefan Buzas for the imposing 'chandeliers' of the airport of Manchester (1961). In the course of the decade and up to the 1980s, the repertoire of modular elements increased progressively, becoming rich with new and varied series, including panels for ceilings, showing yet again the extraordinary quality of the furnace and its technical office in offering solutions to respond to the most varied demands, above all those of the architects, in the field of lighting. These were, for example, hollow elements, generally with a circular or square cross-section, proposed with various surface finishings, among which the rough walled series *bricola* included in the catalogue from 1966.

Side-by-side with these were the aforesaid solid canes or rods that were produced in different cross-sections, such as triangular (*triangolo* series), but also, from the end of the decade, trefoil, used to produce, in addition to various pendant models, numerous installations, among which one particularly evocative one for the auditorium of the Fulda theatre (1978) [11] with its 70,000 canes, this being employed by the designer Gerhard Weber to solve some acoustic problems. There were also heat-moulded models such as the *ghiaccioli* (from 1975 called *eliche*), each composed of three slats joined together and converging towards the centre of the element. Characterised by undulating extremities and lined surfaces on both faces, they were designed not long before the middle of the 1960s and proposed in the catalogue in *cristallo* glass or with a nucleus in amethyst, *pagliesco* or *talpa* glass. An exceptional use of the *ghiaccioli* is to be seen in the theatre of Schweinfurt (1966) where the designer Trude Karrer chose this type, with large-sized elements, for a scenographic installation to be placed in the first-floor foyer. In the design of the modular elements, as well as of various models of lamps, a part was also played by Toni Zuccheri, who had been present in the glassworks since the early 1960s and to whom particularly we owe the design of the *esprit* modular elements in the form of stylised flowers, used in the production of the homonymous spherical pendant lamp that had such a critical success. Overall, however, the greater part of the modular items of these years can be attributed to the work of De Santillana, who nonetheless chose not to appear as the designer except on rare occasions, such as the Venice Biennale 1970 where the *Patchwork* system was exhibited, consisting of 'luminous modular elements with handmade tiles in coloured glass'.[16]

In 1985 the Venini firm was invited to participate in Paris in the exhibition that the Centre Pompidou dedicated to the theme of lighting, *Lumières: Je pense à vous,* which presented an international overview of lighting fixtures from the end of the 19th-century to 1985. The glassworks made a significant contribution by exhibiting a large chandelier with thirty-six lights by Vittorio Zecchin (model no. 2039) and the *Tappeto volante*, a glass structure with ribbons designed by Ludovico Diaz de Santillana the previous year: two different modes and worlds representing the essential elements of a great history.

1 G. Mariacher, *Antichi lampadari vitrei veneziani*, Venice 1957, pp. 7-8.

2 Ivi, p. 30.

3 Ivi, pp. 31-32.

4 Cf. M. Barovier, C. Sonego (edited by), *Vittorio Zecchin: i vetri trasparenti per Cappellin e Venini*, Milan 2017, particularly pp. 461-467.

5 Cf. M. Barovier and C. Sonego (edited by), *Napoleone Martinuzzi Venini 1925-1931*, Milan 2013, particularly pp. 390-411.

6 Cf. M. Barovier, C. Sonego (edited by), *Tomaso Buzzi alla Venini*, Milan 2014.

7 Cf. M. Barovier (edited by), *Carlo Scarpa Venini 1932-1947*, Milan 2012.

8 *Guida della Sesta Triennale*, Milan 1936, p. 142.

9 E. Zorzi, 'Una importante iniziativa veneziana nel campo dell'arredamento: il "Gruppo Arti Decorative"', in *Le Tre Venezie*, July-August, 1939, pp. 237-248.

10 Cf. M. Barovier, C. Sonego (edited by), *Fulvio Bianconi alla Venini*, Milan 2015; M. Barovier, C. Sonego (edited by), *Paolo Venini e la sua fornace*, Milan 2016.

11 Cfr. C. Sonego, *Palazzo Grassi, Headquarters of the Centro Internazionale delle Arti e del Costume*, in this catalogue, pp. 232-234.

12 'A Palazzo Grassi. Il costume ritratto nel tempo' in *Il Gazzettino*, 24 August 1951.

13 'Italia '61 a Torino. Alla Mostra delle regioni, Il Veneto', in *Domus*, August 1961, p. 18.

14 P. Santini, '"Italia 61". La mostra delle regioni' in *Comunità*, 90, 1961, p. 19.

15 'Dalla babele dei dialetti nasce sul Po la più spettacolare sintesi dell'Italia', in *La Stampa*, 26-27 April 1961.

16 *Catalogo della XXXV Biennale Internazionale d'Arte Venezia*, 1st ed., Venice 1970, p. 128.

VENINI: THE PROJECT OF LIGHT IN THE 1930s

Carla Sonego

In an article in *Domus* in February 1929 on the Venini company *Nuovi vetri muranesi*, Gio Ponti pointed out how 'outside the purely aesthetic field interesting new applications for lighting are to be noted, made possible by "pulegoso" glass, glass with minute bubbles created by Venini to achieve, by means of excellent refraction and optimal luminous transparency, the best conditions for modern lighting'.[1]
If on the one hand this observation would seem to indicate the real reasons for the creation of this material, quite apart from any artistic questions, on the other it shows how, at this time also in Murano, responses were being sought to the demands of 'modernity' coming from the sector.
In the 1920s, with the development of lighting engineering in Italy as well as abroad, a debate had started on the possibilities and culture of modern lighting (*lucicultura*).[2]
Faced with the low level of development compared with the international panorama, technical associations were formed to promote the modernisation both of the plant engineers and the world of design.
In Milan in 1926, for example, the ANSI was founded (Associazione nazionale per lo sviluppo dell'illuminazione – National Association for the Development of Lighting) which immediately began publishing an informative bulletin of a monographic kind, which was carried from 1928 as a section in the monthly magazine *Energia Elettrica*.
From 1930 to 1935 the association published the monthly magazine *L'illuminazione razionale* with principal contributions coming from engineers and well known sector experts, such as Carlo Clerici, Giovanni Canesi and Guido Jellinek, but also from architects such as Antonio Cassi Ramelli, who also on several occasions worked with Murano glass. The title of the magazine, a variant of the *L'Eclairage Rationnel* of Paris, sums up many planned aims of the monthly, which did not confine itself to the technical side of the subject but took into consideration 'the principle of the overall quality of the light effect rather than just quantification of the lighting parameters and assessment of the technical characteristics of the fixtures and installations'.[3]
In the late 1920s the topic spread also to magazines connected with the world of architecture and interior design where, beside editorials on the subject, articles by some of the collaborators of *L'illuminazione razionale*, such as the aforementioned Clerici, Canesi, Jellinek, and Cassi Ramelli, were published.[4]
While in one of the first numbers of *Domus* (March 1928) Ponti himself in an editorial pointed out

[1] Projectors and screen in cane glass in the Torre di Maratona in Turin. Period photograph, 1933

[2] Lamp after a design by Michele Marelli, 1930, Venini S.A.

that 'all modern research in the area of lighting is directed at procedures and fixtures that are more frankly in line with the character of electric lighting',[5] shortly afterwards the discussion of the theme was entrusted to Carlo Clerici.

Complete with examples of French lamps and some by Pietro Chiesa, the article emphasises how 'electric light [has] entirely upended the problem of lighting and the recent progress of the industry [...] [has] provided architects with possibilities of an unsuspected value.'[6] However the author observes that few people have realised this because there are those 'who go to excess in the number of lamps that try to make an element of decoration out of means of lighting', so causing the phenomenon of glare; others still who use 'artistic chandeliers already part of the general taste and apply, instead of the soft flames of the candles of yesteryear, powerful dazzling lights'.[7]

The direction advocated by Clerici was that witnessed in the examples shown, which are also a plea to architects to apply themselves to the problem and take 'account of the possibilities and necessities of rational lighting'.[8]

A more ample discussion was offered by Guido Jellinek in 1929 on the pages of *Architettura e arti decorative*.[9] Assuming 'light to be a veritable construction material', the culminating point of the recent conquests in the area of artificial lighting, he proposed a collection of images drawn from the panorama of French (Roux-Spitz, Printz etc.) and German (Riphahn, Grod etc.) lighting. In the 'technique of light' the engineer Jellinek distinguished two 'tendencies': one aimed at redesigning the lighting body – by rethinking the traditional chandelier – by using new models that 'adapt to the architecture of the space';[10] the other at indirect lighting, with the use of luminous sources hidden behind cornices or architectural elements, directing the light flux on to the ceiling. In addition there was also the possibility of producing luminous architectural elements, both for interiors and for facades.

The first results of this debate were seen in 1930 at the 4th Triennale of Monza, which gave ample space to the subject, both in the Furnishing Gallery and the Lighting Gallery, with the intention of 'showing the evolution taking place and speeding up progress towards new developments and refinements'.[11]

'Since the coming into existence of the electric light bulb,' as Ferdinando Reggiori observed, 'only now has the problem been seriously posed; perhaps we are arriving last, but the important thing is to arrive'.[12]

In the fixtures exhibited the bulbs had disappeared from sight and, taking account 'rationally' of the possibilities of electric light, there was an effort to solve or at least to control the problem of the dazzling caused by transparent glass through the use of other materials. The new lamps were therefore characterised by the use of opaline or frosted glass, or the more recent *pulegoso* glass i.e. 'coloured or plated glass of a considerable thickness and, if this should not be enough, the use of special equipment to achieve uniform diffusion of the light over the illuminating surface'.[13]

If in the Lighting Gallery there were few chandeliers with arms in transparent glass, so widely represented in previous Triennali, there were various fixtures using tubular bulbs, mostly screened by cylindrical shields.

Among these fixtures there were those designed by Luigi Piccinato and Michele Marelli for the Venini firm, which here made its debut as a manufacturer (Venini S.A.) exhibiting a small series of table, floor, wall and pendant lamps. In some cases, inspired by French models,[14] they were produced with metal mountings (burnished, nickel-plated or silver-plated) and minimalist diffuser screens in opaque glass, 'muted and elusive in colour', in the form of tubes or truncated-cone-shaped bells.[15] Published repeatedly by *Domus* and *L'illuminazione razionale* and described by the glassworks as 'rational lights of a modern kind',[16] while not being exceptional for the originality of the lines, they exemplified an effort to use Murano glass in a new way thanks to the involvement of two young architects. [2, 3]

Present in the Lighting Gallery also with various fixtures after a design by Napoleone Martinuzzi, the director of the glassworks,[17] there were Venini works to be seen in the entrance hall on the first floor

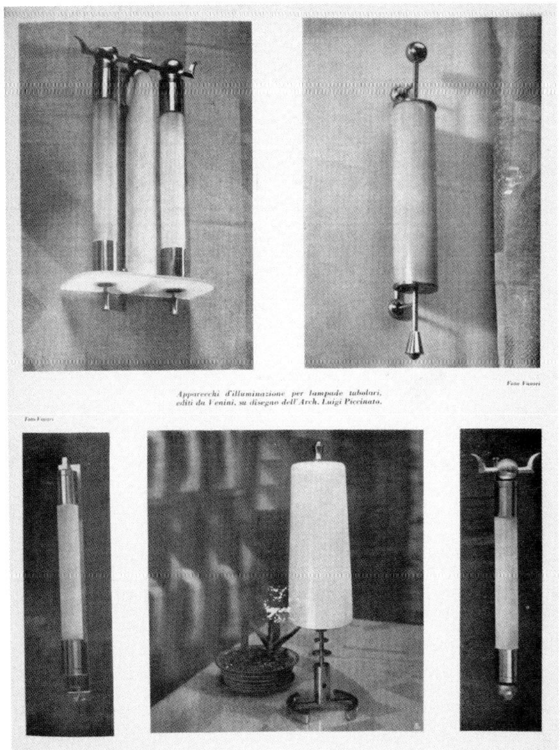

[3] Lamps after a design by Luigi Piccinato, 1929, Venini S.A., in *Domus*, December 1929

[4] Lamps with semi-frosted canes after a design by Paolo Mezzanotte and Giovanni Greppi in G. Canesi, A. Cassi Ramelli, *Architetture luminose e apparecchi per illuminazione*, Milan 1941, 2nd ed., p. 170

and in the stairway leading to the second, with solutions that document the research under way within the glassworks.

With regard to the stairway, these were luminous architectural elements such as the 'mete', a sort of column-obelisk, of a somewhat art-déco kind, produced in 'gold and red' yellow opaque glass which in a certain way seemed reminiscent of the luminous columns placed along the avenida Maria Cristina in Barcelona during the exhibition of 1929. In the entrance hall on the first floor the glassworks positioned a luminous cornice in *pulegoso* glass at the base of the dome, so providing for the indirect lighting of the central area. Made up of a series of glass elements juxtaposed along the circumference and supported by curved brackets in the form of leaves after a design by Martinuzzi, the cornice was one of the first lighting installations with modular elements, a theme that would soon become central for Venini projects.

In this respect, incidentally, it is worthwhile noting how at the 4th Triennale of Monza, the MVM Cappellin glassworks also exhibited, in its room, a straight-line lighting installation with modular elements, consisting of a horizontal metal frame and glass canes 'recessed appropriately at their extremities' with a system which had been patented by the company on 29 May 1929.[18] The system, however, was not used extensively because Giacomo Cappellin's glassworks, which counted among its 'collaborators' the young architect, Carlo Scarpa, closed down for financial reasons in January 1932.

A variant on this solution is constituted by the use of canes of semi-frosted glass for the production of 'lined' diffuser screens, which began to take hold from c. 1931.

The semi-frosted canes of two or three centimetres in diameter and various lengths were placed next to each other and supported by simple metal mountings, generally in anticorodal aluminium, so making it possible to produce fixtures in various shapes, mainly for walls and ceilings. Furthermore, as Cassi Ramelli observed in the pages of *L'illuminazione razionale* in December 1932, 'the Murano tubes, side by side and as it were forming an *indentation* pattern, all the more so if alternating in colour, produce an excellent effect of stretched silk and with their fluting hide the bulbs from sight. A development on this was patented by Venini, where the cane was frosted internally, so obtaining a more regular and a warmer effect'.[19] Among the first productions were the articulated sconces (180 x 86 cm), after a design by Giovanni Greppi, executed by the glassworks for the Banca Popolare of Milan (opened on 8 December 1931), which Cassi Ramelli, by way of illustration, published both as a support to the said article of 1932 and in the volume authored together with Giovanni Canesi titled *Architetture luminose e apparecchi per illuminazione*.[20] In this volume they were presented together with the high sconces (180 x 27 cm) designed by Paolo Mezzanotte for the Stock Exchange Building of Milan, officially opened in 1932. [4] Featuring a semi-cylindrical body, they were characterised by the elegant lower extremity of the metal mounting which, as in the lamp designed by Greppi, was enhanced by the presence of a metal sphere. For the same building, Mezzanotte also used the semi-frosted canes for ceiling lamps, consisting of semi-cylinders side by side with luminous squares or rectangles, and for the cylindrical fixtures of the restaurant with their more 'technical' design, composed of 'long luminous tubes [...] striped in red and amethyst' hanging from the ceiling, which were combined with a Richard Ginori ceramic covering after a design by Gio Ponti.[21]

Included in the glassworks catalogue in various models, particularly as wall but also as pendant lamps, (e.g. nos. 5210-5211, Blue Catalogue), this type of glass was repeatedly adopted by the architects Angiolo Mazzoni and Roberto Narducci who were active at Office 5 of the Ministry of Communications, which in the course of the 1930s developed various post office buildings and railway stations, in compliance also with government initiatives to tackle unemployment (Decree 10102 of 8 July 1930).[22]

Napoleone Martinuzzi may be considered to be the intermediary between the glassworks and Mazzoni because as a sculptor he had often been involved directly by the Bolognese architect in the decoration of his buildings, starting with the Dopolavoro ferroviario of Rome (1930), for which the Venini firm

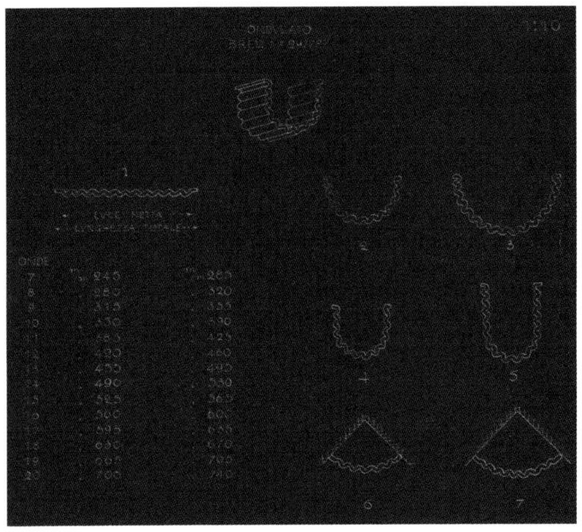

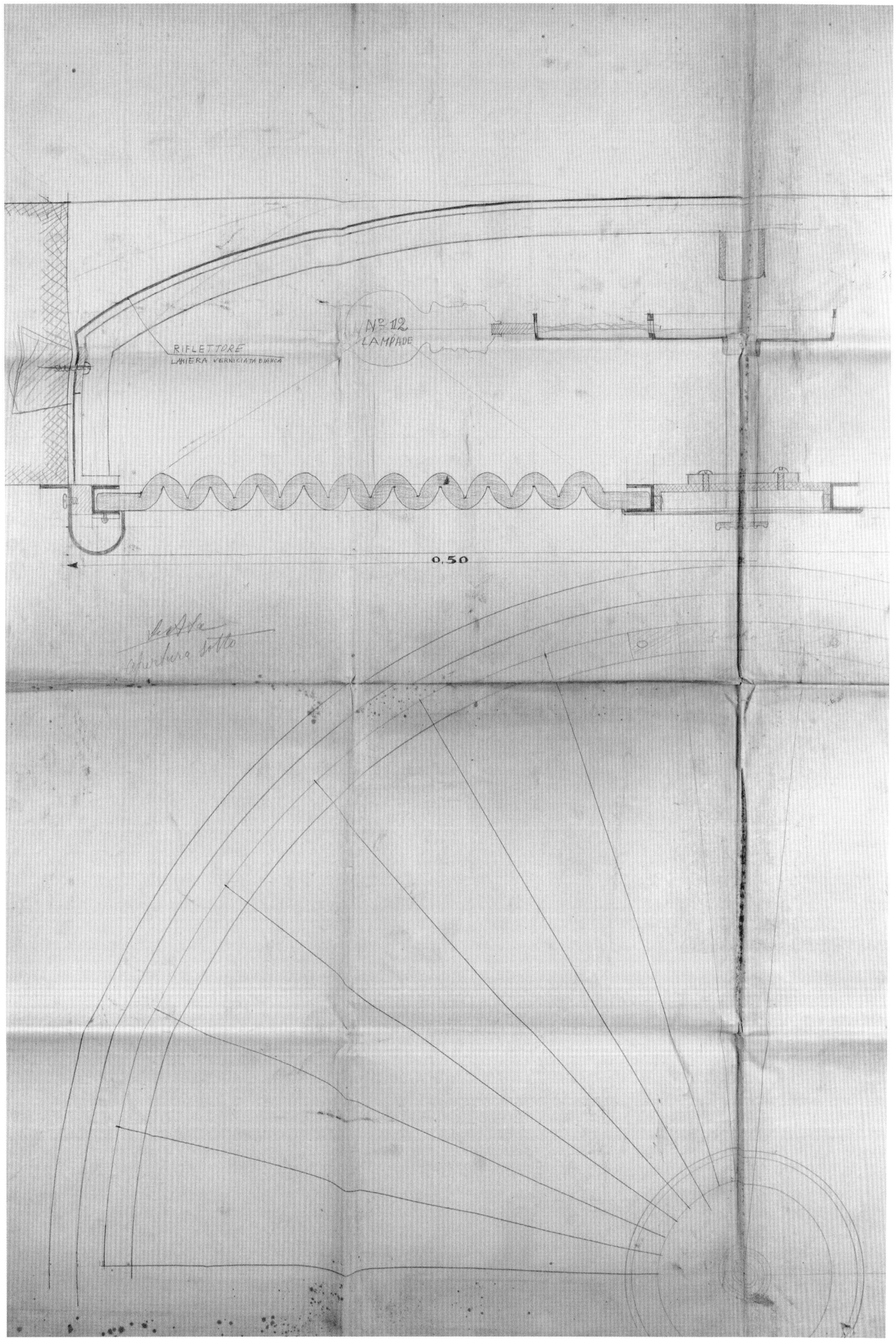

[5] Page C with profiles of *ondulato* glass, patent no. 297789, Blue Catalogue

[6] Drawing for a ceiling lamp in *ondulato* glass, Siena railway station, after a design by Angiolo Mazzoni

[7] Lamps with semi-frosted canes in the Post Office building of Grosseto, after a design by Angiolo Mazzoni. Period photograph, 1932

[8] Royal room with a luminous ribbon in *ondulato* glass, Siena railway station, after a design by Angiolo Mazzoni. Period photograph, 1935

produced various lighting fixtures in *pulegoso* glass and in cased glass after the design of Martinuzzi. This was one of the first instances of collaboration between the Murano glassworks and the Office's designer, who continued to avail himself of the glassworks into the second half of the decade, progressively reaching a sort of standard type of lighting installation, thanks to the use of modular systems of a kind to satisfy the functional and representational demands made by the Ministry of Communications and the fascist state.

A turning point here was the case of the Post Office of Bergamo, inaugurated in 1932, where in addition to new lamps in cased glass of an art-déco inspiration, after the design of the Murano sculptor, Mazzoni also chose fixtures with semi-frosted canes both for the exterior and the interior (correspondence room). The first were large cylindrical fixtures, positioned in corners and with shapes suggesting the lictor beams; the second, mixtilinear wall lamps which, while ensuring efficient lighting, with their discreet presence seemed almost to blend in with the stone pillars.

In other projects, as in the Post Office of Grosseto (1932), [7] Massa (1933) and La Spezia (1933), in Latina (post office and railway station, 1932) and in the accessory services building of the railway station of Santa Maria Novella in Florence (c. 1933), the architect used only the new 'technical' lamps, in many cases box-shaped wall lamps with rounded corners, which stood out on the brick or marble structure on which they were fixed, establishing a kind of dialogue with it.[23]

In Bergamo there were also other lamps with modular elements, such as the wall lamps in *ondulato* glass which the Venini firm had patented with an application of 2 April 1931 (patent no. 297787).[24] [5] This was a new option which presumably had been studied by the glassworks at the request (and with the involvement?) of Mazzoni who made great use of it, even especially favouring it, in the projects completed between 1932 and 1936.

The effort to reduce the loss of light caused by the various materials in use ('semi-transparent, frosted or translucent multifaceted glass') to shield the light sources, led to, as the text of the patent indicates, a 'light diffuser formed of perfectly transparent glass, in which the diffusion or dispersion of the rays coming from the light source is determined by the fact that the layer of glass the rays must pass through is undulating on the two faces'.[25] This diffuser was produced by 'grouping together several elements each formed of a strip of undulating glass' straight or curved. Fixed on to a metal frame the elements – ten centimetres in width and up to eighty in length – could 'form casings of a prismatic, cylindrical, globoid, or any other form of surface of revolution, suitable for enclosing variously shaped light sources.'[26] Offered also in coloured glass with delicate hues, these *ondulato* glass items not only satisfied technical lighting demands but also, as emphasised by Cassi Ramelli in the pages of *Architettura*, 'offer[ed] a great many plastic and chromatic decorative resources'.[27]

While noting the affinities with 'certain French colleagues', the architect remarked on the quality of the *ondulato* glass pieces which, as in the case of the fixtures with semi-frosted canes, 'if they are not entirely illuminated, react with brilliant and lively surfaces to simple contact with natural light'.[28]

In Bergamo, as in the post office of Gorizia (officially opened in 1932), Mazzoni used *ondulato* glass for a series of sconces on very minimalist lines with somewhat accentuated semi-cylindrical bodies framed in the metal mounting. In the following years this system was used by the architect with great nonchalance in the production of luminous ceiling cornices, very large pendant lamps, circular ceiling lamps, [6] luminous ribbons with concealed supply systems, luminous wall and ceiling tubes etc., establishing with the glassworks a sort or repertoire of solutions which he adopted both for interiors and exteriors. Notable, among others, are the projects at the post office of Palermo (1934) and at the station of Siena (1935) where the Venini firm produced a considerable number of fixtures demonstrating the versatility of *ondulato* glass which Mazzoni, particularly interested in the qualities of the materials and the relationship between them, adopted also because of their chromatic characteristics. [8] An example is the arrangement of the Royal Room in the Siena station, lit by a long concealed ribbon (910 x 84 cm) of which the curved extremity followed the course of the partially glazed wall.

[9] Pavilion of the industrial port of Venezia-Marghera at the Fair of Padua after a design by Brenno Del Giudice, detail. Period photograph, 1932

[10] Torre di Maratona, Turin, after a design by Brenno Del Giudice. Period photograph, 1933

To produce this, as an exception, use was made of green glass with *bollicine*, a material – a further development of the *pulegoso* type but with a clearer appearance – which softened the light and 'contrasted' with the mosaic decoration of crimson tesserae of the ceiling and floor (execution Sarim) and with the black marble of the walls crossed by bands of Verde Issorie marble.[29]

Ondulato glass was also chosen by many other designers, starting with Marcello Piacentini, who from the 1920s onwards called upon the services of the glassworks for lighting projects and who used the new type of glass for the execution of lighting as an architectural component, such as the 'lantern' of the Torre della Rivoluzione and the crest of the Istituto Nazionale delle Assicurazioni building, both overlooking the Piazza della Vittoria in Brescia, officially opened on 1st November 1932. Among the architects was also the Venetian architect Brenno Del Giudice, who exploited the peculiarities of the patent, associated with plates of *alluman* (an alloy of aluminium and magnesium) to characterise as a 'very modern' construction the pavilion of the industrial port of Venezia-Marghera at the Fair of Padua in 1932.[30] In particular in the 'tower' at the centre of the building, he designed a luminous ribbed structure in *ondulato* glass giving reflections that were amplified by the metal covering. [9] He adopted a similar solution, articulated in a different way, for the Torre di Maratona in Turin that marked the entrance to the sporting complex, the 'Stadio Mussolini', inaugurated on 14 May 1933 on the occasion of the Littoriali della Gioventù games.[31] Built in reinforced concrete, the construction was equipped with a lighting system in *ondulato* glass and glass with amethyst canes, [1] juxtaposed or inserted in the facade or side elevations to make the tower visible from afar during the night and in harmony with it the sporting complex promoted by the regime. [10]

The Turin project, which involved other designers and included also the execution of luminous architraves for the stadium building, documents the different possibilities for the use of the patent and also allowed the glassworks, as did other contracts, to overcome the difficulties linked to the economic crisis which, after 1930 but particularly in 1932, had a heavy impact on the Murano glass sector.

In January 1933 in a letter to Fernanda Ojetti, Paolo Venini related how 'in 1930 Murano had exports of a value of 8 million and in 1932 of a value of 800,000 liras [...]; in 1930 8,000 workers were employed and in 1932 800; [...] With the help of the Turin work, I am continuing with the reduced production of last year and hope to survive. Now I have the time to prepare all the new production and for the Triennale."[32]

With a view to the said event – the fifth, which having been transferred from Monza to Milan, was held in the new Palazzo dell'Arte in May 1933 – the glassworks sent various architects a letter which allows us to understand the working procedures generally used in its relationships with the different designers: 'Our production is entirely at your disposal for whatever you might need for the Triennale: whether simply to implement the models designed by you or to collaborate with you in the design of these models or to submit to you projects of ours based on indications supplied to us.'[33]

There were various outcomes to these 'collaborative projects', among which should particularly be mentioned that with the architects Angelo Bordoni and Angelo Carminati who, together with Mario Sironi, designed sculptural 'hanging lamps in bronze' (h 450 cm), using *ondulato* glass, for the ceremonial hall. [12] This glass, which here saw its official 'consecration', had also been used for the striking luminous structure of the entrance hall of which Gio Ponti noted the characteristic 'effect', 'silvery and trilling', whether with the light on or off.[34] [11] The architect, in fact, while not disdaining the possibilities offered by the innovations in lighting, criticised their influence on the quality of the fixtures which, when turned off, could appear 'without the interest of any form or substance'.[35]

Ponti also, in May 1933 in *Domus*, had reported the presence in the glassworks of Carlo Scarpa together with Tomaso Buzzi,[36] noting also 'the return of the rich chandelier' which progressively reaffirmed itself, as evidenced by the works that can be ascribed to the Lombard architect, but also to the work of the young Venetian, associated with Venini since the closure of the Cappellin company. Along the

[11] Luminous structure in *ondulato* glass, entrance hall, 5th Triennale of Milan. Period photograph, 1933

[12] Lamps in *ondulato* glass after a design by Angelo Bordoni, Angelo Carminati and Mario Sironi, ceremonial hall, 5th Triennale of Milan. Period photograph, 1933

same lines was also the large chandelier designed by Antonio Cassi Ramelli in 1932 for the Salone del Cielo of the Luna Park of the Lido di Venezia, with which the architect 'wished to make use in a modern way of one of the many possibilities that the Murano industry could offer [him]'.[37] Featuring a series of ribbed tapes, folded downwards to hide the body of the lamp made up of a series of frosted plates, the chandelier was included in the glassworks catalogue with a model on a smaller scale (no. 5278). [13]
The continuing research on new solutions led in the following years to the registration of another patent (no. 321982 of June 1934) and its supplement (no. 333411 of 19 February 1935):[38] this was lined scored glass which made it possible to create continuous luminous structures consisting of elements with a cylindrical cross-section and otherwise, obtained by moulding, 'with round internal and external mouldings, or just on one side, and ending on both sides with edges turned inwards and possibly equipped with notches to accommodate heads'.[39] In this way the necessity for a metal frame for fixtures in *ondulato* glass, which interfered with the structure and caused areas of shadow, was avoided. To improve lighting efficiency, the inside of the modular element was finished with close-packed incisions. As can be seen in the Blue Catalogue, compiled on an on-going basis from the 1930s, the scored glass was proposed, in addition to the aforesaid 'lined scored' version, also in 'ashlar' and 'wavy' with elements having six 'cable decorations' of a width of 10 centimetres. For *ondulato* glass the catalogue itemises 38 shapes, while for this new patented model there are 104 profiles, pointing to the greater flexibility and compositional possibilities of the system in the definition of which – as is documented by a considerable *corpus* of archive designs – Carlo Scarpa played a part.
Among the projects completed with scored glass there was also a series of public works commissioned by the regime and its constituent structures, such as the Colonia marina femminile dei fasci italiani all'estero [Female summer holiday camp of the Italian fasces abroad] in Tirrenia, designed by Giulio Pediconi and Mario Paniconi (inaugurated in 1935) and the much larger complex of the Scuola di applicazione per la Regia areonautica (aeronautics training school) of Florence, designed by Raffaello Fagnoni (1937-38).[40] In the latter in particular, the system was used in the implementation of a sort of luminous architrave surrounding the Aula Magna. Below it, in the vaulted entrance hall, a series of chandeliers of a markedly decorative kind was placed, like those with a metal structure and applied elements, designed by Scarpa, which were exhibited at the Triennale of 1936 and in the Italian pavilion at the Exposition Universelle of Paris in 1937.
Besides the fixtures with modular elements designed particularly for public contracts, the glassworks continued to develop new models of extremely elegant lamps intended both for domestic and ceremonial settings, also because of its active involvement in 'an important Venetian initiative in the furnishing field: the "Gruppo Arti Decorative"'.[41] Promoted by the Unione Fascista degli Industriali, the Federazione degli Artigiani and the Istituto Veneto per il Lavoro, the initiative had resulted in the constitution of a group of entrepreneurs who represented Venetian excellence in the field of the decorative arts and which had come together to implement projects in this area.
Among the projects completed, of particular importance was the work done on the banqueting hall of the Principi di Piemonte Hotel of Turin (1937),[42] where the glassworks took care of both the lighting and decoration of the hall, organised by the technical office of the firm with the involvement of Carlo Scarpa.[43]
Structured on three sides by a series of alcoves, the hall was lit by elegant chandeliers having diffuser screens with flowers and paterae, [14] the richness of which was reflected in the mosaic decoration of the alcoves covered with golden tesserae having decorations in glass that, with their reflecting surfaces, contributed to striking light effects.
The quality of the wide-ranging research of the glassworks in the period is also documented by a series of elaborate diagrams attributable to Scarpa. [15] In one case it is an undated proposal, probably of the late 1930s and early 1940s, for a series of outdoor lamps, presumably lampposts, where the originality of the design goes together with specific technical lighting solutions. In the other case

[13] Model no. 5278

[14] C. Scarpa, lamp with applied elements, Banqueting Hall, Principi di Piemonte Hotel, Turin. Period photograph, 1937

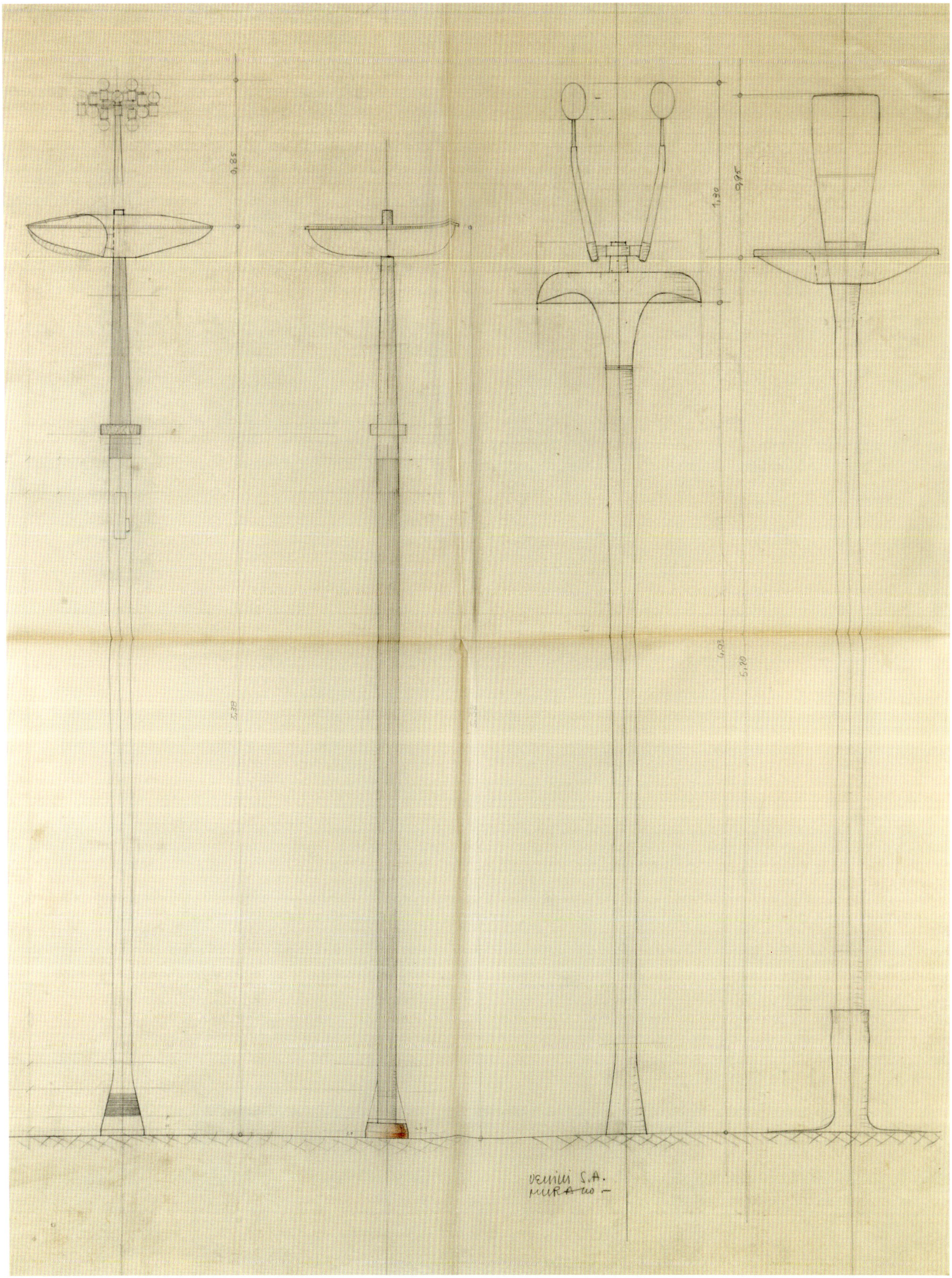

15 C. Scarpa, drawing for street lamps, [1930s-40s]

a small collection of sheets illustrate the lighting proposals for the staircase of the Palazzo della Civiltà Italiana in the EUR district after the design of Giovanni Guerrini, Ernesto Lapadula and Mario Romano, the construction of which began in 1938. One of these proposals provides for the creation of a monumental luminous spiral column in ashlar glass towering, with appropriate fasteners, up to the top of the central stairwell (h 60 m). An alternative consisted of an equally colossal luminous pillar with a central section in diamond-point-etched patterned glass, silvered inside, and with wings in ashlar glass. [16] Two carefully designed projects, which in their two different ways, like the works of this decade respond in a spirit of 'modernity' to the various demands of lighting.

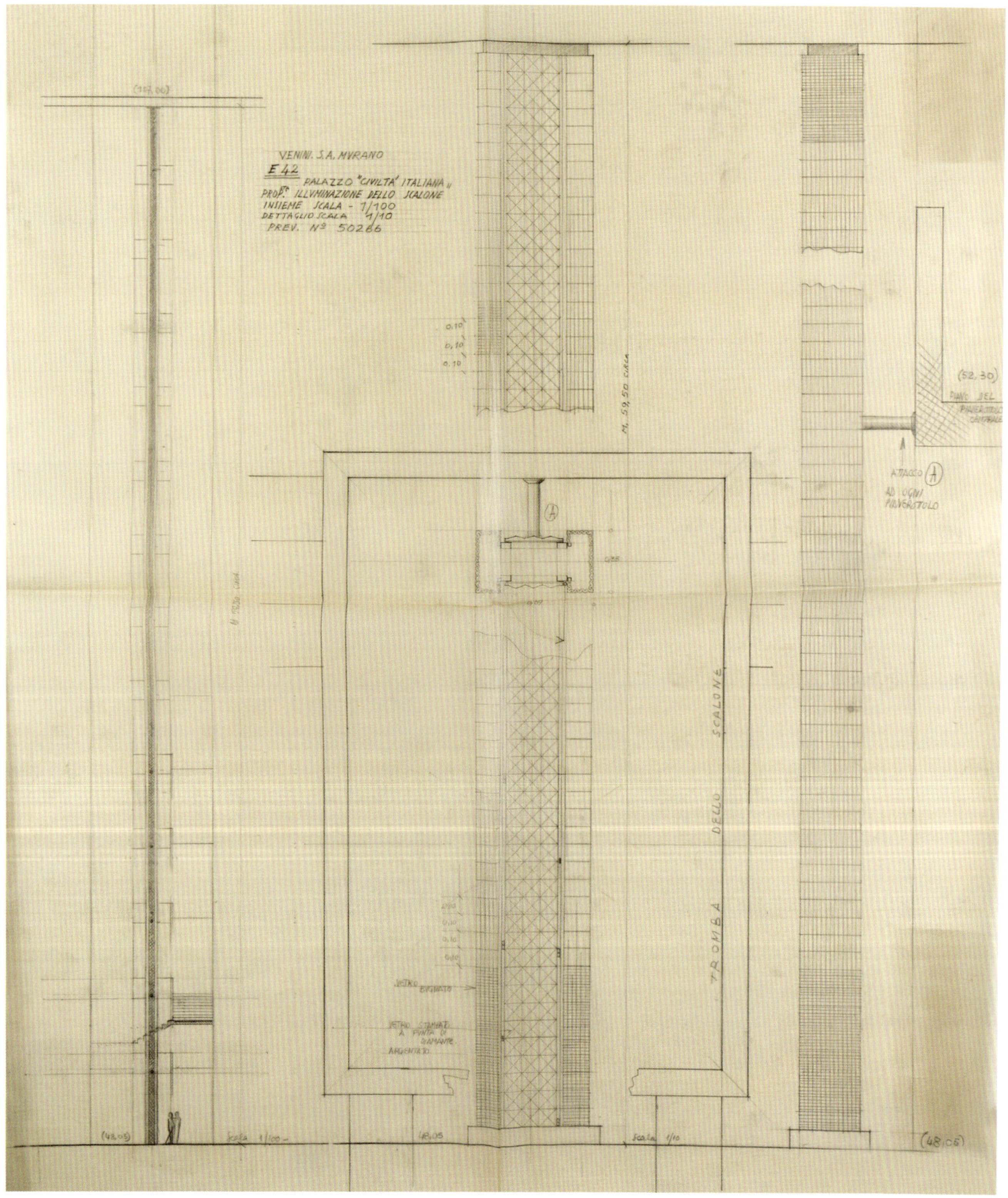

[16] C. Scarpa, proposal for lighting of the staircase, Palazzo della Civiltà Italiana, late 1930s

1 Dir. [G. Ponti], 'Nuovi vetri muranesi', in *Domus*, February 1929, p. 33.

2 C. Biagini, M. Fabbrini, 'Verso un'architettura della luce: la "lucicultura in Italia negli anni '20', in *Bollettino ingegneri*, 8/9, 2009, pp. 14-20.

3 Ivi, p. 16.

4 Cf., for example, *Domus* [G. Ponti], 'Orientamenti del gusto nell'arredare la casa', in *Domus*, March 1928, p. 41; C. Clerici, 'Architetture moderne ed illuminazione', in *Domus*, May 1928, pp. 32-33, 46-47; G. Marangoni, 'L'illuminazione e la sua nuova estetica', in *La Casa bella*, June 1928, pp. 11-14; G. Canesi, 'Tendenze moderne nell'illuminazione', in *Rassegna di Architettura*, May 1929, pp. 176-185; G. Jellinek, 'Luce e architettura', in *Architettura e arti decorative*, October November 1929, pp. 61-72; A. Cassi Ramelli, 'Si cerca un lampadario', in *La Casa bella*, February 1930, pp. 45-49.

5 Domus [G. Ponti], 'Orientamenti del gusto...', op. cit., p. 41.

6 C. Clerici, 'Architetture moderne...', op. cit., p. 33.

7 Ivi, p. 47.

8 Ibid.

9 G. Jellinek, 'Luce e architettura...', op. cit.

10 Ivi, p. 66.

11 *Catalogo Ufficiale della IV Esposizione Triennale Internazionale delle arti decorative ed industriali moderne*, Milan, 1930, pp. 221-222. Cf., inter alia, A. Cassi Ramelli, 'L'illuminazione alla Triennale di Monza, in L'illuminazione razionale', June-July 1930, pp. 43-47.

12 F. Reggiori, 'La Triennale di Monza. IV mostra internazionale delle arti decorative', in *Architettura e arti decorative*, July 1930, p. 512.

13 C.A. Felice, *Arte decorativa 1930 all'esposizione di Monza*, Milan 1930, p. 43.

14 Cf., e.g., 'Le XIX salon des artistes decorateurs', in *Art et decoration*, January 1929, p. 25; 'Le mobilier et les arts décoratifs au salon d'automne', in *Art et décoration*, November 1929, pp. 177-179.

15 The fixtures after the design of Luigi Piccinato had already been presented in 1929 in E. L. [Lancia], 'Apparecchi moderni di illuminazione', in *Domus*, December 1929, pp. 42-43. Cf. also C.A. Felice, *Arte decorativa...*, op. cit., p. 44; G. Canesi, A. Cassi Ramelli, *Architetture luminose e apparecchi per illuminazione*, Milan, 1941, 2nd ed., pp. 154, 180.

16 Cover, *Domus*, November 1930; 'Per la vostra casa moderna', in *Domus*, January 1934, p. 31; A. Cassi Ramelli, 'L'illuminazione alla Triennale...', op. cit., pp. 44-46, 47; *Mostra di vetri, ceramiche e merletti d'arte moderna italiana. Tentoonstelling van glas, aardewerk en kant, van moderne italiaansche kunstnijverheid*, exhibition catalogue, Milan 1931, p. 14.

17 Cf. 'Illuminazione 1926-31', in M. Barovier (edited by), *Napoleone Martinuzzi Venini 1925-1931*, exhibition catalogue, Milan 2013, pp. 406-408.

18 C. Sonego, 'Carlo Scarpa dall'architettura al vetro', in M. Barovier, C. Sonego (edited by), *La vetreria M.V.M. Cappellin e il giovane Carlo Scarpa 1925-1931*, exhibition catalogue, Milan, 2018, p. 38.

19 A. Cassi Ramelli, 'Apparecchi di illuminazione muranesi', in *L'illuminazione razionale*, December 1932, p. 272. The patent referred to by Cassi Ramelli is not known.

20 G. Canesi, A. Cassi Ramelli, *Architetture luminose...*, op. cit., p. 170.

21 G. Marussig, 'Le arti decorative nel nuovo palazzo delle borse', in *Rassegna di Architettura*, March 1933, pp. 119-121.

22 Cf., inter alia, F. Businari, *L'architettura nei palazzi per le poste e telegrafi costruiti e da costruirsi a cura dell'amministrazione delle ferrovie dello stato*, 2nd National Congress of Italian Engineers Rome 1931, Milan-Rome 1931.

23 Cf., inter alia, M. Cozzi, E. Godoli, P. Pettenella (edited by), *Angiolo Mazzoni (1894-1979) Architetto Ingegnere del Ministero delle Comunicazioni*, Milan 2003.

24 C. Sonego, 'Carlo Scarpa nell'ufficio tecnico della Venini', in M. Barovier (edited by), *Carlo Scarpa Venini 1932-1947*, exhibition catalogue, Milan 2012, p. 48.

25 *Brevetto 297787* in Central State Archive Rome, Ministry of Industry and Commerce and Craftsmanship, Italian Patents and Trademarks Office, Inventions series (hereinafter ACS MICA).

26 Ibid.

27 [A. Cassi Ramelli], 'Nuovi aspetti e nuove applicazioni del vetro muranese di Venini', in *Architettura*, May 1933 no page number. The architect expressed himself similarly also in the aforementioned article in the *Illuminazione razionale*, A. Cassi Ramelli, 'Apparecchi di illuminazione...', op it., p. 272.

28 Ibid.

29 'Le nuove stazioni ferroviarie di Siena e Reggio Emilia. Ing. Angiolo Mazzoni', in *Architettura*, March 1937, pp. 134-135.

30 P. Ma. [Marconi], 'Il Padiglione per il porto industriale di Venezia-Marghera alla Fiera campionaria di Padova', in *Architettura*, July 1932, p. 365.

31 Ga. Mi. [Minnucci], 'La torre di Maratona, il campo di atletica leggera e la piscina allo stadio Mussolini di Torino', in *Architettura*, January 1934, pp. 31-34.

32 *Lettera di Paolo Venini a Fernanda Ojetti*, 10 January 1933, in Galleria Nazionale di Arte Moderna, Fondo Ojetti, cass. 76 7 (I).

33 *Lettera della Venini S.A. a Tomaso Buzzi*, 10 December 1932, in Archivio Buzzi Scarzuola, Arti Applicate, folder 48.

34 G. Ponti, 'I vetri d'arte italiani alla Triennale', in *Domus*, July 1933, p. 236.

35 Ibid.

36 G. Ponti, 'I vetri d'arte italiani alla Triennale', in *Domus*, May 1933, p. 236.

37 A. Cassi Ramelli, 'Il "Luna Park" del Lido di Venezia', in *L'illuminazione razionale*, October 1932, pp. 211.

38 C. Sonego, 'Carlo Scarpa nell'ufficio tecnico...', op. cit., pp. 53, 55.

39 *Brevetto 333411* in ACS MICA.

40 'Colonia marina femminile dei fasci italiani all'estero a Tirrenia. Architetti Mario Paniconi e Giulio Pediconi', in *Architettura*, December, 1936, pp. 577-589; R. Fagnoni, 'La scuola di applicazione per la R. Aeronautica a Firenze', in *Architettura*, June 1938, pp. 329-369.

41 E. Zorzi, 'Una importante iniziativa veneziana nel campo dell'arredamento: il "Gruppo Arti Decorative"', in *Le Tre Venezie*, July-August 1938, pp. 237-248.

42 Ivi, p. 248.

43 Realised after a design by Vittorio Bonadè Bottino, with interior design by Giovanni Chevalley, the building was constructed in the context of the reconstruction of the second section of via Roma, on the initiative of the Agnelli family and was opened officially on 23 December 1937. Cf., inter alia, 'Il ministro Thaon di Revel inaugura il grande albergo "Principi di Piemonte"', in *La Stampa*, 24 December 1937.

EVEN MORE DIFFICULT! ARTIFICIAL LIGHT

Alberto Campo Baeza

BUSHEL BASKET

'Nor do they light a lamp and then put it under a bushel basket; it is set on a lampstand, where it gives light to all in the house' (Matthew 5: 13-16). These words from Holy Scripture could almost have been written with Venini in mind. Because artificial light is one of the most difficult architectural materials to work with but, at the same time, it is absolutely essential for life and architecture. In fact, I would even go as far to say that it has been handled skilfully when it disappears and all that we can perceive are its wonderful effects.

I have tried to say it in every possible way that LIGHT is the key theme in architecture. [1] Natural LIGHT. *Architectura sine luce, nulla architectura est* is the title of my most significant text on LIGHT – written so long ago. For the title of my latest, rather more recent work, I turned to Galileo and his expressive *Eppur si muove!* to underline that natural LIGHT is a material in movement. So obvious, yet disregarded by most people. Especially by architects, it seems.

What about artificial light? I will tell you right now that, for architects, artificial light is one of the most difficult materials to work with. That simple gesture of inserting a plug into a socket and switching on a light is far from simple to manage.

Like the shortlist of players for a great football team, Venini's 'final selection' comprises a large number of rather famous names, accompanied by the number of the glass pieces – lights – designed. Carlo Scarpa (23), Ettore Sottsass (13), Gae Aulenti (1). But also Alessandro Mendini, Gio Ponti, Ron Arad, Tadao Ando, Tapio Wirkkala, Tobia Scarpa and many more. Among them are two friends of mine, Massimo Vignelli, the creator of the Helvetica font, and Giorgio Vigna.

At this stage of the game – to stay with the football metaphor – I also designed a table light. The Triaedrus is a lamp composed of four lines.

[1] The Robert Olnick Pavillion at Magazzino Italian Art Museum By Alberto Campo Baeza in collaboration with Miguel Quismondo © Magazzino Italian Art Foundation, Cold Spring, NY 2022

TRIAEDRUS

I recently perfected the design of a light called the Triaedrus lamp, the outcome of my research into the geometry of the trihedron. [3]
The three half-lines forming the corners of the trihedron are made from slender stainless steel tubes. The idea was to place a led strip at the right height to aid reading once lit.
Supporting this strip, which is always horizontal, is a vertical line joined to a base formed by two horizontal lines orthogonal to each other.
The three lines of the support form a trihedron ensuring complete stability, which is further reinforced by the lead core of the two tubes resting on the table.
Inside the lamp – which may contain a line with a 10-mm diameter – is a USB rechargeable battery which causes the device to emit LIGHT, artificial light, as if by a miracle. A miraculous light like that of the oil lamps made from clay by primitive humans, so far and so near!
This lamp is 'almost nothing', a trihedron. Which is why I called it TRIAEDRUS. [2]
I think that it clarifies what I wrote: the best thing that could possibly happen is for VENINI to fall in love with my TRIAEDRUS and to decide to produce it. It would be an honour.

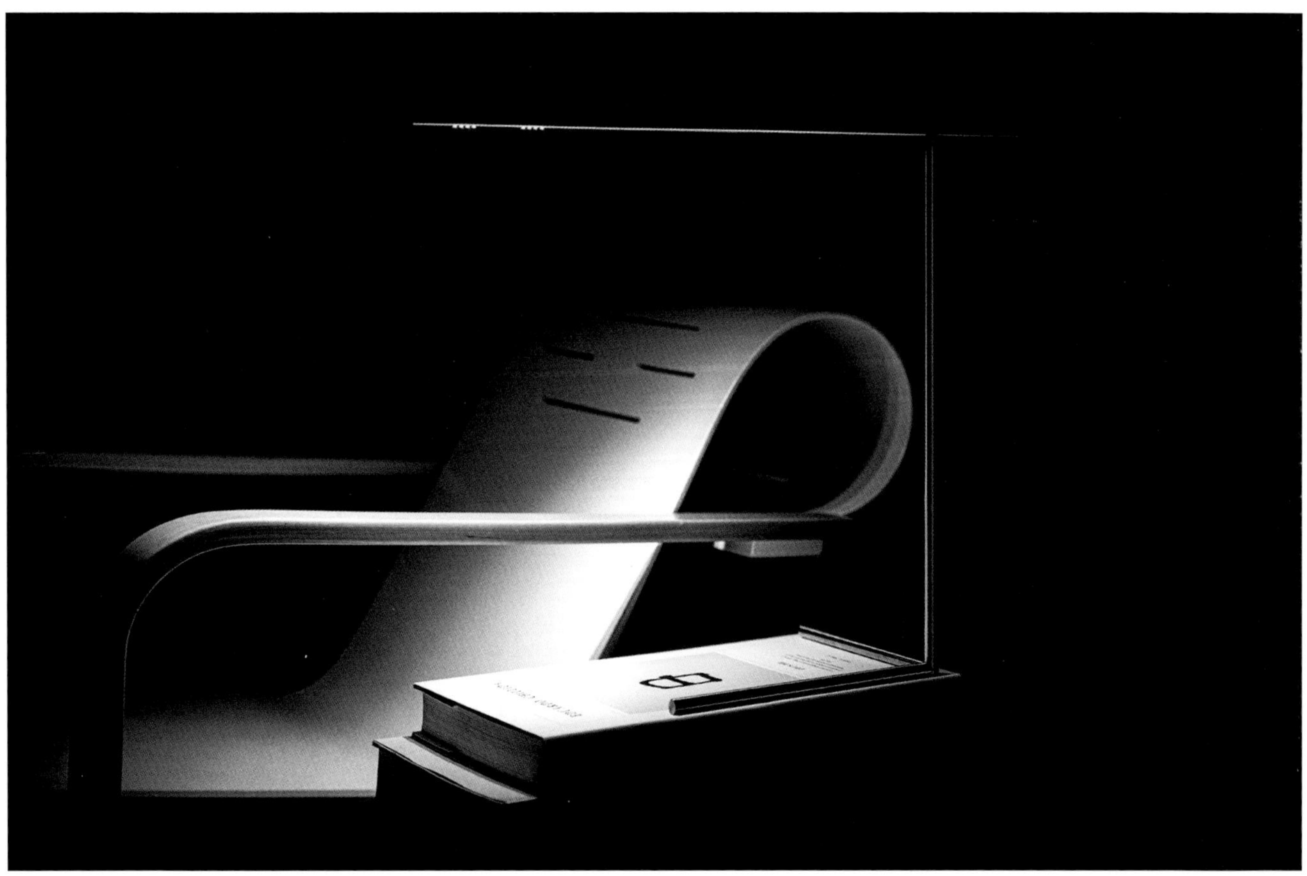

[2] *Triaedrus* lamp. Courtesy Alberto Campo Baeza

[3] Study for a *Triaedrus* lamp, 2019. Courtesy Alberto Campo Baeza

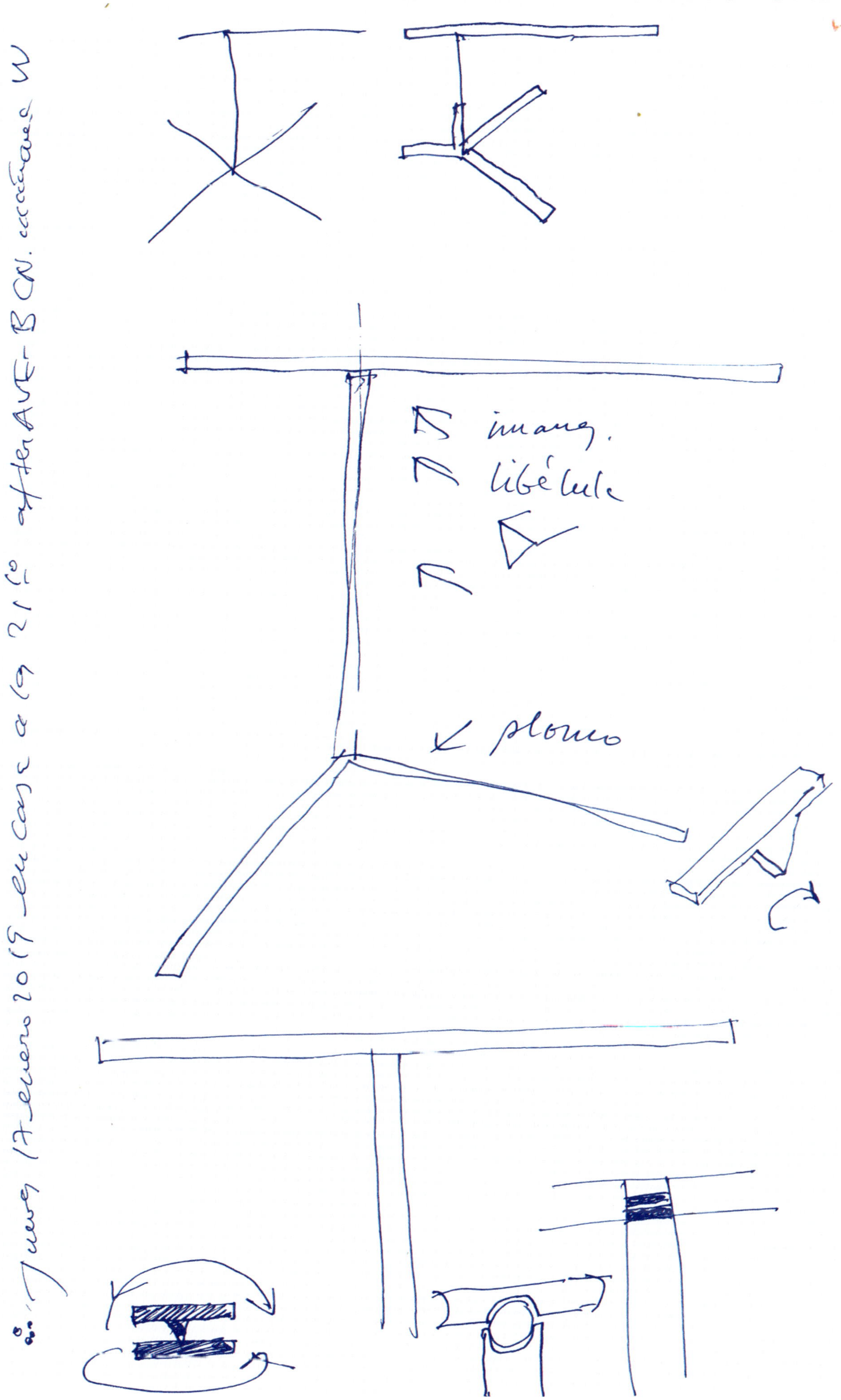
libélule
plomo

VENINI

ARCHIVAL SYSTEMS AT THE SERVICE OF HISTORY: VENINI LIGHTING THROUGH THE PERIOD CATALOGUES

Simona Larghi

Thanks to the analysis of the materials stored in the Venini archive it is possible to find a great deal of period evidence, particularly drawings and photographs, which have been used to describe the vast number of lighting projects implemented by the furnace between the 1920s and 1980s and so try to reconstruct the history of Venini production in this context. The results contained in the catalogue are the fruit of an experience that saw constant comparison between these primary sources and the documentary sources available. The study of the official Venini catalogues has proved fundamental for structuring a comprehensive analysis of the types of lighting which were designed and produced over these decades, whether for normal retail sales or for *ad hoc* projects. These documents, each of them reflecting a specific 'Zeitgeist', whether for the style of the units presented or the catalogue graphics used, were printed by the Venini firm several times and then mainly used internally, having already been distributed to retailers in Italy and abroad.

The reference point for the 1920s is the Venini catalogues containing the sconces and chandeliers with arms of Vittorio Zecchin and Napoleone Martinuzzi. [2] A selection of these models is to be found later in the Blue Catalogue, where models are documented for a period stretching from 1921 to 1942. In this catalogue, ongoing for all of the 1930s and up to 1942, some items can be identified as being the work of Tomaso Buzzi, Carlo Scarpa, Giulio Gatti Casazza and Antonio Cassi Ramelli.

The Red Catalogue, which covers lamps and chandeliers from 1948 to 1966, also includes some models from the Blue Catalogue and at the same time presents new solutions, such as the floor lamps of Fulvio Bianconi or the sconces and pendant lamps in *zanfirico* glass.

The end of the 1950s constitutes a crucial moment for the innovation of Venini lighting in so far as, at the same time as the serially produced lamps, an important modular type was created which would then make an important contribution to the years ahead. These were the *polyhedrons*, a famous series of sectional units of which very early evidence is to be found in a technical booklet, probably for internal use and intended for the furnace, which contains worksheets of these early models initially referred to as 'prisms'. This untitled document contains precious specifications about the number of elements in glass and of the 'remainder' (metal part) to be produced for each type of polyhedron lamp, including models nos. 5591 and 5592 which were exhibited at the Exposition Universelle et Internationale of Brussels and at the Vienna exhibition *Venedig Zeigt Glas aus Murano*, both in 1958. [3] The

[1] *Venini lighting catalogue*, 1969, cover

[2] Model no. 2033 with eighteen flames after a design by Vittorio Zecchin, Venini catalogue, 1920s

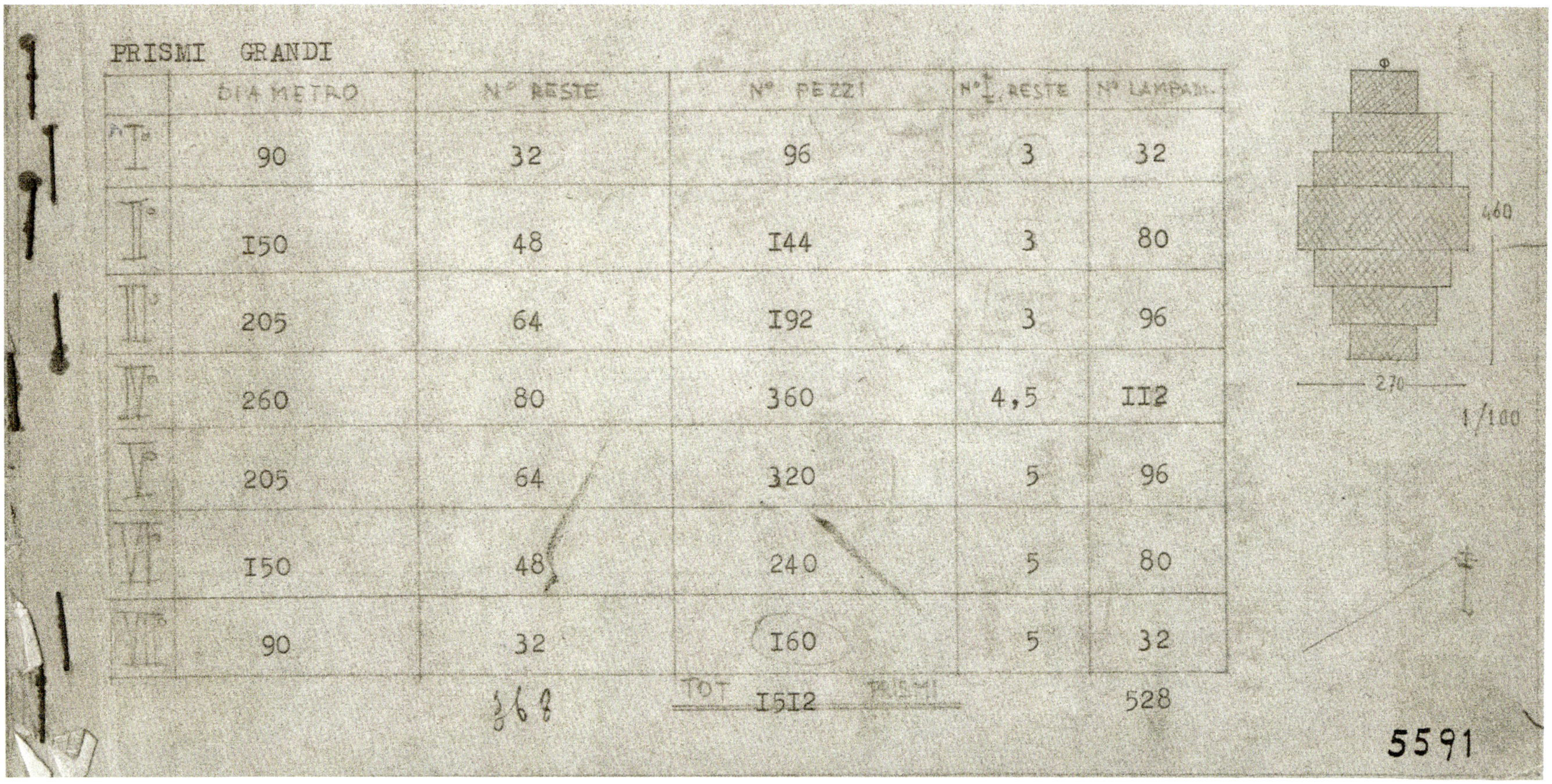

PRISMI GRANDI

	DIAMETRO	N° ASTE	N° PEZZI	N° ½ ASTE	N° LAMPAD.
I°	90	32	96	3	32
II°	150	48	144	3	80
III°	205	64	192	3	96
IV°	260	80	360	4,5	112
V°	205	64	320	5	96
VI°	150	48	240	5	80
VII°	90	32	160	5	32
		368	TOT 1512 PRISMI		528

[3] Technical sheet for the polyhedron chandelier (model no. 5591) exhibited at the Exposition Universelle of Brussels, Venini booklet, c. 1958

[4] Manchester Airport in *Venini impianti di illuminazione 2*, [1963], AHL

[5] View from below of the chandelier designed by Ignazio Gardella for the Olivetti store in Dusseldorf in *Venini impianti di illuminazione 2*, [1963], AHL

catalogue *Venini lighting* also belongs to the second half of the decade and included technical sheets for the lamps designed by Massimo Vignelli.
Another reliable support for the study of 1950s production is represented by two catalogues promoted by the Venini retailers in the United States. Around 1955 the catalogue *Contemporary Italian Lighting* was printed for the Altamira store founded in New York, and official Venini retailer in America. [6] Here can be found, for example, lamps *a fasce di colore* by Massimo Vignelli as well as the lamp designed by the BBPR group for the Olivetti store in New York (1954). A similar catalogue, also for the United States market, was published in the early 1960s under the title: *Venini LTD* (from the name of the company registered in the United States). [7]

The numerous catalogues of the 1960s and 1970s may be classified in two groups: on the one hand, the firm produced catalogues and booklets in which the models were included in accordance with their serial sequence and type, while on the other, a series of catalogues was published containing the sheets with the most important 'architectural lighting' projects. To this latter group belong: *Venini impianti di illuminazione* [1961] and *Venini impianti di illuminazione 2* [1963] in which one finds, for example, the sheets concerning the velarium of Palazzo Grassi (1951), the chandeliers produced for the Manchester Airport (1961) and the chandelier, designed by Ignazio Gardella, for the Olivetti store in Dusseldorf (1960-61). [4, 5] To the first category belongs the *Venini lighting catalogue*, printed in October 1966 after a design by the Bellavitis & Valle firm. This was the first publication in which a selection of catalogued chandeliers and lamps was presented (e.g. lamp no. 800.2 designed by Franco Albini in 1954 for the auditorium of the Triennale of Milan) to which was added a section dedicated to modular compositions (e.g. the series *bricole*, *ghiaccioli*, *poliedri* and *triangolo*). Each model is presented in the form of a technical sheet which includes information about the type of glass, the colours and the mounting used. An updated catalogue of the same kind was printed in 1969: also entitled *Venini lighting catalogue* and designed by Bellavitis & Valle, it remains a reference point for the analysis of the production, in series and modular, previous to the 1970s. [1, 9] In the section *Venini architectural lighting catalogue* the modules *fiorito*, *esprit*, *trilobi*, *totem* and *cheerio* are presented for the first time. Some table lamps, excluded from this catalogue, are however present in the 1969 Green Catalogue.
Also from the 1960s there are at least two booklets to be considered which show the different types of patterned glass then in production (*Venini*, 1965, and *Tabella Venini*, 1969), such as *bambù* glass, *cerchi* glass and *stellare* glass. [8] Some of these types of patterned glass were already well represented in the production of the previous decades and were taken up again here and produced with new variations.

In January 1970 *Venini illuminazione d'architettura*, a collection of 'architectural lighting' projects, was published; [10] a few years later, following the same principle, *Venini lavori di illuminazione 1973* (1972) and *Venini illuminazione d'architettura 1974* (1973) came out. In 1973 *Venini nuovo catalogo di illuminazione 73* was printed, which included the technical sheets for the lamps *Ninfea*, *Omotto*, *Membrane* and *Farfallone* designed by Toni Zuccheri and the Venini lamps *Car 70* for Pierre Cardin. A complete overview of the models that came into production in the early 1970s can be found in *Venini 75: Catalogo di illuminazione* which is divided into three sections: *Lampade*, *Lampadari* and *Sistemi per forniture*. Some of the designers are mentioned here, among whom Pierre Cardin, Toni Zuccheri and Mario Ticcò, who collaborated in those years in the creation of new lighting units. [12] The last section (*Sistemi per forniture*) is dedicated to the types of glass with which it was possible to create new fixtures in different forms and sizes (cfr., *Venini 75 Catalogue: Sistemi per Forniture*, in this catalogue, pp. 609-615) . Throughout the decade catalogues of different kinds were printed, such as the *Venini* catalogue [1970] with the lamps of Roberto Menghi, Ornella Noorda [11] and Sergio Asti, the *Venini* card catalogue [1972-73], the *Venini* poster (1974), the *Luce 76* brochure (1976), the *Venini illuminazione d'archittetura* catalogue [1978] and the booklets *Venini 1929/1978 catalogo vetri* (1978) and *Venini. Catalogo di illuminazione* (c. 1978).

The catalogue of the 1980s with the most information is called *Venini* and is a large ring binder with a selection of the most interesting modular pieces produced for 'architectural lighting' of the previous decades. Printed in 1985, it is subdivided into 15 sections, each of which is dedicated to a specific category. There are, for example, the sections: *Asta*, *Canne*, *Poliedri*, *Alga*, *Esprit* etc. [13] In this context certain terms are revised according to the use of the time: in particular, the terms *asta*, *canna* and *tubi* are differentiated. In the section *Lampadari* new versions of chandeliers in vogue in the 1930s and 1940s are proposed. Worthy of mention among the other catalogues of the same period is the catalogue *Venini,* a ring binder with a light blue cover, containing lamps designed by Ludovico Diaz de Santillana (*Tricorno*, *Tolboi*, *Smolboi*, *Victor Victoria*, *Alabastro*), Alessandro Diaz de Santillana (*Ustorio*) and Laura de Santillana (*Sigul*).

[6] *Contemporary Italian Lighting*, catalogue of the Altamira store in New York, [c. 1955]

[7] Pendant lamps, *Venini LTD* catalogue for the United States market, 1960s

[8] Sconce in *bambù* glass, *Venini*, 1965, booklet

[9] '1969 New Ideas on lighting by Venini', *Venini lighting catalogue*, 1969

[10] *Palazzo Uffici Olivetti, Venini illuminazione d'architettura*, 1970

[11] *Light-Ice* table lamp (model no. 817.1) after a design by Ornella Noorda, *Venini,* [1970]

[12] *Car 70* lamps (series no. 820), *Venini 75: Catalogo di illuminazione*, 1975

[13] 'Sezione 2 / Canna', *Venini*, 1985

altamira
BENAVEDE, INC.
125 East 55th St.
New York 22, N. Y.
Telephone: PLaza 3-7644
Cable: Altamira, New York
Contemporary Italian Lighting...
AR-12128 Triennale floor lamp.
Polished brass or polished chromium tripod base, stem and arms. Shades and handles in choice of red, black, white, blue, yellow or gray; custom colors at slight additional expense. Shades and arms are adjustable. 62½" high stem; 45" maximum width. Foot
are included. Shipped partially assembled.
AV-4040BV table lamp.
Blue and white table lamp shown.
(Display Box Not Part of Lamp)
AV-5457 lamp.
Multi-pastel shown.
(color combination #3)
All glass lighting shown in this brochure is hand-blown and hand-rolled Venetian glass created by Venini of Murano, Venice, Italy. Because of limitations in color photography, we cannot guarantee the exact shades of various colors. No two glass
will ever be precisely the same and the occasional presence of a small bubble or other variation is not a

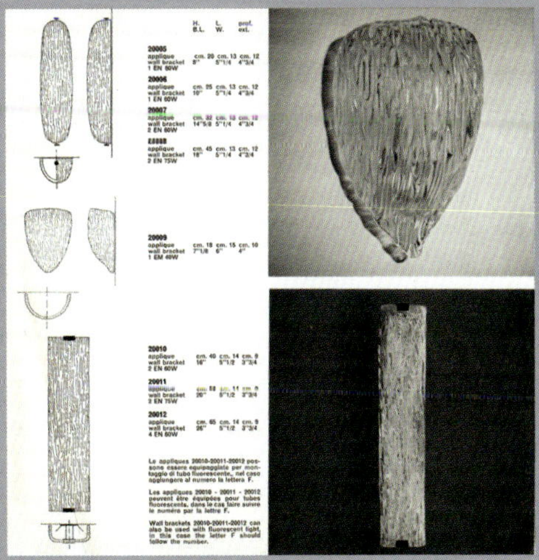

LIGHT-ICE
Design: Ornella Noorda

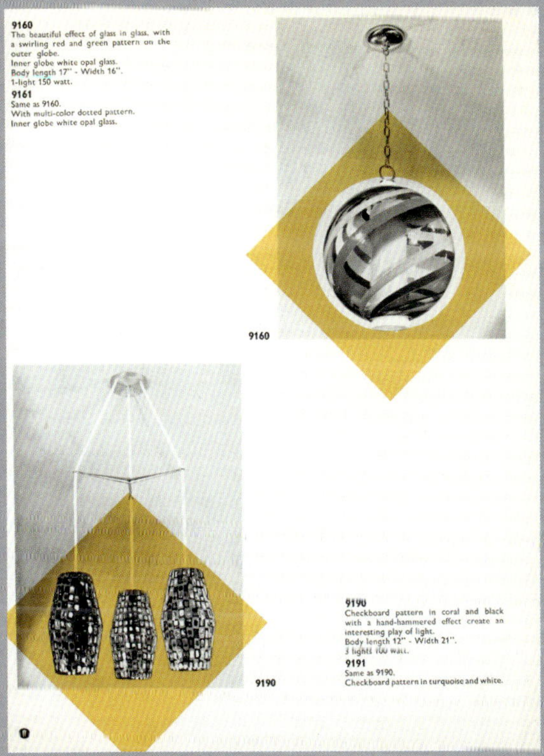
9160
The beautiful effect of glass in glass, with a swirling red and green pattern on the outer globe.
Inner globe white opal glass.
Body length 17" - Width 16".
1-light 150 watt.
9161
Same as 9160.
With multi-color dotted pattern.
Inner globe white opal glass.
9160
9190
Checkboard pattern in coral and black with a hand-hammered effect create an interesting play of light.
Body length 12" - Width 21".
9191
Same as 9190.
Checkboard pattern in turquoise and white.
9190

VENINI
ARCHITECTURAL
LIGHTING
CATALOGUE
81/91
1969 New Ideas on lighting by Venini
May we draw your attention to some of our new ideas on lighting.
In our complete line you will find chandeliers, pendants, floor and table lamps, wall-brackets; all in the most sophisticated and refined VENINI glass techniques and colours.
If you wish more informations about these models, and many more, please ask for our general lighting catalogue.
We are also at your disposal for special designs and for architectural lighting projects. Our long experience with installations all over the world enables us to design just the type of fixture you need for your particular location.
If you would like us to help you, give us information as to sizes desidered, shape selected, room dimensions, and maximum wattage available.
963.8

820
car 70

Olivetti, Palazzo Uffici, Ivrea, 1964
Soffittatura vano scale, in elementi corrugati esagonali da 40 cm., massima dimensione ml. 13.
Lighting ceiling on the staircase well hexagonal corrugated glass elements (16"), maximum size 45'.
Deckenbekleidung für Treppenhaus aus sechseckigen gerunzelten Elementen à 40 cm., Höchstlänge 13 m.
Venini, Venezia, 1967
Soffitto luminoso in lastre ondulate di vetro «impasto» (cm. 90 x 25).
Lighting ceiling in ondulated glass «impasto» (36" x 10").
Deckenbeleuchtung aus wellenförmigen «impasto» - Glasplatten (90 x 25 cm.).

Sezione 2/Canna
Scheda 2.0

PROJECTS 1921-1985

Marino Barovier and Carla Sonego

A chronological overview is presented here of the lighting projects completed by the furnace between 1922 and 1985 and of which there is evidence in the Venini archive. The works have been arranged on the basis of the handwritten chronology drawn up in the 1970s by Emma Lanci (employed in the glassworks since the 1920s and 'historic' associate of Paolo Venini) from the lists of works present in the catalogues *Venini lavori di illuminazione 1973* (1972) and *Venini* (1985), and also from the documentation coming from the archive of the Caliari firm, the Venini retailer in Turin. The chronologies have been verified, and where possible amplified, by cross-checking between published sources and archive materials. The period photographs and drawings published, where not otherwise specified, come from the Archivio Storico Venini, Murano.

LIST OF ABBREVIATIONS PHOTOGRAPHIC ARCHIVES

AC	Caliari Archive, Turin
AHL	Howard Lockwood Archive, Fort Lee (NJ – USA)
AMH	Marc Heiremans Archive, Brussels
MART	Mart, Archivio del '900, Fondo Angiolo Mazzoni, Rovereto
MAXXI	MAXXI Museo nazionale delle arti del XXI secolo, Roma. Collezione MAXXI Architettura

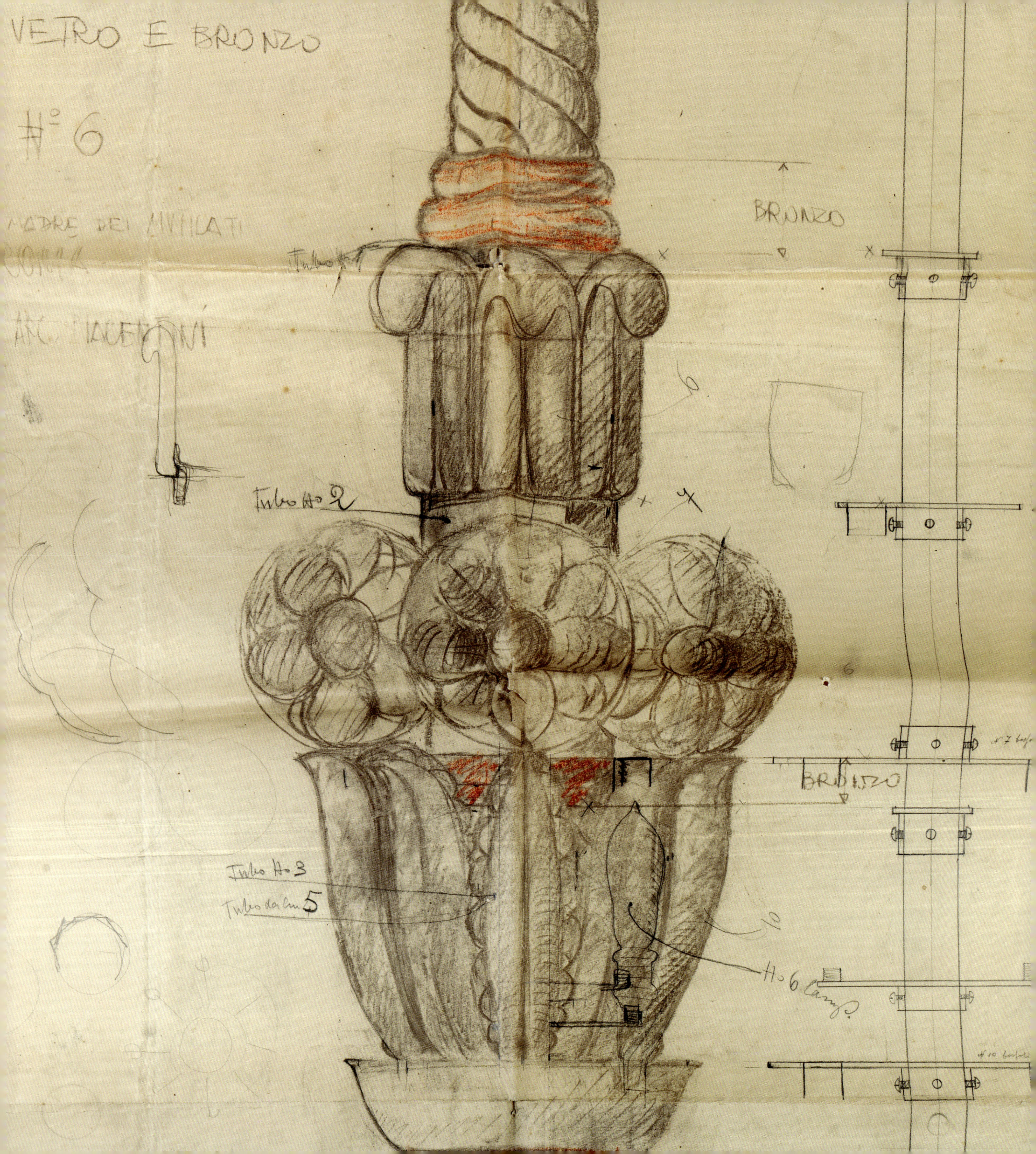
VETRO E BRONZO
N° 6
BRONZO
BRONZO

1920s

1922

MILAN (IT)
MILAN FAIR
DESIGN V. ZECCHIN

WITH ARMS
PENDANT

The debut of the glassworks V.S.M. Cappellin Venini & C. at a public event took place through participation in the third edition of the Milan Fair. Together with dinner services and decorative items, some examples of chandeliers in the style of old oil lamps were also presented.

1922

VENICE (IT)
XIII ESPOSIZIONE INTERNAZIONALE D'ARTE DELLA CITTÀ DI VENEZIA
DESIGN V. ZECCHIN

WITH ARMS

On the occasion of the Venetian event the glassworks presented a large chandelier after the design of Vittorio Zecchin, in the vestibule of the Central Pavilion.

1923

MONZA (IT)
I MOSTRA INTERNAZIONALE DELLE ARTI DECORATIVE
DESIGN V. ZECCHIN

WITH ARMS

On the occasion of the first Monza exhibition the V.S.M. Cappellin Venini & C. exhibited a series of glass pieces and some chandeliers after the design of Vittorio Zecchin, which were placed in different areas. Five chandeliers (entered in the catalogue under no. 2036) were located in the foyer of the first floor; on the same floor there was a chandelier in room 2, reserved for the Book Fair (model no. 2033), in room 17 reserved for glassworks (model no. 2028), in room 19, with various exhibitors (model no. 2035), in room 47 with table glassware, and in room 25 dedicated to the textile products of Cotoniere Meridionali (model no. 2013).

>
I MOSTRA INTERNAZIONALE DELLE ARTI DECORATIVE
Chandeliers in the foyer of the first floor. Period photograph, 1923

>>
I MOSTRA INTERNAZIONALE DELLE ARTI DECORATIVE
Chandeliers in the foyer of the first floor. Period photograph, 1923

«
I MOSTRA INTERNAZIONALE DELLE ARTI DECORATIVE
Chandelier in Room 2, Book Fair. Period photograph, 1923
›
I MOSTRA INTERNAZIONALE DELLE ARTI DECORATIVE
Chandelier in room 19. Period photograph, 1923

1924

VENICE (IT)
XIV ESPOSIZIONE INTERNAZIONALE D'ARTE DELLA CITTÀ DI VENEZIA
DESIGN V. ZECCHIN

WITH ARMS
PENDANT

The V.S.M. Cappellin Venini & C. participated in the Venetian event by exhibiting in an area adjoining the Rotonda, vases, 'street lights' and chandeliers.

1925

MONZA (IT)
II MOSTRA INTERNAZIONALE DELLE ARTI DECORATIVE
DESIGN V. ZECCHIN

WITH ARMS

On the occasion of the second Monza event, the last in which Giacomo Cappellin and Paolo Venini appeared as associates, the glassworks participated by exhibiting, among other things, chandelier models after the design of Vittorio Zecchin.Some of these (model no. 2042) were located in the foyer on the first floor, others (model no. 2039) were in the Dining Hall, while a further luminaire was placed in the foyer of the second floor.

>
II MOSTRA INTERNAZIONALE DELLE ARTI DECORATIVE
Chandelier no. 2039, in G. Marangoni, *Le arti del fuoco: ceramica, vetri, vetrate*, Turin 1927, plate 110

>
II MOSTRA INTERNAZIONALE DELLE ARTI DECORATIVE
Chandelier in the foyer of the first floor. Period photograph, 1925

>>
II MOSTRA INTERNAZIONALE DELLE ARTI DECORATIVE
Chandeliers in the foyer of the first floor. Period photograph, 1925

1925

PARIS (FR)
EXPOSITION INTERNATIONALE DES ARTS DÉCORATIFS ET INDUSTRIEL MODERNES
DESIGN V. ZECCHIN

WITH ARMS

On the occasion of the Paris event the V.S.M. Cappellin Venini & C. produced, for the Italian pavilion, a large chandelier in eight tiers (h 470 cm, max Ø 200 cm) designed by Vittorio Zecchin and described by the critic Ugo Nebbia as 'a jaunty Murano glass rocket' (*Emporium*, July 1925). It consists of a three-tiered pendant lamp with thirty-six lights and arms and corollas in smoked-coulored glass with finishings in green glass. The upper level, which is purely decorative, is characterised by forty-eight swirls of transparent green glass. The model is entered in the V.S.M. Venini & C. catalogue in the variant with six to twelve lights (no. 2066) and a version with fifty-four lights is to be found in that of M.V.M. Cappellin & C. (no. 1908). The chandelier belongs to the collection of the Musée des Arts Decoratifs in Paris.

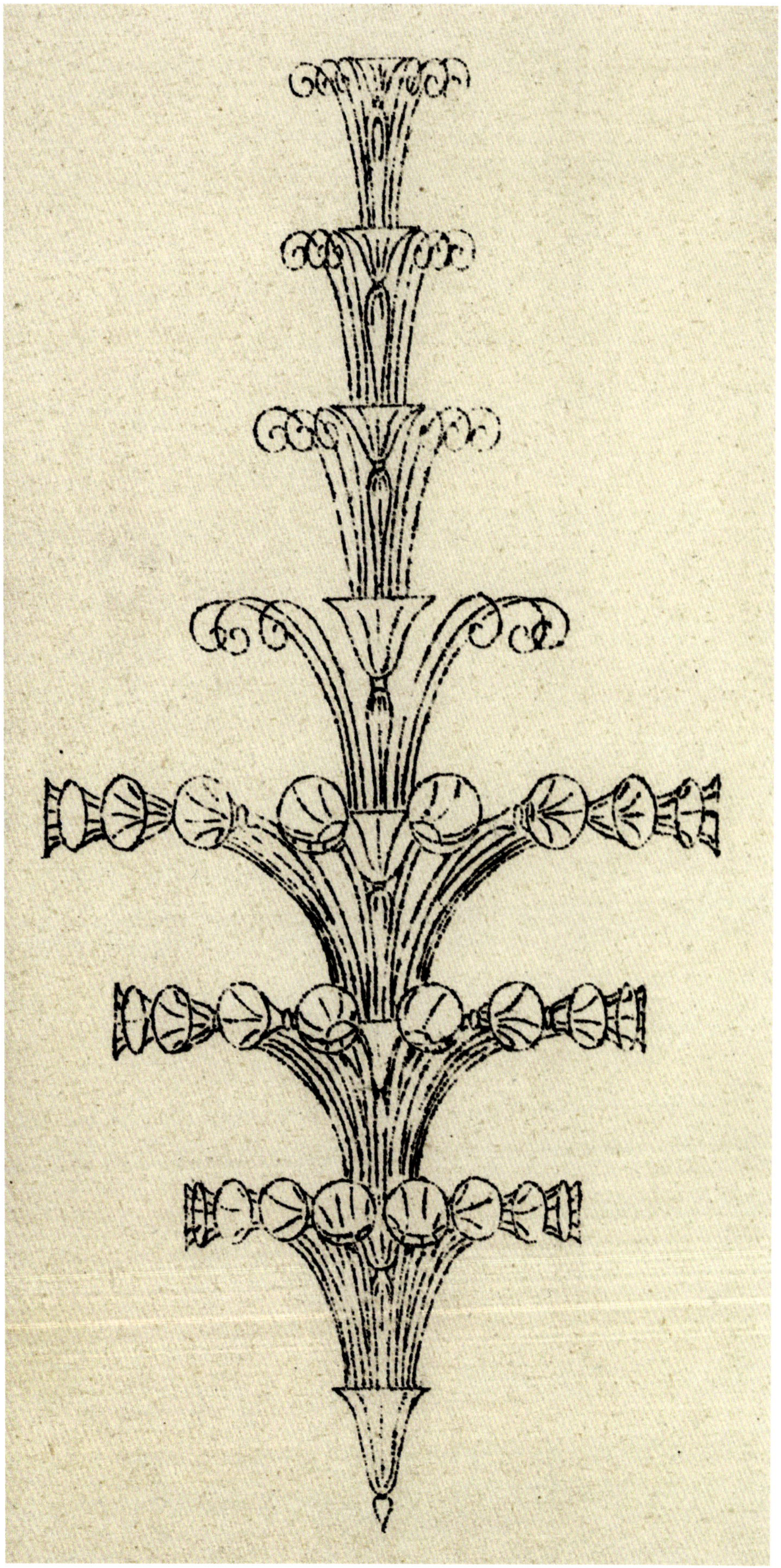

>
EXPOSITION INTERNATIONALE DES ARTS DÉCORATIFS ET INDUSTRIEL MODERNES
Drawing for chandelier with fifty-four lights in the M.V.M. Cappellin & C. catalogue

>>
EXPOSITION INTERNATIONALE DES ARTS DÉCORATIFS ET INDUSTRIEL MODERNES
Chandelier with thirty-six lights in the Italian pavilion.
Period photograph, 1925

G.TOLLERI

1926

FLORENCE (IT)
CAPPELLA ALLA MADRE ITALIANA
DESIGN N. MARTINUZZI

WALL LAMPS

The Madre Italiana votive chapel or Capponi chapel, in the left transept of the Chiesa di Santa Croce [Holy Cross Church], was inaugurated on 4 November 1926. In the area, on which Libero Andreotti worked, the Venini glassworks supplied four wall lamps with nine arms in transparent amethyst glass (the model is entered in the catalogue under no. 2129).

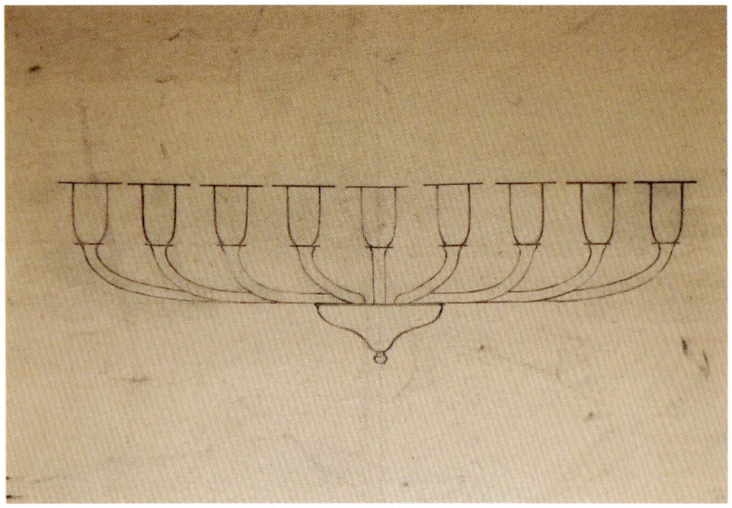

>
CAPPELLA ALLA MADRE ITALIANA
Drawing for the nine-light wall lamp, c. 1926

1926

ROME (IT)
ARGENTINA THEATRE
DESIGN N. MARTINUZZI

WITH ARMS

For the restoration overseen by Marcello Piacentini (1926), the Venini glassworks created several lighting systems for the 18th-century theatre building, already restructured several times in the 19th century. The Venini intervention consisted in particular of chandeliers with twenty-four lights after a design of Napoleone Martinuzzi (model entered in the catalogue under no. 2083, h 150 cm) and corresponding wall lamps with five lights (no. 2131), positioned in the colonnaded foyer. For the theatre auditorium numerous three-light wall lamps in ribbed glass were produced, placed at the five levels corresponding to the tiers of the boxes (no. 2132). These last mentioned are still *in situ*.

>
ARGENTINA THEATRE
Chandeliers and wall lamps with arms in the foyer.
Period photograph, c. 1927

>>
ARGENTINA THEATRE
Lighting of the auditorium with wall lamps having three lights.
Period photograph, c. 1927

1926

ROME (IT)
ALBERGO DEGLI AMBASCIATORI

WITH ARMS

Lighting project for the building designed by the architect Marcello Piacentini in collaboration with the artist Emilio Vogt. The contribution of the glassworks is documented, inter alia, by a drawing in the Venini archives with a design for *cesendello* lamps in iridised *cristallo* with thin *rigadin* ribbing to be placed in the lobby of the hotel. On this occasion chandeliers with twelve lights were produced (entered in the catalogue under no. 2091, Black Book, Venini) and wall lamps, model 2148, probably designed by Napoleone Martinuzzi.

1926

VENICE (IT)
XV ESPOSIZIONE INTERNAZIONALE D'ARTE DELLA CITTÀ DI VENEZIA

DESIGN N. MARTINUZZI

WITH ARMS

For the Venetian event, apart from vases and a glass fountain, the glassworks produced a large chandelier in transparent amethyst glass which was installed in the rotunda decorated by Galileo Chini (room 2). Both the chandelier (indicated in the catalogue under no. 2067), and the other Venini artefacts followed the design of Napoleone Martinuzzi, at the time Artistic Director of the V.S.M. Venini e c.

>
ALBERGO DEGLI AMBASCIATORI
Model no. 2091 for twelve lights chandelier

>>
XV ESPOSIZIONE INTERNAZIONALE D'ARTE
DELLA CITTÀ DI VENEZIA
Chandelier in transparent amethyst glass. Period photograph, 1926

1926-30 GARDONE RIVIERA (IT)

VITTORIALE DEGLI ITALIANI

DESIGN V. ZECCHIN, N. MARTINUZZI

WITH ARMS
WALL LAMPS
PENDANT
TABLE

A trusted adviser of Gabriele D'Annunzio, Napoleone Martinuzzi was involved personally as an intermediary between the poet and the glassworks for the creation of various lighting systems for the Vittoriale, D'Annunzio's imposing residence. From 1926 to about 1930 several lights intended for the Prioria and Casseretto (residence of the architect Gian Carlo Maroni) arrived in Gardone whether commissioned by the poet or as a gift from the sculptor. In some cases these were chandeliers already present in the catalogue and designed by Vittorio Zecchin, in others were original artefacts designed specifically by Martinuzzi for the Poet. Examples of the first case are the chandelier in *cristallo* and dark-blue glass (model no. 2001) located in the Stanza del Mappamondo [Globe Room] and the chandelier in transparent green glass (model no. 2026) in the guests' bathroom. In particular, the Murano artist was the author of the highly colourful luminous pumpkins in yellow and light-blue cased glass, located in the Music Room and produced around 1927-28. Between 1928 and 1930 the cornucopia chandelier in *lattimo* cased glass and smoked glass with application of gold leaf and in *ghiaccio* glass for the Stanza del Mascheraio [Mask-Maker's Room] were created.

>
VITTORIALE DEGLI ITALIANI
Cornucopia chandelier in the Stanza del Mascheraio. Archive photograph

>>
VITTORIALE DEGLI ITALIANI
Chandelier in the Stanza del Mappamondo. Archive photograph

>
VITTORIALE DEGLI ITALIANI
Luminous pumpkin in the Stanza della Musica. Archive photograph

>>
VITTORIALE DEGLI ITALIANI
Glass pieces after a design by Napoleone Martinuzzi in the Stanza della Musica. Archive photograph

TENERA'

1927

MILAN (IT)
ALLA PENNA D'OCA RESTAURANT

TUBE-SHAPED

For the refurbishing of the Milanese restaurant, carried out by the Il Labirinto group, the Venini firm created a few lighting systems. These were tubular in opaline glass probably designed by Tomaso Buzzi.

1927

MONZA (IT)
III MOSTRA INTERNAZIONALE DELLE ARTI DECORATIVE

DESIGN N. MARTINUZZI

WALL LAMPS
PENDANT

In this third recurrence of the Monza exhibition, V.S.M. Venini e c. participated by exhibiting glass pieces and various lighting systems which were installed in different areas. Mostly these were lamps designed by the new Artistic Director, Napoleone Martinuzzi, such as the pendant lights (model no. 2097) installed in the lobby of the first floor. Also attributable to the sculptor were a chandelier located in Room 42, reserved for the Jesurum firm, the lamps in Room 44, where Il Labirinto exhibited, and the chandelier and some wall-lamps with arms and nine lights (model no. 2149) in the main hall. As documented by the exhibition catalogue, other fixtures were installed in Room 72, various exhibitors ('lamp'), and on the second floor in the lounge curated by Luisa Lovarini, Room 94 ('chandelier'). Finally, in the bedroom furnished by Giovanni Berardi, Room 128, a 'chandelier' and a 'lamp' were installed.

>
III MOSTRA INTERNAZIONALE DELLE ARTI DECORATIVE
Venini wall lights and glass pieces in the main hall.
Period photograph, 1927

1927

ROME (IT)
II MOSTRA NAZIONALE D'ARTE MARINARA
DESIGN N. MARTINUZZI

WITH ARMS

The glassworks took part in the Rome exhibition with the installation, not only of a fountain in the so-called 'Nido delle sirene' room , but also a chandelier with fifteen lights, with ribbed cups and in three tiers of ribbed bands with curled extremities. The fixture was catalogued under no. 5001.

>
II MOSTRA NAZIONALE D'ARTE MARINARA
Model no. 5001, Blue Catalogue

>
II MOSTRA NAZIONALE D'ARTE MARINARA
Fifteen-light chandelier in transparent glass.
Period photograph, 1927

>
II MOSTRA NAZIONALE D'ARTE MARINARA
'Nido delle sirene' room. At the back the Venini chandelier can be seen. Period photograph, 1927

1928
1936

ROME (IT)
CASA MADRE DEI MUTILATI

WALL LAMPS
PENDANT
FLOOR

Inaugurated on 4 November, on the occasion of the 10th anniversary of the end of the First World War, the monumental building was constructed after a design by the architect Marcello Piacentini. The Venini firm was called upon to produce several lighting fixtures arising out of the collaboration between the architect and Napoleone Martinuzzi, in his role as Artistic Director of the glass-works. These were six chandeliers in green *pulegoso* glass installed in the alcoves of the vestibule above the main stairway and are documented by an archive drawing dated 20 January 1928. On the first floor there was a *cesendello* chandelier in transparent glass. A second intervention took place in 1936 in which lamps of two different sizes were placed in the stairwell. These fixtures are still *in situ*.

>
CASA MADRE DEI MUTILATI
Main staircase with *cesendello* lamp on the first floor.
Period photograph, 1928

>>
CASA MADRE DEI MUTILATI
Main staircase. Period photograph, 1928

MCM XXVIII

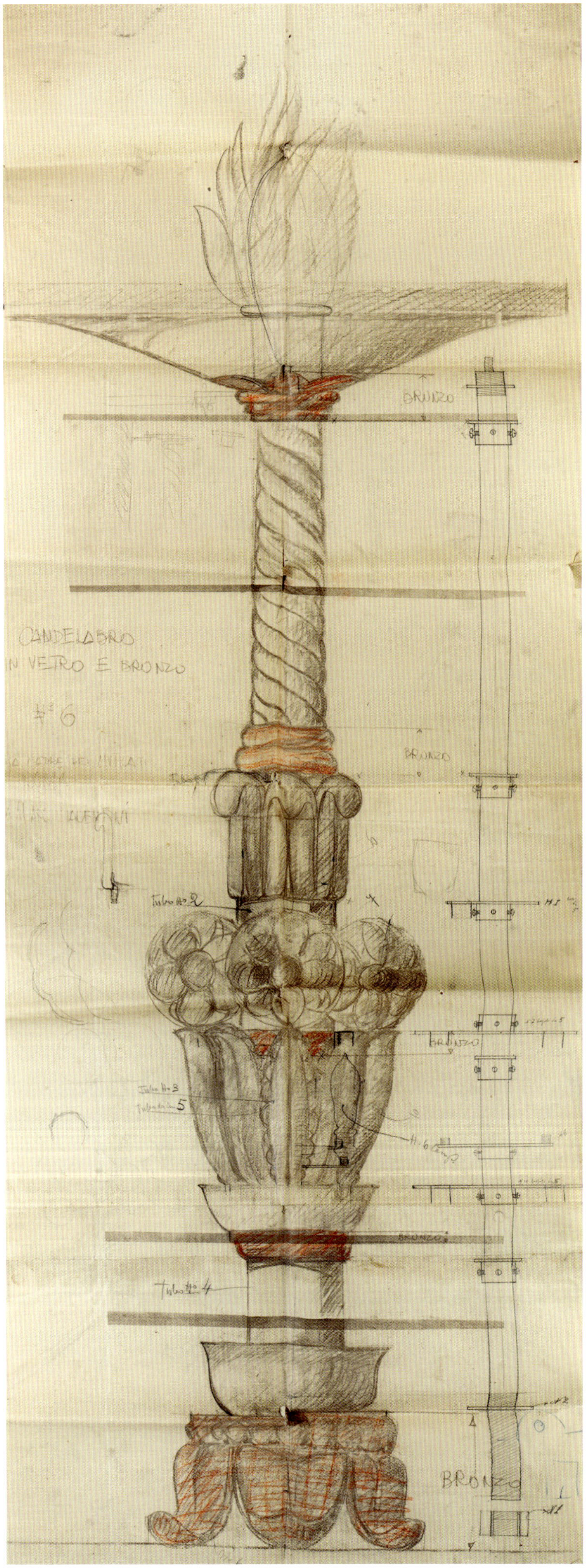

›
CASA MADRE DEI MUTILATI
Drawing of the candelabrum in green *pulegoso* glass, 1928

›
CASA MADRE DEI MUTILATI
Candelabrum in green *pulegoso* glass. Period photograph 1928

1929 BARCELONA (ES)

EXPOSICIÓN INTERNACIONAL DE BARCELONA

WALL LAMPS
PENDANT
FLOOR

On the occasion of the Spanish event, the glassworks participated by exhibiting chandeliers and lamps in transparent glass, mostly designed by Napoleone Martinuzzi. From left to right can be seen: a *cesendello* chandelier with ribbed elements (no. 5007), a nine-light wall lamp (no. 2149), a fifteen-light chandelier (no. 5001), a two-light wall light (no. 2156), a lamp with three superimposed upside-down bells in *cristallo pulegoso* glass (of the no. 5026 type) and a chandelier with six lights (no. 2028). Among these, models 2149 and 5001 were exhibited for the first time respectively at the 3rd International Exhibition of Decorative Arts of Monza (1927) and the 2nd National Maritime Art Exhibition of Rome (1927).

1929 FLORENCE (IT)

MODERNISSIMO CINEMA

Lighting project for the Florence cinema.

1929 MILAN (IT)

UNIVERSITÀ CATTOLICA DEL SACRO CUORE

WALL LAMPS

For the premises designed by the architect Giovanni Muzio, the glassworks contributed lighting systems which are documented by archive drawings. These included a group of wall lamps 'a prisma' [prism-shaped] in *cristallo* glass and a lamp in *pulegoso* glass illustrated in a document dated 26 September 1929.

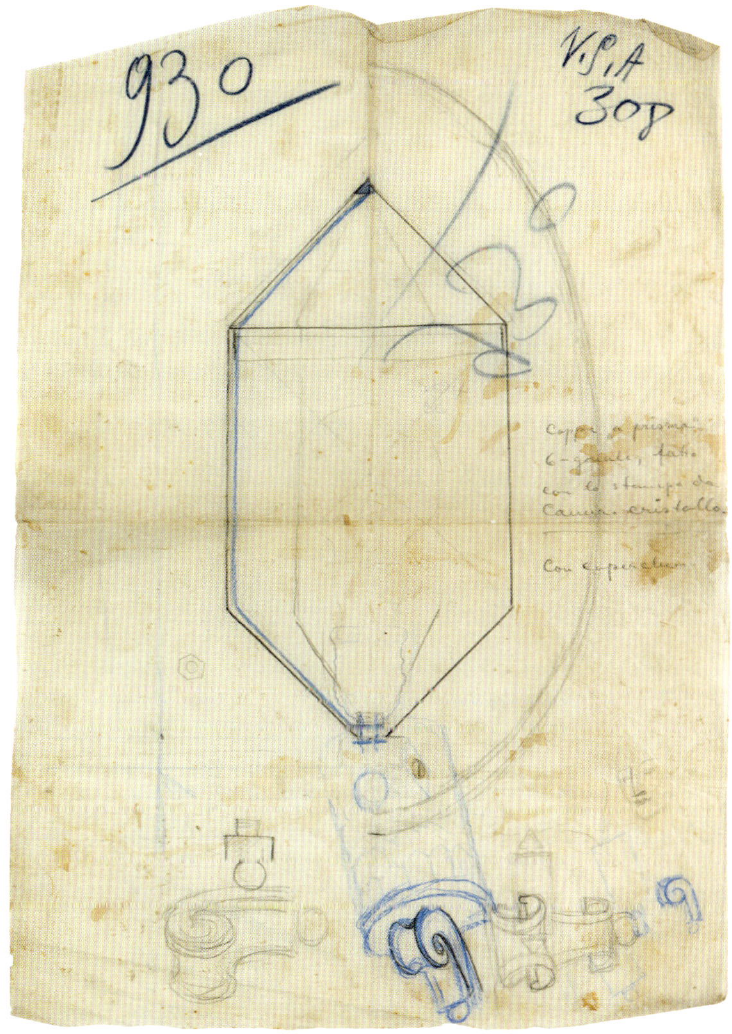

›
EXPOSICIÓN INTERNACIONAL DE BARCELONA
Venini Showcase. Period photograph, 1929

›
UNIVERSITÀ CATTOLICA DEL SACRO CUORE
Design for six *a prisma* lights, c. 1929

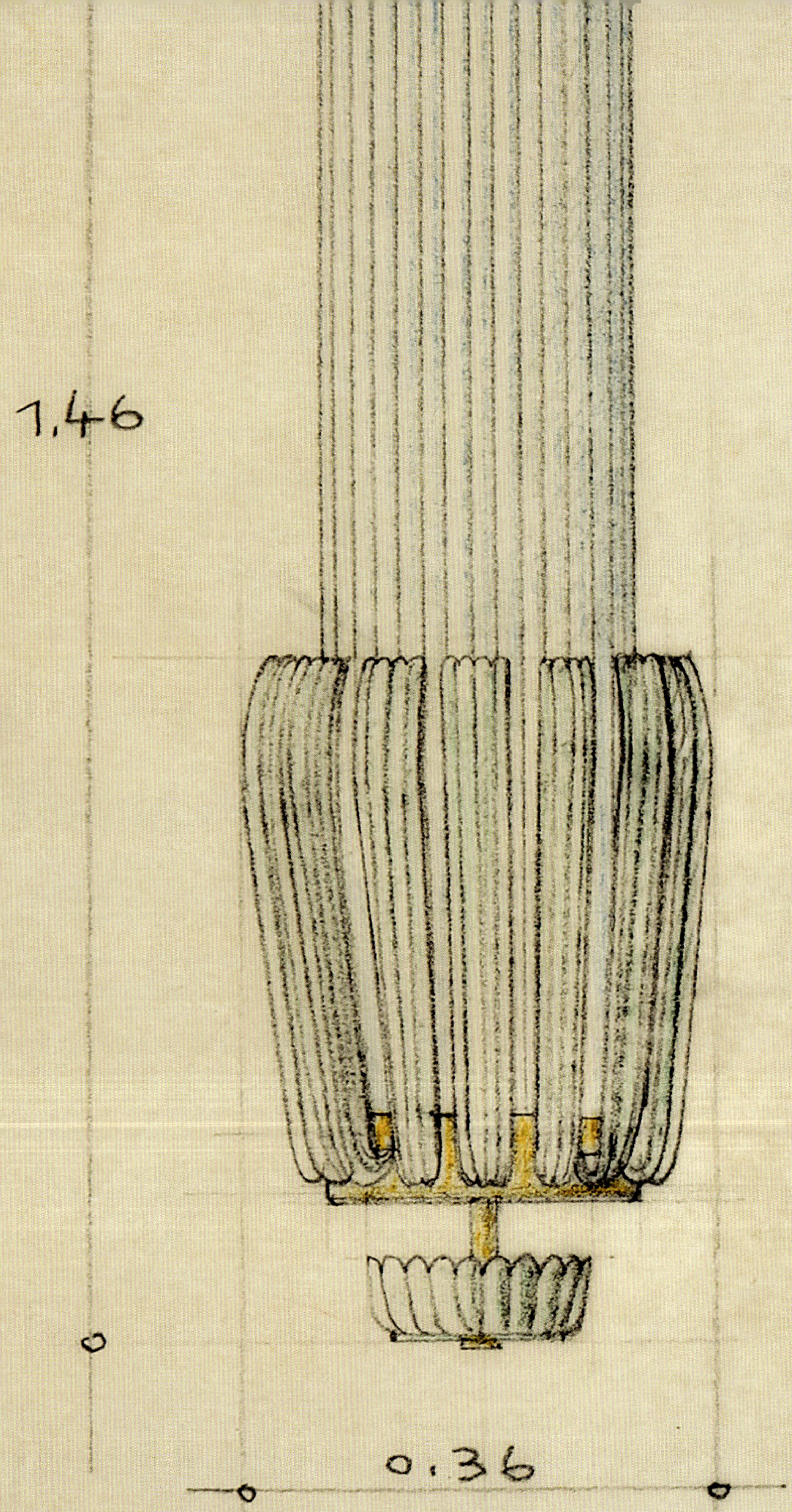

1,46
0.36

1930s

1930

FERRARA (IT)
POST OFFICE BUILDING
DESIGN N. MARTINUZZI

WALL LAMPS
TABLE

After a troubled construction history, the building, designed by Angiolo Mazzoni starting in 1926, was inaugurated on first of June 1930. The glassworks were involved particularly in the public hall with the installation of six sconces and two luminous 'fountains' after a design by Napoleone Martinuzzi, to whom we also owe the stuccowork of the lintels and vault, dedicated to the myth of Phaeton. The sconces, in the form of urns with covers, are in smoked-coulored cased glass with finishings in turquoise glass. The same colours are also used in the two 'fountains' (h c. 120 cm) formed by the superimposing of five ribbed bell-shaped elements on top of which a polychrome glass fruit is placed. Installed above the high desks, the light source of the 'fountains' is at the base and hidden by a metallic screen.

>
POST OFFICE BUILDING
Corner of the hall with wall lamp and luminous 'fountain'. Period photograph, MART

>
POST OFFICE BUILDING
Public hall. Period photograph, MART

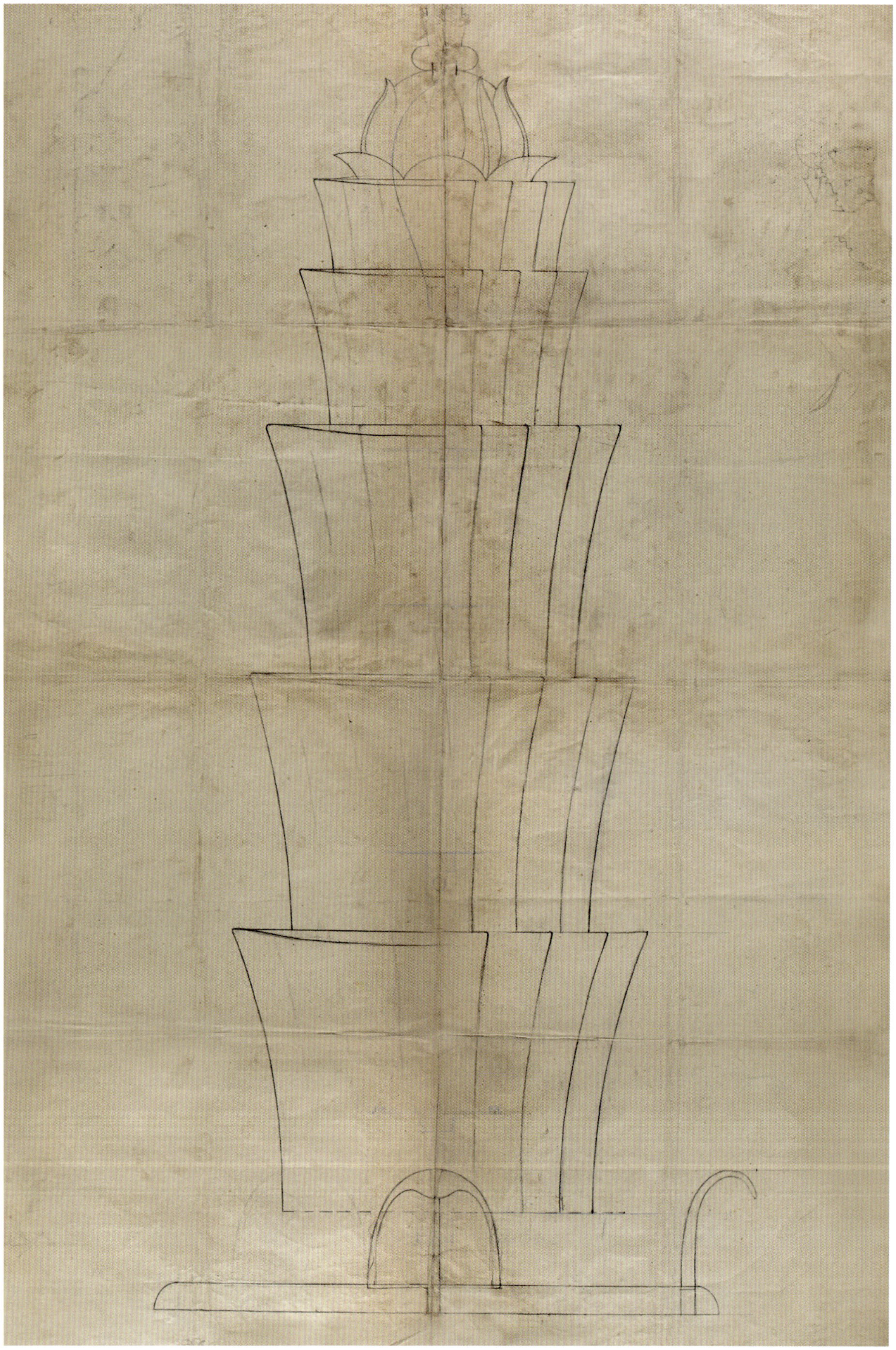

>
POST OFFICE BUILDING
Design for luminous 'fountain', c. 1929

>
POST OFFICE BUILDING
Sconce in cased glass. Archive photograph

>>
POST OFFICE BUILDING
Public hall with luminous 'fountain'. Archive photograph

1930

MONZA (IT)
IV ESPOSIZIONE TRIENNALE INTERNAZIONALE DELLE ARTI DECORATIVE ED INDUSTRIALI MODERNE

WALL LAMPS
CEILING
PENDANT
TABLE

On the occasion of the fourth Monza exhibition the V.S.M. Venini & C. participated by exhibiting, apart from a series of glass pieces, numerous lighting fixtures for the most part after the design of the Artistic Director, Napoleone Martinuzzi. Worthy of particular attention among these are the luminous 'milestones' in yellow cased glass, located in the entrance staircase, and the luminous cornice in white *pulegoso* glass placed at the base of the entrance hall dome. The latter space is lit also by four chandeliers composed of superimposed upside-down bells, also in white *pulegoso* glass. Various lamps (wall lights, ceiling lights, hanging lights, table lights) are to be found on the second floor in various areas of the Furniture Gallery (studio, designed by Paolo Buffa and Antonio Cassi Ramelli; library, designed by Roberto Papini etc.), in the Glass and Ceramic Gallery and in the section that the Triennale dedicated for the first time to the theme of light (Lighting Gallery). Apart from some hanging lamps and original 'torch holders' with sheets in *pulegoso* glass and unusual table lamps with bases consisting of a sort of aquarium, after the design of Martinuzzi, here there were also lights designed by Michele Marelli and Luigi Piccinato in metal and cased glass. Other lamps are present in the 'Casa del dopolavorista' [workers' free-time club], which was developed in the park after a design by Luisa Lovarini. Some of these pieces were exhibited the following year at the glass, ceramic and lace exhibition of Amsterdam.

>
IV ESPOSIZIONE TRIENNALE INTERNAZIONALE DELLE ARTI DECORATIVE ED INDUSTRIALI MODERNE
Entrance hall. Period photograph, 1930

>>
IV ESPOSIZIONE TRIENNALE INTERNAZIONALE DELLE ARTI DECORATIVE ED INDUSTRIALI MODERNE
Luminous 'milestones' in the stairway. Period photograph, 1930

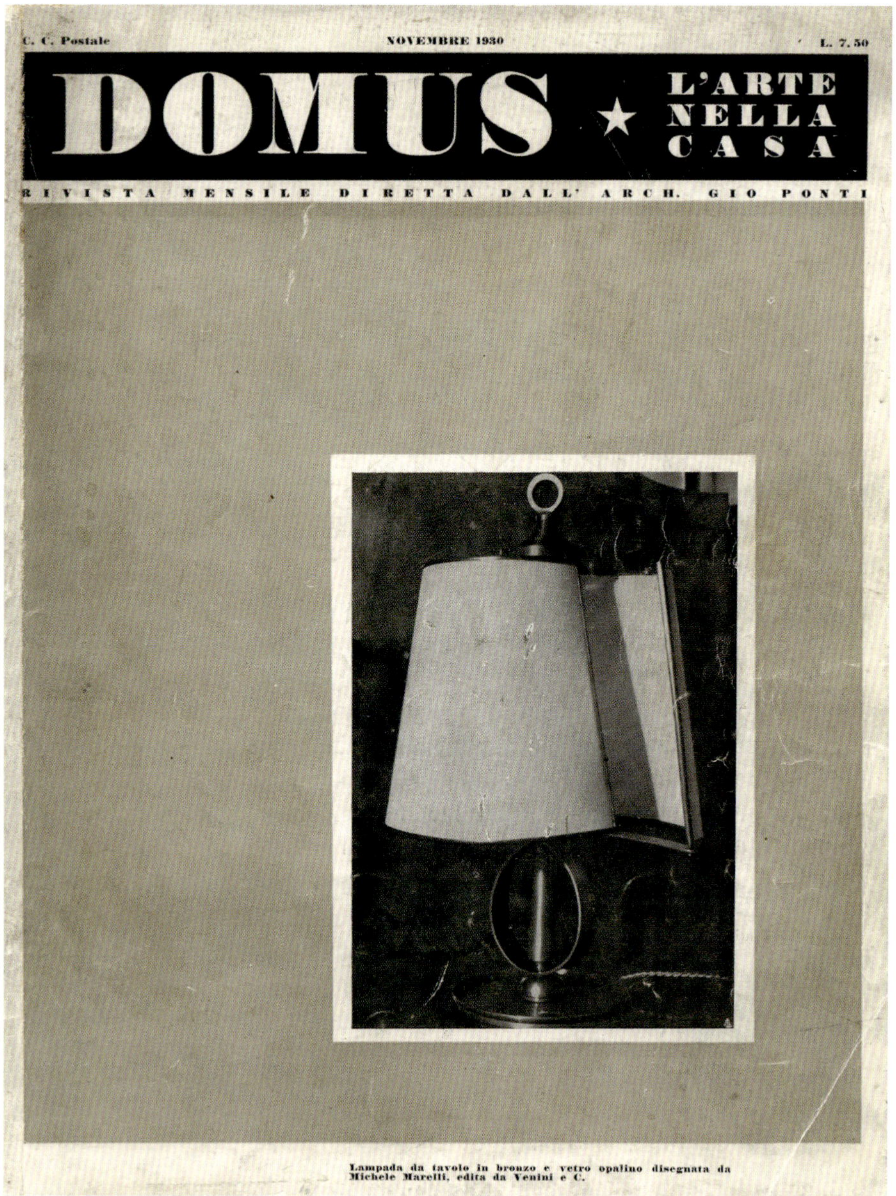

C. C. Postale NOVEMBRE 1930 L. 7,50

DOMUS ★ L'ARTE NELLA CASA

RIVISTA MENSILE DIRETTA DALL' ARCH. GIO PONTI

Lampada da tavolo in bronzo e vetro opalino disegnata da Michele Marelli, edita da Venini e C.

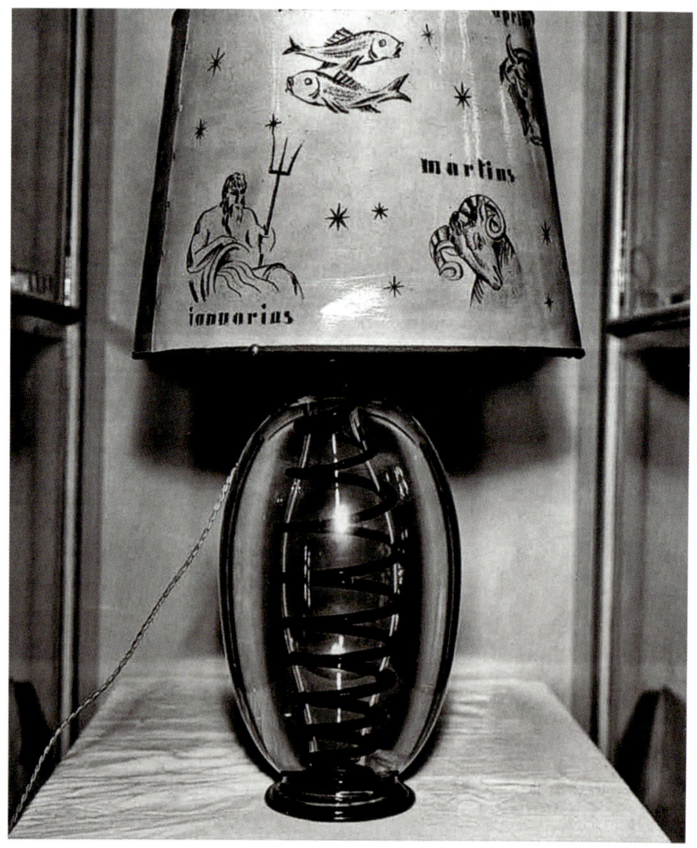

>
IV ESPOSIZIONE TRIENNALE INTERNAZIONALE DELLE ARTI DECORATIVE ED INDUSTRIALI MODERNE
Table lamp after a design by Michele Marelli, in *Domus*, November 1930

>
IV ESPOSIZIONE TRIENNALE INTERNAZIONALE DELLE ARTI DECORATIVE ED INDUSTRIALI MODERNE
Chandelier after a design of Napoleone Martinuzzi in the Lighting Gallery. Period photograph, 1930

>
IV ESPOSIZIONE TRIENNALE INTERNAZIONALE DELLE ARTI DECORATIVE ED INDUSTRIALI MODERNE
Table lamp with aquarium base. Period photograph, 1930

>
IV ESPOSIZIONE TRIENNALE INTERNAZIONALE DELLE ARTI DECORATIVE ED INDUSTRIALI MODERNE
Wall lamp after a design by Napoleone Martinuzzi in the Glass Gallery. Period photograph, 1930

1930

ROME (IT)
WORKERS' FREE-TIME CLUB
DESIGN N. MARTINUZZI

WALL LAMPS
CEILING
PENDANT

The project at the 'Dopolavoro ferroviario' of Rome was one of the first of a series of works carried out by the glassworks for the Ministry of Communications and particularly in association with the architect-engineer Angiolo Mazzoni, active at Office 5 of the ministry. The free-time club building, designed by the said Mazzoni together with Efisio Vodret (1925-1930) and opened on 1st June 1930, consisted of a comprehensive complex including a theatre (known as the Teatro Italia) with adjoining areas, offices, a library, 'le palestre' [gyms] and a hotel with restaurant. As documented by period photographs and various drawings from the Venini archive, the glass furnace produced numerous lighting fixtures after the design of Napoleone Martinuzzi. Among these we can identify hanging lamps in transparent glass based on the classical *cesendello* and chandelier no. 2068 located in the library. The lighting fixtures for the theatre are different: for example the superimposed bell-shaped wall lamps in white *pulegoso* glass installed in the entrance hall. Ribbed lights in green glass (wall lamps and lamps over the architraves) were placed in the gallery, while for the hall superimposed cup-shaped sconces in varying forms and sizes produced in cased glass were used.

>
WORKERS' FREE-TIME CLUB
Lamps in *pulegoso* glass in the entrance hall of the theatre.
Period photograph, MART

>
WORKERS' FREE-TIME CLUB
Lamp in ribbed glass in the gallery of the theatre.
Period photograph, MART

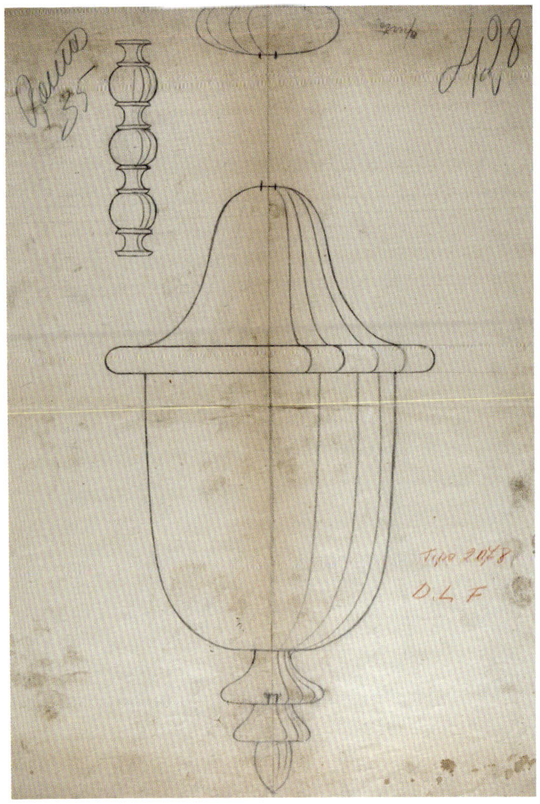

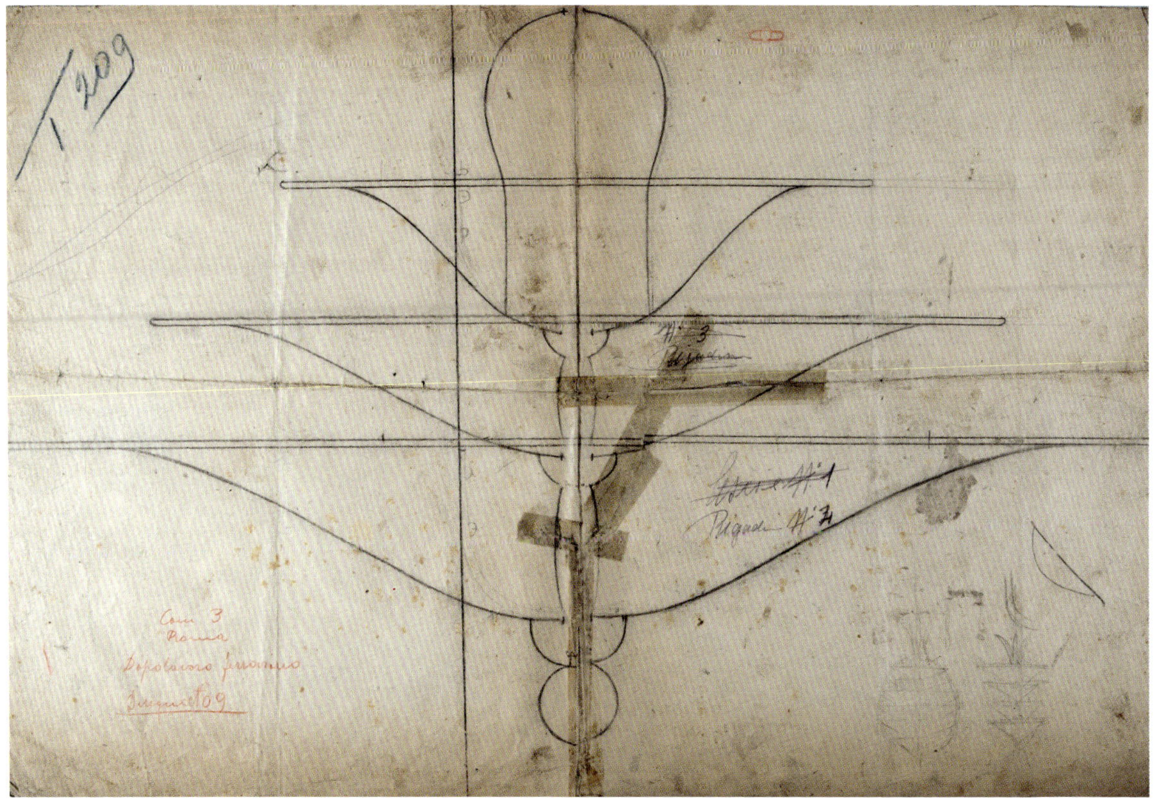

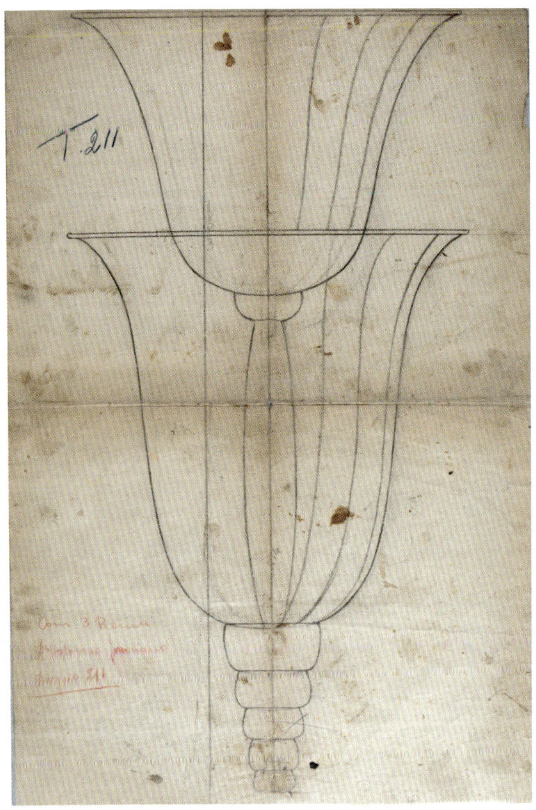

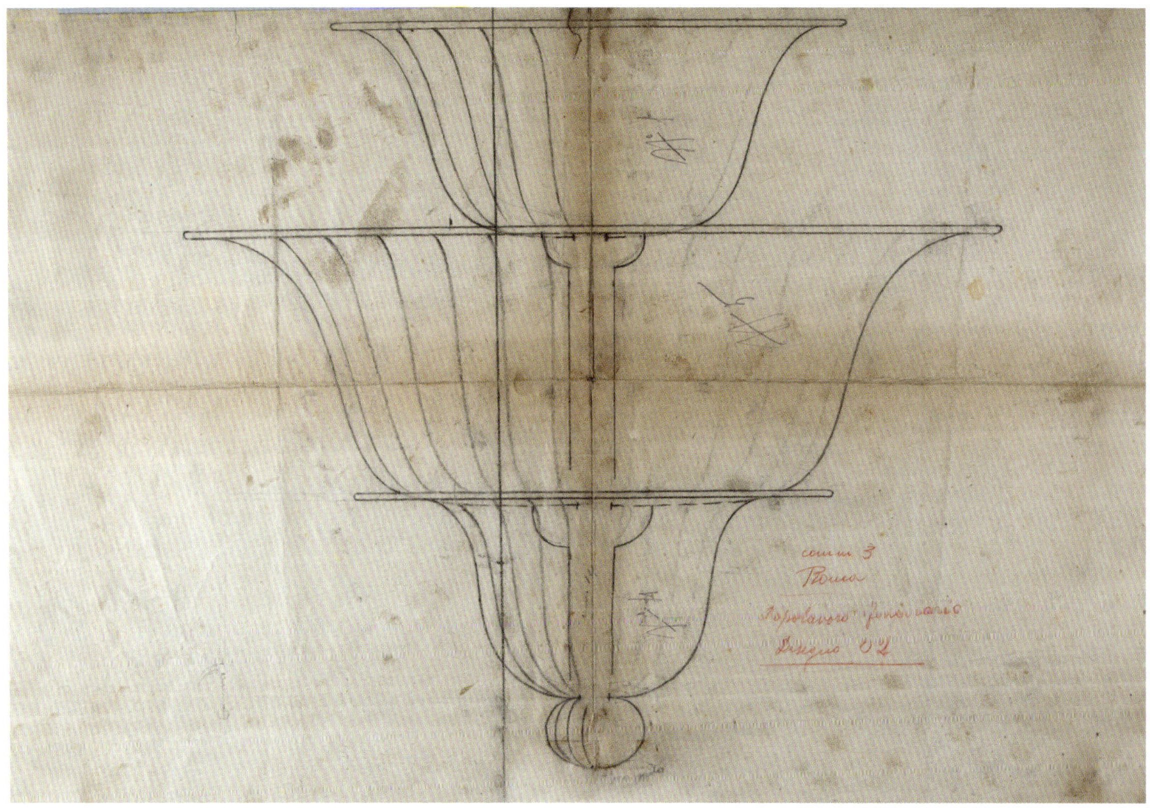

>
WORKERS' FREE-TIME CLUB
Drawing for *cesendello*

>
WORKERS' FREE-TIME CLUB
Drawing for sconce for the theatre auditorium

>
WORKERS' FREE-TIME CLUB
Drawing for superimposed bell-shaped sconce

>
WORKERS' FREE-TIME CLUD
Drawing for superimposed bell-shaped sconce

1930

TRIESTE (IT)
CALIFORNIA STEAMER
DESIGN A. BUCCI

WALL LAMPS

Lighting project for a ship, with interiors designed by the painter Anselmo Bucci. The project consists of large lanterns with components in wrought iron produced by the Caussi company of Trieste.

1930

ROME (IT)
PALAZZO DEL VIMINALE

CEILING

In the halls of the Presidenza del Consiglio [Prime Minister's Office] fitted out by the architect Giovanni Michelucci, ceiling lights were used, like the bell-shaped one in white *pulegoso* glass present in the 'saletta delle statistiche' [statistics room].

1930

TRIESTE (IT)
TIMAVO STEAMER
DESIGN A. BUCCI

WALL LAMPS
CEILING

For the vessel of the Navigazione Libera Triestina, with interiors designed by the painter Anselmo Bucci, the glassworks produced wall and ceiling lights in coloured and white opaline glass for some of the principal rooms, among which the entrance hall, the Pomona Room, the Acquarium Bar and the Music Room.

>
PALAZZO DEL VIMINALE
Statistics Room in the offices of the Prime Minister in Domus, November 1930

>
TIMAVO STEAMER
Music Room. Period photograph, 1933

1931 MILAN (IT)

BANCA POPOLARE DI MILANO

DESIGN G. GREPPI

SEMI-FROSTED GLASS CANES

In the bank building designed by the architect Giovanni Greppi and opened on 8 December 1931, the glassworks produced a series of wall lights, designed by the same architect. These were articulated sconces, with metallic mounting and diffuser screen in semi-frosted lined canes.

1931 TRIESTE (IT)

CONTE DI SAVOIA TRANSATLANTIC LINER

Lighting project for certain rooms of the ship designed by Gustavo Pulitzer and launched in October 1931.

1931 TRIESTE (IT)

DUCHESSA D'AOSTA STEAMER

DESIGN N. MARTINUZZI

WALL LAMPS
CEILING

For the ship, with interiors designed by the painter Anselmo Bucci, the glassworks created, among other things, sconces designed by Napoleone Martinuzzi for the dining room. These were lamps in polychrome glass in the distinctive form of baskets of fruit.

>
BANCA POPOLARE DI MILANO
Sconce with semi-frosted canes. Period photograph, 1931

>
DUCHESSA D'AOSTA STEAMER
Dining room. Period photograph, 1931

1931

ROME (IT)
I QUADRIENNALE D'ARTE NAZIONALE
DESIGN N. MARTINUZZI

LUMINOUS FOUNTAIN

On the occasion of the Roman event, Napoleone Martinuzzi, acting here also as a member of the organising committee, designed a large luminous fountain for the winter garden designed by Enrico del Debbio. The installation consists of a voluminous, illuminated, tripartite lower part, made up of curved canes in transparent glass from which water gushes out. The upper part, in 'aquamarine opaque glass' with decorative elements in sea-green and sapphire *pulegoso* glass, features a high finial which acts as a focal point for the room.

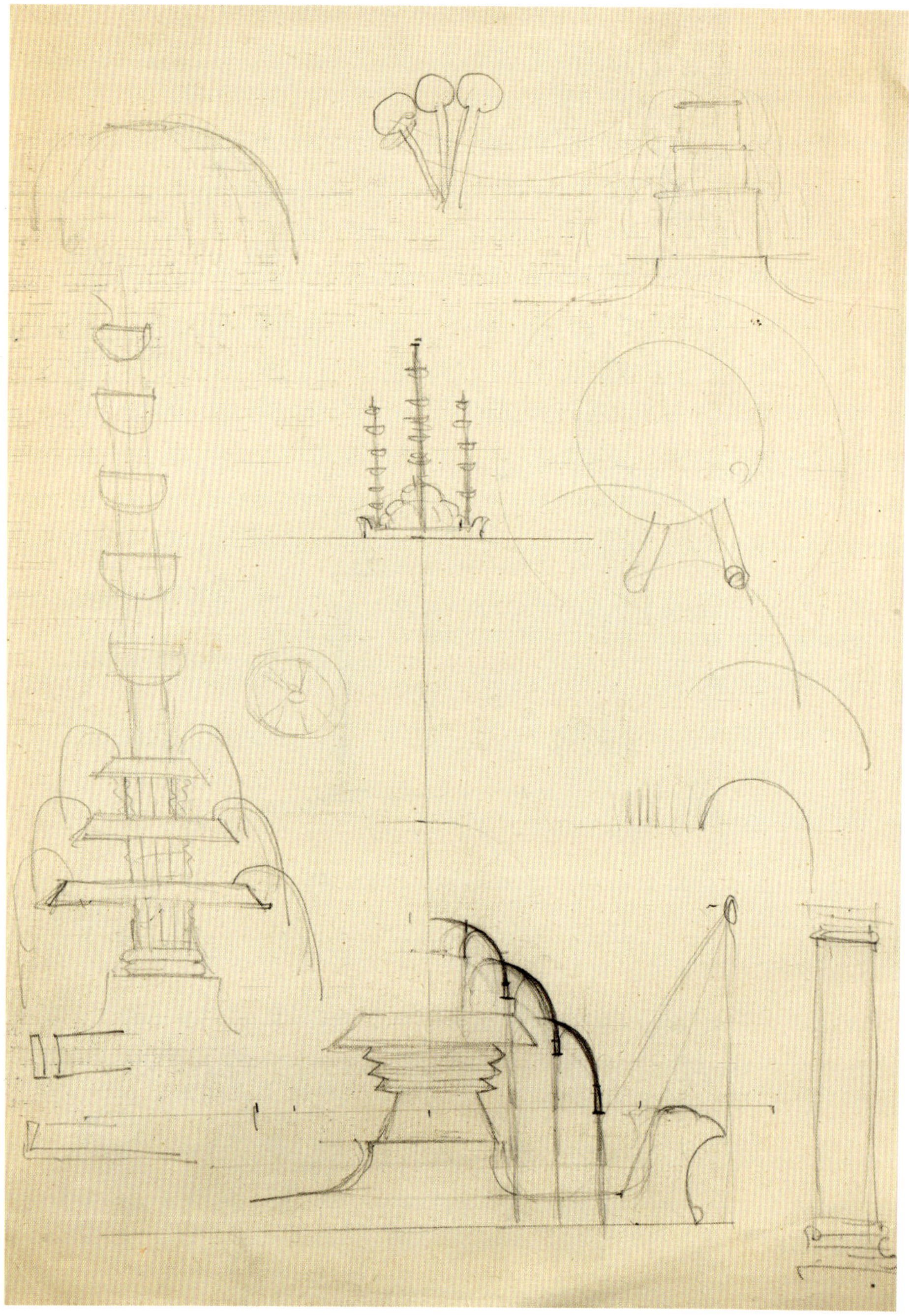

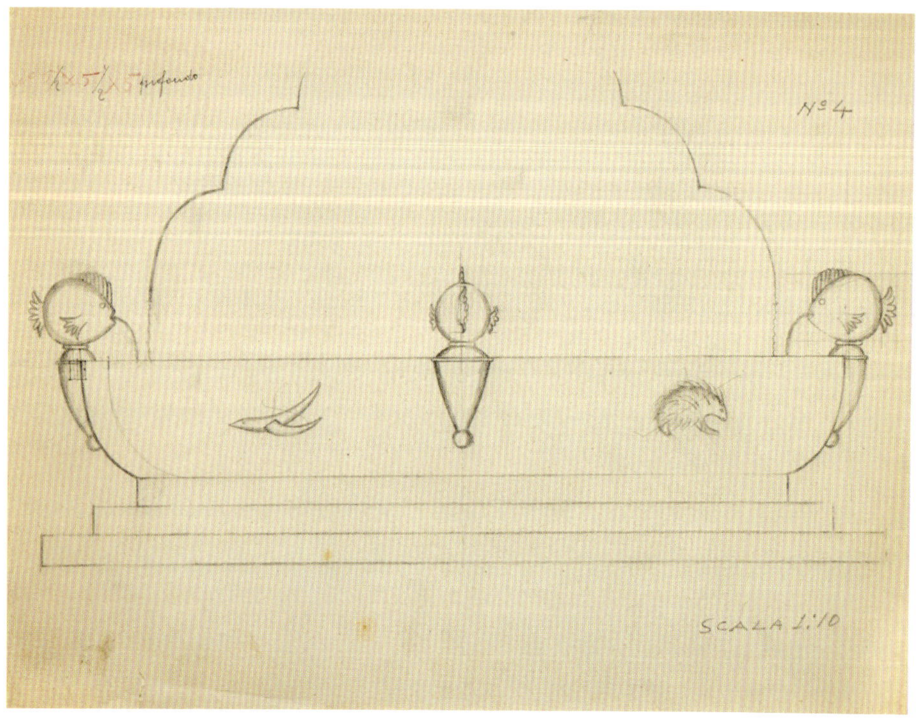

>
I QUADRIENNALE D'ARTE NAZIONALE
Drawing for the luminous fountain to be placed in the winter garden of Enrico del Debbio

>
I QUADRIENNALE D'ARTE NAZIONALE
Variant no. 4 for the design of the pool

>>
I QUADRIENNALE D'ARTE NAZIONALE
Large luminous fountain. Period photograph, 1931

1932

AALBORG (DK)
SAINT MARK'S CHURCH
DESIGN M. BRANDSTRUP

WITH ARMS

For the Danish religious building designed by Einar Pachness, the glassworks produced a series of chandeliers and sconces with arms in *pagliesco* glass after a design by Mogens Brandstrup. The fixtures are still *in situ*.

›
SAINT MARK'S CHURCH
Central nave. Period photograph, 1932

1932

BERGAMO (IT)
POST OFFICE BUILDING
DESIGN N. MARTINUZZI, A. MAZZONI

SEMI-FROSTED GLASS CANES
WALL LAMPS
TABLE
ONDULATO GLASS

Built between 1929 and 1931 and designed by Angiolo Mazzoni, the building was inaugurated officially on 30 October 1932. Renewing the association with Napoleone Martinuzzi, the architect again called upon the glassworks for the creation of a series of lamps and an installation for the entrance hall (cactus in *pulegoso* glass illuminated at the base). Some of the fixtures were created using modular elements like undulating glass and semi-frosted glass canes: the first were used for wall lights for the entrance hall and stairways, the second both for the two large, cylindrical, polychrome lights situated externally near the entrances and for the wall lamps of the correspondence hall. In other cases Martinuzzi was involved in designing lights of a highly decorative nature: these were sconces in the form of urns in yellow cased glass with red finishings beside the entrance hall memorial stone, lamps with arms in the form of cornucopia (from three to seven) resting in most cases over the high desks of the correspondence hall and the money services hall. Here wall lamps were also installed with opaline bell-shaped elements (from one to four), while more rounded shapes characterise the sconces of the telegram hall where in January 1934 two large paintings by Mario Sironi were installed. Many of these fixtures are still *in situ*.

»
POST OFFICE BUILDING
Entrance hall with lamps in cased glass and in undulating glass. Period photograph, c. 1932

»
POST OFFICE BUILDING
Correspondence hall. Period photograph, c. 1932

»
POST OFFICE BUILDING
Wall lamp in yellow cased glass with finishings in red vitreous paste, entrance hall. Archive photograph

CORRISPONDENZE
I POSTELEGRAFONICI
DELLA PROVINCIA DI BERGAMO
CADVTI NELLA GRANDE GVERRA
MCMXV — MCMXVIII
FACCHINETTI ATTILIO
CALLEGARI CARLO
OFFREDI MANFREDO
BOSIO ANTIMO
GERVASONI ANGELO
GERINI CARLO
ROTA BERNARDO
ANNO X

>
POST OFFICE BUILDING
Correspondence hall. Period photograph, c. 1932

>
POST OFFICE BUILDING
Correspondence hall. Period photograph, c. 1932

>>
POST OFFICE BUILDING
Lamp with arms, 'money services' hall. Period photograph, c. 1932

>>
POST OFFICE BUILDING
Lamp with arms, 'money services' hall. Archive photograph

1932

BRESCIA (IT)
POST OFFICE BUILDING, TORRE DELLA RIVOLUZIONE, BUILDING OF THE ISTITUTO NAZIONALE DELLE ASSICURAZIONI

SEMI-FROSTED GLASS CANES
ONDULATO GLASS

Between 1930 and 1932 the centre of Brescia was reorganised by the architect Marcello Piacentini with the creation of the Piazza della Vittoria inaugurated on 1st November 1932. Among the new buildings, there were three important edifices for which the glassworks provided lighting fixtures for both internal and external use, where particular use was made of semi-frosted and undulating glass. More specifically, in the monumental Post Office Building, the focal point at the north of the square, semi-cylindrical lamps in semi-frosted cane glass were used in various areas, such as the public correspondence hall. At the summit of the Torre della Rivoluzione [Revolution Tower], situated to the north-east, a luminous ring-shaped band was created with elements in undulating glass. In this way, the tower was seen as a sort of beacon with a powerful symbolic value. Opposite the tower there is the great high building owned by the INA [National Insurance Institute], called the 'Torrione' (max h 57 m), consisting principally of apartments. Here, on the top floor, next the restaurant with terrace, a lighting system was installed consisting of specifically designed shielded spotlights, with inserts also in undulating glass.

>
POST OFFICE BUILDING
Public correspondence hall. Period photograph, 1932

>
BUILDING OF THE ISTITUTO NAZIONALE DELLE ASSICURAZIONI
The 'Torrione' by day. Period photograph, 1932

>>
TORRE DELLA RIVOLUZIONE
The building photographed by night. Period photograph, 1932

>>
TORRE DELLA RIVOLUZIONE
General view of the building. Period photograph, 1932

RE VITTORIO EMANVELE III
DVCE BENITO MVSSOLINI
BRESCIA FASCISTA
QVESTA PIAZZA VOLLE
A RICORDO DELLA VITTORIA

1932

CATANIA (IT)
IL POPOLO DI SICILIA

CASED GLASS

For the office of the administrative director of the daily newspaper, designed by the architect Francesco Fiducia, the glassworks produced a hanging lamp in chrome-plated metal and cased glass with a diffuser body formed of two superimposed truncated cones.

1932

GORIZIA (IT)
POST OFFICE BUILDING

ONDULATO GLASS

In the Post Office Building officially opened on 28 October 1932 and constructed between 1930 and 1932 after a design by Angiolo Mazzoni, a unique type of wall lamp was adopted using undulating glass modules. These were fixtures with a metal mounting and semi-cylindrical body of different dimensions positioned in the various areas of the building among which the correspondence and parcel hall, the telegram service hall, the money service hall and the stairwell situated inside the tower and frescoed by Guido Cadorin.

›
POST OFFICE BUILDING
Correspondence and parcel hall. Period photograph, 1932

›
POST OFFICE BUILDING
Stairwell in the hall with fresco by Guido Cadorin.
Period photograph, 1932

1932

GROSSETO (IT)
POST OFFICE BUILDING
DESIGN A. MAZZONI

SEMI-FROSTED GLASS CANES

Also for this Tuscan Post Office Building, opened on 13 November 1932 and featuring on the façade a sculptural group by Martinuzzi ('Maremma domata'), Angiolo Mazzoni called upon the services of the Venini firm for the production of certain artistic lights, designed by the architect himself. These were 'lighting fixtures in metal and glass' for internal and external areas based on a single box-shaped model with rounded corners, metal mounting ('bronzed brass' or 'extruded anticorodal') and diffuser screen with vertical semi-frosted canes. The fixtures were delivered and mounted between 2 September and 17 October 1932 (Giacomelli 2013, p. 150). A series of fixtures was positioned in the portico, in the entrance hall, on the brick walls of the spiral staircase at the back of the entrance area and in the public hall. Various lamps are still *in situ*. The same type of lamp was also used by Mazzoni in the external areas of the accessory services building of the Florence train station of Santa Maria Novella (c. 1933).

>
POST OFFICE BUILDING
Entrance hall. Period photograph, 1932

>
POST OFFICE BUILDING
Stairwell with the sculptural group 'La madre' by Domenico Ponzi. Period photograph, 1932

1932

LIDO DI VENEZIA (IT)

CHEZ VOUS, EXCELSIOR HOTEL

DESIGN M. BRANDSTRUP

TABLE

For the renowned fashionable venue of the Excelsior, defined as 'the most elegant dance-hall in the world', original table lamps were produced in the form of a vase containing a branch with stylised inflorescences (spherical elements). As an autographed drawing initialled by the author documents, the model is the work of the Danish artist Mogens Brandstrup who, already active with V.S.M. Cappellin Venini e c., continued to have relationships with the furnace of Paolo Venini in the early 1930s. The model was included in the Venini catalogue under number 9027 and, as documented by archive drawings, was produced also in other variants for later commissions.

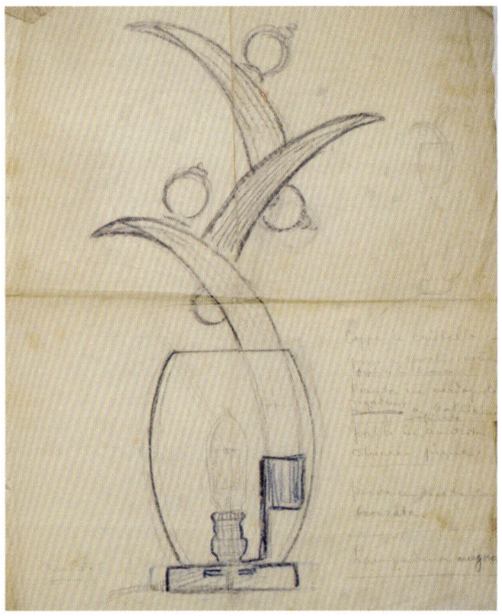

>
CHEZ VOUS, EXCELSIOR HOTEL
M. Brandstrup, study for a luminous plant, variant A

>
CHEZ VOUS, EXCELSIOR HOTEL
'Luminous plant produced for the tables of Chez-vous at the Excelsior of the Lido of Venice', in *Domus*, February 1933, p. 82

1932

LIDO DI VENEZIA (IT)

ENTERTAINMENT BUILDING, LUNA PARK

DESIGN A. CASSI RAMELLI

PENDANT

The central building for the Luna Park of the Lido of Venice is a project of the architect Antonio Cassi Ramelli on behalf of Anonima Luna Park Venezia-Lido. On this occasion, the Venini firm was called upon to produce the large chandelier of the Salone del Cielo, the dance hall on the second floor which took its name from the stucco decoration with stars and planets. Included in the catalogue under the number 5278 (Blue Catalogue), the chandelier (Ø 160 cm) was designed by the architect himself and is distinguished by, among other things, the presence of two disks in 'frosted crystal' to increase the luminosity of the appliance (*L'illuminazione razionale*, October 1932, p. 211).

>
ENTERTAINMENT BUILDING, LUNA PARK
Salone del Cielo, in *L'illuminazione razionale*, October 1932

>>
ENTERTAINMENT BUILDING, LUNA PARK
Detail of the chandelier, in *L'illuminazione razionale*, October 1932

1932

MILAN (IT)
STOCK EXCHANGE BUILDING
DESIGN P. MEZZANOTTE

SEMI-FROSTED GLASS CANES
OPALINE GLASS

In the building of Piazza Affari designed by the architect Paolo Mezzanotte and opened in 1932, the glassworks, in addition to circular ceiling lamps in opaline glass with slight ribbing, produced a series of ceiling and wall lights with a diffuser screen of semi-frosted canes and nickel-plated brass mounting. In the first case they had a square (170 x 170 cm) or rectangular (220 x 115 cm) base. The larger sconces (Ø 27 cm, h 180 cm), on the other hand, are characterised by their semi-cylindrical form with a decorative metal element at the lower extremity. In the restaurant, designed by Gio Ponti and with tiles decorated by Richard Ginori, there are 'long tubes' (*Rassegna di Architettura*, March 1933) in glass with *cristallo* canes having amethyst inserts (Ø 20 cm, l 260 cm).

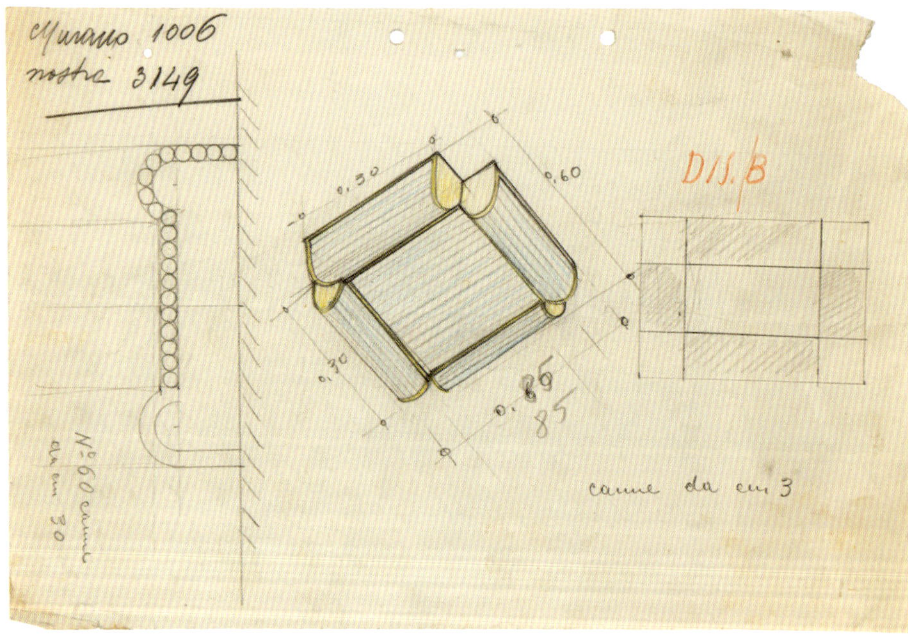

›
STOCK EXCHANGE BUILDING
Lamp with semi-frosted canes. Period photograph, 1932

›
STOCK EXCHANGE BUILDING
Drawing for the lamp with semi-frosted canes

››
STOCK EXCHANGE BUILDING
Restaurant. Period photograph, 1932

DIMENSIONI
0,20 X 2,60

1932

PADUA (IT)

PAVILION OF THE INDUSTRIAL PORT OF VENEZIA-MARGHERA, XIV FIERA DI PADOVA

SEMI-FROSTED GLASS CANES
ONDULATO GLASS

In designing the Fair pavilion, opened in June 1932, Brenno Del Giudice chose to associate the cladding of the building in 'alluman' (an alloy of aluminium and magnesium) with Murano glass. He used undulating glass for the production of three back-lit ribs extending upwards within the tower-like structure positioned at the centre of the pavilion. Screens of cane glass, also back-lit, were inserted in the projection around the entire volume and were also used in the intrados facing the entrance. The use of these solutions produced original chromatic effects, whether with natural or artificial light.

>
PAVILION OF THE INDUSTRIAL PORT OF VENEZIA-MARGHERA, XIV FIERA DI PADOVA
View by night of the pavilion with artificial lighting. Detail of the façade. Period photograph, 1932

>
PAVILION OF THE INDUSTRIAL PORT OF VENEZIA-MARGHERA, XIV FIERA DI PADOVA
Main view. Period photograph, 1932

VENEZIA
MARGHERA

1932

SESTRIERE (IT)

PRINCIPI DI PIEMONTE HOTEL

DESIGN G. CHEVALLEY

PENDANT

Lighting project for the hotel designed by Giovanni Chevalley and Mario Passanti. The involvement of the glassworks is documented by a drawing preserved in the Venini archive and coming from the Chevalley architectural office concerning a hanging lamp for the 'central hall'.

1932-33

TURIN (IT)

STADIO MUSSOLINI AND TORRE DI MARATONA

CANE GLASS
ONDULATO GLASS

The sporting complex, now the Municipal Stadium, was inaugurated on 14 May 1933 on the occasion of the Lictor Youth Games. The construction was the work of many hands, involving the architects and engineers Raffaello Fagnoni, Enrico Bianchini and Dagoberto Ortensi, for the stadium project, and Brenno Del Giudice, Gustavo Colonnetti, Aldo Vannacci and Giorgio Accinelli, for the celebratory tower. The tower, at the entrance to the complex, was built in reinforced concrete and characterised by the presence of back-lit glass inserts. In particular, the façade presented double side ribbing in relief with a screen having vertical slats in undulating glass (50 cm each). Framed by two bands in amethyst horizontal canes, the title 'Stadio Mussolini' stood out, now no longer there, also in canes of the same colour. Two heliographic copies from the Venini archive date the project to December 1932. The glassworks were also involved in the construction of the stadium, producing two luminous architraves, also in undulating glass, positioned in line with the twenty entrances to the stands.

>
STADIO MUSSOLINI AND TORRE DI MARATONA
Access to the stadium. Period photograph, 1932

>
STADIO MUSSOLINI AND TORRE DI MARATONA
Torre di Maratona. Period photograph, 1932

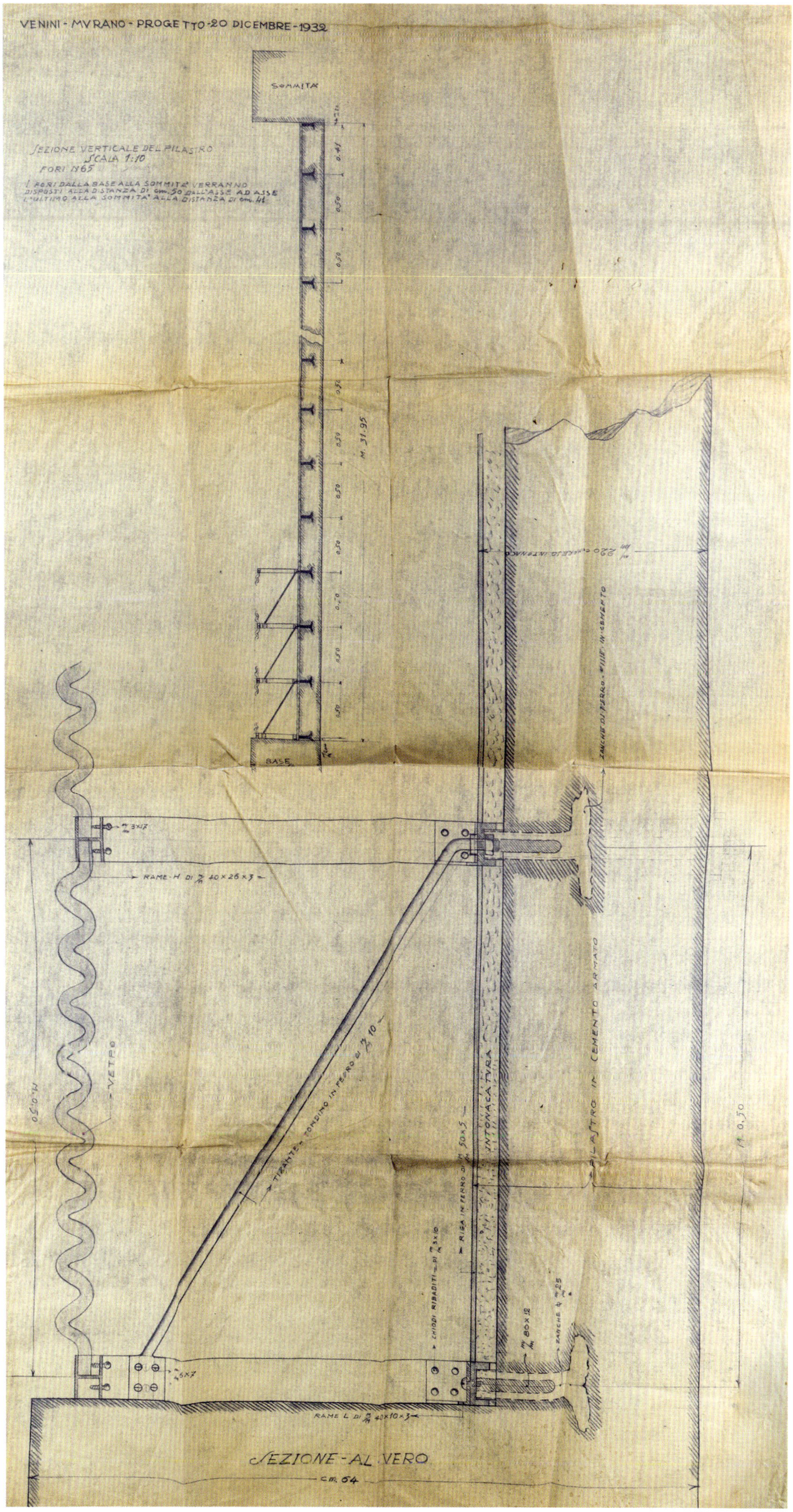

›
STADIO MUSSOLINI AND TORRE DI MARATONA
Vertical section of the ribbing, 20 December 1932

1932
1936

LATINA (IT)
RAILWAY STATION AND POST OFFICE BUILDING
DESIGN A. MAZZONI

SEMI-FROSTED GLASS CANES
ONDULATO GLASS

The train station and Post Office Building of Littoria (now Latina), designed by Angiolo Mazzoni, were inaugurated on 18 December 1932, only a few months after the laying of the first stone (30 June 1932) of the first town founded on the Pontine Marshes. Following the promotion of Littoria to the status of provincial capital (December 1934), both buildings were extended under the guidance of Mazzoni between 1935 and 1936 (official opening on 26 April 1936). On both occasions, the architect renewed his association with the glassworks for the supply of certain lighting fixtures based on his own designs. In the railway station, initially semi-cylindrical wall lamps with a metal (anticorodal) mounting and diffuser screen with semi-frosted canes were adopted, positioned both horizontally and vertically. With the extension, however, 'recessed lights in the ceiling' were produced for the entrance hall, made up of kinds of luminous ribbons and recessed circular ceiling lights with a slatted screen, presumably in undulating glass). For the town Post Office, particularly appreciated by Filippo Marinetti, Mazzoni chose fixtures with semi-frosted canes for the outside and for the inside semi-cylindrical fixtures also with semi-frosted canes, positioned horizontally, like those placed over the various counters. With the extension, the large pendant lamp was added to these, with a long luminous body (l 390 cm) and screen in undulating glass, which was positioned in the centre of the public hall.

>
RAILWAY STATION
Entrance hall of the passengers' building. Period photograph, 1932

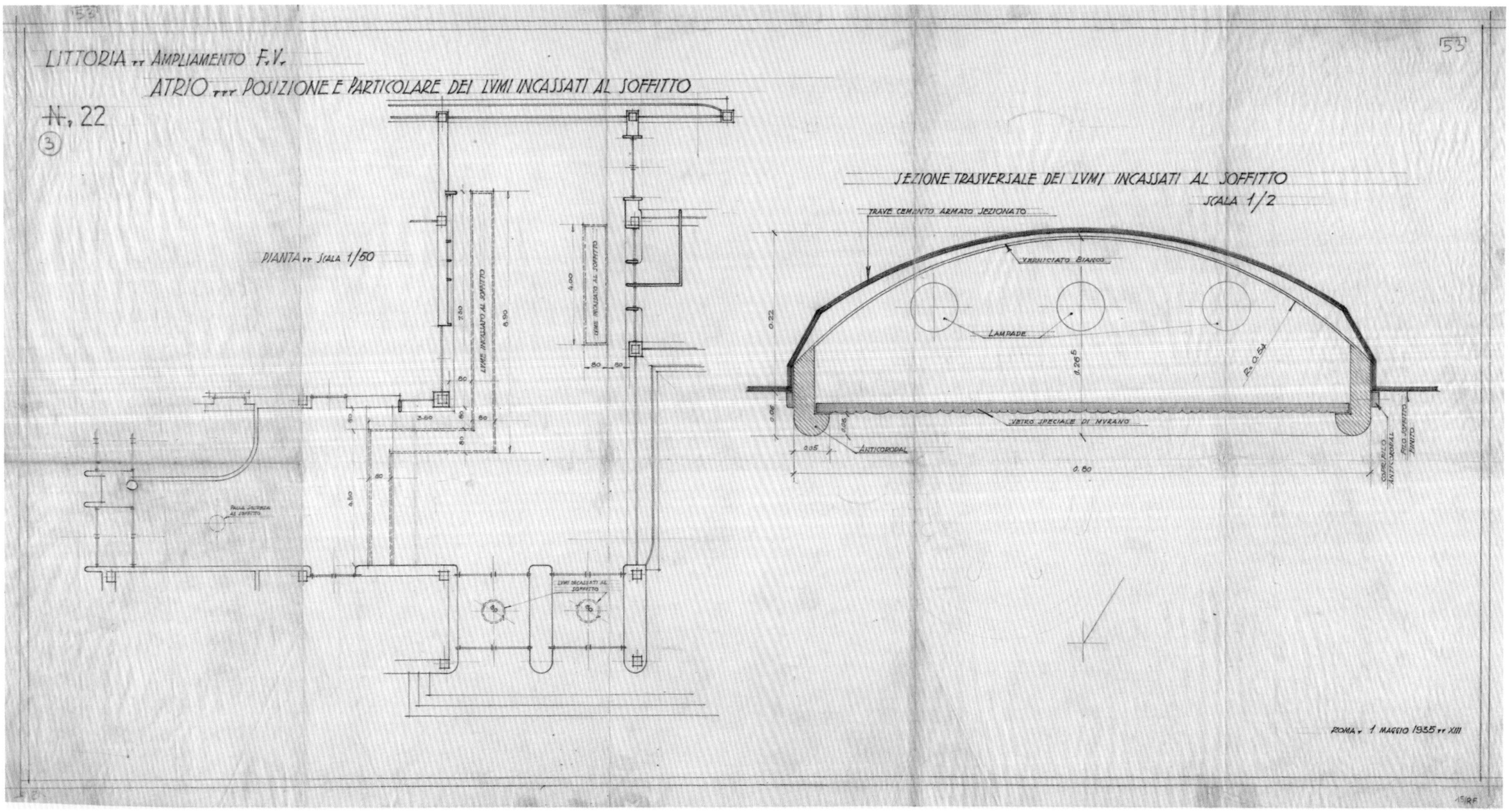
LITTORIA ,, AMPLIAMENTO F.V.
ATRIO ,,, POSIZIONE E PARTICOLARE DEI LUMI INCASSATI AL SOFFITTO
N. 22
PIANTA ,, SCALA 1/50
SEZIONE TRASVERSALE DEI LUMI INCASSATI AL SOFFITTO
SCALA 1/2
TRAVE CEMENTO ARMATO SEZIONATO
VERNICIATO BIANCO
LAMPADE
VETRO SPECIALE DI MURANO
ANTICORODAL
ROMA, 1 MAGGIO 1935 ,, XIII

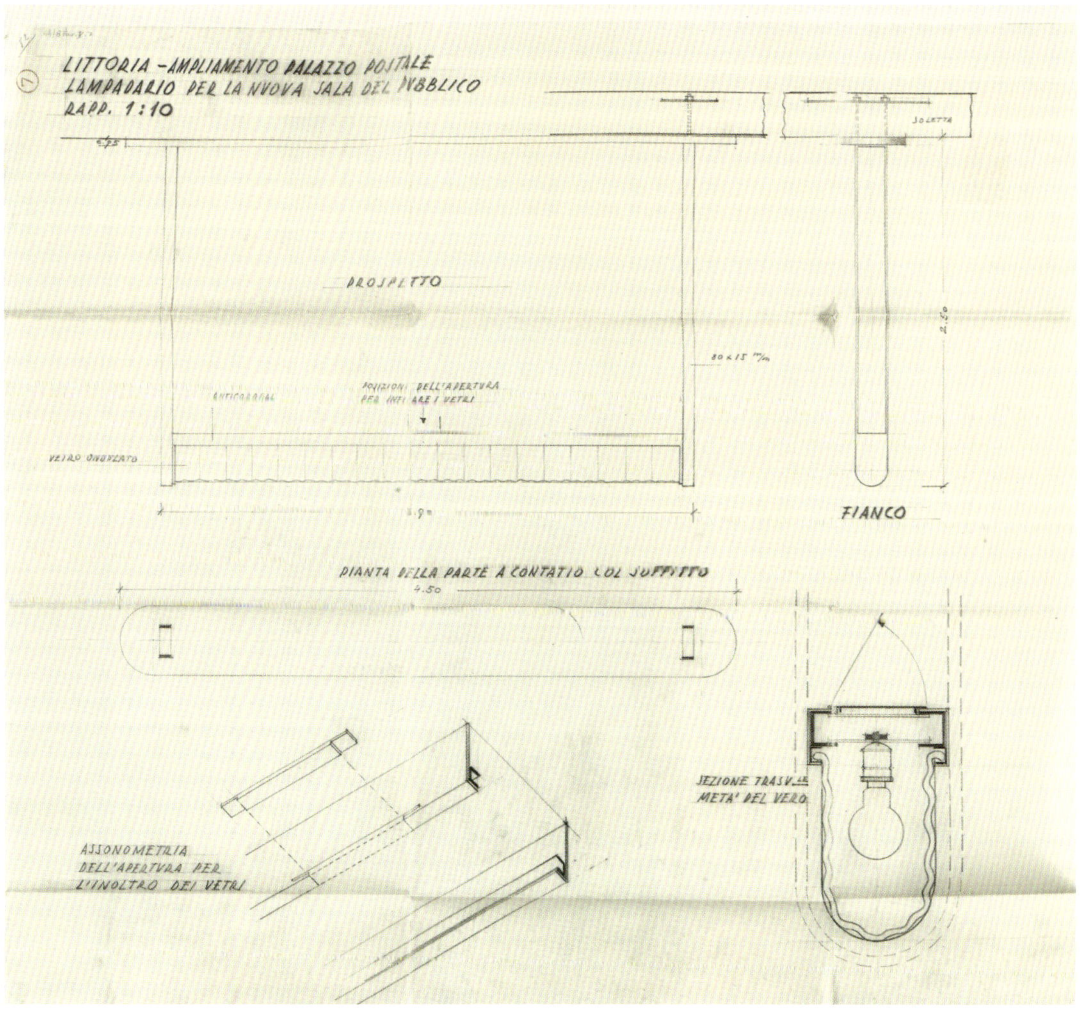

<<
RAILWAY STATION
Writing room. Period photograph, 1932

<<
RAILWAY STATION
Drawing for 'recessed lights in the ceiling', May 1935.
Period photograph, MART

>
POST OFFICE BUILDING
Public hall. Period photograph, 1932

>
POST OFFICE BUILDING
Drawing for hanging lamp in the public hall.
Period photograph, MART

1933

BRESCIA (IT)
ALBERGO DELLA VITTORIA

WITH ARMS

Among the new edifices built at the same time as the construction of the Piazza della Vittoria (1930-33) was this hotel, the layout of which is due to the Brescia architect Egidio Dabbeni. The glassworks were called upon to execute lighting fixtures intended for the common areas. For the banquet hall on the first floor, in particular, a series of chandeliers with arms and curls in *pagliesco* glass was produced, inspired by the model of Vittorio Zecchin displayed at the Exposition Universelle of Paris (1925). The chandeliers and matching sconces are still *in situ*.

>
ALBERGO DELLA VITTORIA
Banquet hall. Period photograph, 1933

1933

LA SPEZIA (IT)
POST OFFICE BUILDING

SEMI-FROSTED GLASS CANES

In the Post Office Building, designed by Angiolo Mazzoni and officially opened on 13 November 1933, as confirmed by two period photographs from the archive of the glassworks, the Venini firm produced a lamp in glass with semi-frosted canes, inserted into the metal structure of the flagpole in front of the façade. For the monumental public hall, a U-shaped luminous ceiling installation was executed with a screen having semi-frosted canes.

>
POST OFFICE BUILDING
Flagpole in front of the façade. Period photograph, 1933

1933

MASSA (IT)
POST OFFICE BUILDING

SEMI-FROSTED GLASS CANES

On 26 September 1933, not long before the official opening of the new Post Office Building designed by Angiolo Mazzoni and inaugurated on 14 November of the same year, the glassworks billed some 'lighting fixtures' (Giacomelli 2013, p. 151). They were probably fixtures for external lighting like those, with a metal mounting and screen with semi-frosted canes positioned on the massive brick flag-bearing structures in front of the entrance, described as 'illuminating pillars' (*Sant'Elia*, no. 6, 1933) which in their design are evocative of the Roman fasces. Other lights, similar to those used at Grosseto, were placed at the sides of the access arch.

>
POST OFFICE BUILDING
'Pilastri Illuminatori' in *Sant'Elia*, no. 6, 1933

1933

MILAN (IT)
MOTTA SHOP

CEILING
PENDANT
FLOOR

The bar-patisserie of Piazza Duomo, occupying two floors connected by a spiral staircase, was arranged following a design by Melchiorre Bega. Here the architect made use of lighting fixtures in original shapes. In the 'bonbonnière room' on the first floor, for example, a hanging lamp (h 146 cm, Ø 36 cm) was positioned, with a circular base and different diameters, included in the catalogue under the number 5259. At the centre of the 'main hall', also on the first floor, there was a chandelier (h 140 cm, 125 x 32 cm) of an 'oblong shape' (*L'Illuminazione razionale*, March 1934, p. 53) in opaline glass with plant motifs in moulded glass and a 'copper framework', included in the catalogue under the number 5267 (*Domus*, March 1934, p. 37). In the same area, near the alcoves with the tables, there were lamps with globes in *mezza filigrana* glass inserted in an unusual decorative structure in cane glass. In the shop there were also many Venini glass pieces and a three-dimensional mosaic panel.

>
MOTTA SHOP
Entrance. Period photograph, 1934

Motta
Motta
PANETTONI

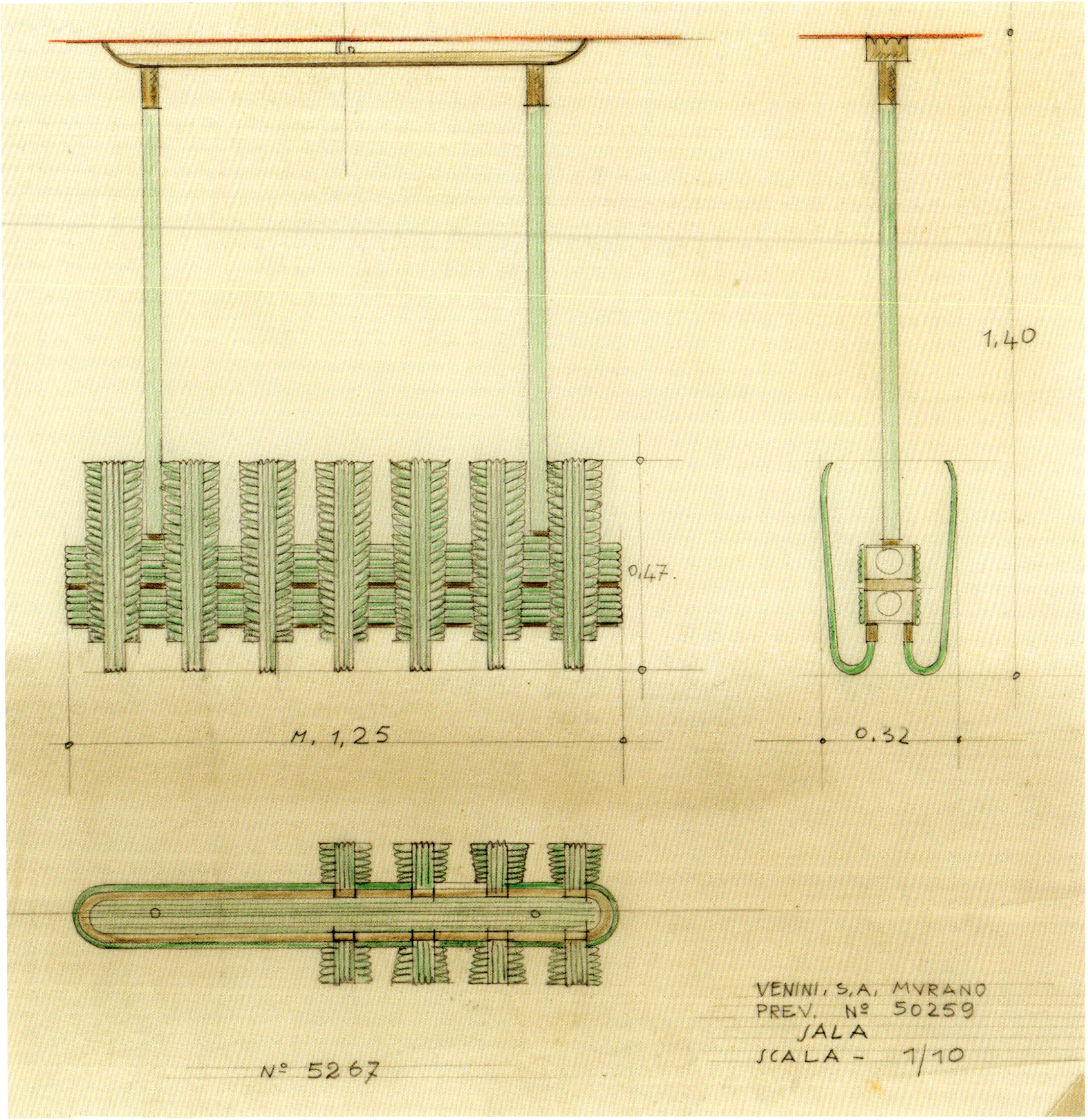

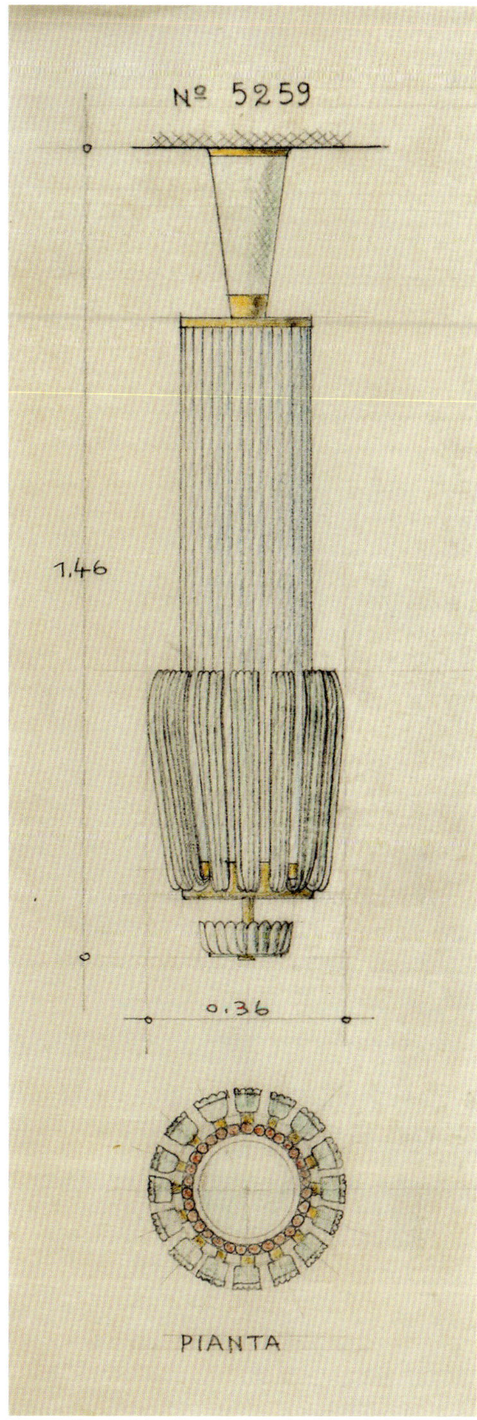

<<
MOTTA SHOP
'Main hall'. Period photograph, 1934

<<
MOTTA SHOP
'Bonbonnière room'. Period photograph, 1934

<<
MOTTA SHOP
'Bonbonnière room'. Period photograph, 1934

>
MOTTA SHOP
Design for the chandelier in the 'main hall'

>
MOTTA SHOP
Design for the pendant lamp in the 'bonbonnière room'

1933

MILAN (IT)
V TRIENNALE DI MILANO

WALL LAMPS
CEILING
PENDANT

The 5th Triennale which opened on 6 May 1933 in the new venue of the Palazzo dell'Arte, designed specifically for the purpose by Giovanni Muzio, saw the glassworks (from 1932 bearing the name Venini S.A.) participate with a wide collection of its production, including also original lighting solutions with contributions in different ways from Tomaso Buzzi and the young Carlo Scarpa, who was active in the technical office of the glassworks. In the vestibule, following the entrance, a large ceiling chandelier was positioned (maximum dimensions 2 x 24 m) consisting of a luminous framework, following a plan formed by two juxtaposed 'U's, in undulating rose-coloured glass (about 500 elements of 10 cm) which was greatly appreciated by the critics (*L'illuminazione razionale*, May 1933). This type of module was also used in the execution of eight imposing 'pendant lamps in bronze and undulating glass' (h 450 cm), after a design by Angelo Bordoni, Antonio Carminati and Mario Sironi, placed in the first-floor Salone delle cerimonie, itself laid out by the same artists. Undulating glass was also adopted for a lighting fixture on a more domestic scale (no. 213) displayed by the Venini firm in the gallery 'Cristalli, metalli, illuminazione' together with other models (wall and hanging lamps, among which nos. 219, 413, 5206, 5207), illustrated in particular on the pages of *Domus*. In addition the said gallery was illuminated by the glassworks with a series of wall lamps formed by a succession of four globes in *reticello* glass. Other fixtures were produced for some areas of the park buildings, such as the Villa di campagna (architects M. Fiocchi, E. Lancia, M. Marelli, G. Serafini), the Casa coloniale (architect L. Piccinato) and Casa media (architect V. Vallot). In the last-mentioned a pendant lamp was installed with four *a reticello* globes hanging from a metal structure, a model of which was included in the catalogue under no. 207.

>
V TRIENNALE DI MILANO
Venini wall lamps in the 'Cristalli, metalli, illuminazione' gallery.
Period photograph, 1933

98.

I VETRI D'ARTE ITALIANI ALLA TRIENNALE

Foto Crimella

Venini - Murano - In alto: Lampadario in vetri a onde - In basso: Lampada a muro in rame con canne di vetro semi-smerigliate e palla superiore in vetro specchiato. Lampada a muro a due coppe in lattimo argentato, color avorio, applique a foglia di cristallo "pulegoso", applique in cristallo a bugna, applique in cristallo a onda

Foto Crimella

3323

380

«
V TRIENNALE DI MILANO
Sala delle Cerimonie.
Period photograph, 1933

›
V TRIENNALE DI MILANO
Venini lighting fixtures, in *Domus*, July 1933

1933

ROME (IT)
CASA DELL'AVIATORE
DESIGN G. GATTI CASAZZA

WALL LAMPS
PENDANT

The aeronautic club (project of Giulio Gatti Casazza), strongly supported by Italo Balbo and opened on 28 October 1933, was located within the Palazzo della Cassa Nazionale Infortuni (CNI, afterwards INFAIL) already designed by the architect Ernesto Brasini (1926-33). The exclusive club, known under the name of Casa dell'Aviatore, was organised over three floors and consisted of guest quarters, the actual club area and the living quarters. It was Gatti Casazza himself who, in collaboration with the glassworks, was responsible for the design of the lighting fixtures. Among these were the characteristic (wall and hanging) lamps made up of a horizontal bundles of canes and conical elements decorated with coloured filaments.

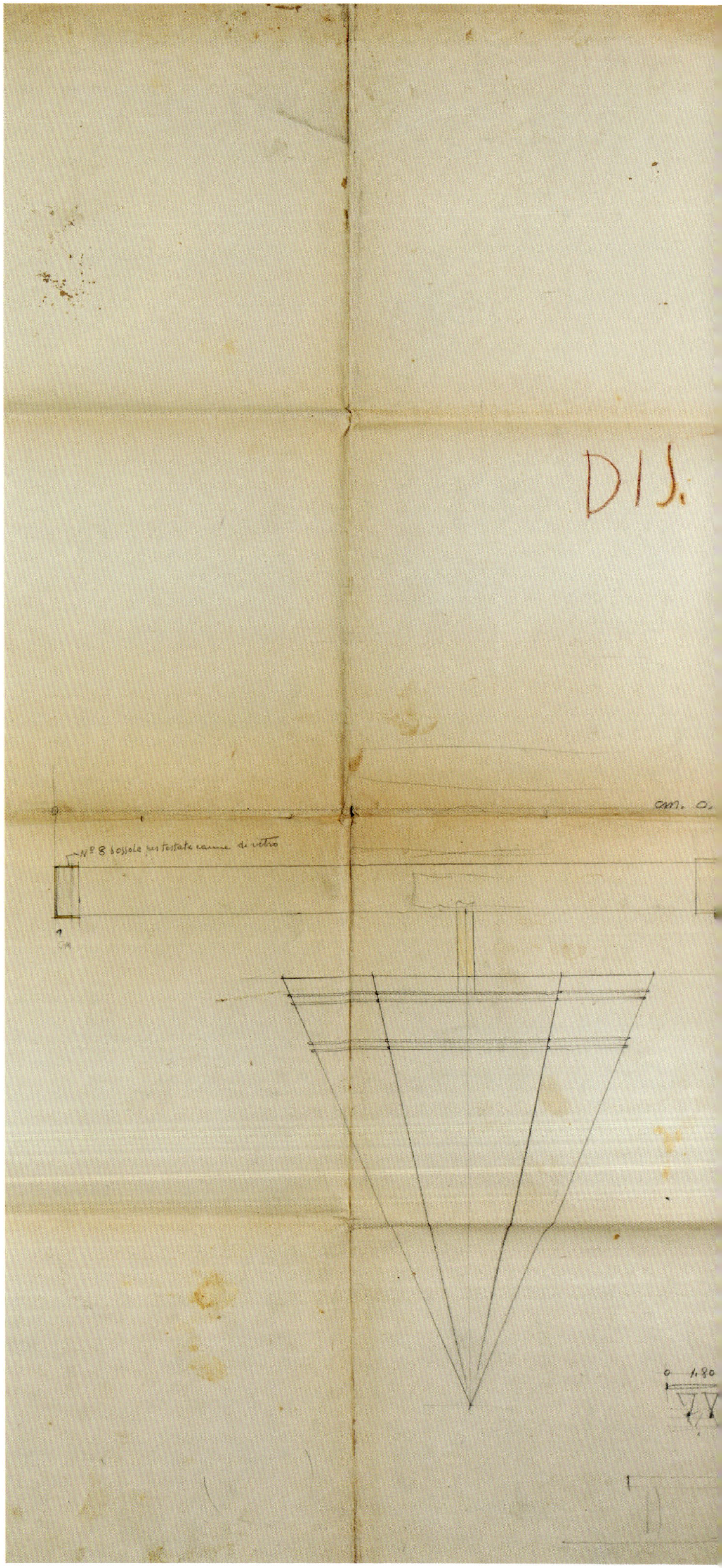

›
CASA DELL'AVIATORE
Wall lamp with conical-shaped elements. Period photograph, 1933

›
CASA DELL'AVIATORE
Proposal for a lamp with conical-shaped elements

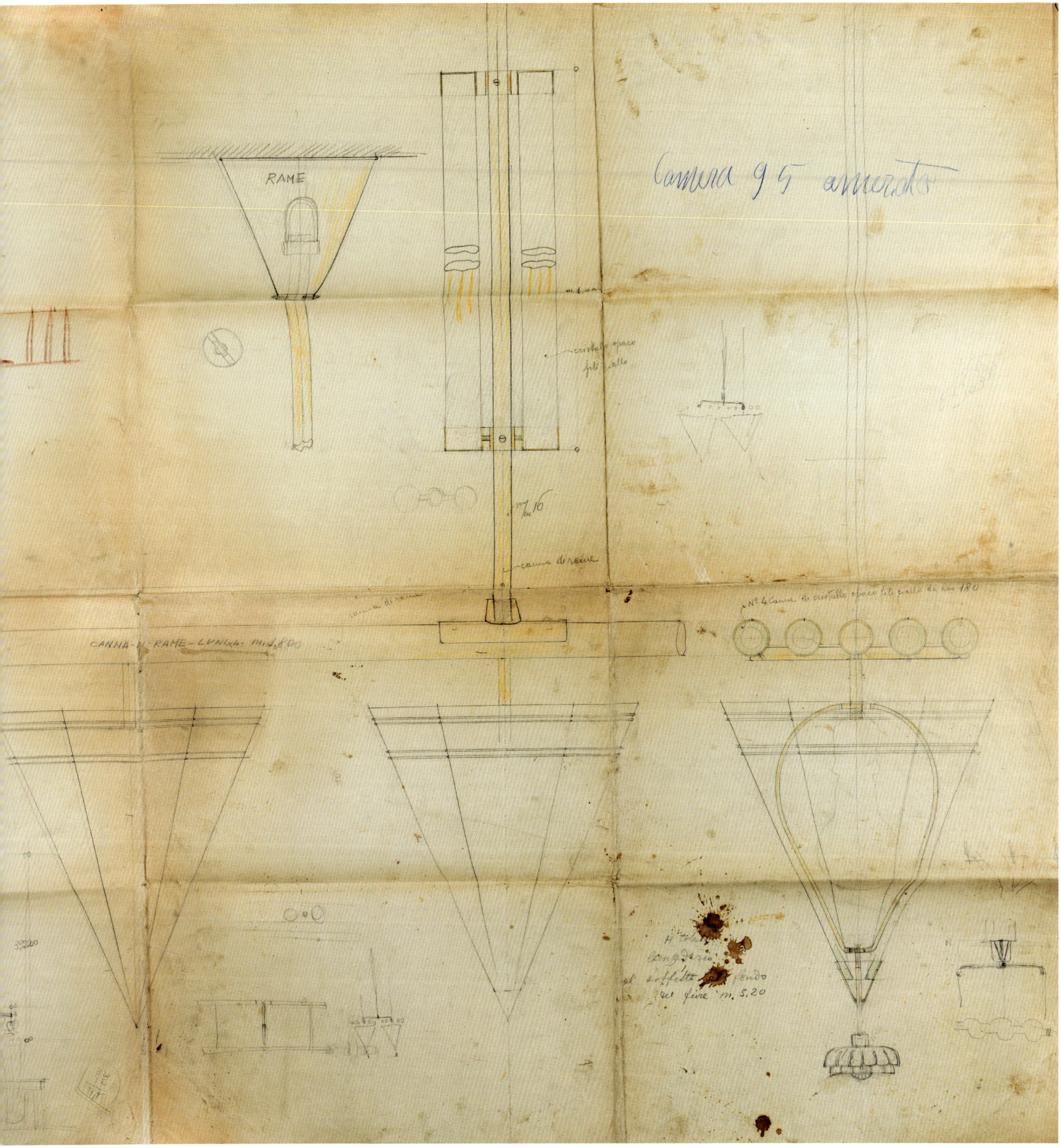
RAME

1933

SAVONA (IT)
POST OFFICE BUILDING

SEMI-FROSTED GLASS CANES
ONDULATO GLASS

This Ligurian Post Office Building was constructed between 1930 and1933 after a design by Roberto Narducci and officially opened on 28 October 1933. The contribution of the Venini firm, documented by an undated estimate (Anna Venini archive) and by period photographs, consisted of the execution of a chandelier in undulating glass (conference hall) and twelve semi-cylindrical wall lamps in semi-frosted cane glass and a metal mounting (public hall and stairwell). On the façade two lamps in undulating glass were installed, formed of semi-cylindrical twin bodies side by side (h 125 x 50 cm), of which a variant with a single body was included in the catalogue under the number 215 (Blue Catalogue).

1933

ROME (IT)
EIAR BUILDING

CASED GLASS
ONDULATO GLASS

For the Roman headquarters of the Ente Italiano per le Audizioni Radiofoniche (EIAR, from 1944 onwards RAI), the glassworks produced fixtures mainly in undulating glass in both ceiling and wall versions. Documented among these are ceiling lamps having a 4-lobed plan, formed by the union of four cylindrical volumes like those of the meeting hall. There is confirmation also of the presence in the main stairwell of a pipe organ in cased glass with finishings in metal.

>
POST OFFICE BUILDING
Postcard 1930s

>
EIAR BUILDING
Meeting hall. Period photograph, 1933

>>
EIAR BUILDING
Stairwell. Period photograph, 1933

ESEGUITE PER L'E.I.A.R.
DI ROMA IN VETRO CURVO ONDULATO

1933

TURIN (IT)
I MOSTRA NAZIONALE DELLA MODA
DESIGN U. CUZZI

SEMI-FROSTED GLASS CANES
ONDULATO GLASS

On 12 April 1933 the first Mostra nazionale della Moda [National Fashion Exhibition] was held in the Parco del Valentino in an articulated building created for the occasion by rearranging the pre-existing Palazzo del Giornale to which were added two new pavilions: those of the Alta Moda [Haute Couture] and the Esposizione-Fiera [Exhibition-Fair]. The principal designer of the complex – which also saw the involvement of Gino Levi-Montalcini, Aldo Morbelli, Maurizio Grandi and Giuseppe Vaccaro – was the architect Umberto Cuzzi, who for the definition of certain of the artificial lighting solutions called upon the Venini firm, particularly for modular elements such as semi-frosted canes and undulating glass. In the large theatre auditorium constructed in the Palazzo del Giornale, for example, seven tall cylinders (h 450 cm, Ø 100 cm) were positioned, in plywood with a central section in semi-frosted canes (Ø 3 cm) which, carefully positioned, descend from the ceiling covered in white muslin (*Casabella*, May 1933, p. 3). In the Alta Moda pavilion, on the other hand, the canes were mounted on a metal frame to form a long luminous band (l 60 cm) running along the ceiling, also in white muslin, for almost the entire length of the building (c. 69 m). Finally, undulating glass was adopted for the vertical luminous panels that acted as a backstage for the mannequins of the 'Milano' exhibition stand.

>
I MOSTRA NAZIONALE DELLA MODA
Auditorium of the theatre. Period photograph, 1933

>>>
I MOSTRA NAZIONALE DELLA MODA
'Milano' stand. Period photograph, 1933

LANO

1933 VENICE (IT)
ACNIL PASSENGER OFFICE

OPALINE GLASS

The headquarters of the water transport company, situated in Riva degli Schiavoni, was designed by the architect Virgilio Vallot (1930-33). The internal works were the first carried out by the Gruppo Arti Decorative (GAD), a company made up of some of the most well known Venetian entrepreneurs (among whom Paolo Venini in the capacity of Vice-President) with the objective of providing a 'turnkey' service. In the passenger office, minimalist wall lamps in opaline glass and brass mounting were installed.

1933-35 VENICE (IT)
ACNIL MOTORBOATS

SEMI-FROSTED GLASS CANES
PULEGOSO GLASS

Between 1933 and 1935 the E. Breda shipyard of Marghera built four motor vessels (Altino, Aquileia, Concordia and Eraclea) for the direct line Venice-Lido, the internal areas of which were designed by the architect Duilio Torres and executed by the Gruppo Arti Decorative. The GAD was a Venetian company which brought together the most important active entrepreneurs in the decorative arts sector (*Le Tre Venezie*, June-July 1939, pp. 247-248). As documented by some period photographs, the Venini firm produced lighting fixtures for the internal rooms (bar, upper and lower covered areas). Among these lamps there were ceiling and wall lamps in glass with semi-frosted canes and sconces with a ribbed bowl in white *pulegoso* glass.

\>
ACNIL PASSENGER OFFICE
Ticket office. Period photograph, 1933

\>
ACNIL MOTORBOATS
Upper covered area. Period photograph, 1933

1934

BARI (IT)
POST OFFICE BUILDING

SEMI-FROSTED GLASS CANES
ONDULATO GLASS

The POST OFFICE building, designed by Roberto Narducci, was constructed between 1931 and 1934 and officially opened on 28 October 1934. The glassworks contributed to certain rooms and to the external areas such as the entrance portico. For the last-mentioned, luminous fasces in glass with semi-frosted canes were placed in specific alternating alcoves at the access doors; on the other hand, at the sides of the entrance stairs leading to the reception hall there were lamps in undulating glass. In the interior of the building, different solutions were used for ceiling or wall lamps in semi-frosted cane glass. Among these were the fixtures positioned in the 'package acceptance hall', 'telegram acceptance hall' and 'American register'. In the counters hall, there was a large dome in glass brick at the base of which was a luminous cornice with 'elements in curved and undulating crystal' (*Architettura*, October 1934, p. 683).

›
POST OFFICE BUILDING
Entrance portico. Period photograph, 1934

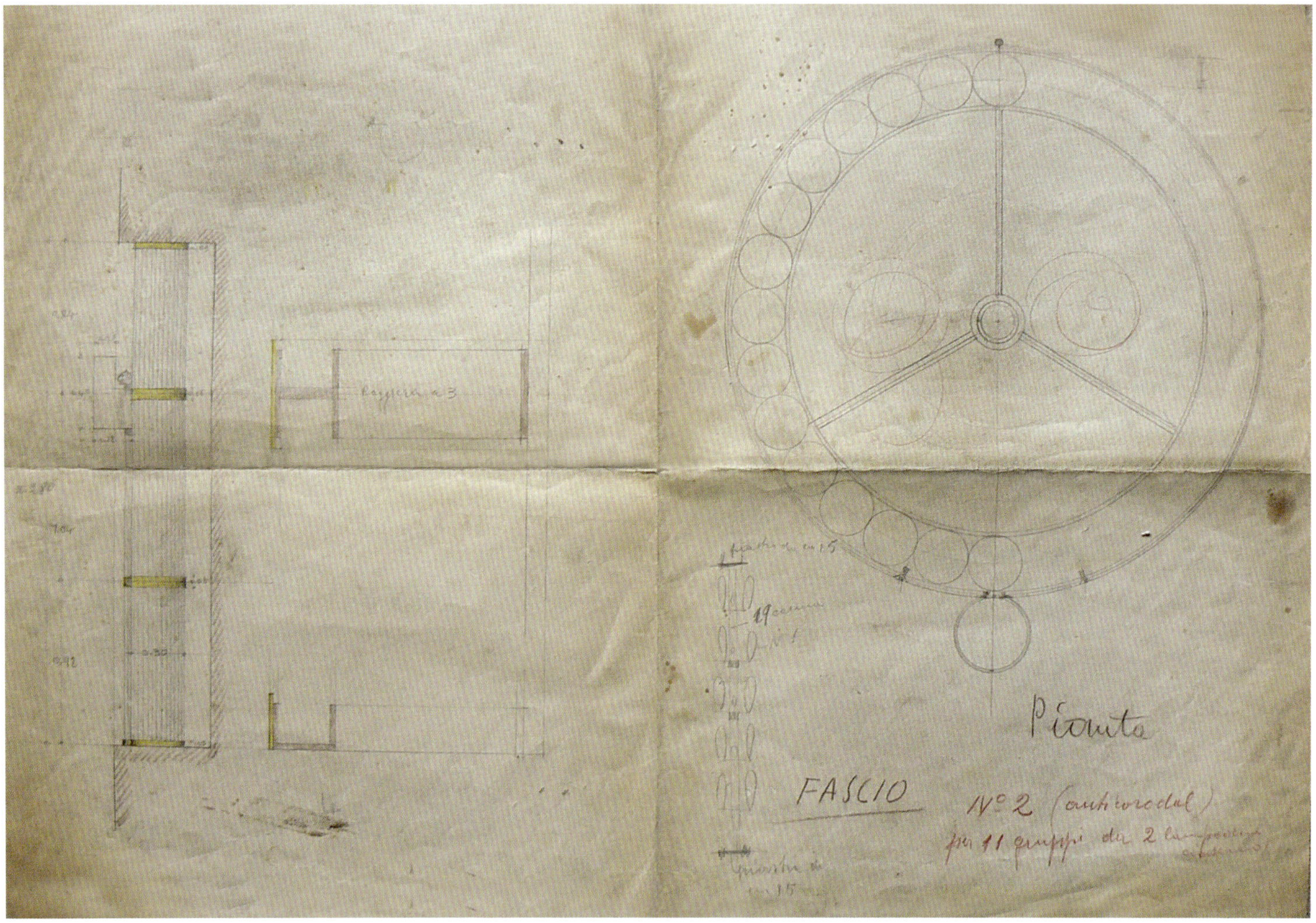

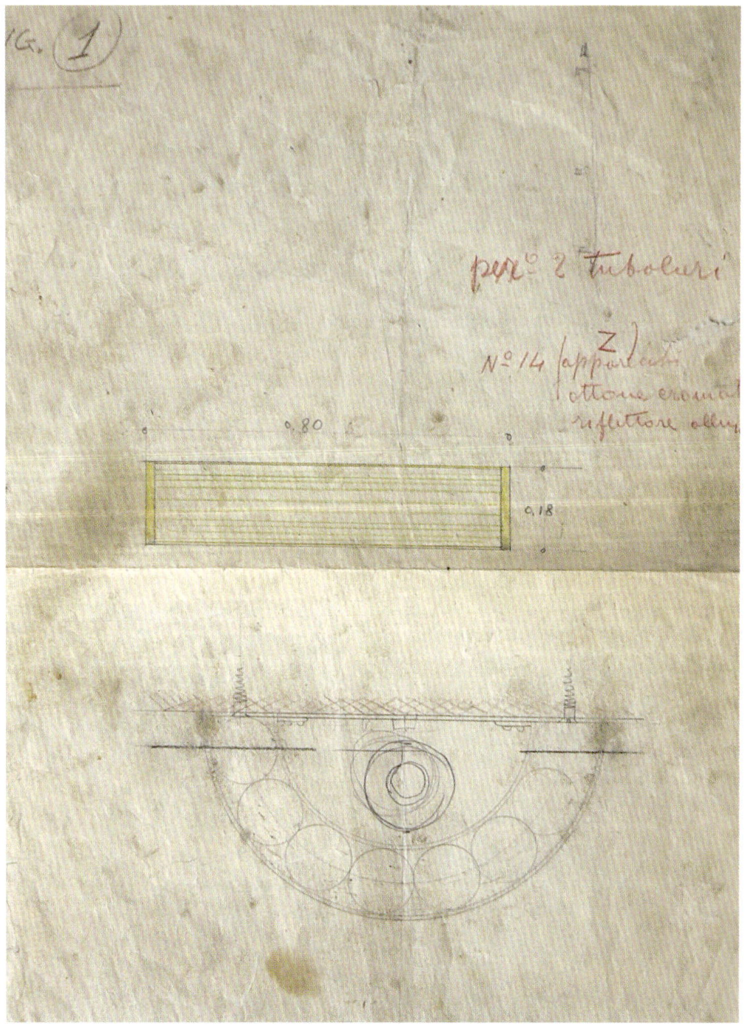

>
POST OFFICE BUILDING
Drawing for luminous fasces in glass with semi-frosted canes

>
POST OFFICE BUILDING
Drawing for ceiling lamp in glass with semi-frosted canes

>
POST OFFICE BUILDING
Package acceptance hall.
Period photograph, 1934

>
POST OFFICE BUILDING
Telegram acceptance hall.
Period photograph, 1934

1934

BOLOGNA (IT)
FOUNTAIN OF THE VICTIMS OF THE DIRETTISSIMA BOLOGNA-FIRENZE
DESIGN G. ARATA

ONDULATO GLASS

In memory of the workers who died during the construction of the fast direct train, Giulio Arata designed a fountain created on the square in front of the Bologna Railway Station. The installation is formed of a large rectangular basin from which a tall marble stele rose, within which elements in undulating glass are inserted to screen the artificial light.

>
FOUNTAIN OF THE VICTIMS
OF THE DIRETTISSIMA BOLOGNA-FIRENZE
Fountain in front of the Railway Station of Bologna.
Period photograph, 1934

1934

BOLZANO (IT)
DUCAL PALACE

SEMI-FROSTED GLASS CANES
PENDANT
FLOOR

The building was constructed between 1932 and 1934 as the residence of the Dukes of Pistoia, members of the Royal Family and representatives of the Italian state in Alto Adige and was opened on 28 October 1934. The designing and construction of the palace were organised by the Civil Engineering Office of Bolzano which availed itself of the services of the architect Ferdinando Forlati for 'all the artistic and decorative part, both for the exterior and for the internal parts' (*Le vie d'Italia*, January 1935). In furnishing the sumptuous 'Villa Roma' (this was its official name) various craftsmen were called upon, including the Venini firm which produced lighting fixtures of different shapes for some of the rooms. Cylindrical sconces in glass with semi-frosted *cristallo* or *pagliesco* canes (positioned horizontally or vertically) were installed in the entrance hall, the vestibule, the the foyer of the ballroom and the ducal chapel. These were solutions proposed by Carlo Scarpa, as a member of the technical office, the designs for which are in the possession of the Venini archive and show how the finishings for these lamps varied. In one of them, the upper metal band is serrated and suggests the shape of a stylised crown. In the vestibule between the entrance hall and the corridor, tall floor lamps with semi-frosted canes were positioned between alcoves, of a design in line with that of the hanging lamp in the 'bonbonnière room' of the Motta shop in Milan (1933). In the smoking room there was a pendant lamp with a central disk, with canes in two colours, on which a crown was set with leaves positioned vertically. The Venini archive also has a drawing of this work.

›
DUCAL PALACE
Entrance hall. Period photograph, 1934

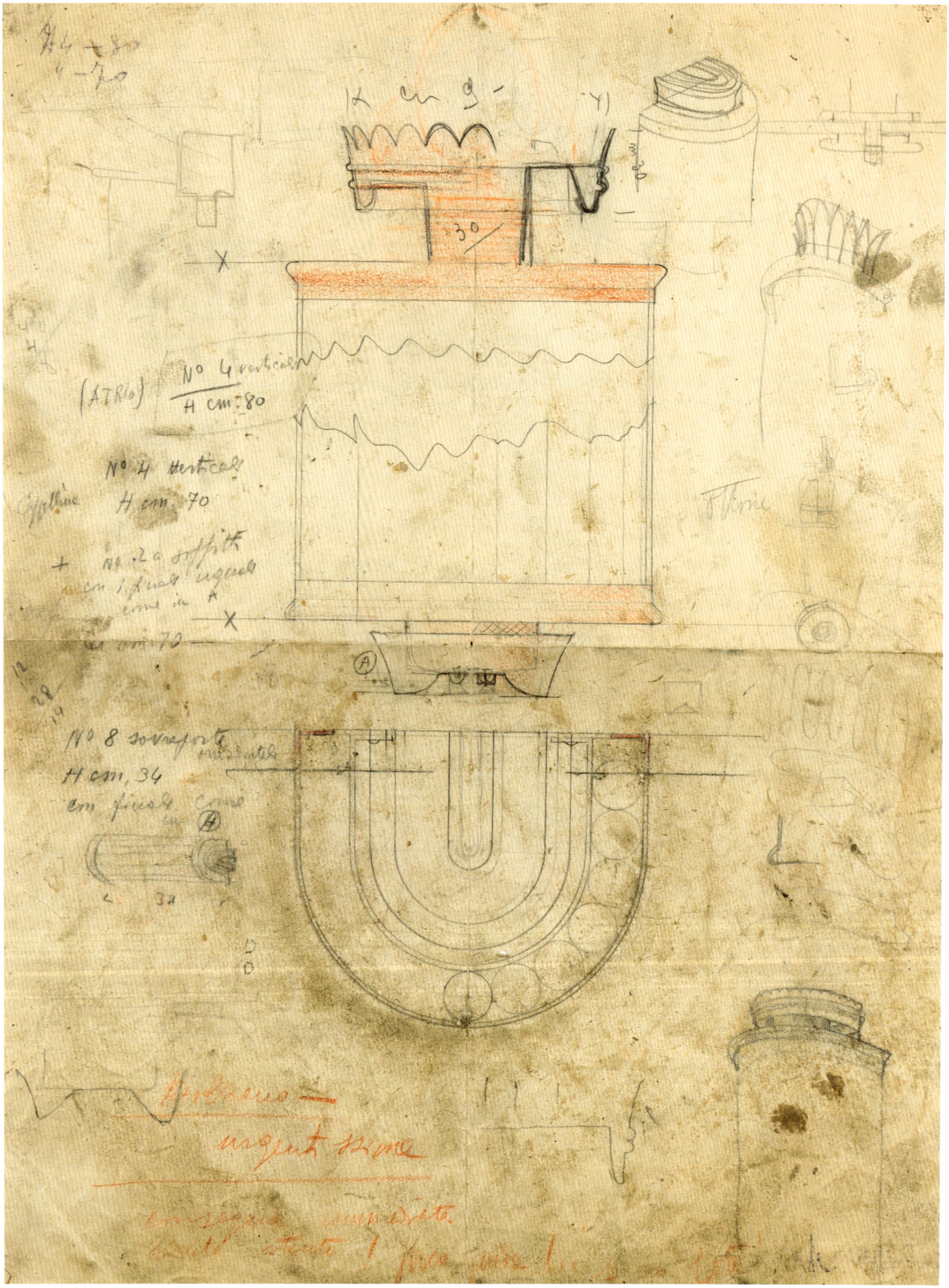

>
DUCAL PALACE
C. Scarpa, studies for cylindrical lamps with semi-frosted canes having finishings in two variants

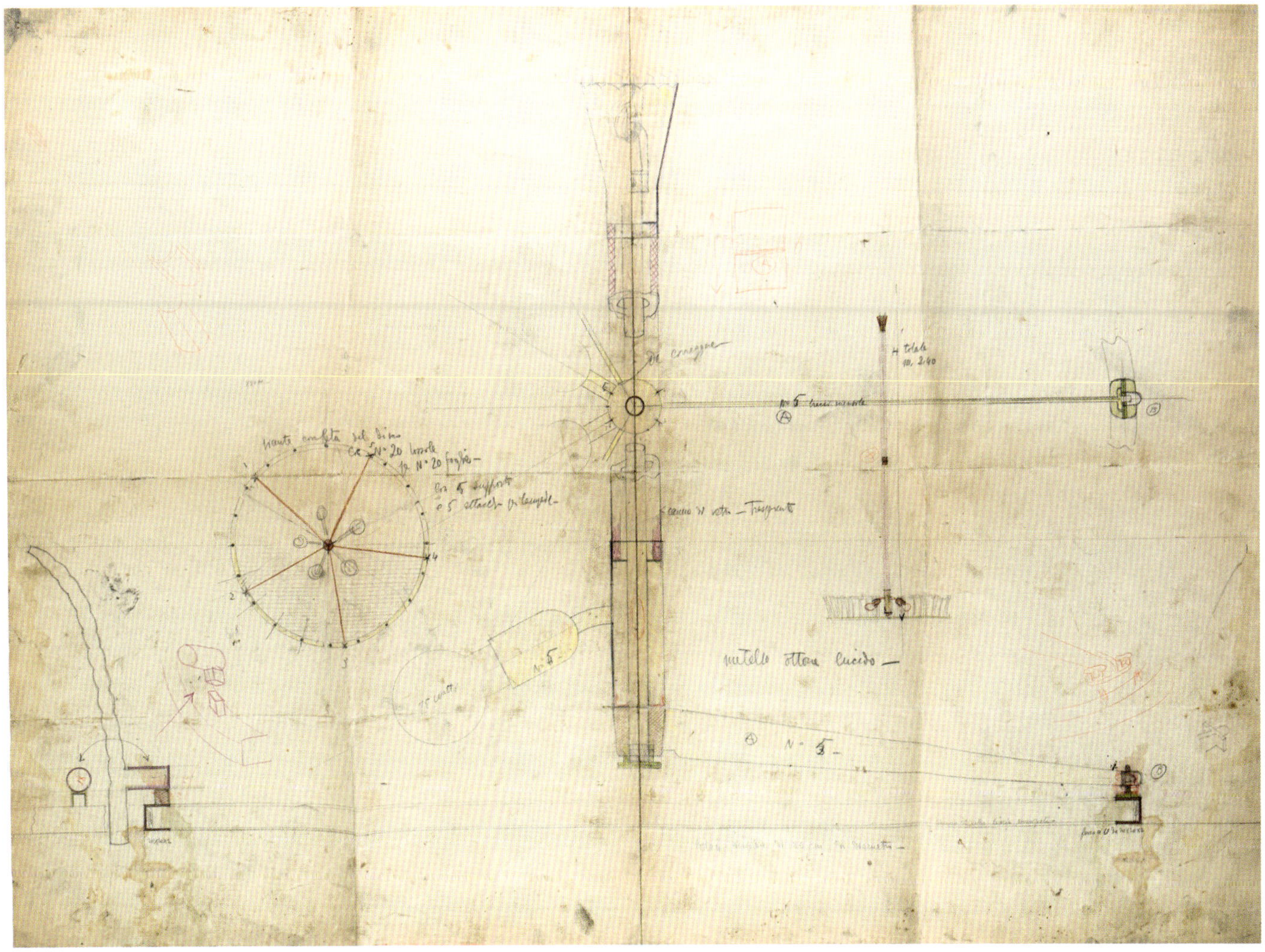

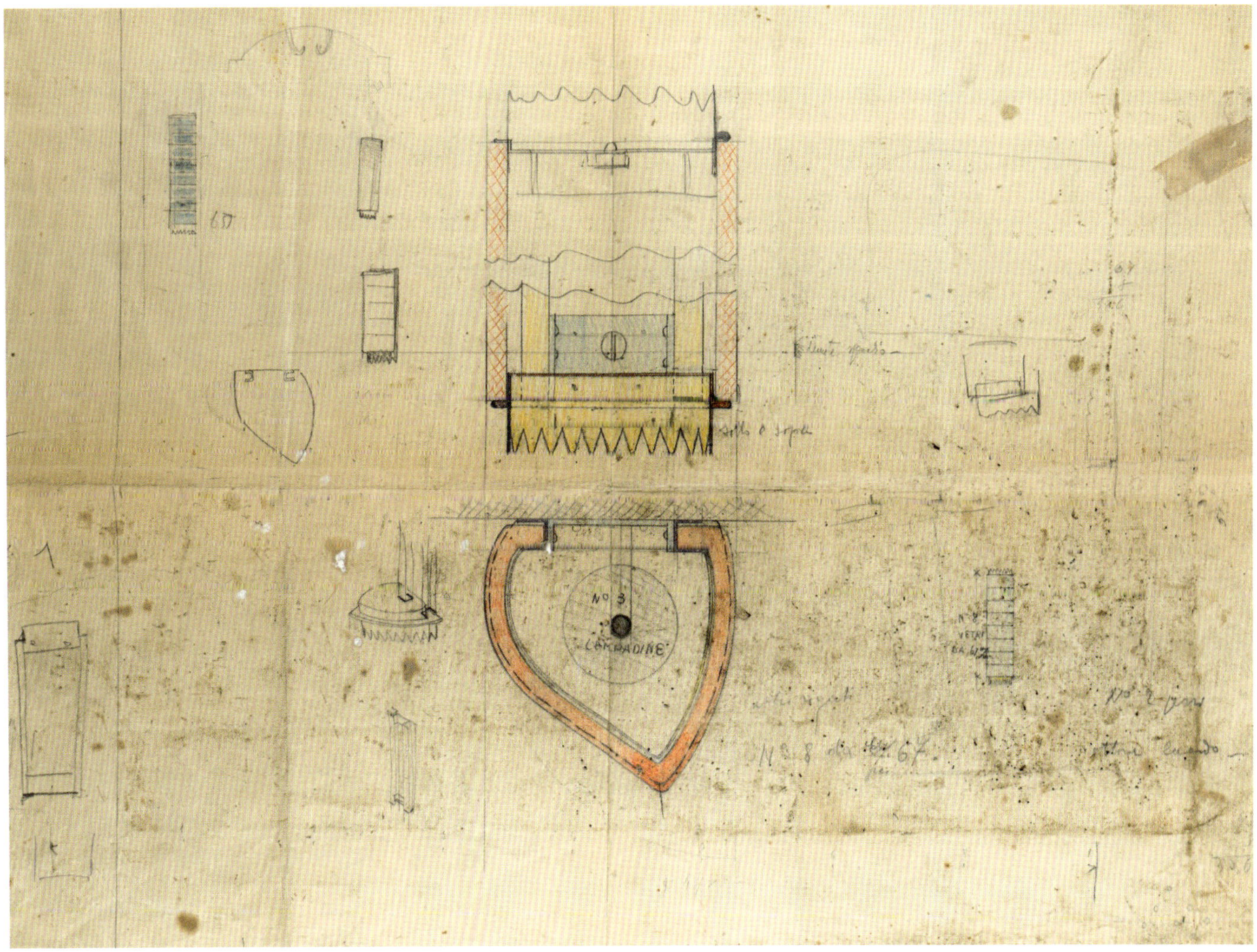

>
DUCAL PALACE
C. Scarpa, drawing of the pendant lamp produced for the smoking room

>
DUCAL PALACE
C. Scarpa, study for sconce in ribbed glass

1934

FERRARA (IT)
PRIMARY SCHOOL UMBERTO I

Lighting project for the public-sector school, now the 'Alda Costa' school, designed by the engineer Carlo Savonuzzi.

1934

LIDO DI VENEZIA (IT)
EXCELSIOR HOTEL

LISTELS
CORDONATO GLASS

In the early 1930s, the entrance hall of the famous Lido hotel (project of Giovanni Sardi, 1908) was renovated after the design of Brenno Del Giudice with works carried out by the Gruppo Arti Decorative on behalf of the Ciga [Italian Hotel Group]. The GAD was a Venetian company which brought together the most important active entrepreneurs in the decorative arts sector (*Le Tre Venezie*, June-July 1939, pp. 247-248). Here the architect used Murano glass both for the lighting fixtures and for decoration of the hall (pilasters with slats in rainbow-hued glass). In particular at the centre of the vault a large oval-shaped ceiling chandelier was placed in a combination of ribbed glass with screens made up of slats. The same solution on a lesser scale was proposed in the side passage. The lighting of the hall is also ensured by the indirect light coming from the luminous cornice in ribbed glass placed at the base of the vault

>
EXCELSIOR HOTEL
Entrance hall. Period photograph, 1934

1934

MILAN (IT)

ASSICURAZIONI GENERALI

DESIGN G. CAVAGLIERI

ONDULATO GLASS

The project is documented by a design in the Venini archive signed by the engineer Giorgio Cavaglieri and dated November 1934. Of particular interest is a ceiling chandelier with a circular base and elements in undulating glass, to be positioned in the entrance hall

1934

MILAN (IT)

NOVUM SHOP

CASED GLASS
ONDULATO GLASS

The Croff store of furnishing fabrics was an installation of Michele Marelli and Gio Ponti (1933-34). Venini fixtures were to be seen on the exterior, in the entrance passage and within, in the large exhibition gallery. In the first case this consisted of a ceiling lamp with a double cover of cased glass included in the catalogue under the number 5405 (Blue Catalogue). In the second case, the ceiling lamps were characterised by a rectangular base and screen in undulating glass.

>
NOVUM SHOP
Entrance. Period photograph, 1934

1934

PALERMO (IT)

POST OFFICE BUILDING

DESIGN A. MAZZONI

SEMI-FROSTED GLASS CANES
CASED GLASS
ONDULATO GLASS

This monumental building was constructed between 1930 and 1934 after a design by Angiolo Mazzoni and officially opened on 28 October 1934. Particular attention was paid to the interior, for which great use was made of, among other things, precious marble coverings. The Venini firm contributed many lighting fixtures after the design of the aforesaid Mazzoni, who used mainly undulating glass, apart from the semi-frosted canes for the various 'lights' designed as integral parts of the various areas. From the outside in, there were Murano fixtures: both in the high colonnaded portico, where there was a series of recessed ceiling lights with cane screens and in the access passage after it, which was lit by a series of wall lamps in metal and undulating glass with screens having five slats with a U profile. While for the entrance and public halls cylindrical wall lamps with semi-frosted canes and metal mounting were used (h 155 cm), various areas were characterised by luminous wall or ceiling inserts in undulating glass (staircase entrance, money services hall, telegram acceptance hall, current accounts hall). In the 'American register' room, on the other hand, the area was enhanced by four more-or-less semi-cylindrical sconces (h 80 cm), also in undulating glass, standing out among the boxes on the marble covering. Particularly noteworthy is the solution for the conference hall where the fixtures in undulating glass contribute to the artistic wealth of the room marked by the presence of the futurist paintings of Benedetta Cappa Marinetti, Tato and Paolo Bevilacqua and by the embroidered curtains of Bruna Somenzi. Here there was a luminous frame running along the ceiling around the perimeter of the room, at the centre of which a long pendant lamp stood out (l. 450 cm) positioned over the marble table. Produced with a metal structure in red copper (body and three supporting rods), it had a diffuser screen in light blue glass with elements having an elongated U-shaped profile. In addition, there was the unusual solution of slats of undulating glass also being used to form the walls of the telephone room. In this Palermo Post Office Building there were also lamps in cased glass of a very decorative kind, inspired by art déco and similar to those of the Bergamo Post Office, which were chosen for the press room. Many of the lamps are still *in situ*.

>
POST OFFICE BUILDING
Conference hall.
Period photograph, 1934

>
POST OFFICE BUILDING
Press room. Period photograph, 1934

>
POST OFFICE BUILDING
Telephone room. Period photograph, MART

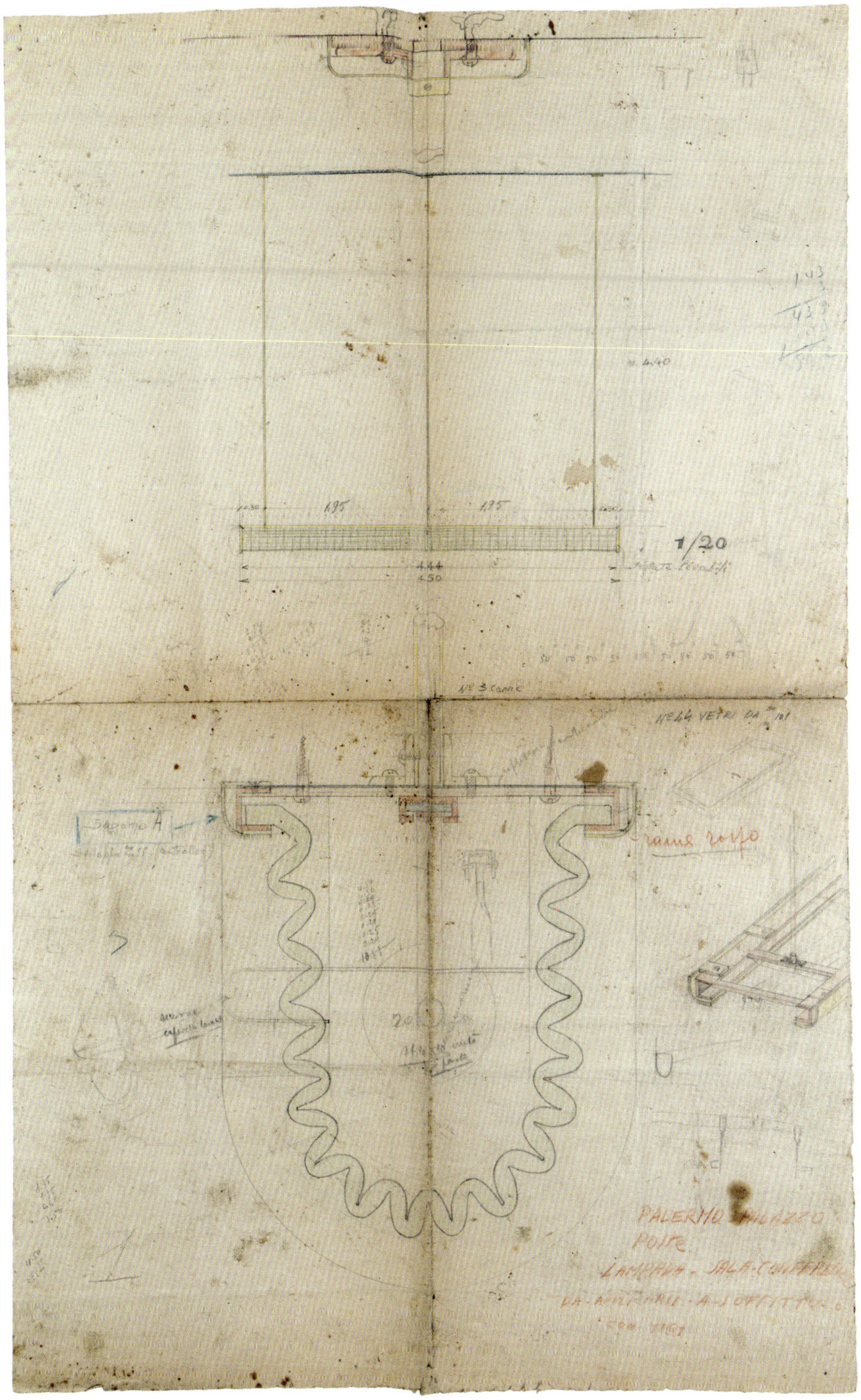

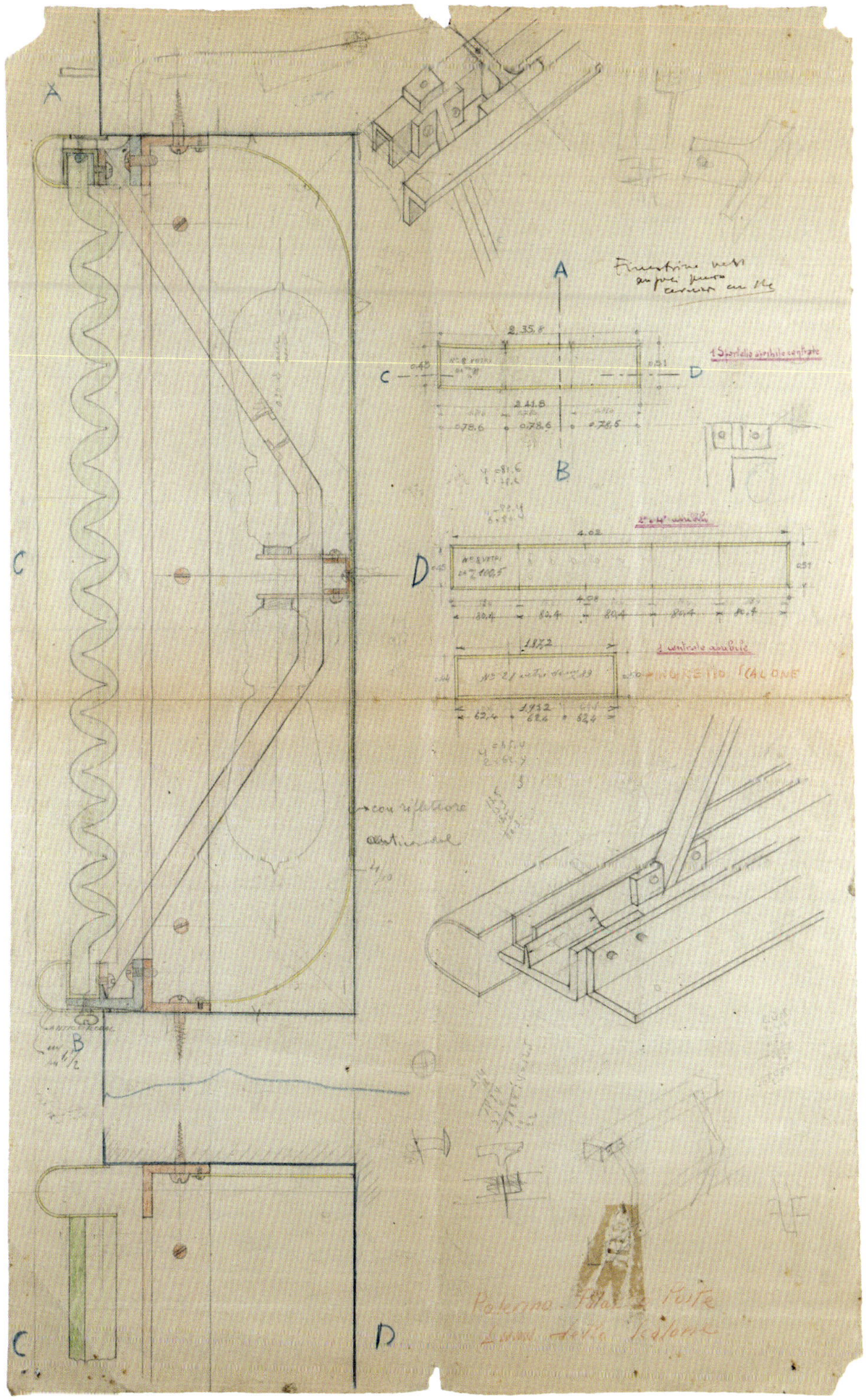

> POST OFFICE BUILDING
Design for a pendant lamp for the conference hall

> POST OFFICE BUILDING
Design for luminous inserts in undulating glass

1934

SABAUDIA (IT)
POST OFFICE BUILDING
DESIGN A. MAZZONI

ONDULATO GLASS

Constructed between 1933 and 1934, the building designed by Angiolo Mazzoni was officially opened on 15 April 1934, as was the town itself. For this commission, the glassworks produced fixtures in undulating glass for the great public hall. These were two luminous bands into which the bulbs were inserted in a concealed way and arranged according to a precise design. The first (l 60 cm) extended over the whole length of the hall (l 24 m) close to the counters and bending on a line with the side entrance. The second (l 32 cm) was placed next to the outer windows. The bands, inserted into the ceiling which was covered in grey ceramic tiles, accompanied members of the public visually as they moved around in the hall. In other areas circular ceiling lamps, also in undulating glass and with concealed bulbs, were installed.

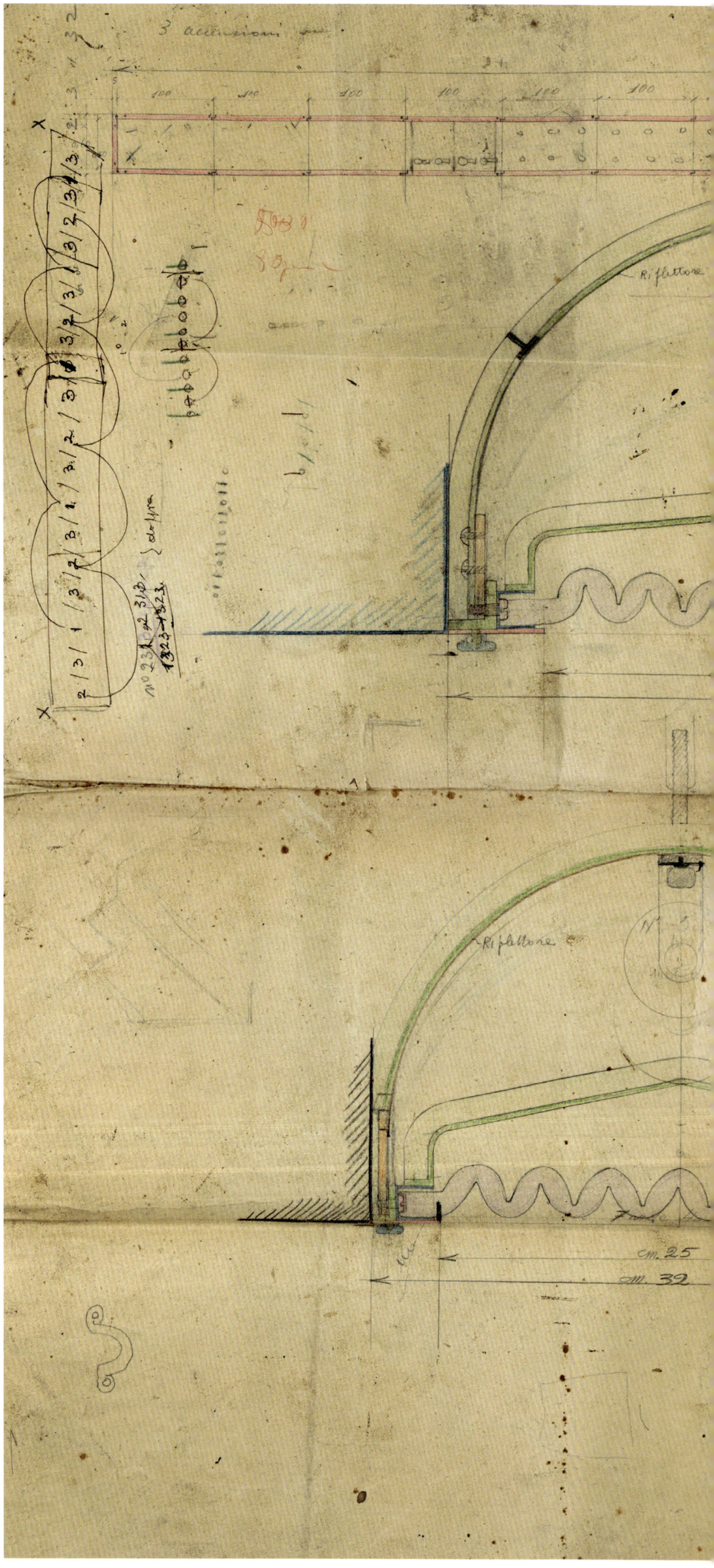

>
POST OFFICE BUILDING
Public hall. Period photograph, MART

>
POST OFFICE BUILDING
Drawing for the luminous bands

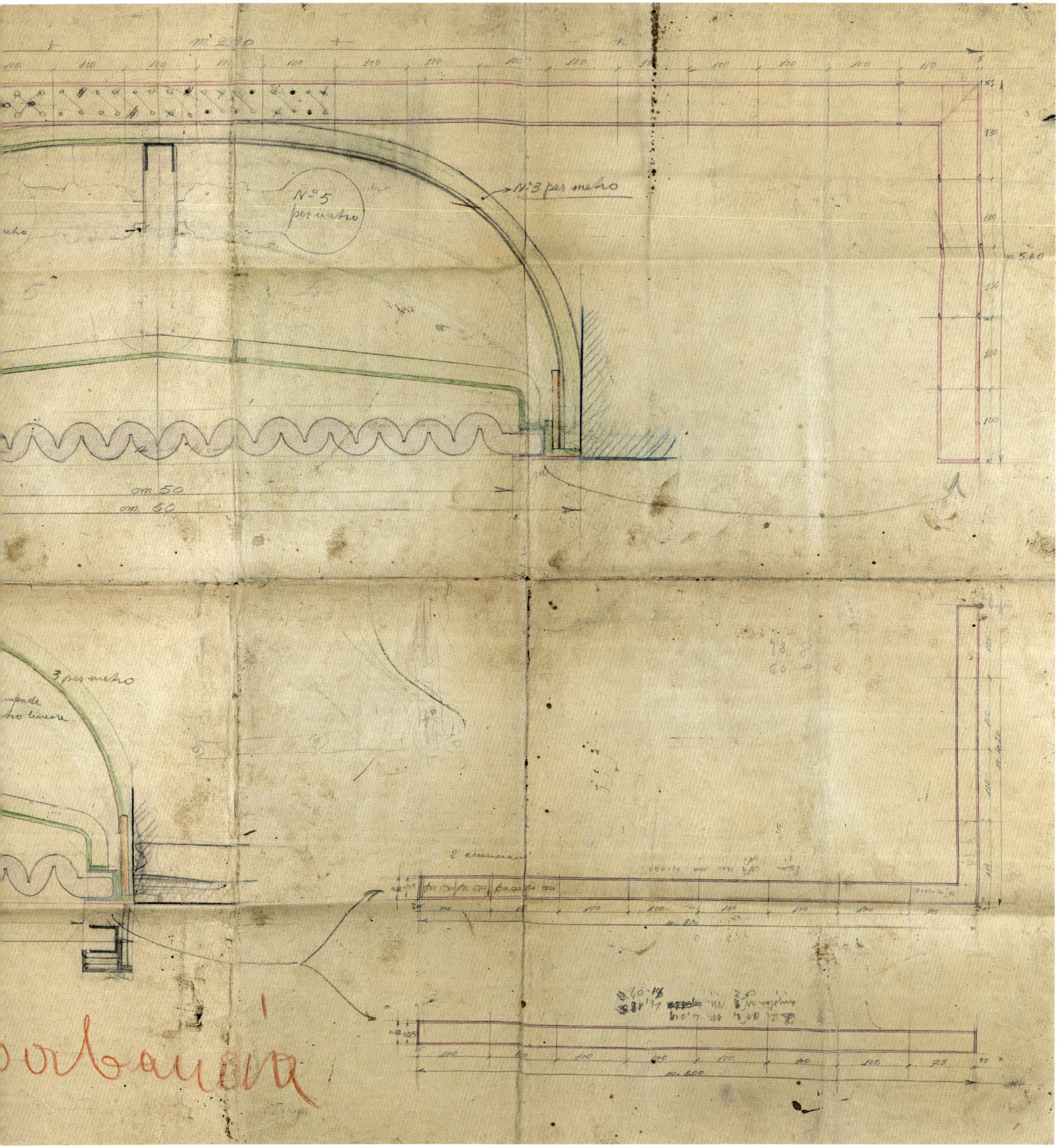
N°3 per metro
N°5 per metro
3 per metro
cm 50
cm 60

1934

TURIN (IT)
DOCK HOTEL

CORDONATO GLASS

For the banquet hall of the hotel building, designed by the architect Nicola Mosso, the glassworks produced a luminous tube in ribbed glass stretching over the whole length of the hall in line with the height differences of the ceiling.

1934

TRENTO (IT)
POST AND TELEGRAPH SERVICES DIRECTORATE-GENERAL
DESIGN A. MAZZONI

CASED GLASS
ONDULATO GLASS

In 1934 the Direzione generale delle poste was officially opened, the work of the architect Angiolo Mazzoni. This was a massive restructuring operation, begun in 1930, which involved the complete renovation of the old Austro-Hungarian Post Office Buildings and of the fragments of the 16th-century 'a Prato' palace, conserving some parts of the latter. In this edifice rich in decorative work, the Venini firm was involved in the execution of lighting fixtures both for the exterior and the interior. At the centre of the courtyard, on which gave the stained-glass windows of Tato and Fortunato Depero which closed the archways overlooking the courtyard, there was a luminous fountain in brick and stone into which was inserted a column in undulating glass. Luminous jambs, also in undulating glass, were placed at the base of the grand staircase, while at the top there was a ceiling lamp, with a screen in undulating glass, which lit the ascent. A similar lamp was to be found also in the four-columned recreational hall. In the portico, over one of the accesses to the post and telegraph recreational club, there was an original lamp in three tiers of cornucopias in cased glass, with a crown of leaves in opaline glass at the base. The Venini archive possesses a collection of drawings and heliographic copies documenting the study for some of the profiles used.

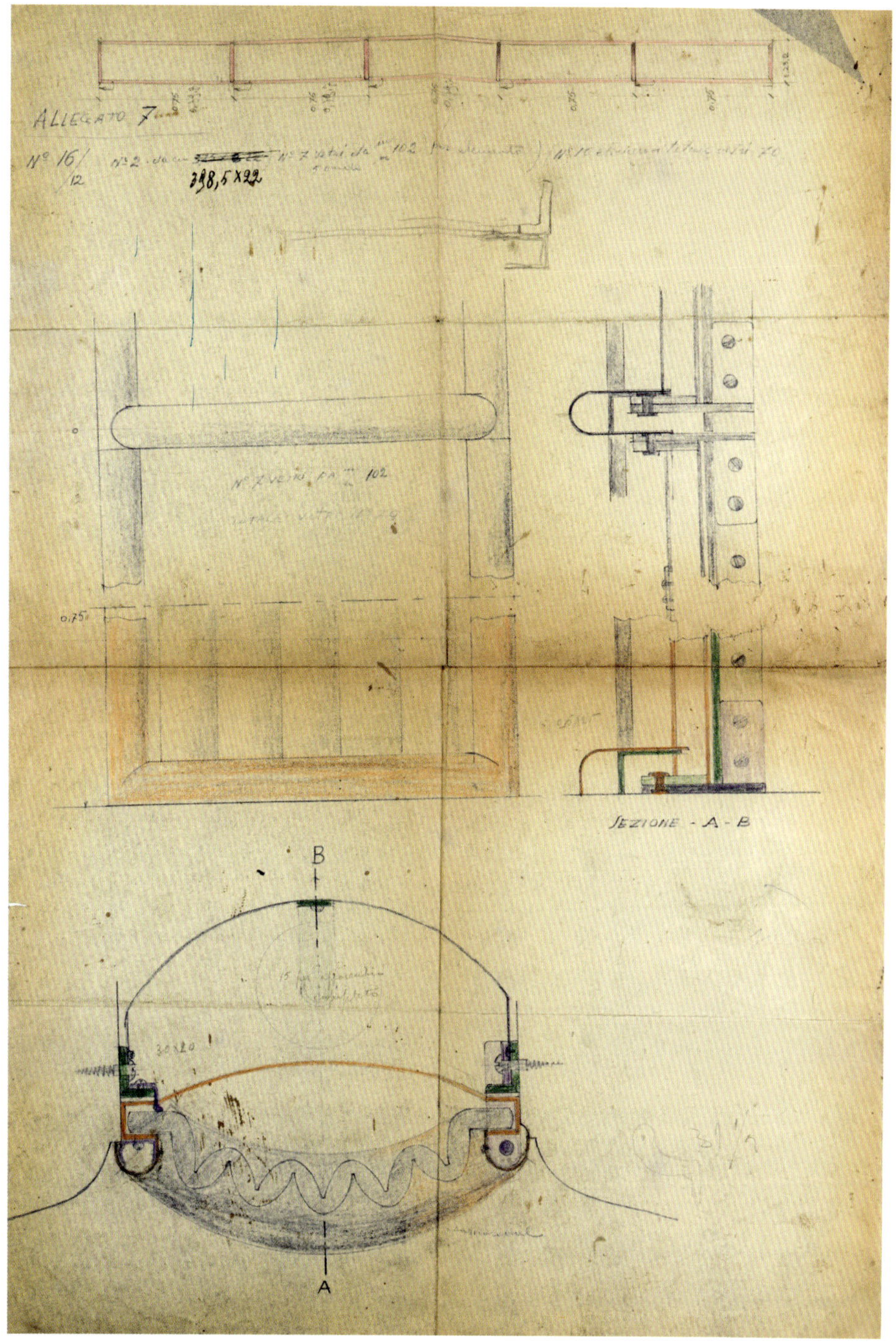

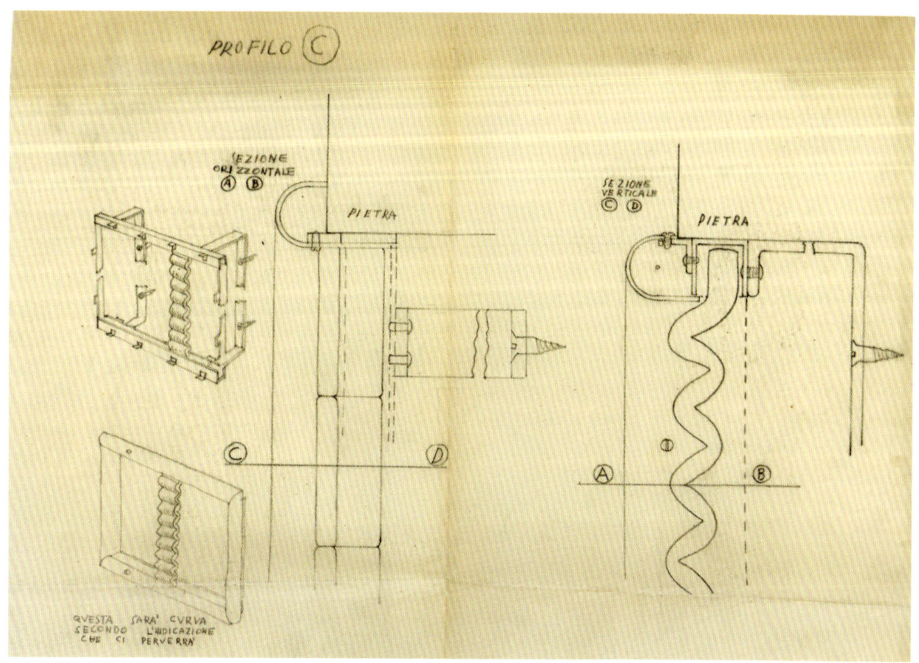

\>
POST AND TELEGRAPH SERVICES DIRECTORATE-GENERAL
Drawing for luminous jambs

\>
POST AND TELEGRAPH SERVICES DIRECTORATE-GENERAL
C. Scarpa, study for wall lamp in undulating glass, profile C

\>>
POST AND TELEGRAPH SERVICES DIRECTORATE-GENERAL
Grand staircase. Period photograph, MART

1934

VENICE (IT)
AMERICAN BAR

PENDANT

In equipping this Venetian venue, Melchiorre Bega used Venini lamps to define the area in a pictorial way. He positioned a series of pendant lamps of a pronounced geometrical design hanging from a series of large circular holes made in the suspended ceiling. This is the model included in the catalogue under the number 5417 after a design by Carlo Scarpa, with a spherical diffuser body and truncated-cone-shaped rod cover, in *mezza filigrana* according to the design, and here produced in *reticello* glass. The same type of solution (large circular hole accompanying model no. 5417) was used by Bega in arranging the Fini store, in Bologna, in the same year.

>
AMERICAN BAR
Model no. 5417. Period photograph, 1930s

>
AMERICAN BAR
Main room. Period photograph, 1934, Università Iuav di Venezia, Archivio Progetti, Fondo Melchiorre Bega

1935

BARI (IT)
INA ISTITUTO NAZIONALE DELLE ASSICURAZIONI

CORDONATO GLASS

Lighting project for the premises of the insurance institution designed by the architect Alberto Calza Bini. This principally involved luminous cornices and ceiling lamps in ribbed glass, of which the Venini archive possesses some drawings dated June 1935.

1935

BOLOGNA (IT)
CASALINI SHOP

WALL LAMPS
PENDANT

For the Bologna store of the Faenza furniture and fittings company, a Venini authorised retailer in 1935, the glassworks archive possesses a drawing also dated 1935 with two proposals for lamps. The first one (solution D) was for a chandelier (h 220 cm, l 180 cm) of an elongated shape, with leaf motifs in moulded glass (variant of no. 5267). The second (solution E) was one with a structure composed of alternating cylinders in glass with semi-frosted canes and *pagliesco* diffuser screen.

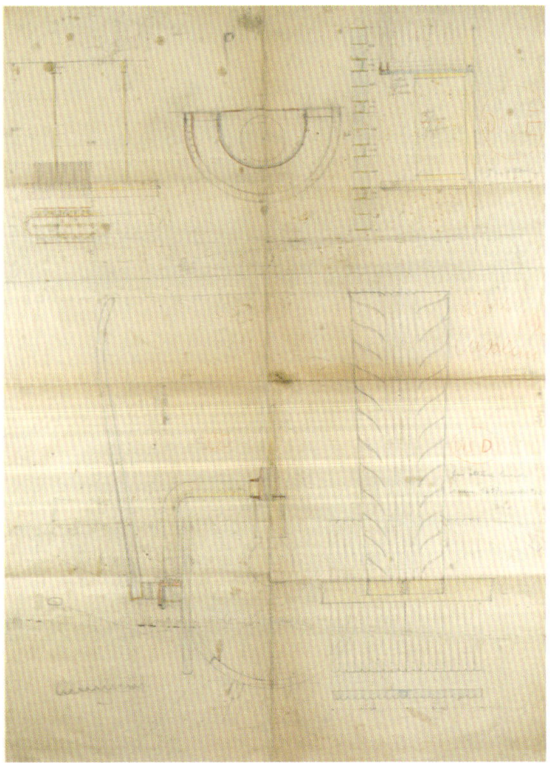

›
CASALINI SHOP
Drawing with lamps for 'Casalini Bologna', solutions D and E

1935

FLORENCE (IT)
SANTA MARIA NOVELLA RAILWAY STATION AND ROYAL PALACE

WALL LAMPS
CEILING
PENDANT
CORDONATO GLASS
ONDULATO GLASS

Officially opened on 30 October 1935, the railway station of Santa Maria Novella was constructed after a design by the Gruppo Toscano, winners in 1933 of a controversial competition. The architect Giovanni Michelucci was head of a 'group' including Pier Niccolò Berardi, Italo Gamberini, Sarre Guarnieri, Leonardo Lusanna and Nello Baroni to which we owe in particular the design of the fittings. The involvement of the glassworks is documented from March 1934, date on which there is a letter from Paolo Venini to Fernanda Ojetti with mention of light tests 'for the canopies of the station', already designed by Angiolo Mazzoni. These were presumably tests made with luminous cornices having modular elements in ribbed glass, patented in June of the same year and probably used in the execution of some of the many cornices present in the passenger building. There were also Venini wall lamps in the left-luggage room, in the first-class waiting room, in the reserved compartment of the first- and second-class restaurant (no. 425, Blue Catalogue). Many fixtures were also produced for the Palazzina Reale [Royal Palace], a building designed by Giovanni Michelucci and situated south of the railway complex. Murano lamps were to be seen in the main vestibule, in the Ministers' room, in the room reserved for the King, where in the ceiling lamp and in the wall lamps (no. 230) the motif of the stylised leaves returns. In the Reception Hall a velarium was also installed, with elements in clear yellow glass, while in the external L-shaped portico there was a series of very large basket-shaped hanging lamps in undulating glass and with a metal structure after a design by Carlo Scarpa. Some of these fixtures are still *in situ*.

»
SANTA MARIA NOVELLA RAILWAY STATION AND ROYAL PALACE
Saletta del Re in the Palazzina Reale in *Architettura*, April 1936

»
SANTA MARIA NOVELLA RAILWAY STATION AND ROYAL PALACE
Drawings for 'ceiling' light and 'sconce' of the 'special room' (room reserved for the King)

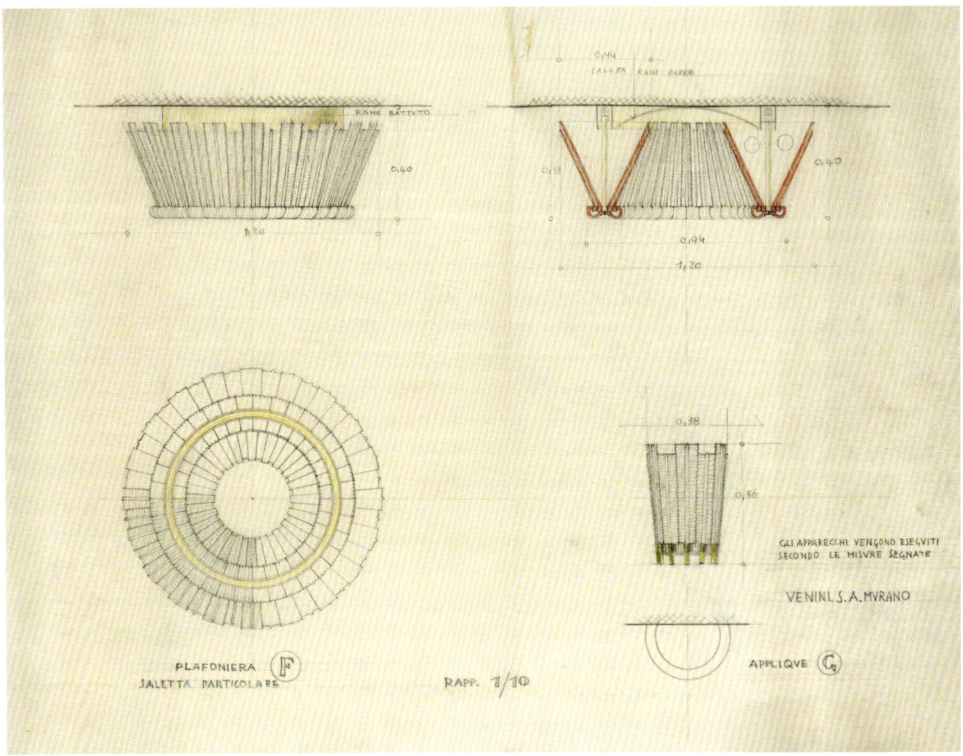
GLI APPARECCHI VENGONO ESEGUITI
SECONDO LE MISURE SEGNATE
VENINI. S.A. MURANO
PLAFONIERA F
SALETTA PARTICOLARE
RAPP. 1/10
APPLIQUE G

>
SANTA MARIA NOVELLA RAILWAY STATION AND ROYAL PALACE
Portico of the Palazzina Reale in *Architettura*, April 1936

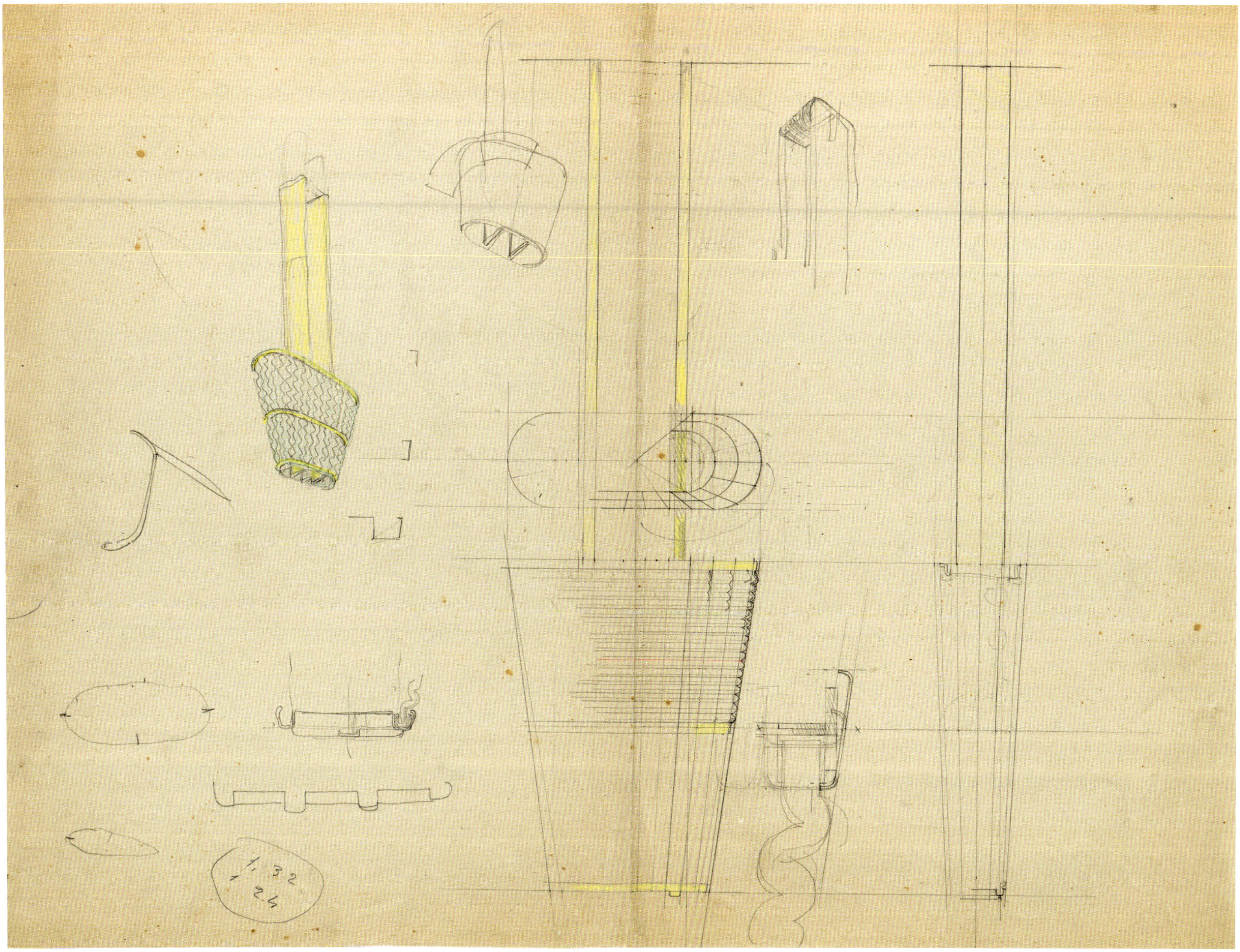

>
SANTA MARIA NOVELLA RAILWAY STATION AND ROYAL PALACE
C. Scarpa, study for the hanging lamp for the portico of the Palazzina Reale

1935

FLORENCE (IT)
UGOLINO GOLF CLUBHOUSE

ONDULATO GLASS

Lighting project for the golf club (1933-35) constructed after a design of the architect Gherardo Bosio. Of particular interest are the ceiling fixtures in undulating glass placed in the entrance hall of the building.

1935

LIDO DI VENEZIA (IT)
GIOVANNI NICELLI AIRPORT

SEMI-FROSTED GLASS CANES
ONDULATO GLASS

The passenger building of the Lido airport (on an area already used for aviation purposes for several years) was constructed after a design by the architect Mario Emmer and officially opened on 4 February 1935. Following the design of the painter Giovanni Nei Pasinetti, the Gruppo Arti Decorative conducted the interior works, in particular the rooms intended for the company Ala Littoria. The GAD was a Venetian company which brought together the most important active entrepreneurs in the decorative arts sector (*Le Tre Venezie*, June-July 1939, pp. 247-248). The Venini firm contributed in various areas, with the positioning of, among other things, ceiling lamps in undulating glass, a luminous cornice in *pulegoso* glass and the luminous screens in cane glass in the mosaic structure in the bar. Some of these works are still *in situ*.

>
GIOVANNI NICELLI AIRPORT
Bar. Period photograph, 1935

>
GIOVANNI NICELLI AIRPORT
Baggage check area. Period photograph, 1935

1935

POLA (HR)
POST OFFICE BUILDING
DESIGN A. MAZZONI

ONDULATO GLASS

The Post Office Building was constructed between 1933 and 1935 after a design by Angiolo Mazzoni and, after building works fraught with certain difficulties, officially opened on 4 November 1935. Considered by the critics as a 'completely futuristic work' (Canali 2001), the Pola building is the last of the Post Office Buildings designed by the architect to have lighting fixtures resulting from the collaboration with the Venini firm. The glassworks archive is in possession of some drawings for this work, some of them dated December 1934, which document the use of 'artistic luminous bodies' in anticorodal and undulating glass. Among them, for example, is the luminous column (h 249 cm) placed between the two glass entrance doors framed by doorposts in pink granite. In the high public correspondence hall there was a long luminous structure with a U-shaped profile (h 479 cm, Ø 38.5 cm) placed near the ceiling, in the convex part in front of the wide stained-glass window running the length of the opposite wall. Above the high desks at the side of the hall there were long lights screened by glass plates. Luminous ceiling tubes, also in undulating glass and in various shapes (T-shaped, L-shaped and I-shaped) were present in the 'packages' public hall, telegram hall and postal order room (l 300 – 500 cm).

>
POST OFFICE BUILDING
Correspondence public hall. Period photograph, MART

>>
POST OFFICE BUILDING
Drawing of the large luminous tube (h 478 cm) in anticorodal and undulating glass for the correspondence public hall

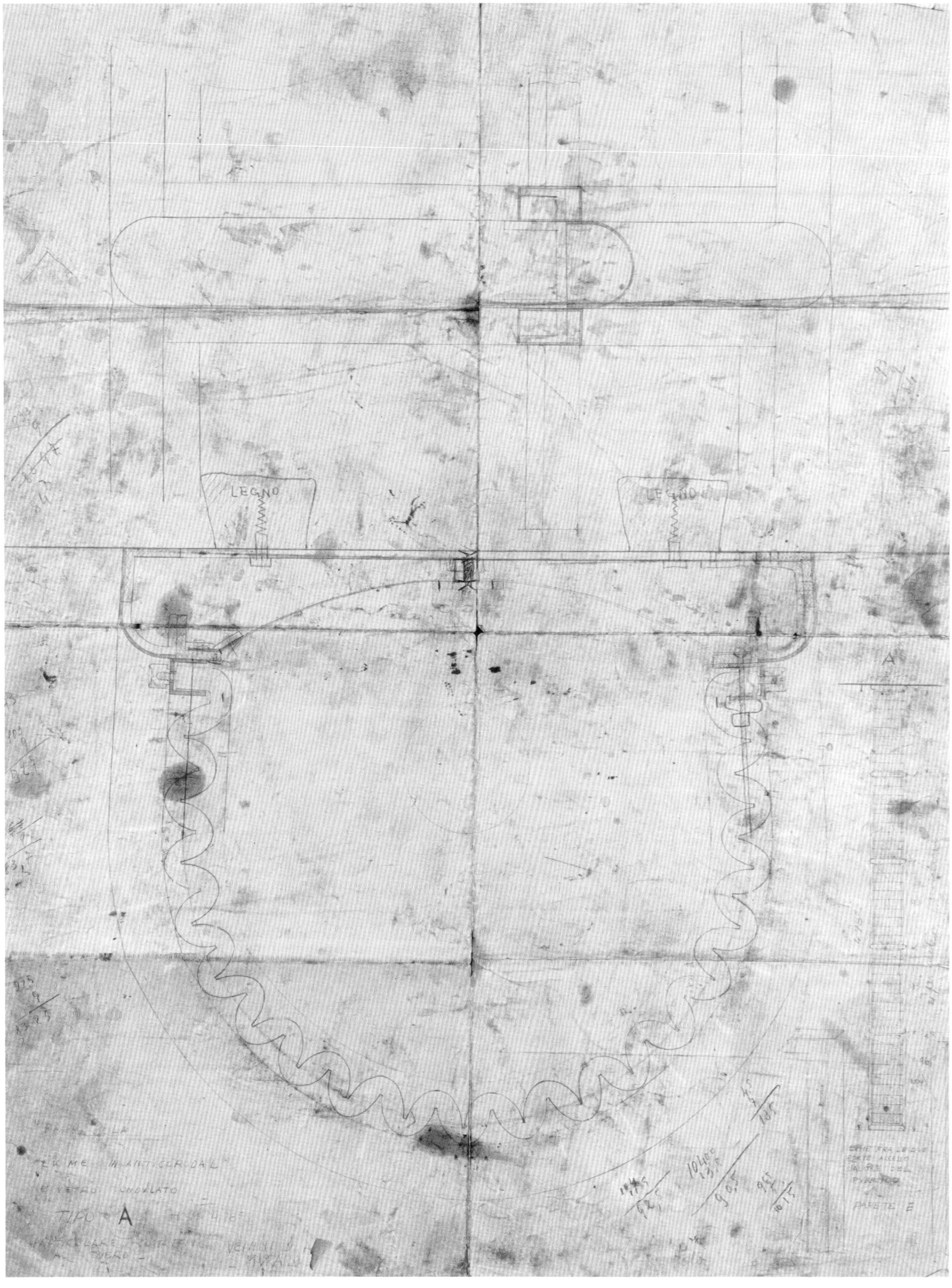
LEGNO
LEGNO
TIPO A

1935

ROME (IT)
BAR, VIA DEGLI SCIPIONI

ONDULATO GLASS

For the little venue designed by the architect Plinio Marconi, the Venini firm used solutions in undulating glass creating pendant lamps with U-shaped profiles.

1935

ROME (IT)
BAR, VIA VIMINALE

ONDULATO GLASS

In addition to the via degli Scipioni commission, Plinio Marconi designed a second bar, in via Viminale. Also in this case the use of undulating glass was preferred to create luminous ceiling beams which, reflected in the surrounding mirrors, created a play of reflections and multiplication effects in the bar areas.

1935

ROME (IT)
S.A.V.A. HEADQUARTERS

WALL LAMPS
CEILING

Lighting project for areas of the Società Alluminio Veneto Anonima in Rome carried out by the Gruppo Arti Decorative. The GAD was a Venetian company which brought together the most important active entrepreneurs in the decorative arts sector (*Le Tre Venezie*, June-July 1939, pp. 247-248).

1935

REGGIO EMILIA (IT)
RAILWAY STATION
DESIGN A. MAZZONI

ONDULATO GLASS

The railway station was built between 1933 and 1935 after a design by Angiolo Mazzoni and was officially opened on 29 October 1935. As is documented also by a handwritten note with the furnace works, the glass-works produced certain fixtures here, particularly types already used in other works by the same architect (Palermo, Pola, Siena etc.). In the entrance hall, for example, there was a dome lamp placed over the high desk in accordance with a solution also used in the Pola post office. The controversial curved volume of the left-luggage room, initially proposed by the architect with a metal frame and curved glass sheets, was executed with inserts in undulating glass, used in a similar manner in the telephone room of the Palermo post office. The enormous raised volume acted as a divide between the arrival and departure zones. Other lamps also in undulating glass were produced for the smaller rooms.

>>
RAILWAY STATION
Entrance hall and left-luggage room. Period photograph, 1935, MART

PARTENZA

1935

SIENA (IT)
RAILWAY STATION
DESIGN A. MAZZONI

ONDULATO GLASS

After a complex planning course, the railway station of Siena was built after a design by Angiolo Mazzoni (1933-35) and officially opened on 25 November 1935. The complex consisted of a series of volumes, intended for different uses, which were connected on the two fronts (towards the square and towards the tracks) by a long station canopy. The artificial lighting was given an equally significant role with solutions aimed at suggesting pathways and characterising the various areas. The greater part of this is due to the significant scale of the Venini contribution which, as documented by a series of working drawings, some of them dated, was developed principally between May and September 1935. Involved here was the production of luminous strips and circular recessed ceiling lights and of a series of semi-cylindrical ceiling and pendant fixtures, all produced in undulating and anticorodal glass, standing out on ceilings largely covered in pâte de verre tiles (done by Sarim). There was a luminous strip with concealed bulbs at the entrance to the 'external caterer', but also and above all in the departures entrance hall next to the counters (800 x 84 cm), as in Littoria, in front of the luggage counter (450 x 84 cm) and in the centre of the area with a triangular end towards the tracks (700 x 84 cm) and in the underground passage between the tracks. Round ceiling lamps were positioned here, and also in the little waiting room between the tracks and outside the entrance. Luminous tubes formed out of the succession of fixtures in undulating glass with U-shaped profiles were positioned here to indicate the paths to follow between, for example, the platform and the exit corridor or to mark out the space belonging to the Royal room or Authorities' room. These areas, as also the 1st class waiting room, were given particular care. While the aforesaid waiting room was characterised by a pendant lamp with an L-shaped body and U-shaped profiles, in the Authorities' room ceiling lamps with concealed bulbs were again chosen, and for the area intended for Royalty there was, unusually, a luminous strip in bubble glass (910 x 84 cm).

>
RAILWAY STATION
Exit. Period photograph, 1935

SCITA
PARTENZE ARRIVI
VIETATO
ATTRAVERSARE
I BINARI

D. Anderson

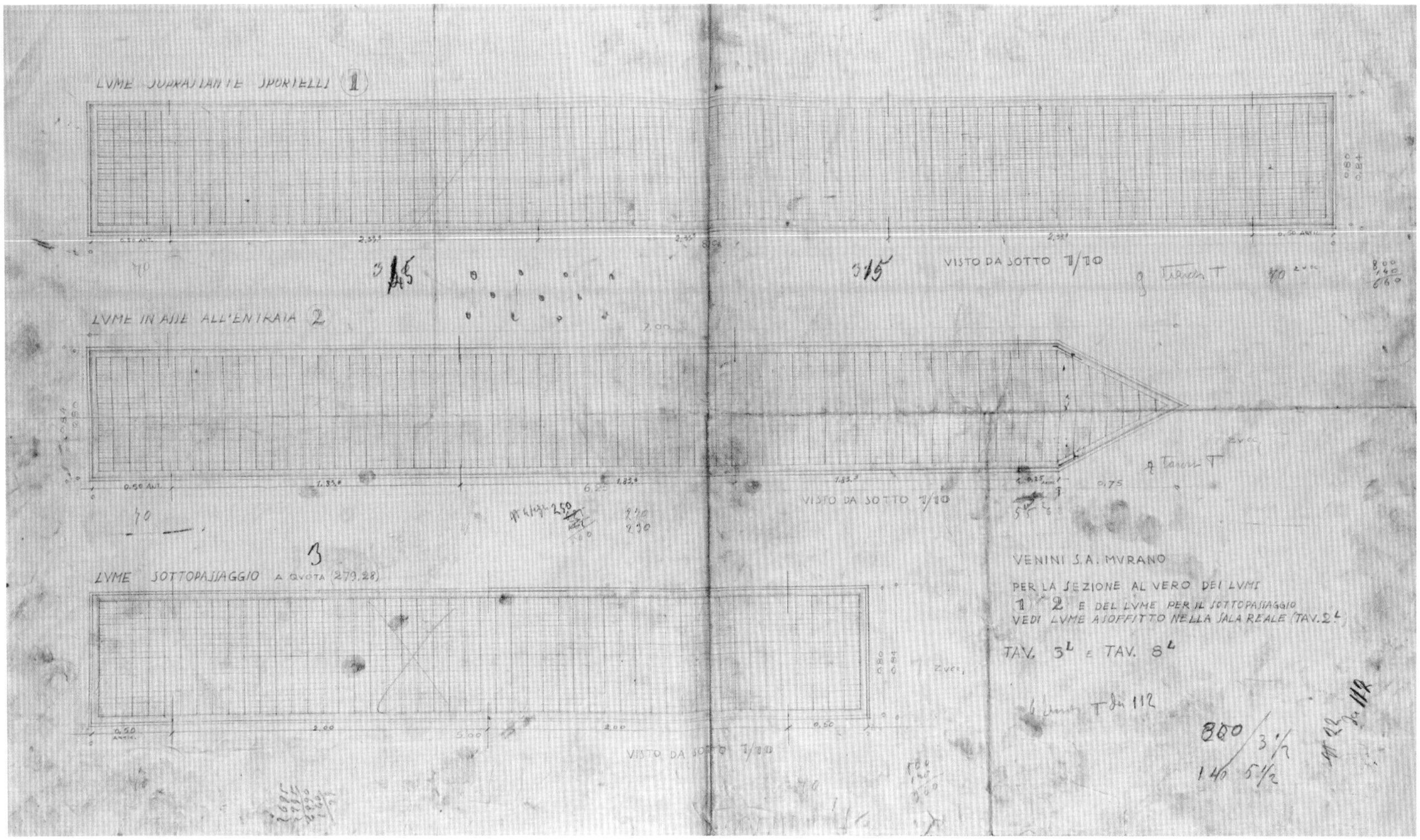

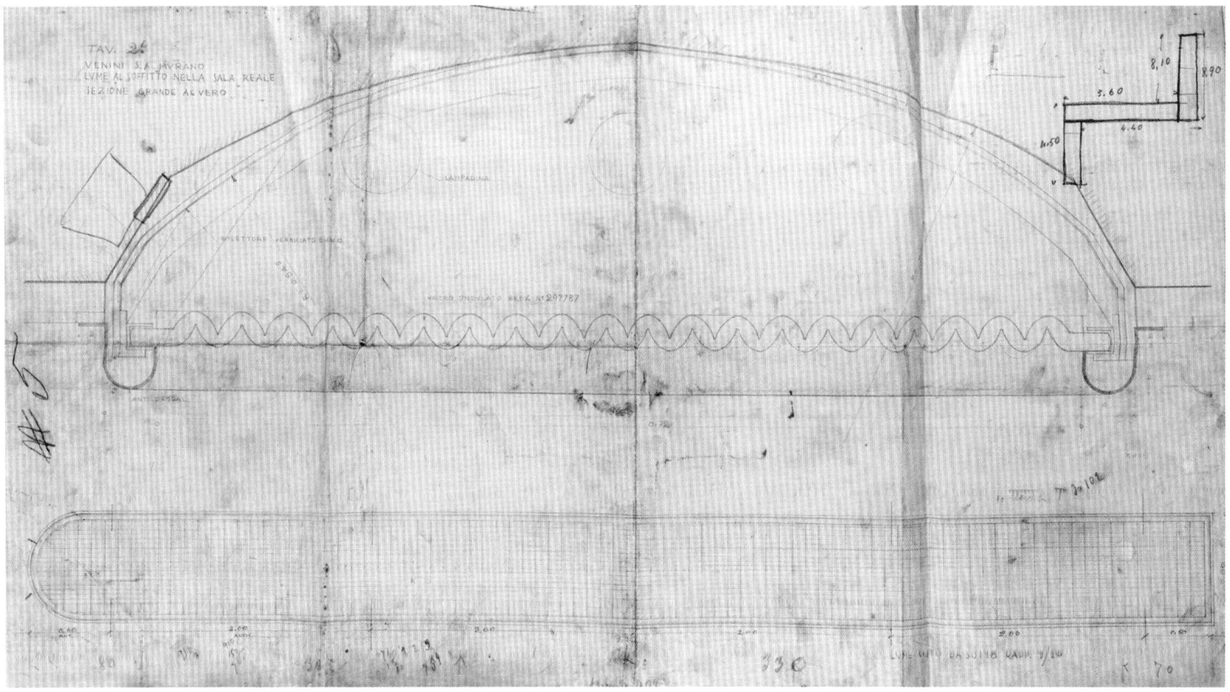

<<
RAILWAY STATION
Exit. Period photograph, 1935

<<
RAILWAY STATION
The Royal room. Period photograph, 1935

>
RAILWAY STATION
Designs for luminous ribbons over the counters, at the entrance and in the underpass

>
RAILWAY STATION
Design for luminous ribbons in the Sala Reale [Royal room]

1935 TIRRENIA (IT)
WOMEN'S HOLIDAY CAMP

CORDONATO GLASS

In the great refectory of the building designed by Mario Paniconi and Giulio Pediconi and officially opened on 6 July 1935, the artificial lighting was ensured by a long pendant fixture running the whole length of the area. This was a luminous tube in ribbed glass, fixed to metal rods and placed in the centre of the area which was glazed on two sides

1936 FORLÌ (IT)
LUIGI RIDOLFI AIRPORT

CORDONATO GLASS

A lighting project for the airport officially opened on 19 September 1936. As is documented by an archive drawing, among the works executed were two luminous pillars, with recessed bulbs, in 'lined ribbed glass' and mounting in nickel-plated brass (h 200 cm).

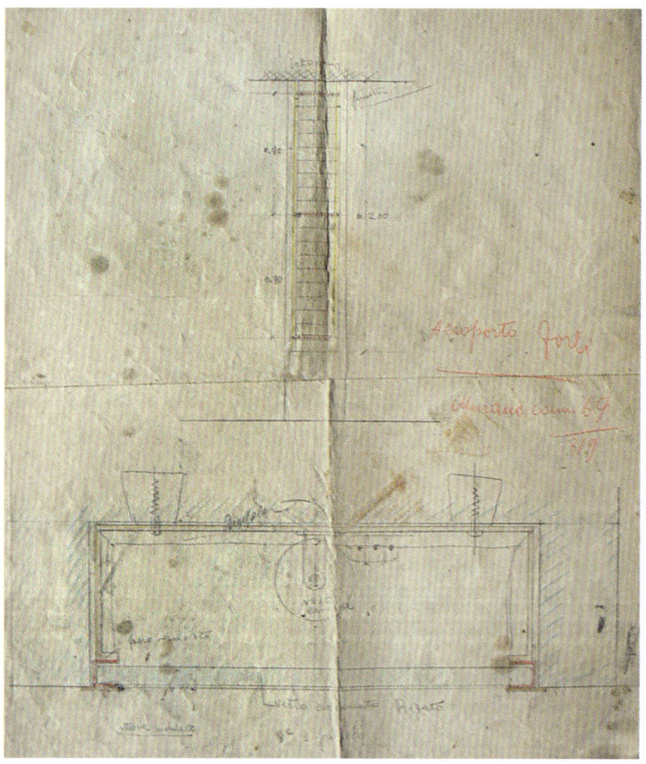

>
LUIGI RIDOLFI AIRPORT
Design for vertical luminous ribbon in ribbed glass

1936 MILAN (IT)
VI TRIENNALE DI MILANO
DESIGN C. SCARPA

WALL LAMPS
PENDANT

On the occasion of the 6th Triennale, the second held at the Palazzo dell'arte of Milan, the glassworks participated both personally with an exhibition room, where it exhibited decorative glass and lamps, and as an active part of the Gruppo Arti Decorative, which organised the creation of the living room included in the Furniture Exhibition (*Le Tre Venezie*, June-July 1939). In the latter setting, arranged after the design of the architect Virgilio Vallot, the Venini glassworks produced small cubic ceiling lamps designed by Vallot himself and installed a hanging loop lamp with a screen having sheets of the 'lastrine brillante' series, the model for which (no. 5286) appears in the Blue Catalogue together with other pendant lamps (no. 5281, 'ribbed', no. 5282, 'with flowers', no. 5283, 'corroded', no. 5284, 'tiles') and sconces (nos. 442, 443) displayed in the dedicated Venini room at the same exhibition. In addition to these models there were no. 5279, with a cylindrical body and 'lastrine brillante', no. 5280 with various sheets, no. 5285, consisting of a dome pendant light in *lattimo* glass together with a wall lamp having a rounded screen (unidentified model). Taken together they are lamps following designs by Carlo Scarpa produced either with vitreous matter also used in decorative glass pieces (e.g. corroded glass, glass with Roman *murrine*) or with a new system consisting of a metal skeleton on which various elements were applied (flowers, paterae, sheets, etc.).

>>
VI TRIENNALE DI MILANO
Venini exhibition room. Period photograph, 1936

venini - murano
STAB. FOT. CRIMELLA MILANO 293.
VI 1936 - A. XIV TRIENNALE D. MILANO

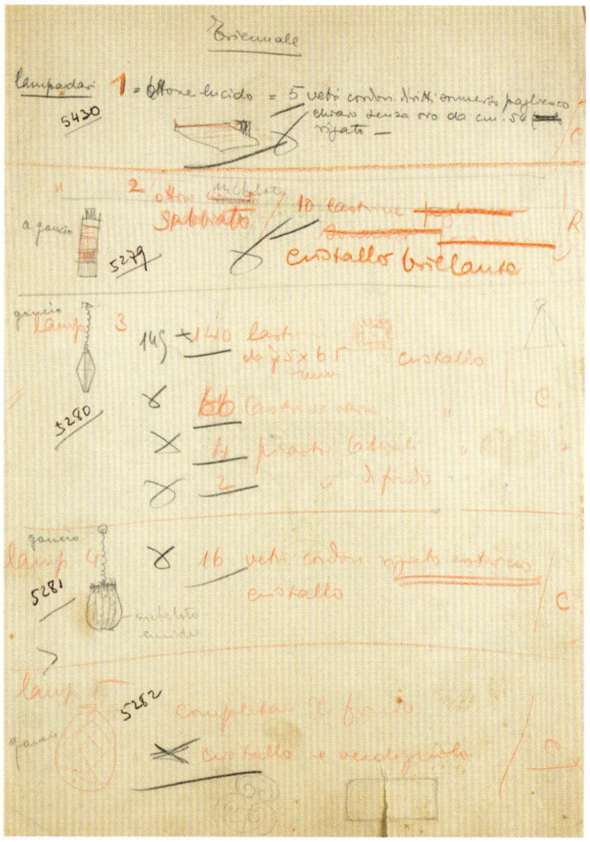

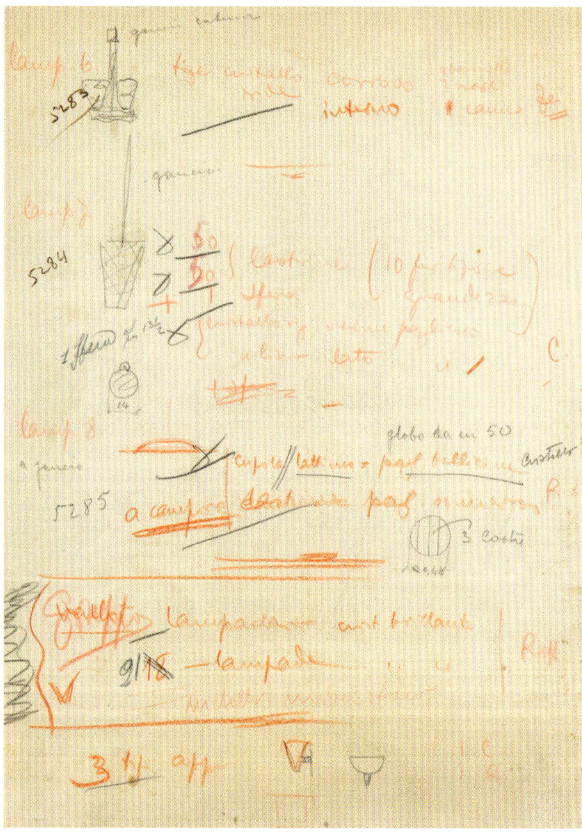

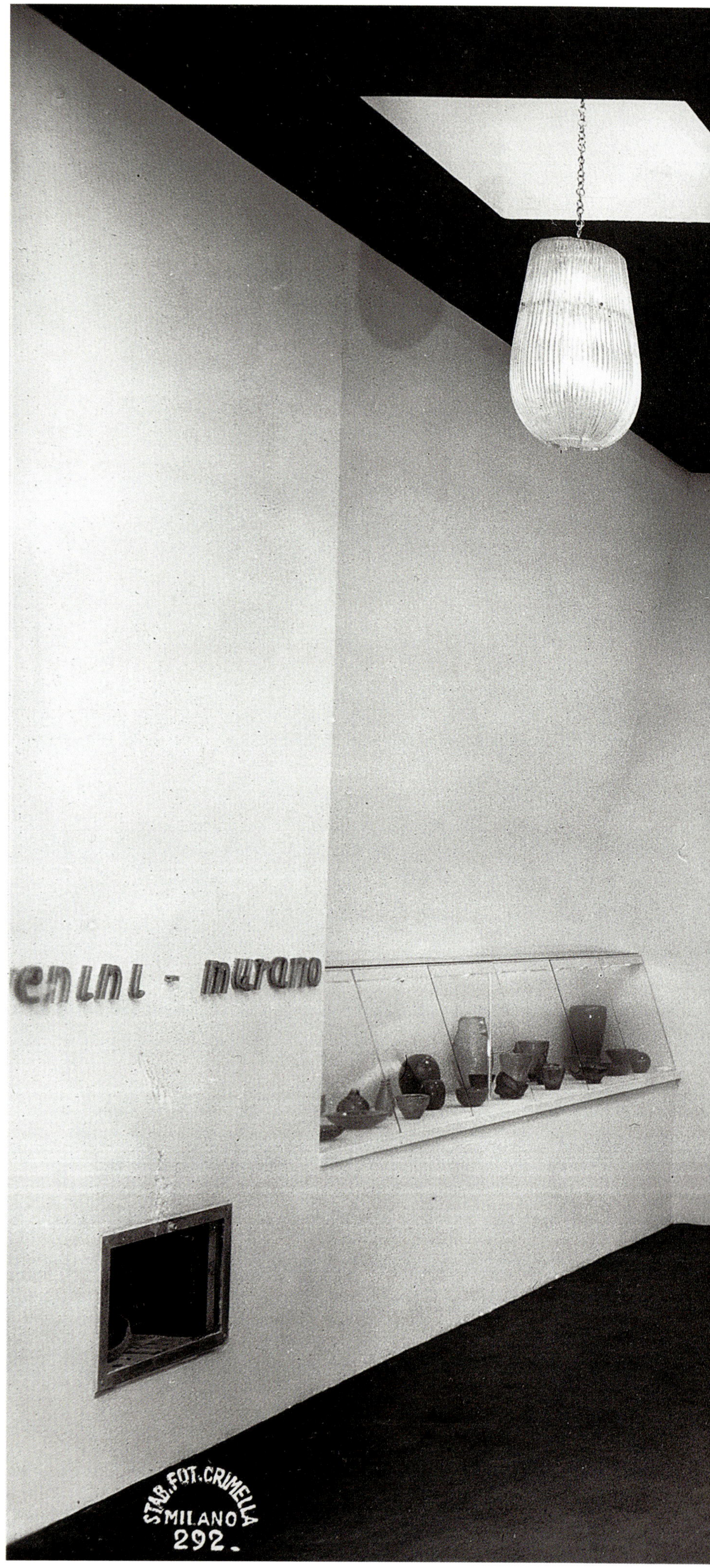

>
VI TRIENNALE DI MILANO
C. Scarpa, P. Venini, list of chandeliers to be exhibited in the glass-works' own room, page no. 1

>
VI TRIENNALE DI MILANO
C. Scarpa, P. Venini, list of chandeliers to be exhibited in the glass-works' own room, page no. 2

>
VI TRIENNALE DI MILANO
Venini exhibition room. Period photograph, 1936. From the left: hanging lights nos. 5281, 5280, 5282, 5279, 5283, 5284, 5285; sconces, not identified, nos. 442, 443

1936-37 VENICE (IT)
UNIVERSITÀ CA' FOSCARI DI VENEZIA
DESIGN C. SCARPA

WALL LAMPS
PENDANT

On the occasion of the restoration organised by Carlo Scarpa (1936-37), the architect used Venini lights for some areas of the university building inaugurated on 25 January 1937. These included pendant lights designed by the architect such as that produced for the Rector's office (no. 5281, Venini catalogue), and sconces in opaline glass with metallic mountings for the ground floor entrance hall and the passage to the first floor.

1937 COMO (IT)
RAVASI SILK FACTORIES

WITH ARMS

Lighting project for the business founded by Guido Ravasi.

1937 MILAN (IT)
SNIA VISCOSA TOWER

Lighting project for certain rooms of the building designed by the architect Alessandro Rimini (1935-37), first Milan skyscraper.

1937 PARIS (FR)
EXPOSITION INTERNATIONALE DES ARTS ET DES TECHNIQUES APPLIQUÉS À LA VIE MODERNE

PENDANT

For the occasion of the Paris exhibition the glassworks produced a large pendant light for the main hall of the Padiglione Italia [Italian Pavilion], on the top floor of the tower designed by the architect Giuseppe Pagano. The fixture, placed in a circular recess in the ceiling, was characterised by its oval shape and the latticed metal structure on which the circular elements ('paterae') were fixed alternating with glass flowers. Examples of this technique are to be found in models nos. 5282 and 5293 (Blue Catalogue).

>
EXPOSITION INTERNATIONALE DES ARTS ET DES TECHNIQUES APPLIQUÉS À LA VIE MODERNE
Main hall, in *Casabella*, July 1937

>>
EXPOSITION INTERNATIONALE DES ARTS ET DES TECHNIQUES APPLIQUÉS À LA VIE MODERNE
Venini chandelier in the main hall. Period photograph, 1937

1937

ROME (IT)
TEATRO DELLE ARTI

CANE GLASS

The headquarters of the Confederazione Nazionale Professionisti e Artisti [National Confederation of Professional People and Artists], which also included the Teatro delle Arti, was officially opened on 5 May 1937, after the design of Carlo Broggi. In the layout of the entrance hall, carried out by the Gruppo Arti Decorative, the Venini glassworks were involved in producing, among other things, an enormous luminous column in *pagliesco* cane glass stretching from the ground floor to the first floor.

1937

ROME (IT)
ELISEO THEATRE
DESIGN L. PICCINATO

ONDULATO GLASS

The lighting project for the Roman theatre, officially opened on 5 January 1938, was carried out by the Venini glassworks following the renovation of the building after a design of the architect Luigi Piccinato (1936-37). This consisted in particular of the production of a series of concealed circular lights with screens in undulating glass positioned in the two-storey-high foyer, and wall lamps, also with undulating glass screens, installed in the lower level of the same foyer.

>
ELISEO THEATRE
Foyer. Period photograph, 1938

1937

SAN SEVERO (IT)
LITTORIO MUNICIPAL THEATRE

WALL LAMPS
PENDANT

The building, nowadays known as the Teatro Giuseppe Verdi, was designed by the Roman architect Cesare Bazzani (1929-1936) and officially opened on 9 December 1937. The same architect also gave directions for the decoration, including the large Venini chandelier (h 460 cm, Ø c. 200 cm) placed at the centre of the vault covering the auditorium. From the available documentation it can be assumed that an initial idea of the architect (Bazzani estate design) was developed in the technical office of the glassworks, also with the involvement of Carlo Scarpa. It was an elegant and complex pendant lamp with a two-tiered body composed of ribbed elements in *cristallo* glass (a kind of leaf). A series of chains of glass spheres connect to a circular structure of slats, ensuring the attachment of the fixture to the ceiling. The Venini archive has an original drawing and the chandelier is still *in situ*. Wall lamps were also designed at the same time.

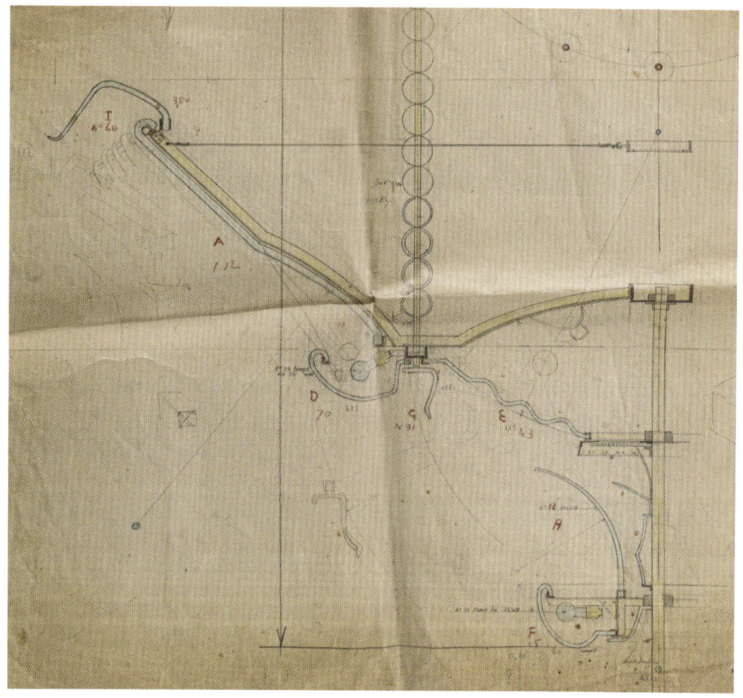

>
LITTORIO MUNICIPAL THEATRE
Drawing for the large chandelier

>
LITTORIO MUNICIPAL THEATRE
Chandelier under construction. Period photograph, 1930s

1937

TURIN (IT)
BANQUETING HALL, PRINCIPI DI PIEMONTE HOTEL

WALL LAMPS
PENDANT
MOSAICI

The hotel represents one of the most important edifices built during the reconstruction of the second section of via Roma and, in particular, of the old isolated S. Antonio da Padova acquired and reconstructed by the Società Anonima Edilizia Piemontese [Non-Profit Piedmont Building Company] (subsidiary of FIAT), according to an overall plan of the engineer Vittorio Bonadé Bottino. To Bonadé Bottino we also owe the design for the 'modern' luxury hotel building, sponsored by the top management of FIAT, not only to respond to the needs of tourism but also to provide the city with appropriate reception environments for celebrations and 'official dinners' (*L'Architettura italiana*, December 1938, pp. 380-381). The interior design ('decoration' and 'setting') was entrusted to the architect Giovanni Chevalley, already designer of the Principi di Piemonte Hotel at Sestriere (1931-32). The construction works were carried out between 1936 and 1937 and the hotel was opened on 23 December 1937. The first floor of the building was intended for a large banqueting hall, accessible on two sides from two galleries and on a third from an adjacent lounge bar or restaurant. For the furnishing of these areas the Gruppo Arti Decorative, a Venetian company, bringing together the most important entrepreneurs active in the decorative arts sector, was called upon (*Le Tre Venezie*, June-July 1939, pp. 247-248). Most probably in agreement with the architect, the GAD participated by creating a sumptuous and original decorative scheme. A good part of the project was carried out by the Venini firm which not only was involved in the lighting of the rooms, but also produced a highly refined mosaic decoration (with grey tesserae and gold inserts) for the walls of the hall and galleries and the nine alcoves along the perimeter of the main area.

>
BANQUETING HALL, PRINCIPI DI PIEMONTE HOTEL
Entertainment room. Period photograph, 1937-38

>>>
BANQUETING HALL, PRINCIPI DI PIEMONTE HOTEL
Niches on the short side. At the centre the set-back niche with the decorative 'Fish' motif can be seen, photograph UNA Esperienze di Torino

In the last-mentioned case this was a mosaic decoration with irregular gold-coloured tesserae above which glass decorations depicting flora (plants and flowers) and fauna (fish, monkey and birds) compositions were applied, where the former were more numerous than the latter. As documented by some preparatory drawings stored in the archives of the glassworks, these compositions were studied by the technical office of the furnace and particularly by Carlo Scarpa, present at the time in the Venini company. The design for the many oval-shaped chandeliers present in the hall can be attributed to Scarpa himself. With metal frames these large lights have screens with flowers and paterae in *cristallo* glass with aquamarine and amethyst finishings. Pendant lamps of a round design with similar motifs were installed in the adjacent areas. In the galleries, on the other hand, there were oblong wall lights with glass tesserae and ribbons, positioned to surround the large mirrors with frames in Murano glass and the infills of the arches, with respective doors, made with 'gold glass sheets'. In the entrance hall containing the cloakroom hanging lights with glass plates, model no. 5284, were used. Some of the decoration and lighting is still *in situ*, while the original ceiling of the banquet hall with 'glass decorations in relief' (little flowers) has been removed.

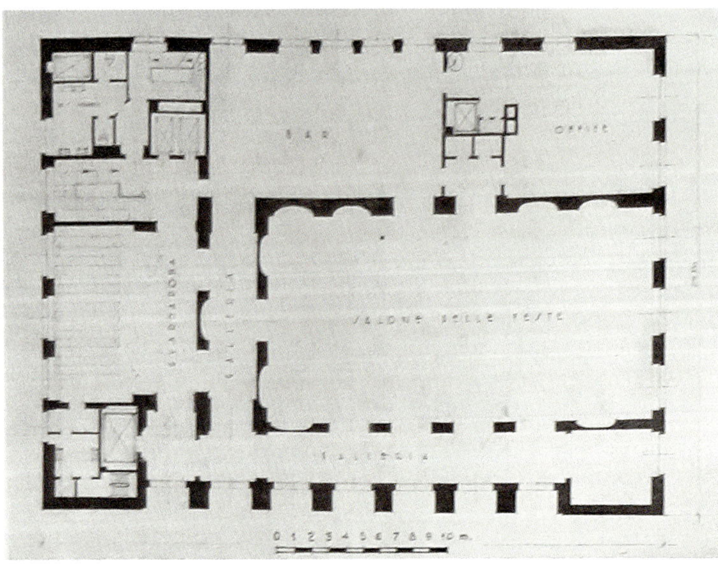

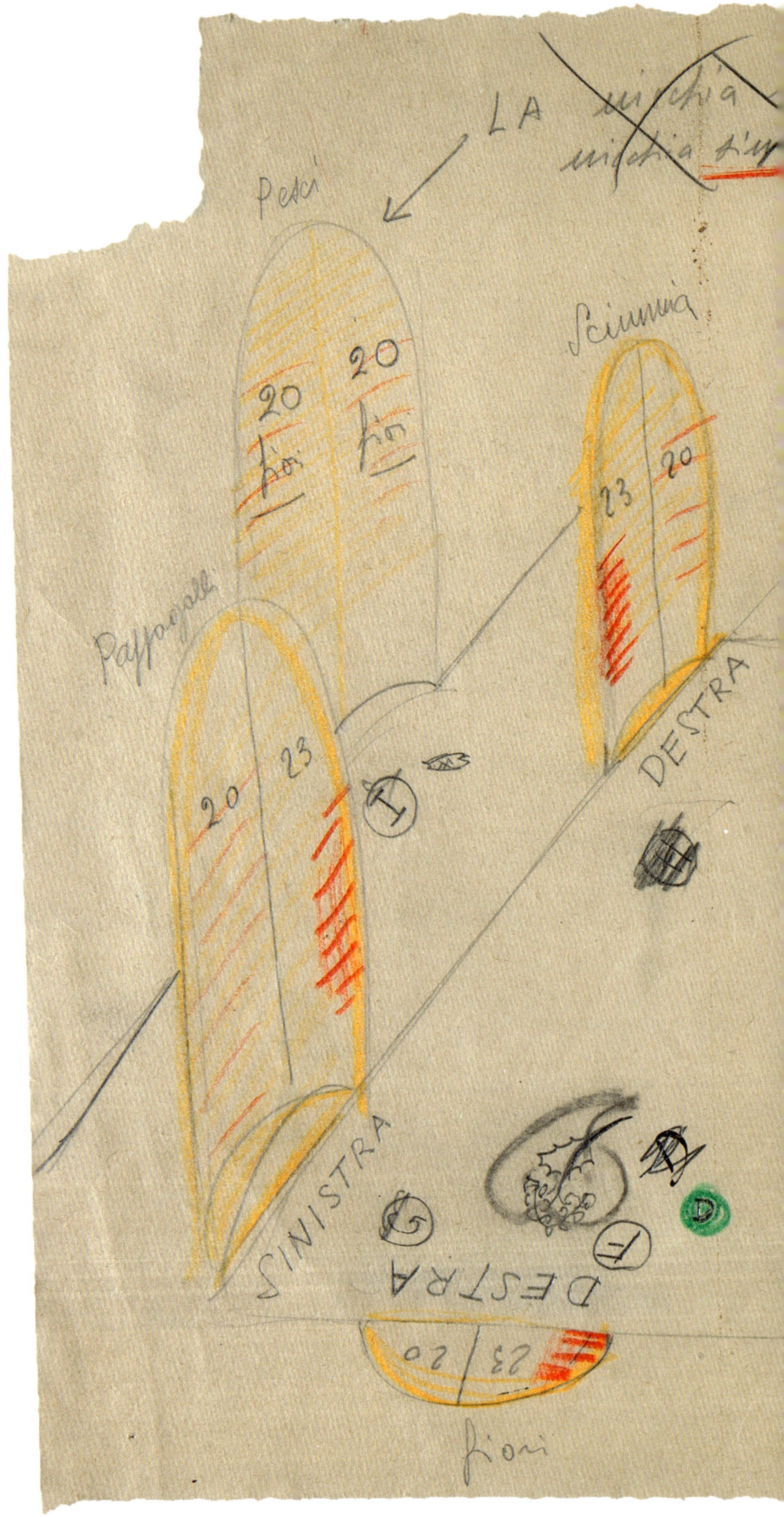

>
BANQUETING HALL, PRINCIPI DI PIEMONTE HOTEL
Plan of the first floor with the Entertainment Room, in *L'architettura italiana*, December 1938

>
BANQUETING HALL, PRINCIPI DI PIEMONTE HOTEL
Plan for the layout of the niches and the various decorative themes

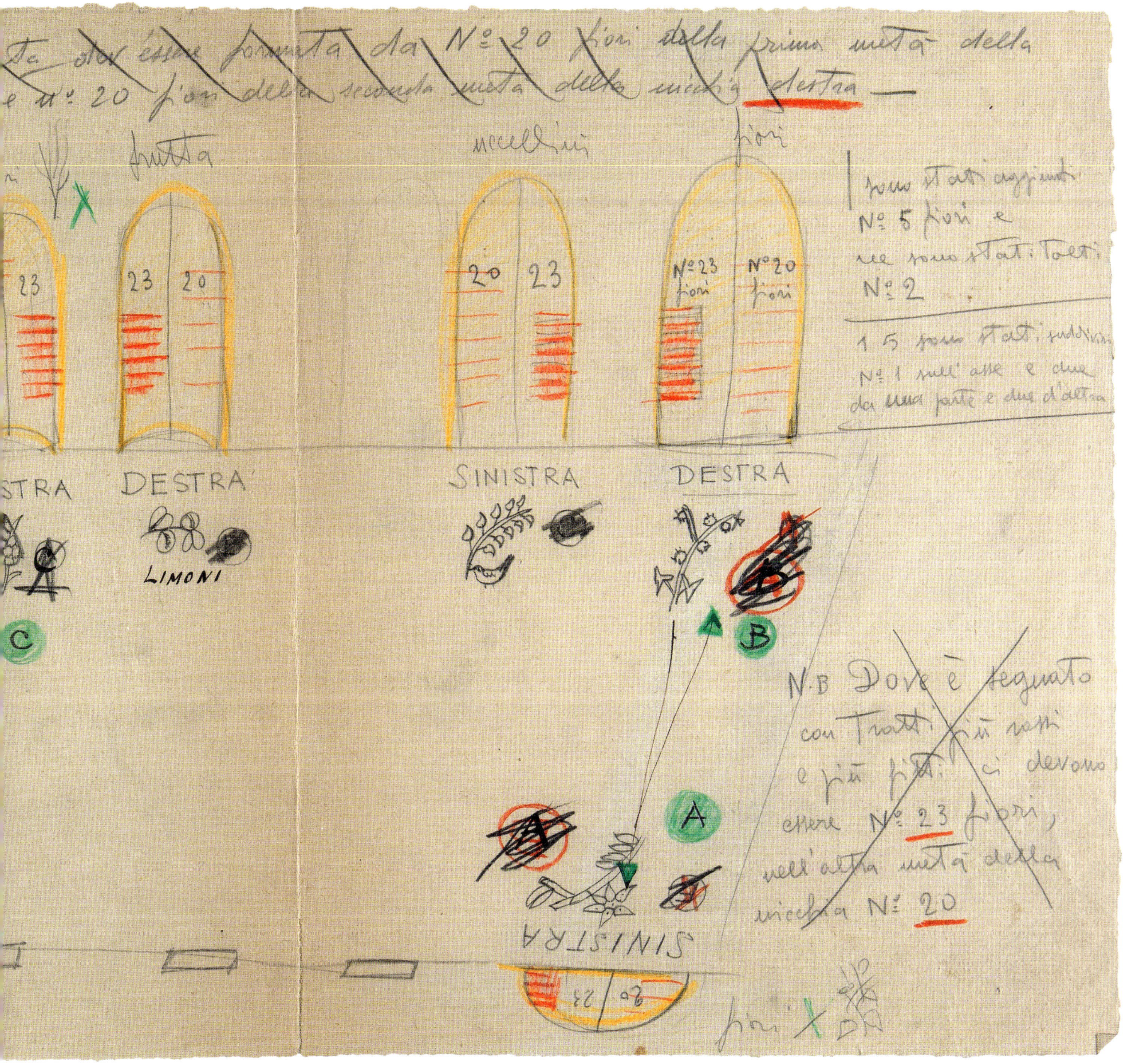
frutta
uccellini
fiori
23 20
20 23
N° 23 fiori
N° 20 fiori
sono stati aggiunti N° 5 fiori e ne sono stati tolti N° 2
DESTRA
SINISTRA
DESTRA
LIMONI
C
B
A
N.B Dove è segnato con tratti più rossi e più fitti ci devono essere N° 23 fiori, nell'altra metà della nicchia N° 20
SINISTRA

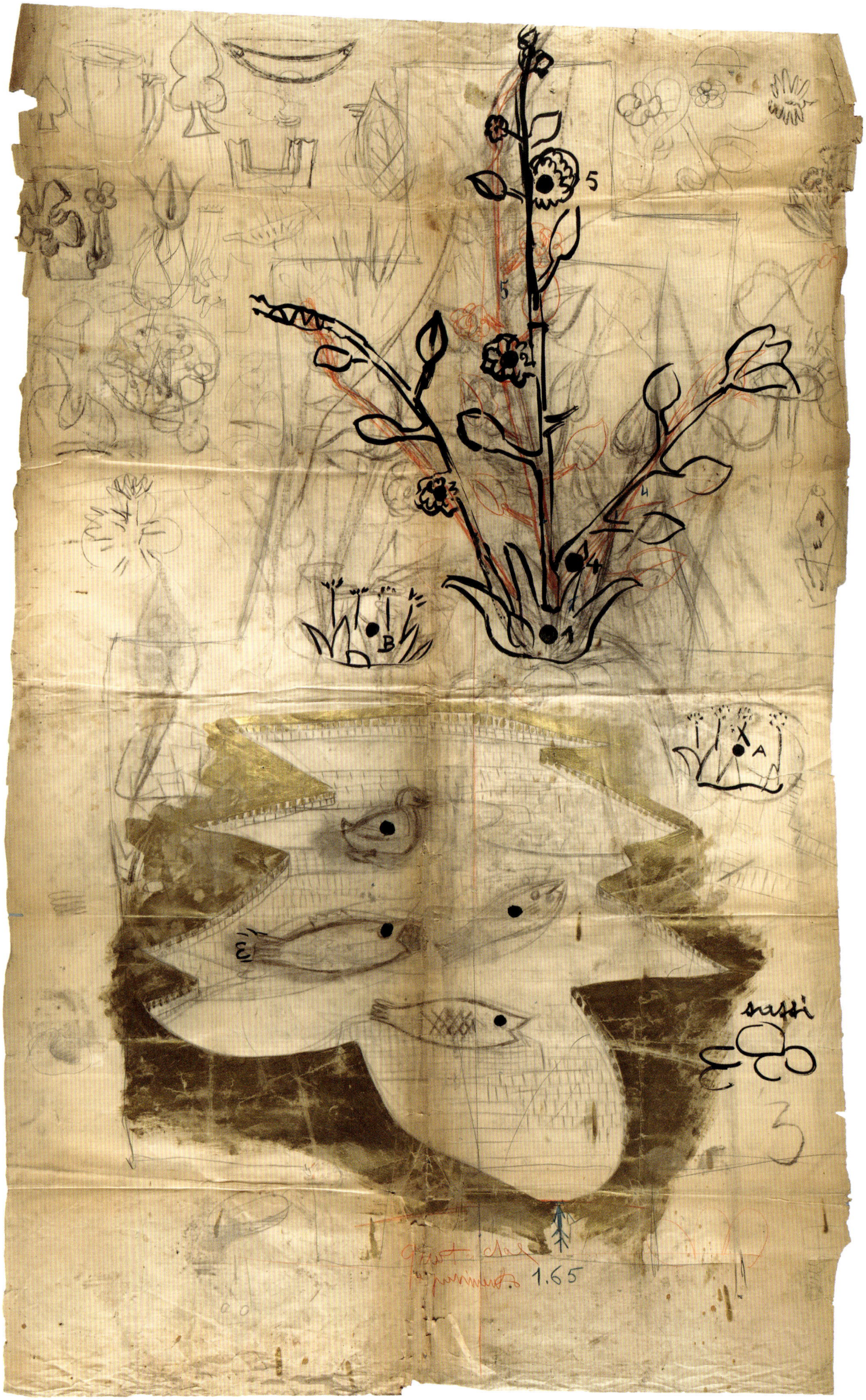

>
BANQUETING HALL, PRINCIPI DI PIEMONTE HOTEL
C. Scarpa, study for glass decoration ('Fish'), side niche, short side
>>
BANQUETING HALL, PRINCIPI DI PIEMONTE HOTEL
Central niche with fish, short side. Period photograph, 1937-38

>
BANQUETING HALL,
PRINCIPI DI PIEMONTE HOTEL
Side niche with flowers (plan B), long side.
Period photograph, 1937-38

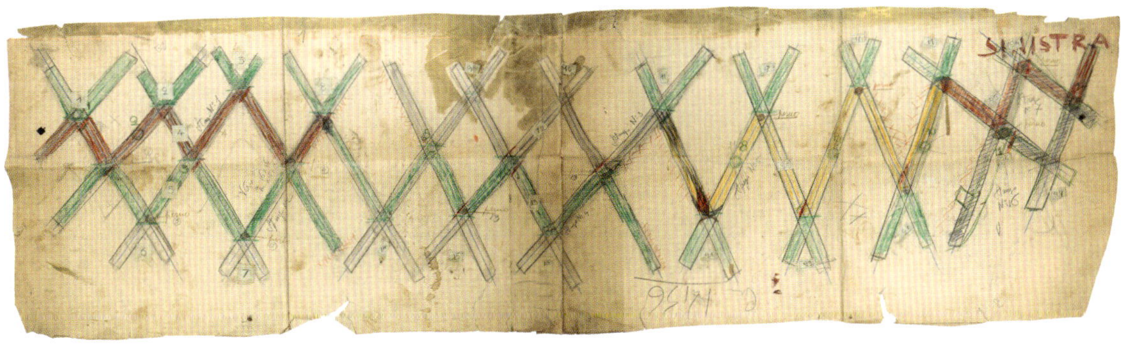

>
BANQUETING HALL, PRINCIPI DI PIEMONTE HOTEL
C. Scarpa, study for glass decoration 'Flowers' plan B), side niche, long side

>
BANQUETING HALL, PRINCIPI DI PIEMONTE HOTEL
Design for glass decoration (fence)

>
BANQUETING HALL, PRINCIPI DI PIEMONTE HOTEL
C. Scarpa, study for glass decoration ('Birds'), side niche, long side

>
BANQUETING HALL, PRINCIPI DI PIEMONTE HOTEL
C. Scarpa, study for glass decoration ('Flowers', plan A), side niche

>
BANQUETING HALL,
PRINCIPI DI PIEMONTE HOTEL
Side niche, long side. Period photograph, 1937-38

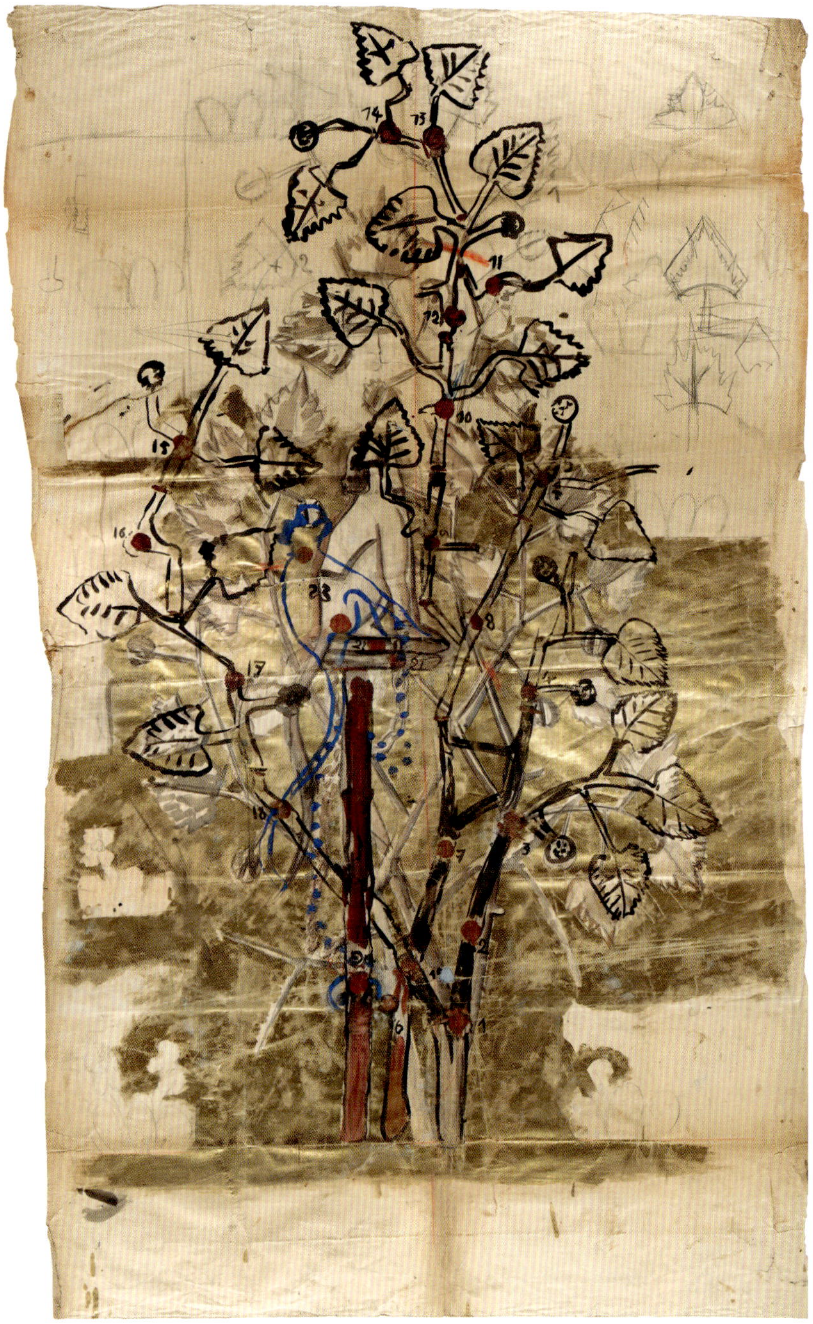

>
BANQUETING HALL, PRINCIPI DI PIEMONTE HOTEL
C. Scarpa, study for glass decoration ('Monkey'), side niche, short side

>
BANQUETING HALL, PRINCIPI DI PIEMONTE HOTEL
C. Scarpa, study for glass decoration ('Flowers/ Plan C'), side niche, long side

>
BANQUETING HALL, PRINCIPI DI PIEMONTE HOTEL
C. Scarpa, study for glass decoration ('Fruit/Lemons'), side niche, long side

>
BANQUETING HALL, PRINCIPI DI PIEMONTE HOTEL
C. Scarpa, study for glass decoration ('Flowers', plan F), side niche, long side. Archive photograph

>
BANQUET HALL, PRINCIPI DI PIEMONTE HOTEL
Side gallery. Period photograph,1937-38

>>
BANQUET HALL, PRINCIPI DI PIEMONTE HOTEL
Wall lamp and detail of the frame of the mirror in the side gallery.
Period photograph,1937-38

1938

CASTROCARO (IT)
CASTROCARO THERMAL BATHS

WALL LAMPS
CEILING
PENDANT

The spa complex, including the Padiglione delle Feste [Entertainment Pavilion], Grand Hotel Terme and Stabilimento Bagni [Spa Grand Hotel and Baths], designed by the architect Diego Corsani with decorative work by Tito Chini, was officially opened in September 1938. In the Padiglione delle Feste the glassworks installed a series of luminous cornices on the ceiling in ribbed glass starting at the entrance (under the circular balcony) and in the theatre (ring-shaped ceiling light in the apse-like area and U-shaped lights at the sides of the same area). In other areas of the Pavilion there are shell-shaped sconces (of which the Venini archive has the original drawing), hanging lamps in ribbed glass (e.g. no. 5291, Blue Catalogue) and a spherical chandelier in white *pulegoso* glass with incorporated stars, with an applied ring motif. Numerous lighting fixtures were then also installed in the rooms of the hotel.

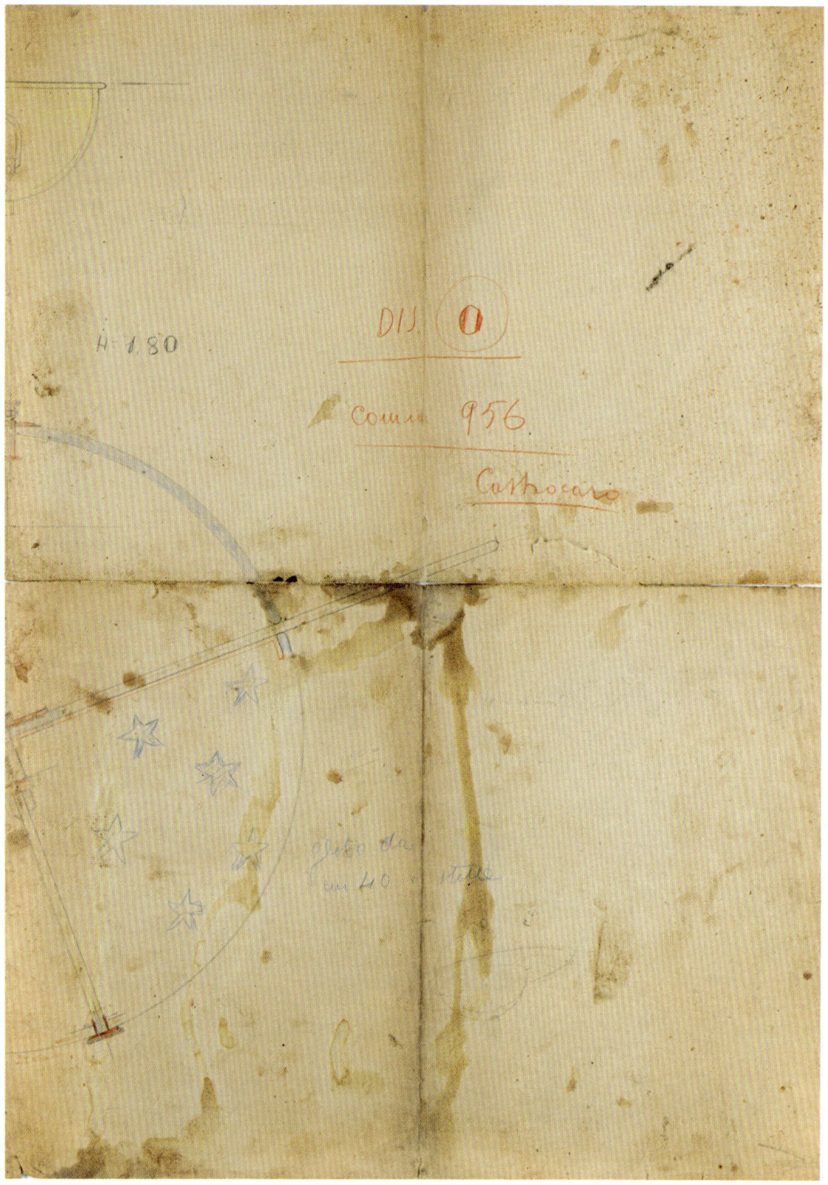

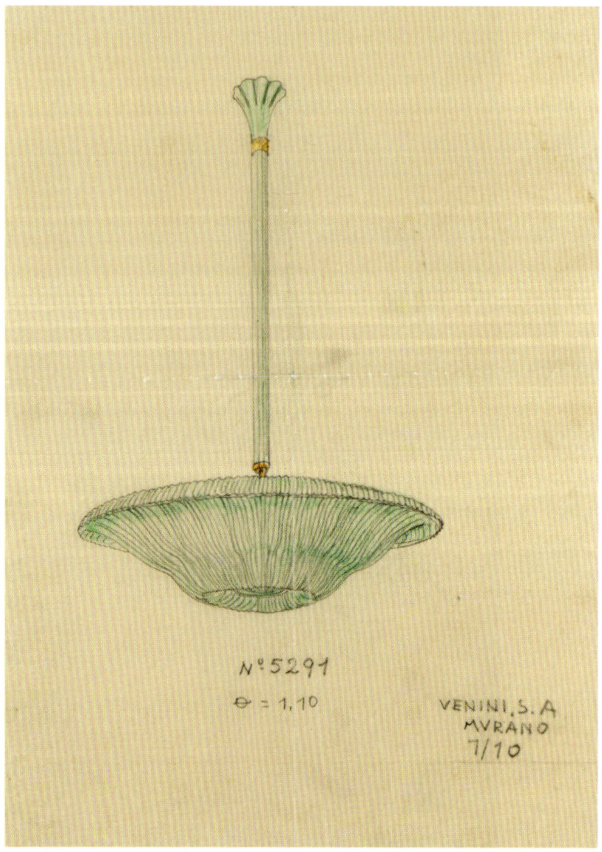

>
CASTROCARO THERMAL BATHS
Drawing for the spherical chandelier with applied ring motif (Saturn type)

>
CASTROCARO THERMAL BATHS
Drawing for the chandelier in ribbed glass, no. 5291

>
CASTROCARO THERMAL BATHS
Entrance, Padiglione delle Feste.
Courtesy Long Life Formula

>
CASTROCARO THERMAL BATHS
Room with coffered ceiling, Padiglione delle Feste. Courtesy Long Life Formula

1938

FERRARA (IT)
CASSA DI RISPARMIO

Lighting project for bank premises.

1938

FLORENCE (IT)
CASSA DI RISPARMIO

Lighting project for bank premises.

1938

FLORENCE (IT)
I.M.E.T. HEADQUARTERS

Lighting project for the Tuscan company producing and maintaining electric and telephonic installations.

1938

FLORENCE (IT)
ITALIAN AIRFORCE TECHNICAL SCHOOL

WALL LAMPS
PENDANT
LUMINOUS FOUNTAIN
CORDONATO GLASS

The imposing training centre for young Air Force cadets, located in an extensive area of 12 hectares in the Parco delle Cascine, was built between 1937 and 1938 after a design by the architect Raffello Fagnoni, for the Central Office of the Demanio Aeronautico [Aeronautical Authority]. This complex of several buildings (headquarters, training, cadets residence, barracks and service area), was completed in record time and inaugurated on 27 March 1938. Apart from the general project, Fagnoni was responsible for the layout of all the interior areas. The Venini firm was called upon by the architect with regard in particular to the production of the lighting for the building intended for teaching. Three luminous fountains composed of back-lit canes in *pulegoso* glass (acting as a slide for the water) were constructed at the south-facing façade of the building. With regard to the interior, Murano lights were positioned in the Aula Magna and in the entrance hall below it. In the case of the Aula Magna long light frames in ribbed glass were placed all along the perimeter of the hall (with the exception of the side behind the speaker's rostrum). In the entrance hall there were ovoid chandeliers in golden glass with applied elements of the 'a fiori' [flowers] series (cf. model no. 5282, Blue Catalogue). Some of the wall lamps (model no. 425, Blue Catalogue) were placed in the areas of the Circolo Ufficiali [Officers' Club].

>>
ITALIAN AIRFORCE TECHNICAL SCHOOL
Luminous fountain in *Architettura*, June 1938

1938

LIDO DI VENEZIA (IT)
CASINO

WITH ARMS
A NASTRI
WALL LAMPS
CEILING

The imposing summer home of the Casino was built after the design of the engineer Eugenio Miozzi, head of the Municipal Technical Office, and opened on 30 June 1938. The building was the largest in the design for a complex of three interconnected buildings (Palazzo del Cinema, Casino and covered swimming pool) of which only the first two were built, one in 1936 and the other between 1937 and 1938. The coordination for the equipping of the gambling house was entrusted to the Gruppo Arti Decorative [Decorative Arts Group] (in the person of Giovanni Nei Pasinetti) and to the Eugenio Quarti company of Milan. Numerous crafts businesses and Venetian and other companies, selected by public competition, took part in the works for the casino.
For the lighting V.S.M. Venini & C., Ferro Toso Barovier, Barovier Toso & C. and the aforesaid Quarti di Milano, were chosen to produce a total of over two hundred chandeliers and six thousand lamps. The glassworks, 'with a project by Pasinetti, Scarpa, Vallot and Venini', produced fixtures for the main rooms on the ground floor, among which the entrance hall, the banquet hall, the bar and the restaurant, while on the first floor it was involved in the Sala da Gioco di Gala [Gala Gaming Room] (private) (*Le Tre Venezie*, June-July 1939). At the centre of the main entrance hall, framed by the marble columns, a circular luminous ceiling was created (Ø 9 m), with a peripheral cornice in green *pulegoso* glass and central chequered area, with opaque squares in gold leaf and translucent squares in *cristallo* glass. Outside the columns, along all the perimeter of the room, two ceiling cornices were placed with leaves in *cristallo* glass. In the bar and restaurant rooms numerous lights were installed, among which the large pendant lamps with 'blown-glass ribbons' in *cristallo* glass with coloured glass finishings after a design by Carlo Scarpa. The chandeliers of the private gaming room were also of an original kind, where the four card suits, used as the decorative motif for the stucco and gold ceiling, occurred again in the long 'chains' that supported the 'classic'-shaped lighting fixtures (h 370 cm) as reinterpreted by Scarpa. Some of these lamps are still *in situ*.

>
CASINO
Main entrance hall. Period photograph, 1938

<<
CASINO
Restaurant and bar with chandeliers in foreground.
Period photograph, 1938

<<
CASINO
Restaurant and bar. Period photograph, 1938

>
CASINO
Project for the layout of the restaurant and bar by Gruppo Arti Decorative, 17 March 1938. At the bottom on the left can be seen the GAD stamp and the signatures of Giovanni Nei Pasinetti and Paolo Venini

>
CASINO
Privè. Period photograph, 1938

>>
CASINO
C. Scarpa, study for chandelier for the private room on the first floor

>>
CASINO
Chandelier with chains consisting of shapes based on playing card suits. Period photograph, 1938

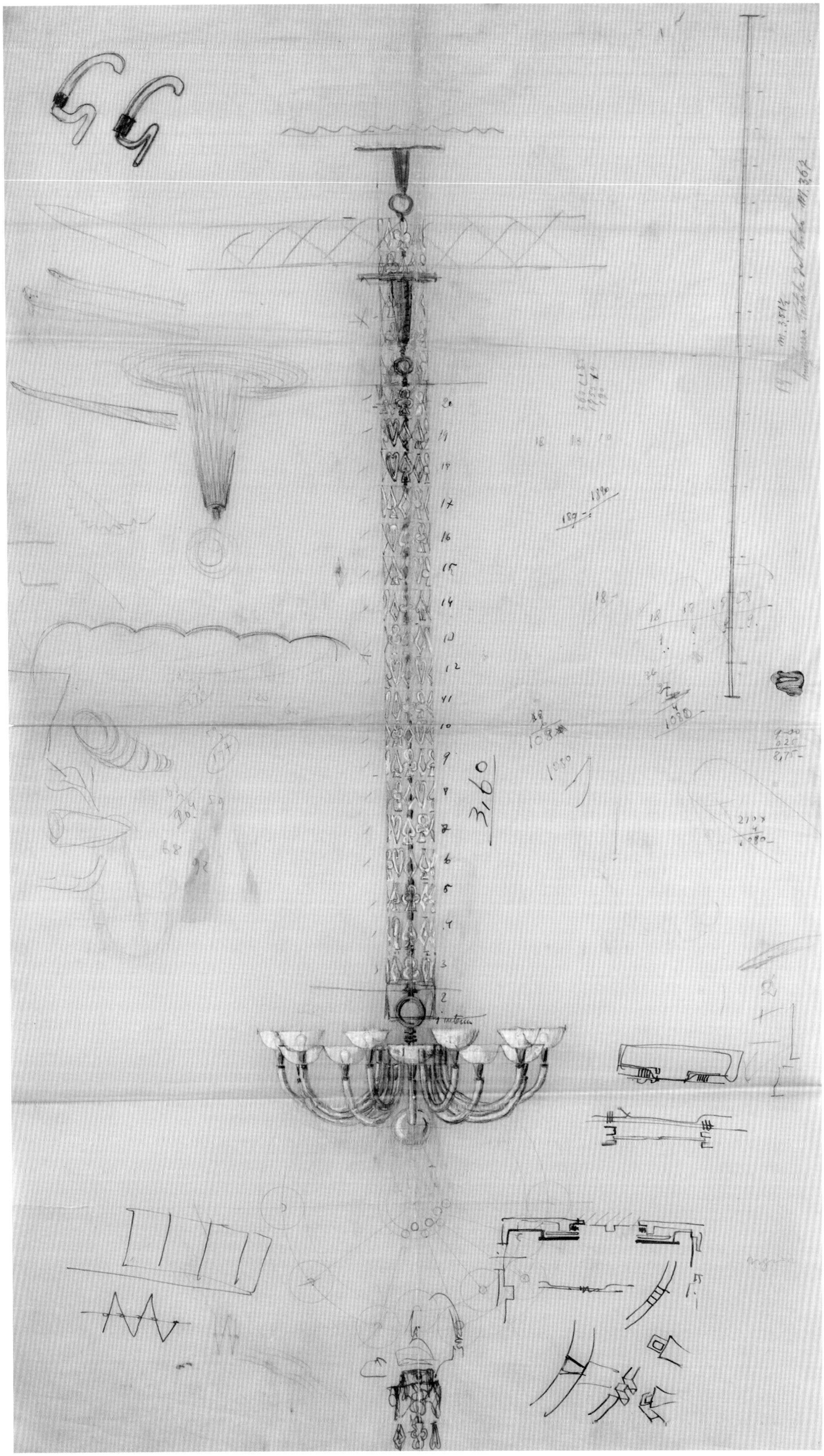

1938 MILAN (IT)
PRINCIPE & SAVOIA HOTEL

Lighting project for a hotel.

1938 ROME (IT)
QUIRINO THEATRE

LEAVES AND FLOWERS

The lighting project for the Roman theatre designed by Marcello Piacentini is documented by an elaborate archive graphic artwork, dated 1938, with studies in his own hand by Carlo Scarpa for a ceiling light with ribbons having leaves and flowers.

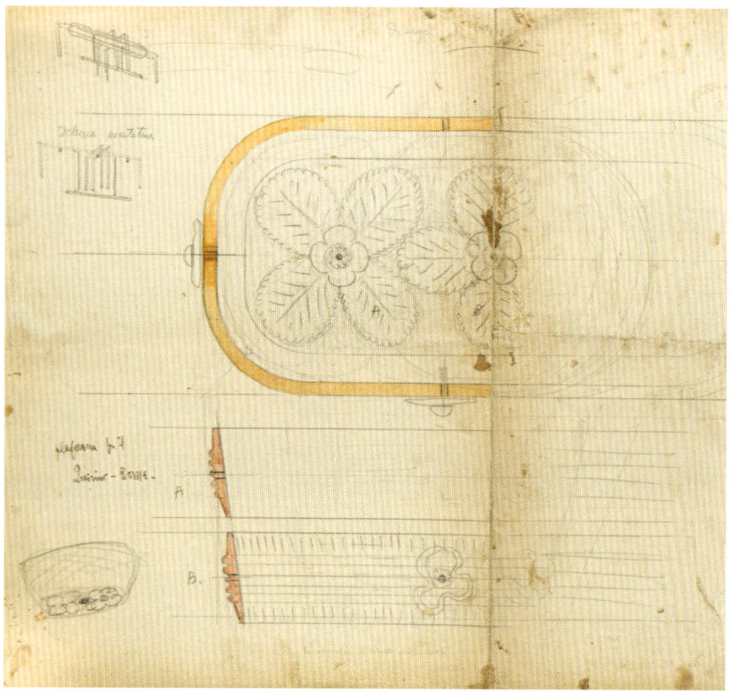

>
QUIRINO THEATRE
Drawing for a ceiling light with leaves and flowers, 1938

1938 VENICE (IT)
CA' GIUSTINIAN

WALL LAMPS
CEILING

The building belonging to the Municipality (and today the venue for the Venice Biennale) was renovated between 1936 and 1938. On the ground floor was the 'Venetian meeting place' with bar and restaurant, laid out by the Gruppo Arti Decorative [Decorative Arts Group] after a design by Nei Pasinetti and Paolo Venini. The GAD was a Venetian company which brought together the most important entrepreneurs active in the decorative arts sector (*Le Tre Venezie*, June-July 1939, pp. 247-248). In the restaurant area, featuring panels, columns and architraves covered with mirrors and glass grids, 'lastrine brillante' sconces of different lengths, of the Model 464 type (Blue Catalogue), were installed. For the bar, wall lamps with a double tier of leaves were used (no. 462, Blue Catalogue). In the adjacent passage large wall lights (no. 461, Blue Catalogue) were chosen with diffuser screens having plant motifs. The Venini firm was also involved on the first floor in the 17th-century style Sala delle Colonne, a new area created during the renovation and now home to the first municipal casino. For this area three ceiling lights were produced: one with a circular base and of a compact size and two having a mixtilinear plan resembling the profile of the coffered ceiling of the central corridor. The lamps had a diffuser screen consisting of a metallic frame on which circular elements of *cristallo* glass ('paterae') and flower elements with centres in greeny and amethyst glass were fixed. Some of these lights are still *in situ*.

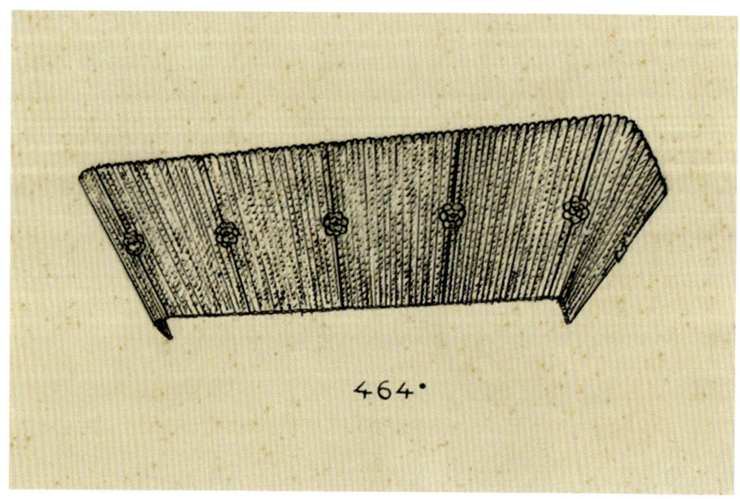

>
CA' GIUSTINIAN
Sconce of the 'lastrine brillante' series, model no. 464, Blue Catalogue

>
CA' GIUSTINIAN
Sala delle Colonne. Period photograph, 1938

>
CA' GIUSTINIAN
Ceiling light with mixtilinear plan, Sala delle Colonne in *Il Vetro*, May 1939

1938 VENICE (IT)
LA FENICE THEATRE

WITH ARMS

Lighting project for a theatre.

1938-39 ROME (IT)
EUR OFFICES BUILDING

WALL LAMPS

The first building to be inaugurated in the context of the vast project of the Esposizione Universale di Roma (EUR) [Universal Exhibition Rome], the building, accommodating the offices of the organisation, was built between October 1937 and the end of 1939 after a design by Gaetano Minnucci. The architect called upon the glassworks for the lighting of the main staircase, called the 'scalone del commissariato' [commissariat stairway], where ten original large wall lamps were installed, supported at the base by a marble corbel. With a metal frame, the sconces had a lateral surface in embossed glass while the front, with a hexagonal profile, consisted of slabs in satin glass. Some of these lamps are still *in situ*.

›
EUR OFFICES BUILDING
'Scalone del commissariato'. Period photograph, 1939

1938-40 ROME (IT)
SWEDISH INSTITUTE

Lighting project for the cultural building designed by the Swedish architect Ivar Tengbom.

1939 PEDAVENA (IT)
PEDAVENA BREWERY

WALL LAMPS

A lighting project for the head office of the Italian Pedavena brewery. This was a series of large wall-mounted lights with a circular base and copper supporting frame. Truncated cone-shaped screen with smoked glass slats. Following their removal, some of them found a new setting in a religious building at Cavallino-Treporti.

1939 ROME (IT)
III QUADRIENNALE D'ARTE NAZIONALE
DESIGN M. PANICONI, G. PEDICONI

LUMINOUS FOUNTAIN

In the 'covered garden' designed by Mario Paniconi and Giulio Pediconi, a fountain designed by the same architects was produced by the glassworks (*L'Architettura italiana*, May 1939). The installation consisted of a terraced structure, covered in pebbles evocative of Italian gardens, on which was mounted a succession of back-lit undulating slabs. The falling water is supplied by tapering elements, also in glass, resting at the top of the said slabs.

»
III QUADRIENNALE D'ARTE NAZIONALE
Luminous fountain. Period photograph, 1939.

1939 TURIN (IT)
RADIO BUILDING, EIAR HEADQUARTERS

Lighting project for the new building of the Radio Authority designed by the architect Alessandro Serangeli (1937-39).

1939-40 ROME (IT)
MEDITERRANEO HOTEL

PENDANT

The lighting project for the hotel designed by the architect Mario Loreti (1939-42) included hanging lights with a circular base and metal frame screened by flowers and paterae in *cristallo* glass.

1939-40 TURIN (IT)
FIAT MIRAFIORI, OFFICE BUILDING

WALL LAMPS
PENDANT

The Palazzo degli Uffici, part of the Mirafiori building complex, designed by Vittorio Bonadè Bottino and by the FIAT technical office and including the manufacturing facility for cars and aeroplane engines and the test track, was built in the period 1939-early 1940. As documented by certain Venini archive drawings and a period photograph from the FIAT archives, the glassworks were involved in 1939 in the design and production of lighting installations for some parts of the Board of Directors and Chairman's areas. In particular, quotations were drawn up for the Chairman's office and the related antechamber and for the boardroom. These were proposals designed by Carlo Scarpa, in the first case for a large and original pendant lamp in two variants – a circular-shaped variant and an oval-shaped variant with arms made of ribbed tubes, in the second case, for a wall lamp also with tubed arms, and in the third case, for 'wall-mounted' lamps (h 250 cm) with stem in 'solid lined ground glass' and curved diffuser screen in embossed glass and ground sheets. In the 'Chairman's Room' a large oval-shaped ceiling lamp was then installed (l max 300 cm) with grey embossed glass slats of 2 cm in thickness.

>
FIAT MIRAFIORI, OFFICE BUILDING
'Chairman's Room'. Period photograph, c. 1940, Centro Archivio Storico FIAT

>>
FIAT MIRAFIORI, OFFICE BUILDING
Quotation 50278 with lamp for the 'Chairman's Room'

>>
FIAT MIRAFIORI, OFFICE BUILDING
Quotation for 'wall lamp for antechamber to Chairman's Room'

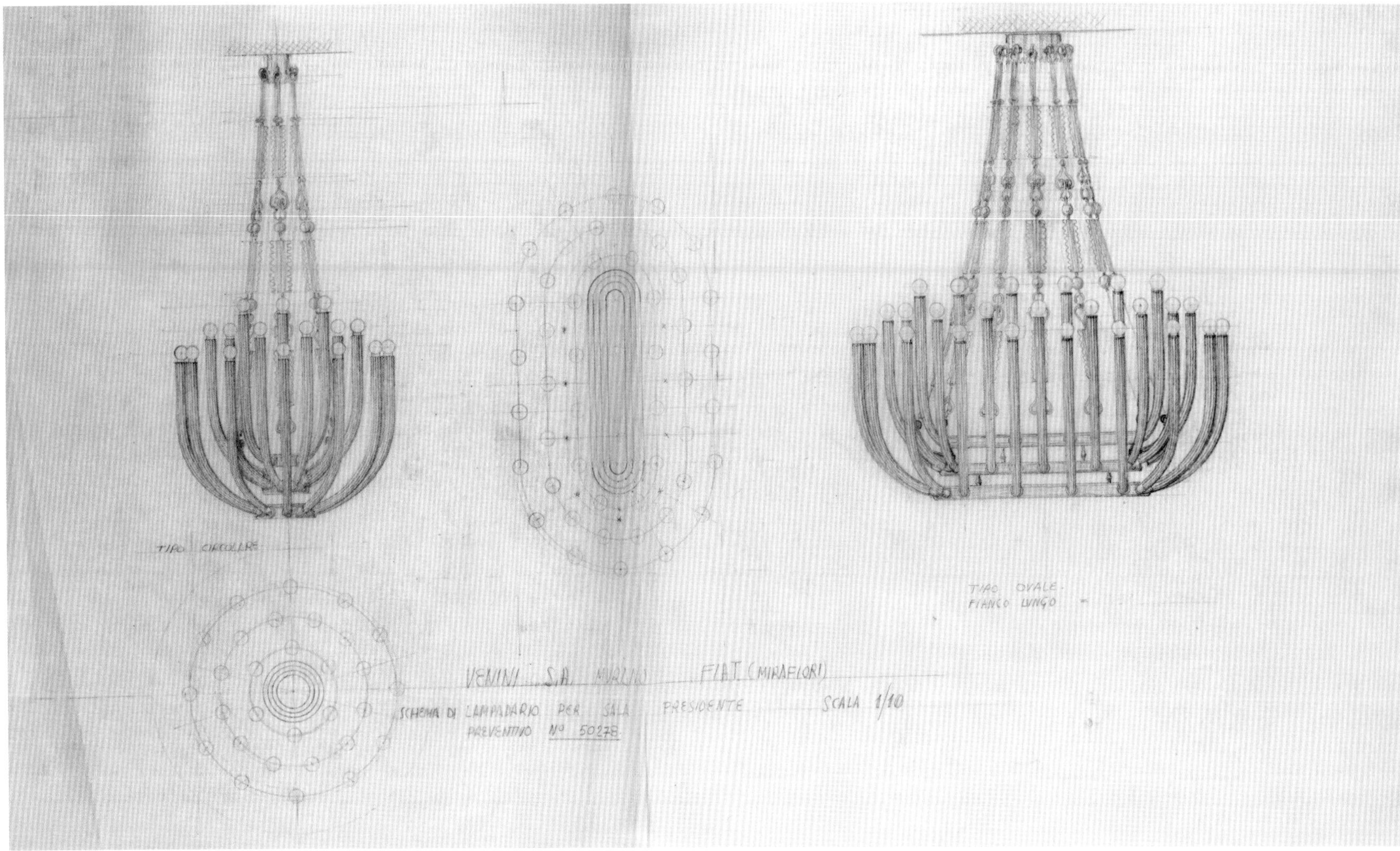
TIPO CIRCOLARE
TIPO OVALE-
FIANCO LUNGO
VENINI S.A. MURANO FIAT (MIRAFIORI)
SCHEMA DI LAMPADARIO PER SALA PRESIDENTE SCALA 1/10
PREVENTIVO N° 50278

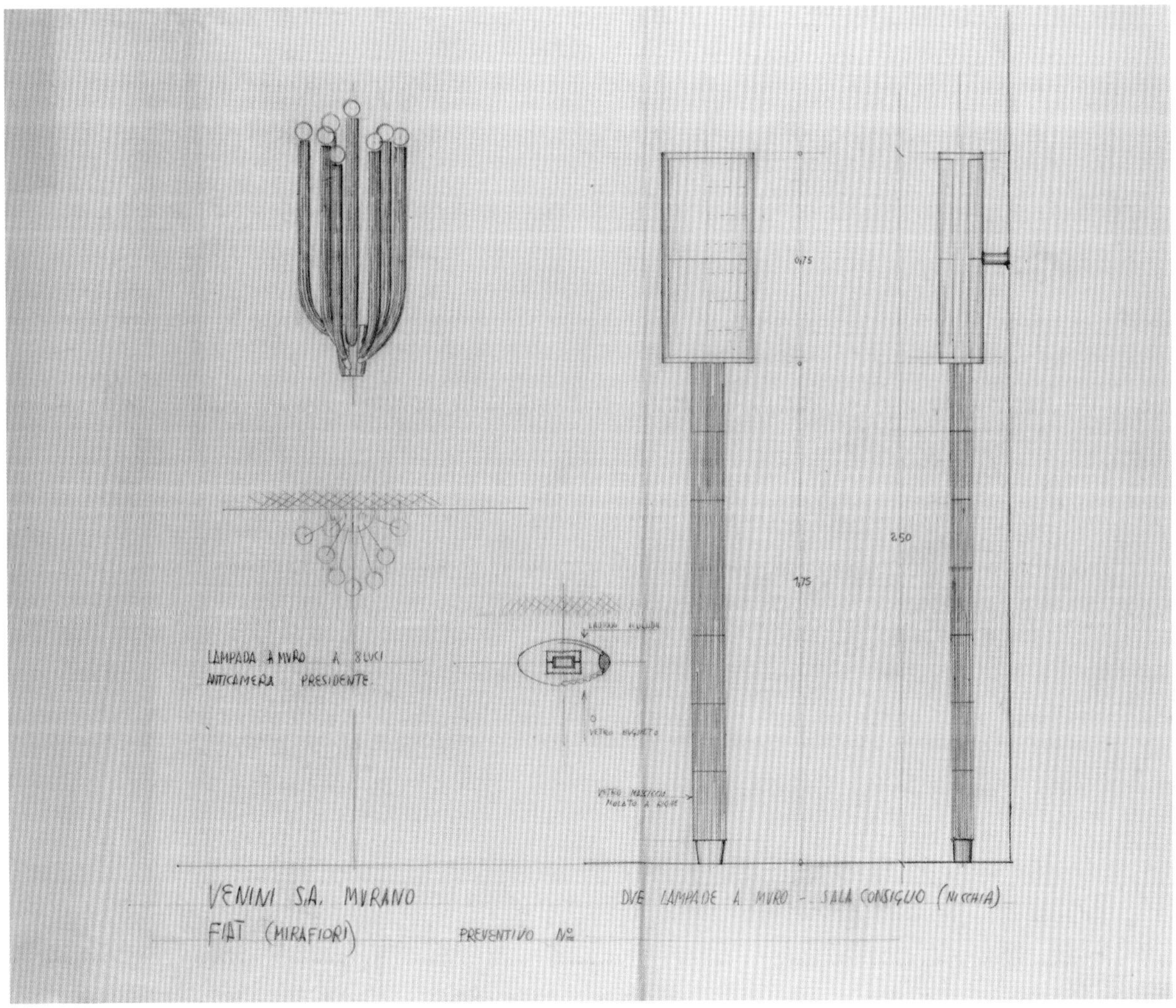
0,75
2,50
1,75
LAMPADA A MURO A 8 LUCI
ANTICAMERA PRESIDENTE
VENINI S.A. MURANO
FIAT (MIRAFIORI)
PREVENTIVO N°
DUE LAMPADE A MURO - SALA CONSIGLIO (NICCHIA)

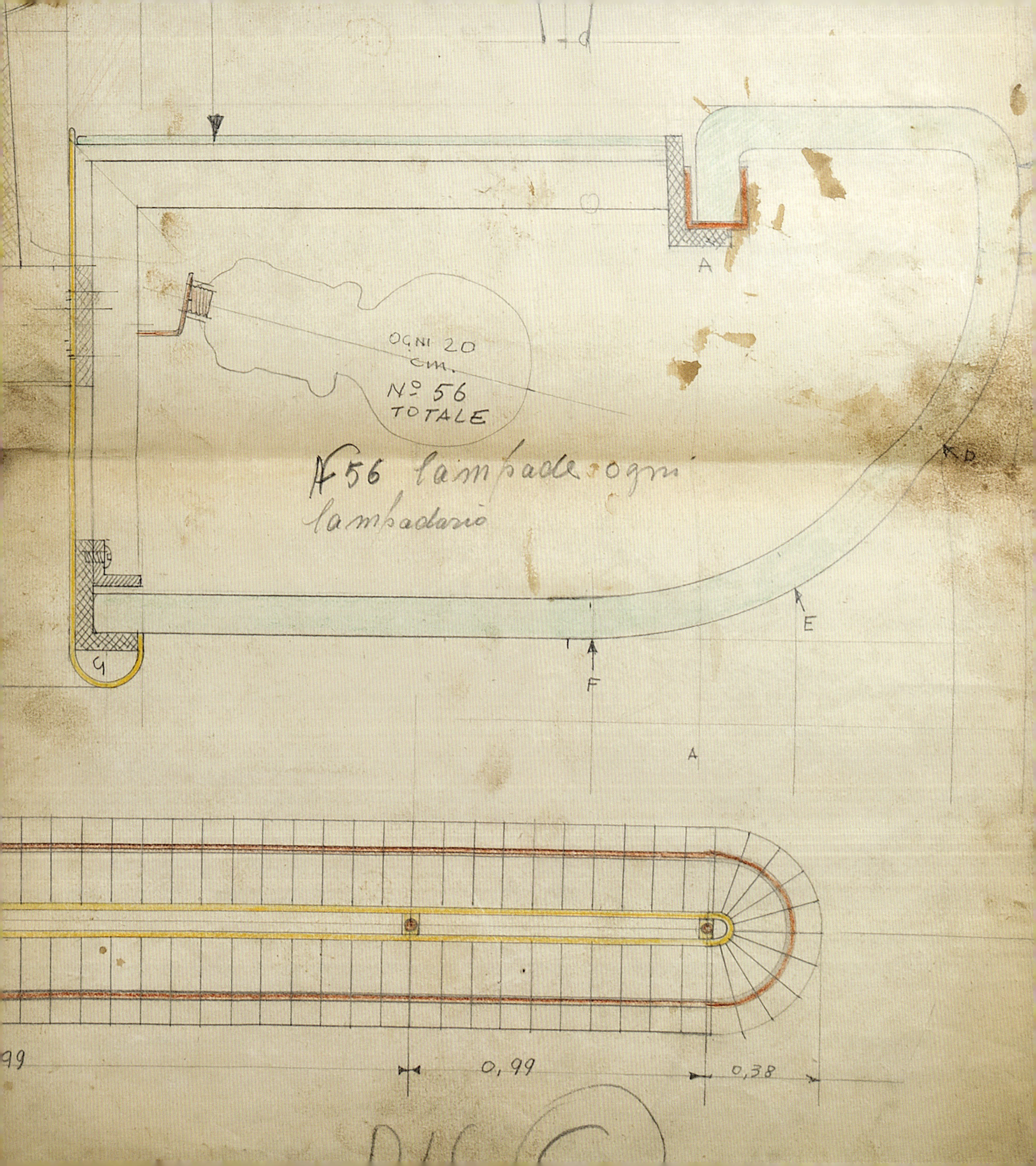

OGNI 20
cm.
N° 56
TOTALE
N 56 lampade ogni
lampadario
A
E
F
G
A
99
0,99
0,38

1940s

1940

AGORDO (IT)
SADE HYDROELECTRIC PLANT

CORDONATO GLASS
PRISM GLASS

In the Agordo power plant designed by the architect Duilio Torres and the engineer Carlo Semenza, the glassworks produced several lighting systems for the external area, and certain internal and underground areas of the building. Among those worthy of note are the light tube (l 123 m) in *cordonato* glass positioned on the ceiling of the access tunnel to the machine room and the minimalist wall lamps in prismatic glass.

>
SADE HYDROELECTRIC PLANT
Access tunnel to the machine room in *Architettura*, April 1942

1940

MILAN (IT)
VII TRIENNALE DI MILANO
DESIGN C. SCARPA

PENDANT

For the Milan event, in addition to new series of glass pieces, a glass table and frames, three new pendant models and a luminous frame for a large mirror after a design by Carlo Scarpa were also displayed. Recognisable among them is model 5315 with twelve arms (Blue Catalogue) in *cristallo* glass and *lattimo* glass, a large lamp with bands and leaves and a basket-like 'white and golden chandelier with ribbons' (Ponti 1940, p. 57).

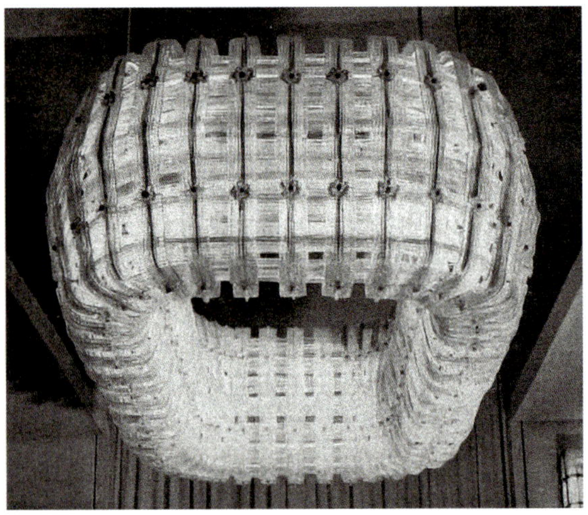

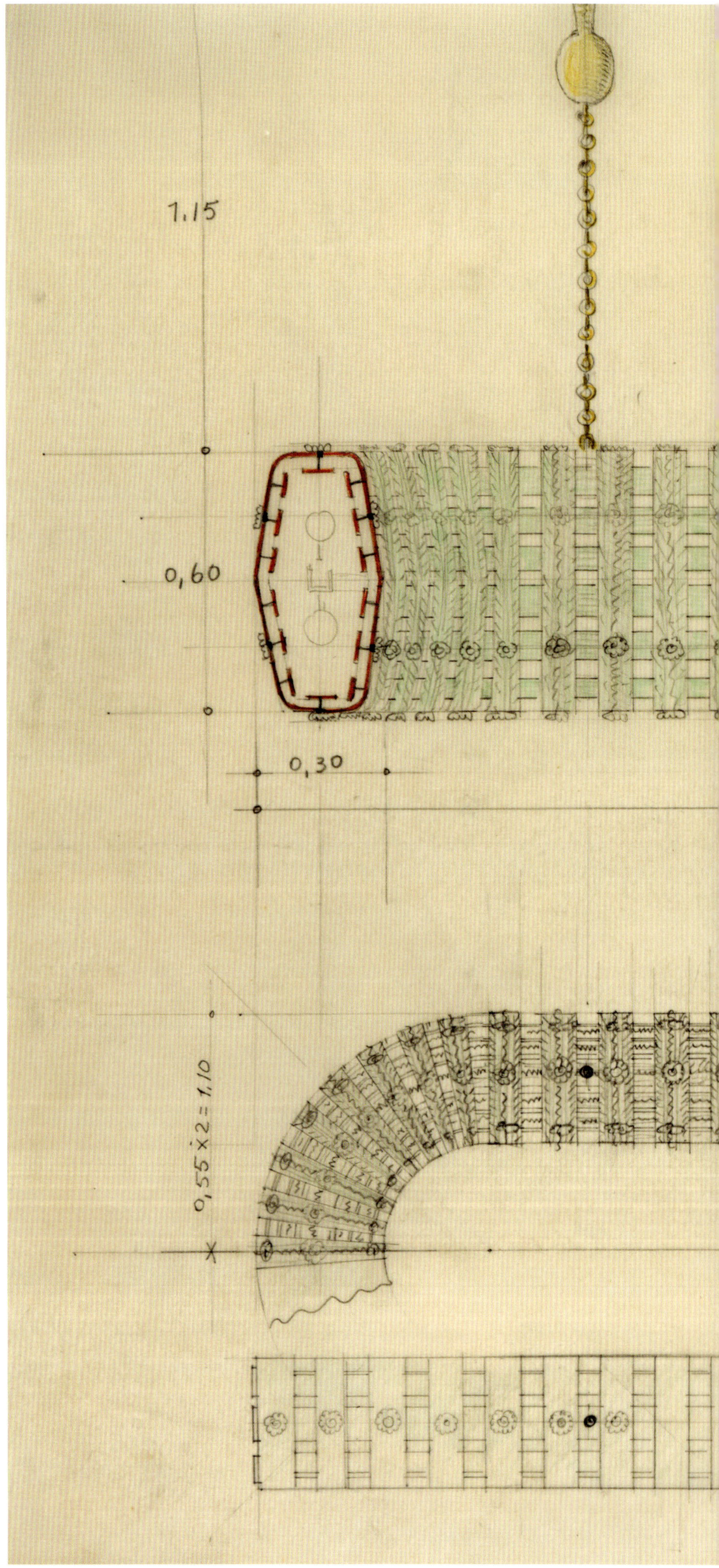

>
VII TRIENNALE DI MILANO
Chandelier with ribbons. Period photograph, 1940

>
VII TRIENNALE DI MILANO
Lamps with bands and leaves. Period photograph, 1940

>
VII TRIENNALE DI MILANO
C. Scarpa, study for chandelier with ribbons, quotation no. 50253, c. 1940

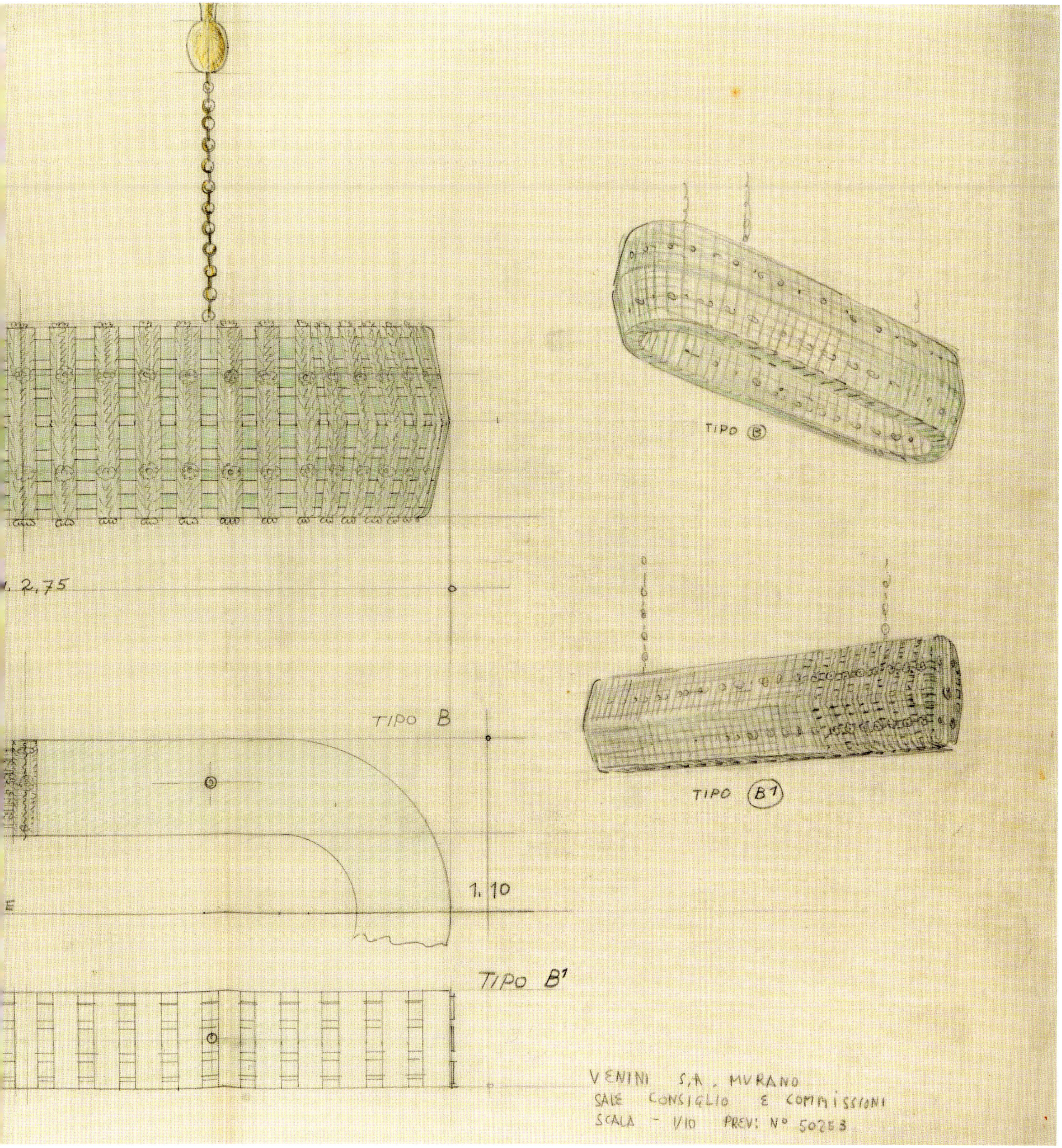
2,75
TIPO B
1.10
TIPO B'
TIPO (B)
TIPO (B1)
VENINI S.A. MURANO
SALE CONSIGLIO E COMMISSIONI
SCALA - 1/10 PREV: N° 50253

LUCE

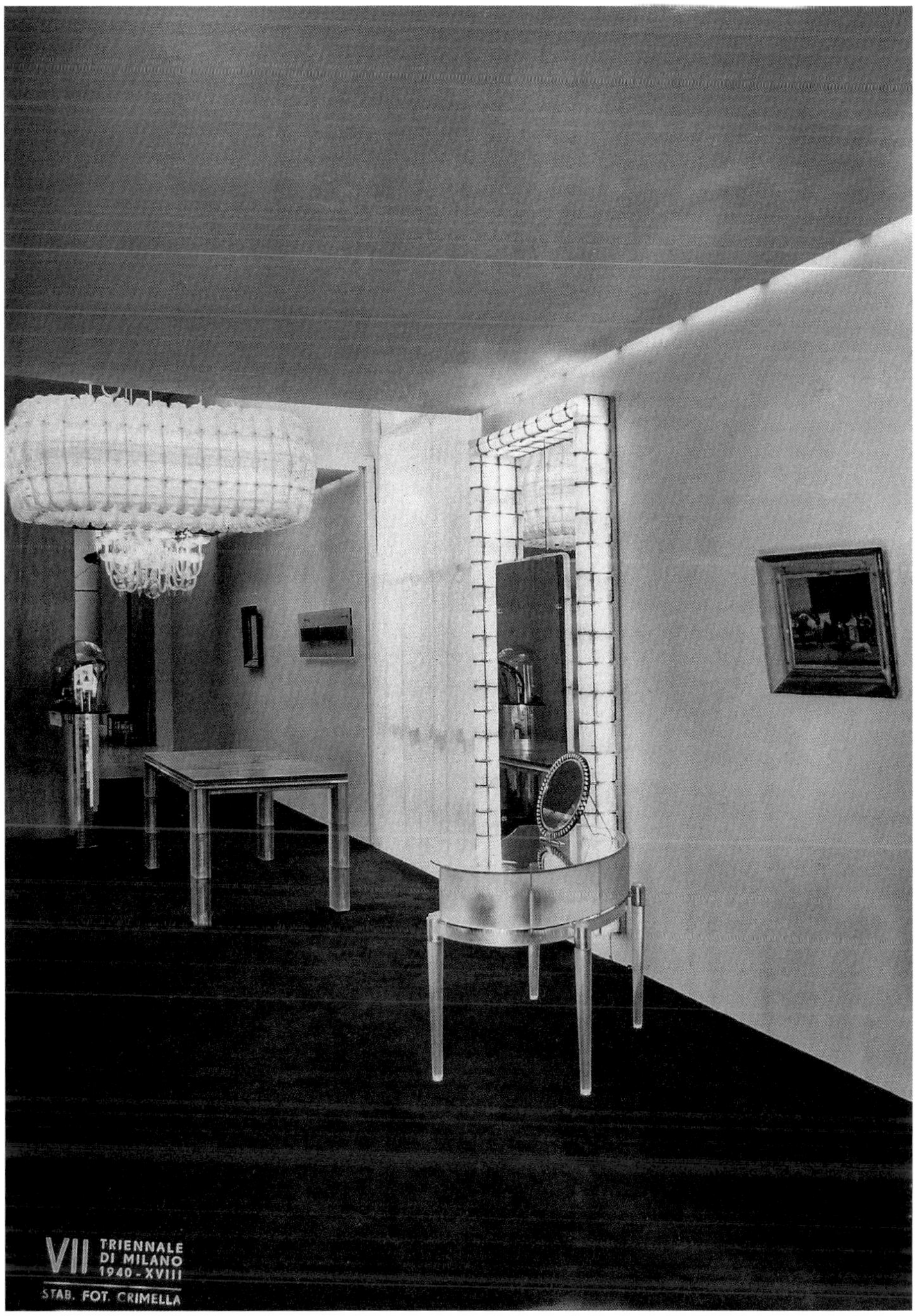

<<
VII TRIENNALE DI MILANO
Mounting of the chandelier no. 5315, in *cristallo* and *lattimo* glass.
Period photograph,1943, Istituto Luce

>
VII TRIENNALE DI MILANO
Venini Room. Period photograph, 1940

>
VII TRIENNALE DI MILANO
Venini Room. Period photograph, 1940

1940

VENICE (IT)
XXII ESPOSIZIONE BIENNALE INTERNAZIONALE D'ARTE

PENDANT

On the occasion of the Venice event, in the area reserved to it, the glassworks exhibited a pendant light in addition to a series of goblets, plates, vases and a table in glass. This light was of a decidedly decorative kind, characterised by polychrome flowers of glass with long undulating stems.

>
XXII ESPOSIZIONE BIENNALE INTERNAZIONALE D'ARTE
Study for a chandelier with floral elements, c. 1940

>
XXII ESPOSIZIONE BIENNALE INTERNAZIONALE D'ARTE
Venini showcase. Period photograph, 1940

235
234
233
232
230
231
229
228
226
224
225
227
223
220
213
211
218
221
201
202
203
205
208
212
216
217
219
240
239
236
237

1940

ROME (IT)
SAVOIA HOTEL

Lighting project for hotel premises.

1940

VENICE (IT)
BANCA D'ITALIA

Lighting project for the bank premises housed in the Palazzo Dolfin Manin.

1940

MILAN (IT)
LAW COURTS

WALL LAMPS
CORDONATO GLASS

Lighting project for the building (1932-40) designed by the architect Marcello Piacentini in collaboration with the architect Ernesto Rapisardi. This consisted, among other things, of a series of lamps 'in gilded metal and Murano striped glass' (*Architettura*, January-February 1942, p. 51) positioned in the entrance hall of the Civil Court. The project is documented in the Venini archive by several drawings such as that for a long pendant lamp in *cordonato* glass (a proposal?) and that for ceiling lights in *cordonato* glass.

>
LAW COURTS
Entrance hall of the Civil Court. Period photograph, 1940

>>
LAW COURTS
Drawing for a ceiling lamp in *cordonato* glass, c. 1940

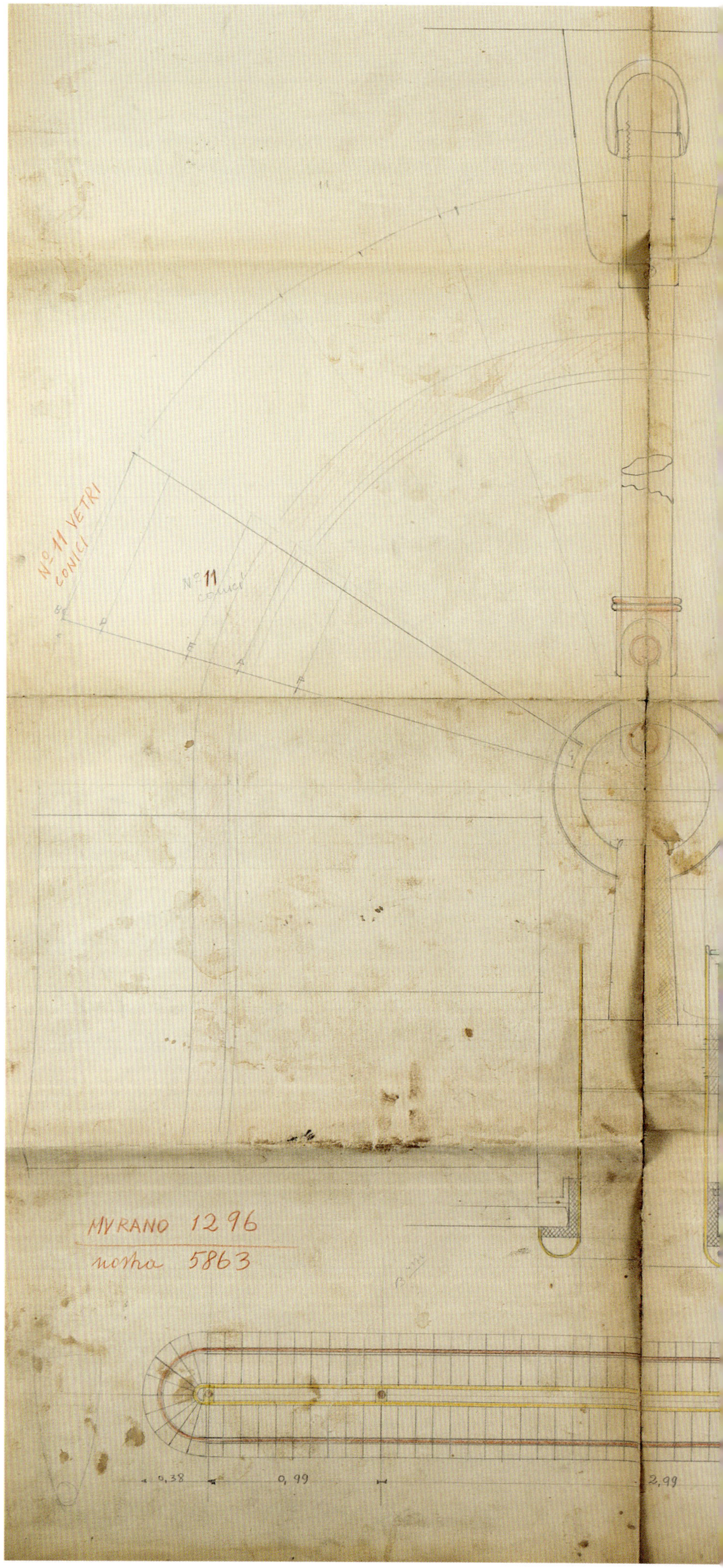

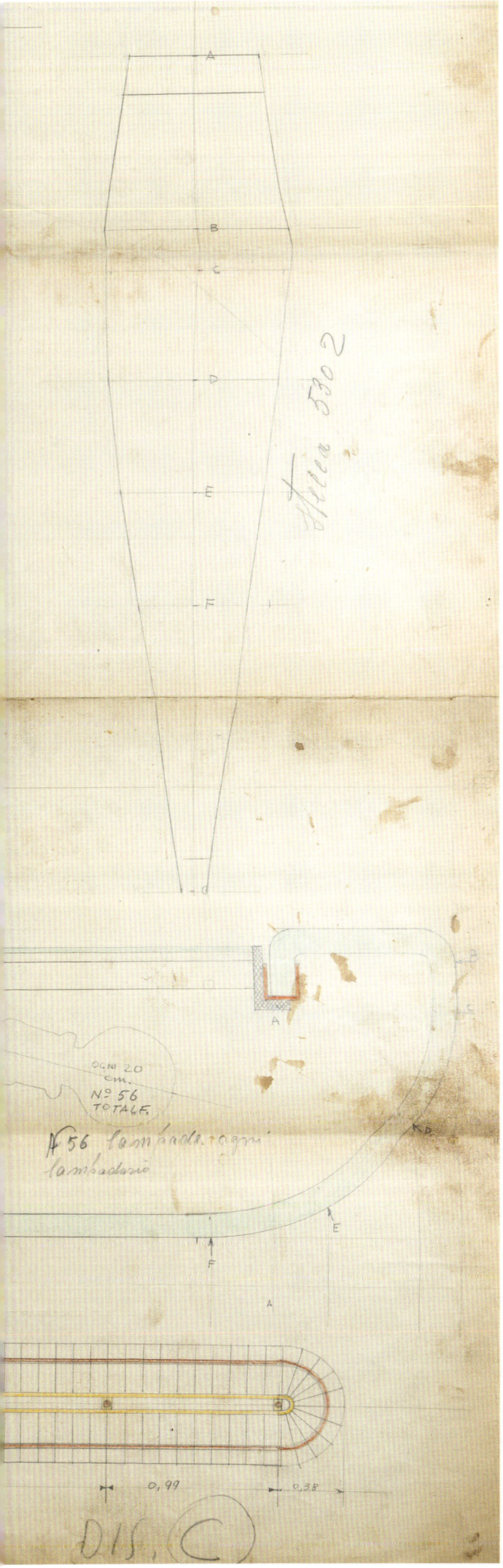
OGNI 20
cm.
N° 56
TOTALE
0,99
0,38
DIS. C

1940
1942

PADUA (IT)
UNIVERSITÀ DEGLI STUDI DI PADOVA

WITH ARMS
WALL LAMPS
PENDANT

On the occasion of the restoration of some of the university buildings, among which the Palazzo del Bo (designed by Ettore Fagiuoli), and the construction of the Palazzo Liviano (designed by Gio Ponti, who also took charge of the interior design of the two buildings) the Venini firm produced a series of lighting systems. In the Palazzo del Bo the glassworks were responsible for, among other things, the lighting of the hall of the Academic Senate (chandelier model 5315, Blue Catalogue, design by Carlo Scarpa) and the professors' room (wall lamps with three arms in opaline glass). For the Baldo degli Ubaldi library chandeliers were produced with a cylindrical base, in two tiers and in engraved *cristallo* glass, to be used also in the Sala dei Giganti in Palazzo Liviano. The initiator of this important renovation project was Carlo Anti, at the time rector of the Padua University. Some of these lights are still *in situ*.

›
UNIVERSITÀ DEGLI STUDI DI PADOVA
Sala dei Giganti, Palazzo Liviano. With the permission of the University of Padua - photograph Federico Milanesi

M. BRVTVS

<<
UNIVERSITÀ DEGLI STUDI DI PADOVA
Hall of the Academic Senate, Palazzo del Bo.
Period photograph, 1960s

1941 LIVORNO (IT)
PALAZZO HOTEL

Lighting project for this late-18th-century hotel.

1941 MILAN (IT)
BANCA COMMERCIALE

Lighting project for bank premises.

1941 MILAN (IT)
BIFFI CONFECTIONARY

CORRUGATED GLASS

Lighting project for the historic Milan café situated at the side of the central octagon of the Vittorio Emanuele II Gallery. It consisted of several lighting systems created with strips in corrugated glass.

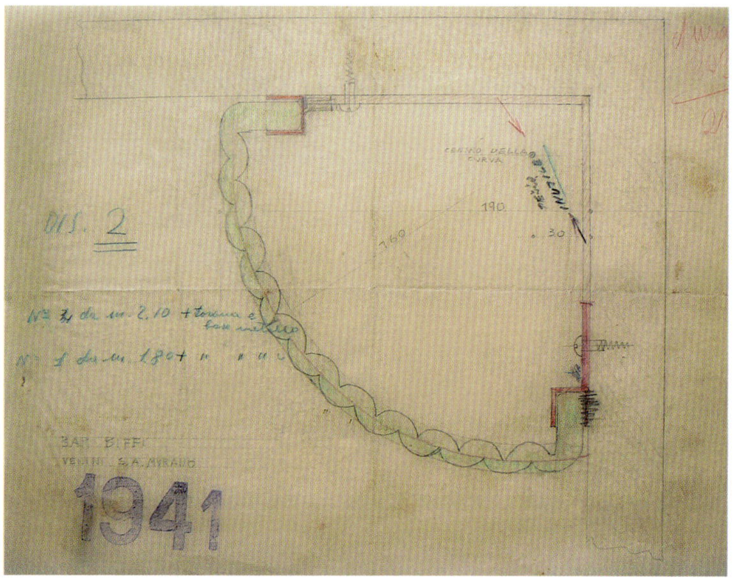

1941 ROME (IT)
EXCELSIOR HOTEL

Lighting project for hotel premises.

1941 ROME (IT)
BANCA D'ITALIA

Lighting project for bank premises.

1942 POCOL (IT)
ARGENTINA HOTEL

WALL LAMPS
CEILING

Lighting project for the mountain hotel in Cortina d'Ampezzo. This was presumably a series of wall and ceiling lights with modular elements in *cristallo* glass.

1942 VERONA (IT)
ASTRA CINEMA

Lighting project for the auditoria of the cinema belonging to the Valerio family.

1946 MILAN (IT)
CITTÀ DI TRENTO BAR

Lighting project for a café.

›
BIFFI CONFECTIONARY
Design for a lamp in corrugated glass, 1941

1946

MILAN (IT)

GRAND HOTEL ET DE MILAN

G. GATTI CASAZZA

PENDANT

The hotel was restored at the end of the war following the damage caused by aerial bombardments. The architect Giovanni Muzio took care of the restoration works, together with the architect Giuseppe Gatti Casazza who was responsible for the furnishings. For some areas of the hotel, the glassworks produced a series of pendant lamps in *cristallo* glass with a leaf motif.

1949

MILAN (IT)

CAPITOL CINEMA

Lighting project for the auditoria of the cinema designed by the architect Enrico Griffini and inaugurated in September 1949.

1949

ROME (IT)

SISTINA CINEMA-THEATRE

Lighting project for the Rome cinema-theatre (1942-49) designed by the architect Marcello Piacentini.

1949

MONFALCONE (IT)

CONTE BIANCAMANO TRANSATLANTIC LINER

DESIGN R. BOICO, A. CERVI, V. FRONDOLI, U. NORDIO

WALL LAMPS
CEILING

For the vessel built in 1924 and refurbished after the war (1948-49) by various designers, such as Gustavo Pulitzer and Gio Ponti, the Venini firm was called upon to produce a series of lighting systems. Among these were the wall lamps for the bar of the first-class veranda (design of June 1949, Venini archive) and the ceiling lamps with modular elements of the second-class gaming hall, designed by a group of Trieste architects (Romano Boico, Aldo Cervi, Vittorio Frondoli, Umberto Nordio) who were involved in the furnishing of several rooms.

>
CONTE BIANCAMANO TRANSATLANTIC LINER
Veranda, first class. Period photograph, 1949

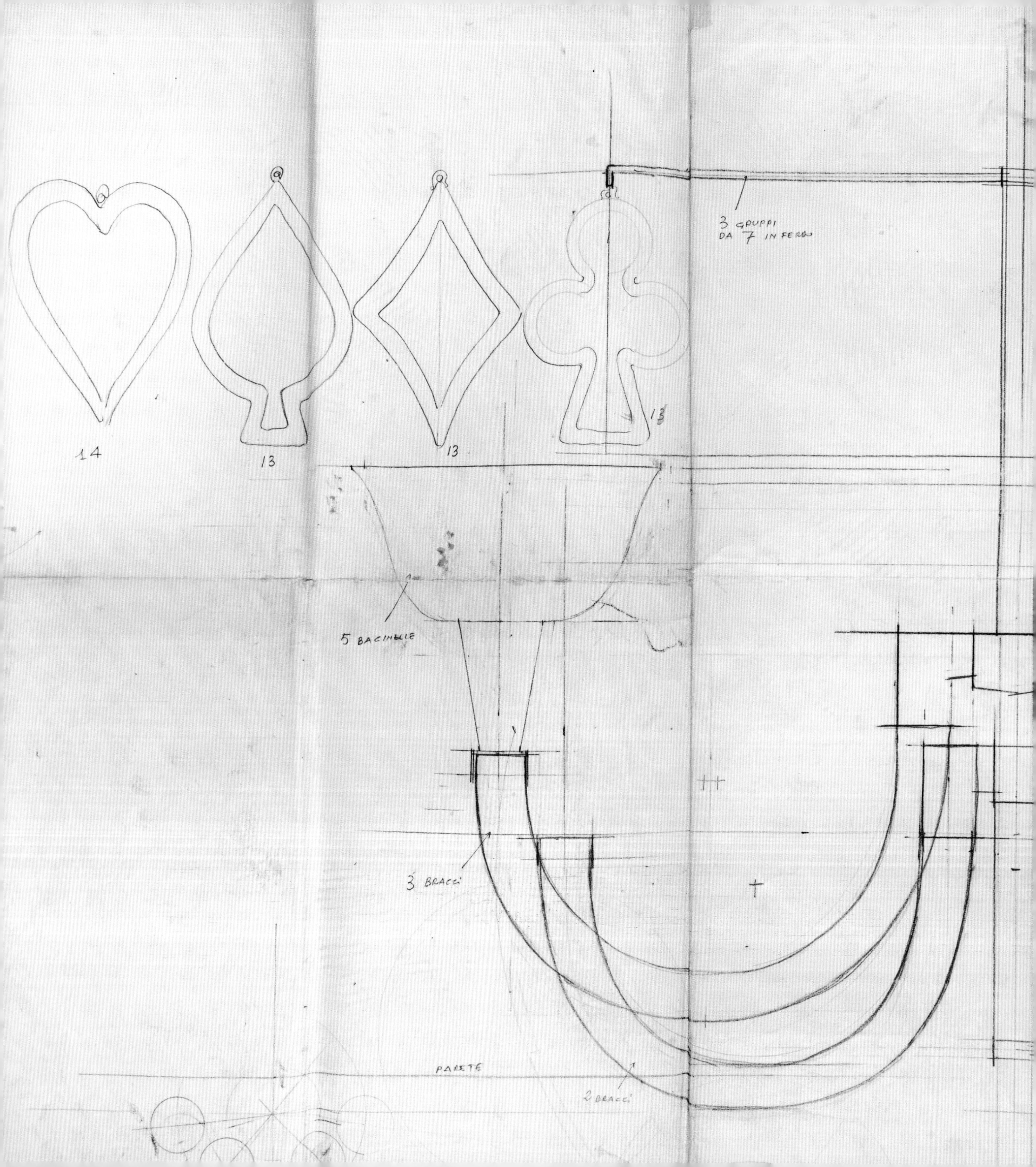

3 GRUPPI DA 7 IN FERRO
14
13
13
13
5 BACINELLE
3 BRACCI
PARETE
2 BRACCI

1950s

1950 FRASCATI (IT)
INA ISTITUTO NAZIONALE DELLE ASSICURAZIONI

Lighting project for premises of the INA.

1950 LIDO DI VENEZIA (IT)
LA PERLA THEATRE, CASINO

Lighting project for the halls of the La Perla Theatre belonging to the Casino of Lido complex.

1950 TURIN (IT)
PRINCIPI DI PIEMONTE HOTEL

WITH ARMS
PRISM GLASS

This is the second project in this hotel, after that completed in 1937. On this occasion the banqueting room was equipped with three large mirrors in a frame of bamboo glass, a console with supports in glass, chandeliers and wall lamps with arms included in the glassworks catalogue and designed by Carlo Scarpa. Flower vases and wall lamps in prism glass were also executed (no. 5797, Red Catalogue).

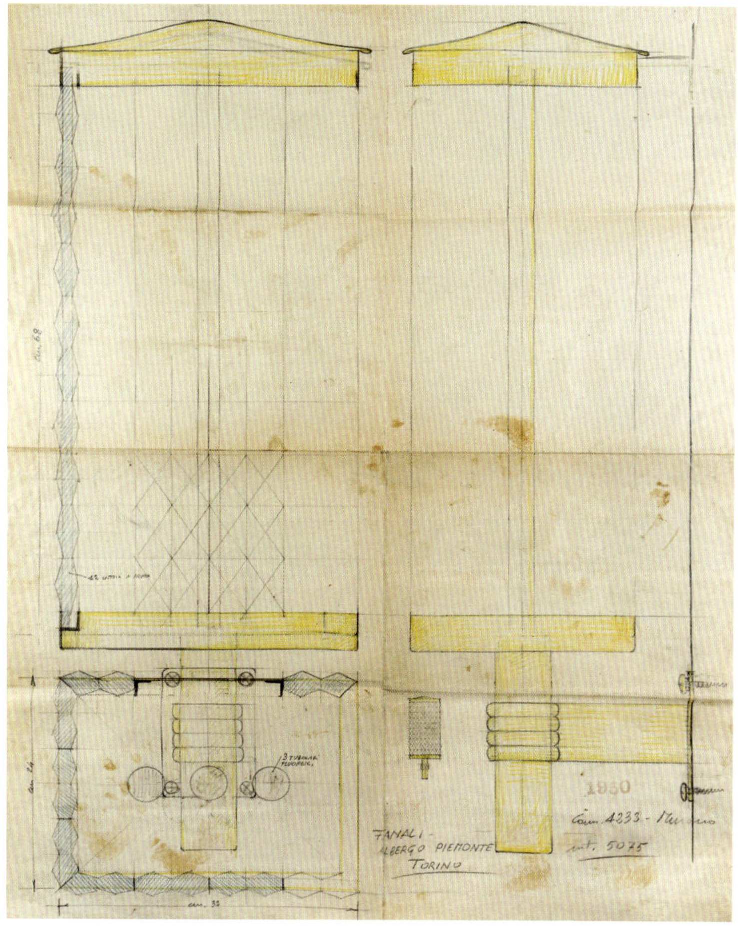

>
PRINCIPI DI PIEMONTE HOTEL
Design for wall lamps in prism glass and metal, 1950

>
PRINCIPI DI PIEMONTE HOTEL
Mirror, console and lamps in the banqueting hall.
Period photograph, c. 1950

>
PRINCIPI DI PIEMONTE HOTEL
Flower box and wall lamp in prism glass and metal.
Period photograph, c. 1950

>
PRINCIPI DI PIEMONTE HOTEL
Venini chandeliers in banqueting hall. Period photograph, c. 1950

1951

LA VALLETTA (MT)
CASINO

Lighting project for the gambling halls of the Maltese casino.

1951

MILAN (IT)
IX TRIENNALE DI MILANO

SPHERES

'Decorative lighting complex' presented at the 9th Triennale of Milan in the lighting section (*IX Triennale di Milano. Catalogue*, 1951). These are six 'streamers' made up of steel cables and spheres in transparent glass, in various colours and sizes, with a *balloton* decoration, which are illuminated from below by three projectors inserted into as many bowls in coloured glass, these also being supported by steel cables.

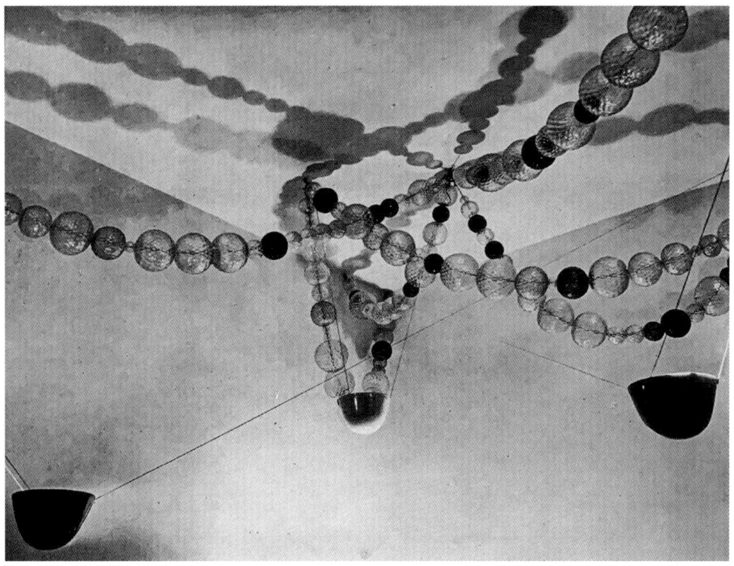

>
IX TRIENNALE DI MILANO
'Lighting complex', in *Forme nuove in Italia*, Milan, 1957

1951

VENICE (IT)
PALAZZO GRASSI, HEADQUARTERS OF THE CENTRO INTERNAZIONALE DELLE ARTI E DEL COSTUME

SPHERES
PRISM GLASS

On 23 August 1951 with the vernissage of the *Mostra del costume nel tempo* and the *Mostra di libri d'arte sul costume*, the new look of the Palazzo Grassi was presented to the public; it had just been restored to become the headquarters of the Centro Internazionale delle Arti e del Costume promoted by Franco Marinotti, the industrialist at the head of the SNIA [Società Navigazione Industriale Applicazione] Viscosa. The layout of the building had been directed by Marinotti's trusted architect, Giuseppe de Min, and by the younger architects Angelo Bianchetti and Cesare Pea, to whom we owe in particular the choices regarding the fitting-out of the spaces, as documented by certain study designs (*Centro Internazionale delle Arti e del Costume. Palazzo Grassi*, 1951). To facilitate implementation of Centro initiatives (exhibitions, fashion shows, congresses) and ensure the possibility of using the whole area of the courtyard, it was decided to install a covering with a skylight in glass screened by a velarium. An initial idea for this velarium is represented in a view of the courtyard initialled by Bianchetti and Pea. Presumably following an exchange of views with the Paolo Venini glassworks and Venini himself, agreement was reached on the work to be realised: a succession of 'streamers' with steel wires and spheres in *cristallo balloton* glass in three different sizes, repeated according to a pre-established pattern. The 'streamers' form part of a rectangular structure (13 x 16 m) the lower section of which is

>>
PALAZZO GRASSI, HEADQUARTERS OF THE CENTRO INTERNAZIONALE DELLE ARTI E DEL COSTUME
View of the velarium of Palazzo Grassi during the preparation of the exhibition *Giuseppe Samonà. 1923-1975. Cinquant'anni di architettura*, project of C. Scarpa. Period photograph, 1975

defined by a frame in prism glass. This material was also used for the rectangular plate forming the summit of the installation on top of which numerous 'streamers' are attached which falling downwards give the idea of four semi-transparent curved partitions: this structure thus hides the skylight above and transforms the courtyard into a 'luminous hall with a ceiling of glass globes' (*Il Gazzettino*, 24 August 1951). In 1985-86, the velarium was removed during the restoration of Palazzo Grassi by the architects Gae Aulenti and Antonio Foscari on behalf of Palazzo Grassi S.p.A. of the FIAT group. From certain graphic evidence in the Venini archive, it is possible to document that the solution of the velarium for Palazzo Grassi was proposed (and implemented?) during the 1950s for other projects, not yet identified: in one case the covering of a ballroom (5 x 15.6 m) (undated design, 1950s) in another a velarium of 3 x 4.84 m (1954).
[*C. Sonego*]

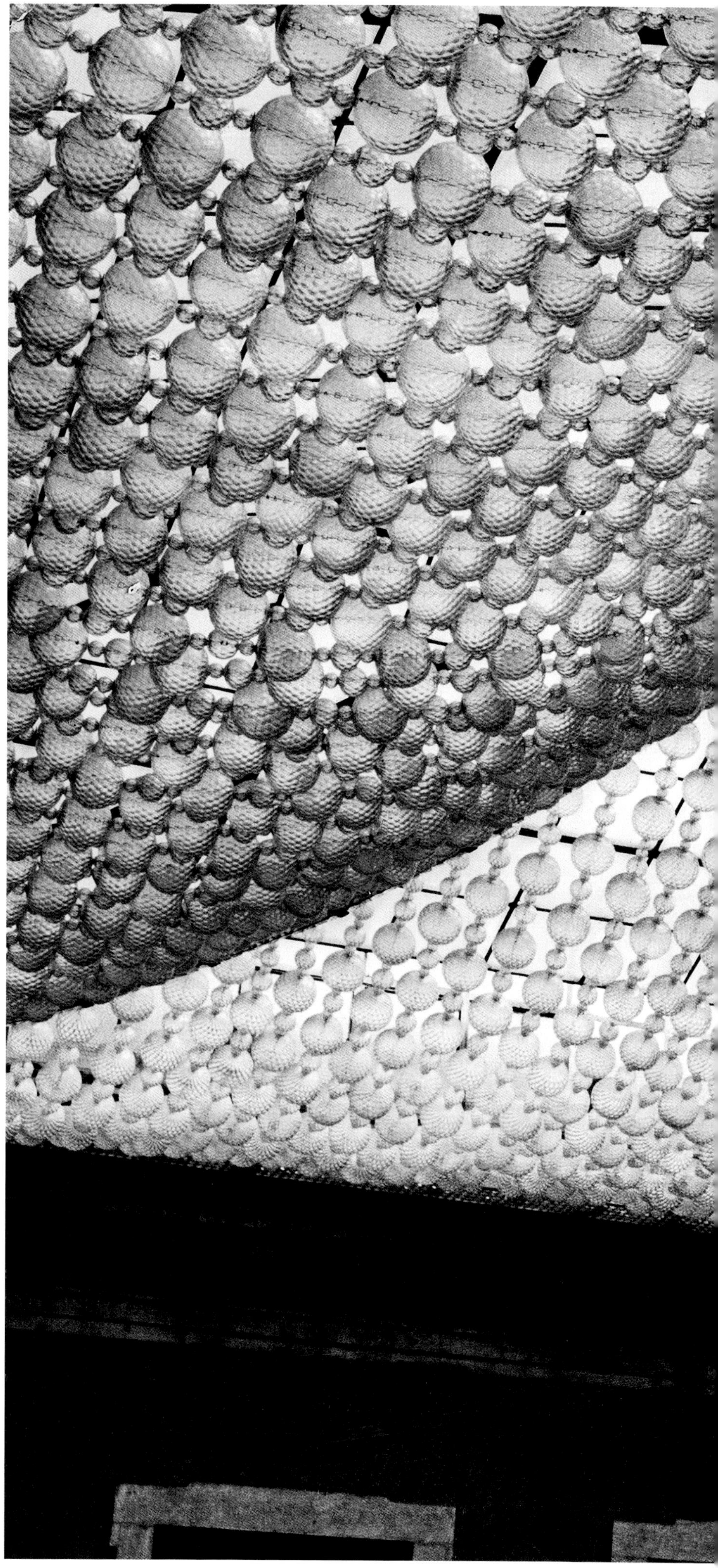

>
PALAZZO GRASSI, HEADQUARTERS OF THE CENTRO INTERNAZIONALE DELLE ARTI E DEL COSTUME
Velarium of Palazzo Grassi in *balloton* spheres and prism glass. Period photograph, 1951

>
PALAZZO GRASSI, HEADQUARTERS OF THE CENTRO INTERNAZIONALE DELLE ARTI E DEL COSTUME
Velarium of Palazzo Grassi in *balloton* spheres and prism glass, detail. Period photograph, 1951

>>
PALAZZO GRASSI, HEADQUARTERS OF THE CENTRO INTERNAZIONALE DELLE ARTI E DEL COSTUME
Velarium of Palazzo Grassi in *balloton* spheres and prism glass. Period photograph, 1951

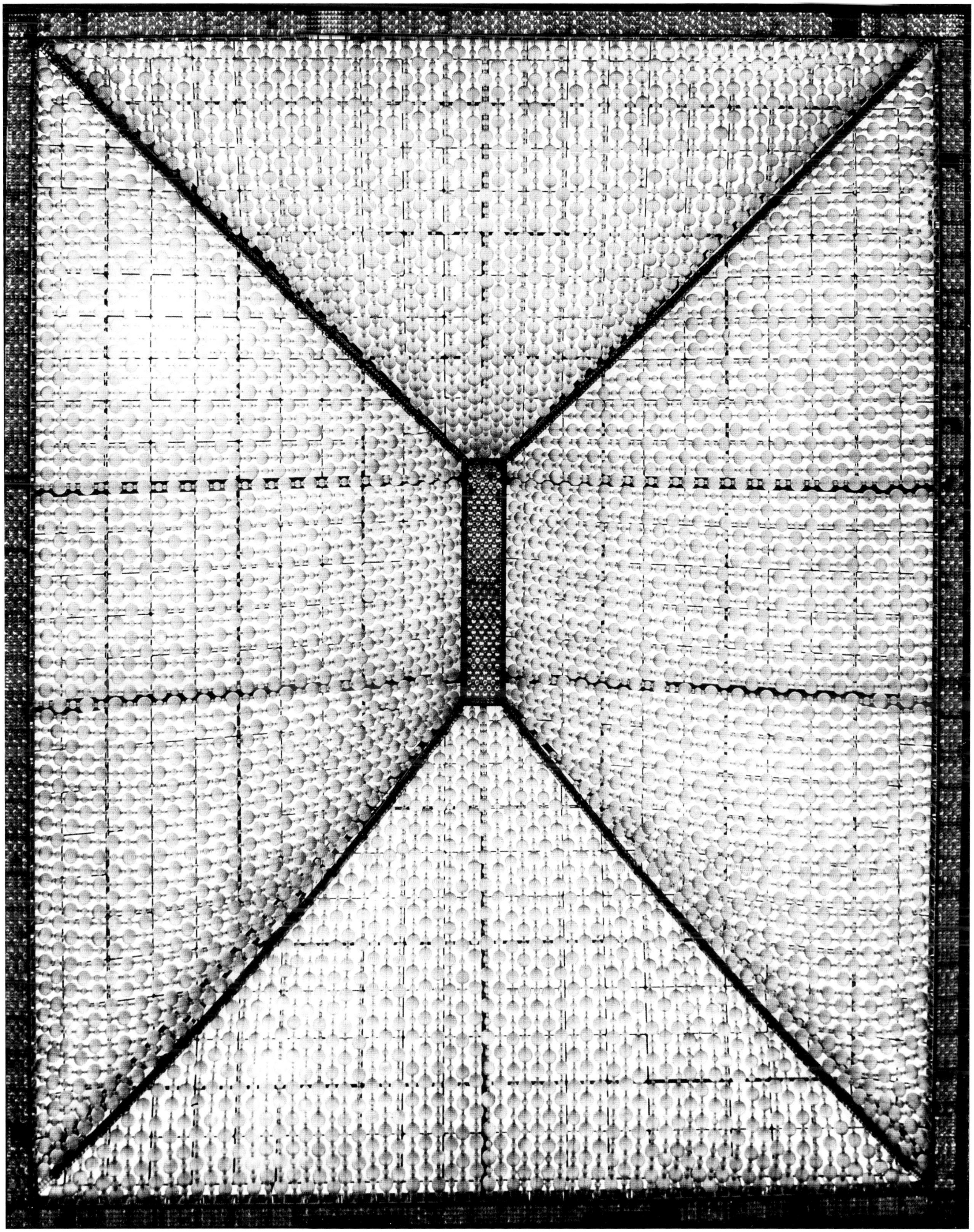

>
PALAZZO GRASSI, HEADQUARTERS OF THE CENTRO INTERNAZIONALE DELLE ARTI E DEL COSTUME
A. Bianchetti, C. Pea, Arrangement of the courtyard of Palazzo Grassi with 'a velarium in Murano glass', in *Centro Internazionale delle Arti e del Costume. Palazzo Grassi*, 1951

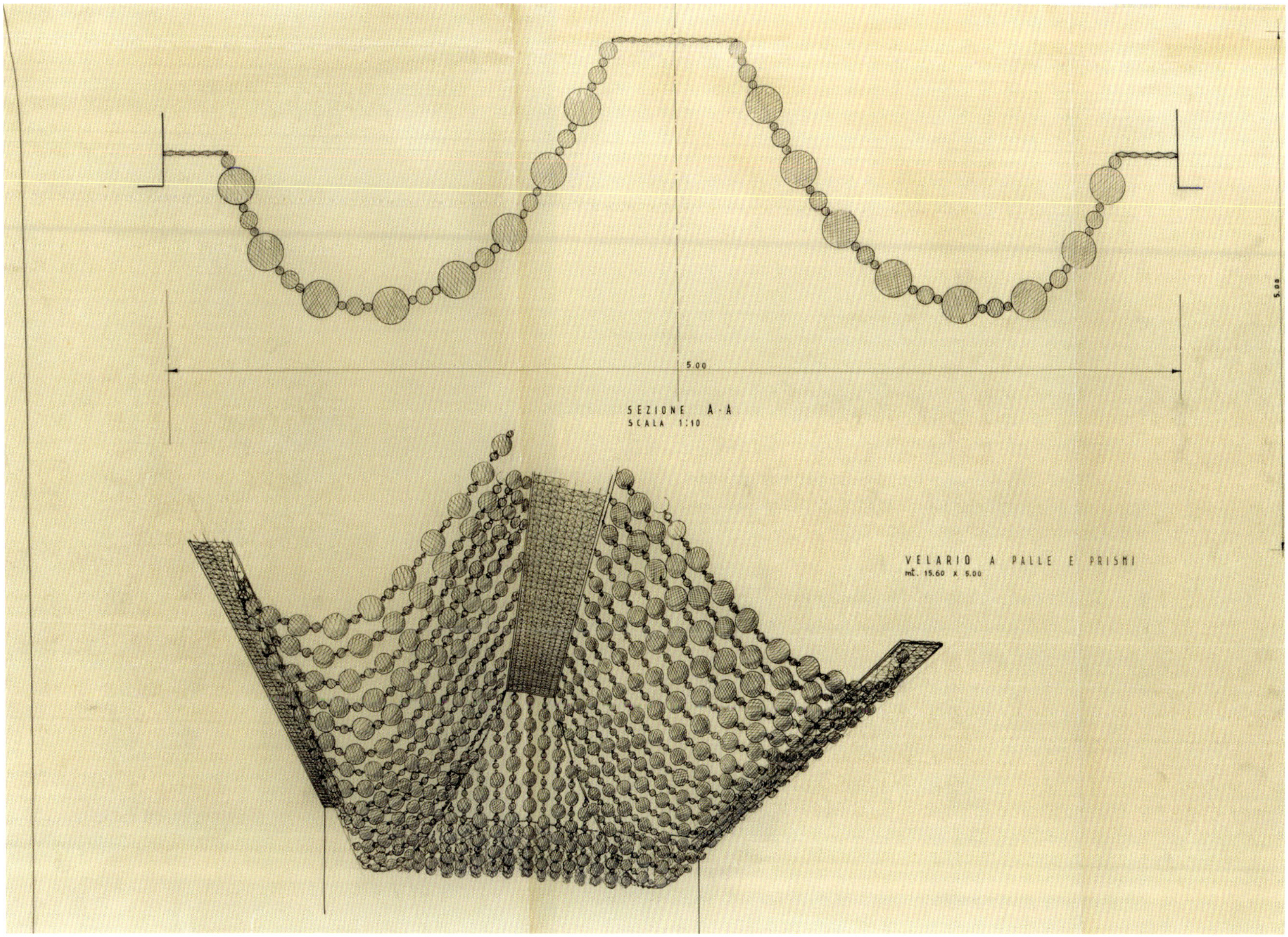

>
Study for the covering of a ballroom with *balloton* spheres, 1950s

1951 YORK (GB)
CITY HALL

WITH ARMS

Lighting project for the town hall of York.

1951-52 BRUSSELS (BE)
THÉÂTRE ROYAL DES GALERIES
DESIGN S. JASINSKI

SPHERES
PRISM GLASS

The Théâtre Royal des Galeries is part of the complex of the Galeries Royales Saint-Hubert designed in 1847 by the architect Jean-Pierre Cluysenaar. In 1951 the theatre was demolished and reconstructed according to the plans of the architect Paul Bonduelle who for the internal areas availed himself of the collaboration of the decorator Stéphane Jasinski. A dome was constructed over the hall, decorated by Magritte with the representation of clouds on a blue background which in the artist's first draft was also studded with a series of rattles. At the centre of the dome a huge chandelier was positioned with a diameter of about six meters, designed by Jasinski and produced with 3384 spheres of different dimensions (from 20 to 3 cm), in transparent glass with a *balloton* decoration. The chandelier is circular in design and the body consists of up of 60 'streamers' made of stainless steel wires and *balloton* spheres. The light source is positioned at the top and along the perimeter of the outermost circle and is screened by plates in prism glass. The perimeter of the chandelier is decorated by a kind of fringe composed of 120 pendants with small *balloton* spheres. The same decoration, with 24 pendants, is also above at the centre of the piece. This monumental chandelier is still *in situ*.

>
THÉÂTRE ROYAL DES GALERIES
Dome frescoed by Magritte and the chandelier with *balloton* spheres, phpto ©Théâtre des Galeries

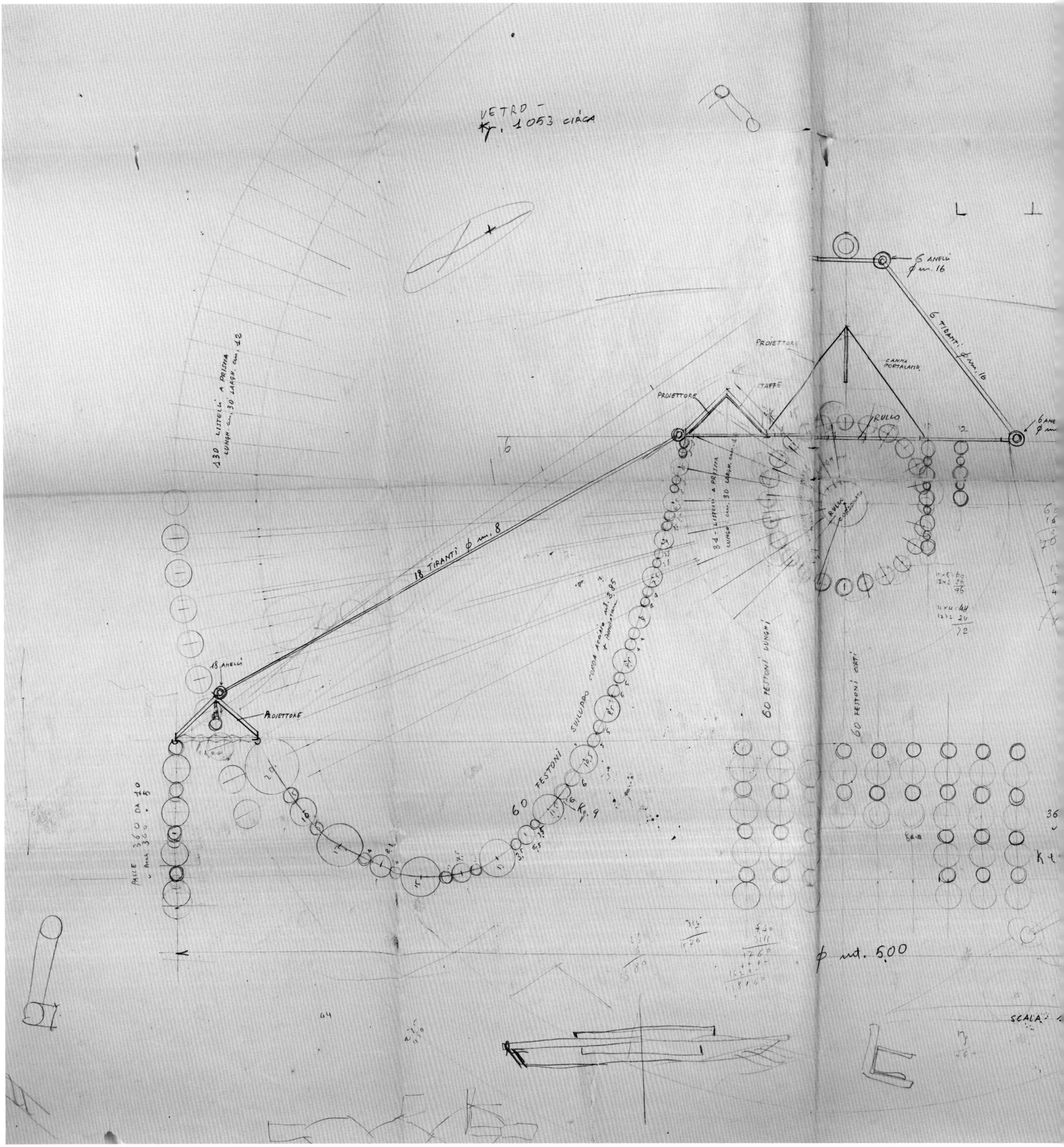
VETRO -
Kg. 1053 CIRCA
130 LISTELLI A PRISMA
6 ANELLI
ø mm. 16
6 TIRANTI ø mm. 16
PROIETTORE
CANNA PORTALAMP.
STAFFE
RULLO
18 TIRANTI ø mm. 8
18 ANELLI
PROIETTORE
60 FESTONI
60 FESTONI LUNGHI
60 FESTONI CORTI
ø mt. 5.00
SCALA

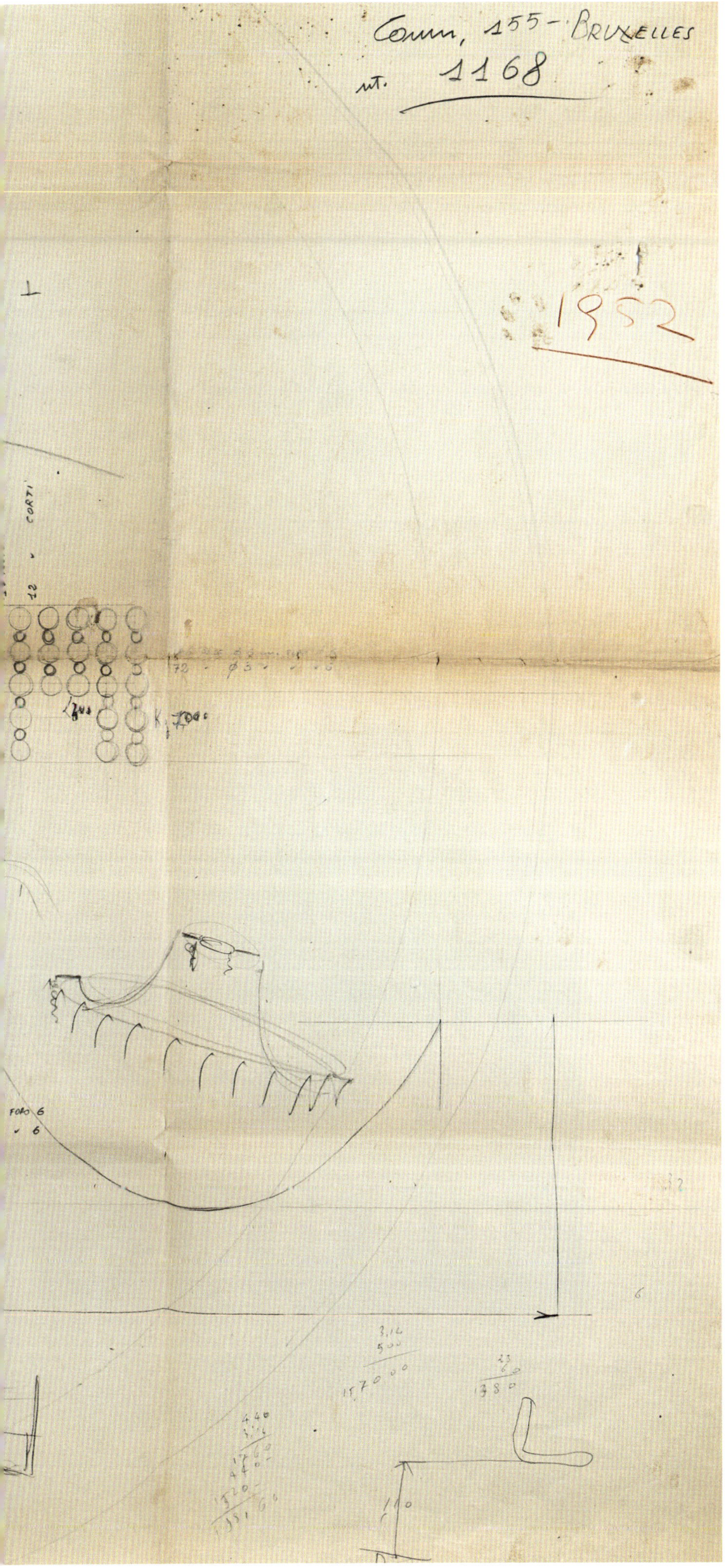

«
THÉÂTRE ROYAL DES GALERIES
Design and studies for the huge chandelier with *balloton* spheres, 1952

›
THÉÂTRE ROYAL DES GALERIES
Chandelier with *balloton* spheres. Period photograph, 1950s

1951-52 FLORENCE (IT)
CHAMBER OF COMMERCE

Lighting project for the Chamber of Commerce building.

1952 FLORENCE (IT)
ODEON CINEMA-THEATRE

Lighting project for the historic Odeon cinema-theatre housed in the Palazzo dello Strozzino after a design, first by Adolfo Coppedè (1914) and later by Marcello Piacentini (1920-22). The Venini project was implemented after the restoration of the building which took place in 1951.

1952 FOLIGNO (IT)
INA ISTITUTO NAZIONALE DELLE ASSICURAZIONI

Lighting project for premises of the INA.

1952 LIDO DI VENEZIA (IT)
CINEMA BUILDING, PORCH

Project for the lighting installations in the *avant-corps* of the Palazzo della Mostra del Cinema designed by the architects Luigi Quagliata and Angelo Scattolin.

1952 MESSINA (IT)
CITY HALL

Town-hall lighting project.

1952 ROME (IT)
BARBERINI CINEMA

Lighting project for the auditoriums of the Barberini cinema.

1952 ROME (IT)
INA ISTITUTO NAZIONALE DELLE ASSICURAZIONI

Lighting project for a building of the INA designed by the architect Manlio Golfarelli.

1952 TURIN (IT)
AUDITORIUM RAI DI TORINO

LEAVES AND FLOWERS
BAMBÙ GLASS
ZANFIRICO GLASS

The building (Auditorium RAI di Torino, now Arturo Toscanini) is the fruit of the renovation of the Teatro Vittorio after a design of the architects Aldo Morbelli e Carlo Mollino. The Auditorium, intended to be the headquarters of the RAI Symphony Orchestra and Choir of Turin, was inaugurated on 16 December 1952. The Venini project included the installation of various wall lamps in glass with *zanfirico* canes for the foyer, for which a long hanging lamp with a motif of leaves and flowers was also executed. There are many other lamps in the accessory areas on the upper floors. Among these are mixtilinear ceiling lamps with borders in bamboo coloured glass and wall lamps with a motif of leaves and flowers (no. 5774, Red Catalogue). Some of these lighting elements are still *in situ*.

>
AUDITORIUM RAI DI TORINO
Ceiling lamp with leaves and flowers in the foyer. Restyling with LED lights by F:L architetti and END architetti, 2019. Ph. © Beppe Giardino

>
AUDITORIUM RAI DI TORINO
Wall lamp with leaves and flowers in areas of the auditorium. Period photograph, 1950s
>
AUDITORIUM RAI DI TORINO
Wall lamp with leaves and flowers and mixtilinear ceiling lamps in parts of the auditorium. Period photograph, 1950s

1953 BIELLA (IT)
SOCIAL THEATRE

Lighting project for theatre complex.

1953 NAPLES (IT)
LUCANIA SHIP
DESIGN G. DE CARLO

CEILING

Circular chandelier with bands in six different colours (Ø 350 cm) for the first-class lounge.

1953 NAPLES (IT)
HAAS SHOP

ZANFIRICO GLASS

Lighting project for retail space.

>
HAAS SHOP
Spherical lamp with a screen with circular elements in *canne di zanfirico lattimo* glass. Period photograph, March 1954

1953 ROME (IT)
QUIRINALE HOTEL

Lighting project for the historic hotel establishment beside the Teatro dell'Opera in Rome.

1953 ROME (IT)
SOCIETÀ ITALIANA SVILUPPO EDILIZIO

Lighting project for a private business.

1953 VENICE (IT)
BANCO DI NAPOLI

Project for bank premises.

1953-54 GENOA (IT)
COLOMBO TRANSATLANTIC LINER
DESIGN R. ALOI

Lighting project for Italian transatlantic liner.

1953-54 KIEL (DE)
DEUTSCHLAND SHIP

Lighting project for German motorboat.

1954 ABANO (IT)
CARE COMPANY

Lighting project for a service company.

1954 MILAN (IT)
X TRIENNALE DI MILANO
DESIGN F. ALBINI

BICHROME OPAL GLASS

On the occasion of the 10th Triennale of Milan an auditorium for conferences was installed in the main hall after a design by Franco Albini and Franca Helg. The lighting of the little amphitheatre was supplied by 'lamps suspended between turquoise-coloured glass bells of "Venini", Murano' (*X Triennale di Milano*, 1954). The model for the lamps designed by Franco Albini (*Domus*, March 1956) was included in the glassworks catalogue under the no. 4023, then nos. 800.2-3 and no. 800.4 (*Venini catalogue*, 1966).

>
X TRIENNALE DI MILANO
Auditorium with lamps after a design by Franco Albini.
Period photograph, 1954

>
X TRIENNALE DI MILANO
Paolo Venini with lamps no. 4023, in *Domus*, October 1959

>>
X TRIENNALE DI MILANO
Design for lamp no. 4023 A

>>
X TRIENNALE DI MILANO
Design for lamp no. 800.2, in *Venini lighting catalogue*, 1966

>>
X TRIENNALE DI MILANO
Lamp after a design by Franco Albini, in *Domus*, January 1956

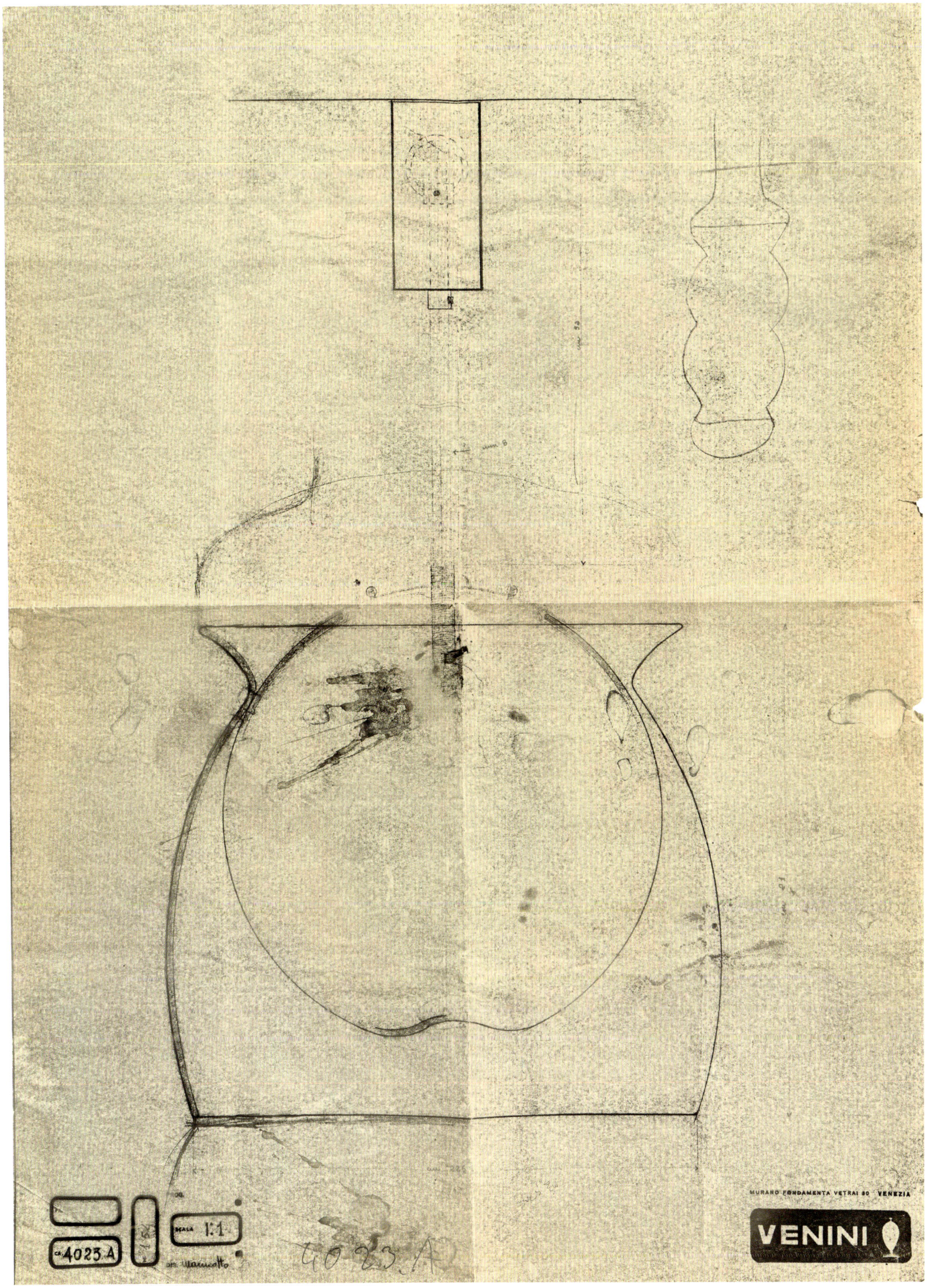
4023 A
SCALA 1:1
MURANO FONDAMENTA VETRAI 50 VENEZIA
VENINI

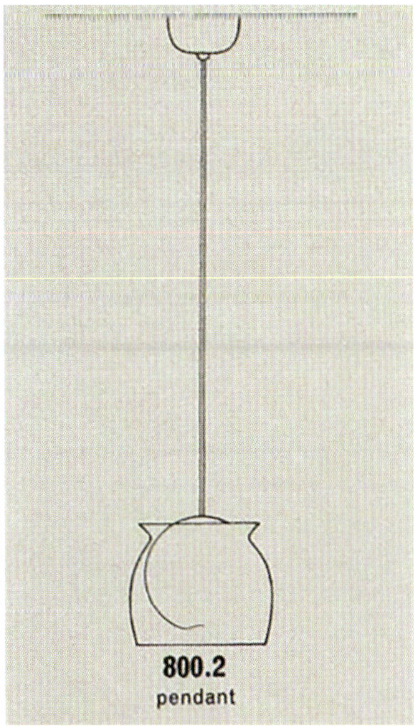
800.2
pendant

1954

NEW YORK (US)
OLIVETTI SHOP
DESIGN BBPR

A FASCE DI COLORE

Entirely BBPR-designed, the exhibition hall for the Olivetti Corporation of America was inaugurated in the summer of 1954 at 584 Fifth Avenue, New York. The materials used by the group of architects were all of great quality and mostly of Italian origin; some examples are the green marble of Runaz, Candoglia marble, and the glass of Murano. The twelve *a fasce di colore* blown-glass lamps, reminiscent of the series of vases of the same name produced by Bianconi, measure 25 cm in diameter and 60 in height (*Domus*, September 1954). Hanging from the ceiling at different heights, the lamps, cone-shaped with a metal band, contrasted with the marble pedestals supporting the type writers. The same model, with different colour variants and carrying the number AV-5457 was later included in the *Contemporary Italian* catalogue [c. 1955] of the Altamira store, the American Venini concessionaire. The store was closed in the 1970s and subsequently demolished.

>
OLIVETTI SHOP
Inside of the store, in *Domus*, September 1954

>
OLIVETTI SHOP
Large bas-relief, paternoster wheel, pedestals and lighting equipment. Period photograph, 1950s

>
OLIVETTI SHOP
A fasce di colore lamps over the pedestals with typewriters. Period photograph, 1950s

1954

ROME (IT)

CONTINENTALE HOTEL

SPHERES

Lighting project for a hotel.

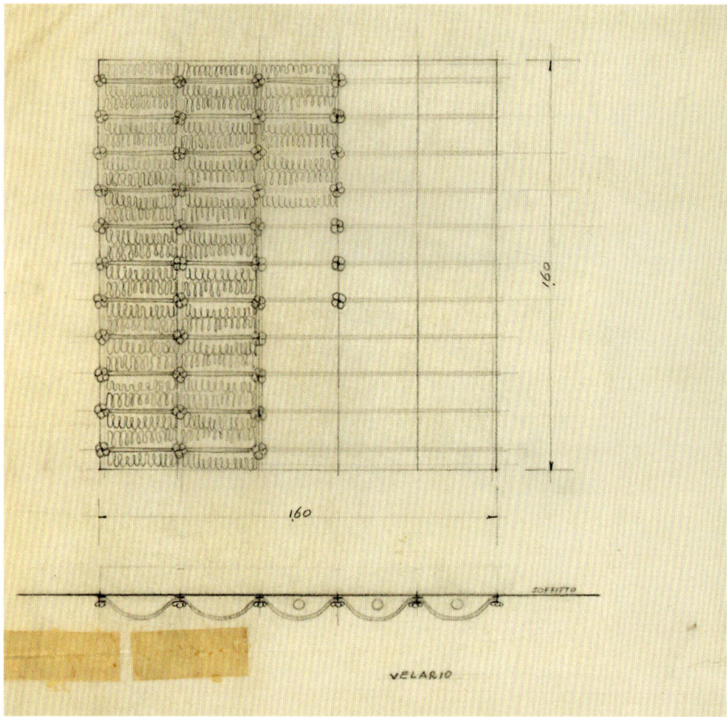

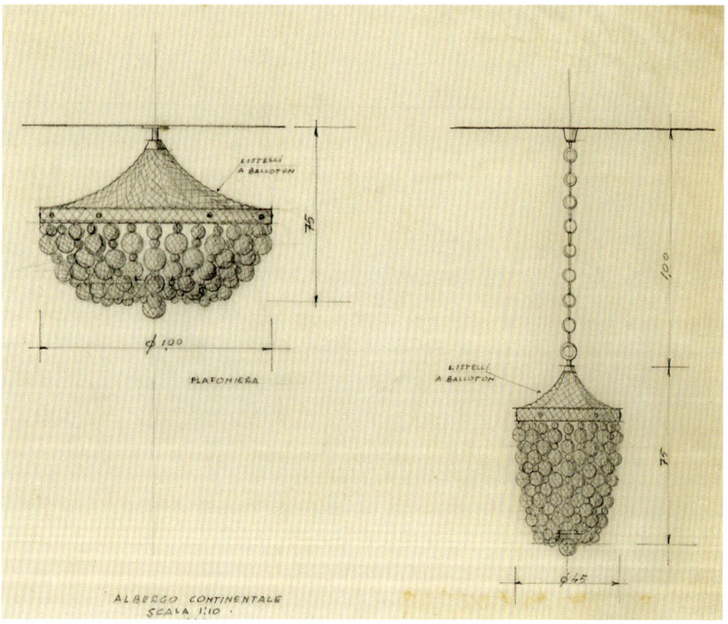

›
CONTINENTALE HOTEL
Design with an estimate for hanging lamps and velarium, details, 1950s

1954

ROME (IT)

SAVOIA HOTEL

Lighting project for a hotel.

1954

ROME (IT)

INA ISTITUTO NAZIONALE DELLE ASSICURAZIONI

Lighting project for the premises of the INA.

1954

SPOLETO (IT)

MUNICIPAL LIBRARY GIOSUÈ CARDUCCI

Lighting elements of the municipal library located in Palazzo Mauri.

1954

TURIN (IT)

AMBROSIO CINEMA

SPHERES
PRISM GLASS

Inaugurated in December 1913, the Cinema Ambrosio at its opening could be considered as one of the great cinemas of Europe. In 1920 it had the largest screen in Italy. In 1923 and again in 1930 it underwent extension and renovation works. In 1954 the architect Aldo Morbelli took charge of rearranging the entrance, designing a new revolving door and redesigning the foyer. In the foyer a new staircase giving access to the gallery was constructed which housed a very large chandelier hung with 'streamers' of *balloton* spheres in *cristallo* glass and contours in prism-shaped glass. The chandelier is still *in situ*.

>
AMBROSIO CINEMA
Entrance hall and staircase with the large chandelier with *balloton* spheres. Period photograph, 1950s

>
AMBROSIO CINEMA
Entrance hall with the large chandelier with *balloton* spheres. Period photograph, 1950s

1954 UDINE (IT)
CASSA DI RISPARMIO

Lighting project for bank premises.

1955 BENEVENTO (IT)
CITY HALL

Lighting project for town hall.

1955 BOLOGNA (IT)
GRAND HOTEL BAGLIONI

Lighting project for luxury hotel.

1955 BOLZANO (IT)
CASSA DI RISPARMIO OF BOLZANO/ SPARKASSE

Lighting project for bank premises.

1955 FROSINONE (IT)
INA ISTITUTO NAZIONALE DELLE ASSICURAZIONI BUILDING

Lighting project for the INA premises.

1955 GENOA (IT)
POLITEAMA THEATRE OF GENOA

Lighting project for the Genoa theatre building destroyed during the Second World War and reconstructed in 1955 after the design of the architect Dante Datta.

1955 LACCO AMENO (IT)
REGINA ISABELLA HOTEL

Lighting project for the hotel complex belonging to the Milan publisher Angelo Rizzoli implemented after the design of the architect Mario Tufaroli Luciano.

1955 PALERMO (IT)
CASSA DI RISPARMIO VITTORIO EMANUELE PER LE PROVINCE SICILIANE

Lighting project directed by the architect Enrico Lenti for the premises of a bank.

1955 ROME (IT)
UNIVERSITÀ DEGLI STUDI DI ROMA

Lighting project for the university premises.

1955 MODENA (IT)
FINI RESTAURANT

CEILING

Lighting project for a restaurant.

›
FINI RESTAURANT
Drawing for a ceiling lamp in coloured glass

1955 URBINO (IT)

UNIVERSITÀ DEGLI STUDI DI URBINO

Lighting project for the university premises.

1955 VENICE (IT)

FONDAZIONE GIORGIO CINI

WITH ARMS

Lighting project for the Fondazione Giorgio Cini of Venice, Isola di San Giorgio Maggiore, Venice.

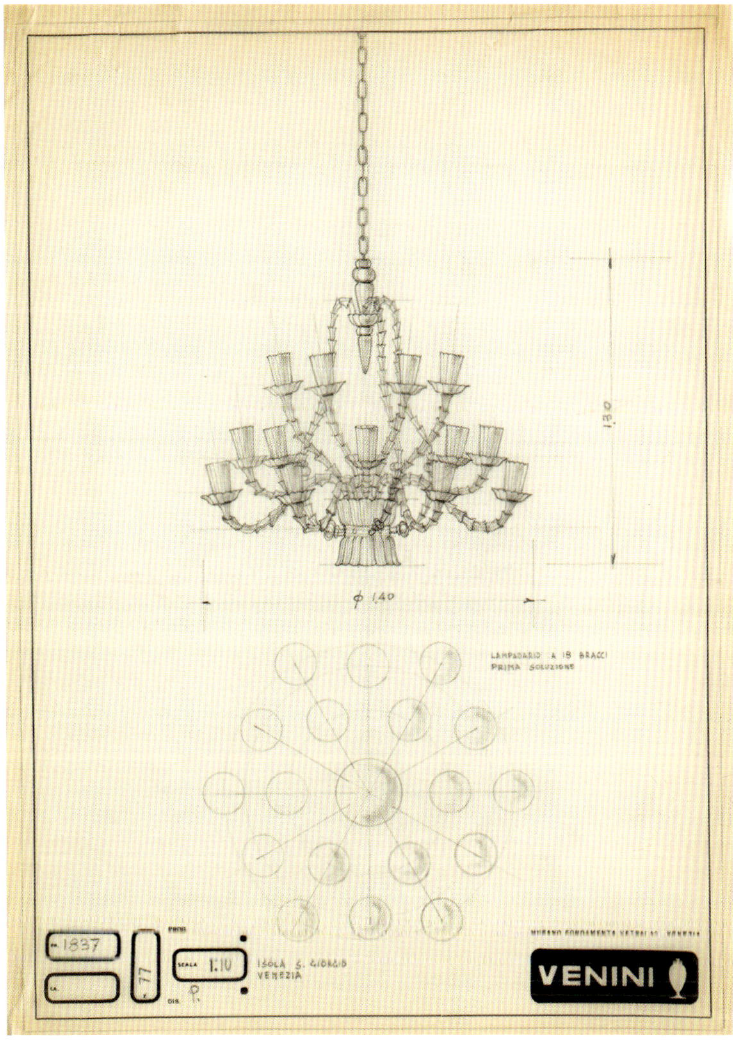

›
FONDAZIONE GIORGIO CINI
Drawing for a chandelier with eighteen arms, first solution

1955 VENICE (IT)

VENICE PROVINCIAL ADMINISTRATION

Lighting project for a public establishment.

1955 VIENNA (AT)

OPERA HOUSE

Lighting project created during the reconstruction of the theatre building which had been severely damaged by the wartime bombings of 1945.

1956 ANKARA (TR)

HILTON HOTEL

Lighting project for a hotel of the Hilton chain.

1956 CAPRI (IT)

QUISISANA HOTEL

Lighting project for a hotel.

1956 COSENZA (IT)

INA ISTITUTO NAZIONALE DELLE ASSICURAZION

Lighting project for premises belonging to the INA.

1956 ISTANBUL (TR)

HILTON HOTEL

Lighting project for a hotel of the Hilton chain.

1956

MILAN (IT)
COMPASSO D'ORO AWARD
DESIGN M. VIGNELLI

CANE GLASS

At the awarding of the third Compasso d'Oro prize two lamps after a design by Massimo Vignelli were mentioned. They were hanging lamp no. 4039, known as *Cipolla*, and table lamp no. 4040, known as *Fungo* or *Zaffiro*, which belong to a rich repertoire shown here below.

>
COMPASSO D'ORO AWARD
Table lamp in white opalino glass with broad canes in red glass, 35 cm high, private collection, Venice

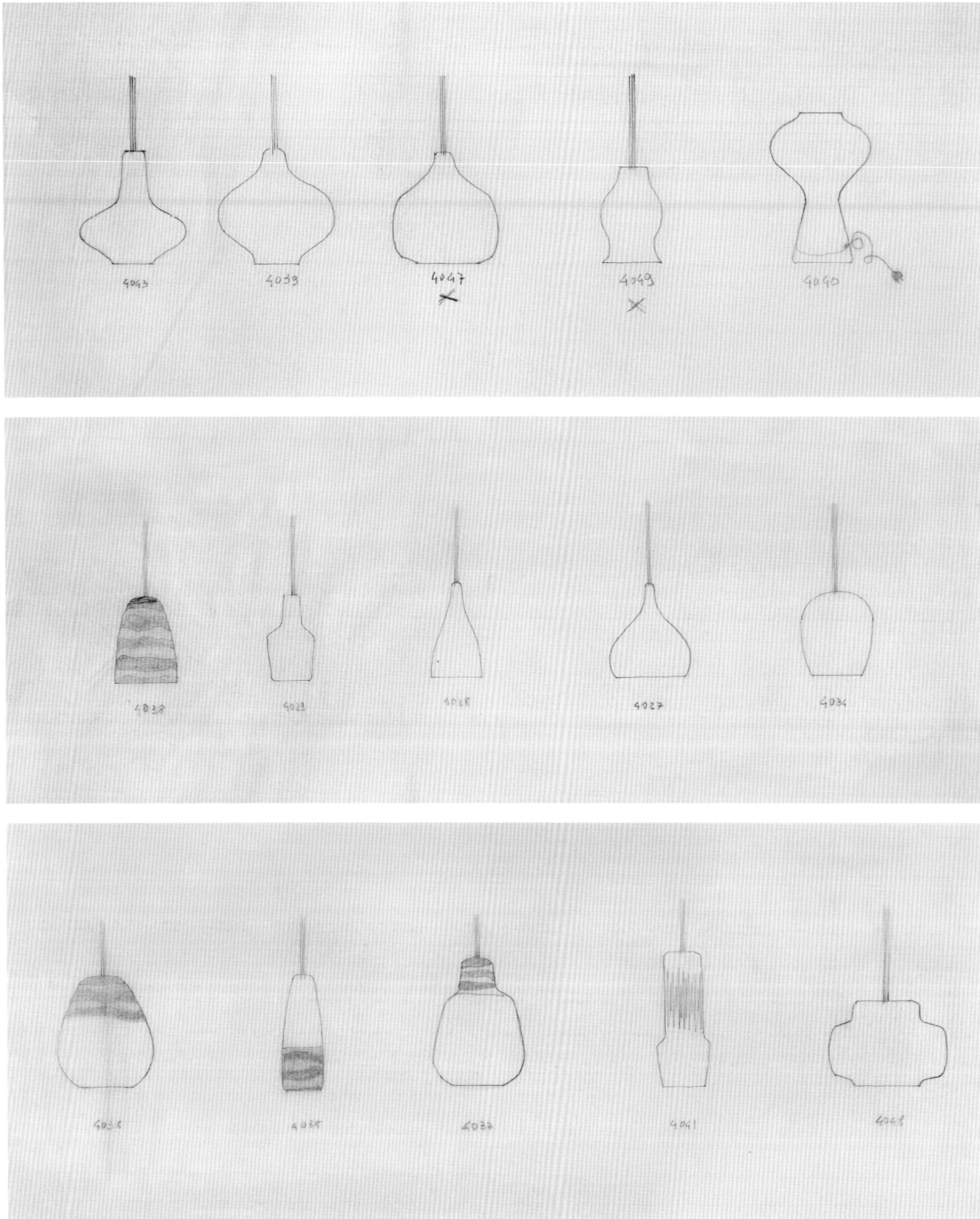

>
Models for hanging lamps after a design by Massimo Vignelli

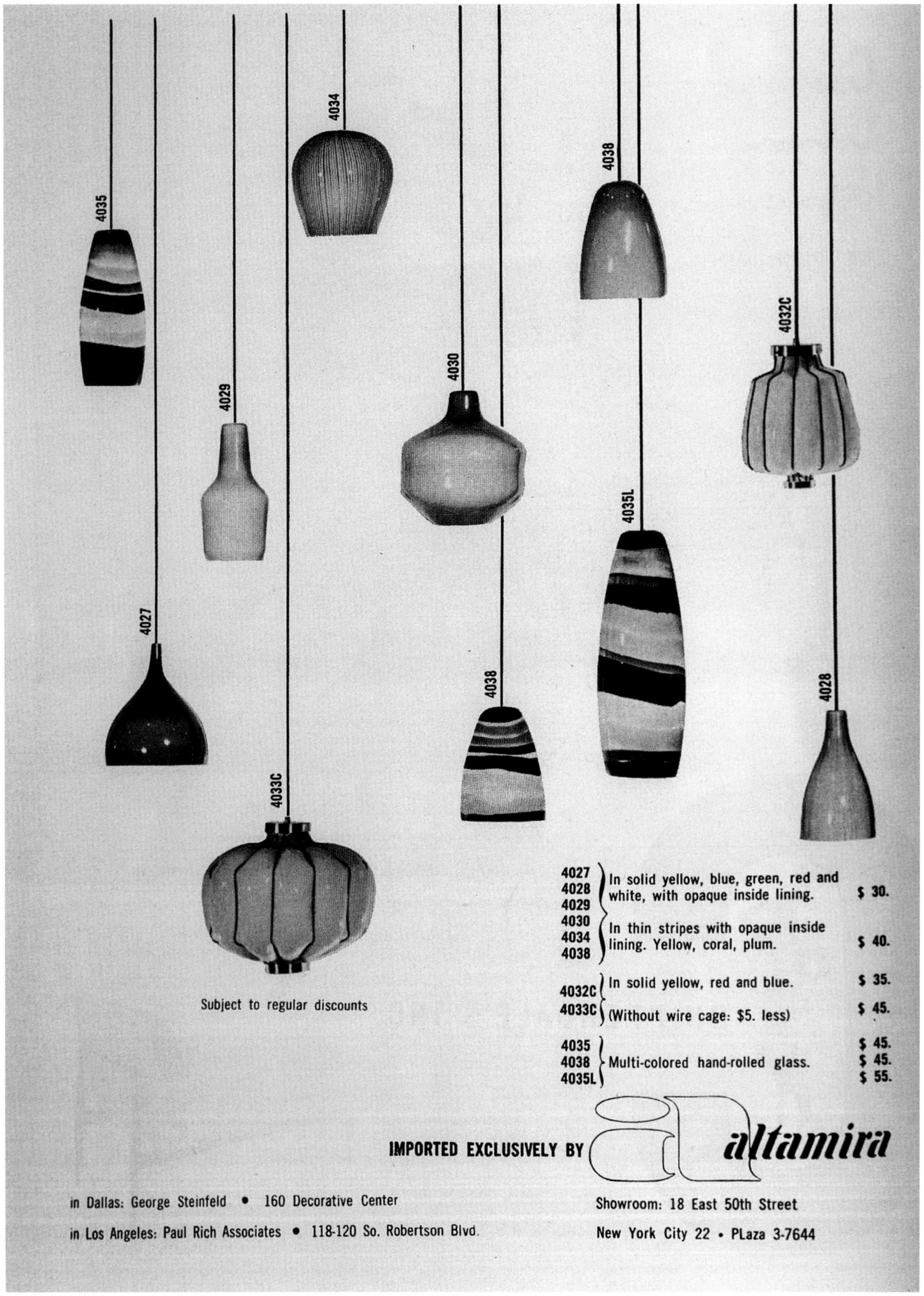

>
Lamps in opaline glass in an advertising page of Altamira, the American Venini retailer, August 1955

>
Lamps after a design by Massimo Vignelli, in the *Contemporary Italian Lighting* catalogue, [c. 1955]

1956 MODENA (IT)

INA ISTITUTO NAZIONALE DELLE ASSICURAZIONI

Lighting project for premises belonging to the INA.

1956 PEDAVENA (IT)

PEDAVENA BREWERY

Lighting project for the headquarters of the Italian Pedavena brand.

1956 ROME (IT)

INA ISTITUTO NAZIONALE DELLE ASSICURAZIONI

Lighting project for premises belonging to the INA.

1956 SASSARI (IT)

SASSARI PROVINCIAL ADMINISTRATIONI

Lighting project for a public establishment.

1956 TRIESTE (IT)

ESTHERITA SHIP

Lighting project for an Italian ship.

1956 VENICE (IT)

XXVIII ESPOSIZIONE BIENNALE INTERNAZIONALE D'ARTE

PENDANT

On the occasion of the 28th Biennale of Venice, the Venini firm, in addition to a series of vases, exhibited a dozen lamps after a design by Massimo Vignelli, among which no. 4035, a model also known as *sigaro*.

1956 VENICE (IT)

PALAZZO DIEDO

Lighting project for school premises.

1956-57 ROME (IT)

SANT'EUGENIO HOSPITAL INSTITUTE

Lighting project for a hospital complex.

1957 LACCO AMENO (IT)

LA REGINELLA HOTEL

This construction, like the Hotel Regina Isabella, was designed by the architect Mario Tufaroli Luciano on behalf of the publisher Angelo Rizzoli. In the 1950s and 1960s, this hotel was the pride of the Isola di Ischia and the reference point of the celebrities of the time who stayed there during the summer months.

1957 LECCE (IT)

INA ISTITUTO NAZIONALE DELLE ASSICURAZIONI

Lighting project for premises belonging to the INA.

1957 MESSINA (IT)

CHAMBER OF COMMERCE

Lighting project for the headquarters of the Chamber of Commerce designed during the 1920s by the architect Camillo Puglisi-Allegra.

1957 MESSINA (IT)

CITY HALL

Lighting project for the town hall.

1957 MILAN (IT)

XI TRIENNALE DI MILANO

DESIGN M. VIGNELLI

CANES

'Chandelier consisting of fifty-four tubes of coloured glass arranged in a spiral' after a design by Massimo Vignelli exhibited at the 11th Triennale of Milan in the Glass section (Pica 1957). This is one of the first examples of lighting fixtures using modular elements. In this case the light source is located at the lower extremity of the tubes and is visible.

>
XI TRIENNALE DI MILANO
Chandelier with coloured canes after a design by Massimo Vignelli.
Period photograph1957

1957 MILAN (IT)

PIA SAN PAOLO BOOKSHOP

DESIGN I. GAREDELLA

BICHROME OPAL GLASS

For the bookshop of the publishers, Edizioni Paoline, furnished by Ignazio Gardella, the glassworks created pendant lights in green opaline glass with a white lower cover (Ø 60 cm) after the design of the architect (*Domus*, June 1957).

1957 MILAN (IT)

PIRELLI AFTER-SCHOOL

Lighting project for areas designed for recreational after-school activities.

1957 NOVARA (IT)

TADINI CLOTHES SHOP

DESIGN V. GREGOTTI, L. MENEGHETTI, G. STOPPINO

PENDANT

Pendant lights designed by the designers of the shop (Vittorio Gregotti, Ludovico Meneghetti, Giotto Stoppino) with the upper part in light green glass and the lower part in white (*Domus*, May 1957).

1957 PADUA (IT)

SADE HYDROELECTRIC PLANT

Lighting project for the Società Adriatica di Elettricità.

1957 RAVENNA (IT)

CHAMBER OF COMMERCE

Lighting project for the building designed by the architect Antonino Manzone and inaugurated in 1957.

1957 ROME (IT)

PALAZZO BRASCHI, MUSEO DI ROMA

Lighting project for Palazzo Braschi, seat of the Museo di Roma from 1952.

1957 ROME (IT)

QUIRINALE PALACE

Lighting project for the official residence of the President of the Italian Republic.

1957 SAINT-VINCENT (IT)

CASINÒ DE LA VALLÉE

TESSUTO

For the Casino of Saint-Vincent a series of cone-shaped hanging lamps were produced with glass textures in different colours: *lattimo-zolfo*, sapphire, black.

1957 TURIN (IT)

CARTIERE BURGO BUILDING

SPHERES
BAMBÚ GLASS

The palace of the Cartiere Burgo in Turin is a business centre – comprising Chairman's and Managing-Director offices, assembly hall, secretariat, administrative and technical offices and experimental laboratory – constructed after a design by the architect Gualtiero Casalegno in the second half of the 1950s (1955-57). The Venini contribution includes a stained glass window and a series of lighting fixtures. Some of these start in the entrance hall and even outside it: a series of wall and ceiling lamps with strips in bamboo glass and with polychrome bands. The same type of glass was used for the production of a perimeter light in the assembly hall and for the long rectangular hanging lamp in the Board Room. To light the grand staircase, a large elongated chandelier with 'streamers' of *balloton* spheres of different sizes and with different details in prism glass was used. Beside the lift doors there was a floor lamp in metal with oval elements with a *balloton* decoration.

»
CARTIERE BURGO BUILDING
Board Room. Period photograph, 1958

>
CARTIERE BURGO BUILDING
Stairwell leading to the assembly hall.
Period photograph, 1958

>
CARTIERE BURGO BUILDING
Assembly hall. Period photograph, 1958

>
CARTIERE BURGO BUILDING
Entrance porch. Period photograph, 1958

1957-58 ROME (IT)
CONVENT OF THE MISSIONARY SISTERS OF THE HOLY GHOST

For the seat of the congregation, Silvio Galizia was responsible for the design of the Mother House and chapel. On this occasion the architect turned to the Venini glassworks for the production of certain lighting fixtures and for the polychrome stained-glass windows of the chapel.

1957-60 LIDO DI VENEZIA (IT)
CASINO

WITH ARMS
PENDANT

From the second half of the 1950s, the Venini firm carried out new lighting projects at the Casino of Lido, documented by some drawings. A study for a lamp with a cane decoration is dated to 1957, while a project for glass streamers and one for wall lamps with arms relate to 1960.

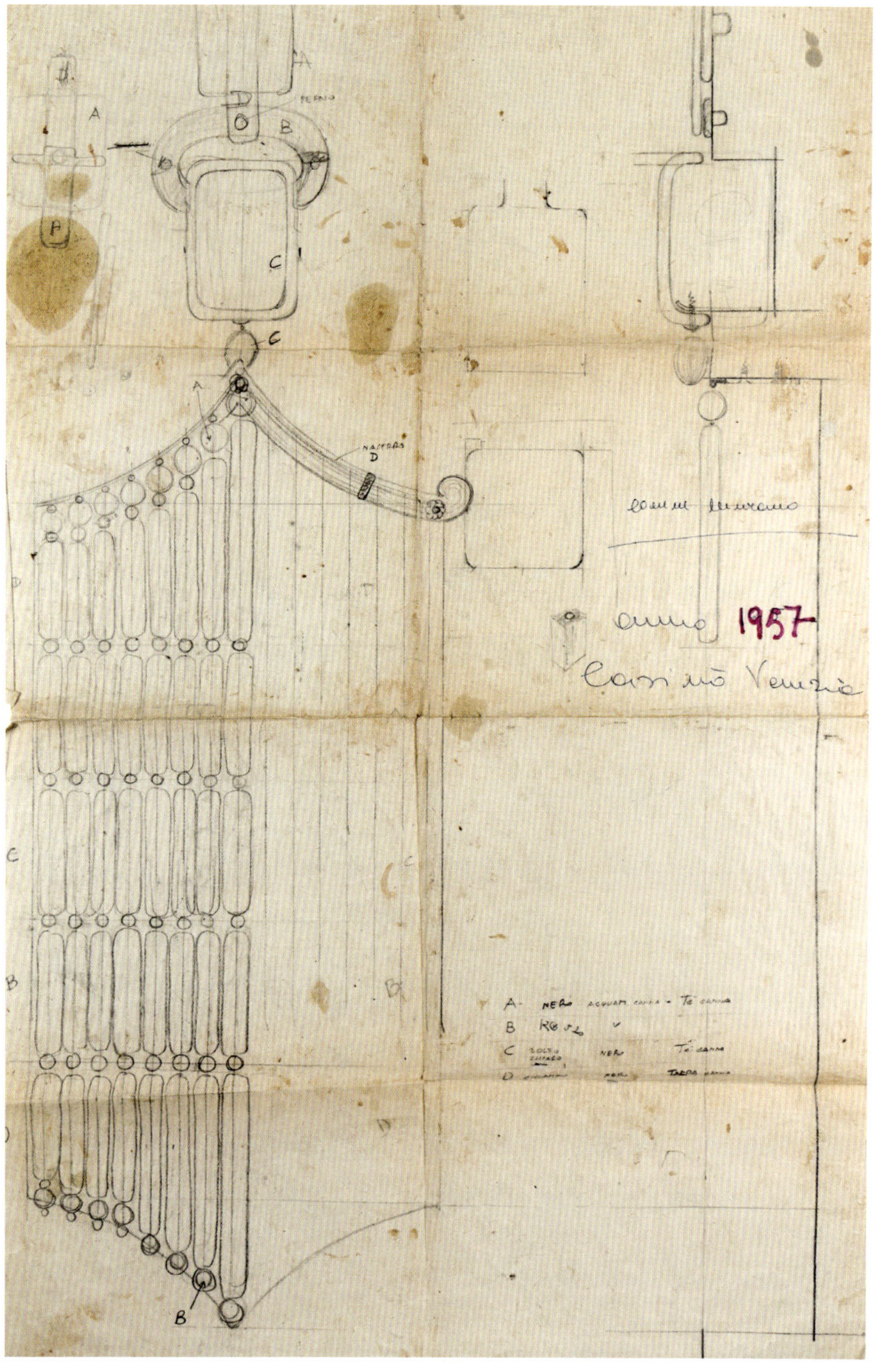

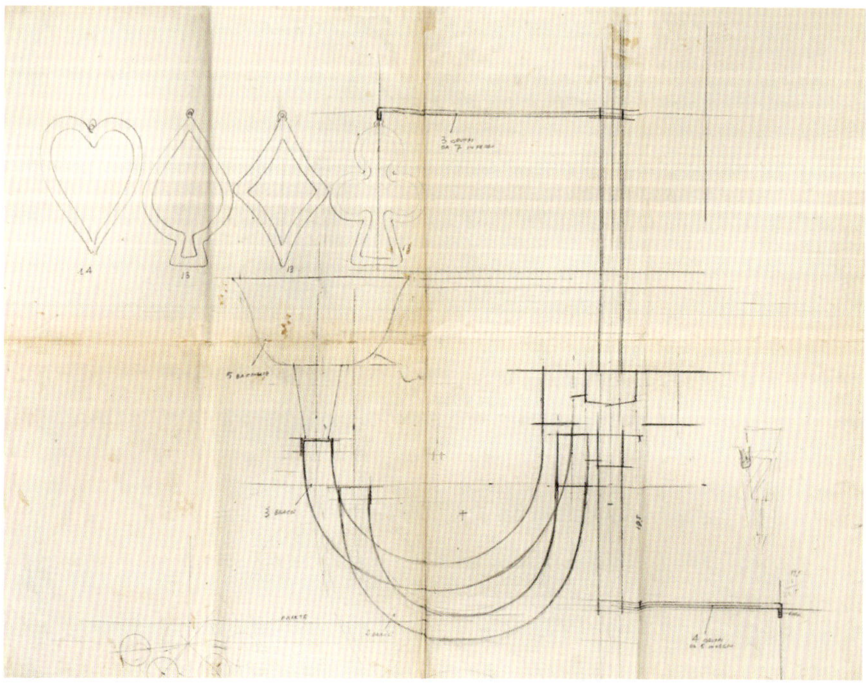

>
CASINO
Study for a wall lamp with polychrome canes, 1957

>
CASINO
Study for glass streamers, detail, 1960

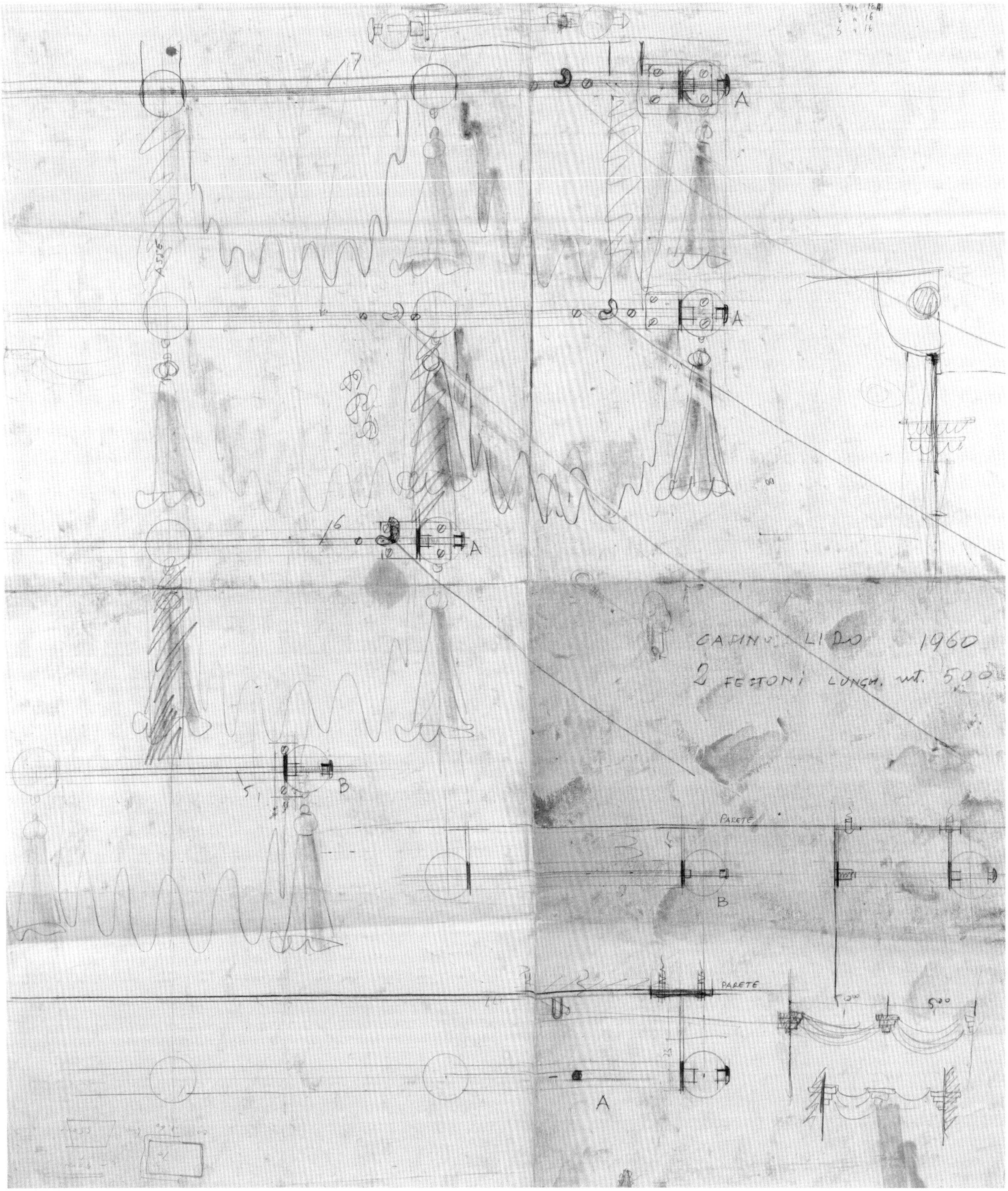

>
CASINO
Design for wall lamps, 1960

1958

BRUSSELS (BE)
ITALIAN PAVILION, EXPOSITION UNIVERSELLE ET INTERNATIONALE DE BRUXELLES
DESIGN I. GARDELLA, P. VENINI, M. VIGNELLI

POLYHEDRONS

Large chandelier composed of 1,500 polyhedrons in bicoloured transparent glass, developed over seven tiers and positioned in the grand entrance hall of the Italian Pavilion on the occasion of the Exposition Universelle of Brussels. The chandelier, one of the first modular examples presented to the public, was installed in the centre of the hall and fixed by means of a series of steel tie rods. The Italian Pavilion was constructed after designs by BBPR, Giancarlo De Carlo, Ignazio Gardella, Giuseppe Perugini and Ludovico Quaroni. At the end of the exhibition, the chandelier was transferred to the Great Mosque of Kairouan, Tunisia.

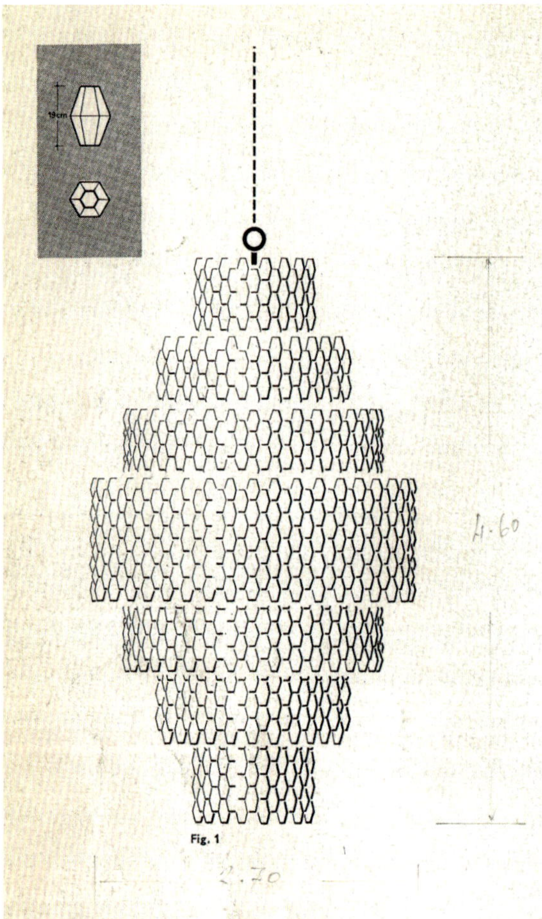

>
ITALIAN PAVILION, EXPOSITION UNIVERSELLE ET INTERNATIONALE DE BRUXELLES
Design for a large chandelier in the *Revue International d'Eclairage*, June 1958

>
ITALIAN PAVILION, EXPOSITION UNIVERSELLE ET INTERNATIONALE DE BRUXELLES
The grand entrance hall with the large chandelier (h 460 cm x Ø 260 cm) and the two stained glass windows produced by the Venini firm. Period photograph, 1958

1958
GÖTEBORG (SE)
PARK AVENUE HOTEL, EXTENSION

Lighting project for a Swedish hotel.

1958
LACCO AMENO (IT)
SPORTING HOTEL, EXTENSION

This facility forms part of the complex of hotel buildings commissioned by Angelo Rizzoli and entrusted to Mario Luciano Tufaroli. The Venini project was carried out on the occasion of the extension of the building.

1958
NAPLES (IT)
NAPOLI SHIP

BRILLANTE GLASS

The Venini lighting project for the dining-room of the 'Napoli' ship. It consists of ceiling lamps produced for the company Stilnovo of Milan.

>
NAPOLI SHIP
Dining-room with ceiling lamps in *brillante* glass plates.
Period photograph, end of 1950s

1958
NEW YORK (US)
PIERRE HOTEL

Lighting project for the ballroom of the Hotel Pierre of New York furnished after the design of the architect Howard Branston (*Vetri Murano Oggi*, 1981).

1958
ROME (IT)
INA ISTITUTO NAZIONALE DELLE ASSICURAZIONI

Lighting project for premises belonging to the INA.

1958
VENICE (IT)
XXIX BIENNALE INTERNAZIONALE D'ARTE EXHIBITION

A FASCE VERTICALI
POLYHEDRONS
BICHROME OPAL GLASS

The Veneto decorative arts exhibition, held at the 29th Biennale of Venice in 1958, also included the lighting sector. At the sector exhibition, where eight glassworks were represented, the Venini firm presented: a 'chandelier with pink and blue pendants', a 'ceiling lamp with grey-purple pendants', a 'floor-standing street light', 'three groups of seven lamps' and a 'white, yellow and brown ceiling lamp' (*29. Biennale Internazionale d'arte*, Venice 1958). Among these lamps can be seen some models after a design by Massimo Vignelli (nos. 4047-4049) and two lamps with polyhedrons in coloured transparent glass like the model illustrated in the exhibition catalogue. In this regard it should noted that this was the first time that polyhedrons were exhibited in a national context.

>
XXIX BIENNALE INTERNAZIONALE D'ARTE EXHIBITION
'Ceiling lamp with grey-purple pendants' (polyhedrons) in the exhibition catalogue. Period photograph, 1958

>
XXIX BIENNALE INTERNAZIONALE D'ARTE EXHIBITION
Venini lamps. Period photograph, 1958

1958

VIENNA (AT)
VENEDIG ZEIGT GLAS AUS MURANO

POLYHEDRONS

On the occasion of the exhibition *Venedig Zeigt Glas aus Murano* (12 May - 15 June 1958), taking place in the rooms of the Museum of Applied Arts in Vienna, a large chandelier with dark-blue and pink polyhedrons was exhibited, developed over three tiers and with a protruding central section. In the same setting two stained-glass windows and display windows with vases and bowls produced by the furnace were installed.

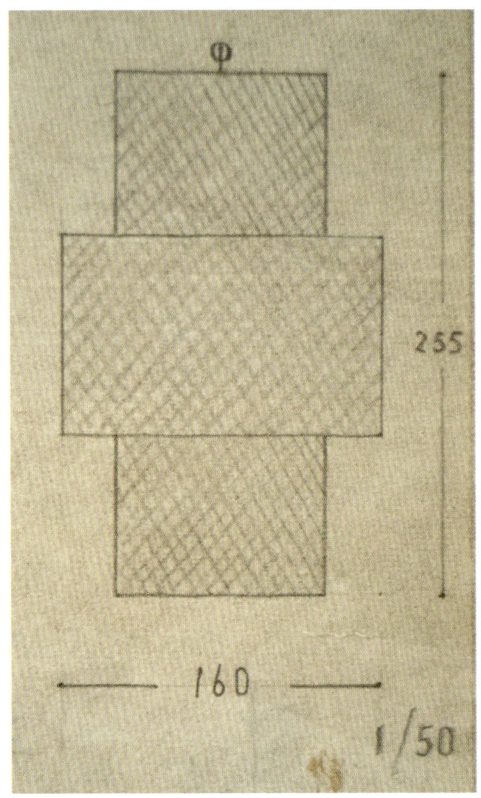

>
VENEDIG ZEIGT GLAS AUS MURANO
Chandelier positioned in the centre of the exhibition hall in the Museum of Applied Arts in Vienna. Period photograph, 1958

>
VENEDIG ZEIGT GLAS AUS MURANO
Outline of the chandelier exhibited at the Viennese exhibition, late 1950s

1958-59 PARIS (FR)

OLIVETTI SHOP

DESIGN F. ALBINI, F. HELG

BICHROME OPAL GLASS

Inaugurated on 8 April 1959, the Olivetti shop in Paris (owned by S.A.M.P.O., then Olivetti France) was situated in the prestigious Rue Fauborg Saint Honoré. The space was designed by Franco Albini with the cooperation of Franca Helg. Playing on the interchange of chromatically contrasting materials (principally aluminium, marble, wood and velvet), the Albini studio produced a luminous space composed of many lamps in the shape of bluebells designed to draw attention to the products on display. The lamps (Ø 45 cm), after a study by Albini and Helg, are in *lattimo* glass with a band in *talpa* grey glass. At the request of Adriano Olivetti himself, the Paris shop was home to numerous pictures by contemporary artists, among which a painting by Paul Klee, to be seen in one of the archive photographs. In 1966, the Olivetti firm decided to renovate the shop, entrusting this task to Gae Aulenti, who decided to dismantle almost all the old installation and remove the Albini and Helg lamps in favour of a new lighting system.

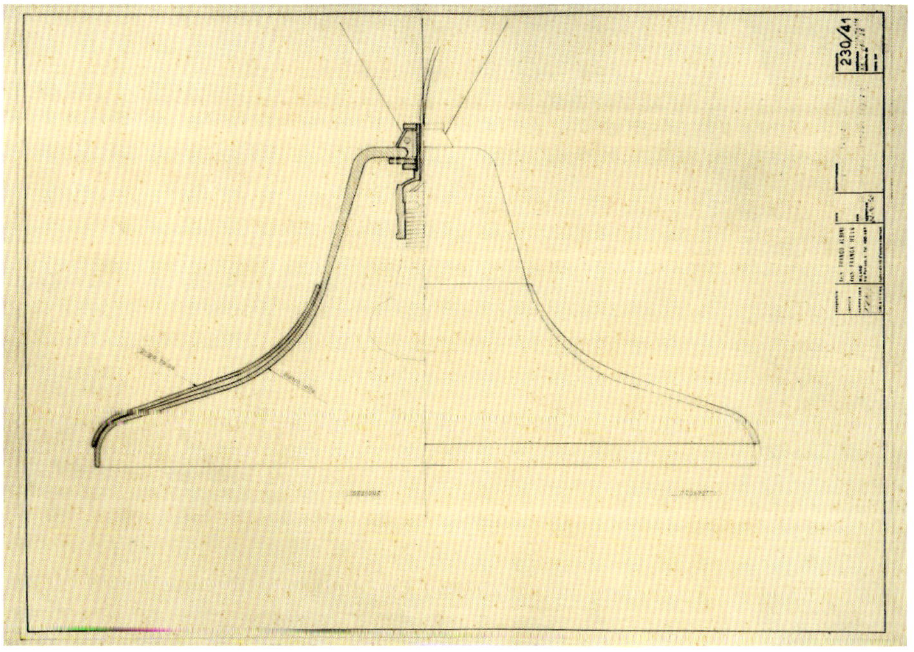

>
OLIVETTI SHOP
Section of the shop dedicated to the display of typewriters. In the background the Paul Klee's painting can be seen. Period photograph, c. 1959

>
OLIVETTI SHOP
Design for a lamp in bicoloured opaline glass proposed by Franco Albini and Franca Helg, October 1958

1959

BELGRADE (RS)

ITALIAN EMBASSY

Lighting project for diplomatic headquarters.

1959

BOLOGNA (IT)

NETTUNO HOTEL

Lighting project for a hotel.

1959

CORNING (US)

GLASS 1959

A FASCE DI COLORE
TESSUTO

On the occasion of the exhibition *Glass 1959* held at the Corning Museum of Glass in Corning, New York, the Venini, among the seven pieces it presented, exhibited also two lamp models after a design by Massimo Vignelli. As documented in the exhibition catalogue, the two pendant models, nos. 4028 e 4029, were to be seen.

1959

MERANO (IT)

FORST BREWERY

Lighting project for production facility.

1959

NAPLES (IT)

OFFICES OF THE PROVINCIAL TOURISM BOARD

CANES

For the offices of the Neapolitan body the Venini firm proposed a model of a pendant lamp having modular elements with canes in two colours, a tapering structure developed over four tiers.

>
GLASS 1959
The pendant lamp no. 4029 exhibited at the *Glass 1959* exhibition, Corning, New York. Period photograph, 1959

>
OFFICES OF THE PROVINCIAL TOURISM BOARD
Chandelier with modular elements, composed of canes with alternating colours. Period photograph, c. 1959

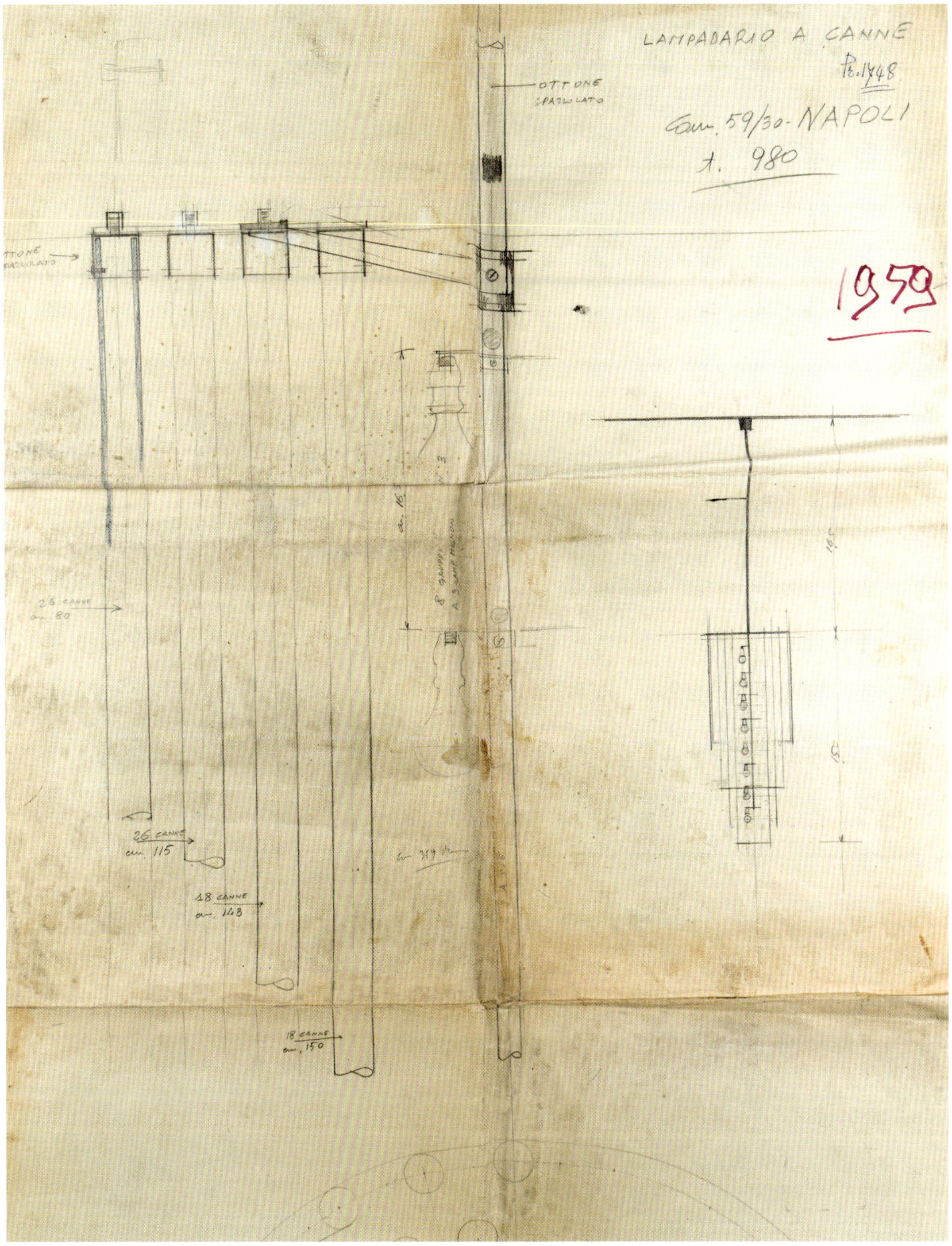

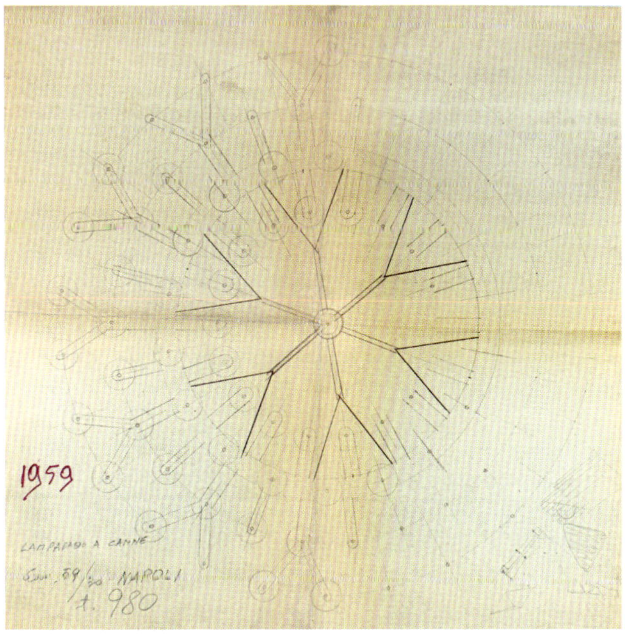

>
OFFICES OF THE PROVINCIAL TOURISM BOARD
Study for a chandelier with canes, having a tapering structure and developed over four tiers, c. 1959

>
OFFICES OF THE PROVINCIAL TOURISM BOARD
Plan of the chandelier with canes, c. 1959

1959 ROME (IT)

CREDITO FONDIARIO

Lighting project for the premises of a bank.

1959 ROME (IT)

FARNESINA PALACE, MINISTRY OF FOREIGN AFFAIRS

DESIGN E. DEL DEBBIO

POLYHEDRONS

Thirteen years after the discontinuation of building on the site of the Palazzo della Farnesina, the headquarters of the Ministry of Foreign Affairs, the result of a complex political and architectural affair commencing in the 1930s, in 1956 the completion of the works was approved and entrusted to the authors of the original project: the architects Enrico Del Debbio, Arnaldo Foschini, Vittorio Morpurgo. In particular Del Debbio, in 1958, was given the task of designing the furnishings, especially those for the formal areas of the Palazzo, which was officially inaugurated on 12 September 1959. Among the furnishings produced, there were certain lighting appliances for which the architect used the Venini polyhedron modular system. This was the system used, for example, for the rounded-shaped chandelier (h 150 cm, Ø 150 cm) situated in the foyer in front of the International Conferences Hall, placed at the centre of the stucco suspended ceiling by Alberto Bevilacqua. On the columns demarcating this area, and the surrounding spaces, there are polyhedron wall lamps, tapering in form and with three tiers (h 120 cm, Ø 50 cm). Similar wall lamps are to be found in the International Conferences Hall, at the centre of which however is positioned a large chandelier in five tiers (h 350 cm, Ø 230 cm) hanging from the vaulted suspended ceiling in majolica ceramics by Pietro Cascella. Other chandeliers of considerable size, with three tiers and in an elongated form (h 225 cm, Ø 150 cm), are to be found in the Sala dei Mappamondi. The lamps are still *in situ*.

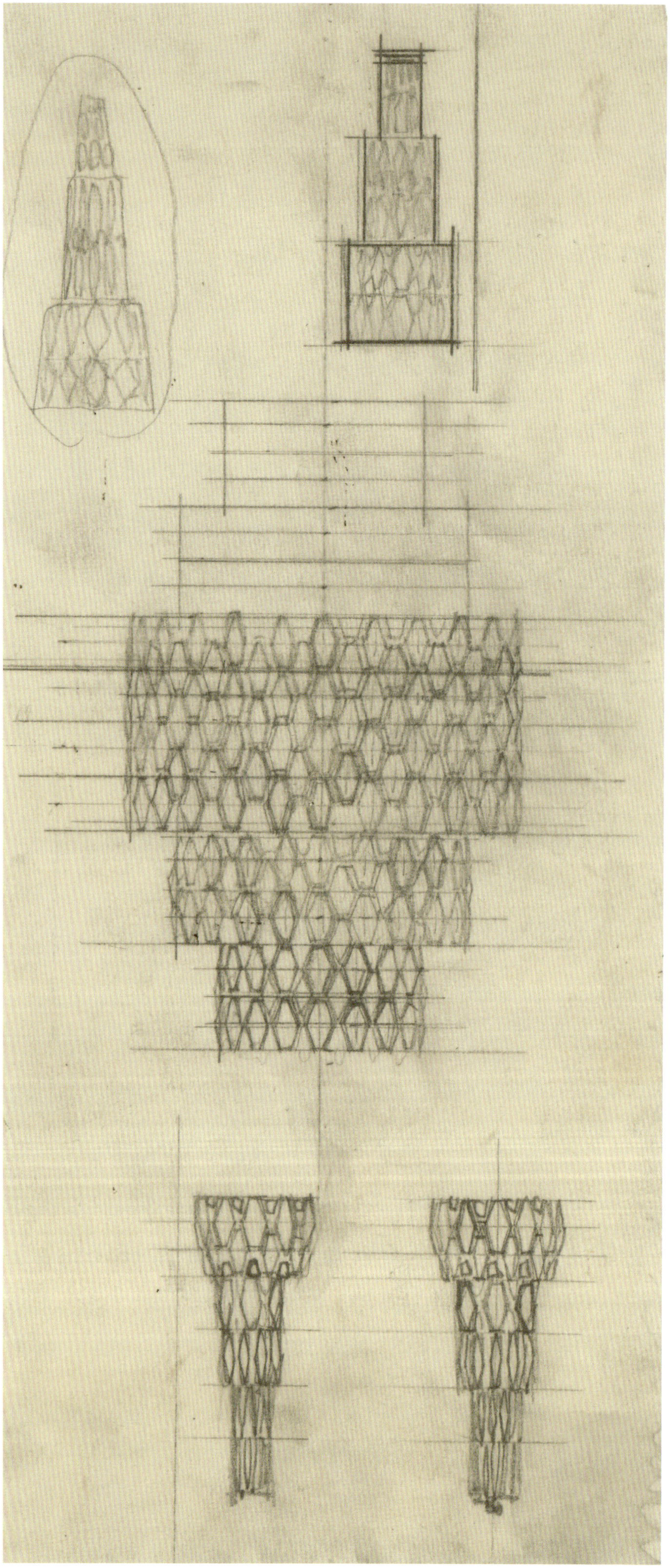

>
FARNESINA PALACE, MINISTRY OF FOREIGN AFFAIRS
E. Del Debbio, study for lamps for the Palazzo della Farnesina, 1958-1959. Rome. MAXXI, Enrico Del Debbio Archive

>>
FARNESINA PALACE, MINISTRY OF FOREIGN AFFAIRS
Foyer of the International Conferences Hall with Venini wall lamps and polyhedron chandelier and suspended ceiling by Alberto Bevilacqua. Period photograph, c. 1960

<<
FARNESINA PALACE, MINISTRY OF FOREIGN AFFAIRS
Sala dei Mappamondi with Venini wall lamps and polyhedron chandeliers. Period photograph, c. 1960

>
FARNESINA PALACE, MINISTRY OF FOREIGN AFFAIRS
International Conferences Hall with Venini wall lamps and polyhedron chandelier and suspended ceiling by Piero Cascella. Period photograph, c. 1960

1959

TURIN (IT)
GALLERIA SABAUDA

MULTICOLOURED STRIPS

After its forced closure during the war, the Galleria Sabauda of Turin reopened to the public on 24 May 1959. The works were directed by the architect Piero Sanpaolesi with the cooperation of the then Director, Noemi Gabrielli. For the occasion, the Venini firm produced a series of wall lamps with multicoloured horizontal stripes.

›
GALLERIA SABAUDA
Wall lamp with multicoloured horizontal stripes.
Period photograph, 1959

1959

TRIESTE (IT)
VICTORIA SHIP
DESIGN G. PULITZER

BICHROME OPAL GLASS

In designing the internal areas of the ship Victoria, the architect Gustavo Pulitzer had recourse to the Venini glassworks, as documented by a drawing for the smoking room dated July 1959. In this solution, Pulitzer uses certain models already designed by Massimo Vignelli and included in the Venini catalogue in the mid-1950s (nos. 4041, 4035) for the creation of minimalist wall lamps.

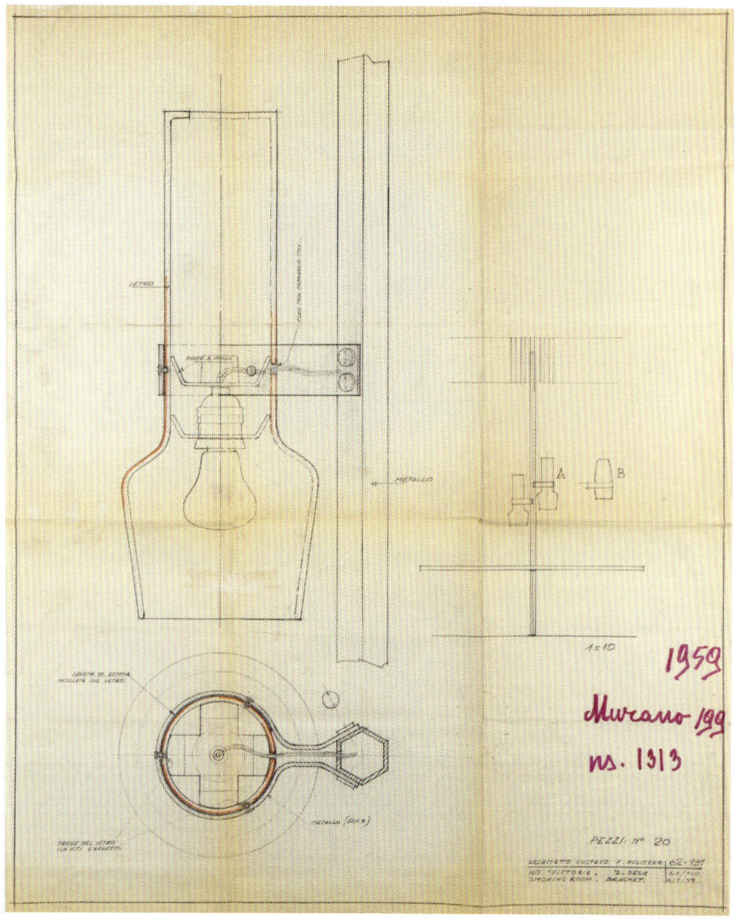

›
VICTORIA SHIP
Design for lamps for the smoking room, 6 July 1959

1959

VENICE (IT)
SOCIETÀ ADRIATICA DI NAVIGAZIONE

POLYHEDRONS

Illuminated panel with little polyhedrons produced for the information office of the Società Adriatica di Navigazione of Venice.

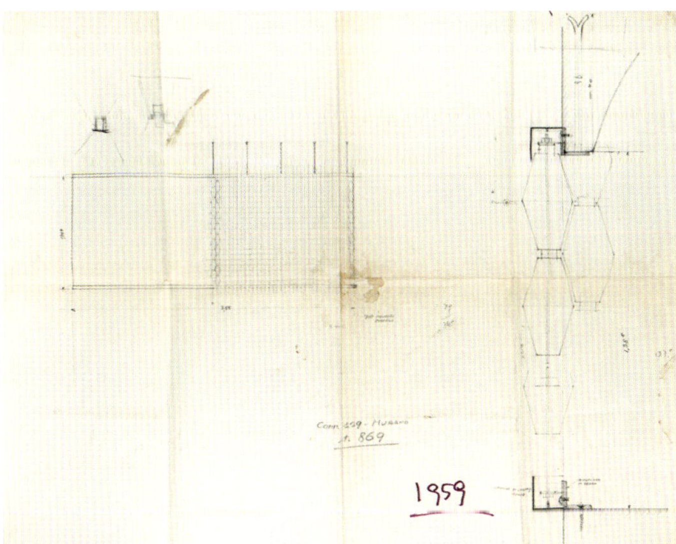

›
SOCIETÀ ADRIATICA DI NAVIGAZIONE
Hall of the information office with an illuminated panel with polyhedrons. Period photograph, c. 1959

›
SOCIETÀ ADRIATICA DI NAVIGAZIONE
Study for the illuminated panel with polyhedrons, 1959

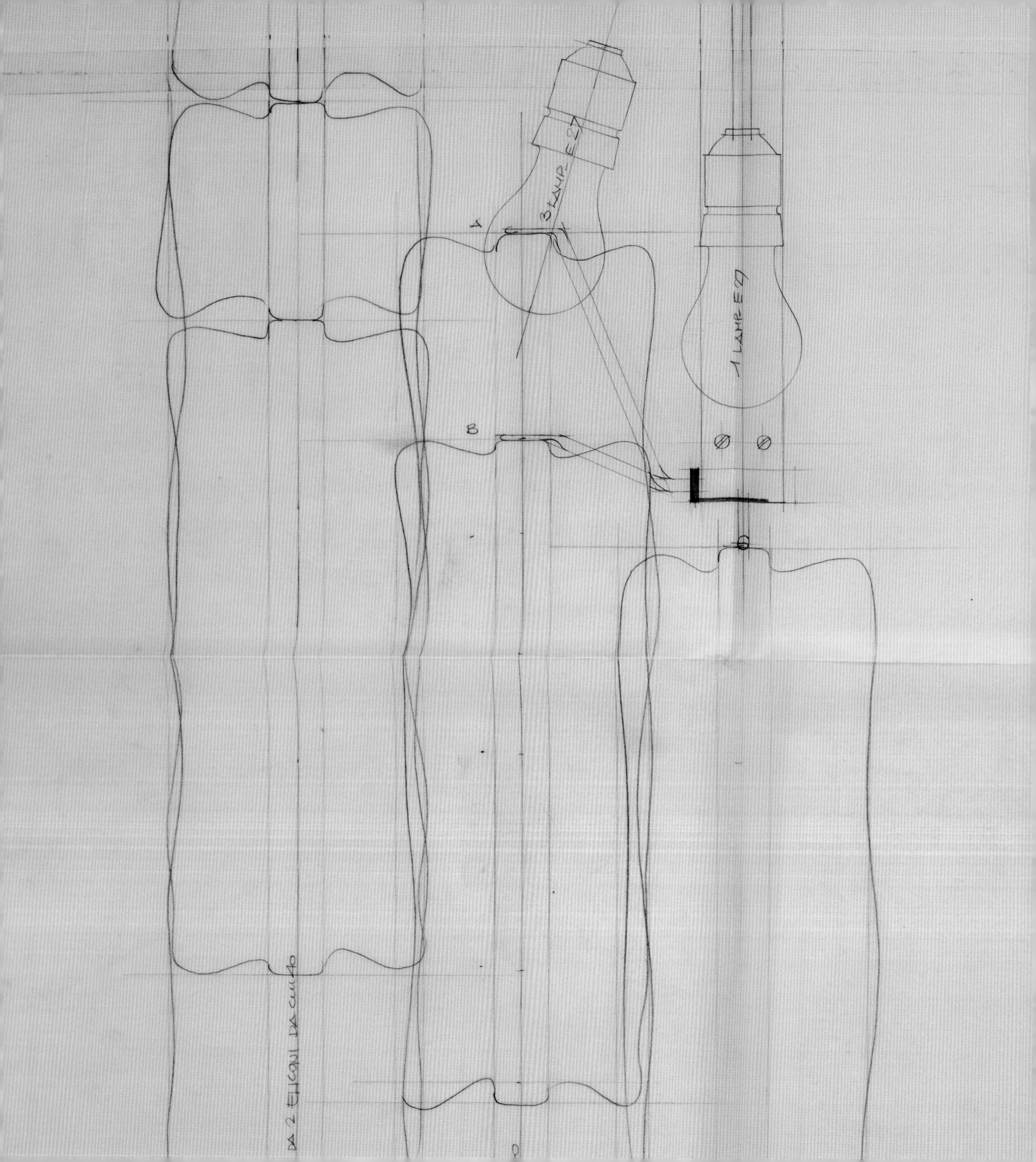
3 LAMP. E 27
1 LAMP. E 27
A
B
DA 2 ELICONI DA CM 40

1960s

1960

LIDO DI VENEZIA (IT)
CHEZ-VOUS, EXCELSIOR HOTEL

DROPS

In the refurbishment of the Chez-Vous, a nightclub in the Hotel Excelsior on the Lido of Venice, Vico Magistretti and Marco Zanuso used a new drop-like modular lighting system to give character to the area of the room with armchairs, coffee tables and the podium for live music. It consists of chandelier-like elements formed by rods (c. 400 in all) of differing lengths with the extremities in the shape of drops. Each single element is fixed to the ceiling with a metal cable in a specific arrangement. The rods, in *cristallo* glass, and in rare instances with coloured *talpa* patches, are housed inside square spaces (180 x 180 cm) created in the false ceiling where the source of the light is also located. In the booklet *Venini impianti di illuminazione* [1961] these luminaires are described as 'lampadari a mazze' [club chandeliers].

<<
CHEZ-VOUS, EXCELSIOR HOTEL
Lighting installation with drop-like elements. Period photograph, c. 1960

>
CHEZ-VOUS, EXCELSIOR HOTEL
Room in the Venetian nightclub with Venini lighting installations.
Period photograph, c. 1960

1960
MILAN (IT)
PAN AM OFFICES

Lighting system for the offices of the American Pan Am airline company located in Torre Velasca and furnished following a design by the architect Ugo Rivolta.

1960
NEW YORK (US)
MARCO POLO CLUB, WALDORF ASTORIA HOTEL

POLYHEDRONS

The project for the Marco Polo club, located in the Hotel Waldorf Astoria, is composed of a series of pendant lamps having polyhedrons with a central projecting section or a tapering structure.

1960
NEW YORK (US)
YARDLEY SHOP

POLYHEDRONS

For the ground floor of the New York shop, the Venini company created a chandelier and some polyhedron wall lamps.

>
MARCO POLO CLUB, WALDORF ASTORIA HOTEL
Polyhedron pendant lamp (h 100 cm, Ø 82 cm).
Period photograph, early 1960s

>>
YARDLEY SHOP
Interior of the shop. Period photograph, 1960s

COTY
YARDLEY
YARDLEY

1960

ROME (IT)
OPERA HOUSE

POLYHEDRONS

Around the mid-1950s, the architect Marcello Piacentini was given the task of reorganising and extending the Opera House, formerly the Costanzi theatre, on which he had already worked in the second half of the 1920s. Among the works, which would conclude in December 1960, was the realisation of a new spacious foyer on the first floor where polyhedron chandeliers in *cristallo* and rose-coloured glass were installed. The chandeliers consisted of three tiers, with a central projecting section (h 190 cm, Ø 110 cm), which are still *in situ*. On the same occasion various polyhedron wall lamps with a tapering structure were installed (h 90 cm, Ø 45 cm).

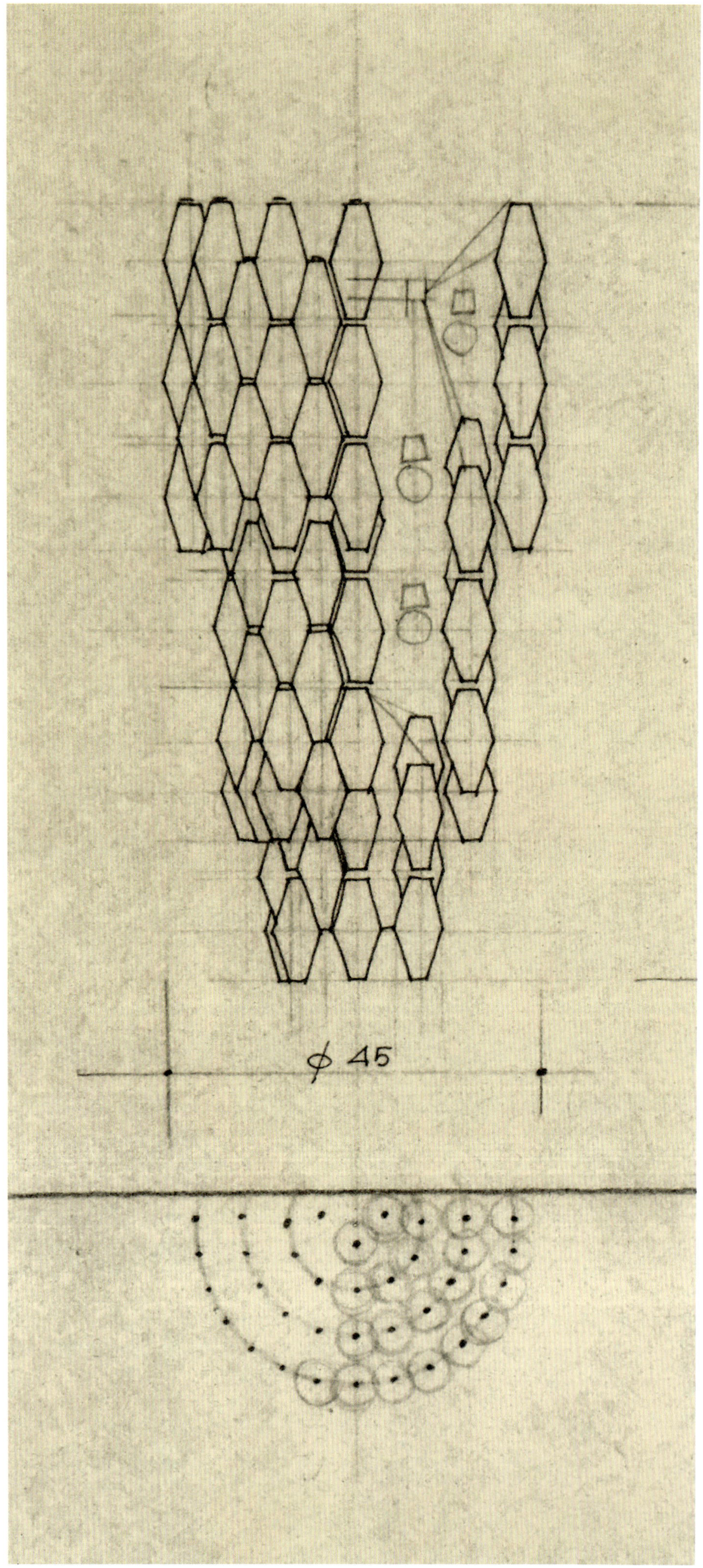

›
OPERA HOUSE
Design for polyhedron wall light, 1959-60, AC

>
OPERA HOUSE
Polyhedron lamps in the foyer of the first floor. Period photograph in *Venini impianti di illuminazione* [1961], AMH

>
OPERA HOUSE
Foyer of the first floor. Photo Yasuko Kageyama-Teatro dell'Opera di Roma

1960

STOCKHOLM (SE)
NORDISKA KOMPANIET

POLYHEDRONS

Lighting project for the executives' dining room of the Swedish department store, Nordiska Kompaniet, in Stockholm. It consists of ceiling lights of various sizes made up of polyhedrons.

>
NORDISKA KOMPANIET
Ceiling lamps with polyhedrons in the executives' dining room.
Period photograph, 1960

1960

TREVISO (IT)
PALAZZO DELLA PROVINCIA

POLYHEDRONS
BICHROME OPAL GLASS

The headquarters of the Provincial Authorities of Treviso was designed between 1953 and 1954 by the architect Luigi Piccinato. Building works were started in 1956 and completed in the early 1960s. It was during the latter period that the intervention of the Venini company took place, creating, among other things, a large ceiling lamp (h 60 cm, Ø 240 cm), a series of wall lamps with polyhedrons (model no. 951.2) for the first-floor areas and the lighting of the Council Chamber with pendant lamps in opaline glass. The young architect Luciano Gemin was also involved in the designing of the lamps.

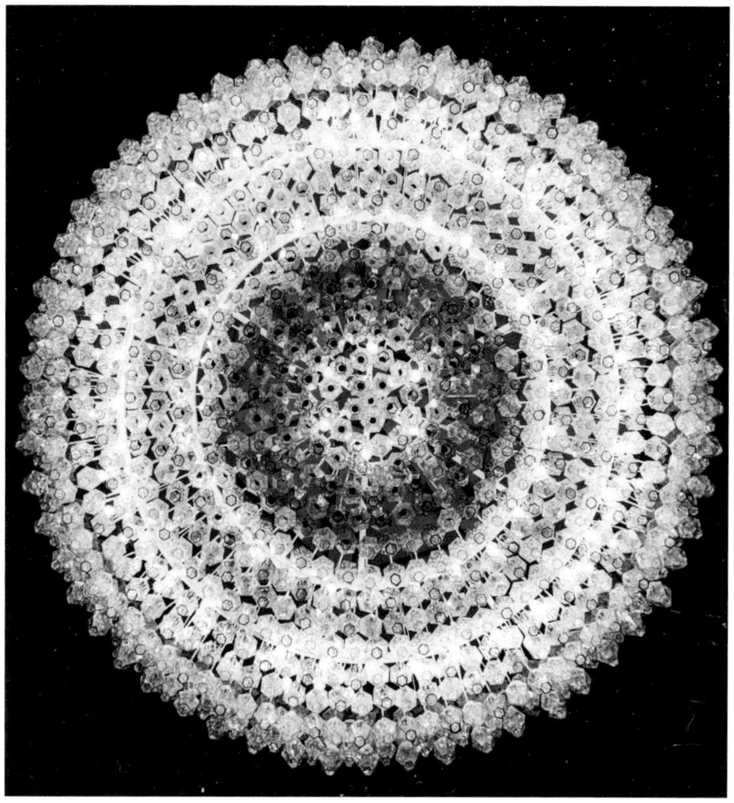

›
PALAZZO DELLA PROVINCIA
The polyhedron chandelier seen from below.
Period photograph, c. 1960

›
PALAZZO DELLA PROVINCIA
Reception hall on the first floor of the building.
Period photograph, c. 1960

>
PALAZZO DELLA PROVINCIA
Council Chamber. Period photograph, c. 1960

1960

VENICE (IT)

EXCHANGE OFFICE, CASSA DI RISPARMIO DI VENEZIA

PLATES
POLYHEDRONS

The lighting for the Exchange Office of the Cassa di Risparmio of Venice, situated near Piazza San Marco, was carried out by combining polyhedron wall lamps with a rectilinear ceiling lamp in bamboo glass.

›
EXCHANGE OFFICE, CASSA DI RISPARMIO DI VENEZIA
Lighting elements. Period photograph, October 1960

1960

VIENNA (AT)

HOTEL EUROPA

PLATES

Lighting project for reception area.

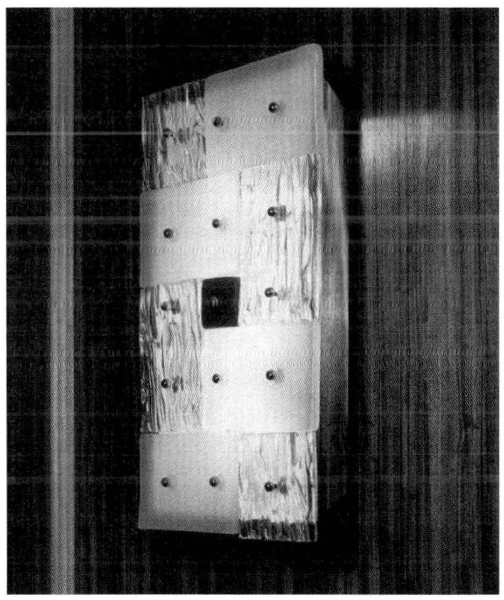

›
HOTEL EUROPA
Wall light with bamboo glass plates, glass with bubbles and opaque glass in the Vienna Hotel Europa. Period photograph in *Venini impianti di illuminazione 2*, [1963], AHL

1960

NÎMES (FR) MUNICIPAL THEATRE

POLYHEDRONS

The work was carried out during the renovation, at the hands of the architect Joseph Massota, of the 'foyer communal', a building in Place de La Calade adapted for theatre purposes following the burning of the Grand Theatre of Nimes. The lighting project consisted in the creation of polyhedron lamps, among which a series of wall lamps and three rounded chandeliers for the first-floor foyer. In the auditorium a large overhead light with a hexagonal shape (l max 400 cm), encased in the ceiling, made up of polyhedrons in two sizes fixed to the ceiling with six-armed metallic structures.

>
MUNICIPAL THEATRE
Auditorium ceiling lamp. Period photograph, 1960s

>
MUNICIPAL THEATRE
Chandeliers and wall lamp in the first-floor foyer.
Period photograph, 1960s

1960-61 DÜSSELDORF (DE)
OLIVETTI SHOP
DESIGN I. GARDELLA

SQUARE RODS

Between the 1950s and 1960s Olivetti opened numerous branches throughout the world. The shop in Düsseldorf was designed in 1960 by Ignazio Gardella and officially opened on 10 April 1961. The centrepiece of this area, structured over a long and narrow space (h 4 x 6 x 30 m), is a chandelier with coloured solid square rods (h 150 cm, Ø 65 cm). This modular element is used to obtain luminous cylinders at different levels. The idea proposed by Gardella is documented by a drawing of the shop from 1960 where one can already see the lighting inset which will then be produced by Venini, together with the knobs of the entrance doors.

>
OLIVETTI SHOP
Detail of the display window in *Domus*, September 1962

>
OLIVETTI SHOP
'Il negozio di notte' [The shop by night] in *Domus*, September 1962

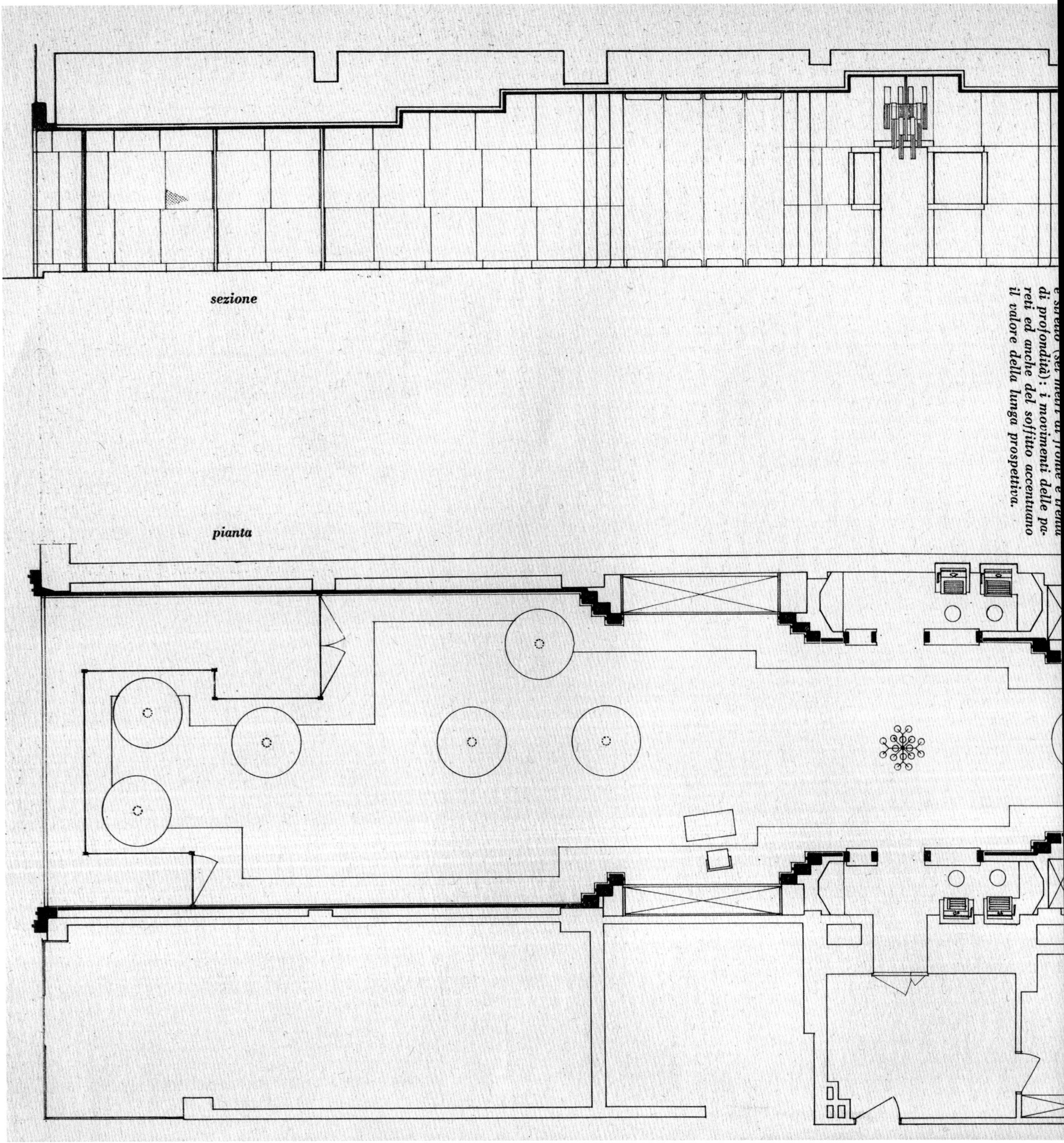
sezione
pianta
di profondità): i movimenti delle pa-
reti ed anche del soffitto accentuano
il valore della lunga prospettiva.

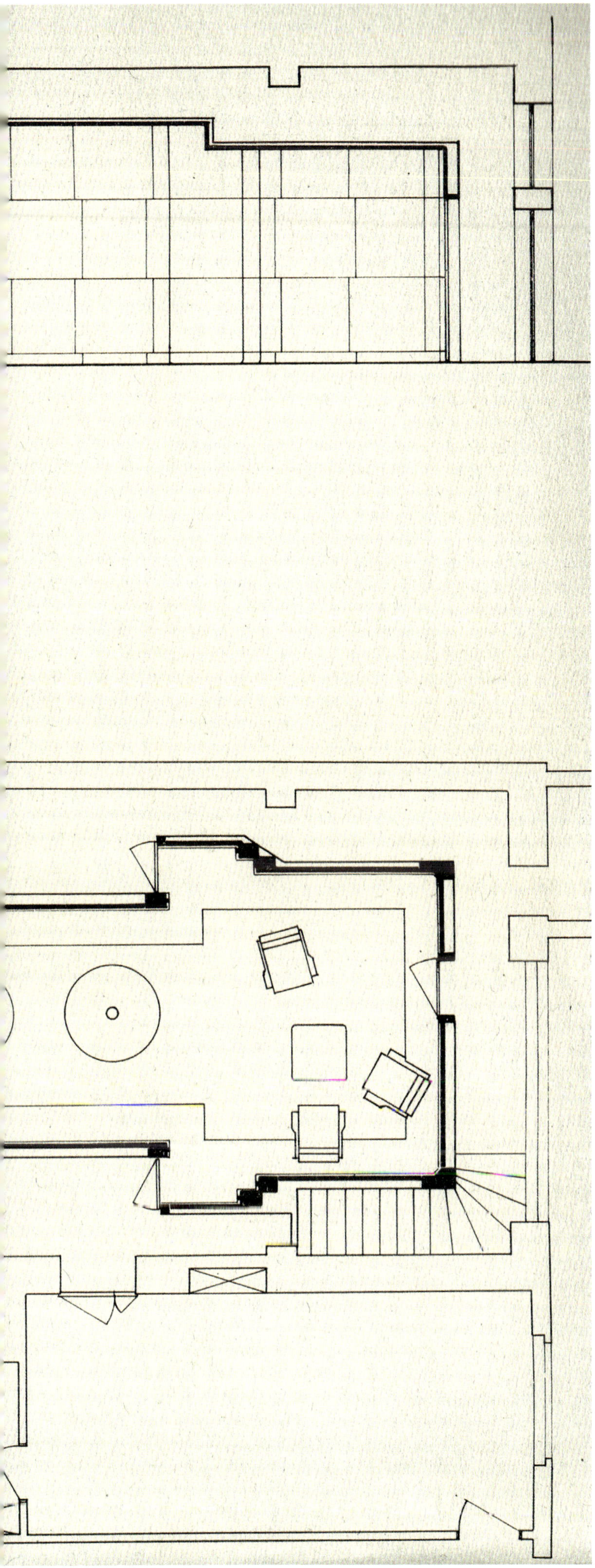

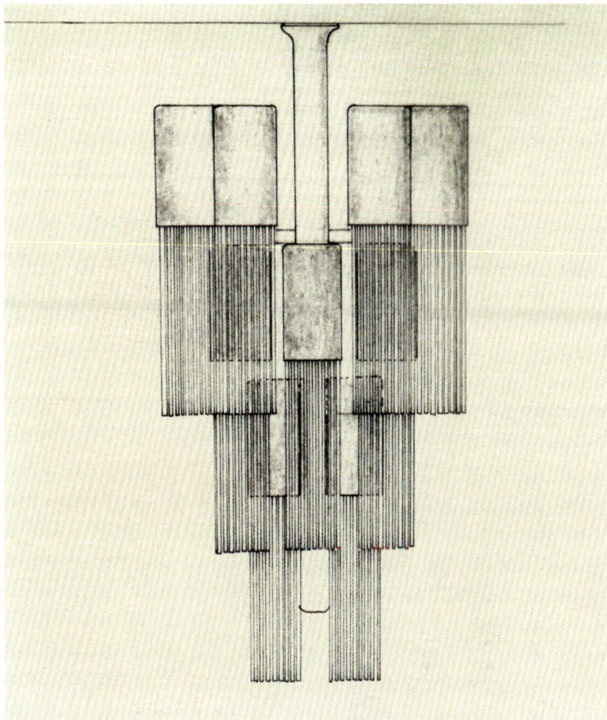

«
OLIVETTI SHOP
I. Gardella, general plan and cross-section, in *Domus*, September 1962
›
OLIVETTI SHOP
Design for the chandelier with solid square rods
›
OLIVETTI SHOP
Interior of the shop. Period photograph, 1960s

1960
1966

FLORENCE (IT)
MUNICIPAL OPERA HOUSE

SQUARE RODS
CUBES
OLIVE
COLOURED PATCHES
POLYHEDRONS

The Venini project took place in the early 1960s at the time of a further restoration of the Municipal Opera House, a 19th-century building which had already undergone significant alterations in the 1930s and in the immediate post-war period, and which has been the venue of the *Maggio musicale Fiorentino* [Florentine May Music Festival] since its beginning (1933). Started in 1958, work on this project of the engineer Alessandro Giuntoli and architect Corinna Bartolini lasted for three years and the theatre reopened on 8 May 1961.

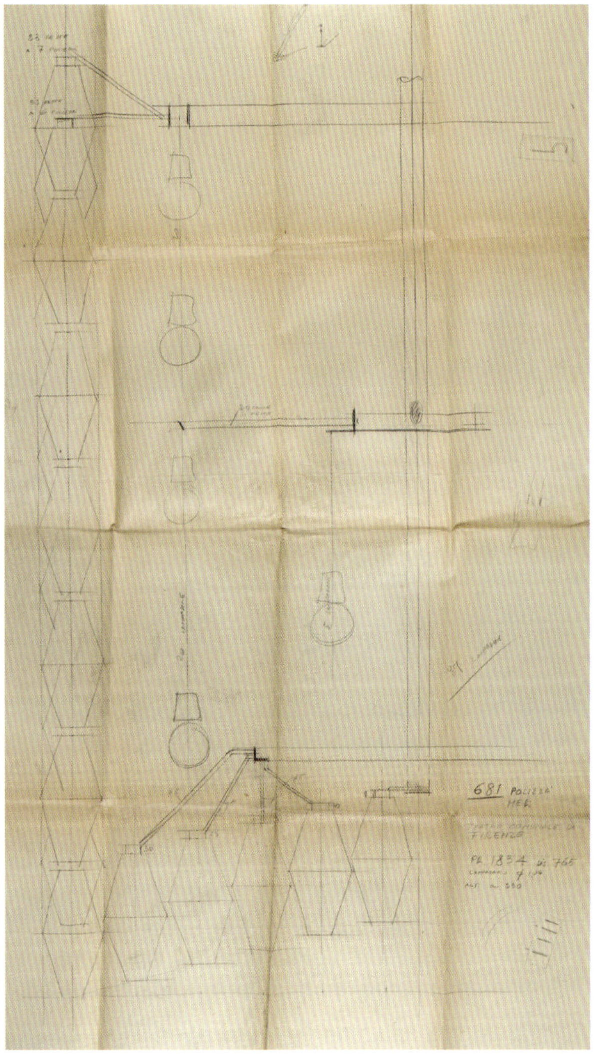

>
MUNICIPAL OPERA HOUSE
Design for one of the cylindrical polyhedron chandeliers for the foyer of the stalls, 1960-61

>
MUNICIPAL OPERA HOUSE
Polyhedron chandeliers (h 230 cm, Ø 100 cm), foyer of the stalls. Period photograph, 1961

For the lighting fixtures mainly modular systems were used, like the solid square rods and polyhedrons used particularly for the large lights in the more extensive areas (entrance hall and foyer). As documented by various period photographs and the booklet *Venini impianti di illuminazione* [1963], for the smaller ceiling lights, polyhedrons with a quadrangular cross-section, cube-shaped elements, ceiling lights with 'background patches of colour' and lamps with ovoid ('olive') elements were used. Following the damage caused by the flood of 4 November 1966, the theatre was renovated yet again in the later months of the same year, still after a design by Alessandro Giuntoli. It was on this occasion that a series of pendant lamps was installed, composed of cylindrical elements in transparent glass with several layers of colour, arranged in groups of three.

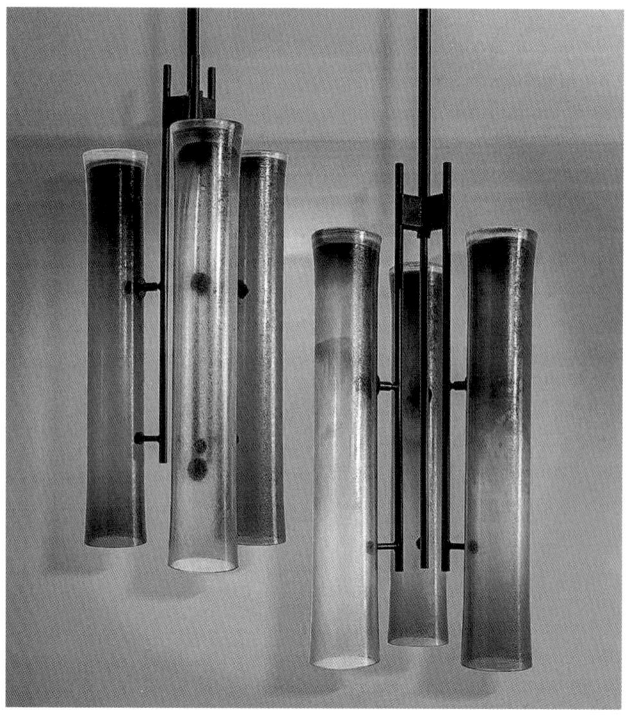

>
MUNICIPAL OPERA HOUSE
Chandelier with coloured solid square rods (h 200 cm, 120 x 120 cm), main foyer. Period photograph, 1961. The pendant model represents a reworking of the lamp designed by Ignazio Gardella for the Olivetti shop in Düsseldorf

>
MUNICIPAL OPERA HOUSE
Lamps in transparent glass with several layers of colour corroded superficially (h 250 cm, 40 x 80 cm), 1966. Private collection, Germany

>>
MUNICIPAL OPERA HOUSE
Ceiling lighting with elements having a quadrangular cross section, boxes. Period photograph in *Venini impianti di illuminazione*, [1961], AMH

>>
MUNICIPAL OPERA HOUSE
Chandelier with 'olives' in opaque glass (Ø 100 cm). Period photograph, 1961

>>
MUNICIPAL OPERA HOUSE
Cube-shaped ceiling lamps (28 x 28 cm), basement foyer. Period photograph, 1961

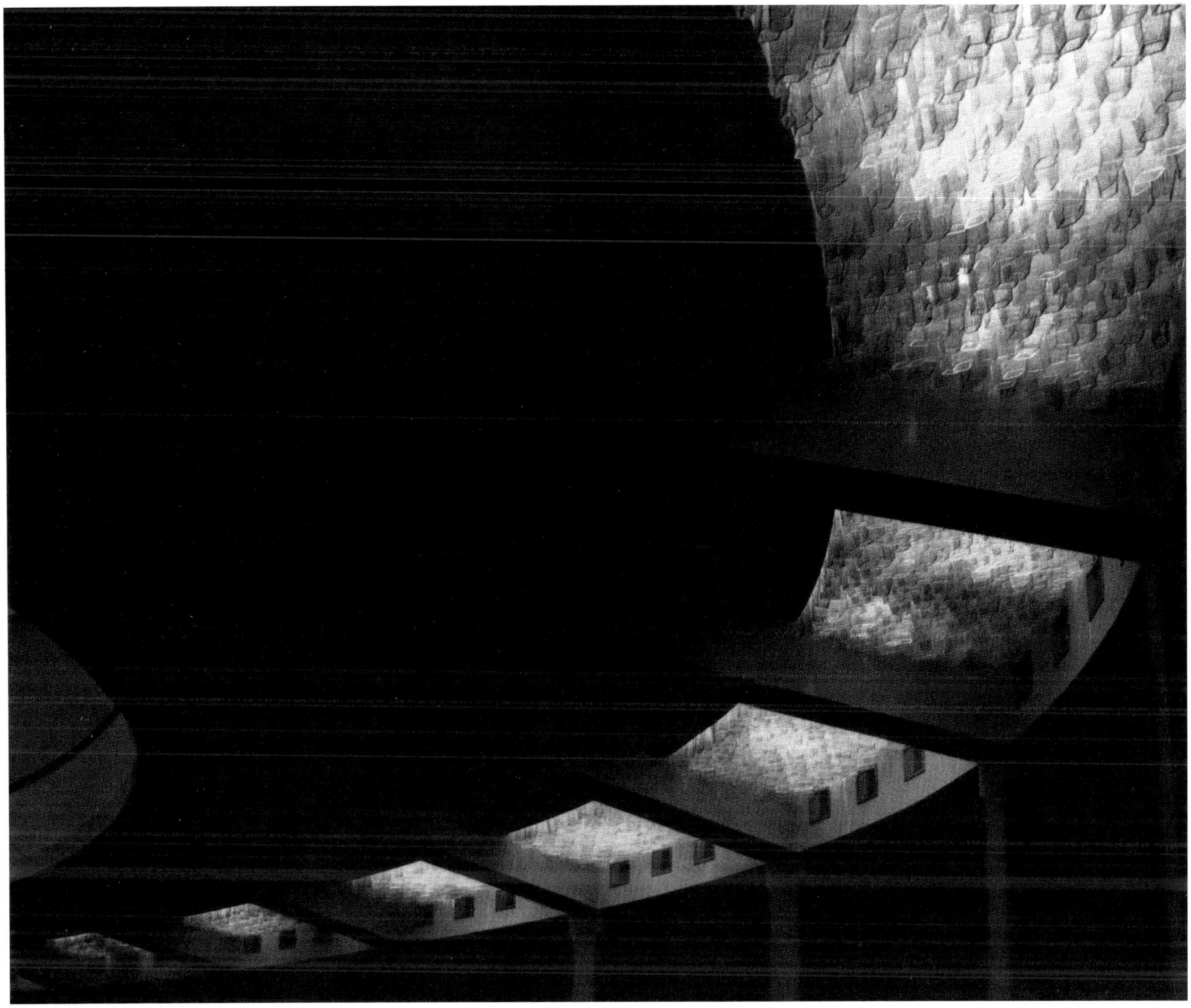

1961

MANCHESTER (GB)
MANCHESTER AIRPORT
DESIGN S. BUZAS

DROPS

For the main lounge (now Terminal 1) of the Manchester airport (built after a design by James Cubitt and Partners), the glassworks created four impressive lighting installations, designed by the architect Stefan Buzas (July 1961). These are in the nature of large chandeliers (250 x 250 cm, max height 500 cm) consisting of 1,300 rods of various heights with the extremities in the shape of a drop, made in *cristallo* glass and to a lesser extent in grey *talpa* glass. Each separate element is attached very precisely to the ceiling with a steel cable so as to produce a voluminous tapering structure. The rods range from 50 to 120 cm and, where the required length is greater than 120 cm, the prolongation is done with empty rods (W 50-100 cm) and small interposed spheres (*Venini lavori di illuminazione 1973*, 1972). The light source is located above the frame supporting the rods. In the production of this work the master glassmaker, Bruno Zanetti, was involved. In 2003 the installations were taken down. At present one of them is in The World of Glass, St. Helens, Merseyside (GB) and another in the Museum of Science and Industry, Manchester (GB).

>
MANCHESTER AIRPORT
Main lounge. Period photograph 1960s

Gates

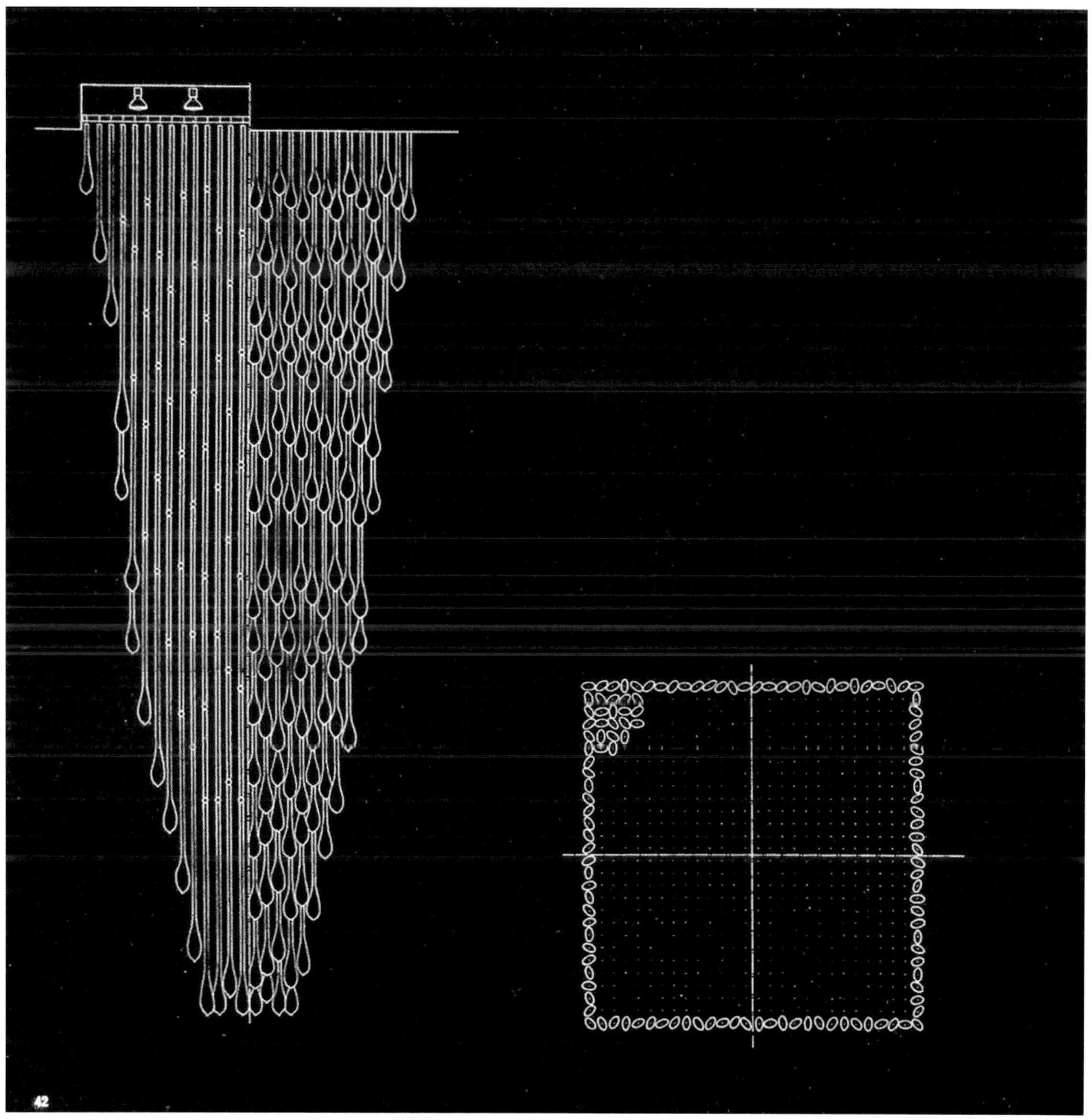

<<
MANCHESTER AIRPORT
Lighting installations with droplets. Period photograph, 1961

>
MANCHESTER AIRPORT
Lighting installation with droplet elements during mounting. Period photograph, 1961

>
MANCHESTER AIRPORT
Lighting installations with droplet elements during mounting. Period photograph, 1961

>
MANCHESTER AIRPORT
Cross section, overview and plan of the lighting installation in *Venini illuminazione d'architettura*, [1978]

1961

PERUGIA (IT)

UNIVERSITÀ DEGLI STUDI DI PERUGIA

Lighting elements for the university designed by the architect Giuseppe Nicolosi.

1961

PARIS (FR)

SALON HELENA RUBINSTEIN

POLYHEDRONS

Series of polyhedron ceiling lights (h 40 cm, Ø 70 cm) produced for the Helena Rubinstein beauty salon in Paris.

>
SALON HELENA RUBINSTEIN
View of the salon. Period photograph, September 1961

1961

PARIS (FR)

FIAT SHOP

SQUARE RODS

For the Fiat Paris showroom in July 1961, the glassworks produced a large illuminated sign in transparent glass placed over the main entrance (h 200 cm). In the interior area, a chandelier with a tapering structure of solid square rods was installed (h 125 cm).

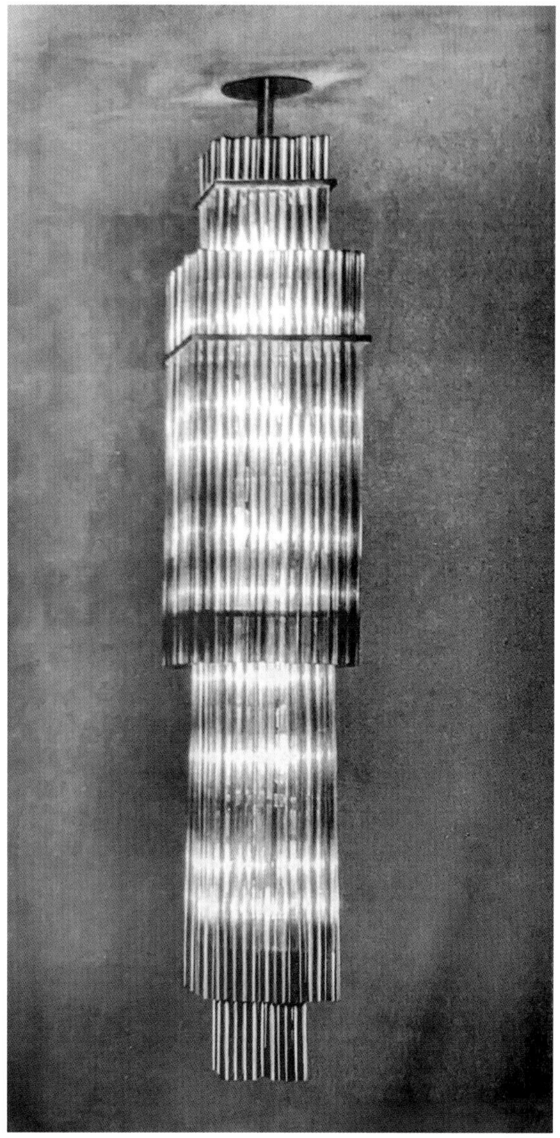

>
FIAT SHOP
Chandelier with square rods, in *Venini impianti di illuminazione*, [1963], AHL

>>
FIAT SHOP
Illuminated sign, in *Venini impianti di illuminazione,* [1963], AHL

FIAT

1961

TURIN (IT)
GRAND HOTEL AMBASCIATORI

RODS
WITH PATCHES OF COLOUR
ON THE CEILING
POLYHEDRONS

The Grand Hotel Ambasciatori was designed by the architect Carlo Alberto Bordogna and opened in 1961. Inside the building there were numerous Venini lighting fixtures, among which chandeliers and wall lights with rods, polyhedrons and variously shaped modules.

>
GRAND HOTEL AMBASCIATORI
Ceiling lights with coloured patches in the entrance hall. Period photograph, March 1964

<<
GRAND HOTEL AMBASCIATORI
Polyhedron ceiling light (h 75 cm, Ø 350 cm) above the staircase connecting the hall with the first floor. Period photograph, March 1964

>
GRAND HOTEL AMBASCIATORI
Luminous cascade with polyhedrons in the stairwell between one storey and the other. Period photograph, March 1964

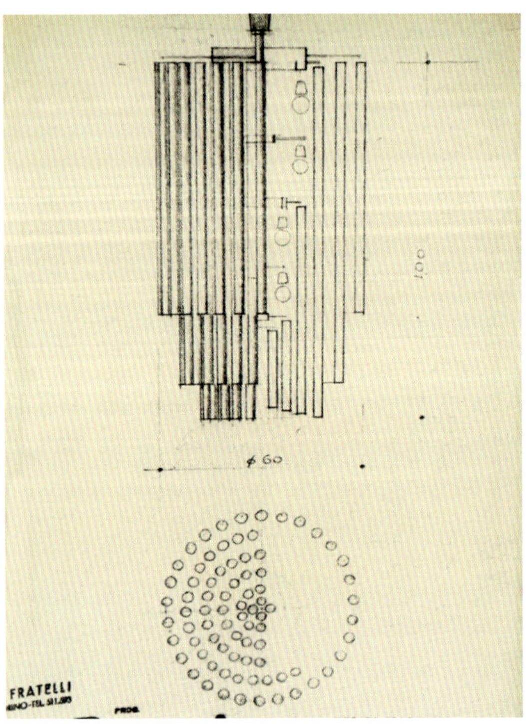

›
GRAND HOTEL AMBASCIATORI
Chandeliers with rods (h 100 cm, Ø 60 cm) in the restaurant area. Period photograph, March 1964

›
GRAND HOTEL AMBASCIATORI
Technical design for the rod chandeliers produced for the restaurant area, AC

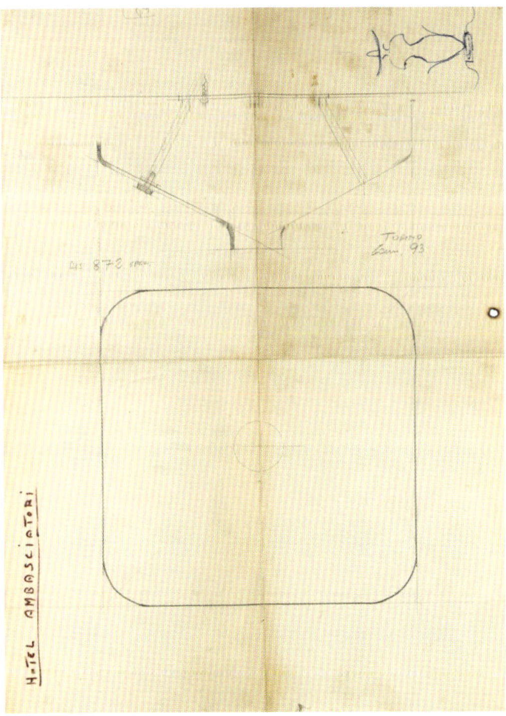

>
GRAND HOTEL AMBASCIATORI
Cone-shaped modular blocks for one of the dining rooms. Period photograph, March 1964

>
GRAND HOTEL AMBASCIATORI
Design of the ceiling light type for the diningroom

1961

TURIN (IT)

VENETO PAVILION, EXHIBITION OF THE REGIONS, ITALIA 61

POLYHEDRONS

Created for the Exhibition of the Regions held as part of the centenary celebrations in Turin of the Unification of Italy, the Veneto pavilion, designed like the others by Nello Renacco, was laid out by Carlo Scarpa and opened, as was the exhibition, on 6 May 1961.
The themes 'rule of the waters' and 'sense of colour' assigned by the organising committee were developed by the Venetian architect through the construction of an impressive space made up of elements and materials of considerable evocative power: water, mosaic, glass, metal, reproductions of works by Venetian painters etc. In an area in the form of a square (32 x 32 m), Scarpa positioned a series of items (a perforated wall with a mosaic decoration by Mario De Luigi, stained glass panes by Salviati, a curvilinear sculpture in sheet iron from which water gushed, a model of the Vajont dam, water basins, some reproductions of works by Venetian painters, some display cases etc.) which interacted figuratively, alluding to the themes covered and defining the spatial hierarchies required by the pathways within the space itself. The nucleus of the composition was 'the immense paradoxical central chandelier, quickly oblivious of its own function, [...] a streaming cascade of gently vibrating light and colour enlivening the space, and enhancing the basin below filling it with myriads of reflections' (Santini 1961, p. 19). This was an extraordinary installation created with over 3,000 polyhedrons of different colours and delicate shades, located behind the wall that separated the entrance area intended for projections from the rest of the pavilion. Characterised by a square base, with lines of polyhedrons on the ceiling extending both towards the rear wall and sideways towards the showcase with the red robe worn by the Doge, the installation consists principally of a structured volume resembling an upside-down truncated pyramid extending downwards over the water basin.

>
VENETO PAVILION, EXHIBITION OF THE REGIONS, ITALIA 61
South-west view of the 'chandelier'. Period photograph, 1961. On the left the display cabinet with the Ducal robe is visible, while on the right the large metallic sculpture after a design by Carlo Scarpa can be made out.

Because of its position the large 'chandelier', 'an enormous stalactite' (*Domus*, August 1961), was visible on three sides and through studied foreshortened views and so while seen from the front, with the mosaic wall at the back, it was impressive in its symmetry, laterally and from an angle the body was characterised by its oblique profile and tapering complex structure, the contour of which seemed to allude to the irregular fall of water perceived from within its spaciousness.

«
VENETO PAVILION, EXHIBITION OF THE REGIONS, ITALIA 61
North-east view of the 'chandelier'. Period photograph, 1961. At the back the wall with the mosaics of De Luigi and stained glass windows of Salviati

›
VENETO PAVILION, EXHIBITION OF THE REGIONS, ITALIA 61
Front view of the 'chandelier'. Period photograph, 1961. Università Iuav di Venezia, Archivio Progetti, Fondo Giorgio Casali

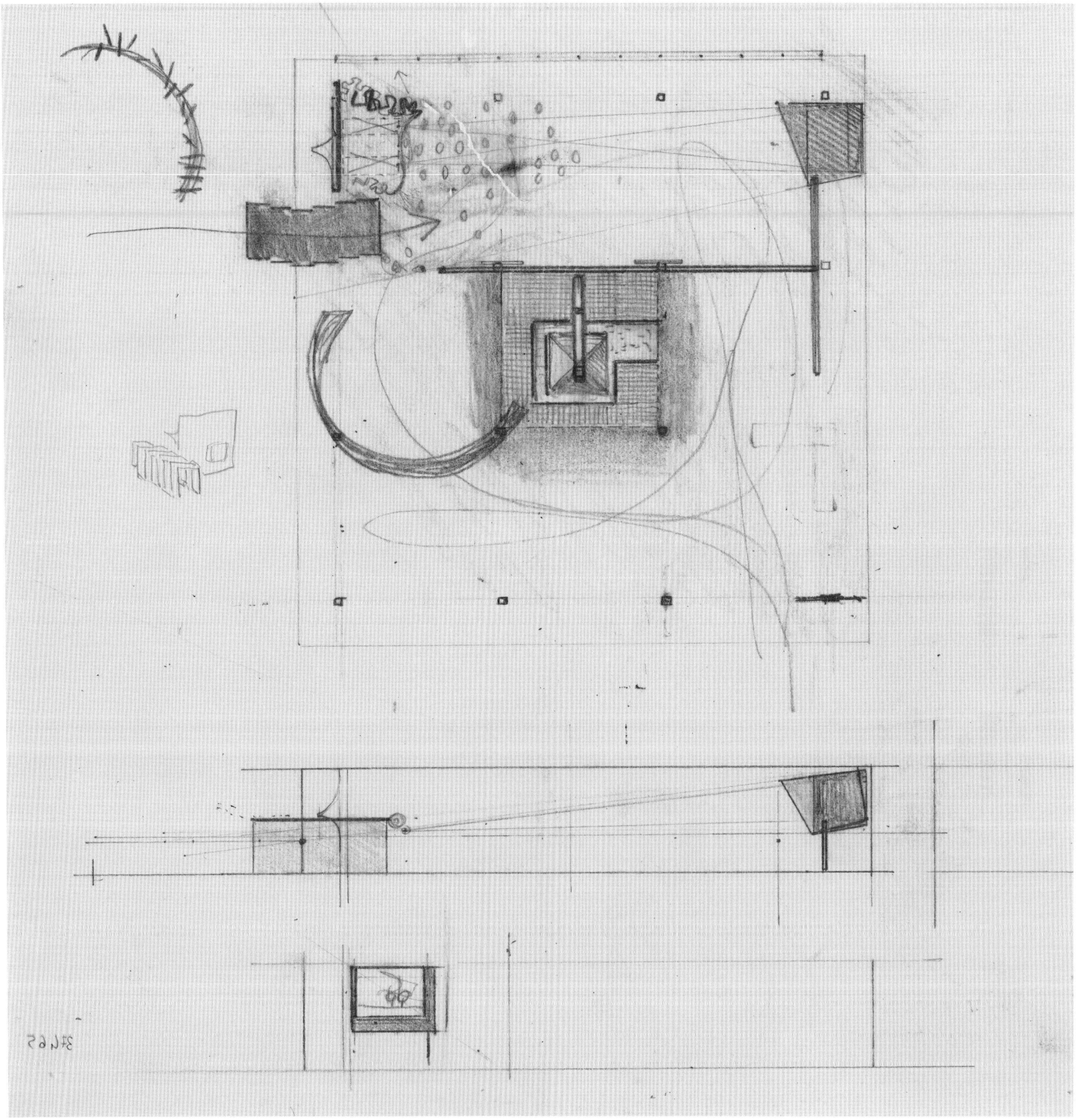

<<
VENETO PAVILION, EXHIBITION OF THE REGIONS, ITALIA 61
Detail of the 'chandelier'. Period photograph, 1961

>
VENETO PAVILION, EXHIBITION OF THE REGIONS, ITALIA 61
C. Scarpa, planimetric study of the pavilion and itineraries, 1961.
MAXXI, Carlo Scarpa Archive
At the centre the plan of the polyhedron installation and grating surrounding it can be seen.

<<
VENETO PAVILION,
EXHIBITION OF THE REGIONS, ITALIA 61
'Chandelier' detail. Period photograph, 1961

>
VENETO PAVILION,
EXHIBITION OF THE REGIONS, ITALIA 61
View of the installation from the south-east. Period photograph, 1961

1961

TURIN (IT)
LABOUR BUILDING, INTERNATIONAL LABOUR EXHIBITION, ITALIA 61

RODS

Among the projects realised on the occasion of Italy 61, an event organised for the first centenary of Italian unification, was the production of a huge wall light placed in one of the parking areas of the Palazzo delle Nazioni, called the Palazzo del Lavoro in the project by Pierluigi Nervi, which housed the Esposizione Internazionale del lavoro [International Labour Exhibition]. It was a retro-illuminated wall lamp with a metallic structure and diffuser screen made of rods in light green and *pagliesco* glass (w 450 cm, max h 60 cm). In the booklet *Venini impianti di illuminazione* [1961], the lamp is described as a 'wall lamp with organ pipes'.

›
LABOUR BUILDING, INTERNATIONAL LABOUR EXHIBITION, ITALIA 61
Wall light with glass rods in two colours. Period photograph, 1961

1961

TURIN (IT)
TEATRO NUOVO

OLIVE
POLYHEDRONS

Located in the Parco del Valentino, the Teatro Nuovo is part of the complex Palazzo della Moda e delle Esposizioni [Palace of Fashion and Exhibitions] (later Torino Esposizioni) built in 1938 after the design of Ettore Sottsass Sr. In the post-war period the complex underwent various transformations. In the early 1960s as part of the celebrations of the centenary of the unification of Italy (Italia 61), the Teatro Nuovo was refurbished after a design by the Turin architect Paolo Caliari. On this occasion the architect chose large chandeliers with ovoid elements, called 'olives', with a *balloton* decoration (h 160 cm, Ø 250 cm), for areas such as the entrance hall or foyer, while for the ceiling of the 'sala grande' [audito-

>
TEATRO NUOVO
Ceiling lamps with polyhedrons in the 'sala grande'.
Period photograph, c. 1961

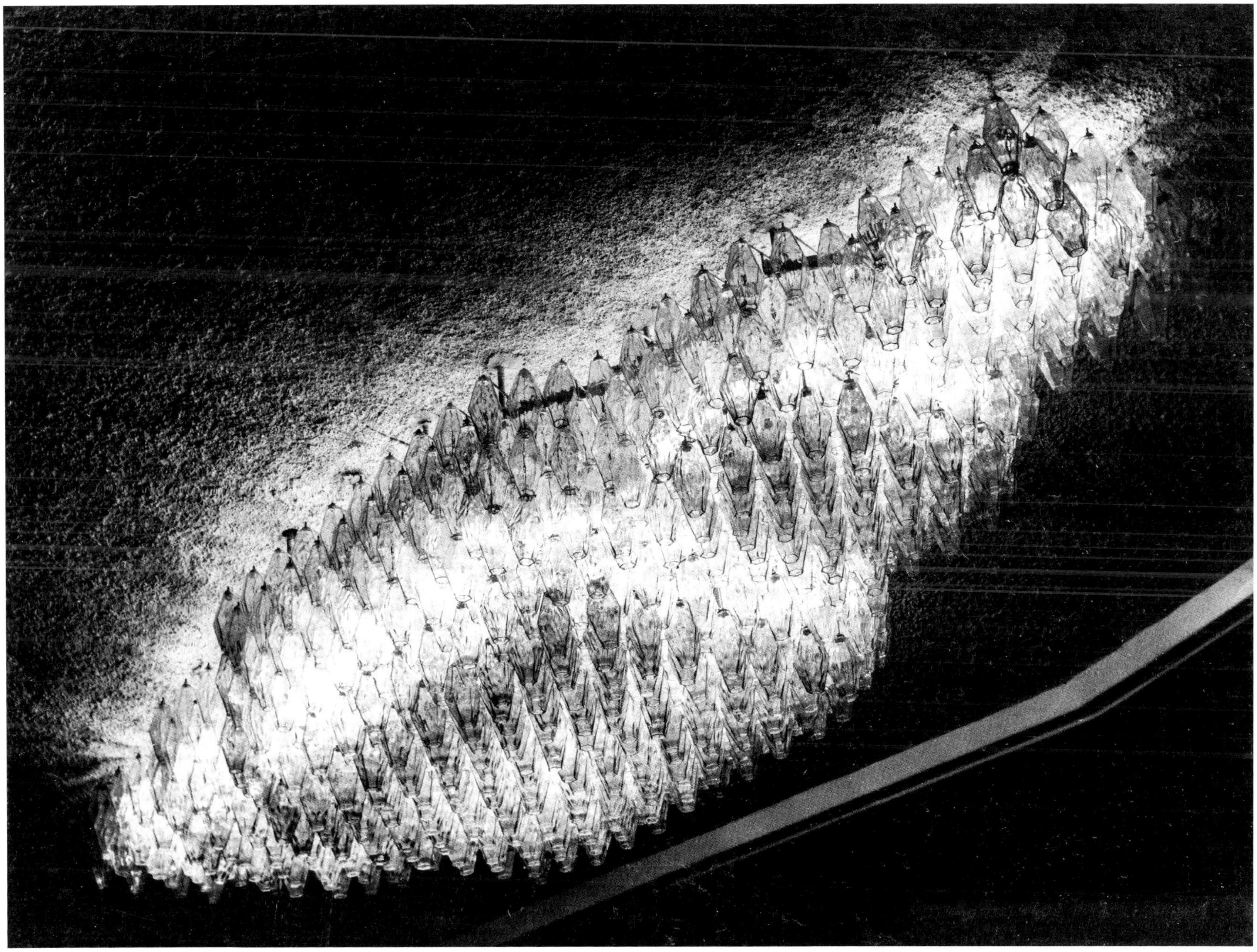

rium] original ceiling lamps were created in an elongated shape made up of polyhedrons (400 x 127 cm). These lamps are still *in situ*. Finally, a series of wall lamps of significant size with a tripartite structure (h 300 cm, Ø 110 cm) were also produced.

>
TEATRO NUOVO
Wall lamps with polyhedrons. Period photograph, c. 1961

>>
TEATRO NUOVO
Chandelier with *balloton* 'olives'. Period photograph, c. 1961

1961

TREVISO (IT)

CHURCH OF SAN CAMILLO

RODS

For the church of the Istituto delle Figlie di San Camillo, designed by the architect Roberto Fontana and annexed to the hospital building of the same name, the Venini firm created a chandelier with transparent *cristallo* glass rods described in the booklet *Venini impianti di illuminazione* [1961] as a 'chandelier with organ pipes' (h 160 cm, Ø 120 cm). The fixture had a symmetrical structure, in three tiers and with a circular plan and protruding central section. The building has been demolished.

›
CHURCH OF SAN CAMILLO
Chandelier with rods. Period photograph, c. 1961

1961

WASHINGTON D.C. (US)

SHERATON PARK HOTEL

Lighting project for the imposing hotel building in the capital of the United States.

1961

ZURICH (CH)

FINTER BANK ZÜRICH

PLATES

The project for the headquarters of the Swiss Banking Institute (June 1961) consisted in the creation of minimalist wall lamps and an illuminated cornice. In both cases sheets of moulded glass with the so-called *stellare* decorative motif were used.

›
FINTER BANK ZÜRICH
Venini lamps in an area of the Zurich headquarters. Period photograph, c. 1961

1961-62 ROME, EUR (IT)

RESIDENCE GARDEN HOTEL

PENDANT
TABLE
FLOOR

The Hotel Residence Garden was constructed after the design of the architect Attilio Lapadula. Within it, various elements of Venini lighting are included.

›
RESIDENCE GARDEN HOTEL
Floor lamp no. 2242 *a fasce orizzontali* carried out after a design by Fulvio Bianconi and included in one of the hotel bedrooms. Period photograph, c. 1962.

›
RESIDENCE GARDEN HOTEL
Room with pendant lamp no. 4039, designed by Massimo Vignelli and table lamp. Period photograph, c. 1962

1961-63 ROME (IT)
ISTITUTO BANCARIO SAN PAOLO DI TORINO

RODS
SOLID RODS

For the Roman headquarters of the Istituto Bancario San Paolo di Torino (now Intesa Sanpaolo), designed by the young architect Tommaso Valle, the Venini firm produced some wall lamps with blown-glass rods and solid rods for various settings, among which the entrance, the landing on the first floor, the waiting room and the boardroom.

>
ISTITUTO BANCARIO SAN PAOLO DI TORINO
Waiting room, blown-glass rods on the first floor, wall lamps with blown-glass rods (h 60 cm x 360 cm) in *Venini illuminazione d'architettura*, 1970. Period photograph, 1960s

>
ISTITUTO BANCARIO SAN PAOLO DI TORINO
Waiting room on the first floor. Period photograph, 1960s

1962 AMSTERDAM (NL)
CHAMBER OF COMMERCE

POLYHEDRONS

The project for the Chamber of Commerce of Amsterdam (October 1962) consisted principally of the lighting of the meeting hall, where a series of polyhedron chandeliers was installed, arranged centrally in a row. The chandeliers (h 150 cm, Ø 75 cm) are structured in three tiers, with a circular plan and protruding central section. The metal support structure is made with bars fixed at the extremities to cylindrical elements.

>>
CHAMBER OF COMMERCE
Meeting hall. Period photograph, c. 1962

1962

AOSTA (IT)
GIACOSA CINEMA-THEATRE

POLYHEDRONS

The project for the historic cinema-theatre, situated within the municipal complex of the capital of the Valle d'Aosta, consisted of the installation of various luminaires with polyhedron modular elements. Among these are a series of polyhedron wall lamps and ceiling lamps in light-blue glass (corridor and balcony, first floor) and pendant chandeliers whether in the variant with light-blue polyhedrons or with *pagliesco* polyhedrons, all compact in size. The exceptions are two large paired 'chandeliers' (h 350 cm, Ø max 60 cm), with a telescopic structure in five parts, each in a different colour (light blue, crystal, light *pagliesco*, *pagliesco*, red), which are placed in the doubly-height areas near the stairs (entrance).

>
GIACOSA CINEMA-THEATRE
Polyhedron chandelier in different colours. Archive photograph

>
GIACOSA CINEMA-THEATRE
Polyhedron chandelier in different colours. Private collection, Milan

>
GIACOSA CINEMA-THEATRE
Polyhedron chandelier in different colours, detail of the tip. Private collection, Milan

1962

BOLOGNA (IT)
TOWN HALL

POLYHEDRONS

The project in the Palazzo Comunale [town hall] of Bologna (November 1962) consisted in the production of a series of chandeliers with polyhedrons of various shapes and dimensions placed on the first floor in the areas belonging to the Mayor's Office (entrance hall, antechamber of the mayor's office, various offices).

>
TOWN HALL
Polyhedron chandelier (h 108 cm, Ø 120 cm) in the entrance hall. Period photograph in *Venini impianti di illuminazione*, [1963], AHL

>
TOWN HALL
Polyhedron chandeliers (h 160 cm, Ø max 70 cm) in the antechamber of the mayor's office. Period photograph in *Venini impianti di illuminazione*, [1963], AHL

>>
TOWN HALL
Polyhedron chandelier (h 108 cm, Ø 120 cm) in the entrance hall. Period photograph in *Venini impianti di illuminazione*, [1963], AHL

1962

GÖTEBORG (SE)
RESTAURANT I.K.A.

POLYHEDRONS

For the lighting of the principal room of the Swedish restaurant (October 1962) large circular ceiling lights with polyhedrons in transparent bichrome glass were used.

1962

THE HAGUE (NL)
MINISTRY OF AGRICULTURE

POLYHEDRONS

The project at the Dutch Ministry of Agriculture (October 1962) saw the Venini firm produce some lamps for the offices, among which the office of the minister. Here polyhedron chandeliers in three tiers with a circular plan and projecting central part were place; a supporting metal structure made up of rods fixed at the extremities to cylindrical elements.

1962

LIDO DI VENEZIA (IT)
DE LAURENTIIS STAND, 23RD VENICE INTERNATIONAL FILM FESTIVAL

POLYHEDRONS
TRIANGLE

For the stand of the De Laurentiis film producers, set up in the Lido di Venezia for the 23rd Venice International Film Festival, wall lamps and lamps with polyhedrons and solid triangular rods of different shapes and dimensions were installed.

>
RESTAURANT I.K.A.
Polyhedron ceiling lamps. Period photograph, 1962

>
MINISTRY OF AGRICULTURE
Minister's office. Period photograph, 1962

>
DE LAURENTIIS STAND,
23RD VENICE INTERNATIONAL FILM FESTIVAL
Installation with polyhedrons. Period photograph, 1962

1962

LONDON (GB)
J. HENRY SCHRÖDER WAGG & CO. LTD BANKING CORPORATION

BICHROME OPAL GLASS

In the London headquarters of the J. Henry Schröder Wagg & Co. Ltd. bank, designed by Stefan Buzas, there are a group of lamps in opaline glass.

\>
J. HENRY SCHRÖDER WAGG & CO. LTD BANKING CORPORATION
Public hall. Period photograph, 1960s

1962

STUTTGART (DE)
KLEINES HAUS

POLYHEDRONS

Part of the Staatstheater complex of Stuttgart, the Kleines Haus (drama theatre) was destroyed during the Second World War and entirely reconstructed after the design of Hans Volkart, Kurt Pläcking and Bert Perlia between 1958 and 1962. On this occasion the glassworks intervened with the installation of some luminaires in the new building, which was opened on 5 October 1962. Among these were the cylindrical chandeliers with *cristallo* polyhedrons (h 150 cm, Ø 50 cm) in the foyer of the first floor.

\>
KLEINES HAUS
Cylindrical pendant lamp with polyhedrons.
Period photograph, 1962

\>\>
KLEINES HAUS
Pendant lamps with polyhedrons in the foyer of the first floor. Period photograph, 1962

1962-63 MONTREAL (CA)
GRANDE SALLE, PLACE DES ARTS
DESIGN F. LEBENSOLD

PLATES

The first building completed in the performing arts complex of Place des arts, the Grande Salle was erected between 1961 and 1963 and opened on 21 September 1963. The theatre, renamed Salle Wilfried-Pellettier in 1966, was built after a design of the Canadian architects Ray Affleck, Guy Desbarats, Dimitri Dimakopoulos, Fred Lebensold, Jean Michaud and Hazen Sise to accommodate events such as symphony concerts, operas, ballet and musicals with a capacity of 3,000 seating places. The interior was designed, in particular, by Fred Lebensold and the decorator Henri Beula who set out to create 'the warm atmosphere of the European halls' (Cha 2006, p. 49). It was Lebensold who designed the original ceiling lamps with their elongated rhomboid structure (l max 750 cm, h max 120 cm) executed by the Venini firm with plates in amber corrugated glass. The lamps follow one another at equal intervals in the horse-shoe space surrounding the hall both on the first floor (foyers of the stalls) and on the first floor, called the 'piano nobile'. In particular, at this level, the luminaires engage in an ideal way with *Les Anges radieux*, a sculpture in bronze by the Canadian artist Louis Archambauld placed over the curved wall of the central staircase. During the reconstruction works on the building in 2013, the lamps underwent changes and the glass elements were removed.

›
GRANDE SALLE, PLACE DES ARTS
Staircase of the 'piano nobile' with the ceiling lamps and the sculpture *Les Anges radieux*. Period photograph, 1963

<<
GRANDE SALLE, PLACE DES ARTS
Side foyer of the 'piano nobile'. Period photograph, 1963

>
GRANDE SALLE, PLACE DES ARTS
Ceiling lamps with amber corrugated glass plates.
Period photograph, 1963

1963

HOUSTON (US)
PETROLEUM CLUB
DESIGN W. PARKER MCFADDEN

WITH ARMS

For the Texan club, designed by George Pierce, the glassworks produced the illuminated bodies in ground glass of some lamps with arms, with a structure in aluminium, designed by William Parker McFadden. The design of the lamps is inspired by that of oil lamps.

1963

FRANKFURT (DE)
IHC HOTEL INTERCONTINENTAL
DESIGN O. APEL

POLYHEDRONS

On 6 June 1963 the Hotel Intercontinental of Frankfurt was opened, which at that time could be considered the biggest hotel in Germany. For this building, designed by the architectural firm ABB Architekten founded by Otto Apel, the Venini glassworks produced a ceiling lamp of a considerable size (Ø 400 cm) for the main dining-room - Ristorante dell'Arte (*Deutsche Bauzeitung*, April 1964; *Rivista Internazionale d'Illuminazione*, June 1964) designed by Apel himself. This is a circular lamp with modular polyhedron elements, fixed to the ceiling with four metal rods.

>
IHC HOTEL INTERCONTINENTAL
Ristorante dell'Arte. Period photograph, 1963

1963

IVREA (IT)
ISTITUTO EUROPA

Lighting project for a cultural building.

1963

LONDON (GB)
SALON ROGER AT VIDAL SASSOON

RODS

The beauty salon Roger at Vidal Sassoon was built between 1962 and 1963 by Gordon and Ursula Bowyer, English architects chosen by Sassoon, a prominent hair stylist of the time. The salon was located in Park Lane, London, on the ground floor of the Grosvenor House hotel. In this commercial area, the Venini firm placed a chandelier with rods of different lengths intended to connect the area between the raised floor and the entrance.

>
SALON ROGER AT VIDAL SASSOON
Interior of the beauty salon Roger at Vidal Sassoon. Period photograph, mid-1960s

1963 NAPLES (IT)
RAI PRODUCTION CENTRE

POLYHEDRONS

For the bar-room of the Rai production centre of Naples, a complex designed by Mario De Renzi, Renato De Martino and Raffaele Contigiani and opened on 7 March 1963, the glassworks carried out a series of luminous ceiling polyhedron insets of 35 and 16 cm in height. The ceiling is hexagonal in plan, within which rows of polyhedrons in the two dimensions alternate.

>
RAI PRODUCTION CENTRE
Ceiling with polyhedrons in two dimensions. Period photograph, 1963

1963 PARIS (FR)
REVILLON FRÈRES SHOP

DROPS

For the fur shop Revillon Frères of Paris, the Venini firm produced a lighting installation consisting of elements in the form of drops. The rods, in *cristallo* glass and a dark colour (amethyst?), are inserted in a circular compartment at the top of which the light source is situated. The installation is reminiscent of the solution used by the Chez-Vous club of the Hotel Excelsior of Venice designed by the architects Magistretti and Zanuso.

>
REVILLON FRÈRES SHOP
Chandelier with drops (h 200 cm, Ø 120 cm), in *Rivista Internazionale d'Illuminazione*, February 1969

1963 ROME (IT)

CAVALIERI-HILTON HOTEL

Lighting project for the luxury hotel situated in Monte Mario.

1963 TURIN (IT)

ISTITUTO BANCARIO SAN PAOLO DI TORINO

Lighting project for some areas of the Palazzo Turinetti di Pertengo, headquarters of the Istituto Bancario San Paolo di Torino. The building, seriously damaged during the war, was renovated after a design of the architect Arturo Midana (1954), helped by and later replaced by Mario Dezzutti (1960-63). The building was opened on 31 October 1963.

1963 VENICE (IT)

ALL'ANGELO HOTEL

Lighting project for the historic establishment frequented by artists and painters.

1963 VIENNA (AT)

CHAMBER OF COMMERCE

POLYHEDRONS

Lighting project for the Vienna headquarters, consisting largely in the production of polyhedron lamps.

>
CHAMBER OF COMMERCE
Polyhedron pendant lamp in *Venini impianti di illuminazione*, [1963], AHL

1963-64 HONG KONG (HK)
THE PENINSULA HONG KONG HOTEL

POLYHEDRONS

During the restoration of the hotel (1961-63), after the design of the architects Walter Marmorek and Peter Womersley, the Venini firm produced a lighting installation composed of three large polyhedron 'tents' over the reception desk.

›
THE PENINSULA HONG KONG HOTEL
Reception. Period photograph, c. 1964

1963-64 SAVONA (IT)
GABRIELLO CHIABRERA THEATRE

POLYHEDRONS

The lighting project for the municipal theatre is evidenced principally by two designs showing polyhedron wall lamps.

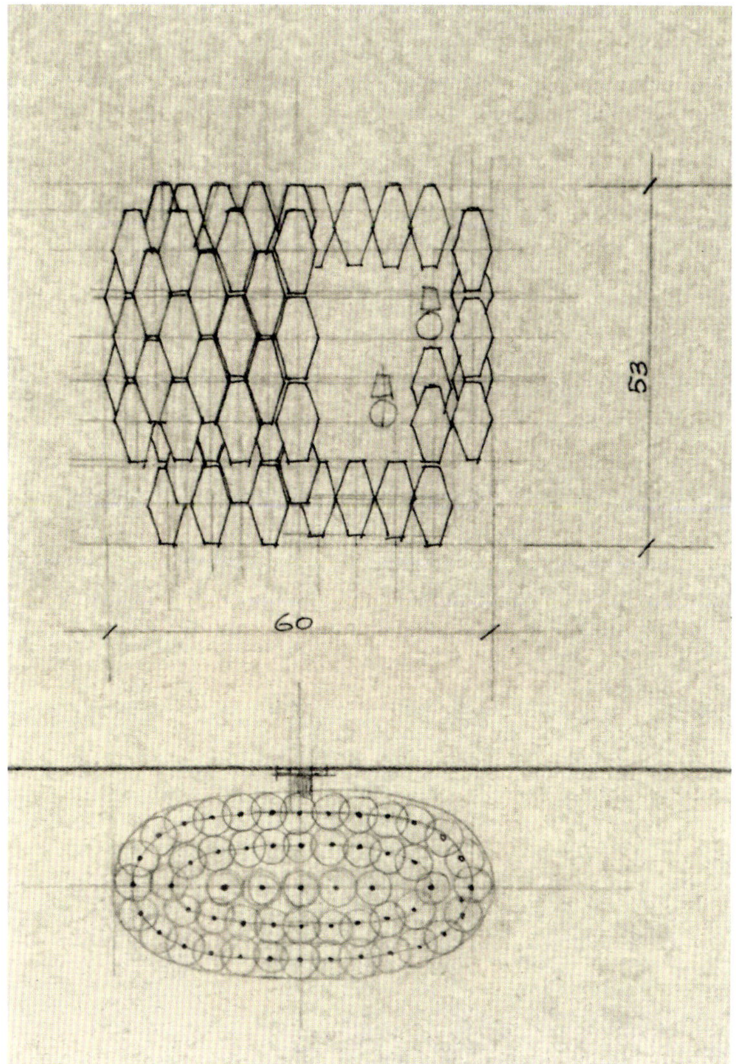

›
GABRIELLO CHIABRERA THEATRE
Design with a polyhedron wall lamp (h 53 cm, Ø 60 cm), AC

1963-65 GENOA (IT)
MICHELANGELO TRANSATLANTIC LINER
DESIGN I. GAMBERINI, A. PSACAROPULO, G. PULITZER

PLATES
POLYHEDRONS
SPHERES

For some areas in the first class of the Michelangelo transatlantic liner (initial project of Nicolò Costanzi), constructed by the Ansaldo shipyard of Sestri Ponente (Genoa), the Venini firm produced various lighting elements. Among others, there was a group of chandeliers 'in blown moulded globes' (*Venini illuminazione d'architettura,* 1970) for the theatre (installation Alessandro Psacaropulo), ring-shaped polyhedron ceiling lamps for the dining-room (installation Gustavo Pulitzer) and a chandelier having plates with *murrine* placed in the entrance hall (installation Italo Gamberini).

1963-65 TRIESTE (IT)
RAFFAELLO TRANSATLANTIC LINER
DESIGN A. LAPADULA

RODS
ICICLES
BAMBOO GLASS

Launched only a few months after her twin-ship Michelangelo, the Raffaello transatlantic liner (initial project by Nicolò Costanzi) was built by the San Marco shipyard of Trieste. The Venini firm produced a series of chandeliers using modular elements such as rods and icicles and bamboo glass. Among these, of particular note are the blown rods of the first-class hall (installation Attilio Lapadula).

>
MICHELANGELO TRANSATLANTIC LINER
Ring-shaped polyhedron ceiling lamps (h 30 cm, Ø 150 cm) for the first-class dining-room. Period photograph, c. 1965

>
MICHELANGELO TRANSATLANTIC LINER
Chandeliers 'in blown moulded globes' (*Venini illuminazione d'architettura,* 1970) for the first-class theatre.
Period photograph, c. 1965

>>
MICHELANGELO TRANSATLANTIC LINER
Chandelier having plates with *murrine* (h 30 cm, Ø 300 cm) for the first-class entrance hall. Period photograph, c. 1965

1964

ABANO (IT)
PLAZA HOTEL

HEXAGONAL ELEMENTS
OCTAGONAL ELEMENTS
SQUARE ELEMENTS
ESPRIT

The project for the hotel saw the glassworks use different solutions for the lighting of areas such as the huge entrance hall and the dining-rooms. For the entrance hall, octagonal (Ø max 40 cm) and square (8 x 8 cm) modules were used, partially inserted into the false ceiling. Produced by blowing in moulds, in two different colours (*pagliesco* and grey-green), the modules are combined following a structured design so as to obtain a more intense light at the entrance, where the luminous surface is more extended, and a more diffuse light in the two wings of the entrance hall, where the ceiling is dotted with small but numerous aggregations of modules. With regard to the dining areas, in the main double-high dining-room, three large chandeliers (Ø 240 cm) and Esprit wall lamps, from which the lamps take the name, were placed, after a design by Toni Zuccheri. These luminaires are still *in situ*. For the second single-floor dining-room, a triangular luminous false ceiling was installed, made up of backlit hexagonal modules.

>
PLAZA HOTEL
Entrance. Postcard 1960s, private collection

tel plaza

>
PLAZA HOTEL
Entrance hall with module-based luminous ceiling.
Period photograph, 1965

>
PLAZA HOTEL
Luminous module-based false ceiling in the small dining-room of the restaurant.
Period photograph, 1965

>
PLAZA HOTEL
Esprit chandeliers in the main-dining room of the restaurant.
Period photograph, 1965

1964 ABANO (IT)

SANAT THERMAL BATHS

Lighting project for thermal resort.

1964 FERRARA (IT)

CHAMBER OF COMMERCE BUILDING

Lighting project (1959-64) for the Ferrara headquarters, following the refurbishment of the internal areas after a design by the architect Ico Parisi.

1964 GENOA (IT)

BANCO DI ROMA

Lighting project for the premises of a bank.

1964 CATANIA (IT)

CHURCH OF SANT'EUPLIO

FULL RODS
ICICLES

Very seriously damaged by the bombardments of 1943, the Church of Sant'Euplio was reconstructed and opened in 1964, after a design by Giacomo Leone. For the occasion, in addition to a polychrome stained-glass window, the Venini firm produced a series of pendant lamps with solid-rod elements, in the body of the church, and with icicles at the four sides, the latter intended to draw attention to the sacred nature of the setting.

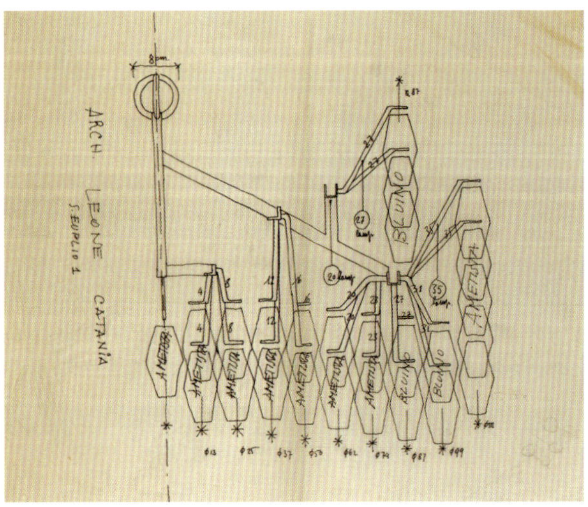

>
CHURCH OF SANT'EUPLIO
First solution proposed, with amethyst and light-blue polyhedrons

>
CHURCH OF SANT'EUPLIO
Interior. Period photograph, c. 1964

1964

IVREA (IT)
OLIVETTI OFFICE BUILDING
DESIGN M. NIZZOLI

HEXAGONAL ELEMENTS

The Olivetti Office Building (Chairman's Office, Executive Board and corporate General Services) was designed by Annibale Fiocchi, Marcello Nizzoli and Gian Antonio Bernasconi, architects to whom the task was entrusted after the death of Adriano Olivetti (1959). The three were chosen by the management group who took over after Adriano and who intended in this way to emphasize the continuity of the Olivetti signature style. The task was assigned in May 1960, works began in February 1961 and ended by 1964. It is to Marcello Nizzoli, in particular, that we owe the design of the skylight produced by the Venini firm over the grand staircase, focal point of the original plan with three arms that functions as a distribution hub for the entire structure. The skylight in hexagonal *corrugati* elements (l 40 cm) has a hexagonal plan (maximum size 13 m) and extends over two staggered altitudes. The skylight is still *in situ*.

>
OLIVETTI OFFICE BUILDING
Stairwell of the Olivetti Office Building with skylight composed of hexagonal *corrugati* elements. Period photograph, c. 1964

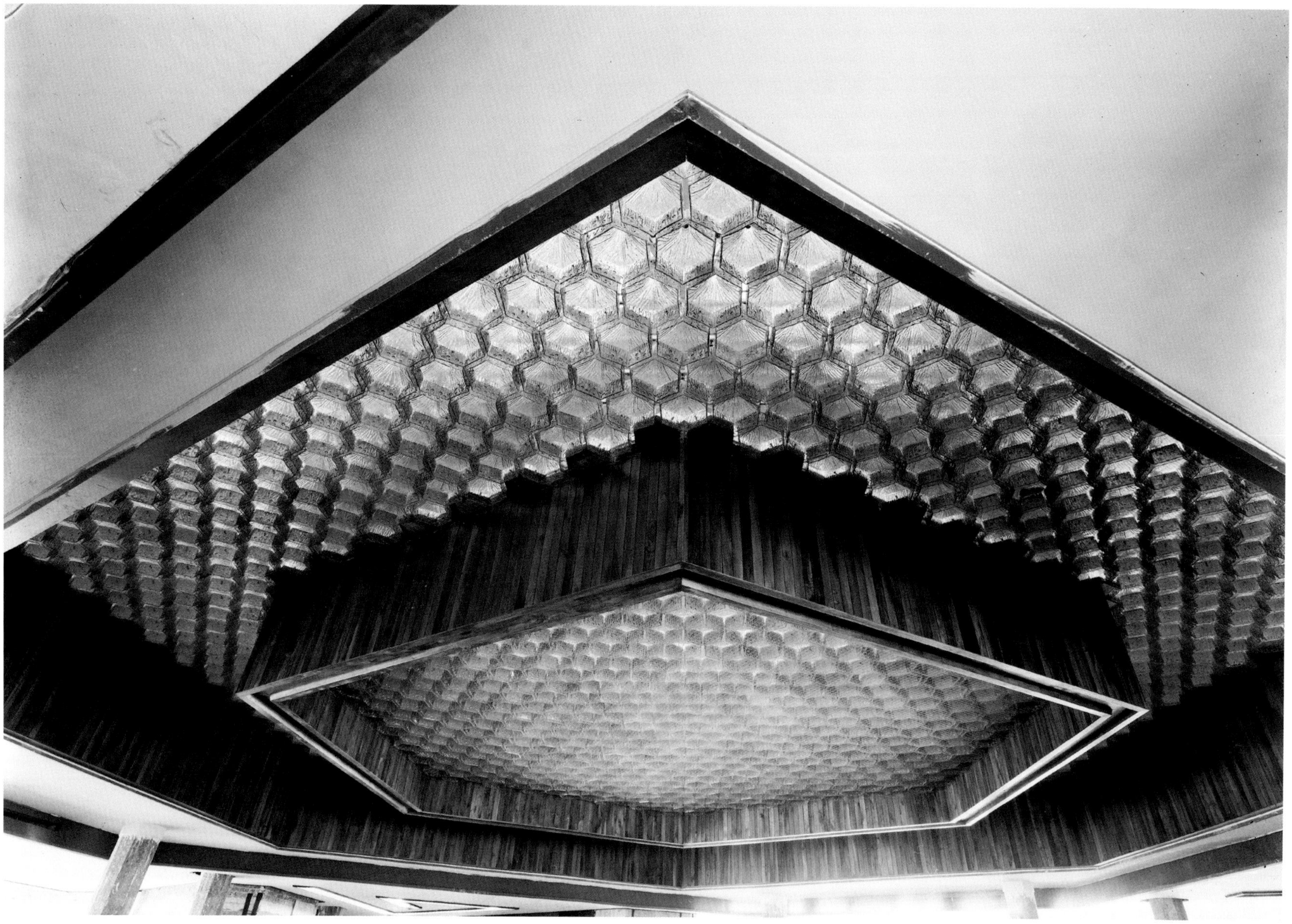

>
OLIVETTI OFFICE BUILDING
Detail of the skylight in which the two staggered altitudes are visible. Period photograph, c. 1964

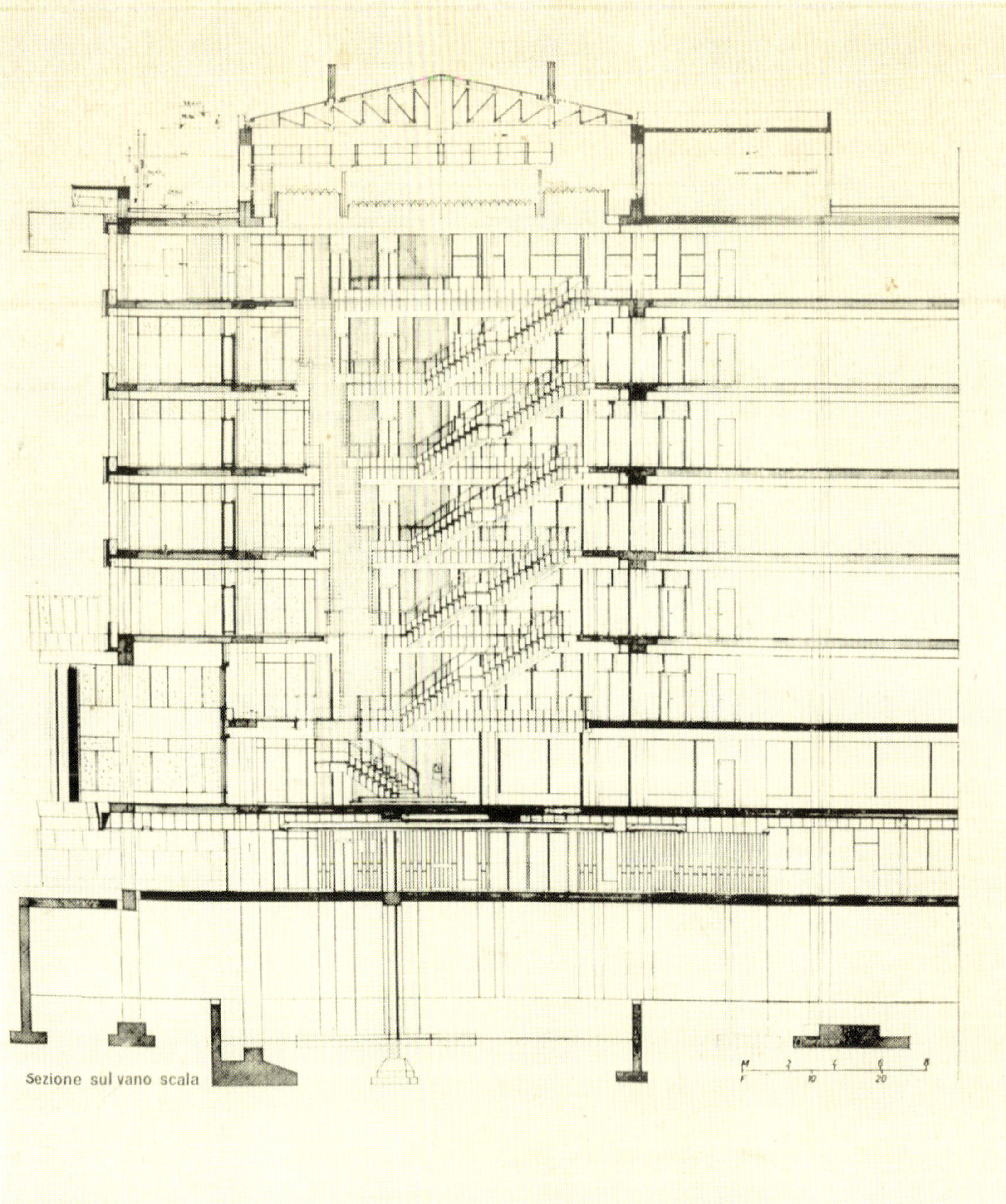

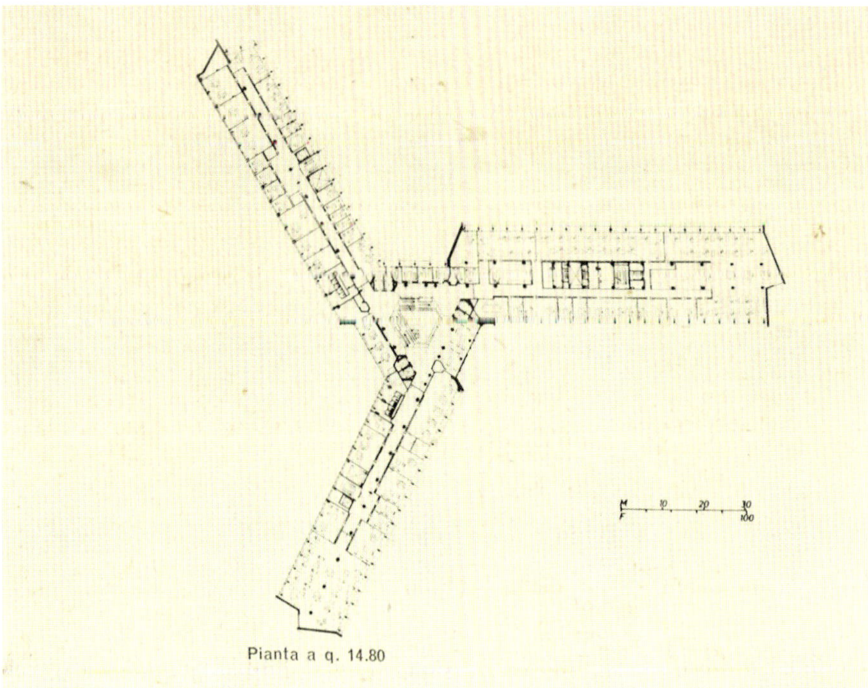

>
OLIVETTI OFFICE BUILDING
Vertical section in *L'architettura. Cronache e storia*, August 1966

>
OLIVETTI OFFICE BUILDING
Three-arm plan in *L'architettura. Cronache e storia*, August 1966

1964 MESTRE, VENICE (IT)
AMBASCIATORI HOTEL

POLYHEDRONS

For the dining-room of the Hotel Ambasciatori of Mestre, the Venini firm produced a group of ceiling lamps and wall lamps with polyhedrons.

1964 PADUA (IT)
CASSA DI RISPARMIO DI PADOVA E ROVIGO

PLATES

The project consisted of thc production of some ceiling lamps for the president's room located in the extension of the bank building designed by Gio Ponti. These are circular ceiling lamps with a diffuser screen made of sheets of thick glass with incorporated polychrome rods. The decorative motif is a repetition of one of those to be found in the sheets used for the production of the two large stained-glass windows placed in the same setting, the fruit of the collaboration between the Milan architect and Toni Zuccheri. The lamps are still *in situ*.

›
CASSA DI RISPARMIO DI PADOVA E ROVIGO
Ceiling lamps and large stained-glass window in the president's room, Intesa Sanpaolo Collection. Photograph Enrico Fiorese 2021

1964 ROME (IT)
POLICE CORPS ACADEMY

Lighting project for the Police Corps Academy, opened in 1964.

1964 SESTRI LEVANTE (IT)
MIRA GUESTHOUSE

Lighting project for hotel premises.

1964 TAORMINA (IT)
CASINO

Lighting project for the gaming halls of the Sicilian casino.

1964 TREVISO (IT)
CHURCH OF SS. REDENTORE

In the church of the SS. Redentore, constructed after a design by the architect Roberto Fontana, the artificial lighting of the presbytery was produced by a cylindrical polyhedron chandelier.

1964-65 CAGLIARI (IT)
UNIVERSITÀ DEGLI STUDI DI CAGLIARI

Lighting project for areas designed by the architect Luciano Deplano. Among these is the library.

1964-65 HONG KONG (HK)

THE MANDARIN HOTEL

DESIGN D. ASHTON, D. PHILIPS

SQUARE RODS
DROPS
SPHERES
OBELISKS
POLYHEDRONS

The Mandarin Hotel (now Mandarin Oriental) was designed by the architect John Howart on behalf of the firm Leigh & Orange; the designers Don Ashton and Derek Phillips were responsible for arranging the interior. In the halls there were various Venini luminaires, among which: chandeliers with drops and golden spheres (h max 300 cm, 250 x 100 cm), chandeliers (h 90 cm, Ø 40 cm) and wall lamps (h 75 cm, Ø 40 cm) with 'falling obelisks in solid glass' (*Venini illuminazione d'architettura 1973,* 1972), ceiling lamps with polyhedrons and a chandelier with solid square rods (h 600 cm, Ø 120 cm).

>
THE MANDARIN HOTEL
Stairwell with bands of solid square rods 'con anima a fiamma rossa' [with a red flame spirit], in *Venini illuminazione d'architettura 1973*, 1972. Period photograph, mid-1960s

<<
THE MANDARIN HOTEL
Entrance hall with droplet chandeliers and golden spheres.
Period photograph, mid-1960s

<<
THE MANDARIN HOTEL
Bar with polyhedron cylindrical ceiling lamps. Period photograph, mid-1960s

>
THE MANDARIN HOTEL
The *Supper Club*. Night Club with chandeliers and wall lamps produced with 'cadute di obelischi in vetro massiccio' [falling obelisks in solid glass], in *Venini illuminazione d'architettura 1973*, 1972.
Period photograph, mid-1960s

1965

ABANO (IT)
GARDEN HOTEL

PENDANT
POLYHEDRONS

Lighting project for a thermal resort hotel. It consists principally of pendant lamps among which lamp no. 802.1 (*Venini lighting catalogue*, 1966), with a band of colour, and a series of large polyhedron-shaped lamps.

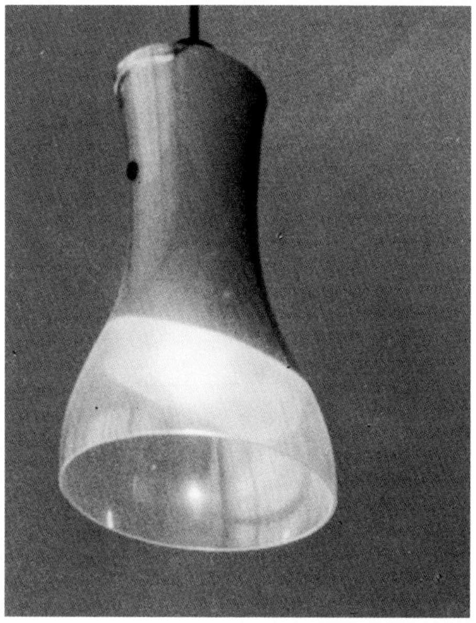

>
GARDEN HOTEL
Pendant lamps. Period photograph, c. 1965

1965

ABANO (IT)
MIONI PEZZATO HOTEL

ICICLES
TRIANGLES

Lighting project for a thermal resort hotel. It consists, among other things, of chandeliers with icicles in different shapes and dimensions and a luminous column having solid triangular rods with a tapering structure. Some of these lamps are still *in situ*.

>
MIONI PEZZATO HOTEL
Luminous column with solid triangular rods.
Period photograph, c. 1965

>
MIONI PEZZATO HOTEL
Reception. Period photograph, c. 1965

1965 BARDONECCHIA (IT)
GRAND HOTEL RICKY

PENDANT

This Piedmont hotel was constructed between 1964 and 1965 after a design by the architect Amedeo Albertini. The Venini firm had the task of supplying pendant lamps of different colours, with an elongated shape and cylindrical metal attachment.

GRAND HOTEL RICKY
Pendant lamps. Period photograph, 1965

1965 CERVIA (IT)
TOWN HALL

Lighting project for the municipal headquarters.

1965 KUWAIT CITY (KW)
GENERAL TRADING

Lighting project for a private company.

1965 MILAN (IT)
FIRENZE RESTAURANT

Lighting project for a restaurant.

1965 MILAN (IT)
SNIA VISCOSA

Lighting project for premises belonging to the historic company active in the area of artificial and synthetic fibres, textiles and the chemical sector.

1965 NAPOLI (IT)
GRAND HOTEL VESUVIO

Lighting project for hotel premises.

1965

NEW YORK (US)
SALON VIDAL SASSOON

TRIANGOLO

Designed by Gordon and Ursula Bowyer, the same architects who in 1963 worked on the London shop, Roger at Vidal Sassoon, the New York beauty salon was opened in June 1965. The shop was commissioned by Richard Salomon, the then Director and Chairman of the Lanvin-Charles of the Ritz. Here a chandelier of very large dimensions was proposed (h 400 cm) with solid triangular rods. Each single element is fixed to the ceiling with a metal cable.

>
SALON VIDAL SASSOON
Interior of the shop. Period photograph, mid-1960s

1965

PARIS (FR)
CRÉDIT INDUSTRIEL ET COMMERCIAL
DESIGN P. GAUTIER-DELAYE

RODS

In 1965 the Venini firm produced an enormous luminous band with coloured rods for the wall above the counters of the Crédit Industriel et Commercial of Paris. The project was implemented by Pierre Gautier-Delaye, an interior designer who frequently resorted to luminous solutions in order to mark out the passage-way from one floor to another. The wall lamp, 12 metres long, was also clearly visible to passers-by: the huge glass slabs used for the facade of the building enabled enjoyment of this installation also from outside.

>
CRÉDIT INDUSTRIEL ET COMMERCIAL
Detail of the luminous band with rods affixed to the ground floor (h 80 x 1200 cm). Period photograph, 1966

>
CRÉDIT INDUSTRIEL ET COMMERCIAL
Entrance side. Period photograph, 1966

>
CRÉDIT INDUSTRIEL ET COMMERCIAL
Maquette of the project proposed by Pierre Gautier-Delaye, Yves Bresson / Musée d'art moderne et contemporain de Saint Etienne Métropole © Adagp, Paris

>
HENRY À LA PENSÉE SHOP
Interior of the shop. Period photograph, 1960s

1965 PARIS (FR)

HENRY À LA PENSÉE SHOP

POLYHEDRONS

For the lighting of the haute couture shop, Henry à la Pensée, a series of round-based ceiling lamps (h 30 cm, Ø 200 cm) was used with polyhedrons of different colours arranged in alternating bands.

1965 REGGIO CALABRIA (IT)

BANCA D'ITALIA

Lighting project for the premises of a bank.

1965 ROME (IT)

CASA DI CURA MATER DEI

Lighting project for a healthcare facility.

1965 SINGAPORE (SG)

SENG UP ELECTRIC CO.

Lighting project for a private company.

1965 TURIN (IT)

GOBETTI THEATRE

Lighting project (1963-65) for a theatre building on the occasion of restoration after a design by the architect Ada Bursi.

1965 UDINE (IT)

BANCA MEDIOCREDITO

Lighting project for the premises of a bank.

1965 TREVISO (IT)

CONFEZIONI ALTA MODA SHOP

SQUARE RODS

For the retail space Confezioni Alta Moda of Treviso, the Venini firm produced a ceiling lamp (h 250 cm) with solid square rods, in three tiers and with a tapering structure.

>
CONFEZIONI ALTA MODA SHOP
Chandelier with solid square rods. Period photograph, c. 1965

1965-66 ANGOULÊME (FR)
MUNICIPAL THEATRE OF ANGOULÊME

POLYHEDRONS

Constructed in the second half of the 19th century (1866-70) after a design by Antoine Soudée, the theatre underwent various modernisation and restoration works in the course of the 20th century. One of these, carried out around the mid-1960s and finished in 1966, allowing for the return of shows on 5 May of the same year, saw the Venini firm intervene with the production of numerous polyhedron lamps for the lighting of the various areas. The project consisted of the implementation of various wall lamps, among which those in the entrance hall and the balconies giving over the stalls, and of pendant lamps such as the one with a circular plan in the entrance hall. At the centre of the painted ceiling of the main auditorium, a circular chandelier with coloured polyhedrons and a tapering structure was placed (h 100 cm, Ø 250 cm). In 1997 the building underwent renovation works leading to the removal of the luminaires. Some of these, among which the chandelier of the auditorium, were installed in the annexes of the Château des Ombrais in Saint-Projet-Saint-Constant, near to Angoulême.

>
MUNICIPAL THEATRE OF ANGOULÊME
Chandelier with coloured polyhedrons in the auditorium.
Period photograph, c. 1966

>
MUNICIPAL THEATRE OF ANGOULÊME
Chandelier and wall lamp with polyhedrons in the entrance hall.
Period photograph, c. 1966

>>
MUNICIPAL THEATRE OF ANGOULÊME
Chandelier and wall lamp with polyhedrons in the auditorium. Period photograph, c. 1966

1965-66 BARCELONA (ES)
ALCAZAR CINEMA

POLYHEDRONS

Lighting project (1965-66) for the interior areas of the historic Barcelona cinema belonging to the Balaña Group. The cinema was renovated after a design by Antoni and Tomas Bonamusa and reopened on 10 April 1966. For the stairwell, the Venini firm produced an enormous chandelier with polychrome polyhedrons (h max 700 cm, Ø 90 cm) with an elongated and slightly helical structure.

>
ALCAZAR CINEMA
Stairwell with the great polyhedron chandelier.
Period photograph, c. 1966

1965-66 ROME (IT)
BANCO DI ROMA

Lighting projects for some bank branches.

1966 AVEZZANO (IT)
PRINCIPE HOTEL

POLYHEDRONS

Lighting project for an Abruzzo hotel consisting of the supply of ceiling lamps and wall lamps with polyhedrons.

1966 CASTROCARO (IT)
CASTROCARO THERMAL BATHS

SOLID RODS
POLYHEDRONS

Having already been involved in work on this thermal resort hotel in the 1930s, the glassworks produced a series of lamps and chandeliers with modular elements such as polyhedrons and solid rods.

1966 GENOA (IT)
SANTA MARIA DELLE GRAZIE CHURCH

POLYHEDRONS

For the church of Santa Maria delle Grazie, in the Genovese quarter of Sampierdarena, the Venini firm produced a group of polyhedron pendant lamps, in three tiers and with a projecting central part. The lamps are still *in situ*.

1966 GODIASCO SALICE TERME (IT)
THERMAL BATHS

Lighting project for a spa establishment.

1966

MONTEGROTTO (IT)
BERTHA HOTEL

CHEERIO
PLATES
TOTEM

For the spa hotel of Montegrotto, modular systems were mainly used, such as for example the plates with patches of colour which were used to produce lamps for the walls and for the bright cupola over the entrance. For the breakfast room, totem modules were used to decorate the pillars. Cheerio lamps (no. 811.3, *Venini lighting catalogue,* 1969) were placed over the bar in the bar-room.

›
BERTHA HOTEL
Entrance. Period photograph, c. 1966

›
BERTHA HOTEL
Bar-room. Period photograph, c. 1966

1966
NUORO (IT)
BANCA D'ITALIA

Light installation for bank premises.

1966
PESCARA (IT)
FIAT

BRICOLE

The lighting project for the Pescara branch is documented by, among other things, a drawing dated 1966 of a pendant lamp with *bricole* [mooring posts]. The lamp (h 49 x 82 x 82 cm) has a square form and tapering structure.

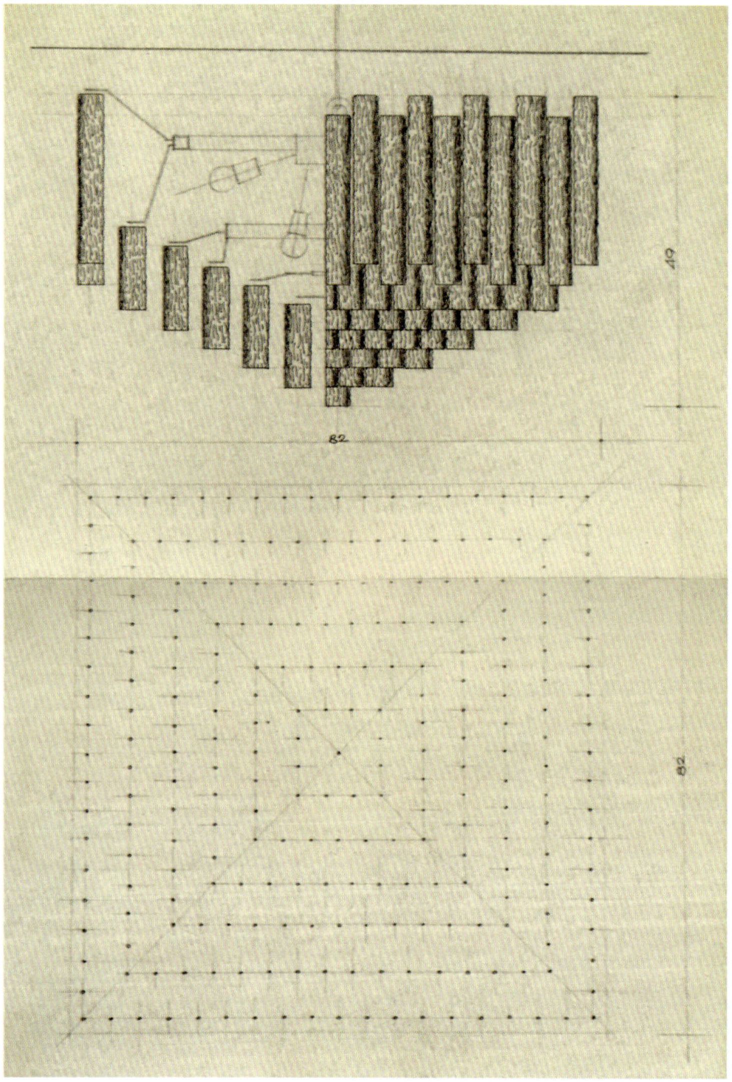

›
FIAT
Drawing for pendant lamp with *bricole* for Fiat, Pescara branch, 26 April 1966, AC

1966
PIACENZA (IT)
BANCO DI ROMA

Project for bank premises.

1966
ROME (IT)
CASSA DI RISPARMIO

Lighting project for bank premises.

1966
SCHWEINFURT (DE)
MUNICIPAL THEATRE
DESIGN T. KARRER

CEILING
PENDANT
ICICLES
DROP
TRIANGOLO

Built after a design by the architect Erich Schelling (1961-66), the theatre was opened on 1 December 1966. The design of the interior was developed by Trude Karrer, Schelling's wife, who turned to the Venini firm creation of lighting fixtures (hanging and ceiling lamps) and above all of two large lighting installations which she designed herself. Of interest is the 'free volume of light in the form of gigantic icicles' (*Venini illuminazione d'architettura*, 1970) located in the foyer of the first floor in front of the staircase giving access to the hall and the mural by Karl Fred Dahmen. The lighting is an arrangement (max l 25 m, max h 3 m) using large (h 60 cm) modular elements in *cristallo* glass (h 60 cm) suspended in groups of seven. Also of great interest is the lighting installation in the auditorium which uses rods with drops at the extremities, of variable lengths, fixed to the ceiling by a metal structure. This composition (max l 20 m, max h 2.5 m), like that in the foyer, was created not just with aesthetics in mind but also acoustics. In the lounge furthermore numerous ceiling lights with square bases in *cristallo* glass were installed. The bar area, on the other hand, was lit with a series of lamps of a smaller size with solid triangular rods. The installations are still *in situ*.

»
MUNICIPAL THEATRE
Foyer with lighting installations having 'gigantic icicles'.
Period photograph, March 1967

>
MUNICIPAL THEATRE
Foyer with lighting installations having 'gigantic icicles'. Period photograph, March 1967

>>
MUNICIPAL THEATRE
Auditorium with lighting installation having drops. Period photograph, March 1967

1966 SIENA (IT)
MONTE DEI PASCHI DI SIENA

Lighting project for bank premises.

1966 TERNI (IT)
CASSA DI RISPARMIO

Lighting project carried out during the extension of the historic headquarters of Palazzo Montani Leoni.

1966 VENICE (IT)
SALONE CAROL'S
DESIGN FT. ZUCCHERI

TROFEI

The lighting project for the Salone Carol's of Venice consisted in the production of a series of ceiling lights in *stracciato* glass with ribbing in relief, after a design by Toni Zuccheri. The lamps correspond to model no. 807.2 of the Trofei series (*Venini lighting catalogue*, 1966)

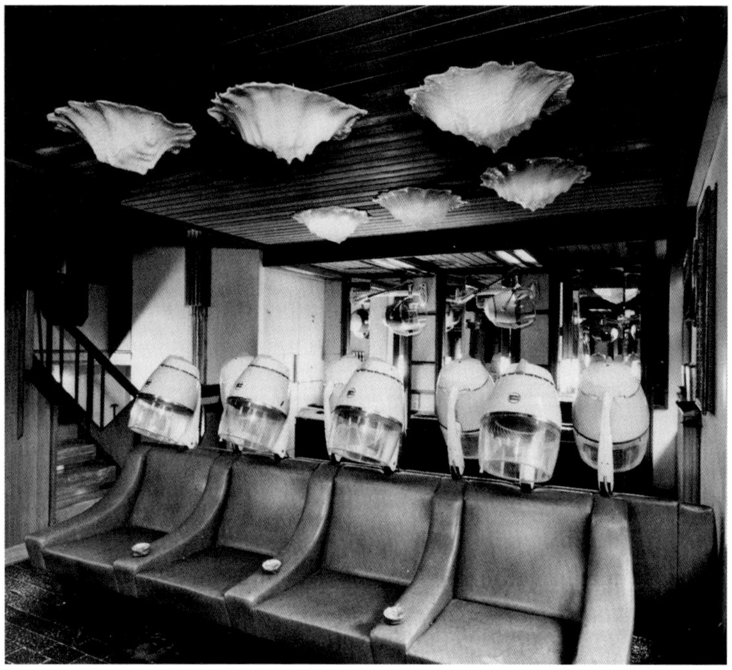

>
SALONE CAROL'S
View of the salon. Period photograph, c. 1966

1966-67 ABANO (IT)
RITZ HOTEL

Lighting project for the hotel and thermal resort complex opened in 1967.

1966-68 TURIN (IT)
RAI DIRECTORATE, VIA CERNAIA

CHEERIO

Lighting project for the new premises of the RAI offices, designed by Aldo Morbelli and Domenico Morelli, the construction of which we owe to the latter of these two as, in the meantime, Aldo Morbelli had died. A design dated October 1966 documents Morelli's intention to use the plates of the Cheerio series for the creation of some of the lights.

1967 CROTONE (IT)
BANCA POPOLARE COOPERATIVA

Lighting project for bank premises designed by the architect Giorgio Volpato.

1967 KUWAIT CITY (KW)
AL ARZ CO.

Lighting project for a private company.

1967 LA VALLETTA (MT)
KURSAAL

Lighting project for a tourist facility.

1967 MESTRE, VENICE (IT)
URBAN POLICE CORPS

Lighting project for the local police station.

1967

MILAN (IT)

MONTE DEI PASCHI DI SIENA

POLYHEDRONS

In the renovation of the premises of the Monte dei Paschi di Siena in via Santa Margherita right in the centre of Milan (opened in June 1967), the architect Pietro Portaluppi adopted a modular polyhedron system. Large circular ceiling lighting with polyhedrons in *cristallo* glass positioned both in the entrance hall and on the street side (a line of six) and in the mezzanine above the access stairway (two). This lighting system has since been removed.

>
MONTE DEI PASCHI DI SIENA
Polyhedron ceiling lights in the lobby on the street side (h 40 cm, Ø 180 cm). Period photograph, 1967

1967

NEW YORK (US)

SPERRY & HUTCHINSON GREEN STAMPS

POLYHEDRONS

Lighting project for the executive canteen of Sperry & Hutchinson Green Stamps in New York. Polyhedron ceiling lights with ring.

>
SPERRY & HUTCHINSON GREEN STAMPS
Executive canteen. Period photograph, 1960s

1967

PARIS (FR)
AMERICAN EMBASSY

RODS

The project for the American Embassy in Paris consisted mainly of the creation of a group of chandeliers with coloured rods (h 120 cm, Ø 60 cm) positioned in the columned portico. The fixtures are three-tiered and with a downward tapering shape.

›
AMERICAN EMBASSY
Portico with chandeliers having coloured rods.
Period photograph, c. 1967

›
AMERICAN EMBASSY
Chandelier with coloured rods. Period photograph, c. 1967

1967

ROME (IT)
FLEMING HOTEL

Lighting project for hotel premises.

1967

ROME (IT)
BANCA FEDERALE DI AMATRICE

Lighting project for the bank's premises.

1967

ROME (IT)
BANCA NAZIONALE DEL LAVORO

Lighting project for bank premises.

1967

ROME (IT)
EDILIZIA MILVIA

Lighting project for a private company.

1967

ROME (IT)
LATERAN MAJOR SEMINARY

POLYHEDRONS

The project consists of the lighting of the seminary chapel designed by the architect Egisto Ercadi. Polyhedron pendant lamps in *cristallo* glass and amber glass were produced, arranged in alternate lines with a lozenge-shaped motif evoking the ribbing of the ceiling. The lighting fixtures are characterised by their original upside-down mushroom shape, obtained with modular components like the polyhedrons. The lamps have recently been removed.

>
LATERAN MAJOR SEMINARY
Polyhedron lamps in the chapel. Period photograph, c. 1967

1967

VENICE (IT)
VENINI SHOP

STRACCIATO GLASS

In the shop in calle XX marzo an imposing retroilluminated false ceiling was installed with undulating sheets (90 x 25 cm each) in *stracciato* glass, a technique studied and used by Toni Zuccheri.

>
VENINI SHOP
Interior of the shop. Period photograph, c. 1967

1967-72 ROME (IT)

LEONARDO DA VINCI HOTEL

DESIGN A. LAPADULA

RODS
ESPRIT

The Leonardo da Vinci Hotel (1963-74), belonging to the Jolly Hotels chain, was designed by the architect Attilio Lapadula. For this building, the Venini firm produced several Esprit chandeliers for the hall adjacent to the entrance, as well as rod lighting fixtures in different shapes and colours for the breakfast room and ballroom.

›
LEONARDO DA VINCI HOTEL
Hall adjacent to the entrance with Esprit chandeliers 'in *cristallo* with a yellow parch 60 cm in diameter', in *Venini*, 1985.

1968 BAIA DOMIZIA, SESSA AURUNCA (IT)

VILLAGGIO DEGLI SVEDESI

Lighting project for the Caserta tourist village opened in 1968 and managed by the Società Riva del Sole of Castiglione della Pescaia.

1968 BARI (IT)

PALACE HOTEL

Lighting project for a hotel establishment.

1968 FOGGIA (IT)

BANCA D'ITALIA

Lighting project for bank premises.

1968 LONDRA (GB)

BRITISH PETROLEUM

TRIANGOLO

For the board-room of the English company operating in the energy sector, the Venini firm created a series of lamps (h 75 cm, Ø 90 cm) with solid triangular rods.

›
BRITISH PETROLEUM
Lamps with solid triangular rods. Period photograph, c. 1968

1968

MADRID (ES)
MORRISON CAFETERIA

POLYHEDRONS

For the Madrid venue the Venini firm created an enormous polyhedron ceiling 'in a free-fall form' (*Venini illuminazione d'architettura 1974*, 1973) above the bar and part of the restaurant.

>
MORRISON CAFETERIA
Polyhedron lighting installation (h 20 cm each). Period photograph, c. 1968

1968

MILAN (IT)
'MARGHERITA' LINGERIE STORE

ICICLES

For the new premises of the legendary Milanese lingerie store, Margherita, opened in 1924 as an artisan corsetry and belonging to the Corti family, the Venini firm produced original 'free-form chandeliers' (*Venini illuminazione d'architettura*, 1970) using a modular system of icicles. In particular, in the area dedicated to the Arredamenti Borsani s.n.c. firm, a long pendant lamp with undulations was positioned in which the modules in *cristallo* glass with an amethyst nucleus are suspended with steel cables. The design of the lights should probably be attributed to the architect and designer Osvaldo Borsani.

>
'MARGHERITA' LINGERIE STORE
Interior with icicle lamps. Period photograph, 1968

1968

MONTECATINI (IT)
EXCELSIOR THERMAL BATHS, EXTENSION
DESIGN G. GIGLI

CUBES

Between 1964 and 1968 the Excelsior thermal baths were extended with the erecting of a building which partially replaced the neo-Renaissance style complex constructed in the first decade of the century. The project coordinator was Sergio Brusa Pasquè who headed a group of different architects, among whom also Guido Gigli. It is to the latter that we owe the arrangement of the large ground-floor area dedicated to the mineral-water treatments, where the glassworks created structured luminous ceiling (15 x 15 m, max h 250 cm). For the production of this structure, cubes of coloured glass (*cristallo*, *talpa chiaro*, *pagliesco*, amethyst, light blue) were used which were superimposed (from two to nine components) following a predetermined design and interconnected by means of an appropriate coupling.

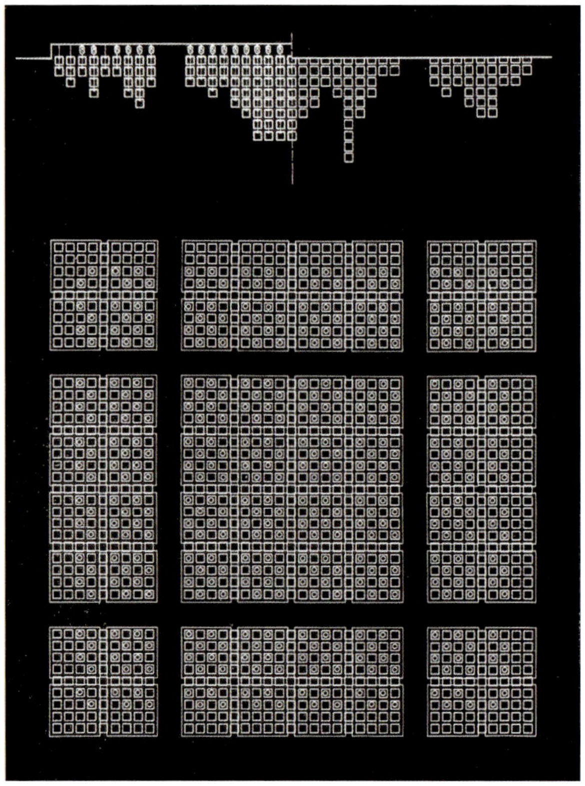

>
EXCELSIOR THERMAL BATHS, EXTENSION
Cross section, overview and plan of the lighting installation, in *Venini illuminazione d'architettura*, [1978]

>
EXCELSIOR THERMAL BATHS, EXTENSION
Luminous ceiling with coloured cubes. Period photograph, c. 1968

1968

NAPLES (IT)
ISTITUTO BANCARIO ITALIANO

Lighting project for the Neapolitan bank headquarters after a design by the architect Cesare Pascoletti.

1968

NEW ORLEANS (US)
INTERNATIONAL EXHIBITION FACILITY

RODS

The exhibition and conference centre, International Exhibition Facility (later Rivergate Convention Center), was designed between 1964 and 1968 by the architectural firm Curtis & Davis. The Venini firm created a large-scale installation for the building. This lighting scheme (max h 150 cm, max w 750 cm) consisted of the formation, according to a precise design, of seven groups each having a corresponding number of lamps. Every individual light source is composed of rods and characterised by a cylindrical body with its lower extremity inclined at 45 degrees. The building was demolished in 1995.

>
INTERNATIONAL EXHIBITION FACILITY
Room with Venini lighting installation. Period photograph, c. 1968

>>
INTERNATIONAL EXHIBITION FACILITY
Chandelier unit at the assembly stage. Period photograph, c. 1968

>>
INTERNATIONAL EXHIBITION FACILITY
Plan of lighting installation, in *Venini. Systems*, n.d.

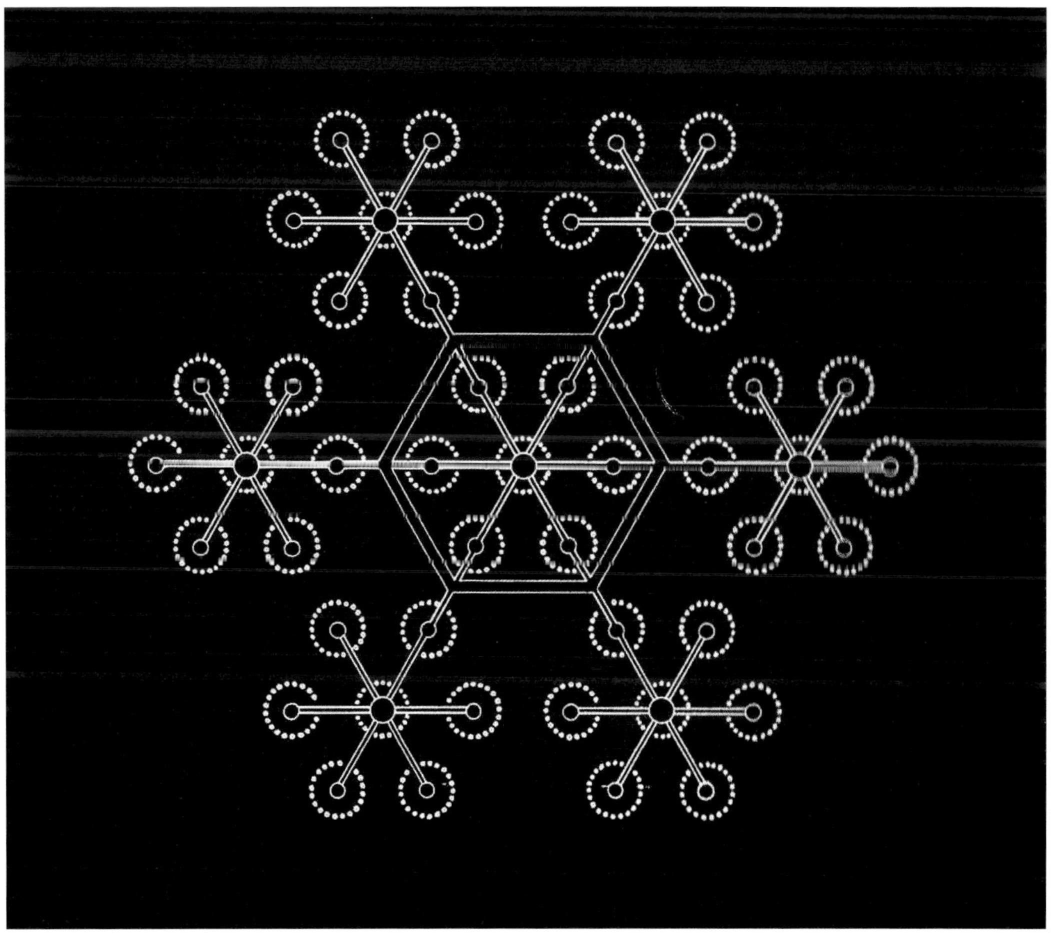

1968

NEW YORK (US)
BURLINGTON INDUSTRIES

DROPS

Lighting project for the New York textile company headquarters. This consists, among other things, in the creation of a chandelier with blown-glass drops (h 120 cm, Ø 90 cm) for the entrance hall of the building.

>
BURLINGTON INDUSTRIES
Chandelier with blown-glass drops. Period photograph, late 1960s

1968

NEW YORK (US)
ZION-EPHRAIM CONGREGATION

POLYHEDRONS

Lighting project for the New York headquarters of a religious institution. This consisted of a series of circular ceiling lamps with *cristallo* polyhedrons (h 150 cm, Ø 240 cm), each with three tiers and a downward tapering outline.

>
ZION-EPHRAIM CONGREGATION
Ceiling lamp with *cristallo* polyhedrons. Period photograph, c. 1968

1968

PALERMO (IT)
BANCA D'ITALIA

Lighting project for bank premises.

1968

ROME (IT)
PALAZZO MONTECITORIO

Lighting project for areas of the official headquarters of the Camera dei Deputati [Chamber of Deputies] and the Italian Parliament.

1968

SAN JUAN (PR)
CARIB HILTON HOTEL

TRIANGLE

Lighting project for one of the hotels of the Hilton chain. It concerned, among other things, a series of large circular ceiling lights with solid triangular rods (h 60 cm, Ø 300 cm), each having three tiers and a downward tapering outline.

›
CARIB HILTON HOTEL
Ceiling lamps with solid triangular rods. Period photograph, late 1960s

1968

TURIN (IT)
LA STAMPA

ON THE CEILING

The work of the Venini firm for the headquarters of the Turin newspaper is documented by, among other things, a drawing from 1968 representing a square-gridded ceiling with multicoloured corrugated elements.

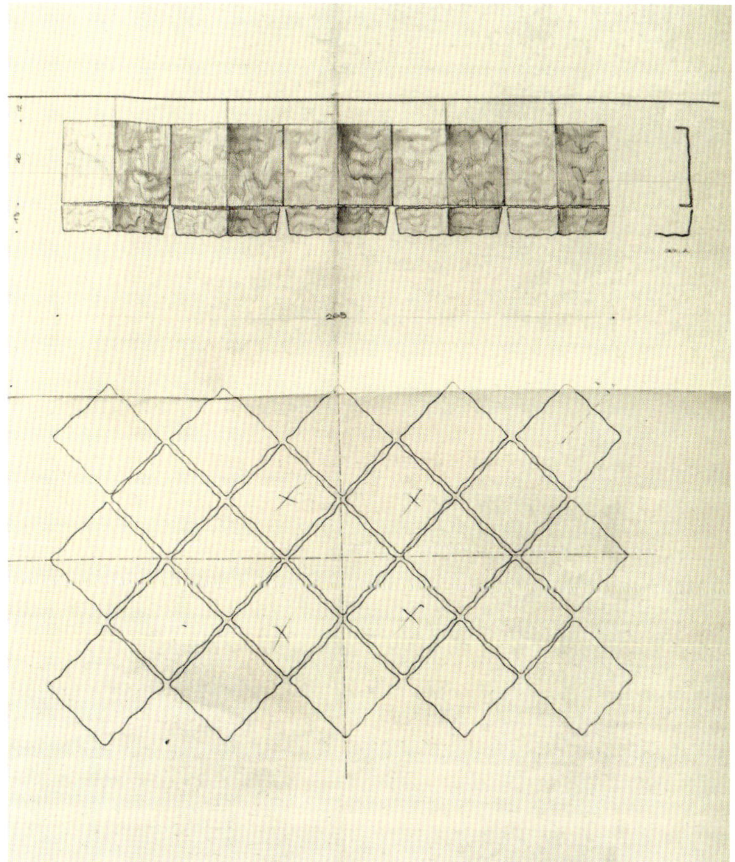

›
LA STAMPA
Drawing with squared ceiling for *La Stampa* of Turin, 24 April 1968, AC

1968 VENICE (IT)
BANCO DI SICILIA

Lighting project for bank premises.

1968 VENICE (IT)
PALAZZO RIO NOVO, ENEL HEADQUARTERS

Lighting project for the company with headquarters in the Rio Novo area, Venice.

1968-69 CALTANISSETTA (IT)
BANCA D'ITALIA

Lighting project for bank premises.

1968-69 CATANIA (IT)
CENTRAL PALACE HOTEL

CUBES
PLATES
TRIANGLE

For the bar of the Catania hotel, designed by the architect Giacomo Leone, the Venini firm created a ceiling composed of cubes of various colours, each with a base of 7 x 7 cm. To give movement to the surface 'cubes' of three different heights were designed and positioned in an alternating way. Ceiling chandeliers were also created with plates, alternating with chandeliers, also on the ceiling, with solid triangular rods, for the large lounge beside the bar.

»
CENTRAL PALACE HOTEL
Hotel bar. Period photograph, c. 1968

1969

SAN MARINO CITY (SM)
PALAZZO DEI CONGRESSI

ICICLES
POLYHEDRONS

The Venini project for the building, known internationally as a venue for cultural and conference activities, consisted in the production of a series of ceiling and pendant lamps using modular elements such as polyhedrons and icicles. The polyhedrons were used for the creation of bicoloured ceiling lights with concentric circles. The icicles, in *cristallo* glass with a nucleus of amethyst glass, were used for the pendant lamps having a downward tapering outline.

›
PALAZZO DEI CONGRESSI
Polyhedron ceiling lamps with concentric circles. Period photograph, c. 1969

1969

LONDON (GB)
STRAND PALACE HOTEL

DROPS
POLYHEDRONS

Lighting scheme for the London hotel restored following a project designed by Dennis Lennon & Partners. The work included, in particular, circular lights with polyhedrons and drop-like elements.

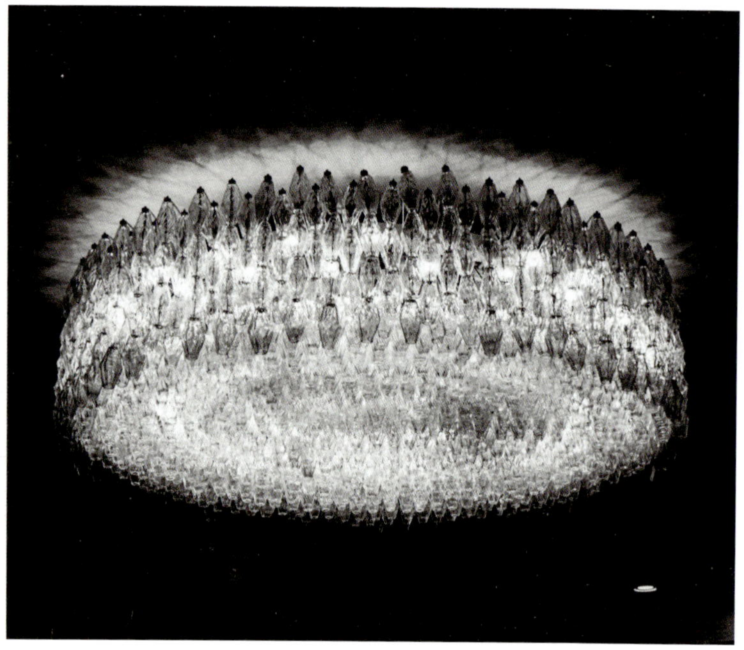

›
STRAND PALACE HOTEL
Polyhedron ceiling lamp. Period photograph, c. 1969

1969

VERONA (IT)
STATE RAILWAY DEPARTMENT

ICICLES

Lighting project for the Verona headquarters of the Compartimento delle Ferrovie dello Stato [State Railway Department], designed by the architect Bruno Ronca. As documented by the presence of a tracing in the Venini archives, the glassworks produced a set of lamps with bichrome icicles.

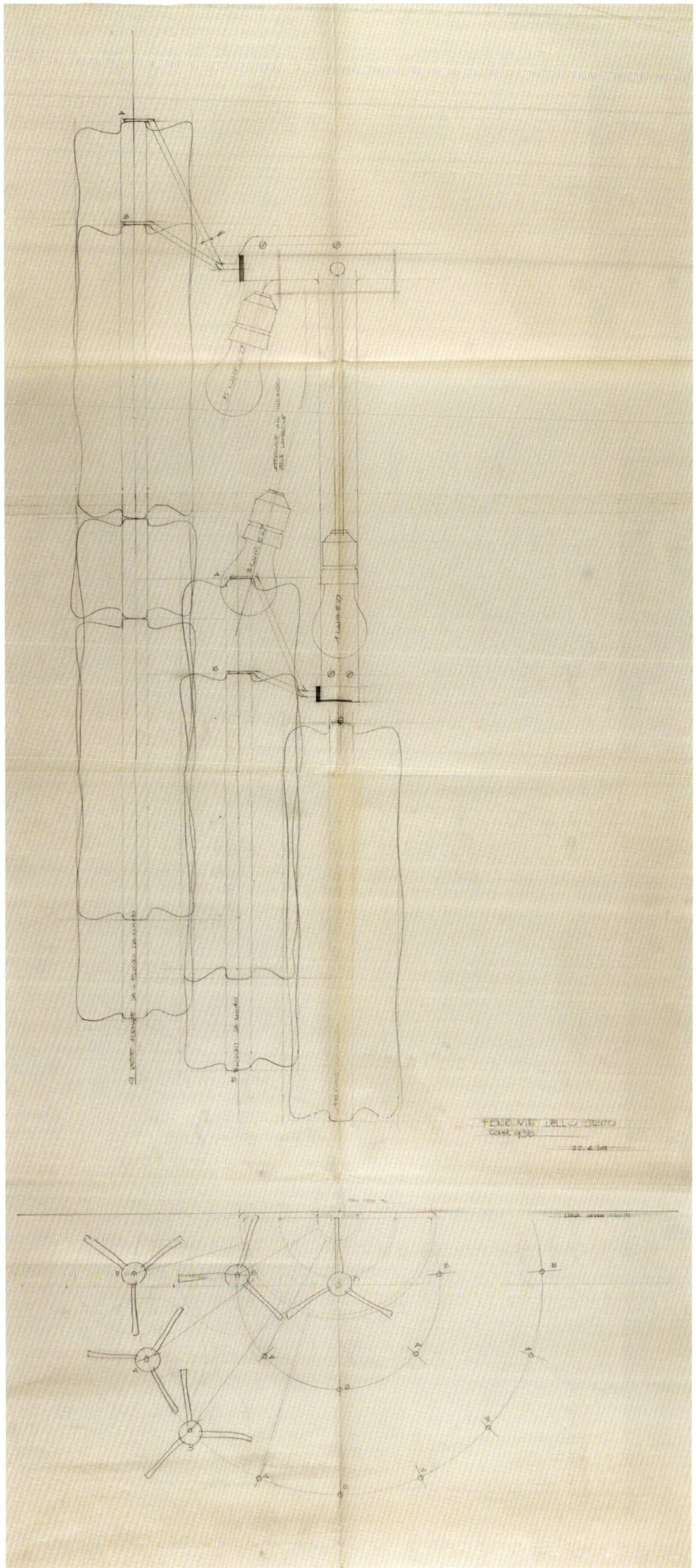

>
STATE RAILWAY DEPARTMENT
Conference room. Period photograph, c. 1969

>
STATE RAILWAY DEPARTMENT
Entrance. Period photograph, c. 1969

>
STATE RAILWAY DEPARTMENT
Design for a wall lamp with icicle elements called 'helicons' for the Ferrovie dello Stato, 22 April 1969

1960s

LONDON (GB)
BALLY SHOP

DROPS

For the London shop, designed by the architect Dennis Lennon, the Venini firm produced a chandelier of blown glass drops.

>
BALLY SHOP
Chandelier of blown glass drops. Period photograph, 1960s

1960s

LONDON (GB)
JAEGER SHOP

POLYHEDRONS

For the London shop, designed by the English architect Dennis Lennon, the Venini firm produced a polyhedron ceiling light.

>
JAEGER SHOP
Polyhedron ceiling light. Period photograph, 1960s

1960s

LOS ANGELES (US)
LOS ANGELES COUNTY MUSEUM OF ART

POLYHEDRONS

Lighting project for the Los Angeles County Museum of Art (now LACMA) consisting, among other things, of a series of ceiling lamps with circular polyhedron bases and a slightly tapering design.

>
LOS ANGELES COUNTY MUSEUM OF ART
Polyhedron ceiling lamp. Period photograph, 1960s

1960s

ORLANDO (US)
FIRST FEDERAL SAVINGS AND LOAN ASSOCIATION OF LINCOLNTON

POLYHEDRONS

For the reception area of the First Federal Savings and Loan Association of Lincolnton, with head-quarters in Orlando, a polyhedron chandelier was commissioned.

>
FIRST FEDERAL SAVINGS AND LOAN ASSOCIATION OF LINCOLNTON
Reception area and counters. Period photograph, 1960s

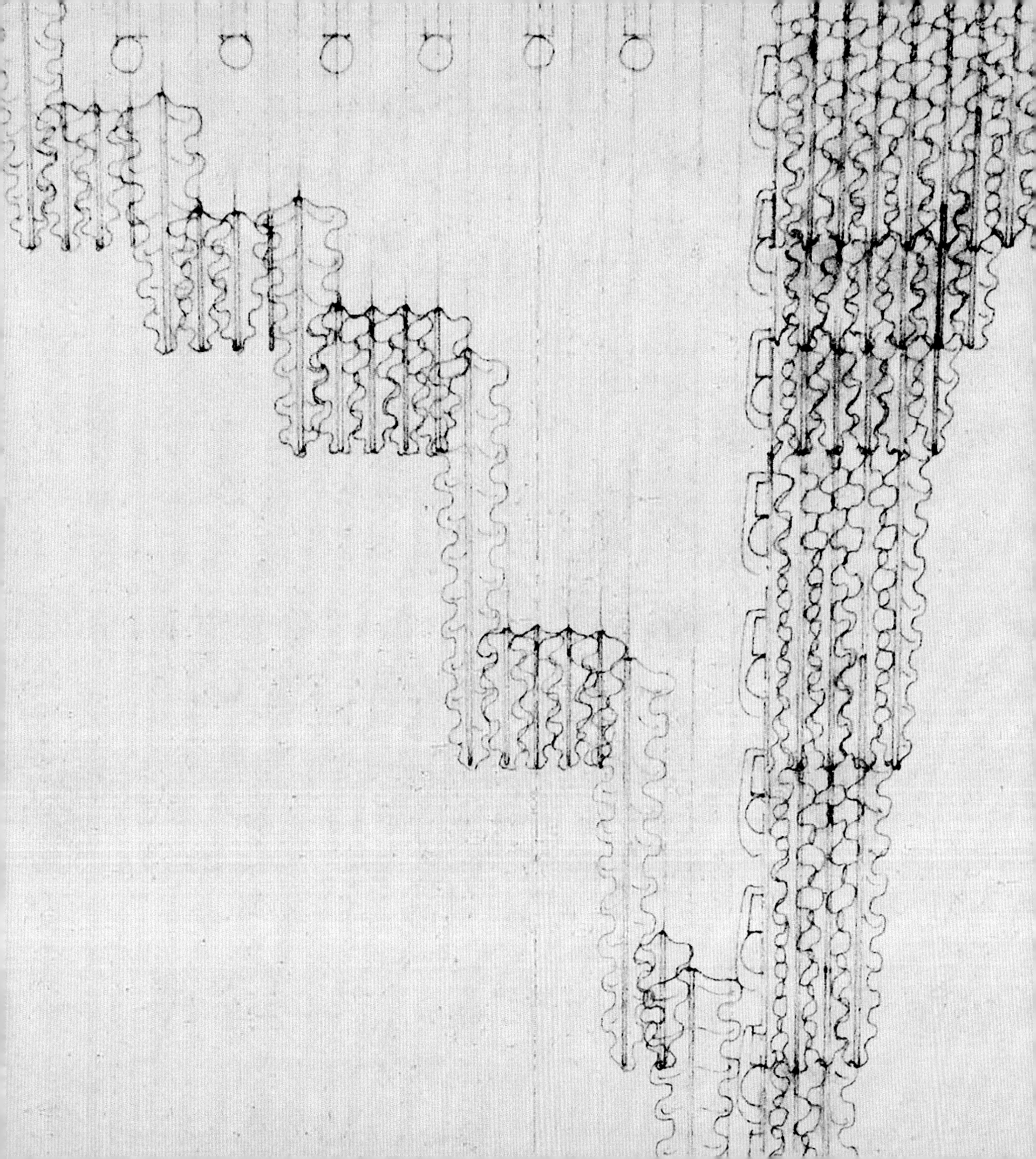

1970s

1970

CENTO (IT)
CASSA DI RISPARMIO DI CENTO

PANELS
PATCHWORK
TRILOBO

For the premises of the financial institution, constructed after a design by the architect Manfredo Vaccari Giglioli, the glassworks was involved in the creation of a complex ceiling light structure for the large public hall, with square panels (45 x 45 cm) having a protrunding part with an oval-shaped cross-section. The panels are in *cristallo* glass and in some cases include patches of teal and *pagliesco* colour at the embossing. In the same area there is also a luminous pillar clad with moulded solid panels (with C and L profiles), produced in *cristallo* glass, with teal and *pagliesco* patches and stone-type finishing, which are mounted on a metallic frame. The light sources are arranged at the base and the summit (*Venini illuminazione d'architettura 1974*, 1973). Again in the public hall two wall compositions (max w 650 cm, max h 150 cm) were positioned, consisting of 42 patchwork-type modular units (no. 952), designed by Ludovico Diaz de Santillana and produced in the A-colour variant (*cristallo*, *pagliesco*, teal). In the stairwell, a large lamp was installed with solid *trilobo cristallo* and light-blue rods having a circular cross-section and a helicoidal structure (h 350 cm, max Ø 80 cm).

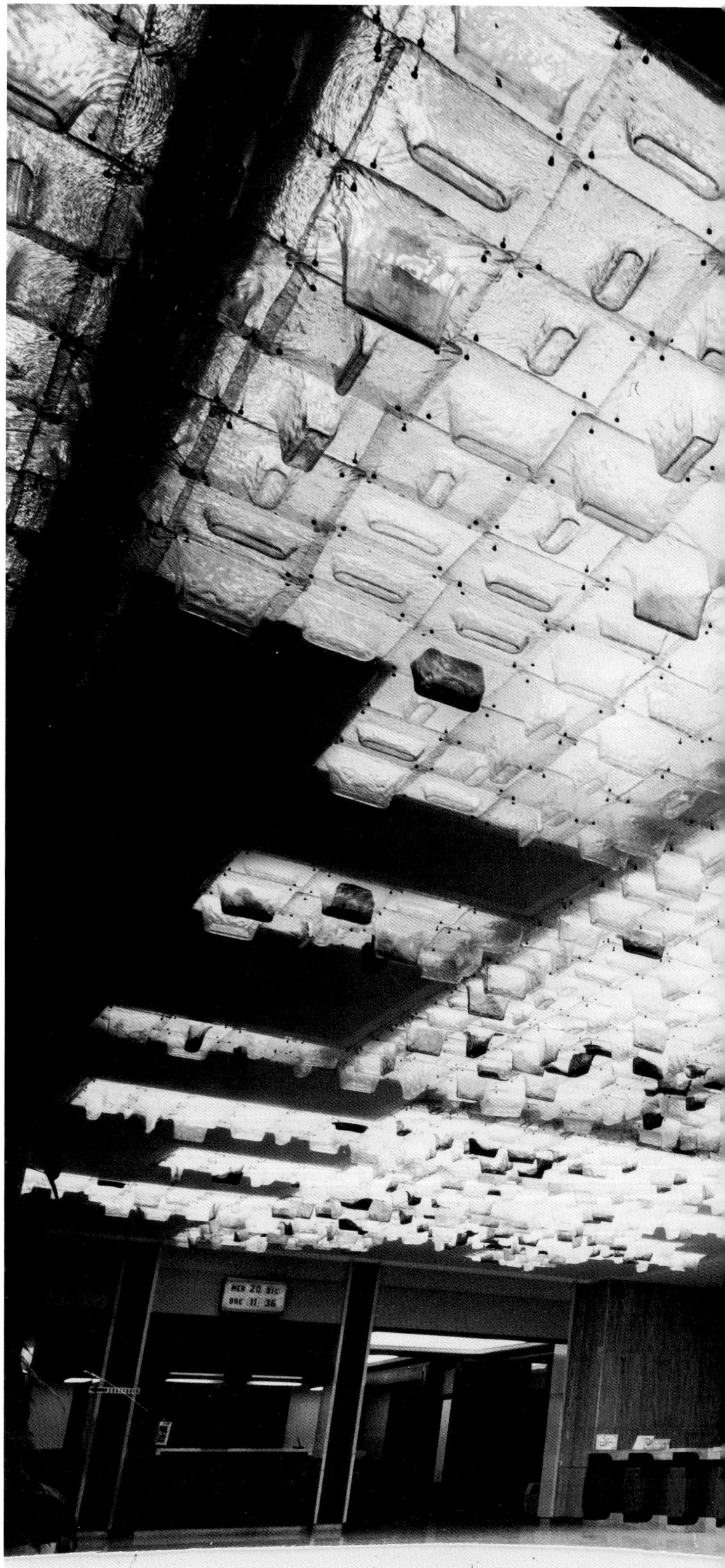

\>
CASSA DI RISPARMIO DI CENTO
Ceiling with moulded panels in the public hall.
Period photograph, c. 1970

>
CASSA DI RISPARMIO DI CENTO
Composition with patchwork elements in the public hall.
Period photograph, c. 1970

›
CASSA DI RISPARMIO DI CENTO
Luminous pillar in the public hall. Period photograph, c. 1970

›
CASSA DI RISPARMIO DI CENTO
Lamp with *trilobo* solid rods in the stairwell. Period photograph, c. 1970

1970

NICE (FR)
VILLA ARSON, ÉCOLE INTERNATIONALE D'ART
DESIGN G. FIDON

POLYHEDRONS

The Villa Arson complex, extending over about two hectares on the Barthélemy hillside and consisting of a series of buildings, among which the main building incorporating the homonymous 18th-century villa, was built in the later 1960s-early 1970s to be the home of the École International d'Art intended not only as a scholastic institute, but also as an Art Centre for International Encounters, a place for exchanges with exhibition areas, accommodation and laboratories for visiting artists. The architectural and landscaping project was developed by the architect Michel Marot, who enrolled a series of collaborators, among whom Georges Fidon. The latter was involved, in particular, in determining the lighting installation to be created by the Venini firm which would be positioned near the monumental cement staircase spanning the main building *(Venini illuminazione d'architettura 1974*, 1973). It consists of a long ceiling light (25 m) with polyhedrons of 35 cm in height, 'in shades of amethyst and *pagliesco cristallo*', arranged to form a sort of succession of clusters which according to Marot evoked a sparkling river or milky way above the rectilinear stairs (Marantz 2021). Beside it an elongated pyramidal polyhedron structure was also installed extended into the adjacent, double-height space. Already in the 1970s the installation was removed, being considered too decorative.

>
VILLA ARSON, ÉCOLE INTERNATIONALE D'ART
Lighting installation beside the stairs in the main building. Period photograph, February 1971

>>
VILLA ARSON, ÉCOLE INTERNATIONALE D'ART
Lighting installation above the stairs in the main building. South-view. Period photograph, February 1971

1970

ROME (IT)
BANCO DI SANTO SPIRITO
DESIGN T. ZUCCHERI

TROFEI

The project for the premises of the Banco di Santo Spirito Directorate General, in piazza del Parlamento (organisation after a design by Giulio Sterbini and Tommaso Breccia Fratadocchi) consisted of the creation of a 'glass curtain made up of conical elements in *cristallo-lattimo "stracciato"*, diameter 50/60 cm' (*Venini*, 1985). The installation, with an almost circular plan (Ø m 10), was produced by superimposing numerous umbelliform elements (model no. 807.4, Trofei series, *Venini lighting catalogue*, 1966), at the centre of which the extremities of the metal support hooks are visible, with the characteristic spiral motif.

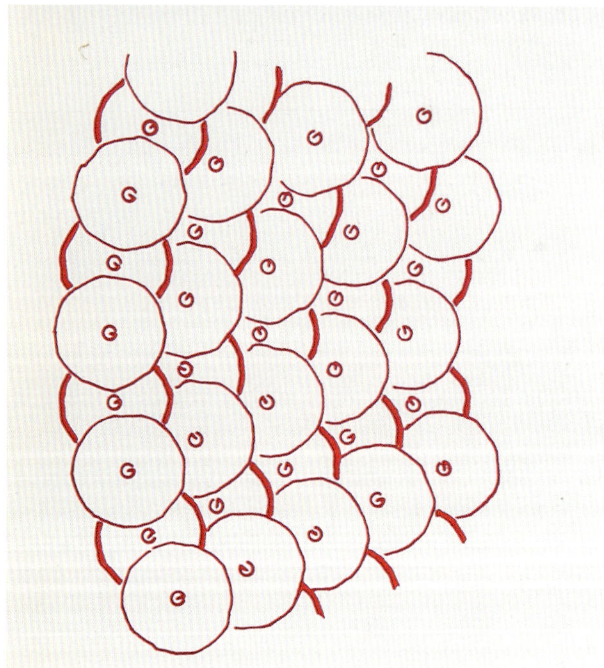

>
BANCO DI SANTO SPIRITO
Curtain with elements in *stracciato* glass. Period photograph, c. 1970

>
BANCO DI SANTO SPIRITO
Sketch of the curtain in *Venini*, 1985

>>
BANCO DI SANTO SPIRITO
Curtain with elements in *stracciato* glass, detail.
Period photograph, c. 1970

1970

ROSEVILLE (US)
HAR-MAR TWIN THEATRE

POLYHEDRONS

For the entrance hall of the cinema-theatre belonging to the Har-Mar shopping centre complex in Minnesota, the Venini firm created three large polyhedron pendant lamps. The lamps have a square base and a pyramidal structure (h 244 cm, 234 x 234 cm).

›
HAR-MAR TWIN THEATRE
Polyhedron lamp. Photo, courtesy Wright

1970-71

VENICE (IT)
MEDIOCREDITO DELLE VENEZIE

DESIGN G. BELLAVITIS, N. VALLE

A PARETE
CEILING
PLATES
TRIANGOLO

For the Venetian bank, with premises in Palazzo Giustinian Pesaro, restored in 1969 after the design of Giorgio Bellavitis and Nani Valle, the glassworks carried out a series of lighting projects documented in the booklet *Venini lavori di illuminazione 1973*, 1972. In the board room an installation was positioned composed of solid triangular rods of various lengths kept in place by steel cables and intended to form a definite design. For this light fixture, the Venini archives contain a drawing dated 9 July 1970. For the stairwell, a ceiling light composed of square panels of the 'quilt' type (no. 825.00, max 45 x 45 cm) in *cristallo* glass and with a teal-coloured band was installed; and in addition there were wall lights in *lattimo* and *cristallo*. For the entrance hall a succession of ceiling lamps were installed Car 70 (no. 820.11, Ø 60 cm).

›
MEDIOCREDITO DELLE VENEZIE
Design of the chandelier of the board room in *Venini lavori di illuminazione 1973*, 1972

››
MEDIOCREDITO DELLE VENEZIE
Board room. Period photograph, c. 1971

>
MEDIOCREDITO DELLE VENEZIE
Stairwell with ceiling installation and glass inset composed of modules of the 'quilt' type. Period photograph, c. 1971

>>
MEDIOCREDITO DELLE VENEZIE
Entrance hall. Period photograph, c. 1971

1971

NEW YORK (US)
SWISS CREDIT BANK

ESPRIT

For the Wall Street branch, a lighting installation was made (h 150 cm, 500 x 500 cm) composed of *cristallo* Esprit elements of variable lengths, from 30 to 90 cm. The composition, positioned in the entrance hall, was also visible to passers-by through the large windows of the entrance.

>
SWISS CREDIT BANK
Entrance hall. Period photograph, c. 1971

1971

SINGAPORE (SG)
THE MANDARIN SINGAPORE HOTEL
DESIGN A. ASHTON

PROFILED ELEMENTS

The Mandarin Singapore hotel (now the Hilton Singapore Orchard) was constructed during the 1960s and opened in the spring of 1971. The designer Don Ashton, who had already worked on The Mandarin of Hong Kong, took charge of the interior. The Venini firm was again present, with the installation of an imposing luminous fountain for the hall of the hotel. This was a square-based structure extending upwards for the entire height of the hall, inserting itself at the top into the ceiling with its golden vaults, while at the base it was surrounded by a series of flower boxes. The great pillar was covered in solid profiled elements cast in corroded *cristallo* glass and mounted on a stainless steel frame. The indirect lighting, above and below, combined with a veil of falling water, together created a very spectacular effect.

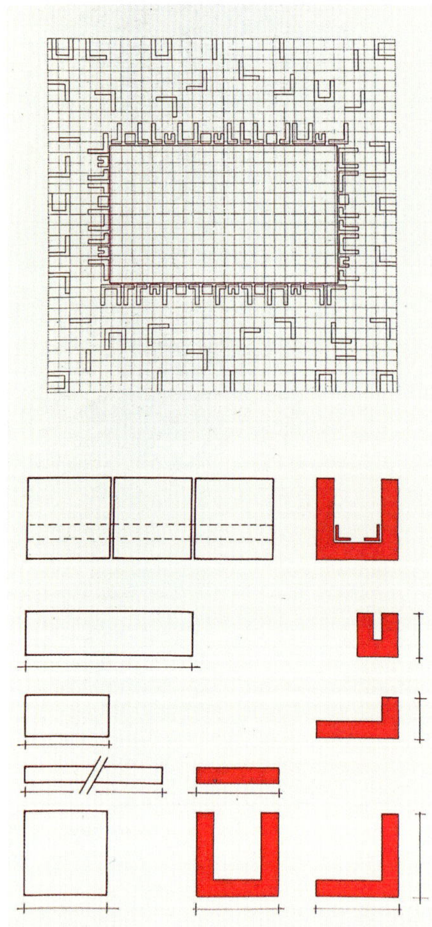

>
THE MANDARIN SINGAPORE HOTEL
Design of the form and arrangement of the sections used for the light installation in *Venini*, 1985

>>
THE MANDARIN SINGAPORE HOTEL
Enormous chandelier (h 900 x 250 x 250 cm) for the entrance. Period photograph, 1971

1971-72 TRIESTE (IT)
REGIONAL COUNCIL BUILDING
DESIGN G. BELLAVITIS, N. VALLE

PENDANT
BRICOLE
CANNE
PLATES

The Trieste building was designed between 1971 and 1972 by the architects Umberto Nordio and Aldo Cervi, while the duo Nani Valle and Giorgio Bellavitis were responsible for furnishing various areas, such as some of the meeting rooms. For the lighting of these rooms, Valle and Bellavitis chose module-based Venini products such as glass with rods, *bricole* and plates. The original solution used for the meeting rooms of the President's office was specifically designed by the architects. This is an oval-based installation composed of a succession of amphora-style pendant lamps, in dark-blue and smoked glass, fixed to a system of concentric rails.

>
REGIONAL COUNCIL BUILDING
Installation in the boardroom. Photo © Fabian Zannini, 2014

>
REGIONAL COUNCIL BUILDING
Installation in the legislative commissions' room, referred to as the 'sala verde' (green room). Photo © Fabian Zannini, 2014

>
REGIONAL COUNCIL BUILDING
Installation in the meeting room of the President's Office, detail. Photo © Fabian Zannini, 2014

>>
REGIONAL COUNCIL BUILDING
Installation in the meeting room of the President's Office. Photo © Fabian Zannini, 2014

1971
1975

SINGAPORE (SG)
SHANGRI-LA HOTEL

PENDANT
ESPRIT

This Singapore hotel, with an interior designed by Bent Severin, was opened in April 1971. Among the projects carried out by the glassworks, of particular note are the large chandeliers for the entrance hall. They are a series of pendant lamps, with a helical metal structure (h 450 cm, Ø 120 cm) from which hang bellflowers and spheres in *cristallo* glass with light-blue patches. In the banqueting hall, at a later time (1975), a group of *cristallo* Esprit chandeliers (Ø 60 cm, *Venini*, 1985) was placed.

>
SHANGRI-LA HOTEL
Banquet room. Period photograph, c. 1975

>
SHANGRI-LA HOTEL
Entrance hall. Period photograph, c. 1971

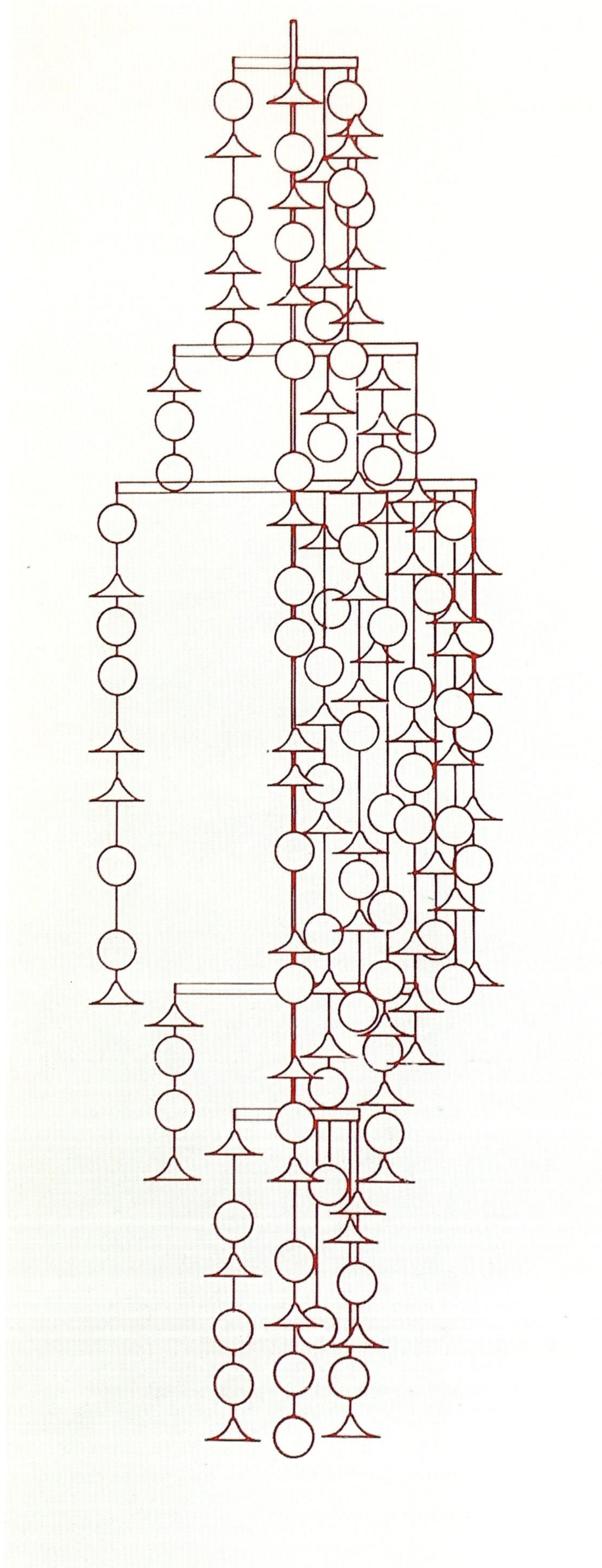

>
SHANGRI-LA HOTEL
Design of the pendant lamp in the entrance hall in *Venini*, 1985

1972

BONN (DE)
BRISTOL HOTEL

POLYHEDRONS

For the German hotel, opened in 1972, after a design by the architect Ernst van Dorp, a series of square-based luminous insets with *cristallo* and amethyst polyhedrons was installed in the ceiling. Each structure is slightly downward tapering in the central section.

1972

FRANKFURT (DE)
FRANKFURT AIRPORT

CALZA

On the occasion of the extension of the airport, on which work ended only a few months before the beginning of the Munich Olympics of 1972, for one of the restaurants the glassworks produced a series of chandeliers (h 180 cm, Ø 80 cm) with *calza* modular elements in *cristallo* glass and with a downward tapering structure. This is one of the first examples of the use of this modular element.

FRANKFURT AIRPORT
Restaurant. Period photograph, c. 1972

1972

SINGAPORE (SG)
COCKPIT HOTEL

DROPS

For this Singapore hotel, designed by the architect Yang Tai Tye and opened in 1972 as an extension of the historic premises, the glassworks produced lamps with blown-glass drops, among which particularly the large chandelier for the stairwell of the hall (h 400 cm, Ø 80 cm).

COCKPIT HOTEL
Stairwell. Period photograph, c. 1972

1972

TORREMOLINOS (ES)
CONFERENCE AND EXHIBITION CENTRE

DROPS

For the cultural centre, the Venini firm produced a chandelier with very large *cristallo* drops (h 600 cm, max Ø 90 cm). The luminaire, still *in situ*, is inserted into a circular false ceiling which functions as a focal point for this enormous hall situated at the entrance to the building.

>
CONFERENCE AND EXHIBITION CENTRE
Entrance, chandelier detail. Period photograph, 1972

>
CONFERENCE AND EXHIBITION CENTRE
Entrance. Period photograph, 1972

1972

VENICE (IT)
CASSA DI RISPARMIO DI VENEZIA

CANNE
CANNE PIENE
PARALLELEPIPEDI
PLATES

In the headquarters of the Cassa di Risparmio, situated in Campo Manin and designed by Pier Luigi Nervi and Angelo Scattolin (1970-72), the glassworks intervened both in the great hall for the public and in the corridors, and also in the offices on the upper floors. In the hall, glass plates were installed made of *cristallo* and *talpa* bamboo glass, partially superimposed to form a fan and inserted into the scenic cover with a cement-based grid designed by Nervi. In the transition area between the ground and upper floors a luminous frame was positioned together with some wall lights in bamboo *cristallo* glass. On the first floor landing there was a circular-based ceiling lamp made of *cristallo* plates and plates in corrugated glass with a *cristallo* and *talpa* V-shaped profile. On the second and third floors, there were ceiling lamps with patterned glass of the 'stone' type in *cristallo* glass with a yellow patch. The latter arrangements were also to be found in the library, office and Chairman's lounge. A pendant lamp with parallelepiped elements having a square cross-section was to be found in the board room. In the designing of the lighting arrangements the architect Antonio Foscari was also involved (*Venini lavori di illuminazione 1973*, 1972). Some of these luminaires are still *in situ*.

>
CASSA DI RISPARMIO DI VENEZIA
Chairman's office. Period photograph, mid-1970s

<<
CASSA DI RISPARMIO DI VENEZIA
Public hall. Photo Archivio Storico Intesa Sanpaolo, photographic section, Carive archives

1973

GENOA (IT)
DORIC SHIP

POLYHEDRONS

Lighting project for the ship belonging to the Home Lines Company. The contribution of the glassworks can be seen in the enormous circular-based chandelier (h 45 cm, Ø 800 cm) with *cristallo* polyhedrons placed in the banqueting hall.

›
DORIC SHIP
Banqueting hall. Period photograph, mid-1970s

1973

LUGANO (CH)
BANCA DEPOSITI E GESTIONI DI CREDITO

ICEBERG

Lighting project for the Lugano bank consisting principally of a large chandelier positioned in the stairwell. This pendant lamp (h 300 cm, Ø 60 cm) consists of a stainless steel structure and iceberg modular elements (*Venini 75: Catalogo di illuminazione*, 1975) in corroded moulded *cristallo* glass.

›
BANCA DEPOSITI E GESTIONI DI CREDITO
Stairwell. Period photograph, c. 1973

››
BANCA DEPOSITI E GESTIONI DI CREDITO
Staircase to upper floors. Period photograph, c. 1973

1973

NEW YORK (US)
WORLD TRADE CENTER

CANNE PIENE
LISTELS
TRIANGOLO
TRILOBO

For several areas of the World Trade Center, opened on 4 April 1973, after a project by the architect Minoru Yamasaki, the Venini firm produced numerous lighting installations, more particularly a group of ceiling lamps with solid triangular *cristallo* rods (h 90 cm, 120 x 120 cm) for the entrances to the Twin Towers (entrance halls of the North and South Towers) and a series of lamps with solid *trilobo cristallo* rods (h 150 cm, Ø 70 cm) for the entrances to the peripheral buildings. Outside, in the Austin Tobin Plaza (called the World Trade Center Plaza), there were lamps with a cylindrical body having slats 'of moulded and patterned glass' (h 200 cm) fixed on stainless steel posts (*Venini*, 1985). In the following years, for the opening of the Marriott World Trade Center Hotel situated between the two principal towers, the Venini firm produced some solid-rod chandeliers.

>
WORLD TRADE CENTER
Entrance hall. Period photograph, c. 1973

>>
WORLD TRADE CENTER
Austin Tobin Plaza, called the World Trade Center Plaza.
Period photograph, 1980s

>>
WORLD TRADE CENTER
Entrance to the peripheral buildings. Period photograph, c. 1973

1973-74 ORLANDO (US)
AMERICAN FEDERAL SAVINGS & LOAN ASSOCIATION

CALZA

For the extension of the bank, the Venini firm produced a large circular-based chandelier with *calza* modular elements (h 450 cm, Ø 300 cm) in *cristallo* and yellow glass with a downward tapering structure.

>
AMERICAN FEDERAL SAVINGS & LOAN ASSOCIATION
Chandelier with *calza* glass elements. Period photograph, c. 1974

1974

KUWAIT CITY (KW)

HILTON KUWAIT HOTEL

POLYHEDRONS

Lighting project for a hotel in the Hilton chain, including among other things ring-shaped ceiling lamps (h 45 cm, Ø 180 cm) with *cristallo* polyhedrons.

>
HILTON KUWAIT HOTEL
Bar-room. Period photograph, mid-1970s

1974

MARSEILLE (FR)
SOFITEL VIEUX-PORT HOTEL

LAGO

The Marseille hotel was opened in 1974 after a design by the architect Guy Daher. For the restaurant room, a large lighting installation was produced of an irregular organic-type design (h 45 cm, max w 1200 cm) with rods of the *lago* (lake) type (*Venini*, 1985). The elements are produced in three shades of blue and placed at different heights.

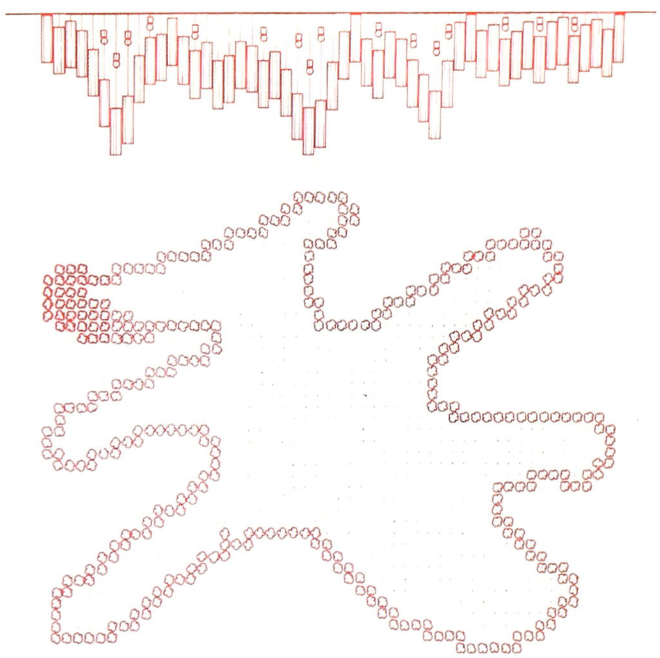

›
SOFITEL VIEUX-PORT HOTEL
Design and cross-section of the lighting system in *Venini*, 1985

›
SOFITEL VIEUX-PORT HOTEL
Restaurant room. Period photograph, c. 1974

1974

TUNIS (TN)
RUSPINA HOTEL

SQUARE RODS

For the hall of the Tunis hotel, the Venini firm produced circular-based chandeliers (h 270 cm, Ø 210 cm) with solid square rods and a downward tapering structure.

1975

LANCASTER (US)
HESS'S RESTAURANT

CERVELLONI

For the American restaurant a luminous column was made with a large cone-shaped capital and luminous rectilinear bands, both made up of *cristallo cervellone* modules. This modular type can be seen in the booklet *Venini 75: Catalogo di illuminazione* (1975) and the project constitutes one of its first uses.

›
RUSPINA HOTEL
Hall. Period photograph, c. 1974

›
HESS'S RESTAURANT
Restaurant room. Period photograph, 1975

1975

RIYADH (SA)

RIYADH INTERCONTINENTAL HOTEL

DESIGN N. A. PRINCE

CANNE QUADRE

The prestigious Saudi Arabian hotel was opened in 1975 after a design by Neal A. Prince, architect and designer of the InterContinental Hotel group. Here the presence of the Venini firm can be seen in the lighting installation designed for the entrance hall. These are large square-based luminaires (h 100 cm, 480 x 480 cm), each consisting of 36 blocks of rods with a square cross-section and *cristallo* glass.

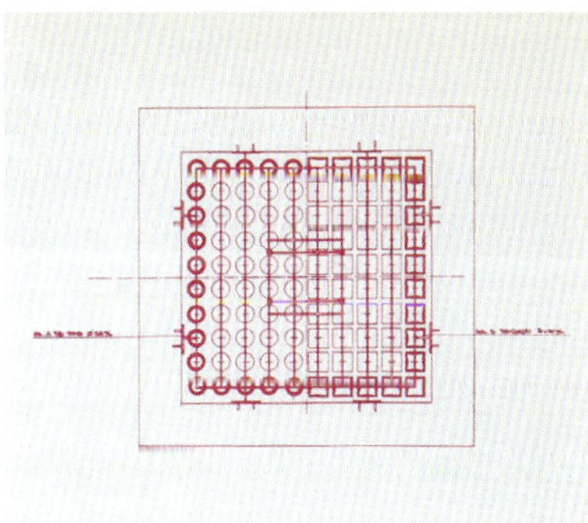

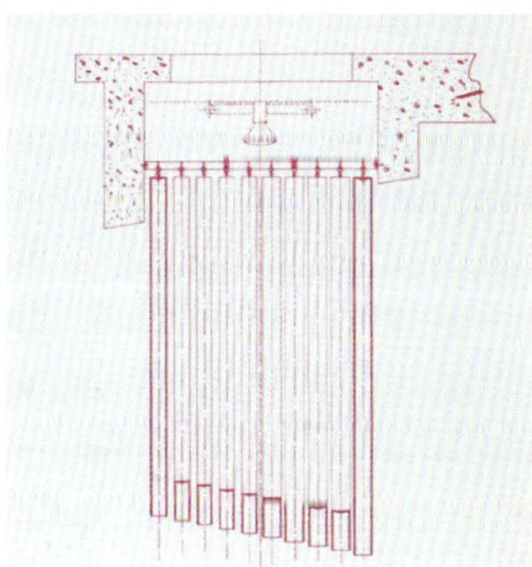

> RIYADH INTERCONTINENTAL HOTEL
Entrance hall. Period photograph, c. 1975

> RIYADH INTERCONTINENTAL HOTEL
Design and cross-section of the modular block in *Venini*, 1985

1976

CERVIA (IT)

MARE & PINETA HOTEL

BOLETUS T
NINFEA

For the Milano Marittima hotel, the Venini firm produced mainly a series of pendant lamps for the day area of the hotel. Among these, there are the Ninfea lamps by Toni Zuccheri for the restaurant room and the Boletus T lamps by Mario Ticcò for one of the public areas. This latter model appeared for the first time in the booklet *Venini 75: Catalogo di illuminazione* (1975).

> MARE & PINETA HOTEL
Restaurant room. Period photograph, 1976

1976

LONDON (GB)
ROYAL CHEMICAL SOCIETY AND GEOLOGICAL SOCIETY, BURLINGTON HOUSE

POLYHEDRONS
TRIANGOLO

At Burlington House, home to five different scientific associations, the Venini firm carried out projects for two of these: the Royal Chemical Society and the Geological Society. For the first, the glassworks produced a chandelier (h 150 cm, Ø 75 cm) with solid triangular rods, positioned at the foot of the monumental staircase. For the second, two pendant lamps were produced (h 120 cm, Ø 75 cm) with *cristallo* polyhedrons and a protruding central structure, intended for the library. The luminaires for the latter area are still *in situ*.

>
ROYAL CHEMICAL SOCIETY, BURLINGTON HOUSE
Hall. Period photograph, c. 1976

1976

MAKATI (PH)
MANDARIN ORIENTAL MANILA HOTEL
A. ASHTON

DORICA

For the Philippines hotel, opened in 1976 after a design by the architect Leandro Locsin and interior by Don Ashton, the glassworks produced a large chandelier made up of solid rods of the *dorica* type for the entrance hall (*Venini*, 1985).

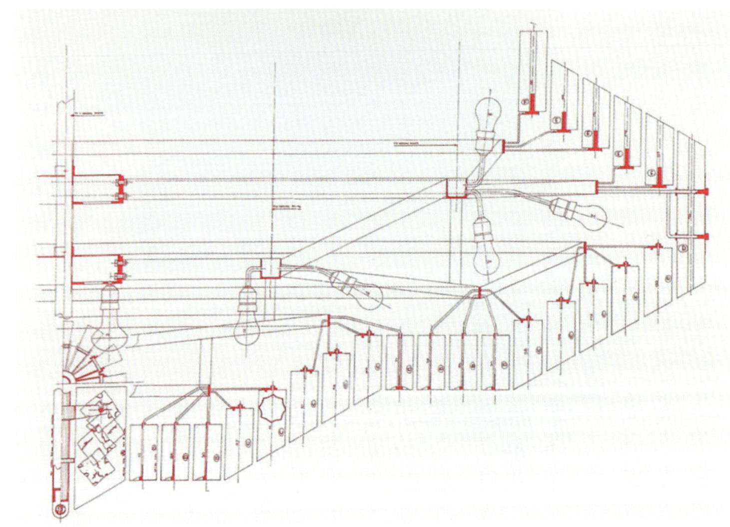

>
MANDARIN ORIENTAL MANILA HOTEL
Entrance hall. Period photograph, 1976

>
MANDARIN ORIENTAL MANILA HOTEL
Outline of the chandelier with modules of the *dorica* type, in *Venini*, 1985

1976

MANCHESTER (GB)
PICCADILLY HOTEL

TRIANGOLO

For the meeting room of the English hotel, designed in 1959 by the firm Covell Matthews & Partners, a series of modular luminaires was commissioned. These were chandeliers (h 180 cm, 105 x 105 cm) with solid triangular *cristallo* rods having a coloured nucleus and lower section cut at 30 degrees. At the same extremity there were pendants made of 'peacock' *murrine* in polychrome glass.

›
PICCADILLY HOTEL
Meeting room. Period photograph, 1976

1977

POVIGLIO (IT)
EUROTRE

ALGA

The lighting project for the Reggio Emilia firm documented by a design of 1977 showing a chandelier with a square base (max h 200 cm, 150 x 150 cm) composed of modular 'seaweed' elements of different lengths.

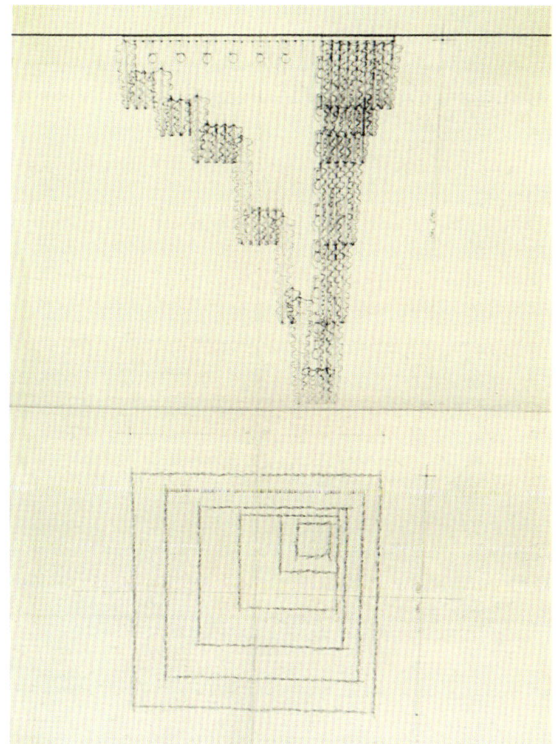

›
EUROTRE
Drawing of a lamp with modular 'seaweed' elements, 25 November1977, AC

1977

TAIF (SA)

MASSARAH INTERCONTINENTAL HOTEL

ALGA
CANNE
CANNE QUADRE
POLYHEDRONS

In the Arabian hotel opened in 1977, the glassworks produced some lighting installations of various modular types. These are mainly crown-type chandeliers (max h 120 cm, Ø 800 cm) with *cristallo* alga modules for the restaurant, chandeliers with hollow square *cristallo* rods having patterned motifs (h 120 cm, Ø 150 cm) for the event room, chandeliers with rods having patterned motifs (h 80 cm, Ø 150 cm) for the cafeteria and ring-shaped chandeliers with an octagonal base with ribbed *cristallo* rods (h 90 cm, Ø 270 cm) for the banqueting room.

>
MASSARAH INTERCONTINENTAL HOTEL
Cafeteria. Period photograph, c. 1977

>>
MASSARAH INTERCONTINENTAL HOTEL
Restaurant. Period photograph, c. 1977

>
MASSARAH INTERCONTINENTAL HOTEL
Restaurant. Period photograph, c. 1977

>
MASSARAH INTERCONTINENTAL HOTEL
Banqueting room during installation. Period photograph, c. 1977

1978

BELLAIRE (US)
5959 WEST LOOP

BRICOLE

For the internal courtyard of the office building of the metropolitan area of Houston, a large chandelier was produced composed of *bricole* modules in *cristallo* glass (h 480 cm, Ø 150 cm). The fixture is characterised by its mirror-image downward tapering structure.

>
5959 WEST LOOP
Internal courtyard. Period photograph, 1978

1978

FULDA (DE)
SCHLOSSTHEATER
DESIGN G. WEBER

TRILOBO

Opened on 6 July 1978 after two years of building works, the Schlosstheater was constructed as an extension and renovation of the theatre-cinema created in the 1950s in the baroque building of the Palace of Fulda winter riding school. The works of the 1970s, carried out after the design of the architectural firm Gerhard Weber & Partners, included also the lighting project of the Venini firm for the entrance hall, foyer and theatre auditorium. In the first two of these, rows of pendant lamps with *trilobo* solid rods (series no. 963) in *cristallo* glass with a teal-coloured nucleus were positioned: the luminaires, with a circular base, have a symmetrical structure with downward tapering extremities (h 270 cm, Ø 60 cm). Each modular element is fixed to the ceiling with a chain. Particularly noteworthy is the ceiling of the auditorium (400 m^2) made up of approximately 70,000 *trilobo* solid rods with 'gradations of colour from teal to straw-yellow' (*Venini*, 1985). This sort of luminous 'false ceiling' is rectilinear for a good part of the length of the auditorium and drops at about 8 metres from the stage to the level of the projector bay and continues sloping towards the proscenium. As indicated in the Weber report, the rod ceiling (each rod h 36 cm), in addition to satisfying the demands of lighting engineering, was designed to cover the overlying trusses, so ensuring the acoustic efficiency of the auditorium (*Schloßtheater Fulda* 1978). The Venini project is still *in situ*.

>
SCHLOSSTHEATER
Luminous ceiling with *trilobo* rods in the auditorium of the theatre seen from the gallery. Photo OSTHESSEN|NEWS/ Carina Jirsch

‹‹
SCHLOSSTHEATER
Luminous ceiling with *trilobo* rods in the auditorium of the theatre seen from the stage. Photo OSTHESSEN|NEWS/ Carina Jirsch

›
SCHLOSSTHEATER
Foyer with pendant lamps having *trilobo* rods.
Photo courtesy Theater Catering Fulda

›
SCHLOSSTHEATER
Pendant lamps with *trilobo* rods in the foyer.
Period photograph, 1978

1978

PARIS (FR)
PARIS FAIR

OCTAGONAL ELEMENTS

On the occasion of the annual fair hosted in the exhibition halls of the Porte de Versailles, the Venini firm produced a large oval looped ceiling light (h 60 cm, Ø 300 x 180 cm) composed of rods with an octagonal cross-section in yellow glass.

›
PARIS FAIR
Entrance hall with oval looped ceiling light. Period photograph, 1978

1978

PARIS (FR)
MOULIN ROUGE

FIORE

For the foyer of the historic Paris venue, an articulated installation with *fiore* rods in *cristallo* glass was produced (max h 190 cm, max Ø 370 x 220 cm). The luminaire is composed of an oval-shaped central body and cylindrical volumes which are reflected on the blue-mirror ceiling. The chandelier is still *in situ*.

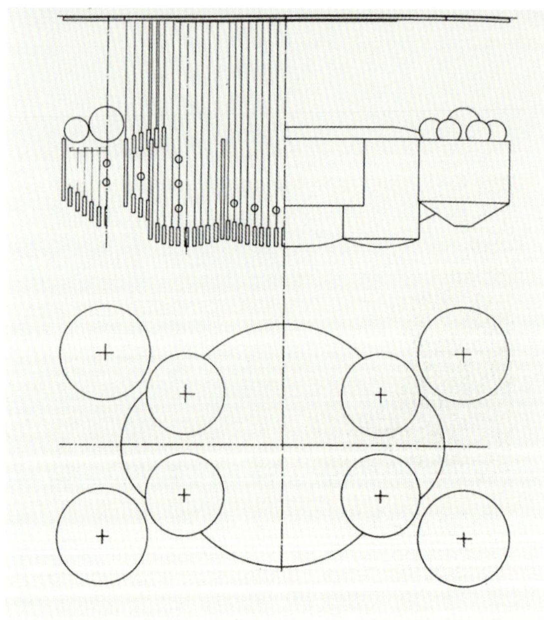

›
MOULIN ROUGE
Chandelier with *cristallo fiore* rods. Period photograph, c. 1978

›
MOULIN ROUGE
Outline of the installation with a symmetrical design in *Venini*, 1985

››
MOULIN ROUGE
Chandelier with *cristallo fiore* rods, seen from below.
Period photograph, c. 1978

1978

TAIF (SA)
SHERATON AL-HADA HOTEL

PLATES

In the Arabian hotel, opened in 1978, the Venini firm carried out lighting projects for the public areas using corrugated glass plates with a V profile, later called taif (*Venini*, 1985). Worthy of note is the roofing of the courtyard with a hexagonal base (Ø 900 cm), at the centre of which a large chandelier was positioned, with a tapering mirror-image structure, in *cristallo* glass with a yellow patch (max h 400 cm). Other smaller pendant lamps with a tapering structure are also documented. The large chandelier is still *in situ*.

>
SHERATON AL-HADA HOTEL
Roofing of the courtyard. Period photograph, c. 1978

>
SHERATON AL-HADA HOTEL
Chandelier with plates called taif. Period photograph, c. 1978

>>
SHERATON AL-HADA HOTEL
Courtyard with chandelier with taif plates.
Le Méridien Al Hada Photos. Photo Abdulrahman AlJabri

1979
1980

RIYADH (SA)
RIYADH HOTEL & CONFERENCE CENTER

CANNE
OCTAGONAL ELEMENTS

In the conference room of the Saudi Arabian building, the glassworks carried out a project for a monumental chandelier, with a circular cross-section and downward tapering structure (h 400 cm, Ø 800 cm), made up of bichrome rods (h 45 cm). Housed within the chandelier there was a 'centralised sound and light system' (*Venini*, 1985). Later a series of chandeliers with a downward tapering structure was supplied, in two different sizes, for the 'banqueting hall' and the 'VIP lounge' (*Venini*, 1985). In the first case, they were chandeliers with a circular base having ribbed rods in *cristallo* glass (h 150 cm, Ø 120 cm; h 210 cm, Ø 150 cm); in the second, luminaires of a square (h 210 cm, 150 x 150 cm) and rectangular (h 90 cm, 180 x 90 cm) design composed of rods with an octagonal cross-section 'with a patterned motif in *cristallo* glass'.

>
RIYADH HOTEL & CONFERENCE CENTER
Conference room. Period photograph, c. 1979

>>
RIYADH HOTEL & CONFERENCE CENTER
Mounting of chandelier for the conference room. Period photograph, c. 1979

>>
RIYADH HOTEL & CONFERENCE CENTER
Banqueting room. Period photograph, c. 1980

>>
RIYADH HOTEL & CONFERENCE CENTER
VIP lounge. Period photograph, c. 1980

1970s

VENICE (IT)

CA' BERNARDO, UNIVERSITÀ CA' FOSCARI VENEZIA

POLYHEDRONS

For the university library, the glassworks produced a group of pendant lamps with *cristallo* polyhedrons and projecting central part.

›
CA' BERNARDO, UNIVERSITÀ CA' FOSCARI VENEZIA
Reading room. Photo Enrico Fiorese 2022

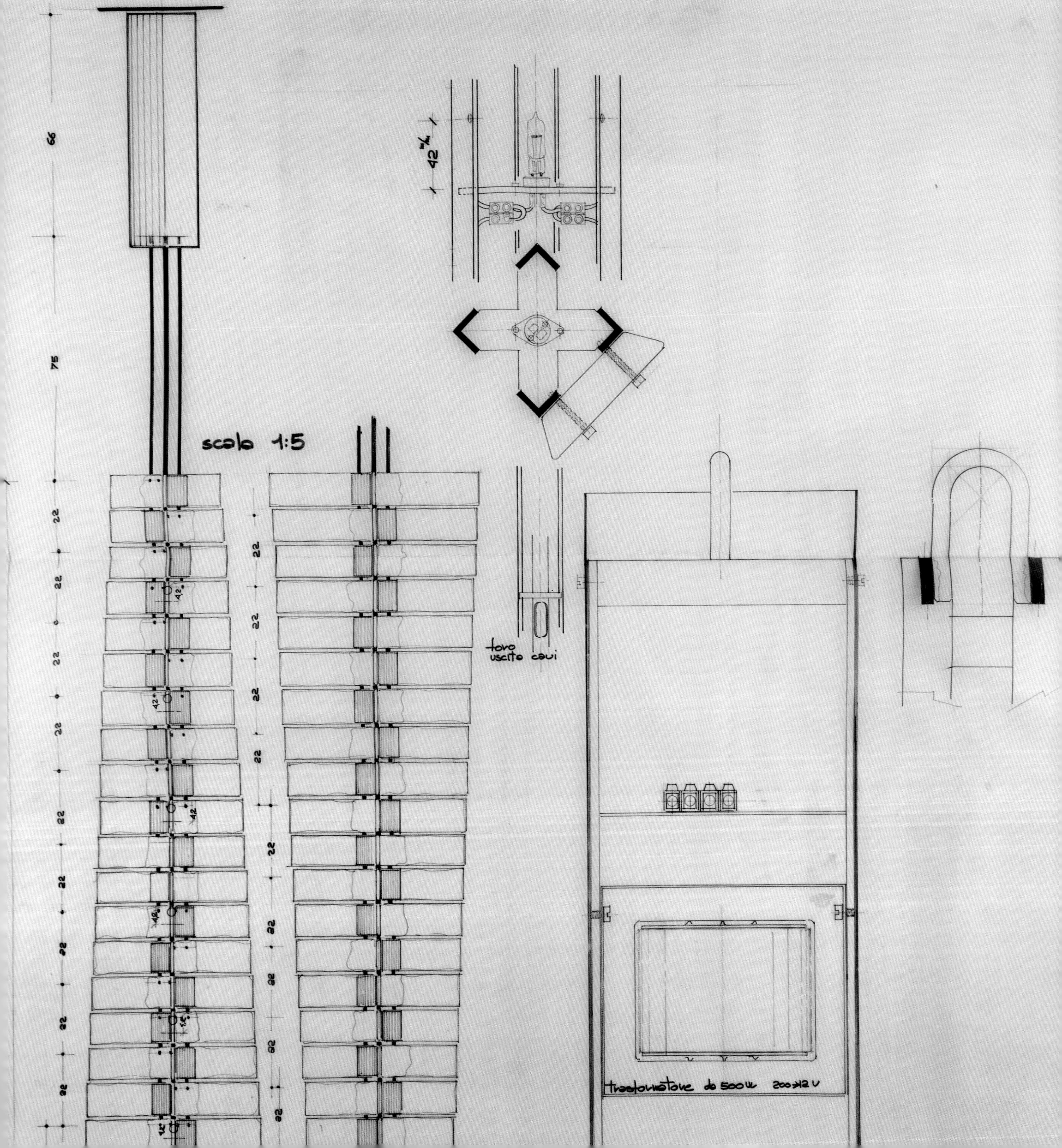

scala 1:5
foro uscita cavi
trasformatore da 500w

1980s

1980

ATHENES (GR)
MERIDIEN HOTEL
J. RIZOS

POLYHEDRONS

In the hall of the Athenian hotel, designed by Jason Rizos and opened in 1980, an enormous lighting installation of 330 m^2 was placed, composed of polyhedron *cristallo*, *talpa* and amethyst glass. The design of the composition (max h 40 cm) reflected the design of the marble floor in slabs of various colours. In the bar of the hotel there was also a flat ceiling with polyhedrons in *cristallo* glass, above the bar counter.

›
MERIDIEN HOTEL
Hall. Period photograph, c. 1980

1980

JUBAIL (SA)
ROYAL SAUDI MILITARY ACADEMY

RODS-SPHERES

Project for the Saudi military academy, consisting of a large lighting installation with modular elements of the rod-sphere type (h max h 75 cm, 200 x 800 cm). The system is composed of six cylindrical bodies called 'drums' (Ø 120 cm) and a 'rectangular screen', of a lower height, with *cristallo* rods-spheres (*Venini*, 1985).

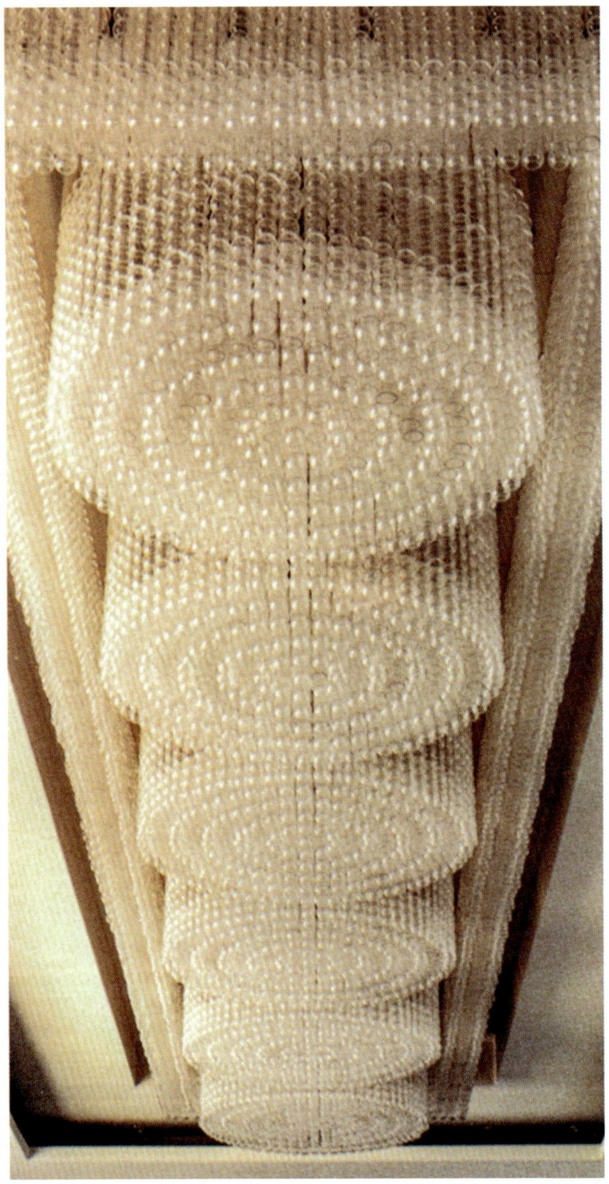

›
ROYAL SAUDI MILITARY ACADEMY RODS-SPHERES
Installation with *cristallo* rods-sphere. Period photograph, c. 1980

1980

LONDON (GB)
HONG KONG AND SHANGHAI BANK, 99 BISHOPSGATE

PANELS

In the lift lobby of the bank housed in the Bishopsgate 99 office building, a large ceiling was installed composed of 'e' type square-based panels (*Venini 75: Catalogo di illuminazione*, 1975). The modules (45 x 45 cm) are mounted on special metallic frames with parallel bands.

›
HONG KONG AND SHANGHAI BANK, 99 BISHOPSGATE
Lift lobby. Period photograph, 1980

1980

TAIF (SA)
ROYAL DIWAN PALACE

CANNE
TRILOBO

In the Saudi Arabian government headquarters, the Venini firm created several lighting systems for areas such as the 'central reception room' and the 'throne room' (*Venini*, 1985). In the first of these, there was a chandelier of significant size (h 150 cm, Ø 300 cm) with solid *trilobo* rods in *cristallo* glass. The large pendant light had a framework with a circular base and tapering shape, ending centrally in a cylindrical structure, also tapering. In the 'throne room', on the other hand, luminous square cornices were installed on the ceiling (h 60 cm, 600 x 600 cm), composed of rods with a triangular cross-section in *cristallo* glass.

›
ROYAL DIWAN PALACE
Throne room. Period photograph, 1980

›
ROYAL DIWAN PALACE
Central reception room. Period photograph, 1980

1980

MILAN (IT)
EUROLUCE

RIBBONS

On the occasion of the September 1980 Euroluce event, for the first time modular systems of the ribbon type were exhibited. In the glassworks' exhibition area a large installation was shown (max h 160 cm, 600 x 600 cm) made up of numerous ribbon chandeliers, in *cristallo* glass, of various sizes, 'organically connected' one with the other (*Venini*,1985).

>
EUROLUCE
Venini Exhibition Area. Period photograph, 1980

1982

MIAMI (US)
PAVILLON HOTEL

Lighting project for the hotel, now InterContinental Miami, belonging to the Miami Center complex opened in 1982 after the design of the architect Pietro Belluschi.

1982

PARIS (FR)
FOURRURES GEORGE V

ALGA

In the Paris fur shop the Venini firm was called upon to produce a series of original decorative solutions. At the centre of the area the enormous central chandelier stood out with its tapering shape composed of *alga* elements (max h 500 cm, Ø 300 cm): also in the central area a mirror was placed which reflected the lights and features of the shop. Below the enormous chandelier a fountain was installed (max 120 cm, Ø 300 cm), with groups of *alga* elements in *cristallo* glass. Near the fountain there was a large wall light, also composed of *alga* elements in *cristallo* glass. Due to a clever play of light made by the glass and the mirrors, the overall display area produced a spectacularly dramatic effect.

>
FOURRURES GEORGE V
Large central chandelier. Period photograph, c. 1982
>
FOURRURES GEORGE V
Fountain with groups of *alga* elements. Period photograph, 1982

1982

RIYADH (SA)
ROYAL SAUDI TELEVISION CENTER

CANNE
NASTRI

In the headquarters of the Saudi Arabian television broadcaster, the Venini firm was involved in two very impressive projects. In the entrance hall, a large chandelier of *cristallo* glass ribbons (h 1050 cm, Ø 180 cm) with a tapering structure, inserted in semicylinders of plexiglass. A larger installation was produced for the twin lateral stairwells: it consisted of a 'chandelier' with rods in *cristallo* glass of the '007' type (*Venini*, 1985) which extended vertically for the entire height of the stairwell (h max 1800 cm). At the top it consisted of the combination of two cylindrical bodies with a pyramid-like extremity while the main structure, which was also cylindrical, tapered progressively downwards. On the sides of the smaller elements were fringes of glass rods.

›
ROYAL SAUDI TELEVISION
Detail of the large chandelier. Period photograph, 1982

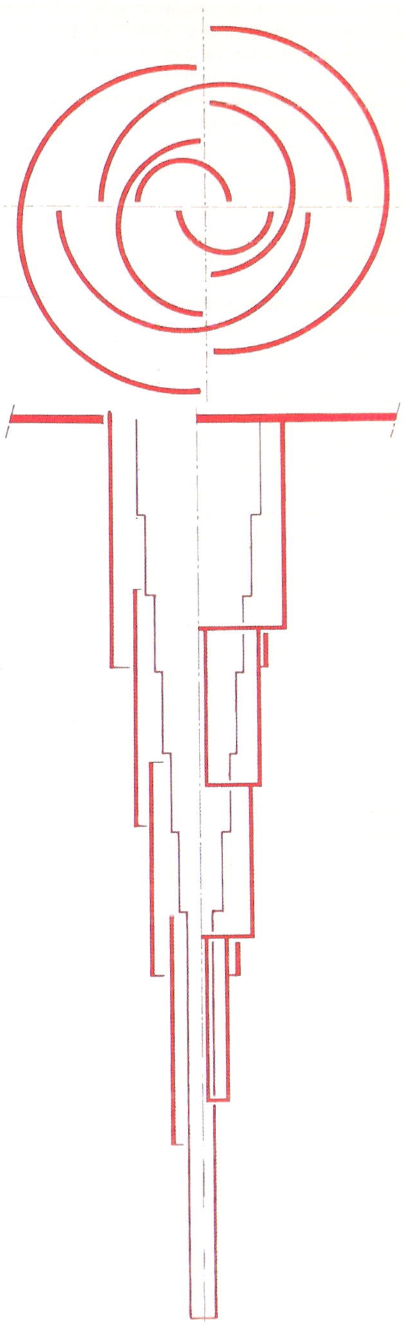

1982

VENICE (II)
BANCO DI SICILIA

FIORE
PLATES

For the banking premises lighting systems were produced for the entrance hall and the adjoining room. The entrance hall had ceiling lighting consisting of plates in *pagliesco* and green, inserted into a metal frame. The adjoining room, on the other hand, contained a group of lamps with a cylindrical base composed of bichrome solid flower rods in *cristallo* and teal.

›
ROYAL SAUDI TELEVISION
Design for the ribbon chandelier for the entrance hall of the building, in *Venini*, 1985

›
ROYAL SAUDI TELEVISION
Detail of the ribbon chandelier with plexiglass semicylinders. Period photograph, 1982

›
BANCO DI SICILIA
Entrance hall with ceiling composed of plates. Period photograph, c. 1982

›
BANCO DI SICILIA
Room with lamps having a cylindrical base and bichrome solid flower rods. Period photograph, c. 1982

1983

HOFUF (SA) AL AHSA GOVERNEMENT CENTER, HOTEL & CONVENTION CENTER

CANNE
PARALLELEPIPED

In the hotel, which contained a conference centre, large lighting systems were created for some of the inner courtyards (*Venini*, 1985). The system included: a parallelepiped chandelier with a square cross-section in *cristallo* and teal glass and with a tapering shape (h 300 cm, Ø 600 cm, single component 40 cm), a chandelier with ribbed rods of the 'cassina' type of various lengths and with gilded spherical ends (max h 350 cm, 450 x 450 cm) and a chandelier with parallelepipeds having a pentagonal cross-section in *cristallo* glass (h 240 cm, Ø 600 cm).

›
AL AHSA GOVERNEMENT CENTER, HOTEL & CONVENTION CENTER
Courtyard 1. Chandelier with square cross-section parallelepipeds (h 300 cm, Ø 600 cm, single component 40 cm) with tapering shape. Period photograph, 1983

1983

MANAMA (BH) GULF INTERNATIONAL BANK

TRILOBO

For the 'committee room' (*Venini*, 1985) of the banking premises in the capital of Bahrein, a large chandelier with a rectangular base was created, designed with three tapering levels (h 108 cm, 307 x 200 cm), composed of solid *trilobo* rods in *cristallo* glass with a teal nucleus.

››
GULF INTERNATIONAL BANK
'Committee Room', in *Venini*, 1985. Period photograph, 1983

1983

MILAN (IT)

CASSINA SHOWROOM

F. BINFARÈ

CANNE

In the context of the exhibition project *Il fuoco e la casa (o Prometeo)* of Francesco Binfarè for the Brianza firm, Cassina, the designer planned glass cascades which were then produced by the Venini firm. It consisted of a composition made up of heat-folded ribbed rods in *cristallo* glass, with the light source inserted in the lower part. The cascade which covered part of the display areas, created all in all an evocative and dramatic effect.

>
CASSINA SHOWROOM
Setting up of the heat-folded ribbed rods in *cristallo* glass.
Period photograph, 1983

>>
CASSINA SHOWROOM
Cascade of heat-folded ribbed rods in *cristallo* glass.
Period photograph, 1983

MARCATRÉ

1983

SAINT-VINCENT (IT)
CASINÒ DE LA VALLÉE

NUVOLA

For the casino, restored in 1983, the Venini firm was involved again with some ceiling and wall lamps made of plates of the *nuvola* type (*Venini*, 1985) in *cristallo* and purple glass. The restoration of the building was overseen by the architects Cesare Casati and Emanuele Ponzio.

>
CASINÒ DE LA VALLÉE
Wall lamps (h 140 cm Ø 140 cm) above one of the exit doors of the theatre hall. Period photograph, 1983

1983

VENICE (IT)
PALAZZO FERRO FINI
L. PARENTI

DROPS

In the headquarters of the Veneto Region, acquired in 1973 and restored by the architect Luciano Parenti (1977-85), the Venini firm produced an extensive lighting system for the entrance hall of the Regional Council. This is an installation (max h 200 cm, max Ø 300 cm) composed of drops floating in *cristallo* glass with yellow-coloured patches suspended by steel cables which cascade from the brass structure fixed to the highest point of the room. Indirect light is propagated from the ceiling through the lower-lying components.

>>
PALAZZO FERRO FINI
Lobby of the Regional Council Headquarters.
Period photograph, c. 1983

1984

NEW YORK (US)
VENINI: THE SPIRIT OF THE MOMENT
L. DIAZ DE SANTILLANA

NASTRI
PLATES

On the occasion of the exhibition of 27 May 1984 at the Heller Gallery, the glassworks, among its most recent productions, also exhibited two large lighting systems designed by Ludovico Diaz de Santillana, *Tappeto volante* and *Tazebao*. The first, which extended horizontally (600 x 60 cm), was composed of ribbons in *cristallo* glass fixed to a flexible metallic structure suspended by steel cables and with halogen lights. *Tazebao*, on the other hand, with a characteristic vertical structure, was formed from plates in *cristallo* glass with coloured patches of *pagliesco* and light blue.

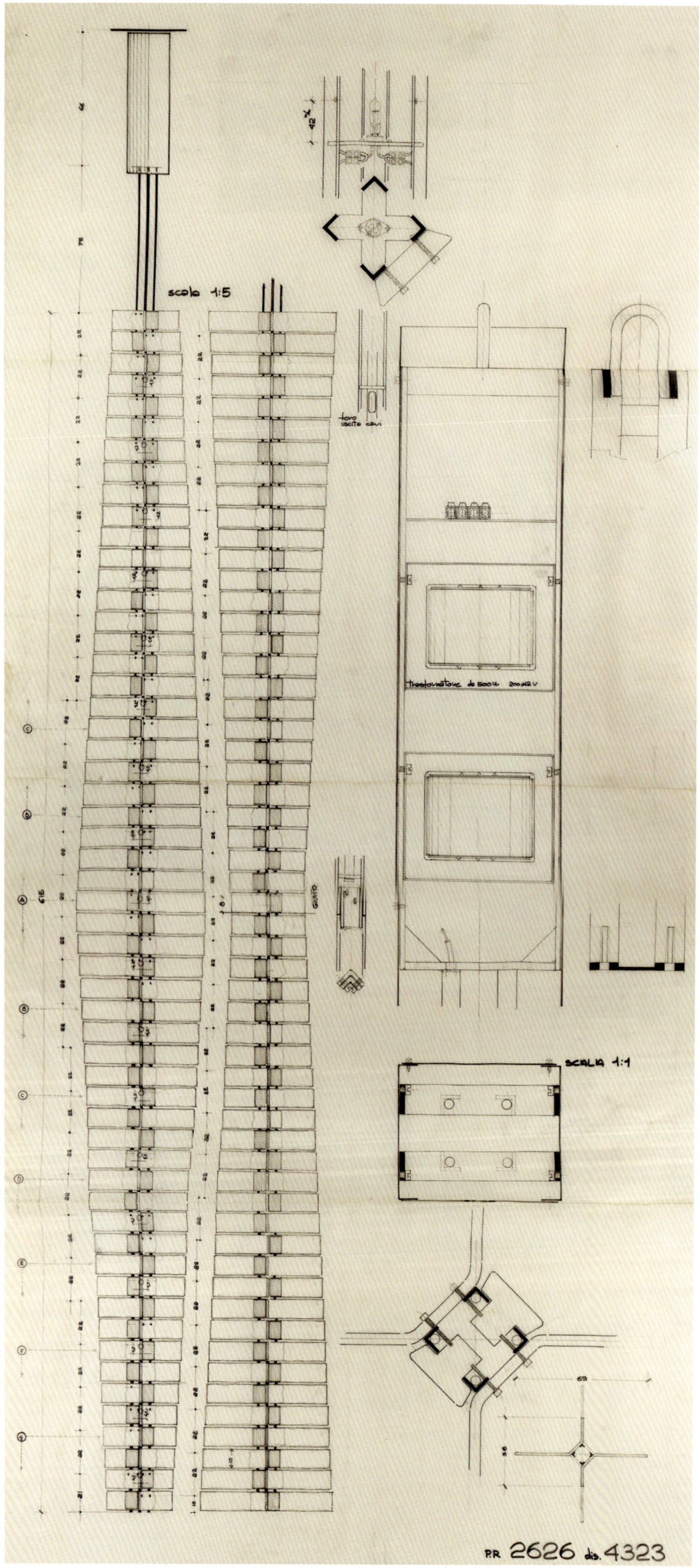

>
VENINI: THE SPIRIT OF THE MOMENT
Tazebao. Period photograph, c. 1984

>
VENINI: THE SPIRIT OF THE MOMENT
Design for *Tazebao* lamp, c. 1984

>>
VENINI: THE SPIRIT OF THE MOMENT
Exhibition area with flying carpet. Period photograph, 1984

VENINI

1984

OSLO (NO)

HOTEL SHERATON

Lighting project for a hotel of the Sheraton chain.

1984

UDINE (IT)

TOWN HALL

N. VALLE

SQUARE RODS

The Council Chamber of the Town Hall, called the Sala Ajace, was an unfinished project by Raimondo D'Aronco (1912, 1929-32) which was completed fifty years later by Nani Valle (1982-84). Here the glassworks were involved in the production of wall lights, designed by Valle, of various shapes and sizes (h 100 cm, w 116 cm; h 140 cm, w 66 cm) composed of solid square rods (3 x 3 cm and 4 x 4 cm) in *cristallo* glass with a *pagliesco* or amethyst nucleus.

1985

MILAN (IT)

NEW ADAM AND EVE (IL CIELO)

WALL LAMPS
PENDANT
FLOOR

Called upon by Ludovico Diaz de Santillana to collaborate in the designing of a new collection, Francesco Binfarè initiated and took charge of the production, coordination and communication activities of a project which took the form of the installation *New Adam and Eve (Il Cielo)* created in the Venini showroom in Milan. Forming part of this installation are the *Aurora* lamps by Paolo Doganello (h 104 cm, Ø 74 cm; h 111 cm, Ø 66 cm), *Pianeta* by Vico Magistretti (h 135 cm, disc Ø 90 cm) and *Miraggi* by Piero de Martini (h max 40 cm, Ø 40 cm), designed for the new collection called *Il Cielo* by Binfarè and exhibited on this occasion.

>
TOWN HALL
Sala Ajace. Period photograph, 1984

>>
NEW ADAM AND EVE (IL CIELO)
Aurora (Version no. 1). Period photograph, 1985

>>
NEW ADAM AND EVE (IL CIELO)
Aurora (Version no. 2). Period photograph, 1985

>>
NEW ADAM AND EVE (IL CIELO)
Pianeta. Period photograph, 1985.

>>
NEW ADAM AND EVE (IL CIELO)
Miraggi. Period photograph, 1985

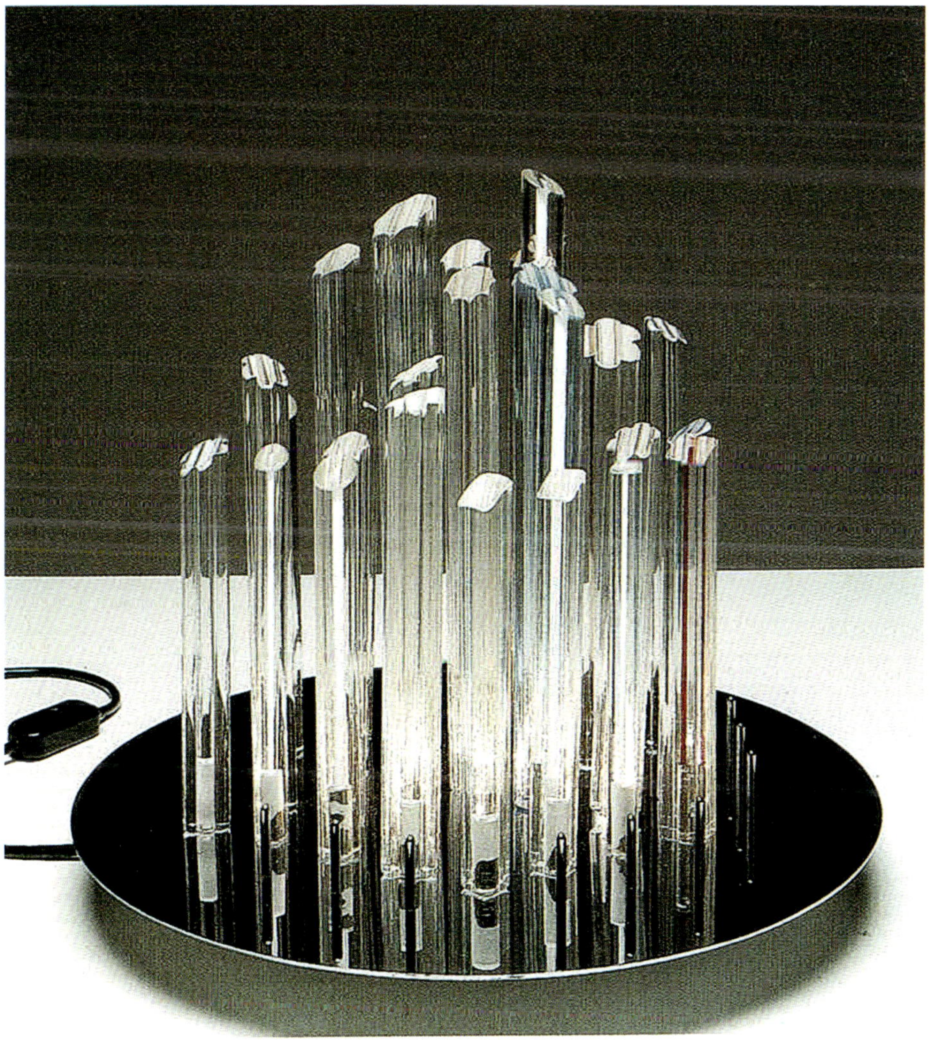

1985

PARIS (FR)
LUMIÈRES, JE PENSE À VOUS

RIBBONS

The glassworks took part in an exhibition opened on 3 June 1985 at the Centre Georges Pompidou, creating a *Tappeto volante* suspended above the escalator at the entrance of the building.

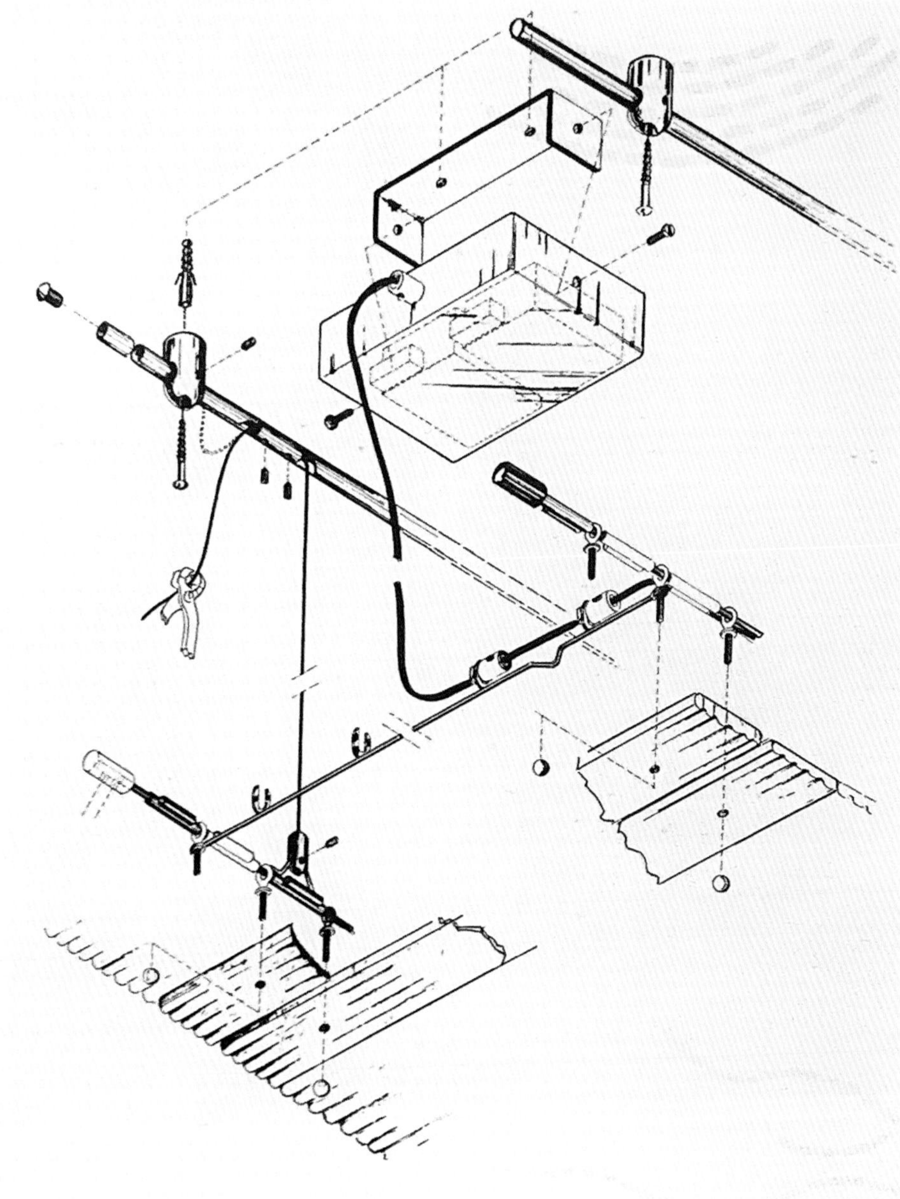

>
LUMIÈRES, JE PENSE À VOUS
Diagram of the mounting of the *Tappeto volante*, in Venini, 1985

>>
LUMIÈRES, JE PENSE À VOUS
Centre Georges Pompidou, entrance. Period photograph, 1985

49

1985

THIENE (IT)
MUNICIPAL THEATRE

BRICOLE
SPHERES

On the occasion of the restoration (1981-85) of the early 20th-century theatre, reopened on 27 March 1985, the glassworks executed a lighting project for different areas of the building. The work included pendant and ceiling lights with *balloton* spheres of various sizes and *bricole* wall lamps.

›
MUNICIPAL THEATRE
Main auditorium. Period photograph, c. 1985

››
MUNICIPAL THEATRE
Access to the halls. Period photograph, c. 1985

DONIZETTI

WORKS ON EXHIBITION

Descriptions follow of the works selected for the exhibition, produced in a time period extending from 1923 to 1984. Complete with a technical sheet, each work is accompanied by a brief description where, in general, the original terminology has been used, whether for the names of the series, the execution technique or the colours. The dates given in each sheet refer to the period in which the series to which the piece belongs was displayed or, if documented, the date of design of the individual artefact. The dating is derived from the analysis of the different catalogues and the illustrated brochures produced by the glassworks, taking account also of the presence of the works in decorative arts exhibitions or their publication in sector magazines. For the installation with *trilobo* canes and for *Pastorale*, the sheets include images taken from the *Venini 75: Catalogo di illuminazione* (1975).

1923

Chandelier in green transparent glass with twelve arms. A similar model was exhibited at the 1st Biennale of Monza in 1923 in Room 19. The chandelier, designed by Vittorio Zecchin, corresponds to model no. 2035 of the Venini catalogue.

210 cm high
150 cm wide
Private collection, Venice

c. 1929

Lamp with three upside-down superimposed bells in green *pulegoso* glass. The lamp, after a design by Napoleone Martinuzzi, corresponds to model no. 5026 of the Venini catalogue.

60 cm high
Valente - Barzaghi collection, Venice

1929

Luminous decorative piece in *pulegoso cristallo* glass in the form of an underwater rock with fish. Finishing in green glass. Base in black lacquered metal containing the light source. The piece, after a design by Napoleone Martinuzzi, corresponds to model no. 9007 of the Venini catalogue.

75 cm high
Fondazione Chiara e Francesco Carraro / Galleria Internazionale d'Arte Moderna di Ca' Pesaro

1929

Luminous decorative piece in *pulegoso cristallo* glass in the form of a fluted column with superimposed vase with leaves. Finishing (mouth of the vase and tips of the leaves) in sapphire glass. The piece, designed by Napoleone Martinuzzi, corresponds to model no. 9001 of the Venini catalogue.

41 cm high
Private collection

1929

Luminous decorative piece in *cristallo pulegoso* glass in the form of a column with superimposed sphere surrounded by a ring. The artefact, after a design by Napoleone Martinuzzi, corresponds to model no. 9004 of the Venini catalogue.

35 cm high
Archivio Storico Venini collection

1929

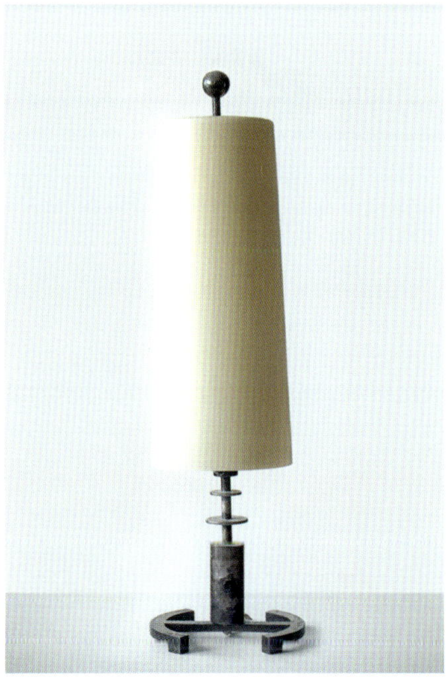

Table lamp with metal structure in bronzed brass and truncated-cone shade in *lattimo* and *pagliesco* cased glass. A similar model was published in *Domus* in December 1929. The lamp was produced after a design by Luigi Piccinato.

58 cm high
Private collection

1930

Table lamp with metal structure in brass and truncated cone-shaped shade in *lattimo* and pagliesco cased [incamiciato] glass. The lamp was designed by Michele Marelli.

48 cm high
Antonello collection

1933

Spherical lamp in *cristallo* glass with, inside, a lamp holder with four lights in the form of a cornucopia. Lamp holder with arms in smoked-coloured glass and bowls in the shape of a truncated cone in white opaline glass. At the centre stylised 'feathers' in smoked-coloured glass. Mounting and truncated-cone-shaped ceiling attachment in metal. The lamp corresponds to a variant of model no. 5299 (Blue Catalogue) after a design by Tomaso Buzzi.

48 cm high
46 cm ø
engraved signature *Venini Murano*
Herat de Nicola collection

1933

Pendant lamp with diffuser screen composed of 'feather'-shaped elements in *cristallo* glass. Metal frame. Ceiling attachment in ribbed glass. With details reminiscent of the style of Tomaso Buzzi, the model was produced by the Venini technical office where Carlo Scarpa was present as draftsman and designer. The light corresponds to model no. 5200 of the Venini catalogue (Blue Catalogue).

147 cm high
Fuori Catalogo Gallery collection, Milan

1933

Ten-light chandelier with cups in embossed glass. Finishings and frame in brass. Central section and arms in ribbed *cristallo* glass. Attached to ceiling with metal rods. A similar model with cups in mirrored glass was exhibited at the Triennale of Milan in 1933. The chandelier corresponds to model no. 5207 of the Venini catalogue (Blue Catalogue).

107 cm high
128 cm wide
Herat de Nicola collection

1933

Pendant lamp with body in corroded *cristallo* glass, decorated with 'leaves' in relief. Cylindrical extremities in glass with jade-green tesserae. Attached to the ceiling with a metal rod. The lamp, after a design by Tomaso Buzzi, corresponds to model no. 5220 in the Venini catalogue (Blue Catalogue).

79 cm high
Private collection, Udine

1933

Table lamp with green ribbed glass and cup in frosted *cristallo* glass decorated with *cristallo* glass 'leaves' in relief. The lamp, designed by Tomaso Buzzi, corresponds to model no. 9030 of the Venini catalogue (Blue Catalogue).

26 cm high
Antonello collection

1933

Floor lamp with diffuser body in the shape of an upside-down bell in *laguna* glass with several layers of colour and application of gold leaf. Shaft and tripod base in metal. The lamp, after a design by Tomaso Buzzi, corresponds to model no. 501 of the Venini catalogue (Blue Catalogue).

178 cm high
Private collection

1933-34

Sconce in *lattimo* cased glass with gold leaf on a ribbed base in amber glass. Small hanging ball in amber *balloton* glass. With details reminiscent of the style of Tomaso Buzzi, the model was produced by the Venini technical office where Carlo Scarpa was present as draftsman and designer. The lamp corresponds to no. 416 in the Venini catalogue (Blue Catalogue).

30 cm high
Private collection, Udine

1934

Hanging lamp with bowl in cased ivory (*lattimo* and *pagliesco*) glass with light application of gold leaf. Spherical pendant with balloton decoration in greenish, *lattimo* and golden glass. Rod in brass and ceiling attachment with horizontal ribbing in greenish, *lattimo* and golden glass. With details reminiscent of the style of Tomaso Buzzi, the model was produced by the Venini technical office where Carlo Scarpa was present in the capacity of designer and planner. The lamp corresponds to the pendant variant of ceiling lamp no. 5413 of the Venini catalogue (Blue Catalogue).

71 cm high
31.7 cm ø
Frederick Iseman Art Trust collection, New York

c. 1934

Chandelier with five lights in green *pulegoso* glass and cups in 'blended' green glass. The chandelier corresponds to model no. 5275 of the Venini catalogue (Blue Catalogue).

80 cm high
80 cm wide
De Albertis Rapett collection

1934

Pendant lamp with spherical body and attachment in the shape of an upside-down truncated cone in *cristallo* and *lattimo reticello* glass. Metallic finishing. Some examples of this model were used by Melchiorre Bega in the furnishing of the American Bar of Venice and in the Fini shoe shop in Bologna. The lamp, after a design by Carlo Scarpa, corresponds to model no. 5417 of the Venini catalogue (Blue Catalogue).

72 cm high
Private collection

c. 1935

Lamp in *lattimo* and smoked cased glass with application of gold leaf and with an ovoid body ribbed horizontally. Finishings and ceiling attachment in the shape of a truncated cone in metal. Some examples of this model were used by Gio Ponti in the furnishing of a Milanese house designed by him (*Domus*, April 1936, pp. 25-33). The light, designed by Carlo Scarpa, corresponds to no. 5254 of the Venini catalogue (Blue Catalogue).

76 cm high
Herat de Nicola collection

1936

Pendant lamp with four lights and a quatrefoil base in *rosato* corroded glass. Diffuser bodies in the shape of an upside-down truncated cone. Strongly iridised surface. A similar model was exhibited at the Triennale of Milan in 1936. The lamp, after a design by Carlo Scarpa, corresponds to model no. 5283 of the Venini catalogue (Blue Catalogue).

63 cm high
45 cm ø
Private collection, Cortina d'Ampezzo

1936

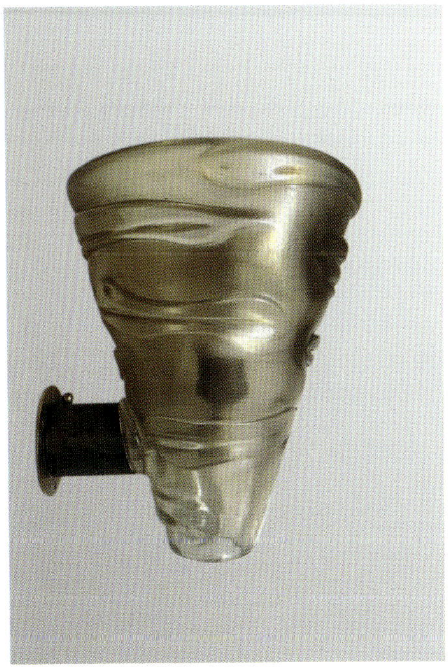

Sconce with body in the shape of a truncated cone in *aurato* corroded glass. Strongly iridised surface. The lamp, after a design by Carlo Scarpa, corresponds to the 'in relief' variant of model no. 443 in the Venini catalogue (Blue Catalogue).

25 cm high
Private collection, Udine

1936

Pendant lamp with upside-down truncated-cone body and diffuser screen with large tesserae in *murrine pagliesco chiaro* glass. Lower globe in *murrine* glass. Nail covers with 'strawberries' *in pagliesco* glass. The construction system consists of a gilded metal skeleton on to which the different elements are applied. A similar model was exhibited at the Triennale of Milan in 1936. The light, designed by Carlo Scarpa, corresponds to model no. 5284 of the Venini catalogue (Blue Catalogue).

50 cm high
Mark Van Wynsberge collection

1936

Spherical pendant lamp in ribbed *cristallo* glass with finishing in metal. The light, after a design by Carlo Scarpa, corresponds to model no. 5294 of the Venini catalogue (Blue Catalogue).

100 cm high
80 cm ø
Private collection

1936

Ceiling light with flared upside-down truncated-cone body in ribbed *cristallo* glass. The light, designed by Carlo Scarpa, corresponds to model no. 5428 of the Venini catalogue (Blue Catalogue).

42 cm high
70 cm ø
Herat de Nicola collection

1934-36

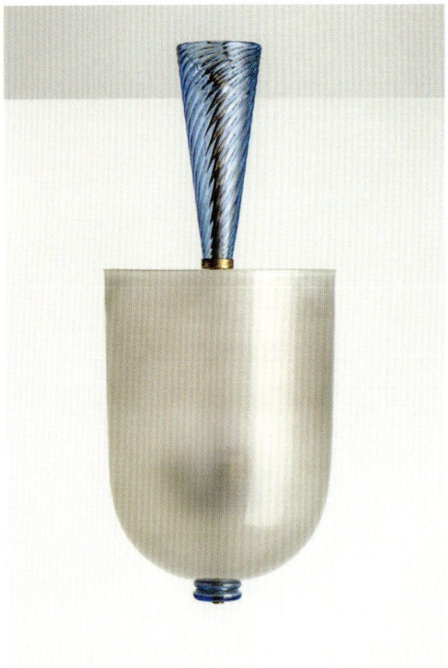

Pendant lamp with body in frosted *cristallo* glass with iridised finish. Truncated cone-shaped stem cover in twisted ribbed *zaffiro* glass. Lower extremity with horizontal ribbing in *zaffiro* glass. The model was produced by the Venini technical office where Carlo Scarpa was present as draftsman and designer.

65 cm high
engraved signature *Venini Murano*
Private collection, Turin

1939

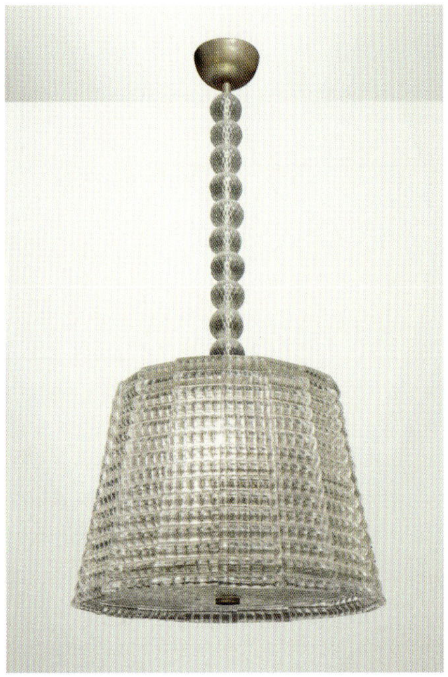

Pendant lamp with a truncated-cone shape and circular base with plates in embossed *cristallo* glass. The light, after a design by Carla Scarpa, corresponds to model no. 5310 of the Venini catalogue (Blue Catalogue).

100 cm high
Private collection, Venice

1940

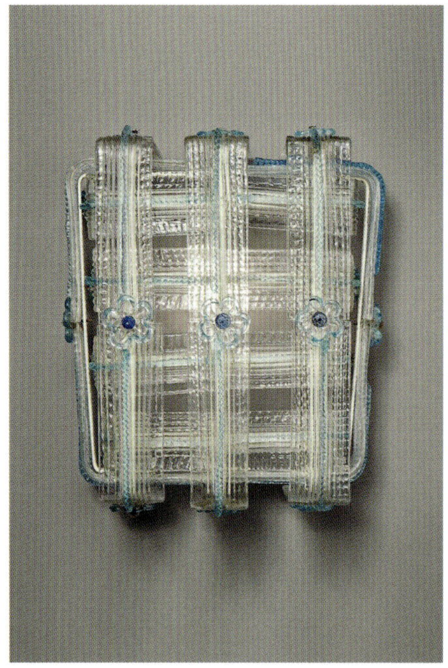

Sconce with blown strips in *cristallo* and aquamarine glass with applied cristallo aquamarine and blue flowers. The sconce belongs to the series 'blown ribbons', after a design by Carlo Scarpa, included in the Venini catalogue (Blue Catalogue).

44 cm high
Galleria Rita Fancsaly collection

1940

Twelve-arm chandelier in *cristallo* glass with arms and spirals in *cristallo* and *lattimo*. Pendants in *cristallo* glass. Finishing in bronzed brass. A similar example was exhibited at the Triennale of Milan in 1940.
The chandelier, after a design by Carlo Scarpa, corresponds to model no. 5315 of the Venini catalogue (Blue Catalogue).

110 cm high
80 cm wide
Private collection, Venice

1938

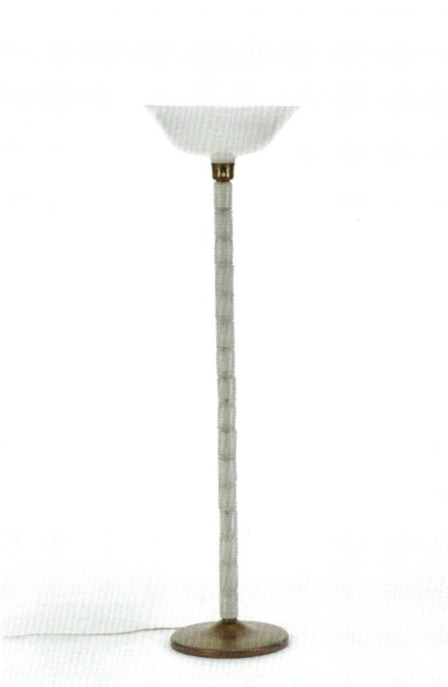

Floor lamp with pole made up of elements in *cristallo* bubble glass with horizontal ribbing. Cup in white *pulegoso* glass with light gold leaf application. Metal mounting. The model was produced by the Venini technical office where Carlo Scarpa was present as draftsman and designer. The lamp corresponds to no. 509 in the Venini catalogue (Blue Catalogue).

178 cm igh
engraved signature *Made in Italy*
Private collection

1942

Floor lamp with stem and foot in *cristallo* glass polished by grinding with brass mounting. The lamp, after a design by Carlo Scarpa, corresponds to model no. 527 of the Venini catalogue (Blue Catalogue).

176 cm high
Private collection

1942

Floor lamp in smoked glass with deep twisted ribbing. Brass metal frame. The lamp, after a design by Carlo Scarpa, corresponds to model no. 529 ('rigato tondo') [round ribbed] of the Venini catalogue (Blue Catalogue).

171 cm high
Private collection, Treviso

1946-48

Chandelier with eight arms in glass of various colours and finishing in *cristallo* glass. The design of the piece was subsequently reworked and the lower rounded element was replaced by a dome-shaped element. The chandelier, designed by Gio Ponti, corresponds to model no. 5557 of the Venini catalogue (Red Catalogue).

68 cm high
Privat collection, Germany

c. 1951

Floor lamp with base and shaft in transparent dark blue glass with opaque red vertical bands. The lamp, after a design by Fulvio Bianconi, corresponds to no. 2241 of the Venini catalogue (Red Catalogue).

171 cm high
Private collection

c. 1951

Floor lamp with base and shaft consisting of stacked elements in *zaffiro* and green glass. The lamp, after a design by Fulvio Bianconi, corresponds to model no. 2242 of the Venini catalogue (Red Catalogue).

190 cm high
Private collection

c. 1951

Floor lamp with base and shaft in *cristallo* glass with green, *zaffiro*, black and red bands. The lamp, after a design by Fulvio Bianconi, corresponds to no. 2243 of the Venini catalogue.

180 cm high
Private collection, Germany

c. 1951

Table lamp in the shape of a truncated cone in blue transparent glass with opaque orange vertical bands. The lamp, after a design by Fulvio Bianconi, corresponds to the variant of model no. 4489 of the Venini catalogue.

height 88 cm
Bischofberger collection, Männedorf-Zurich, Switzerland

1951-56

Large sconce with *lattimo* and aqua-marine canes. Mounting in bronzed brass. The light comes from the Venini shop in Milan.

114 cm high
Herat de Nicola collection

1951-52

Table lamp with base in white opaline glass. Diffuser body in white opaline glass. Mounting in polished brass. The lamp belongs to the so-called 'petroline' series, designed by Paolo Venini, and corresponds to model no. 2706 of the Venini catalogue (Red Catalogue).

44.5 cm high
Private collection

1951-52

Table lamp with base in *verde mela* [apple-green] opaline glass. Diffuser body in *zanfirico lattimo* cane glass. Mounting in polished brass. The lamp belongs to the so-called 'petroline' series, designed by Paolo Venini, and corresponds is a smaller scale variant of model no. 2704 (h 31 cm) of the Venini catalogue (Red Catalogue).

33 cm high
Marcello Moretti Fine Art collection

1951-52

Table lamp with base in red opaline glass. Diffuser body in white opaline glass. Polished brass mounting. The lamp belongs to the so-called 'petro-line' series, designed by Paolo Venini, and corresponds to model no. 2713 of the Venini catalogue (Red Catalogue).

48 cm high
Venini Murano Italia acid stamp
Private collection, Paris

1951-52

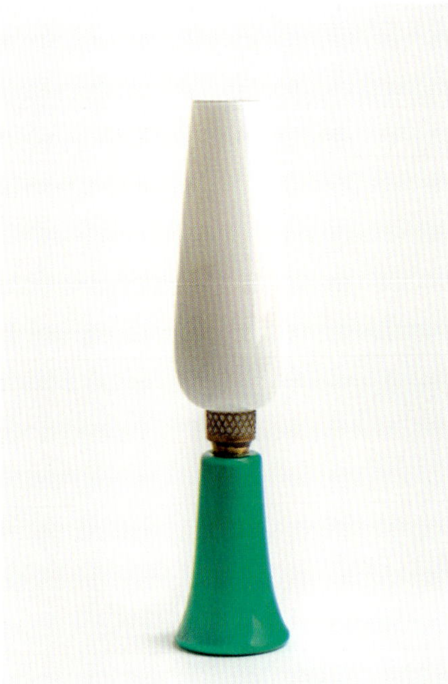

Table lamp with base in green opaline glass. Diffuser body in white opaline glass. Mounting in polished brass. The lamp belongs to the so-called 'petroline' series, designed by Paolo Venini, and corresponds to model no. 2789 of the Venini catalogue (Red Catalogue).

49 cm high
Private collection

1951-52

Table lamp with base in *cristallo* glass with enclosed flower in *lattimo* and *zaffiro*. Diffuser body in white opaline glass. Mounting in polished brass. The lamp belongs to the 'petroline' series designed by Paolo Venini and corresponds to model no. 2786 of the Venini catalogue (Red Catalogue).

42 cm high
Private collection

1954

Table lamp with base in plum-purple composite glass. Metal mounting in brass. The lamp belongs to the 'petroline' series designed by Paolo Venini and corresponds to model no. 2778 of the Venini catalogue.

48 cm high
Murano Italia acid stamp
Marcello Moretti Fine Art collection

1954

Pendant lamp in opaline glass with *fasce di colore* (green, sapphire, black and red). Metal collar and mounting. The lamp, designed by the BBPR group [group of architects], was created for the Olivetti Shop of New York in 1954. The same model, with other colour variants and numbered AV-5457, was subsequently included in the catalogue *Contemporary Italian Lighting* of the Altamira shop, the American dealer for Venini.

66.5 cm high
Antonello collection

1954

Pendant lamp in red and opaline cased glass and internal shade in white opaline glass. A similar model, in turquoise glass, was produced for the small amphitheatre of the Triennale of Milan in 1954. The light, after a design by Franco Albini, is entered in the catalogue under no. 4023, and afterwards nos. 800.2-3 (*Venini lighting catalogue*, 1966).

18 cm high
16 cm ø
Giampaolo Caliari, Oliver Patrick Caliari collection

1955

Pendant lamps in green opaline glass, in *zolfo* opaline glass, in *zaffiro* opaline glass, in tea-coloured opaline glass, in purple opaline glass and in white opaline glass. Three similar pieces, in green opaline, *zolfo* opaline and *zaffiro* opaline were exhibited at the Biennale of Venice in 1956. The lamps, after a design by Massimo Vignelli, correspond to model no. 4029 of the Venini catalogue.

120 cm high
Private collection, Venice

1955

Pendant lamps, one in red opaline glass and the other in white opaline glass, both with a final part in *cristallo* glass with stripes of different colours (black, red, green and *zaffiro*). The lamps, after a design by Massimo Vignelli, correspond to models nos. 4035 and 4041 in the Venini catalogue.

39; 45 cm high
Private collection, Udine

1955

Pendant lamp in white opaline glass with an upper a *fasce di colore* [bands of colour] truncated cone-shaped section in dark amethyst, red, green and *zaffiro*. The lamp, after a design by Massimo Vignelli, corresponds to model no. 4037 in the Venini catalogue.

39 cm high
Private collection

1955

Large pendant lamp in *tessuto* glass with thin white and amethyst canes. The light, designed by Massimo Vignelli, is also known as *Cipolla* and corresponds to a variant on a larger scale of model no. 4039 of the Venini catalogue.

45 cm high
Marco Arosio collection, Milan

1955

Table lamp in opaline glass with thin amethyst canes. A similar example was awarded a mention at the Compasso d'Oro of 1956. The lamp, after a design by Massimo Vignelli, is also known by the name of *Fungo* or *Zaffiro* and corresponds to model no. 4040 in the Venini catalogue.

35 cm high
Gerard Figliola and Mara di Vizia Zanfirico collection, Turin

1955

Table lamp in white opaline glass with broad canes in green glass. The piece, also known as *Fungo* or *Zaffiro*, was awarded a mention at the Compasso d'Oro of 1956. Designed by Massimo Vignelli, it corresponds to model no. 4040 of the Venini catalogue.

28 cm high
Giampaolo Caliari, Oliver Patrick Caliari collection

1957

Wall lamp with square and rectangular bases in bamboo patterned glass with polychrome vertical bands (*cristallo*, amber, *pagliesco*, dark amethyst). Similar examples were produced for the Palazzo delle Cartiere Burgo in Turin.

40 cm high
43; 110 cm wide
Private collection, Belgium

1961-62

Hanging lamp with double *incalmo* technique in opaque anthracite-black glass and a central band in yellow opaline glass. Surface with iridised finish. The lamp belongs to the series *Lines of light*, designed by Thomas Stearns, and corresponds to model no. 4065 of the Venini catalogue.

25 cm high
Private collection

1961-62

Pendant lamp with double *incalmo* technique in opaque antique green and anthracite-black glass with a central band in opaline tea-coloured glass. Surface with iridised finish. The lamp belongs to the series *Lines of light*, designed by Thomas Stearns, and corresponds to no. 4068 of the Venini catalogue.

32 cm high
Private collection

1964

Spherical lamp made up of esprit elements in *cristallo* and tea-coloured glass. The lamp, after a design by Toni Zuccheri, belongs to the series of the same name and corresponds to model no. 959.1 in the Venini catalogue (*Venini lighting catalogue*, 1969).

150 cm high
Pier Francesco Vido collection

1966

Lamps in groups of three elements in transparent glass with several colour strata with surface corrosion and metal mounting. The lights were produced in 1966 for the Teatro Comunale dell'Opera of Florence.

80 cm high
Private collection, Germany

c. 1960

Polyhedron chandelier in smoked and light green glass divided into four tiers with different diameters with a circular base. Metal support frame. The modular elements used belong to the series 951 ('Polyhedrons') of the Venini catalogue (*Venini lighting catalogue,* 1966).

220 cm high
110 cm ø
Enrico Coletti collection

1962

Large multicoloured polyhedron chandelier (bluish, *cristallo,* light pagliesco, pagliesco, red) subdivided into five tapering tiers with a circular base. Metal support frame. The model was created for the foyer of the Teatro Giacosa of Aosta in 1962. The modular elements used belong to the series 951 ('Polyhedrons') of the Venini catalogue (*Venini lighting catalogue*, 1966).

350 cm high
Private collection, Milan

1969

Large chandelier with solid trefoil canes in *cristallo* and tea-coloured glass (detail). The modular elements used belong to the series 963-b ('Trilobi') in the Venini catalogue (*Venini lighting catalogue*, 1969).

250 cm high
Gerard Figliola and Mara di Vizia
Zanfirico collection, Turin

1970

Square-based tiles in *cristallo* glass, with a central relief moulding in transparent glass or glass with coloured patches. Tiles of this type were produced for the Cassa di Risparmio of Cento (Ferrara) in 1970. They belong to the 'pannelli' series present in the Venini catalogue (*Venini 75: Catalogo di illuminazione*, 1975).

41 cm high (module)
42 cm wide (module)
Private collection, Venice

1970

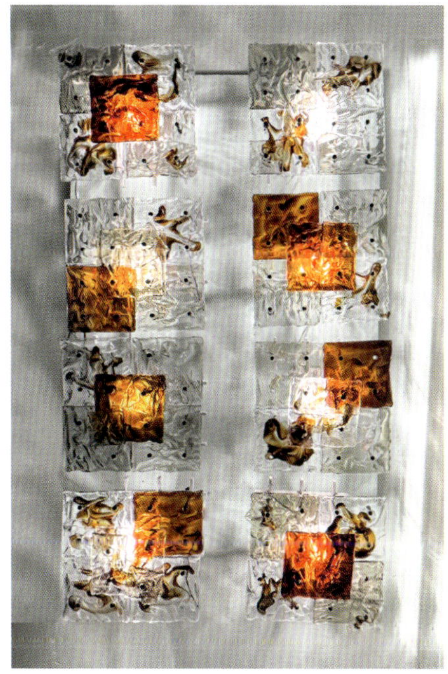

Patchwork, a wall composition with six modules made up of sheets of *cristallo, pagliesco* and tea-coloured patterned glass (variant A). Fixed with a pivot on to a metal grid. The series, after a design by Ludovico Diaz de Santillana, was exhibited at the Biennale of Venice in 1970 and is included in the catalogue under the number 952 (*Venini nuovo catalogo illuminazione 1973*, 1972).

30 cm high (module)
30 cm wide (module)
ROBERTAEBASTA collection

1972-73

Pastorale, composition with blown and hand-shaped elements in *cristallo* glass. Support structure in chrome-plated metal. The artefact corresponds to model no. 966.00 in the Venini catalogue (*Venini nuovo catalogo illuminazione 1973*, 1972).

176 cm high
Mark Van Wynsberge collection

1970-72

Table lamp with shaped body having a circular base in bronze composite glass with a ground edge. Mounting in chrome-plated metal. Exposed light source with silver dome-shaped bulb. The lamp belongs to the series 'Sole' and corresponds to model no. 818.10 in the Venini catalogue (*Venini*, [1972-73], card catalogue).

36 cm high
Gerard Figliola and Mara di Vizia Zanfirico collection, Turin

1972

Table lamp with a globular body in transparent taupe glass containing spheres in *cristallo*, tea-coloured and aquamarine glass. Shaped support base in *cristallo* glass. The lamp belongs to the series 'Pallotta' and corresponds to model no. 821.02 in the Venini catalogue (*Venini nuovo catalogo illuminazione 1973*, 1972).

48 cm high
Mark Van Wynsberge collection

1972

Centoundici, parallelepiped-shaped table lamp in *lattimo* and *cristallo* glass. The lamp, after a design by Mario Ticcò, corresponds to model no. 820.12 in the Venini catalogue (*Venini nuovo catalogo illuminazione 1973*, 1972).

21 cm high
Mark Van Wynsberge collection

1972

Table lamp in *lattimo* glass with inserts in taupe glass. The lamp, after a design by Mario Ticcò, belongs to the series 'Nubolosa' and corresponds to model no. 823.00 in the Venini catalogue (*Venini nuovo catalogo illuminazione 1973*, 1972).

22.5 cm high
Private collection, Belgium

1972

Table lamp in *lattimo* glass with inserts in *cristallo* glass. The lamp, after a design by Mario Ticcò, belongs to the 'Nubolosa' series and corresponds to model no. 823.01 in the Venini catalogue (*Venini nuovo catalogo illuminazione 1973*, 1972).

30 cm high
Mark Van Wynsberge collection

1975

Spherical table lamp in *cristallo* glass and *lattimo* 'canes'. Lacquered metal mounting. The lamp belongs to the 'Anemone' series and corresponds to model no. 831.01 of the Venini catalogue (*Venini 75: Catalogo di illuminazione*, 1975).

40 cm high
Private collection, Germany

1975

Table lamp with base and dome in brown alabaster glass. The lamp belongs to the series 'Alabastro', after a design by Ludovico Diaz de Santillana, and corresponds to model no. 832.00 in the Venini catalogue (*Venini 75: Catalogo di illuminazione*, 1975).

53 cm high
Mark Van Wynsberge collection

1976

Table lamp with ribbed dome in taupe glass. Ribbed stem in *cristallo* glass. Circular base and structure in bronzed metal. The lamp belongs to the series 'Cordonata' and corresponds to model no. 835.00 in the Venini catalogue (*Luce 76*, 1976, booklet).

56 cm high
Mark Van Wynsberge collection

1983

Sigul, floor lamp with base and stem in black lacquered metal and diffuser in black, *lattimo* and green *zanfirico* canes. The lamp, after a design by Laura de Santillana, corresponds to model no. 847.00 of the Venini catalogue (*Venini*, 1983).

187 cm high
Private collection

1983

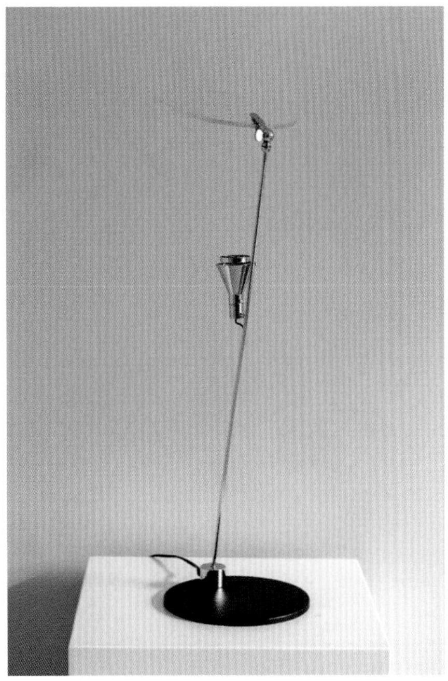

Ustorio, table lamp with a chrome-plated metal structure and orientable diffuser screen in glass with *murrine*, finished at the grinding wheel. The lamp, after a design by Alessandro Diaz de Santillana, corresponds to model no. 847.12 in the Venini catalogue (*Venini*, 1983).

72 cm high
Mark Van Wynsberge collection

1984

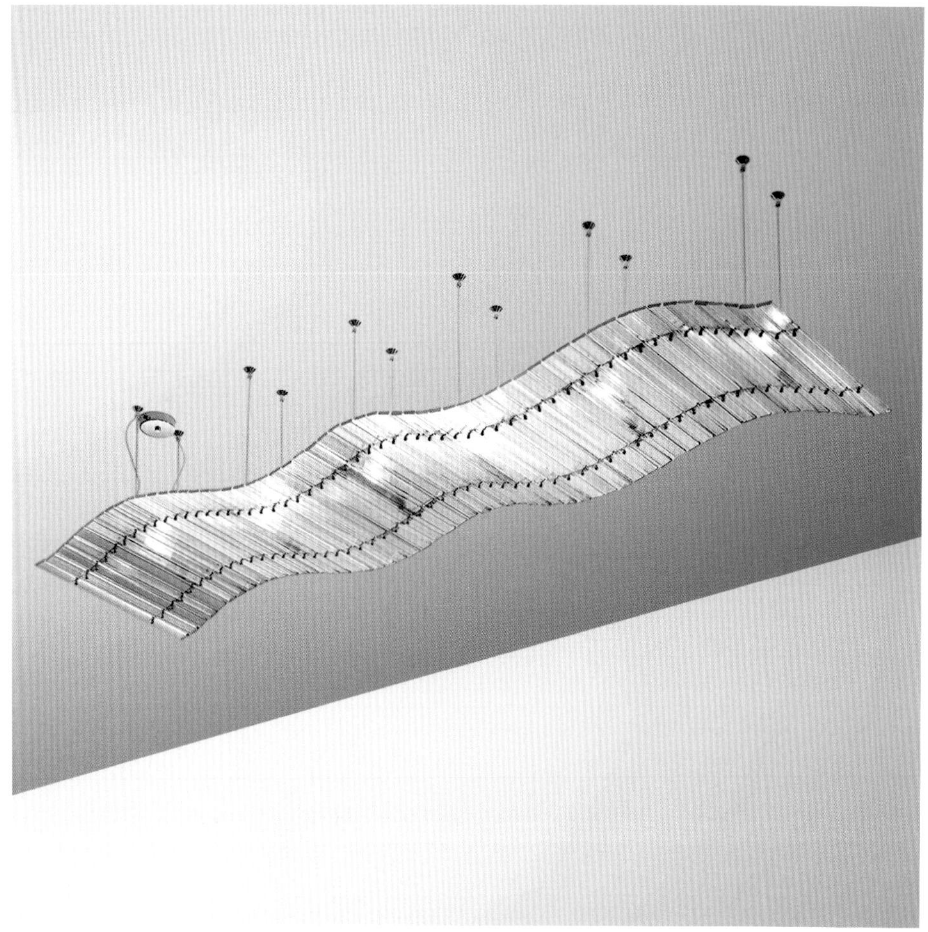

Tappeto volante [Flying carpet] with diffuser screen with *nastri* in *cristallo* glass. Metal support structure. A similar model was exhibited at the Heller Gallery of New York in 1984. The installation, after a design by Ludovico Diaz de Santillana, corresponds to model no. 905.01 of the Venini catalogue (*Venini illuminazione 1987*, 1987).

300 cm lenght
60 cm wide
Private collection

1931-42

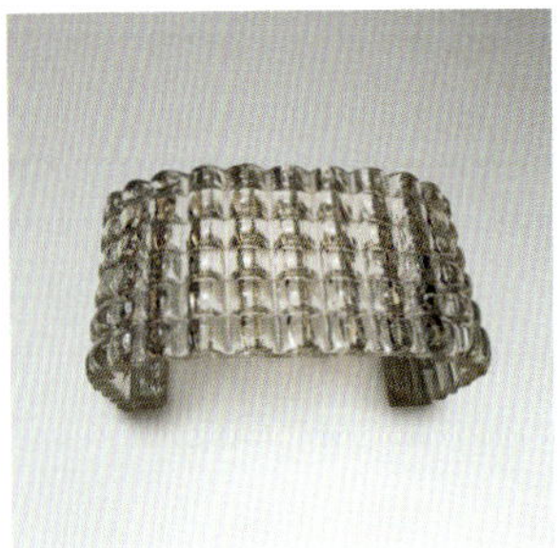

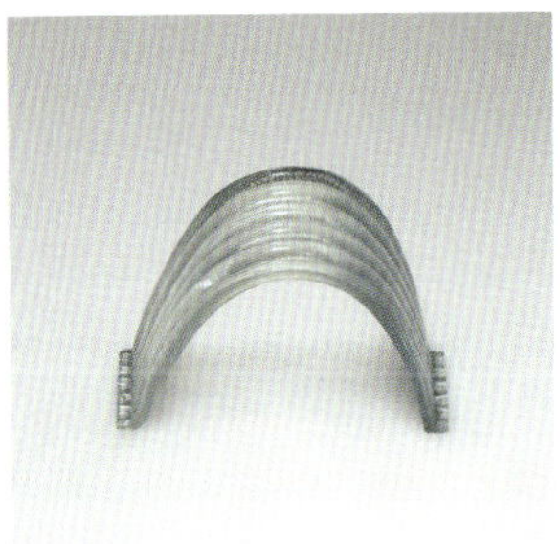

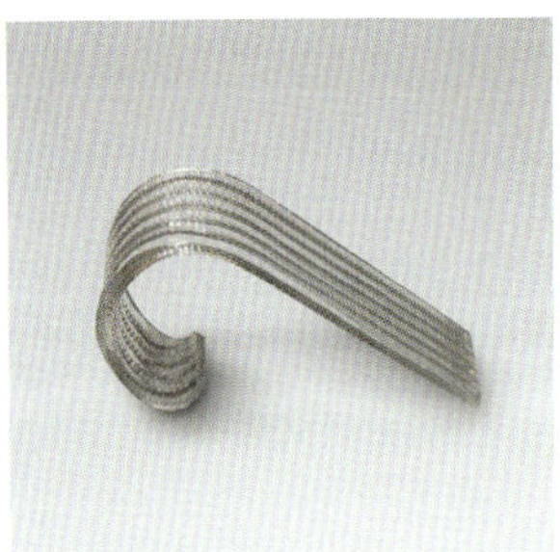

Mouldings with different types of glass (embossed, ribbed, undulated etc.) with which to create modular elements in various shapes and sizes.

from 10 to 15 cm high
from 13 to 48 cm wide
Giampaolo Caliari, Oliver Patrick Caliari collection

1965-69

Sample case with square sheets of *cristallo* glass with various types of patterned glass ('bamboo', 'brain', 'diamond' etc.) produced between the end of the 1930s and the 1960s.

35 cm high (module)
45 cm wide (module)
Marco Arosio collection, Milan

1951

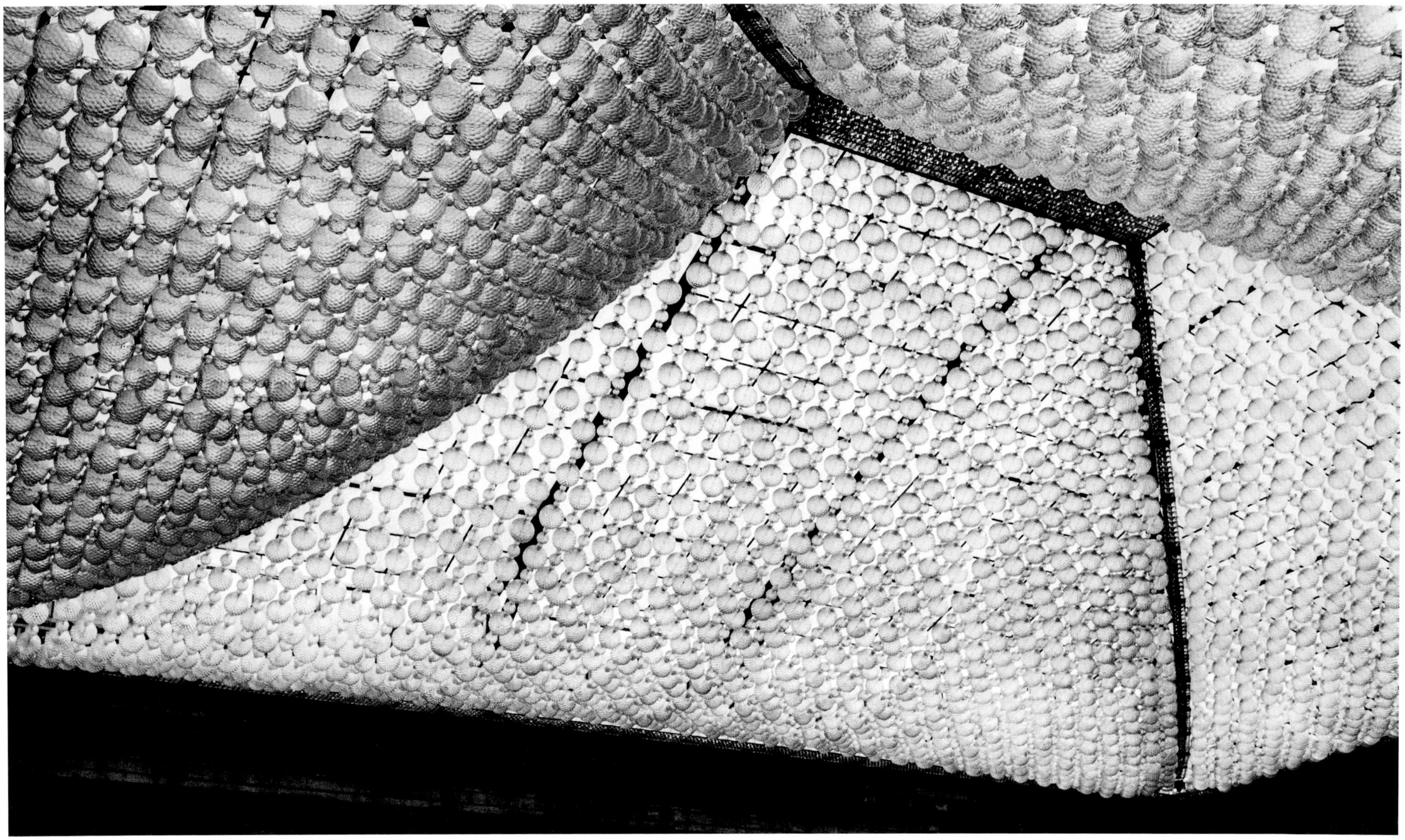

VELARIUM OF PALAZZO GRASSI

Installation with spheres in *cristallo balloton* glass in three different sizes. The work, made with the original spheres for the exhibition VENINI: LIGHT 1921-1985, reproduces on a reduced scale the Velarium made for Palazzo Grassi in 1951, as shown in this period photograph.

950 cm long
700 cm wide
Palazzo Grassi S.p.A. collection

TRIBUTE TO CARLO SCARPA

Installation with polychrome polyhedrons. The work, created for the exhibition VENINI: LIGHT 1921-1985, reproduces, on the basis of original drawings and period photos, the large chandelier designed by Carlo Scarpa for the Veneto pavilion at the Italia 61 exhibition in Turin in 1961, as shown in this period photograph.

424 cm high
550 cm long
520 cm wide

DRAWINGS AND CATALOGUES

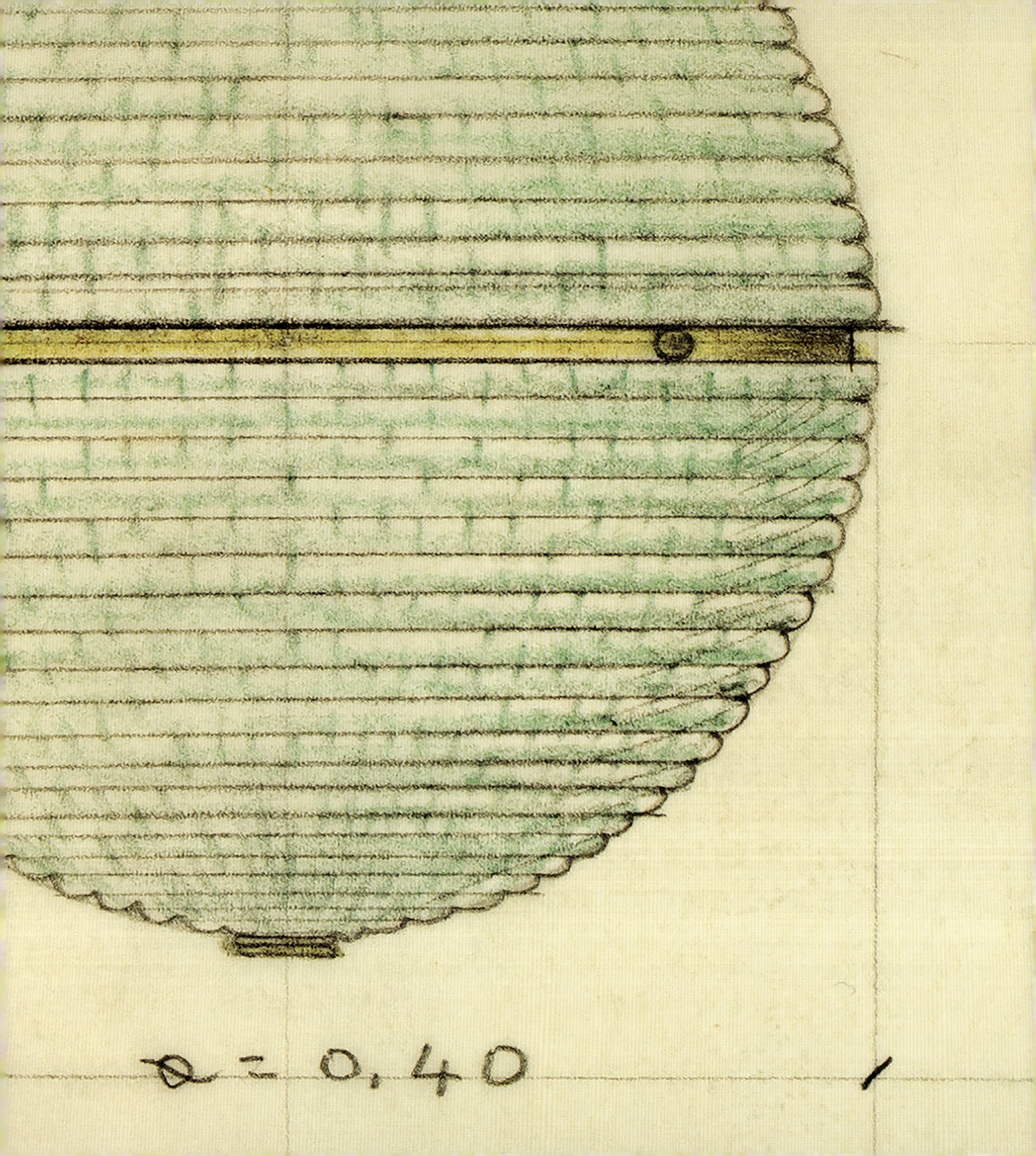
ø = 0,40

DRAWINGS 1930s-1940s

The lamps and chandeliers produced between the 1930s and 1940s are documented in the Venini archive by heterogeneous graphic material. Here a selection is published, consisting principally of tracings, which includes drawings with various numbered models – whether present in the Blue Catalogue or not –, furnace drawings and drawings attached to specific commissions (quotations nos. 50163, 50174, 50253, 50259 and 50262). In most of these the hand of Carlo Scarpa can be detected.

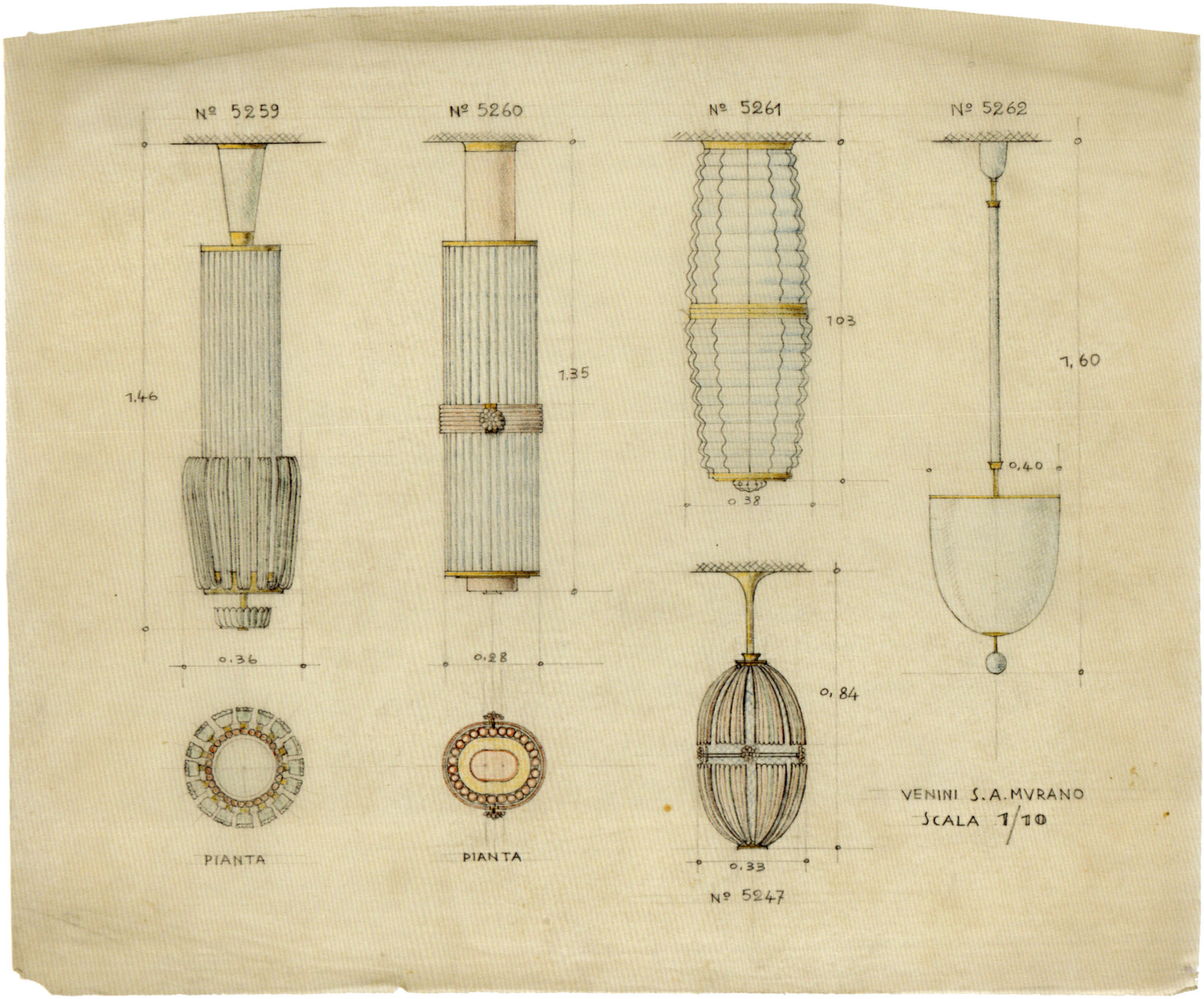

Nº 5259
Nº 5260
Nº 5261
Nº 5262
1.46
1.35
103
1,60
0,40
0.38
0.36
0.28
0,84
PIANTA
PIANTA
0.33
Nº 5247
VENINI S.A. MVRANO
SCALA 1/10

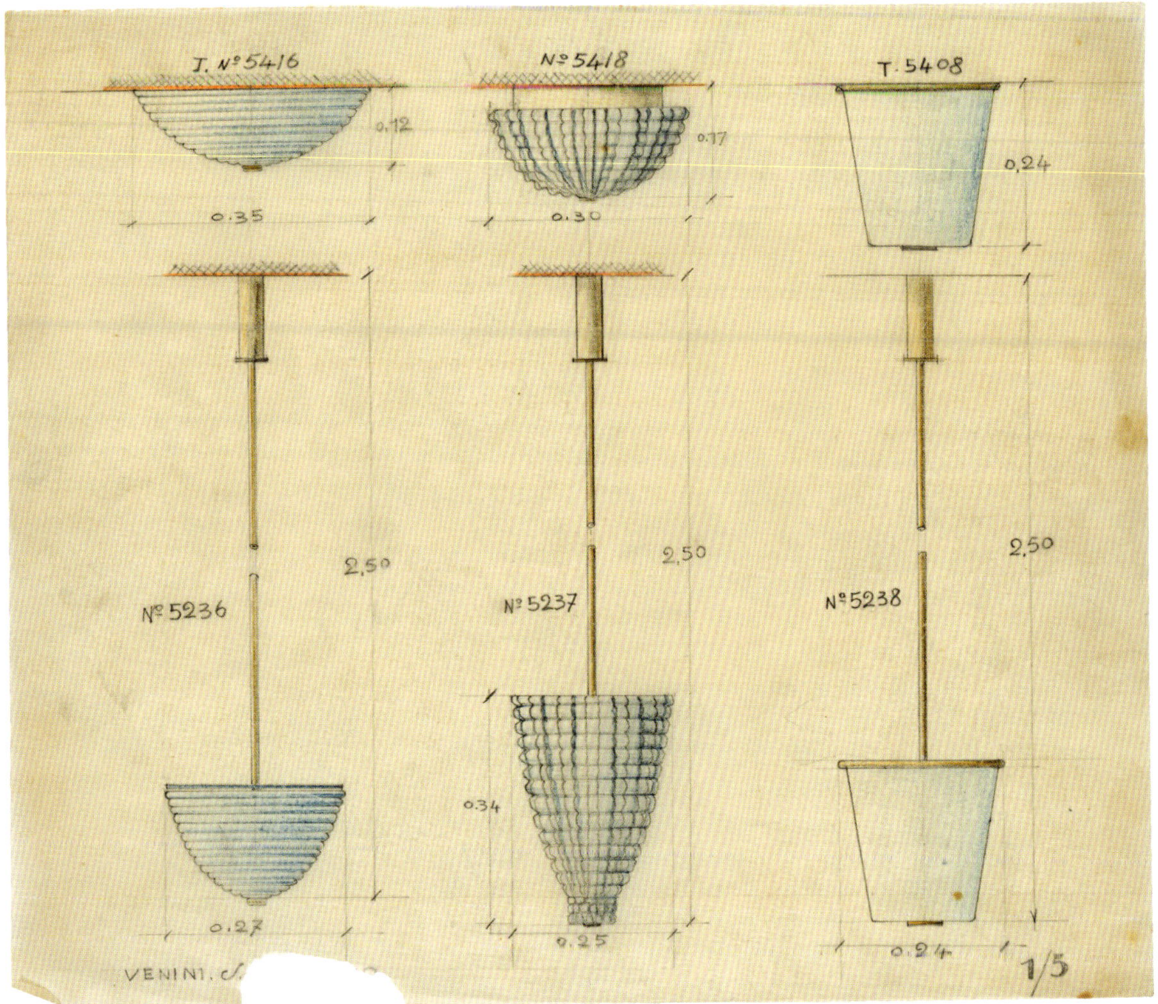
J. Nº5416
Nº5418
T. 5408
0.12
0.17
0.24
0.35
0.30
2,50
2,50
2,50
Nº5236
Nº5237
Nº5238
0.34
0.27
0.25
0.24
VENINI
1/5

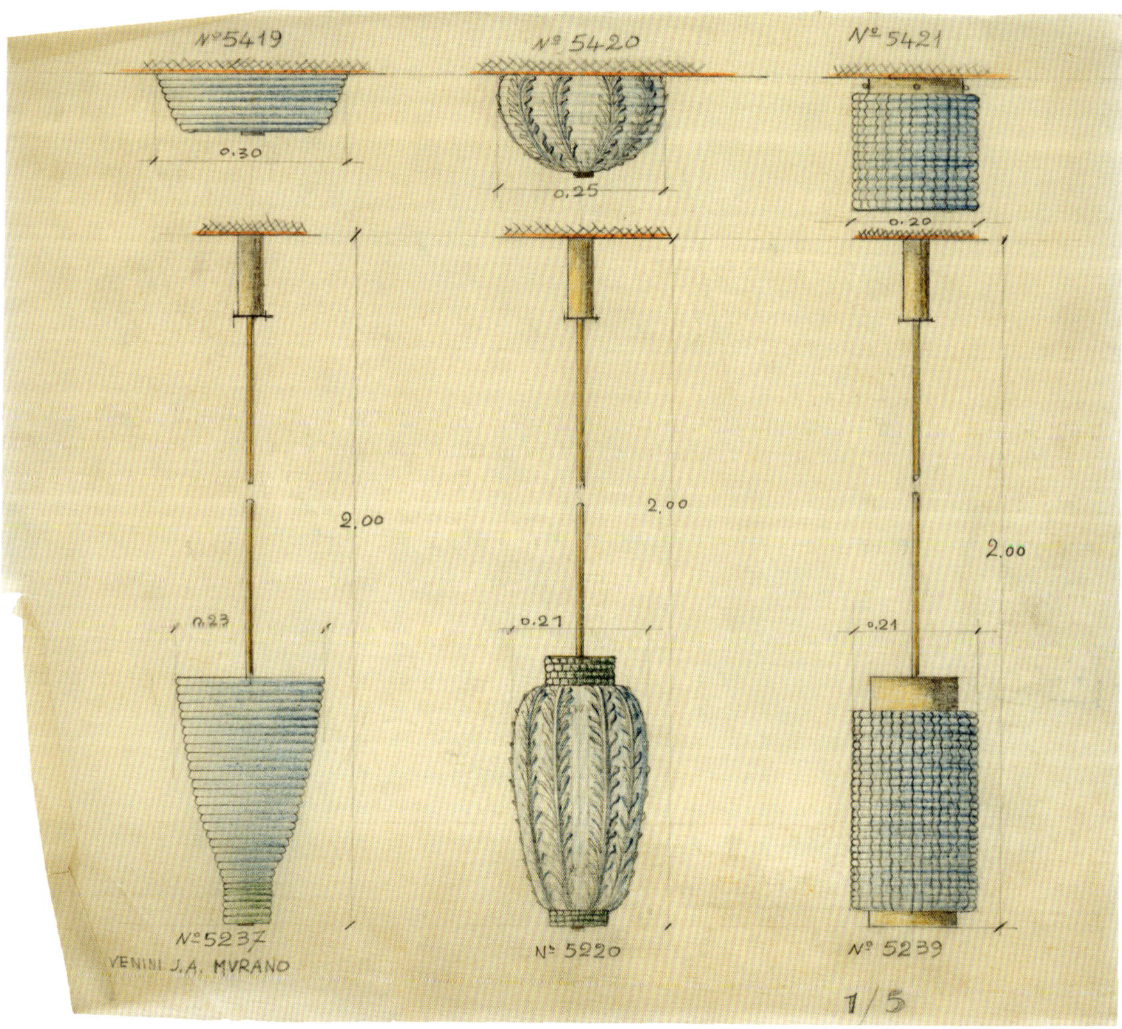
Nº5419
Nº 5420
Nº 5421
0.30
0.25
0.20
2,00
2,00
2,00
0.23
0.21
0.21
Nº5237
Nº 5220
Nº 5239
VENINI S.A. MVRANO
1/5

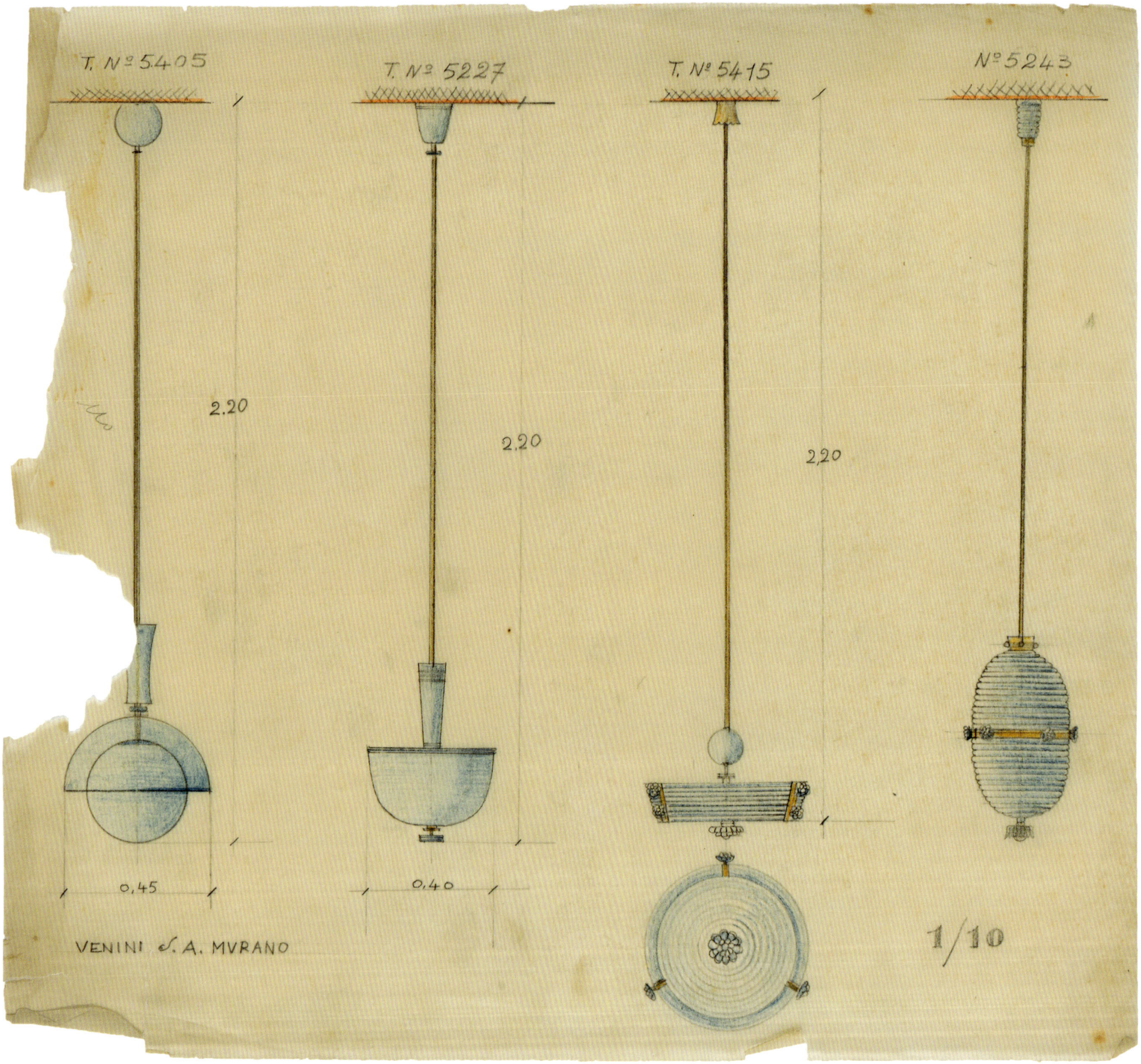
T. Nº 5405
T. Nº 5227
T. Nº 5415
Nº 5243
2.20
2.20
2,20
0,45
0,40
VENINI S.A. MURANO
1/10

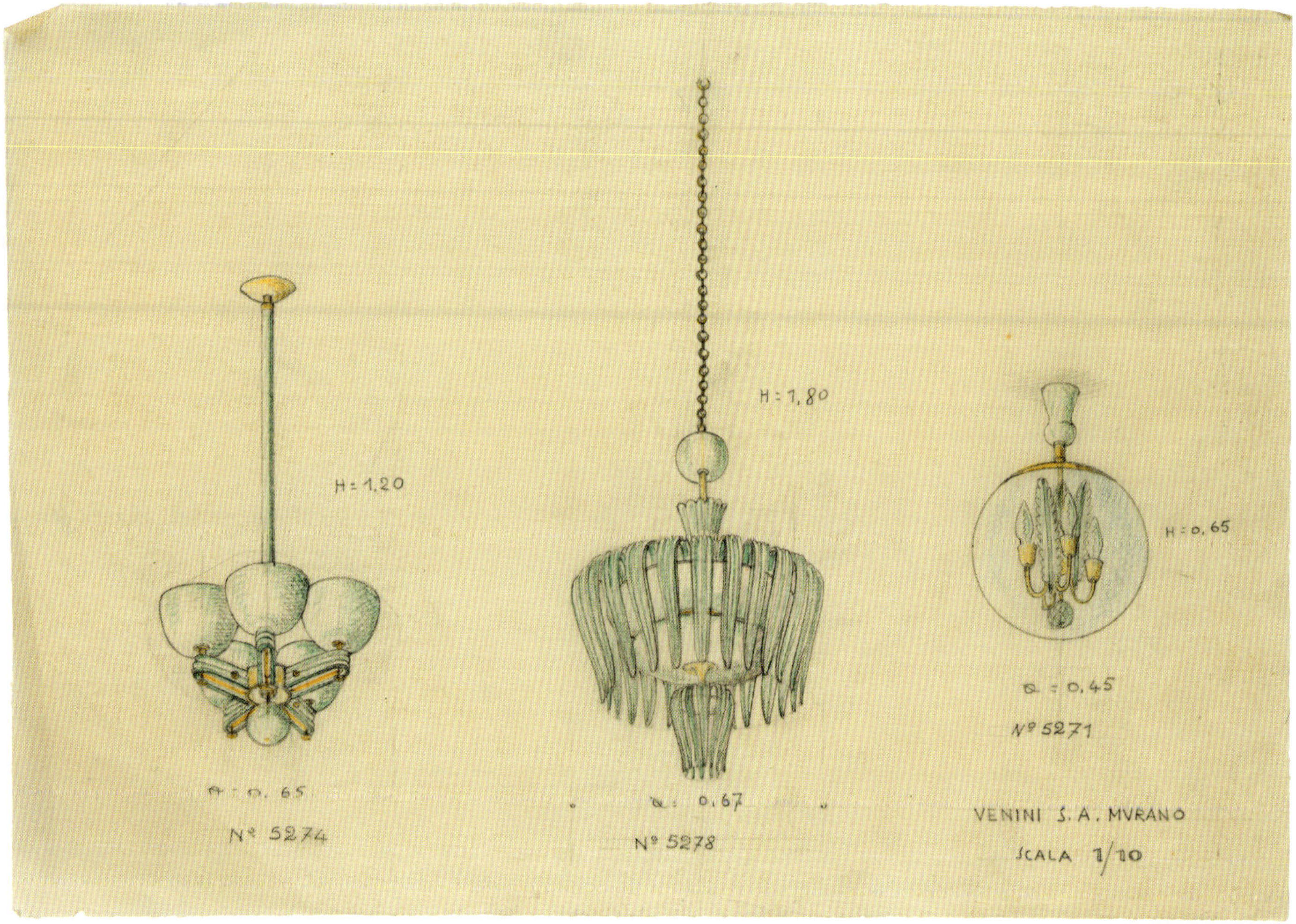
H=1,20
Ø: 0,65
Nº 5274
H=1,80
Ø: 0,67
Nº 5278
H=0,65
Ø=0,45
Nº 5271
VENINI S.A. MVRANO
SCALA 1/10

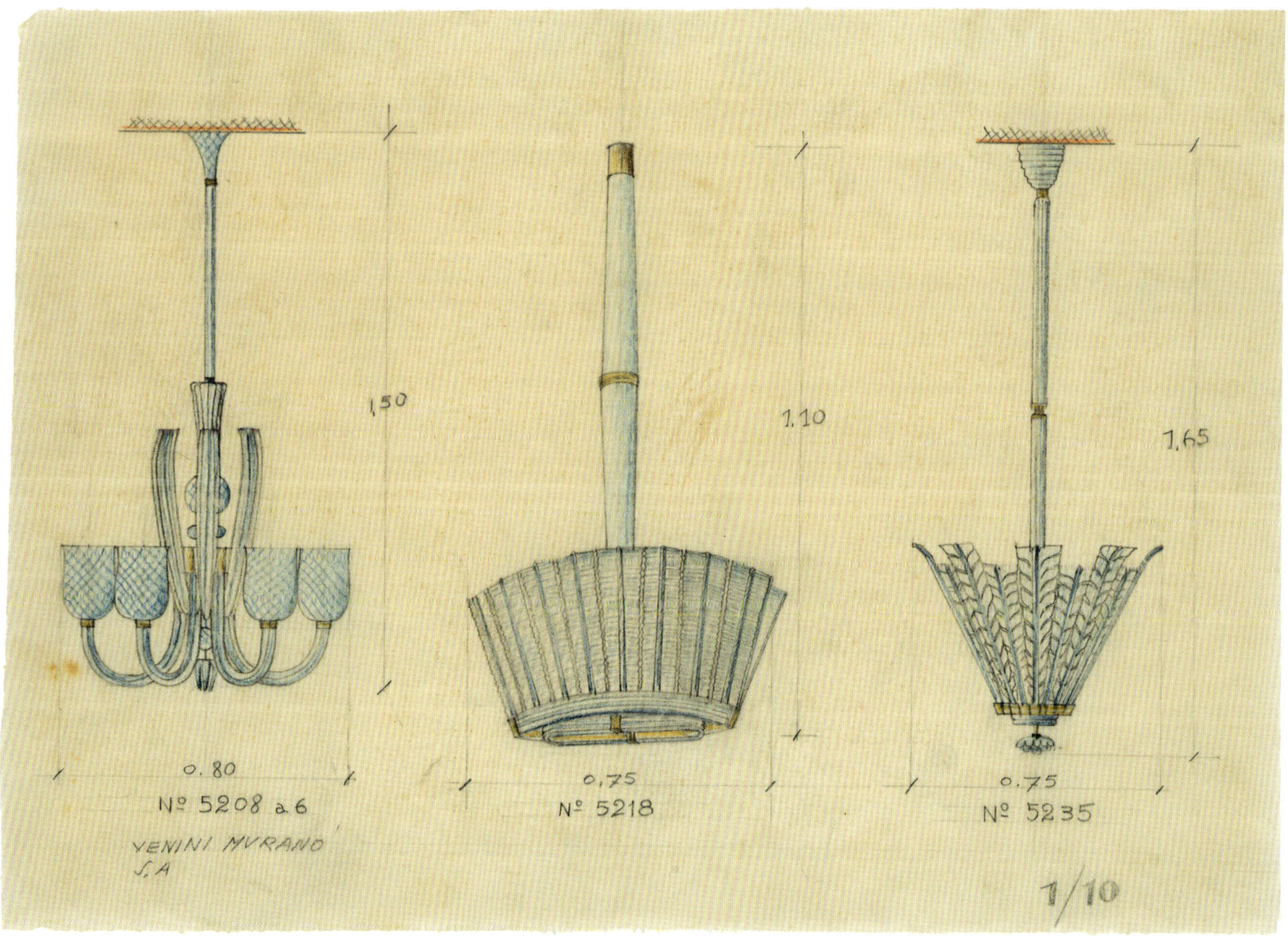
1,50
0,80
Nº 5208 a 6
VENINI MVRANO S.A
1.10
0,75
Nº 5218
1,65
0,75
Nº 5235
1/10

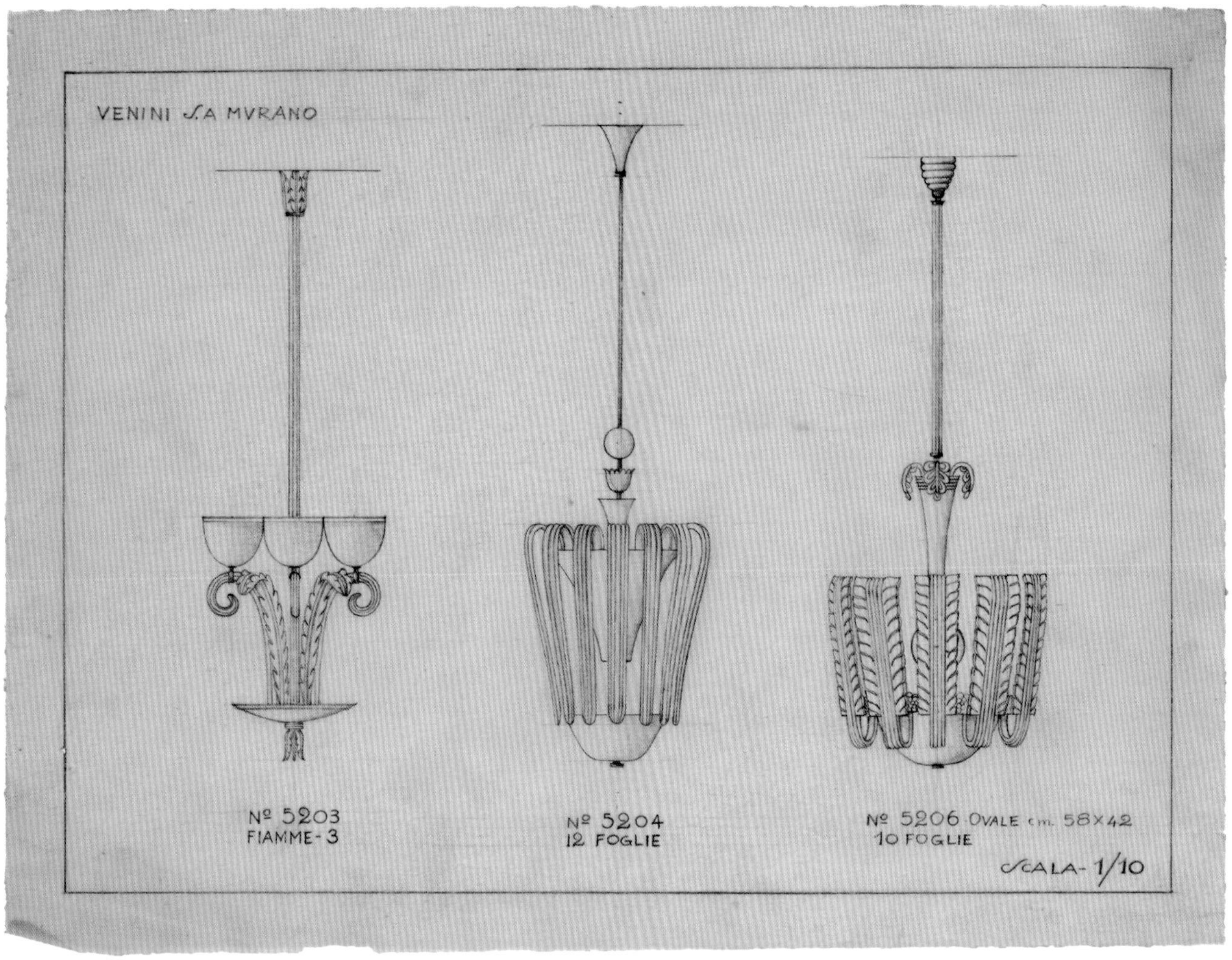
VENINI S.A MURANO
Nº 5203
FIAMME-3
Nº 5204
12 FOGLIE
Nº 5206 OVALE cm. 58×42
10 FOGLIE
SCALA-1/10

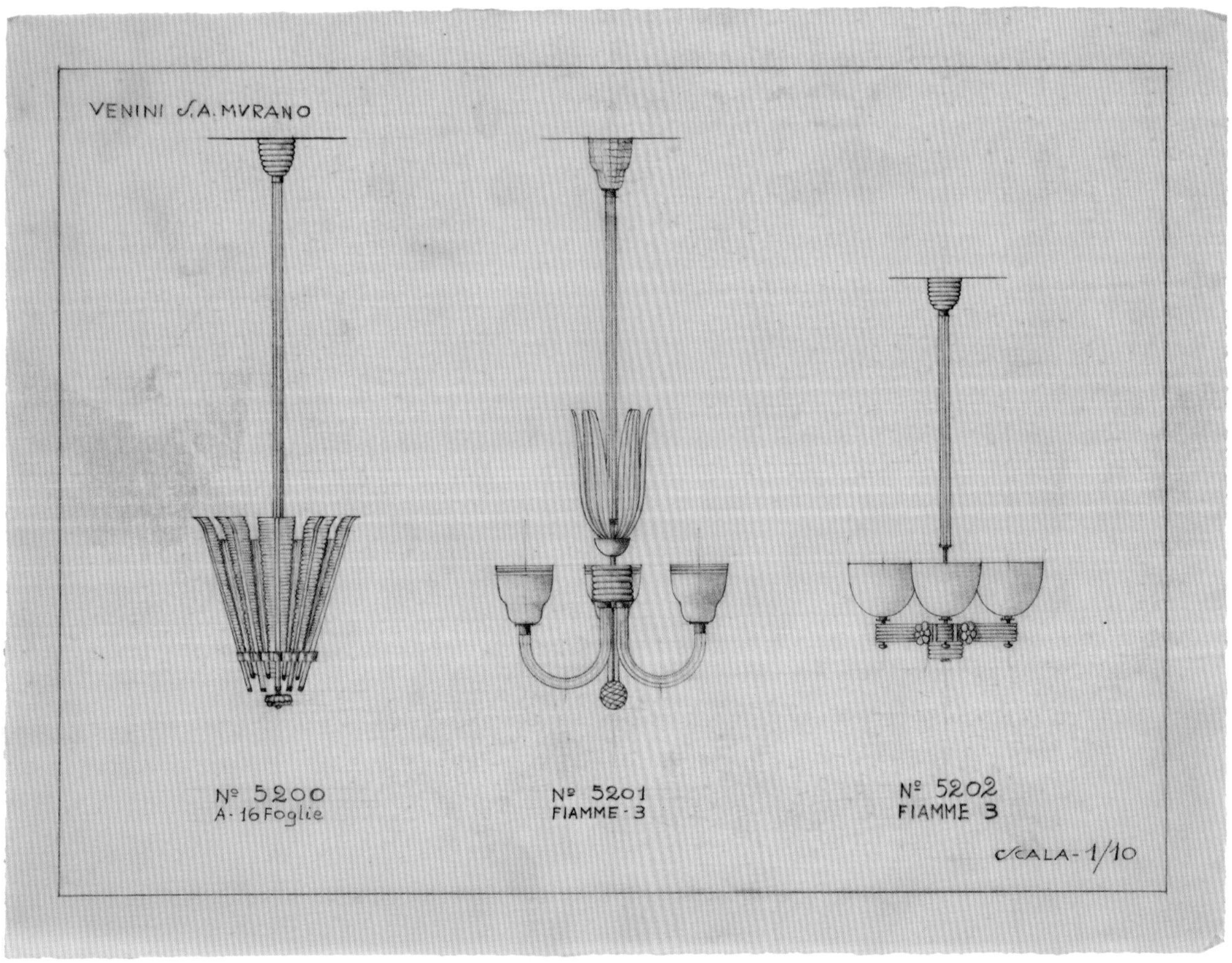
VENINI S.A. MURANO
Nº 5200
A-16 Foglie
Nº 5201
FIAMME-3
Nº 5202
FIAMME 3
SCALA-1/10

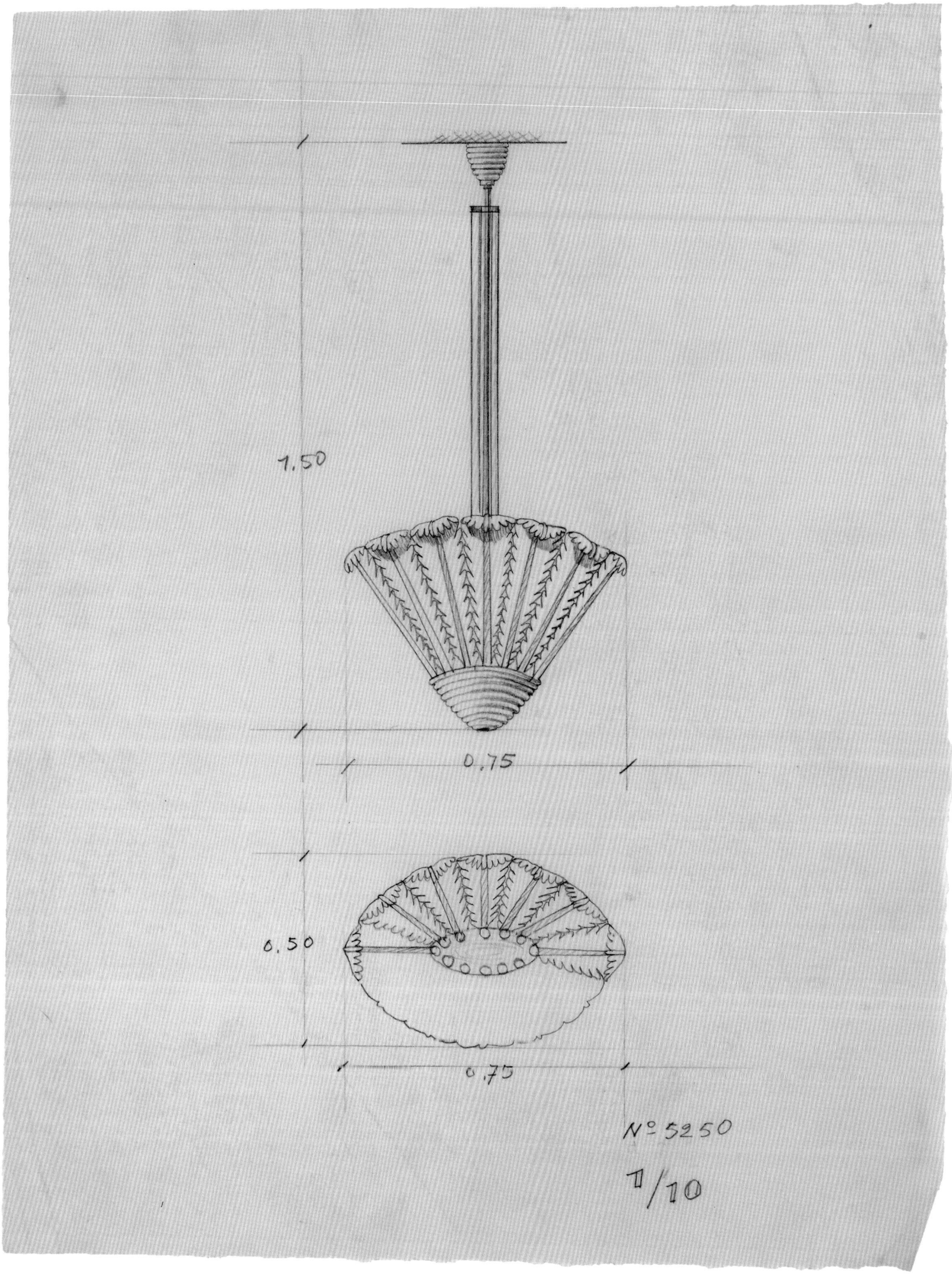
1.50
0.75
0.50
0.75
N° 5250
1/10

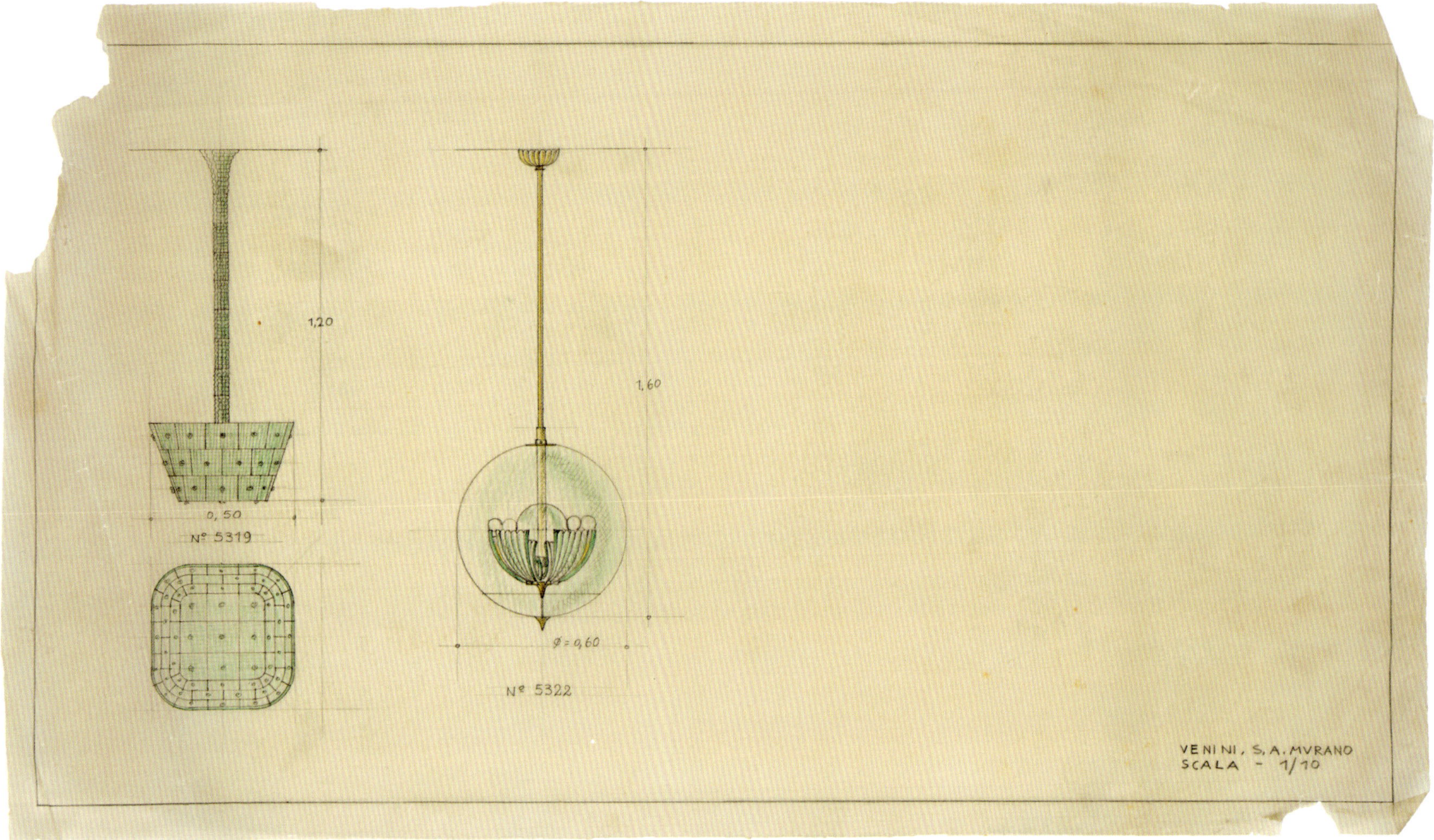
1,20
0,50
Nº 5319
1,60
Ø = 0,60
Nº 5322
VENINI, S.A. MVRANO
SCALA - 1/10

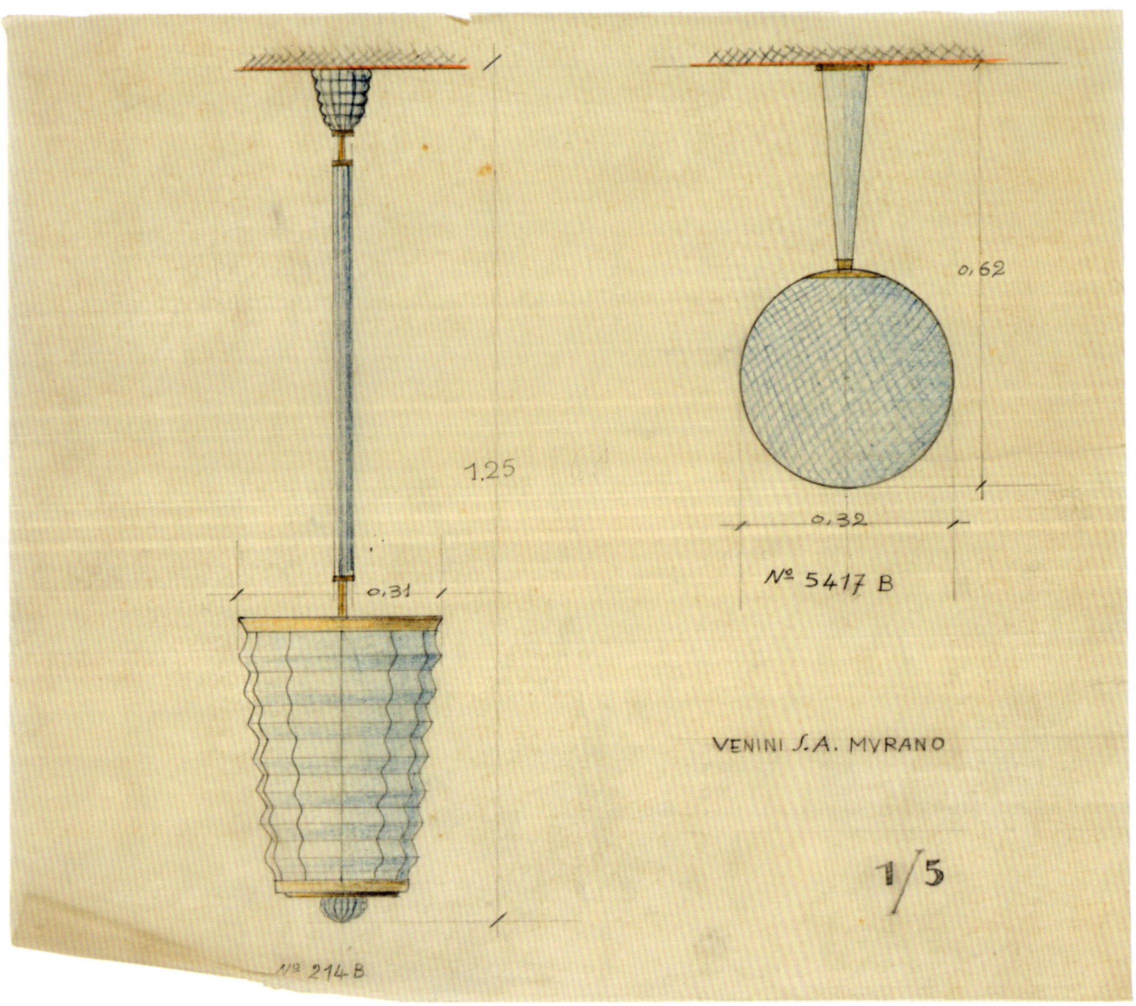
1.25
0,31
Nº 214 B
0,62
0,32
Nº 5417 B
VENINI S.A. MVRANO
1/5

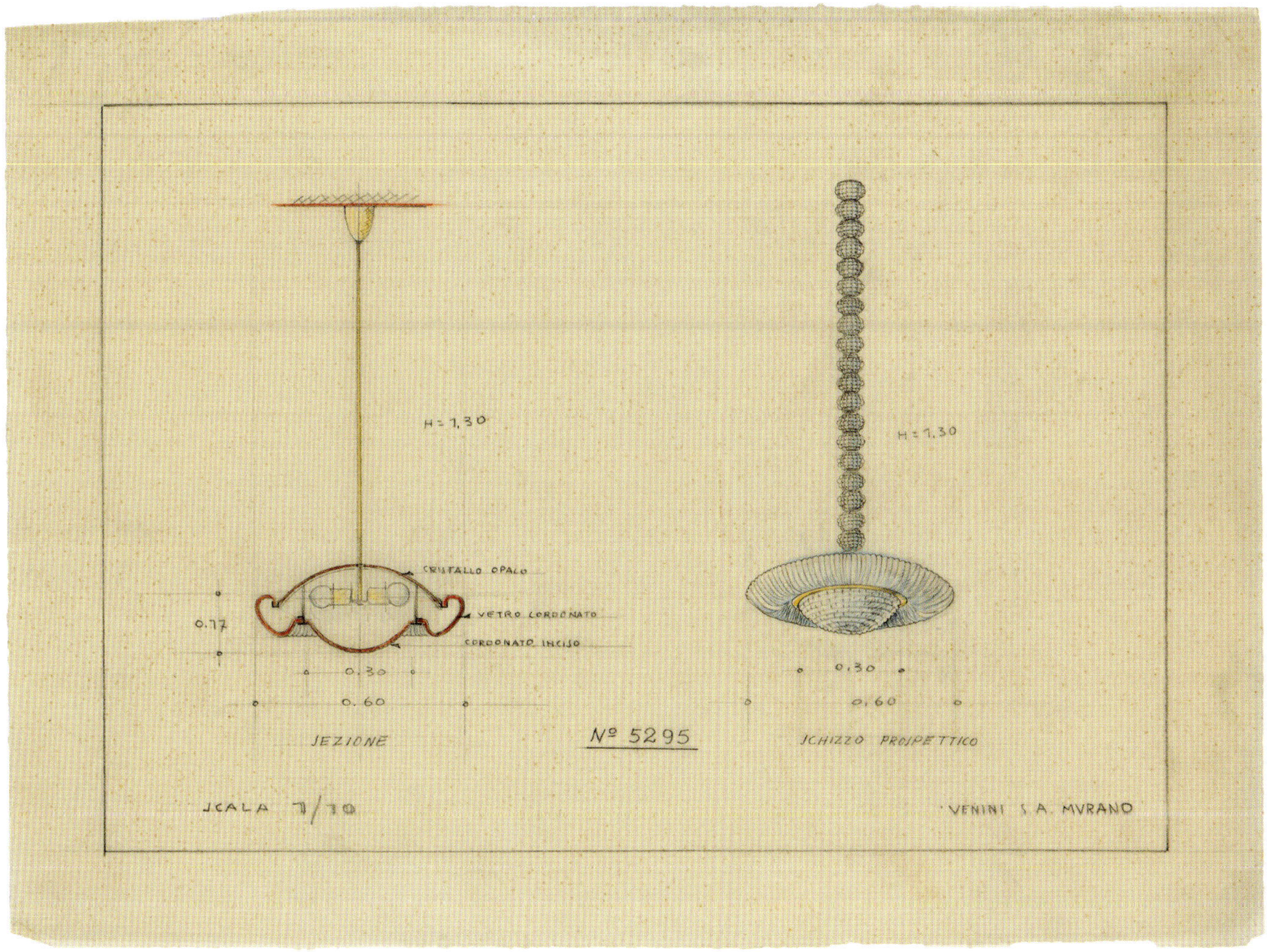
H=1,30
CRISTALLO OPALO
VETRO CORDONATO
CORDONATO INCISO
0,17
0,30
0,60
SEZIONE
Nº 5295
H=1,30
0,30
0,60
SCHIZZO PROSPETTICO
SCALA 1/10
VENINI S.A. MURANO

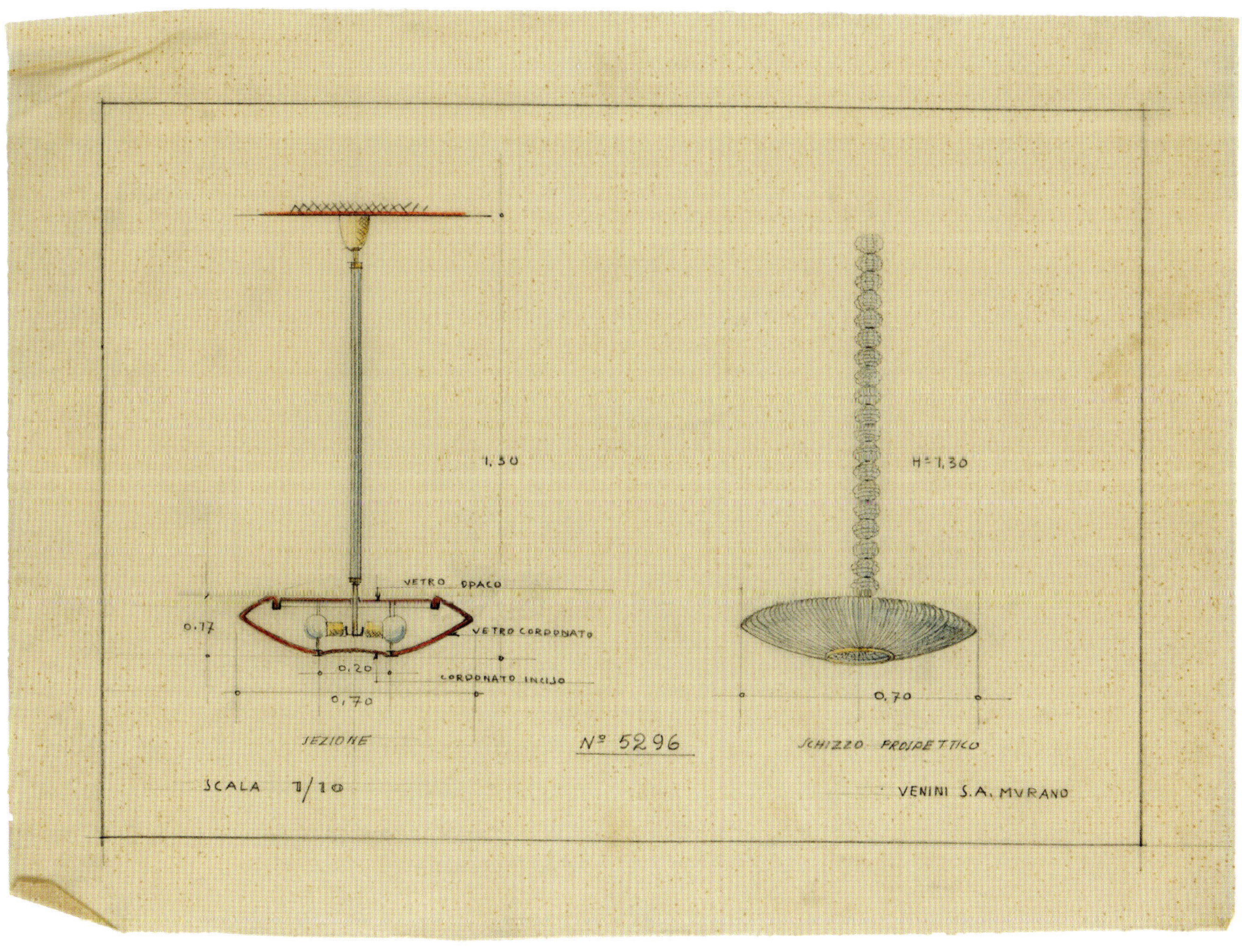
1,30
VETRO OPACO
VETRO CORDONATO
0,17
0,20
CORDONATO INCISO
0,70
SEZIONE
Nº 5296
H=1,30
0,70
SCHIZZO PROSPETTICO
SCALA 1/10
VENINI S.A. MURANO

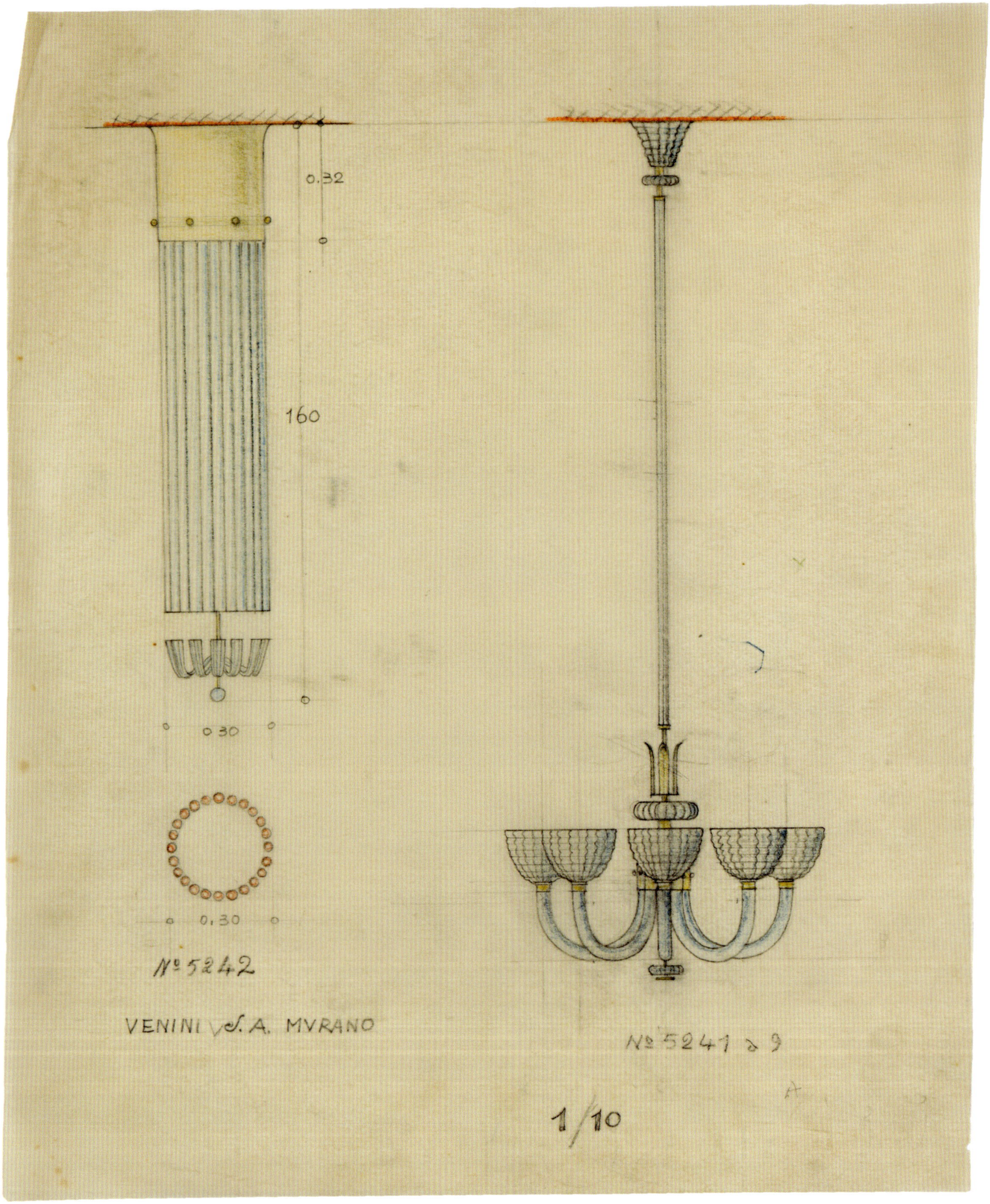
0.32
160
0.30
0.30
Nº 5242
VENINI S.A. MVRANO
Nº 5241 a 9
1/10

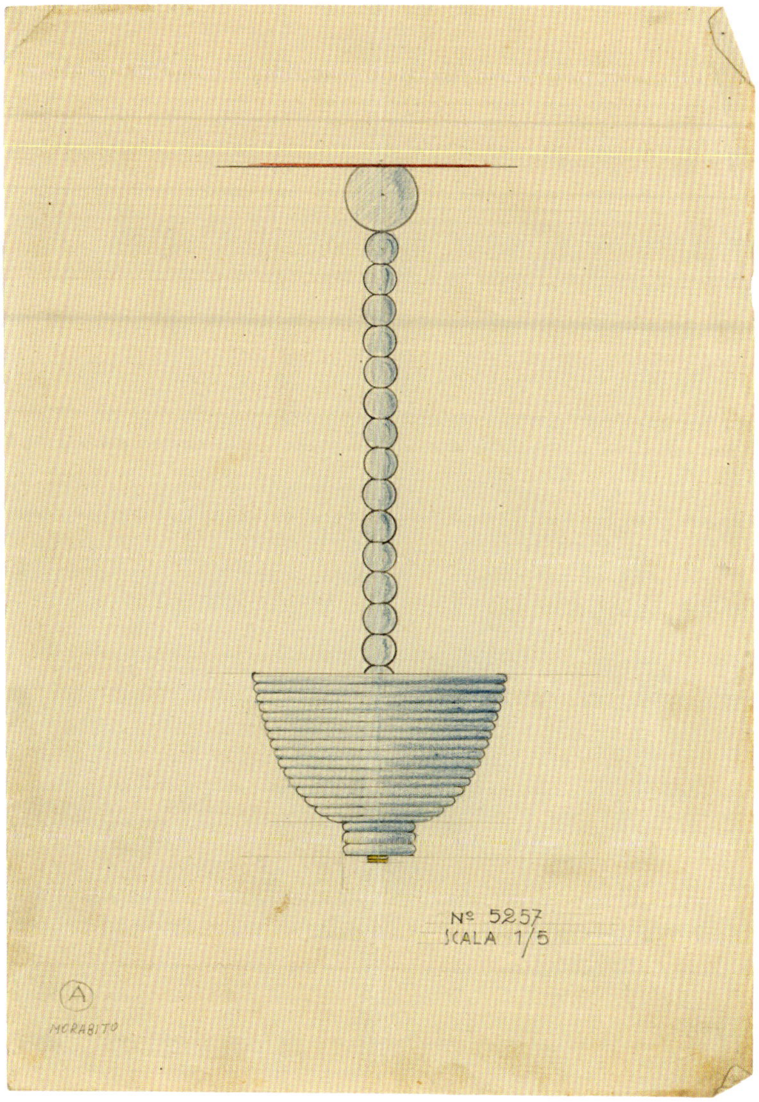
N° 5257
SCALA 1/5
A
MORABITO

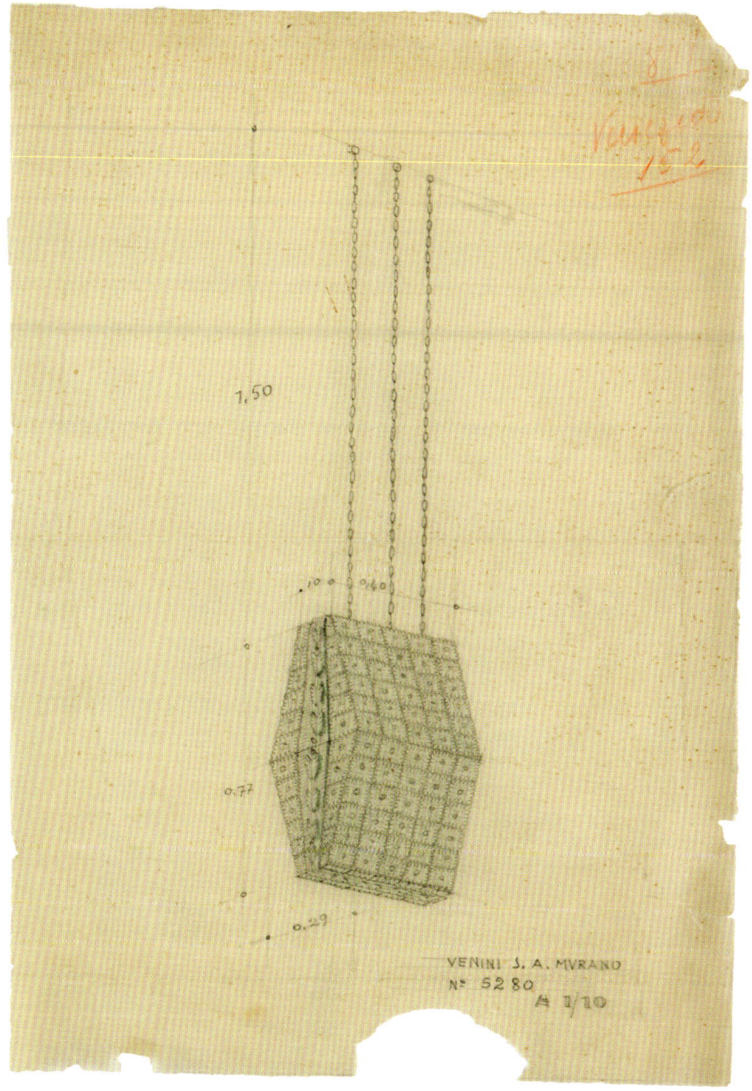
1,50
0,40
0,77
0,29
VENINI S. A. MVRANO
N° 5280
A 1/10

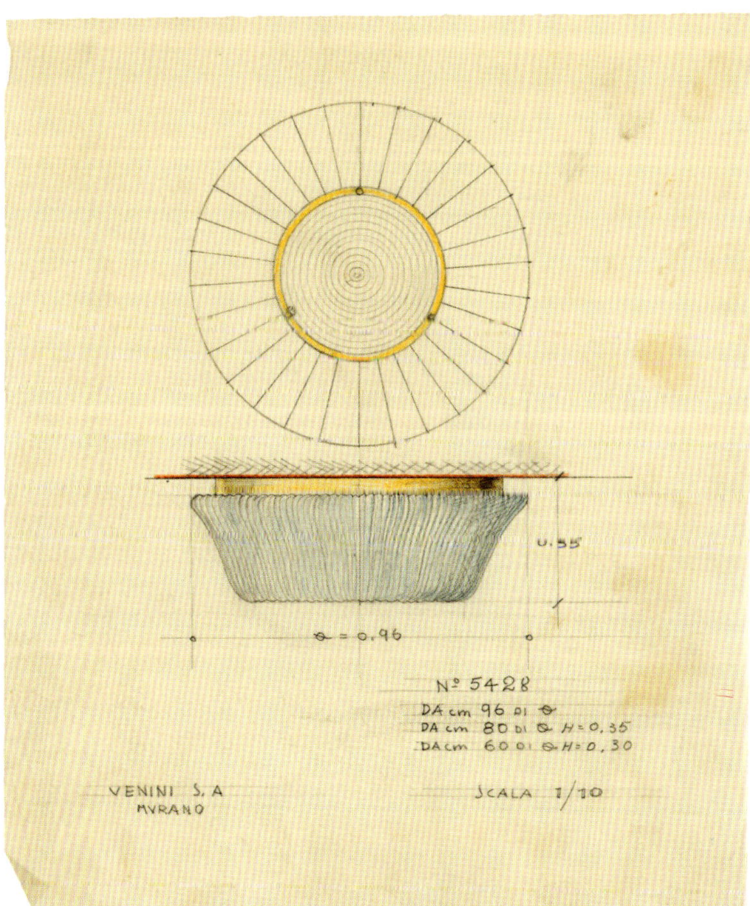
0,35
⌀ = 0,96
N° 5428
DA cm 96 DI ⌀
DA cm 80 DI ⌀ H = 0,35
DA cm 60 DI ⌀ H = 0,30
VENINI S. A
MVRANO
SCALA 1/10

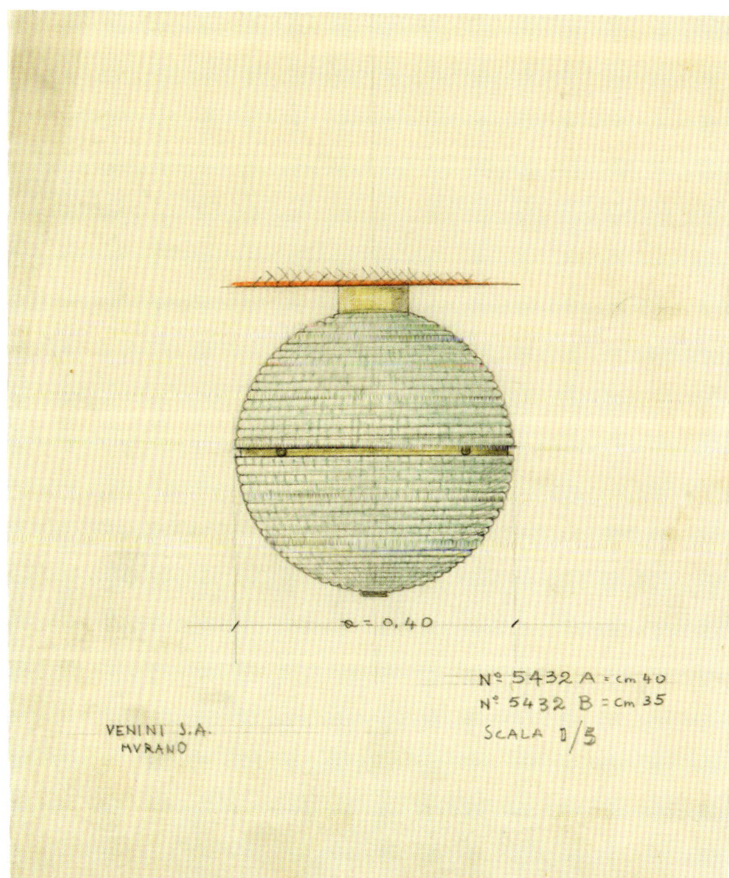
⌀ = 0,40
N° 5432 A = cm 40
N° 5432 B = cm 35
SCALA 1/5
VENINI S. A.
MVRANO

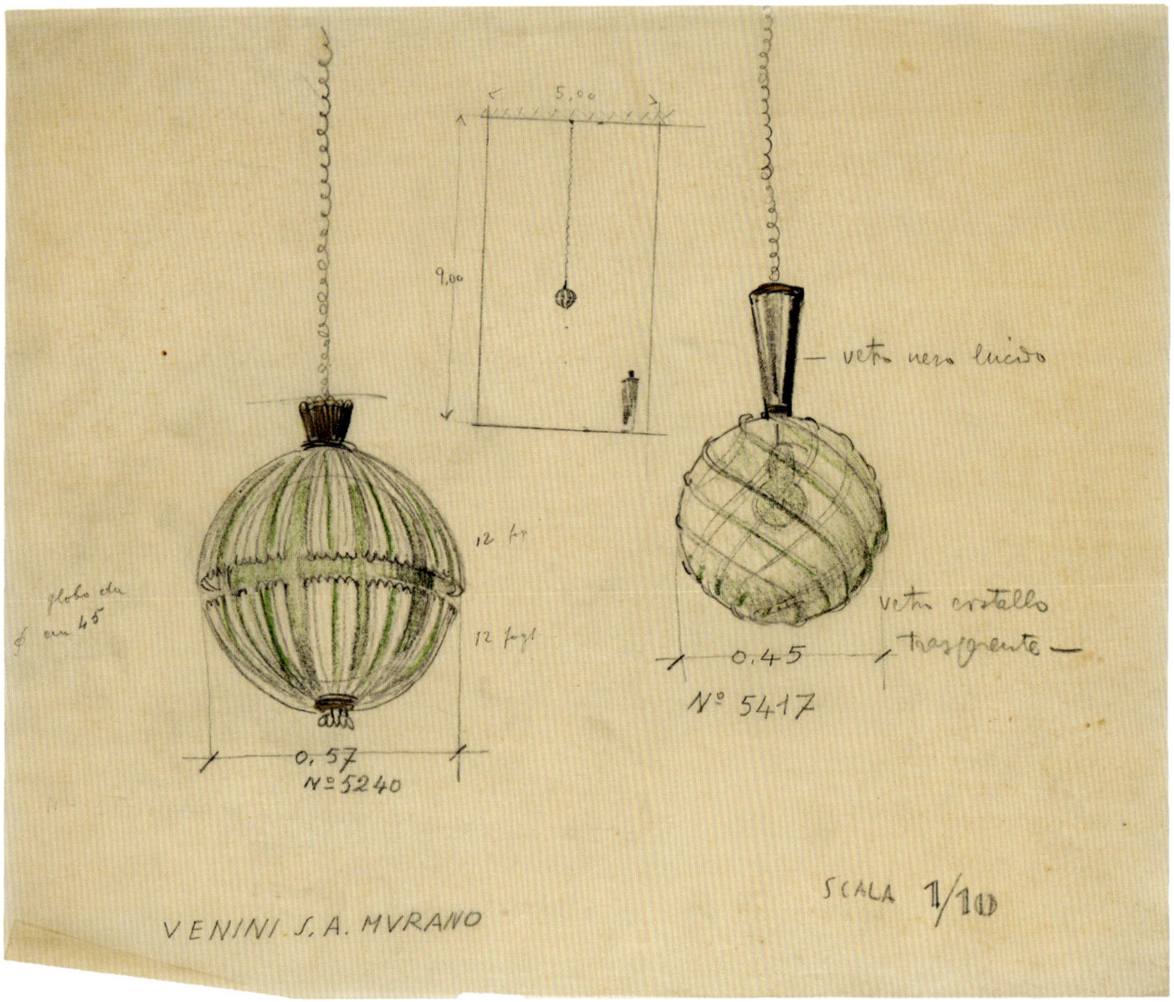
5,00
9,00
vetro nero lucido
vetro cristallo trasparente
0.45
N° 5417
0,57
N° 5240
SCALA 1/10
VENINI S.A. MVRANO

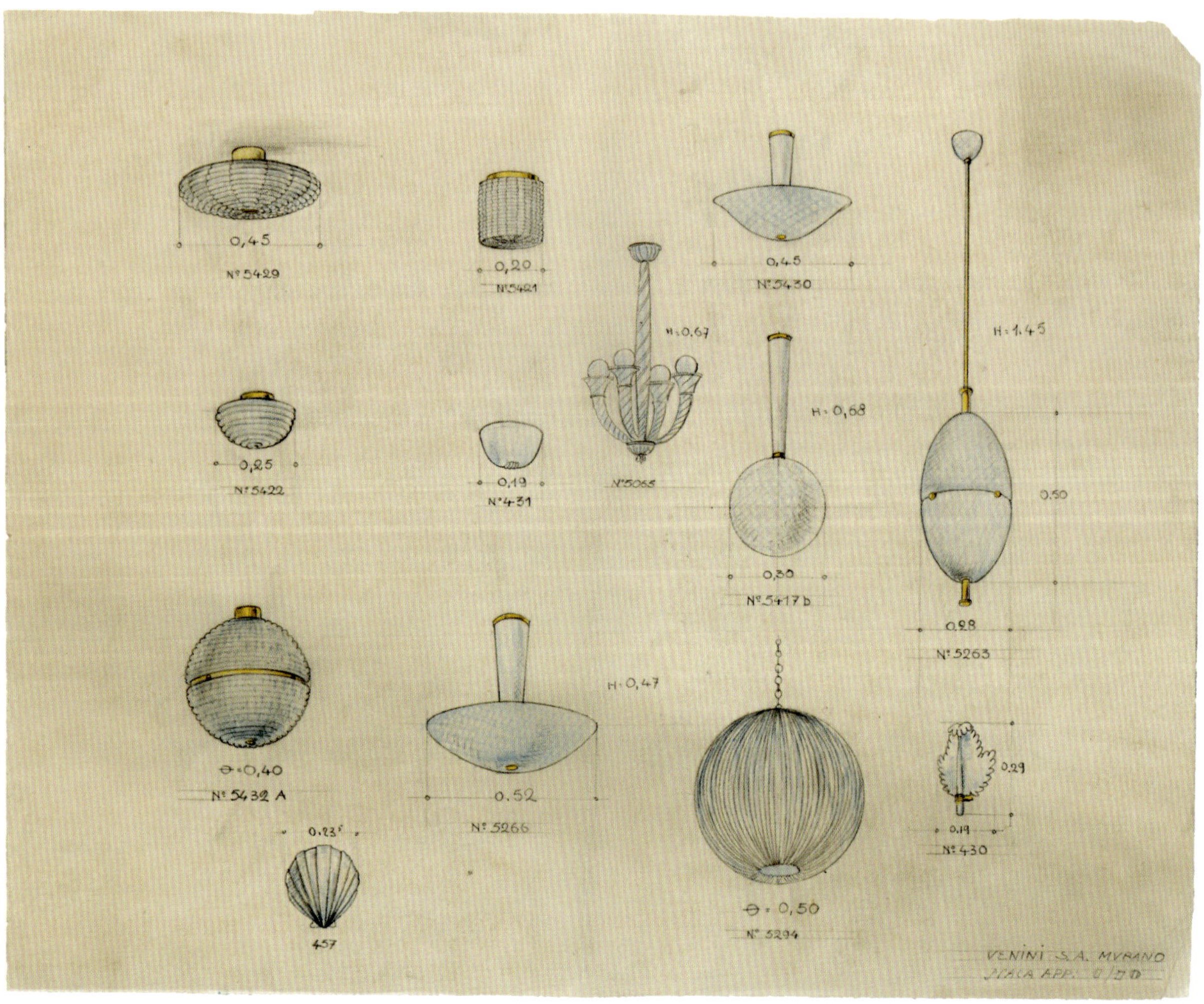
0,45
N° 5429
0,20
N° 5421
0,45
N° 5430
H: 0,67
H: 1,45
H: 0,68
0,25
N° 5422
0,19
N° 431
N° 5065
0,30
N° 5417 b
0,50
0,28
N° 5263
⊖ 0,40
N° 5432 A
H: 0,47
0,52
N° 5266
0,29
0,19
N° 430
0,23
457
⊖ 0,50
N° 5294
VENINI S.A. MVRANO

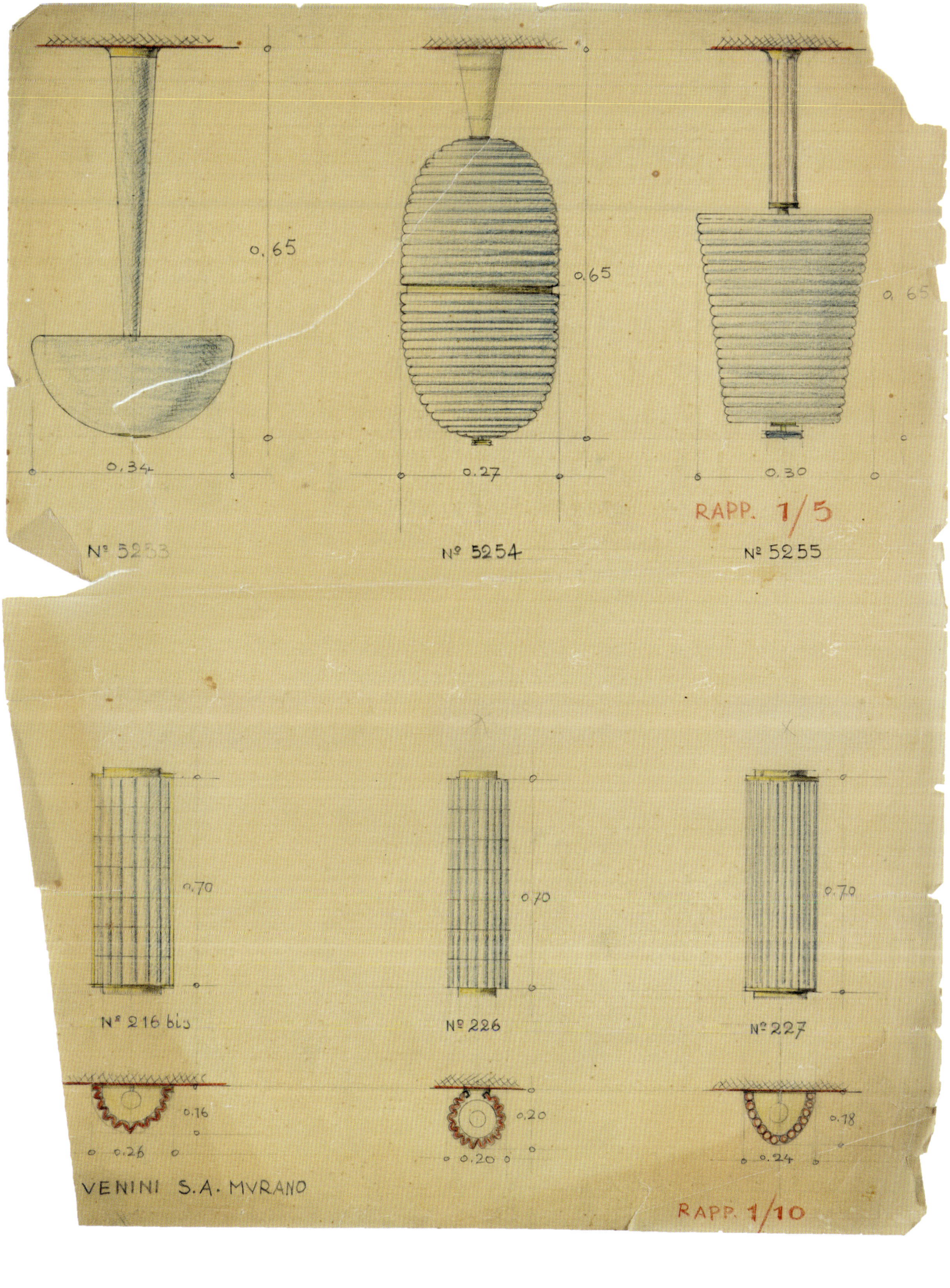
0,65
0,34
N° 5253
0,65
0.27
N° 5254
0,65
0.30
RAPP. 1/5
N° 5255
0.70
N° 216 bis
0.70
N° 226
0.70
N° 227
0.16
0.26
0.20
0.20
0.18
0.24
VENINI S.A. MVRANO
RAPP. 1/10

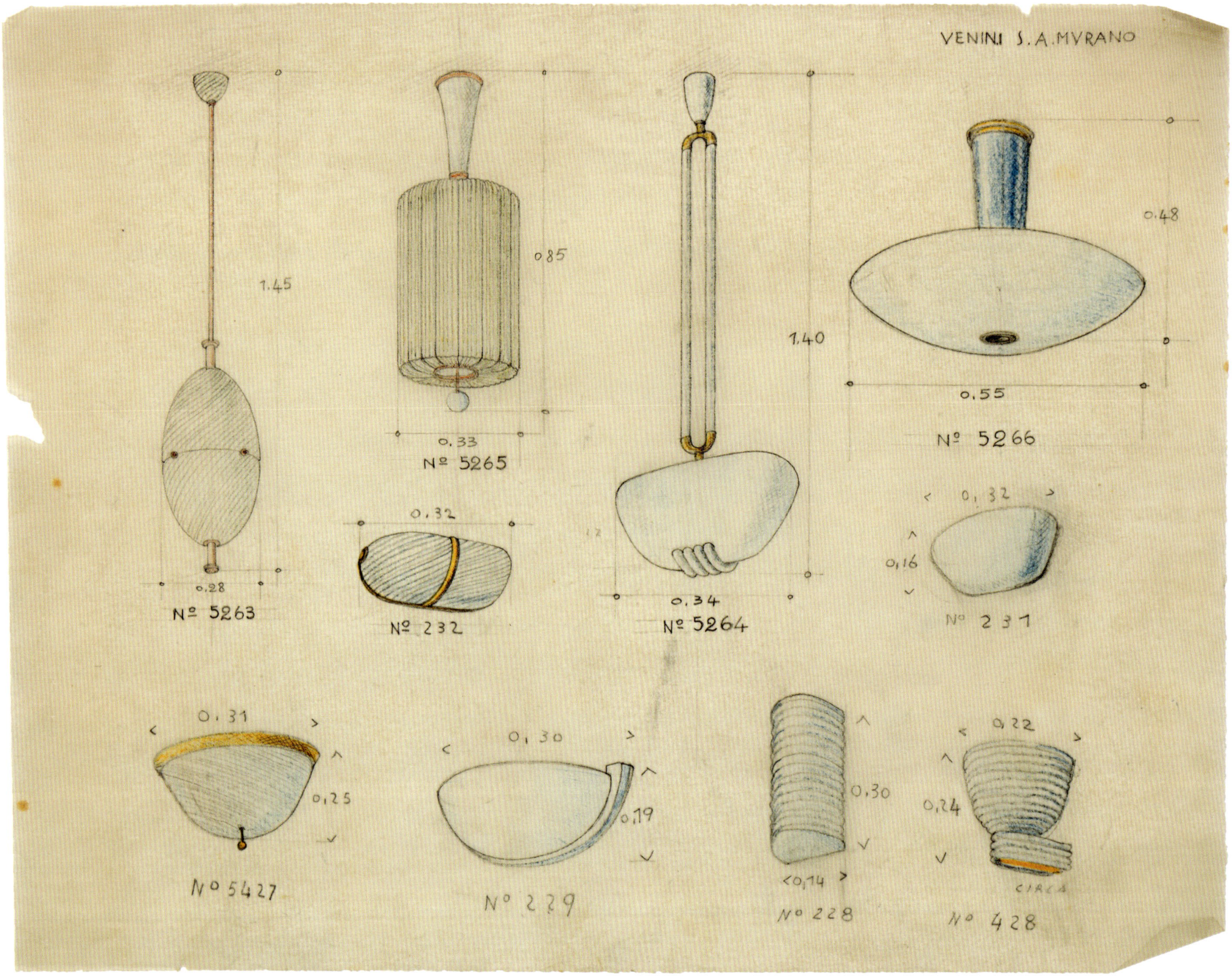
VENINI S.A.MVRANO
1.45
0.28
Nº 5263
0.85
0.33
Nº 5265
0.32
Nº 232
1.40
0.34
Nº 5264
0.48
0.55
Nº 5266
0,32
0,16
Nº 231
0,31
0,25
Nº 5427
0,30
0,19
Nº 229
0,30
0,14
Nº 228
0,22
0,24
CIRCA
Nº 428

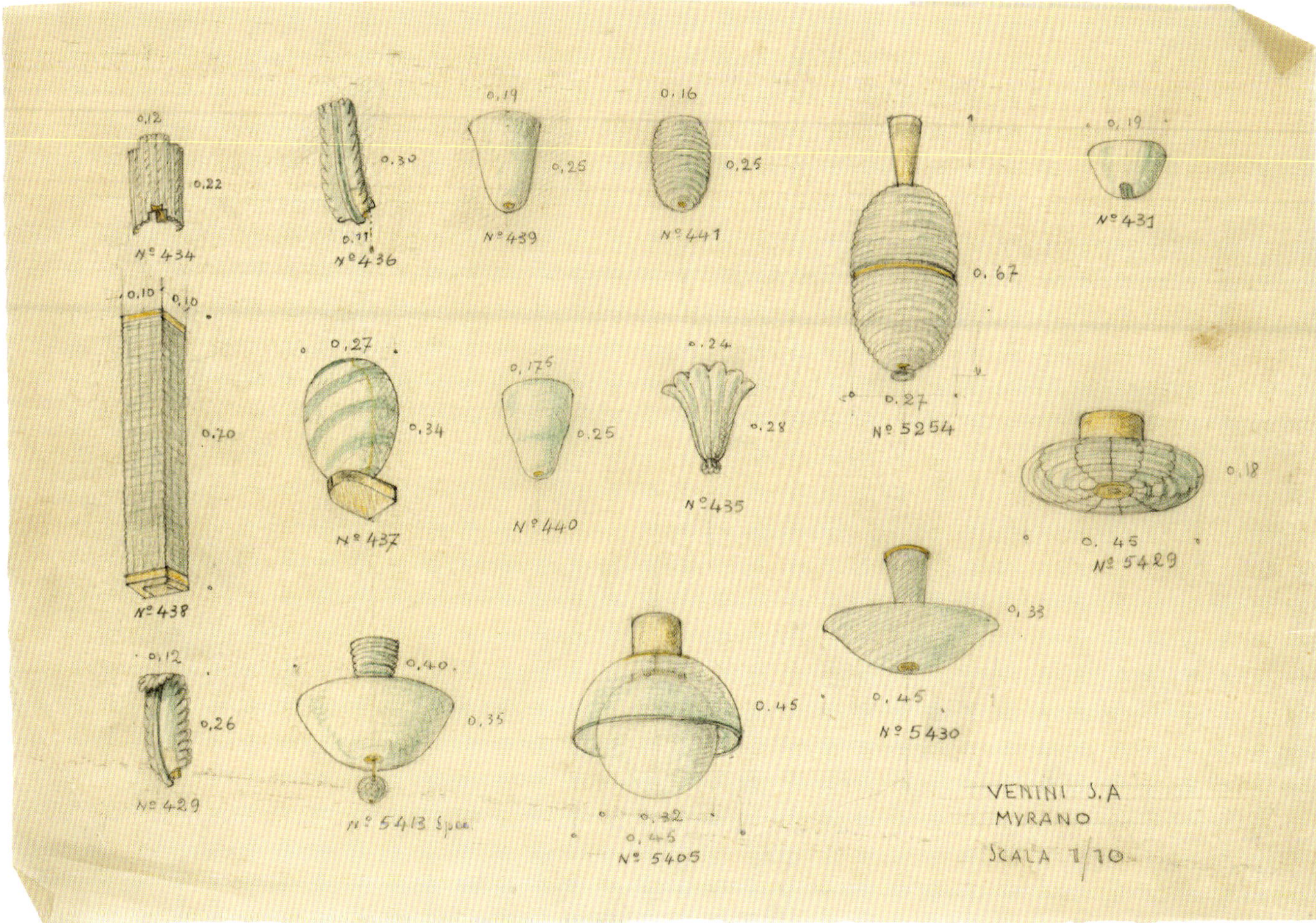
N° 434
N° 436
N° 439
N° 441
N° 431
N° 438
N° 437
N° 440
N° 435
N° 5254
N° 5429
N° 429
N° 5413
N° 5405
N° 5430
VENINI S.A
MURANO
SCALA 1/10

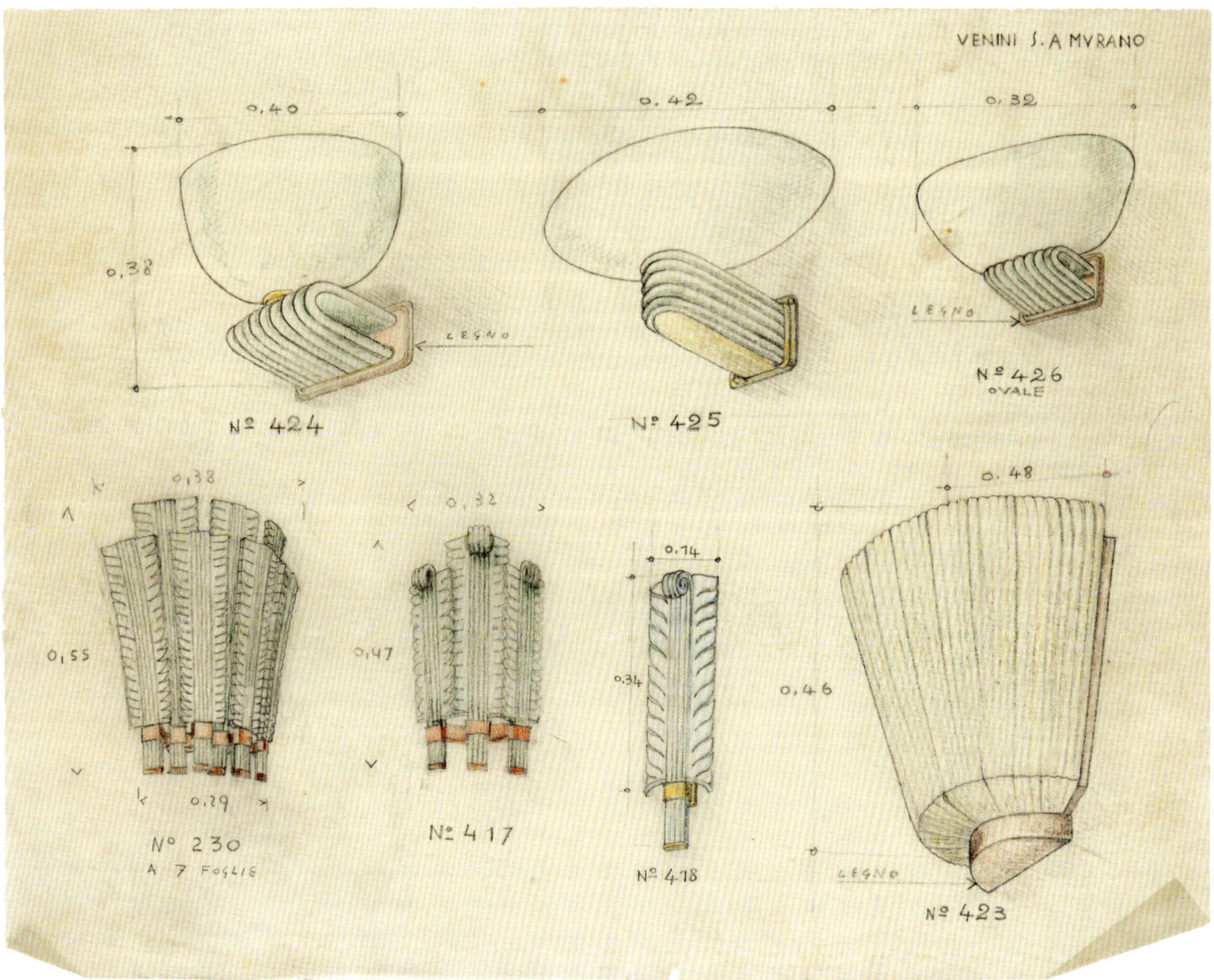
VENINI S.A MURANO
LEGNO
N° 424
N° 425
N° 426
OVALE
N° 230
A 7 FOGLIE
N° 417
N° 418
LEGNO
N° 423

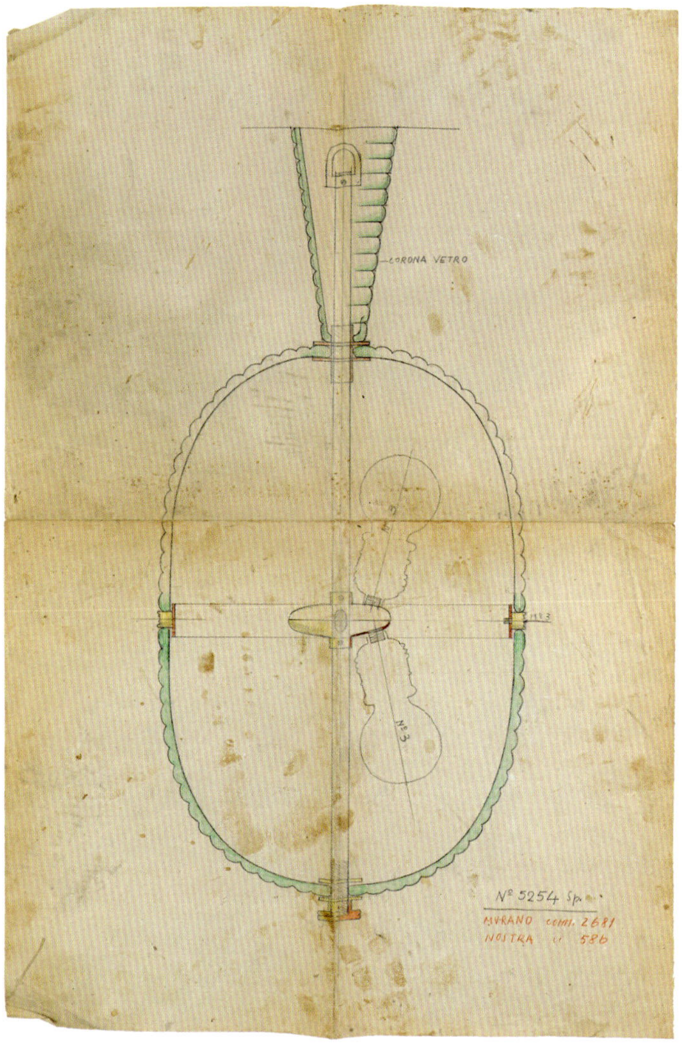
CORONA VETRO
N° 5254 Sp.
MURANO comm. 2681
NOSTRA " 586

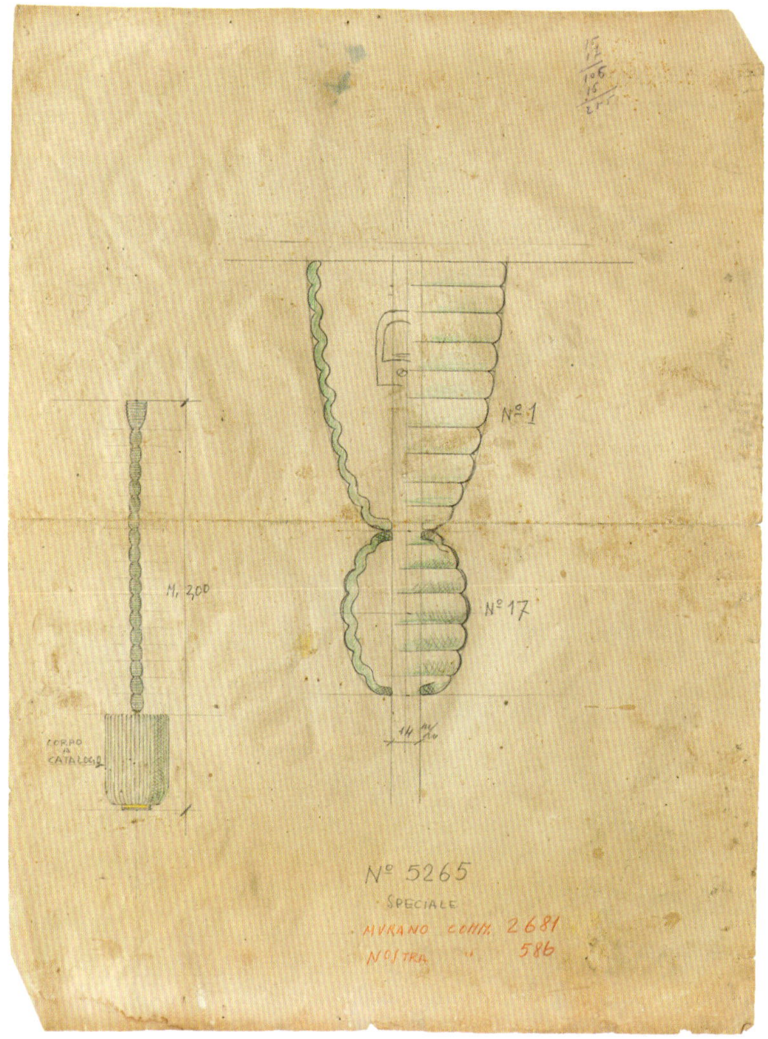
N° 1
N° 17
H. 2,00
N° 5265
SPECIALE
MURANO comm. 2681
NOSTRA " 586

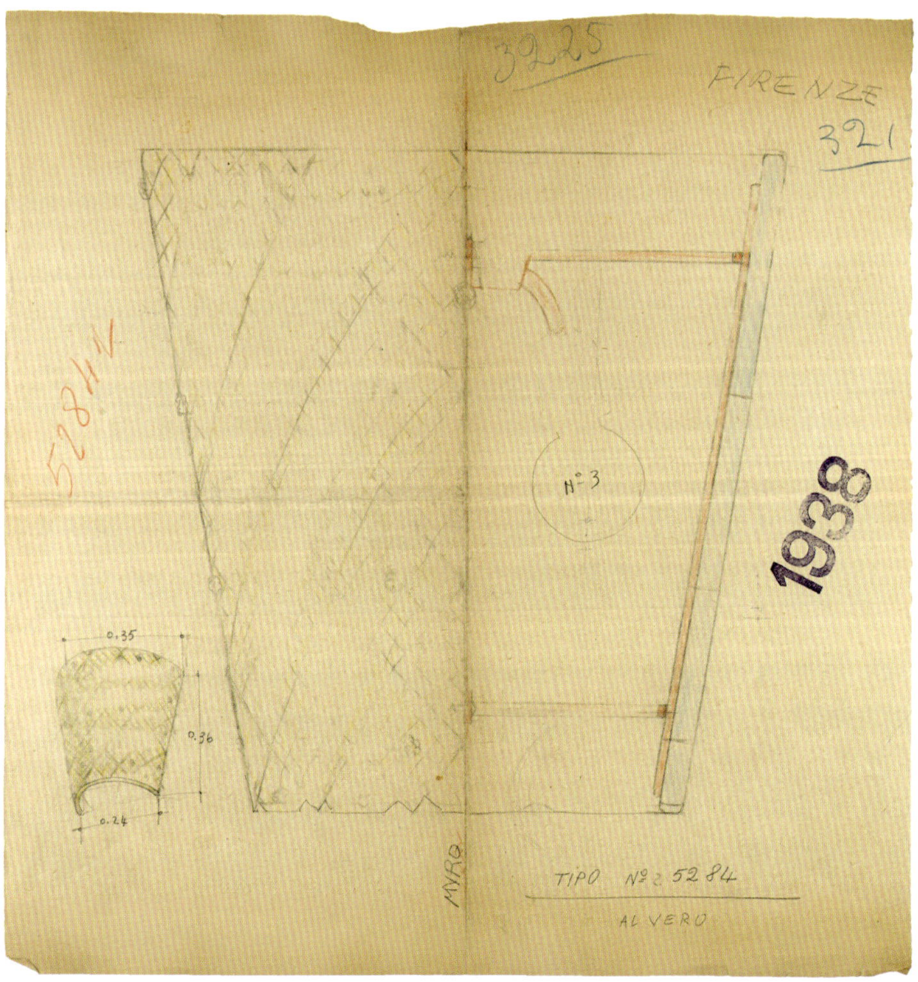
3225
FIRENZE
321
1938
N° 3
0.35
0.36
0.24
TIPO N° 5284
AL VERO

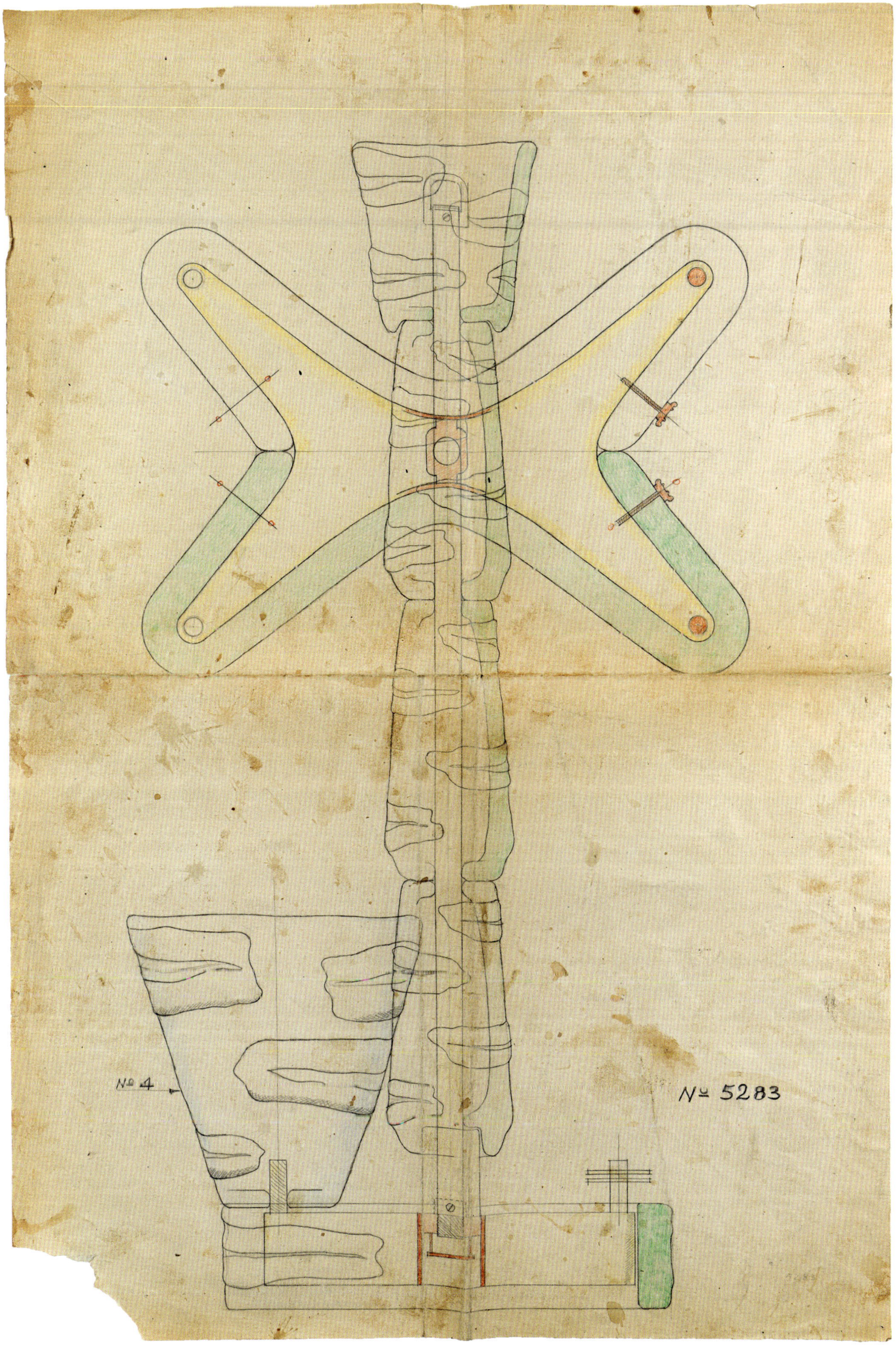
Nº 4
Nº 5283

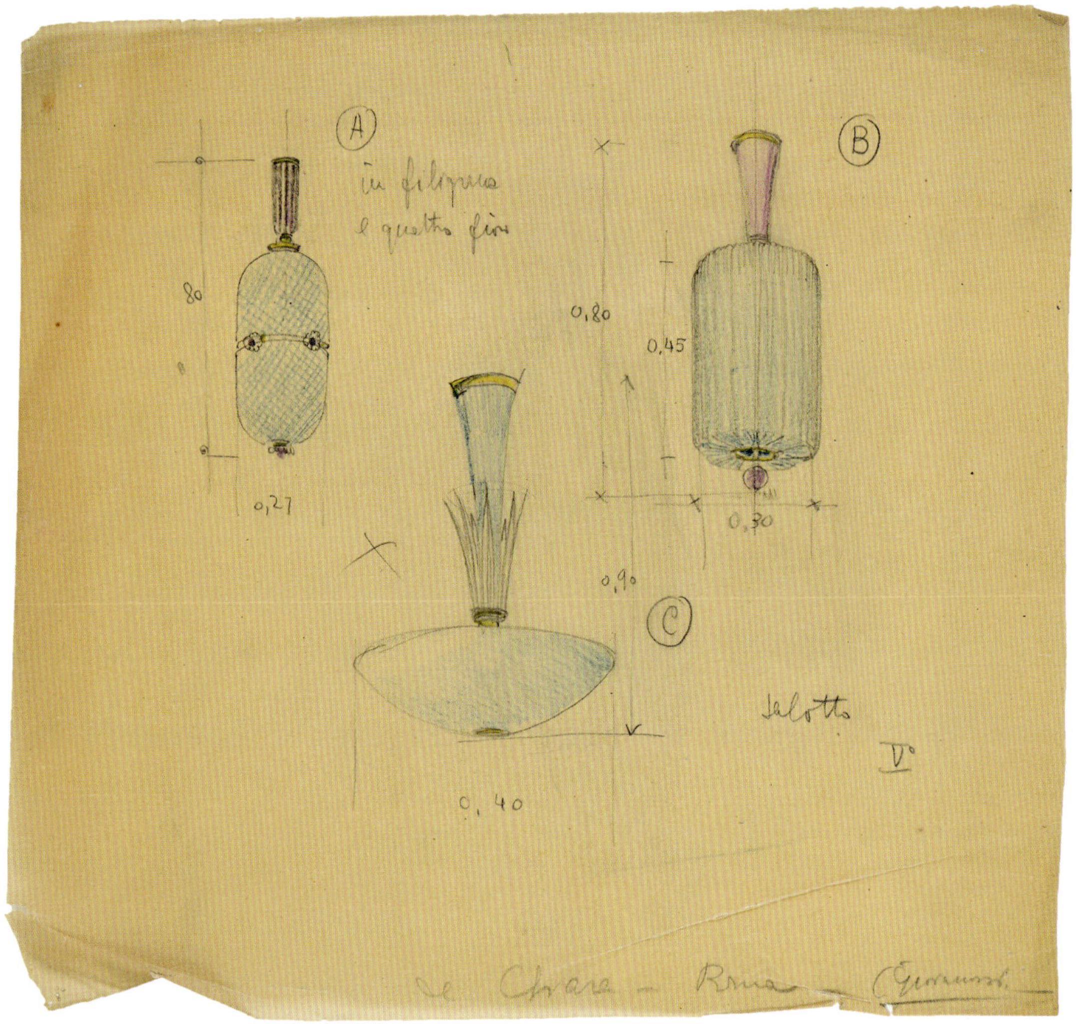
A
B
C
80
0,27
0,80
0,45
0,30
0,90
0,40
V°

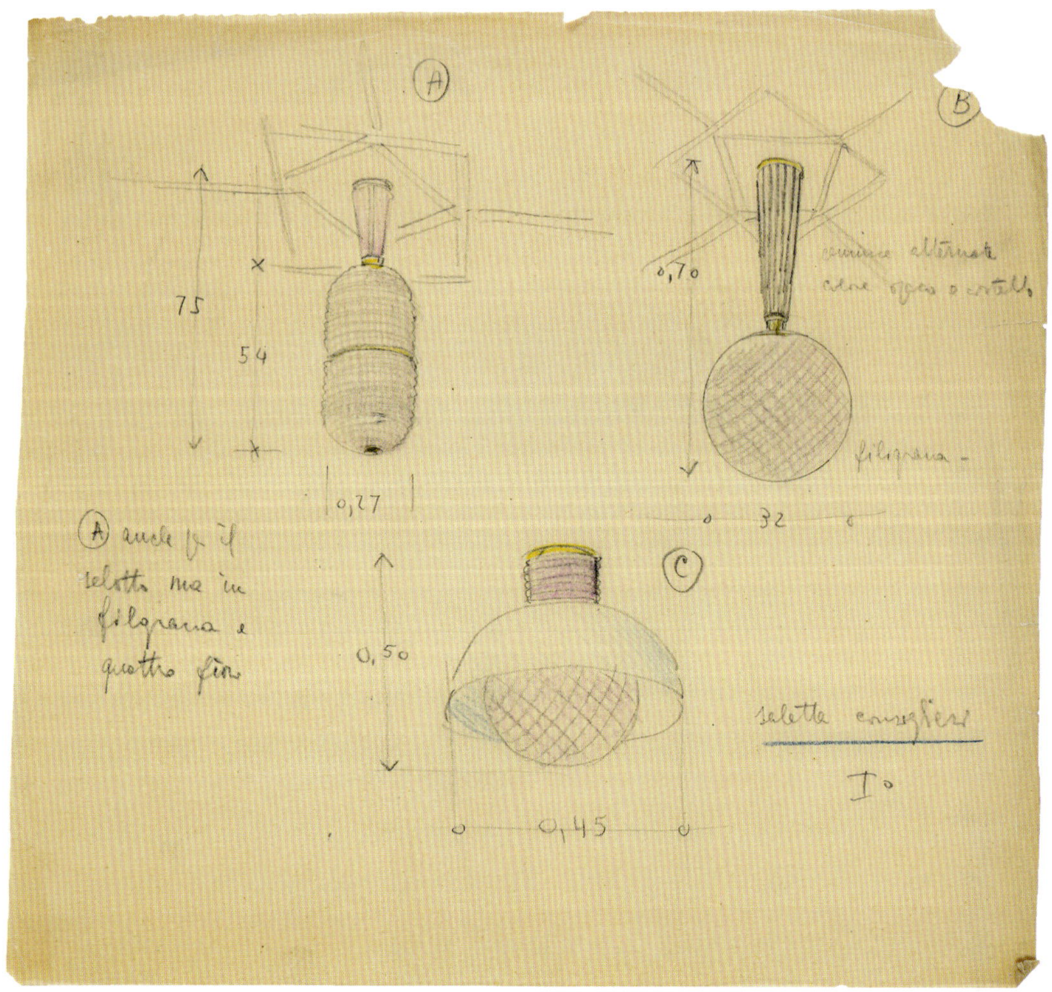
A
B
C
75
54
0,27
0,70
32
0,50
0,45
I°

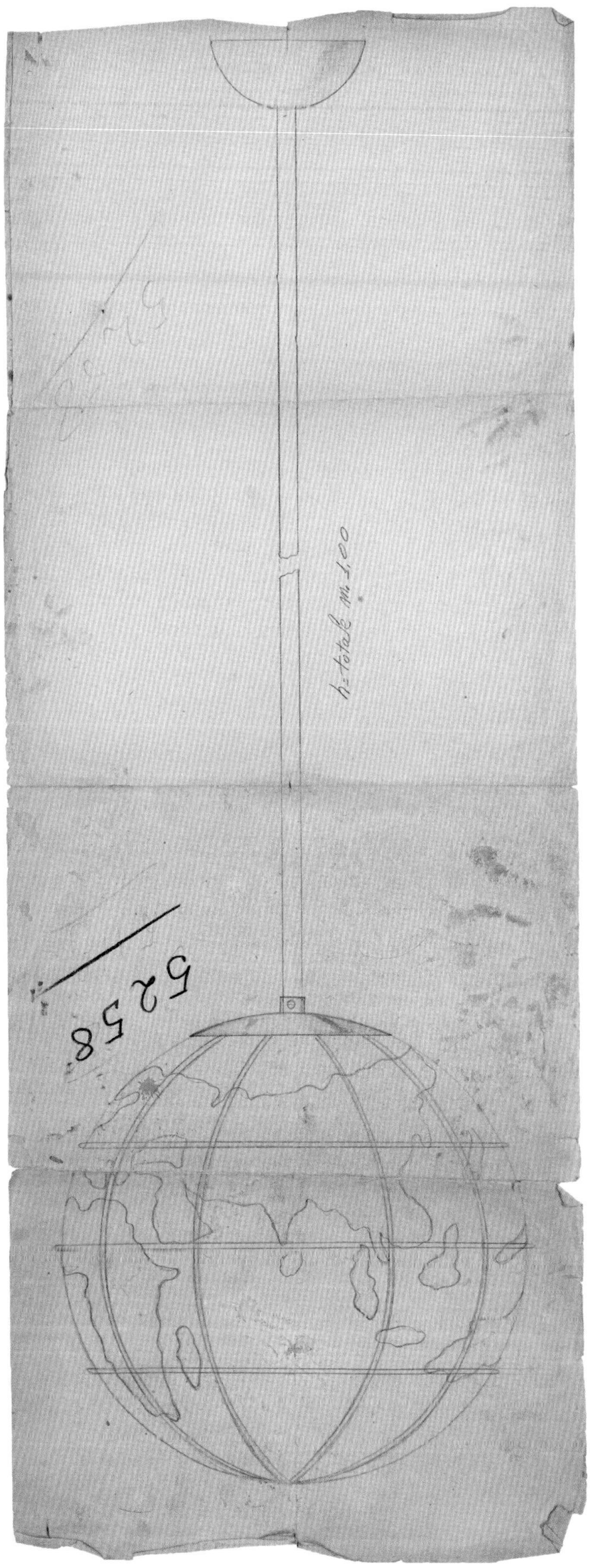

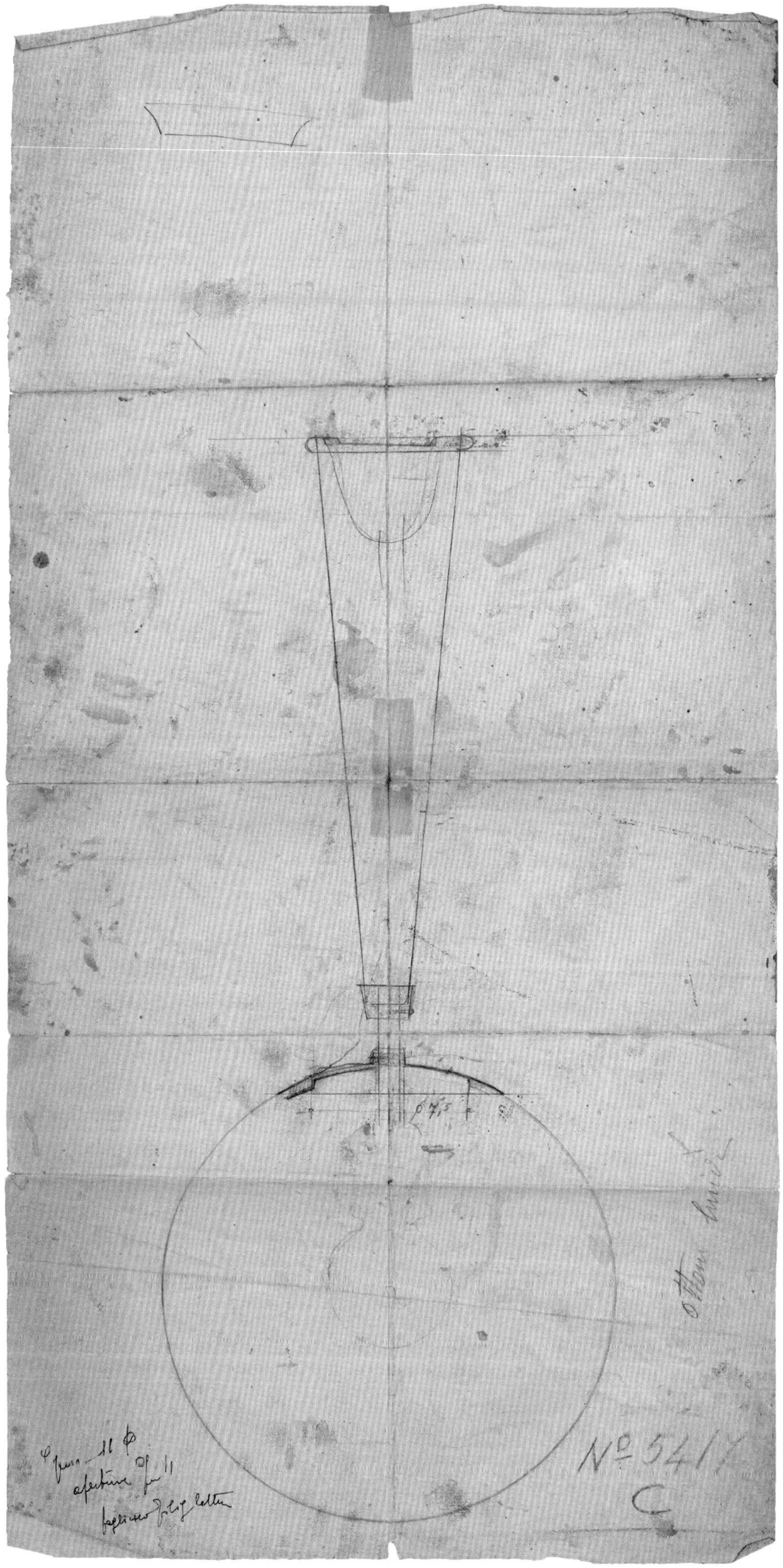

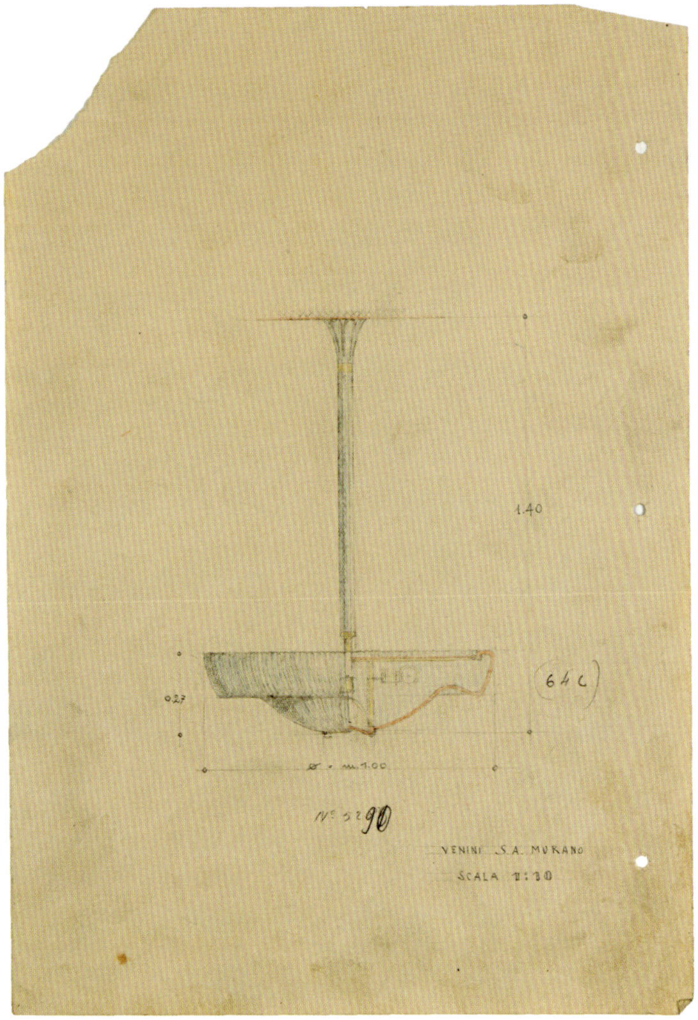
1.40
64 C
VENINI S.A. MURANO
SCALA 1:10

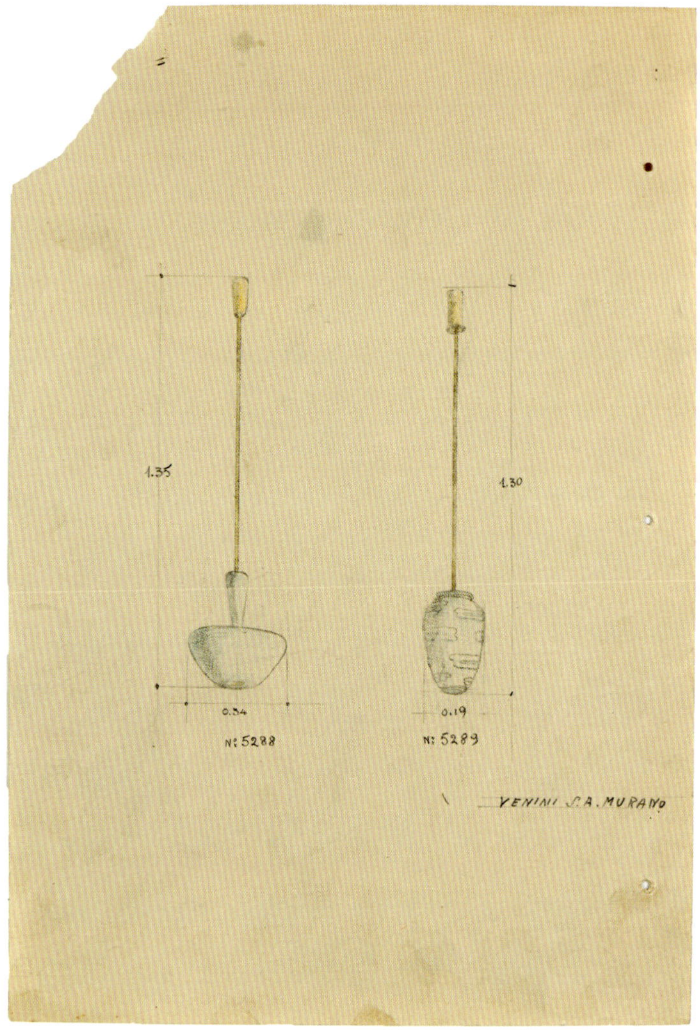
1.35
1.30
0.34
0.19
N: 5288
N: 5289
VENINI S.A. MURANO

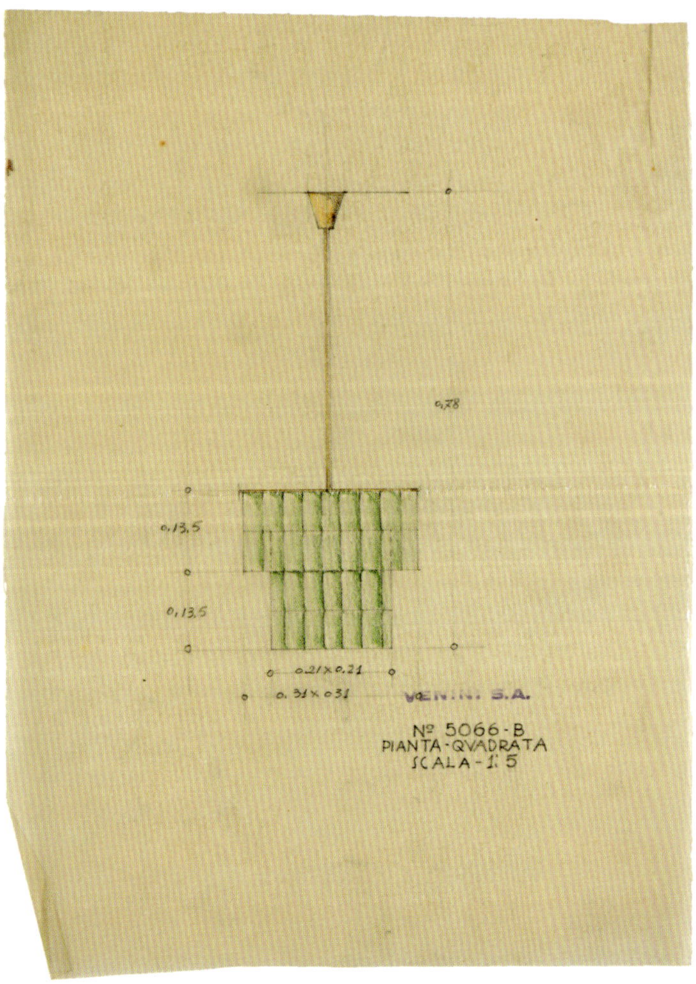
0.13.5
0.13.5
0.21 × 0.21
0.31 × 0.31
VENINI S.A.
N° 5066-B
PIANTA-QVADRATA
SCALA-1:5

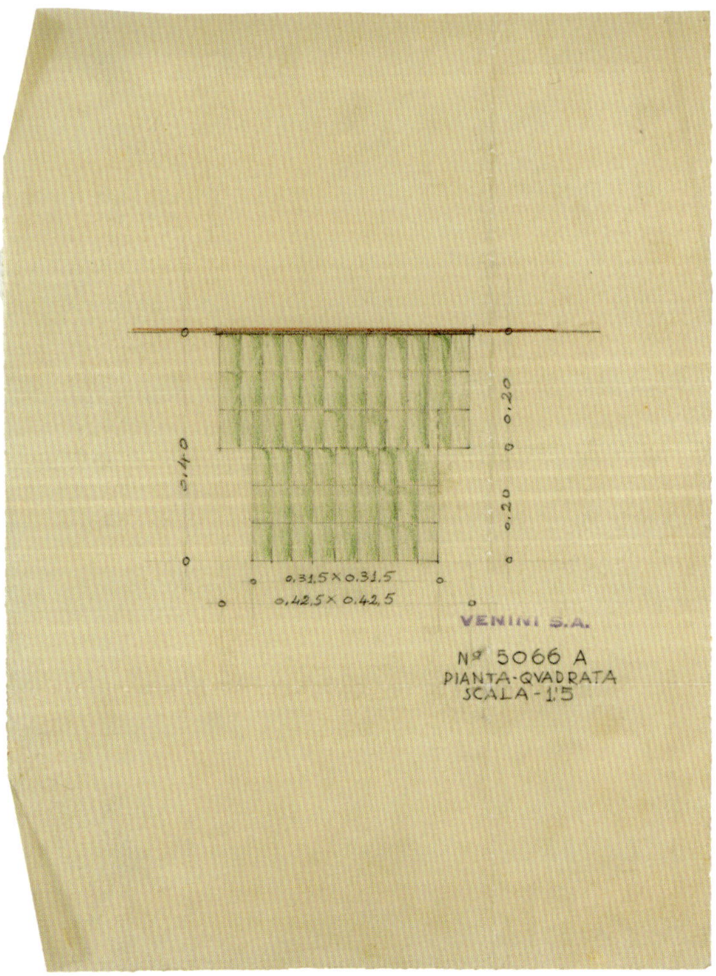
0.40
0.20
0.20
0.31.5 × 0.31.5
0.42.5 × 0.42.5
VENINI S.A.
N° 5066 A
PIANTA-QVADRATA
SCALA-1:5

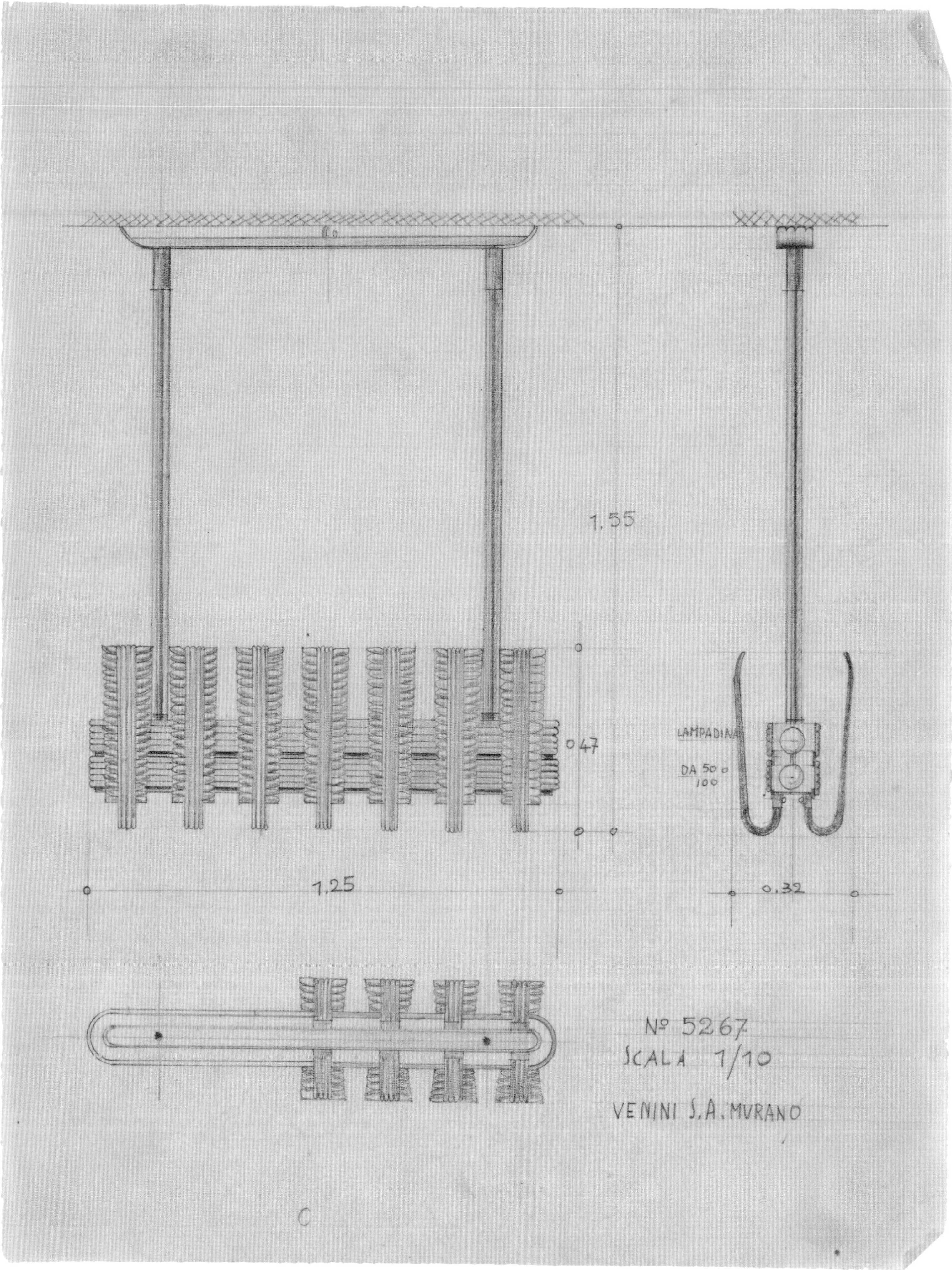
1,55
0,47
LAMPADINA
DA 50 o 100
1,25
0,32
Nº 5267
SCALA 1/10
VENINI S.A. MURANO
C

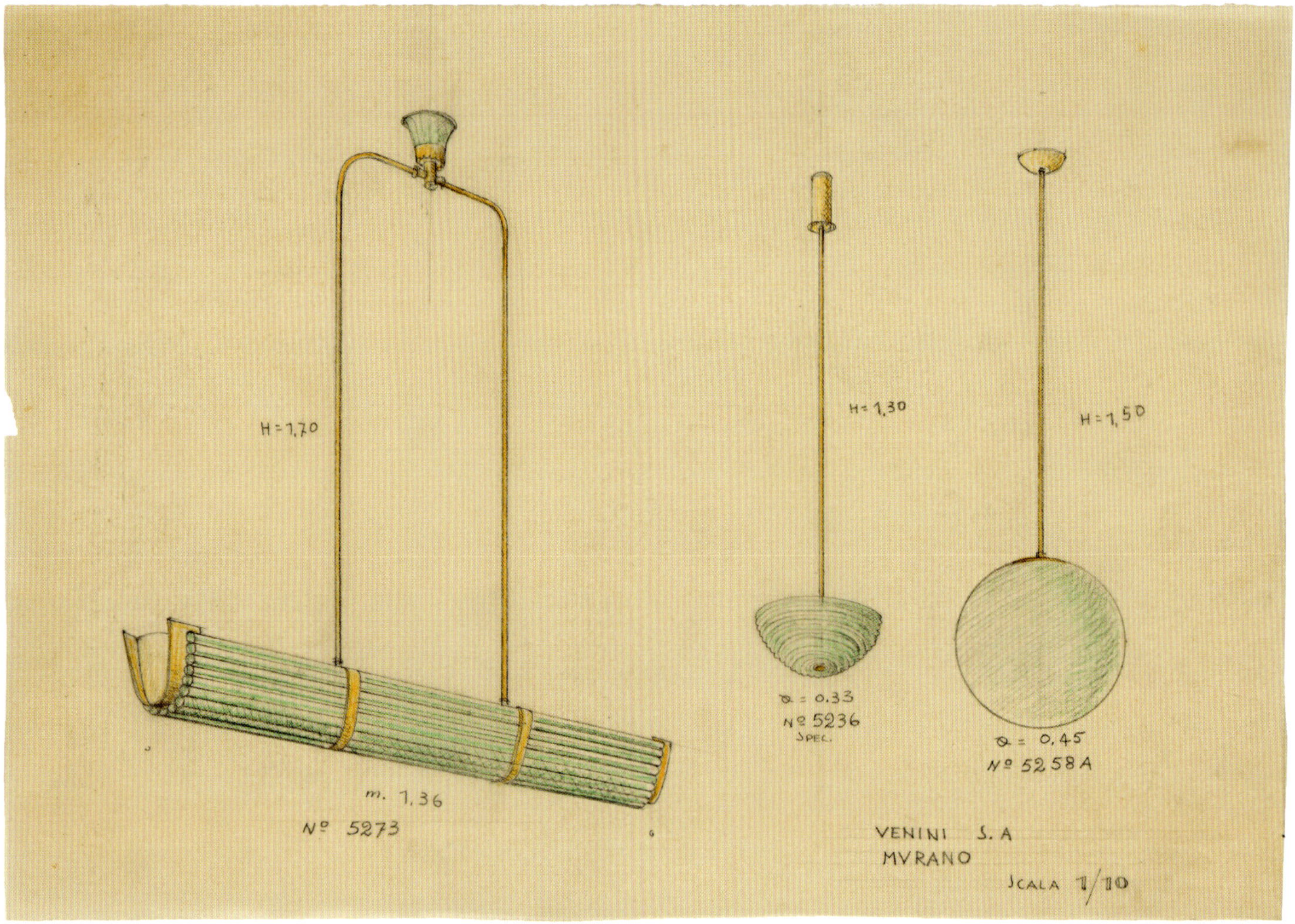
H=1,70
m. 1,36
Nº 5273
H=1,30
ø = 0.33
Nº 5236
SPEC.
H=1,50
ø = 0.45
Nº 5258A
VENINI S.A
MVRANO
SCALA 1/10

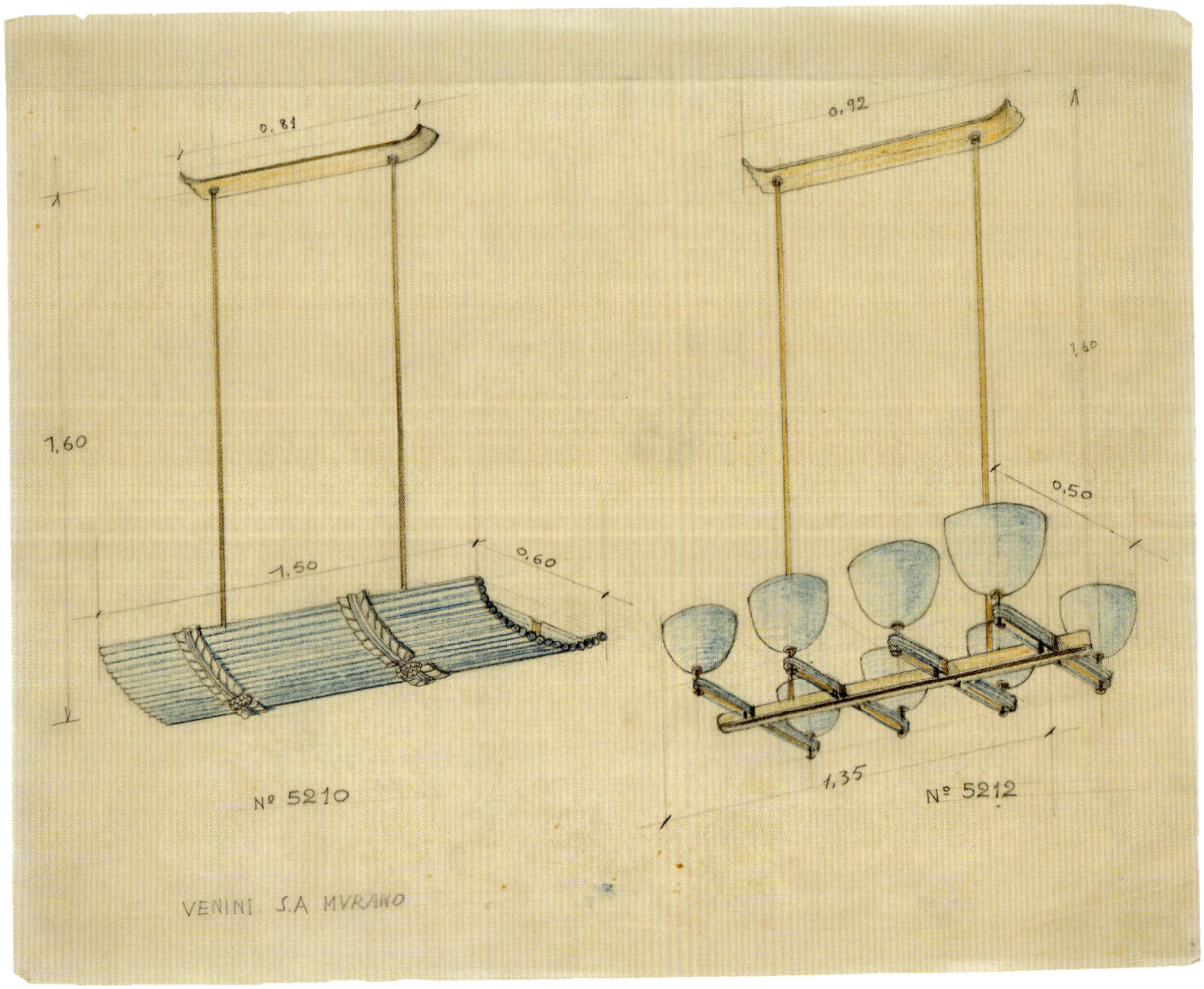
0,81
1,60
1,50
0,60
Nº 5210
0,92
1,60
0,50
1,35
Nº 5212
VENINI S.A MVRANO

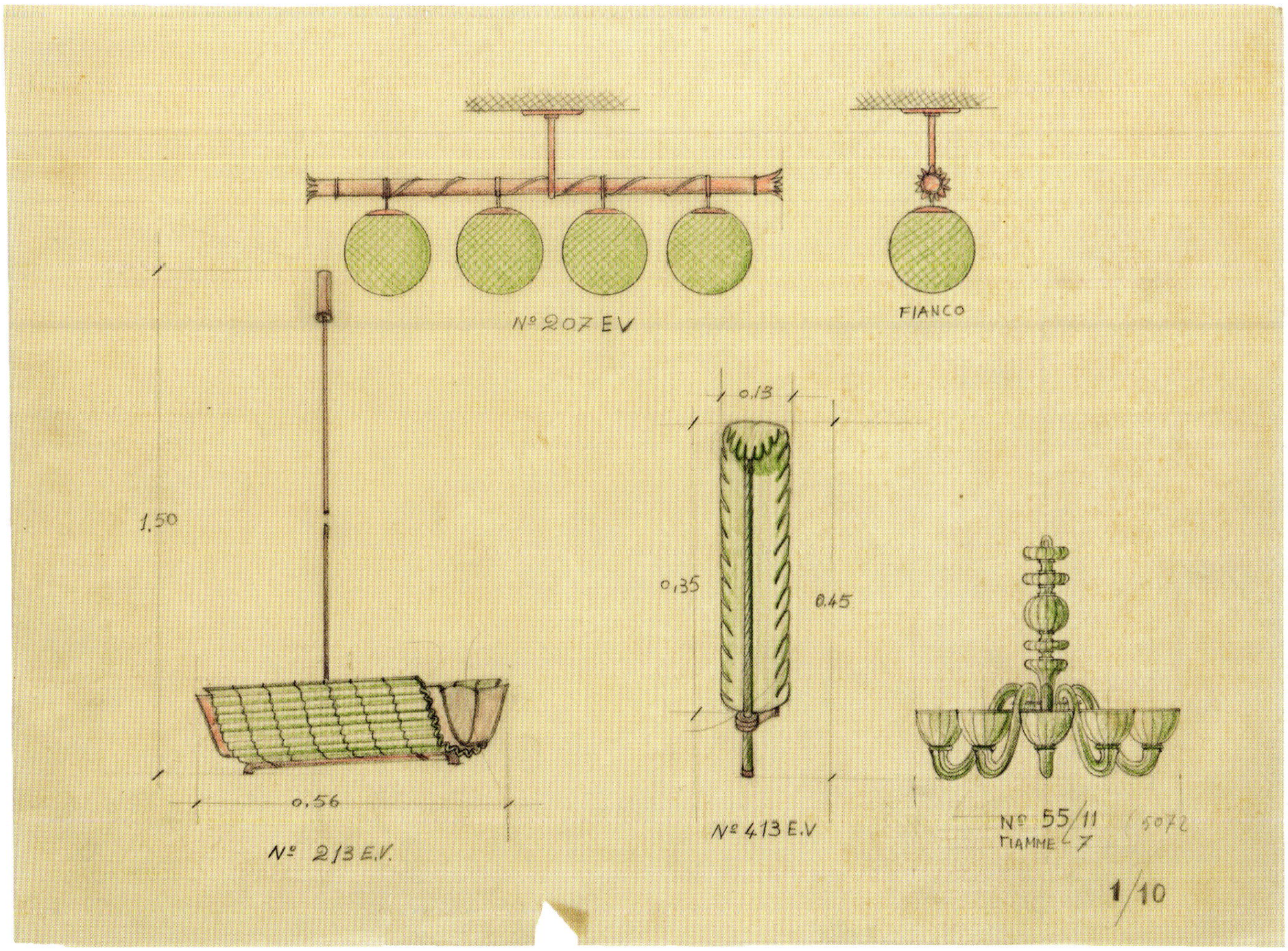
N° 207 E.V
FIANCO
1,50
0.13
0,35
0.45
0.56
N° 213 E.V.
N° 413 E.V
N° 55/11
FIAMME 7
5072
1/10

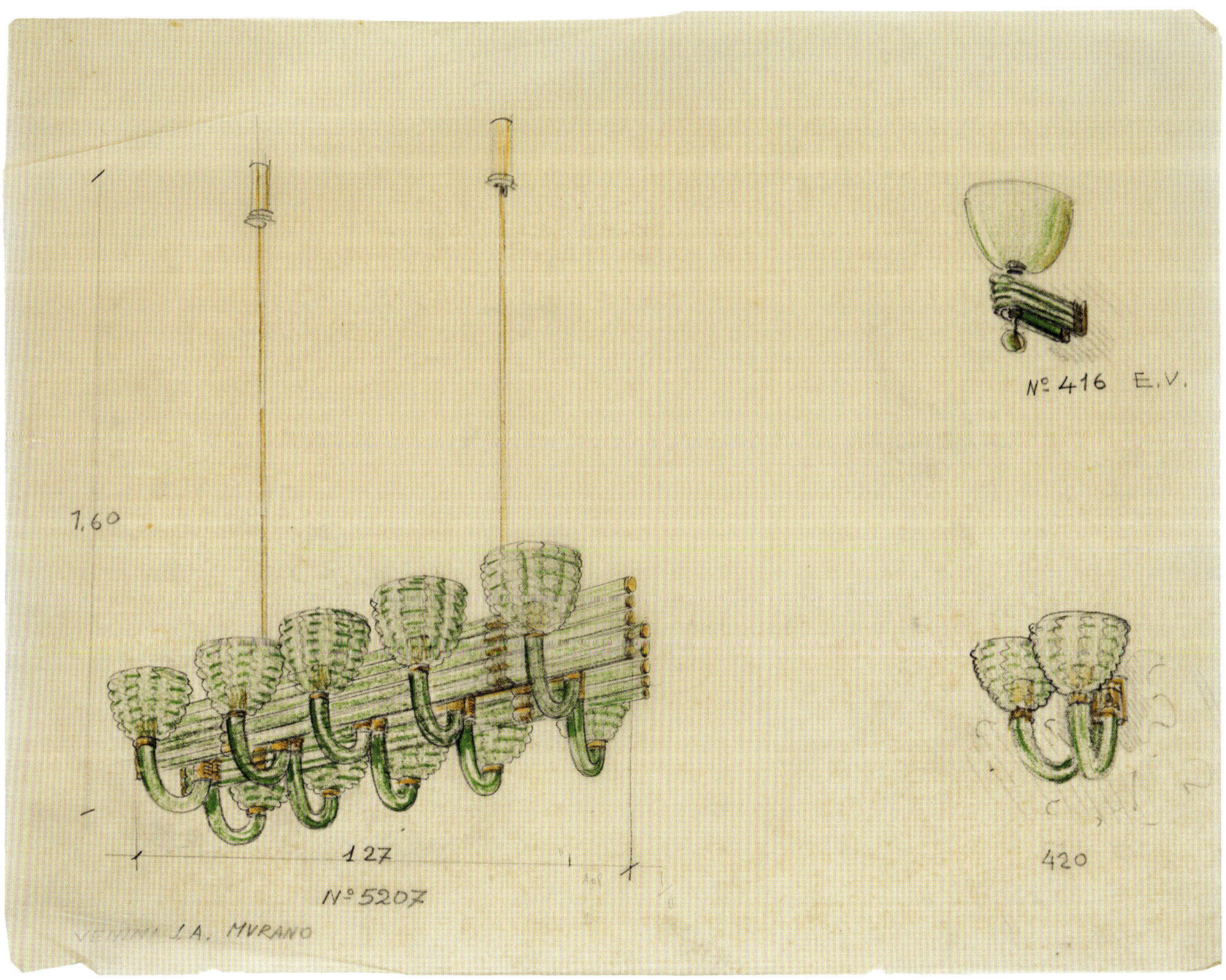
N° 416 E.V.
1,60
1 27
N° 5207
420
I.A. MURANO

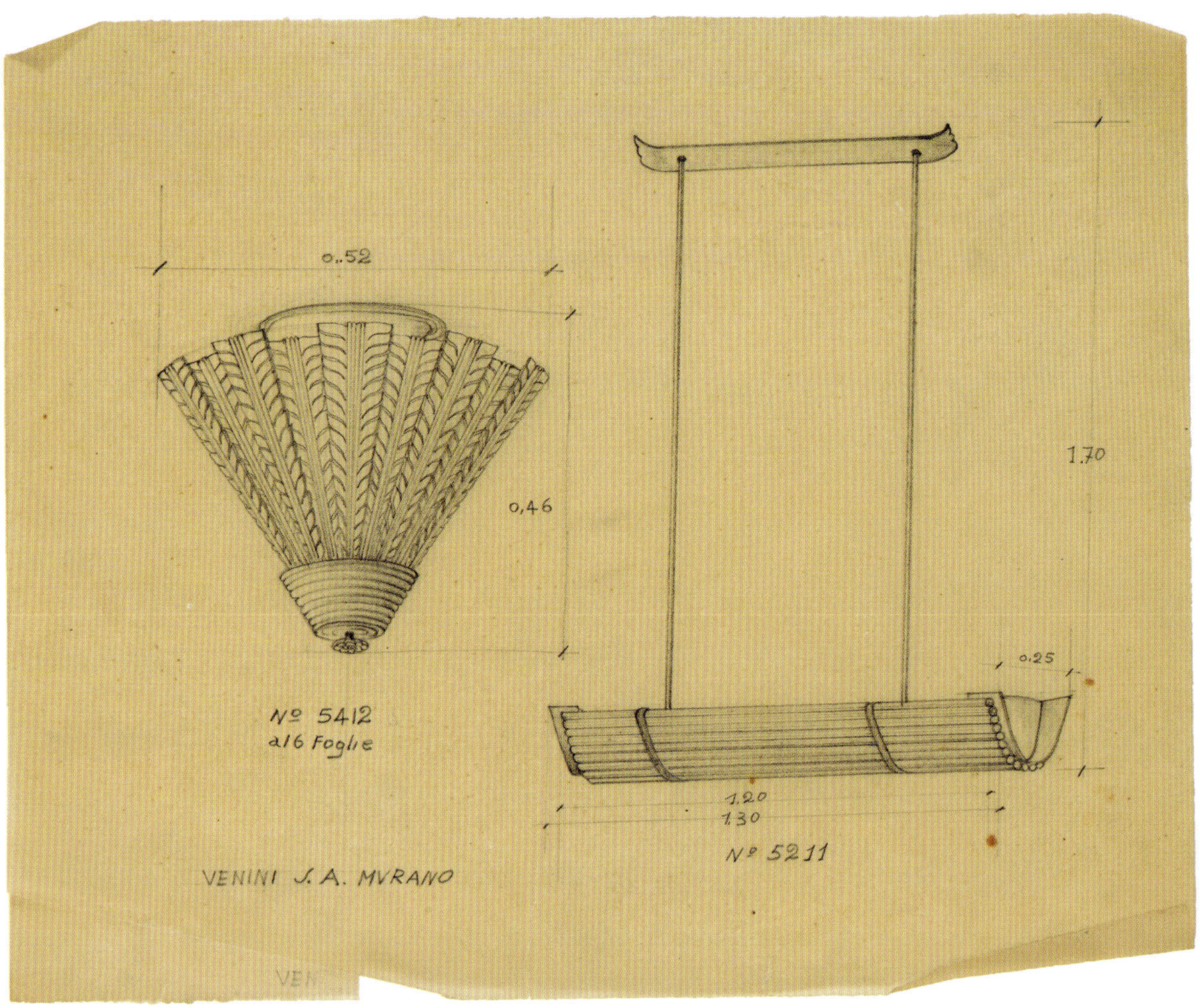
0.52
0,46
Nº 5412
a16 Foglie
1.70
0.25
1.20
1.30
Nº 5211
VENINI S.A. MURANO

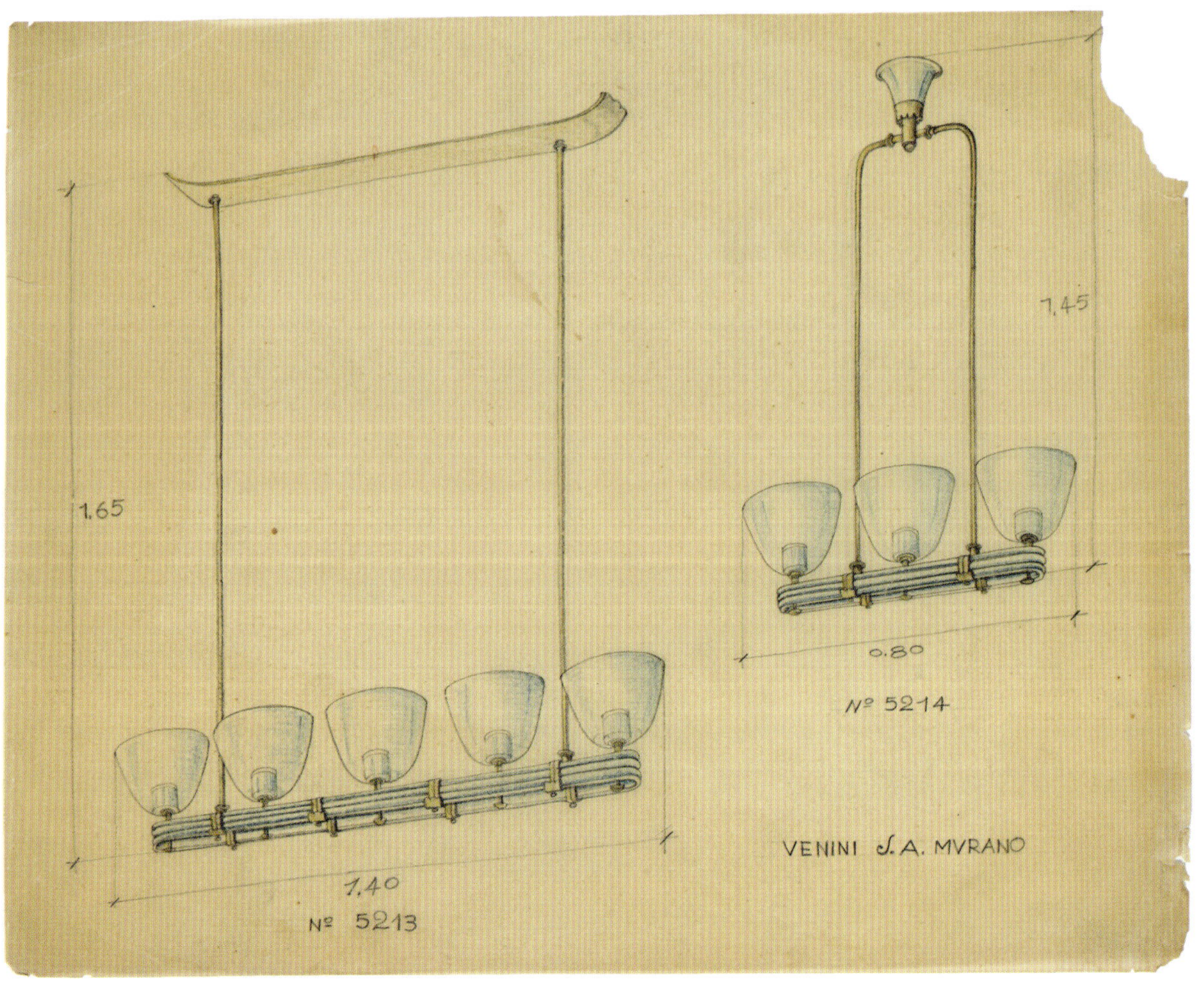
1.65
1.45
0.80
Nº 5214
1.40
Nº 5213
VENINI S.A. MURANO

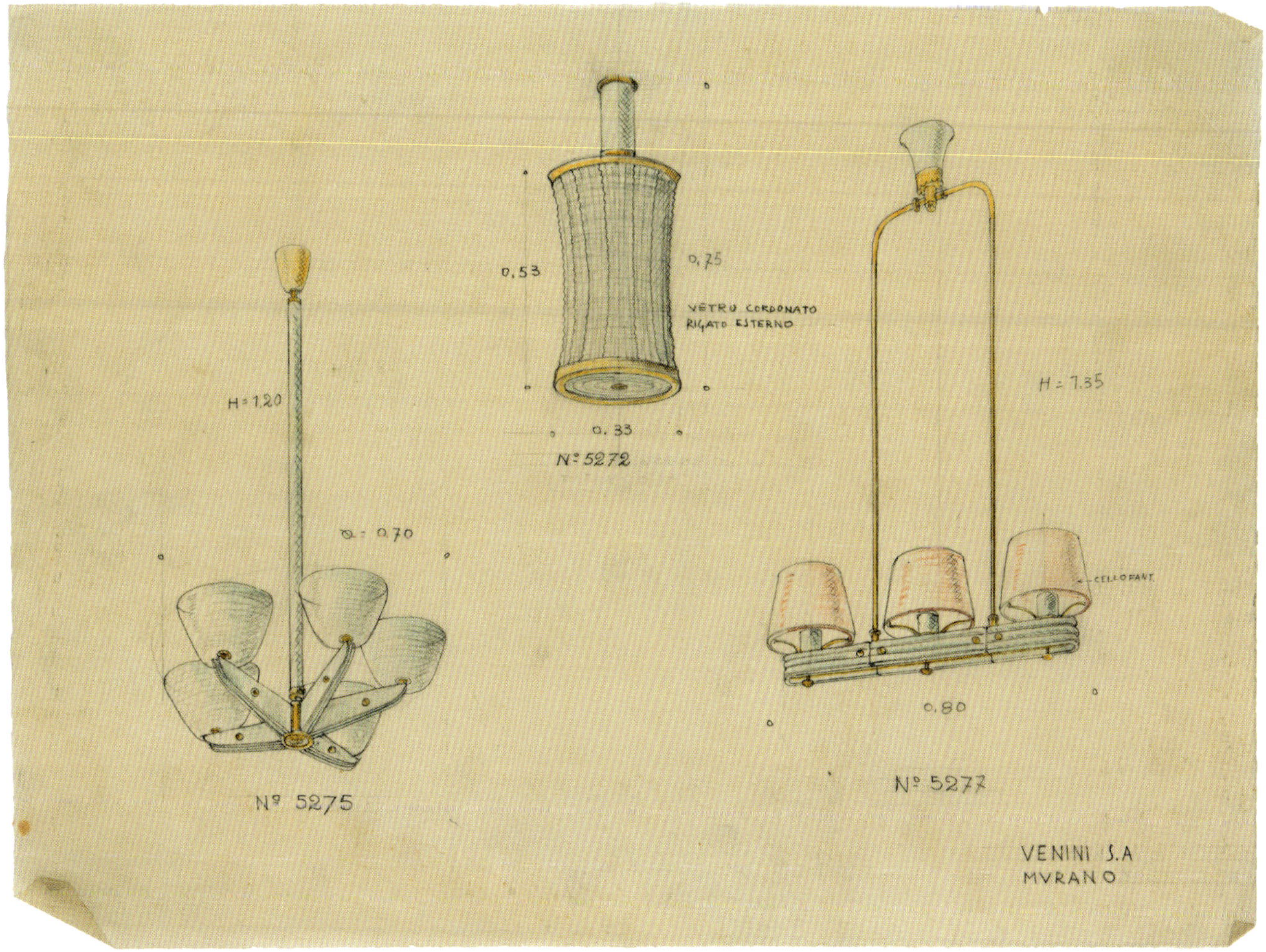
0.53
0.75
VETRO CORDONATO
RIGATO ESTERNO
0.33
N° 5272
H = 1.20
⌀ 0.70
N° 5275
H = 1.35
CELLOPHANE
0.80
N° 5277
VENINI S.A
MURANO

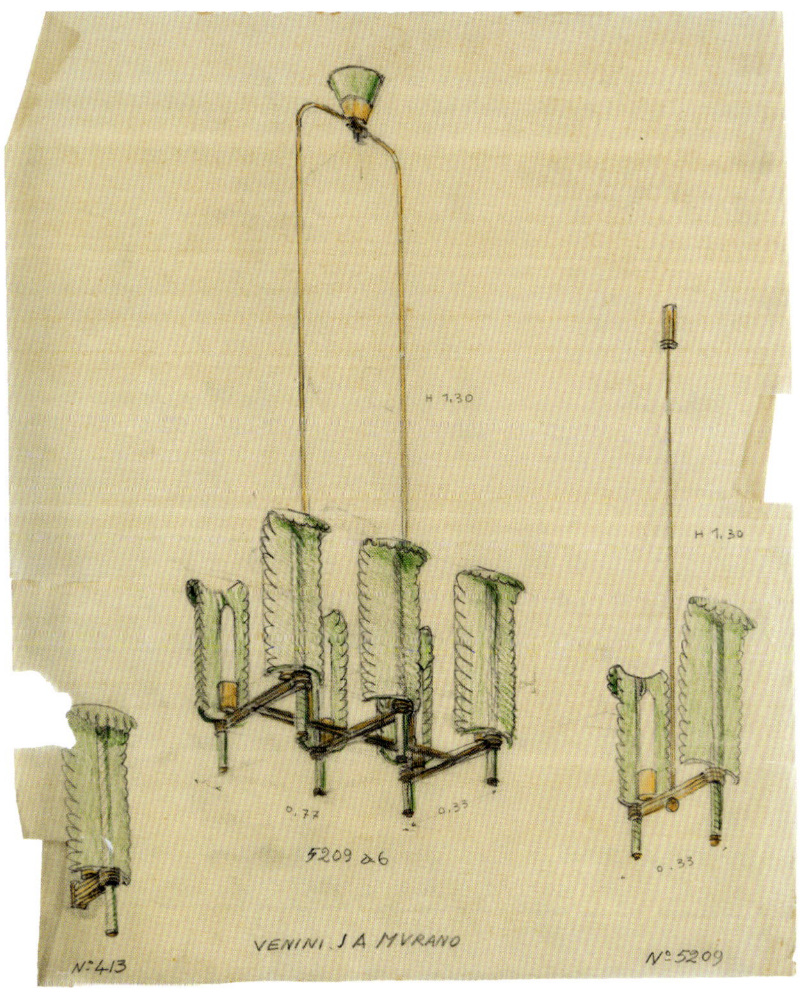
H 1.30
H 1.30
0.77
0.33
5209 a 6
0.33
VENINI S.A MURANO
N° 413
N° 5209

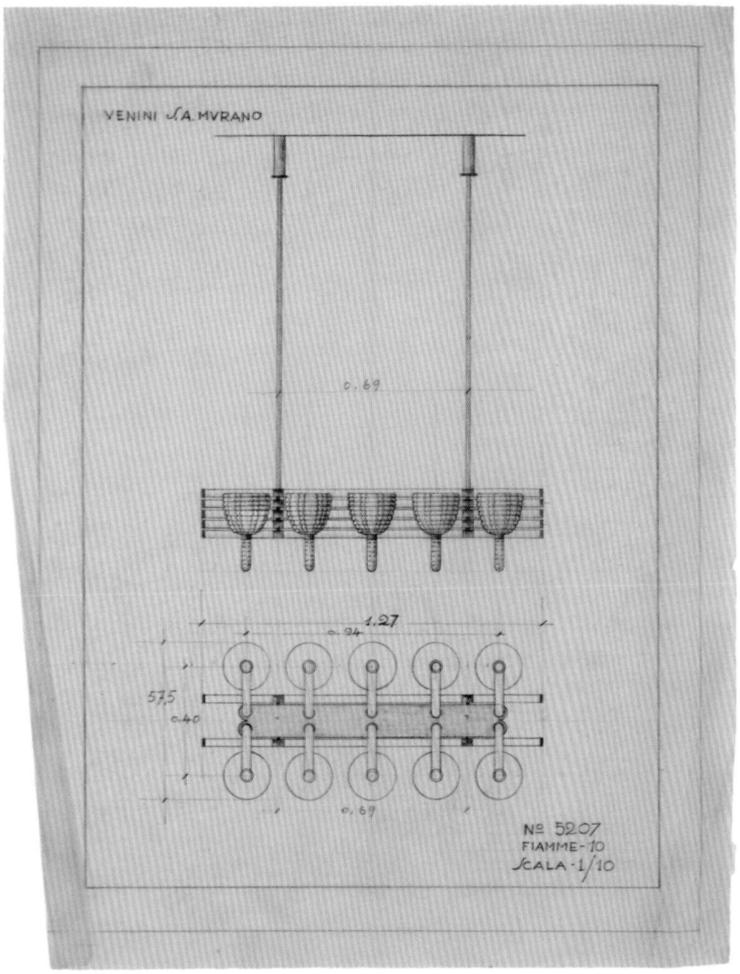
VENINI S.A. MURANO
0.69
1.27
0.94
57.5
0.40
0.69
Nº 5207
FIAMME - 10
SCALA - 1/10

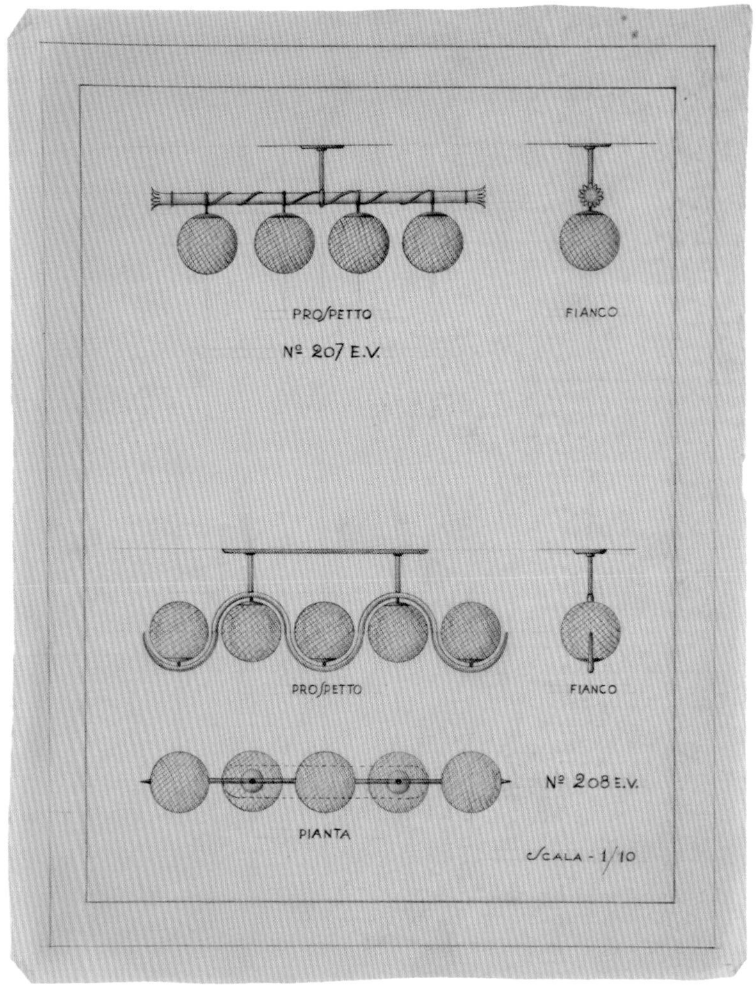
PROSPETTO
FIANCO
Nº 207 E.V.
PROSPETTO
FIANCO
Nº 208 E.V.
PIANTA
SCALA - 1/10

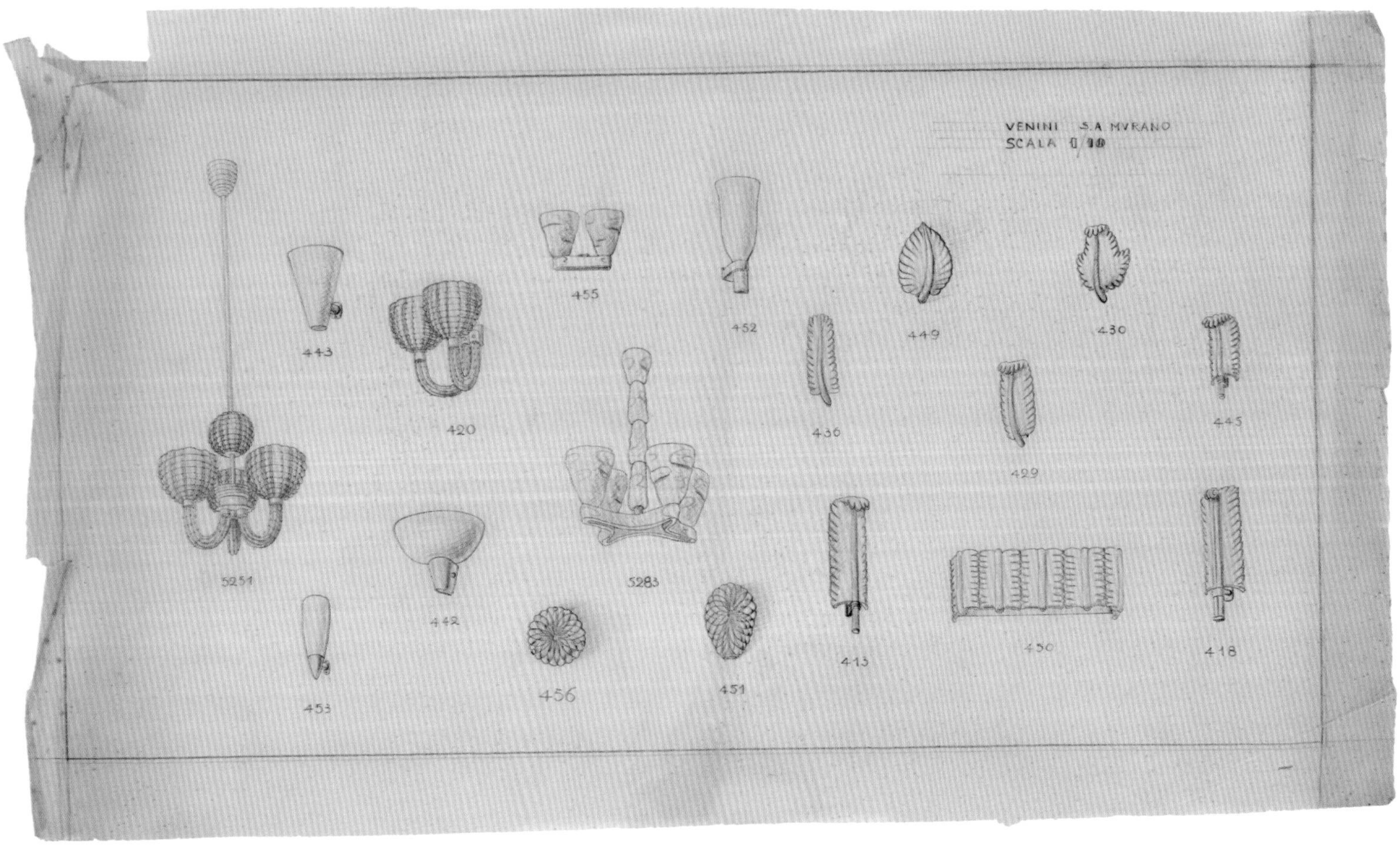
VENINI S.A. MURANO
443
420
455
452
449
430
436
429
445
5251
442
5283
413
450
418
453
456
451

9029
9030
9028
9031
502 EV
501 EV
503 EV
SCALA - 1/10

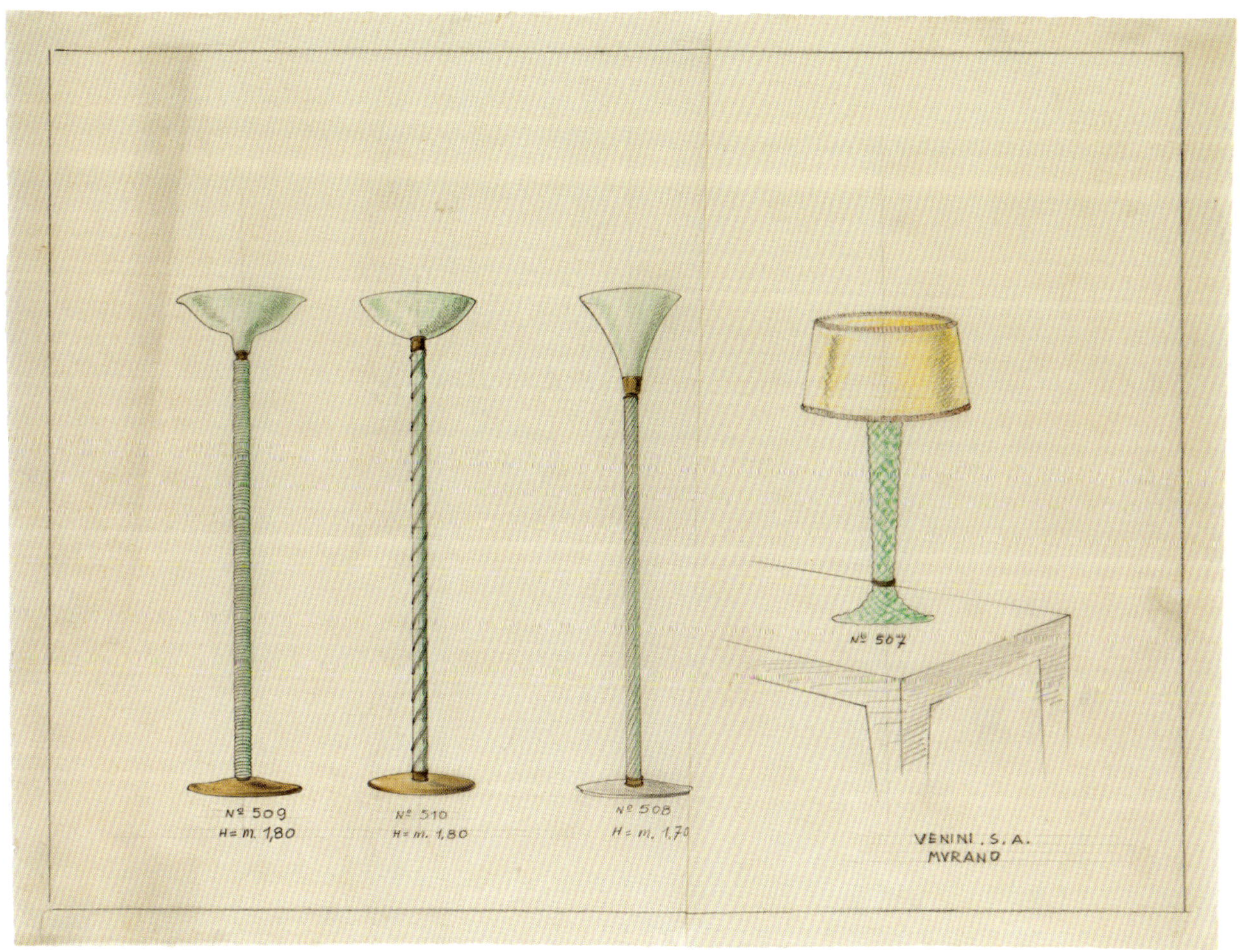
Nº 509
H= m. 1,80
Nº 510
H= m. 1,80
Nº 508
H= m. 1,70
Nº 507
VENINI . S. A.
MURANO

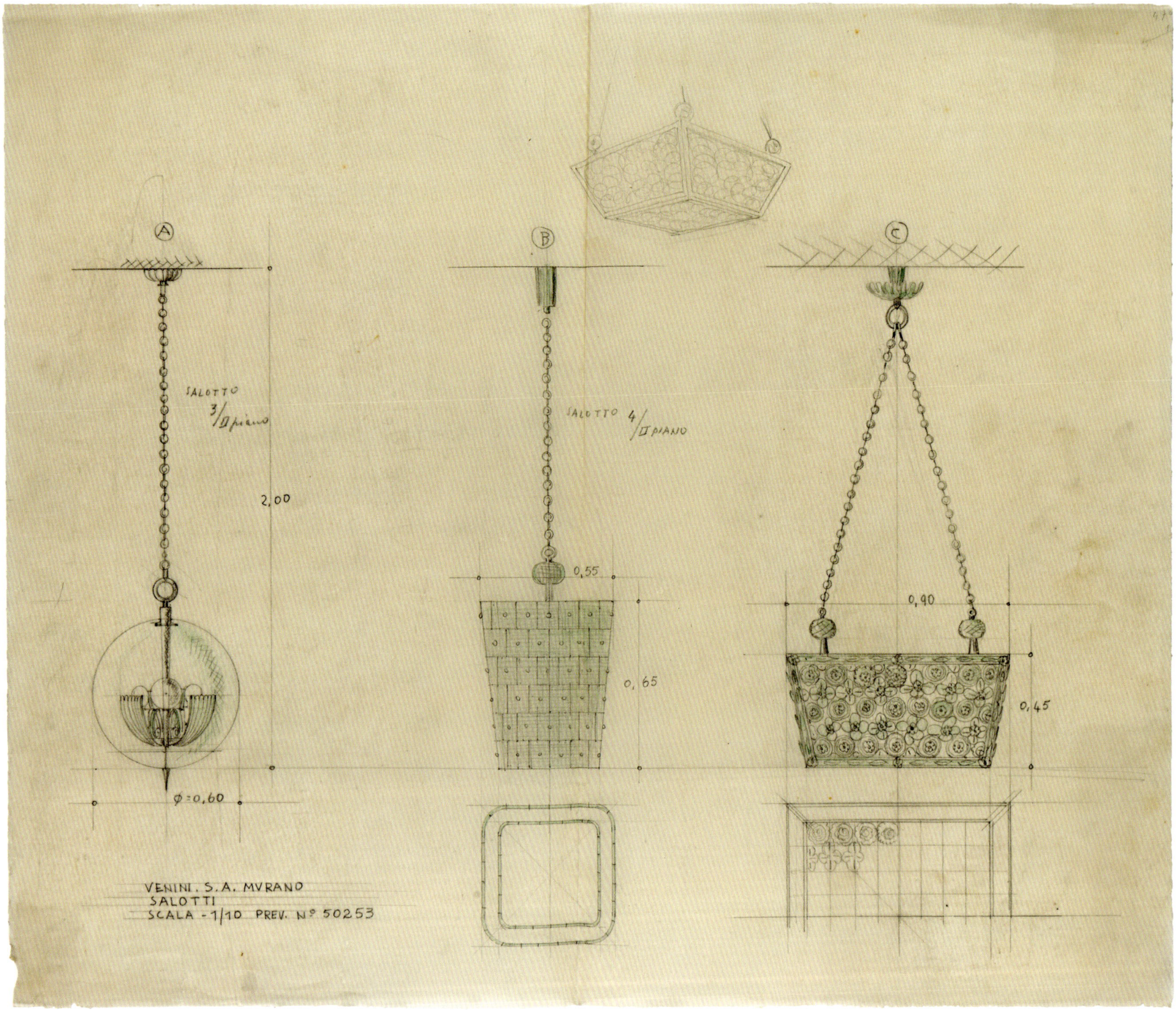
A
B
C
SALOTTO 3/II piano
SALOTTO 4/II piano
2,00
0,55
0,65
0,90
0,45
Φ=0,60
VENINI. S.A. MVRANO
SALOTTI
SCALA - 1/10 PREV. Nº 50253

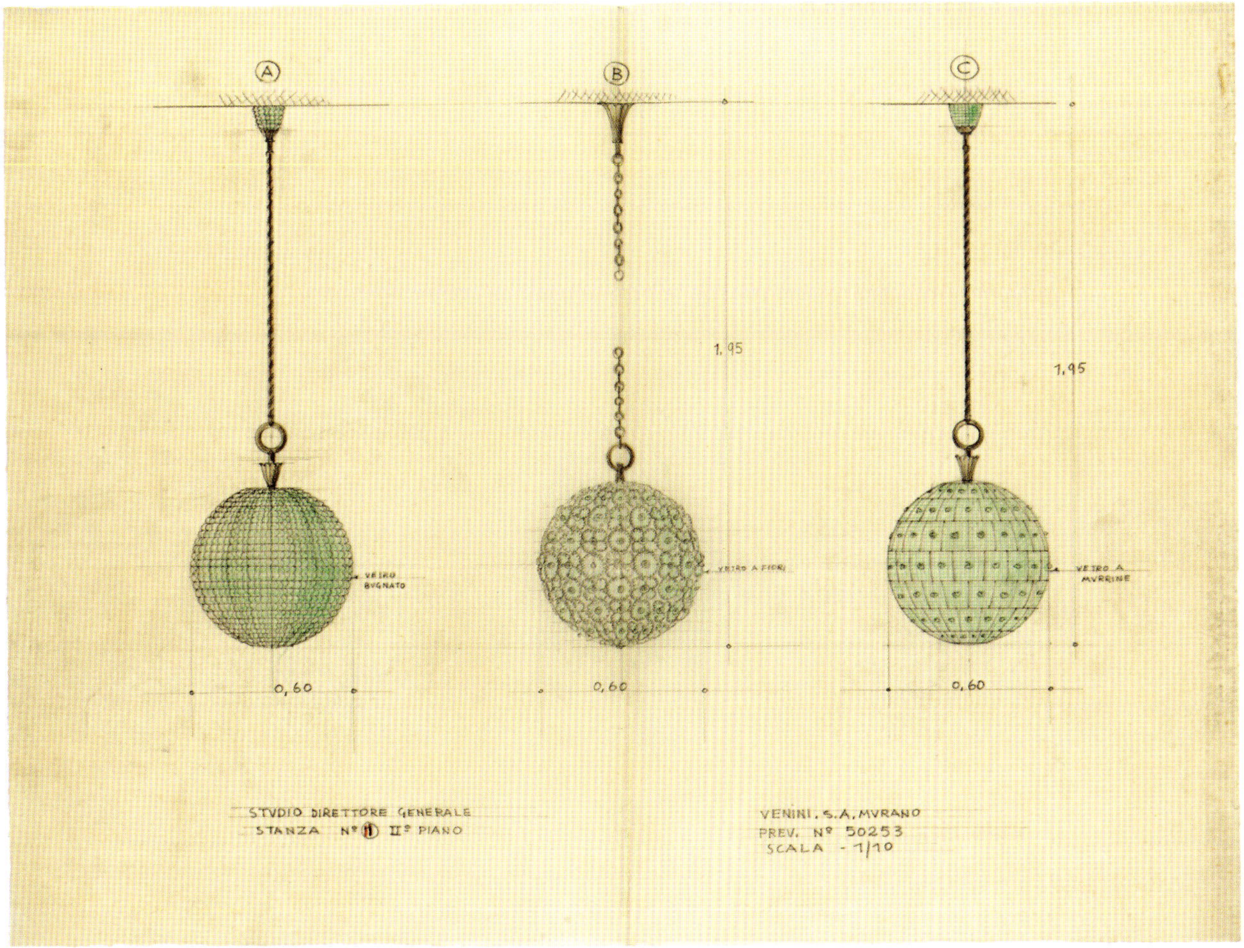
A
B
C
1,95
1,95
VETRO BUGNATO
VETRO A FIORI
VETRO A MVRRINE
0,60
0,60
0,60
STVDIO DIRETTORE GENERALE
STANZA Nº 11 IIº PIANO
VENINI. S.A. MVRANO
PREV. Nº 50253
SCALA - 1/10

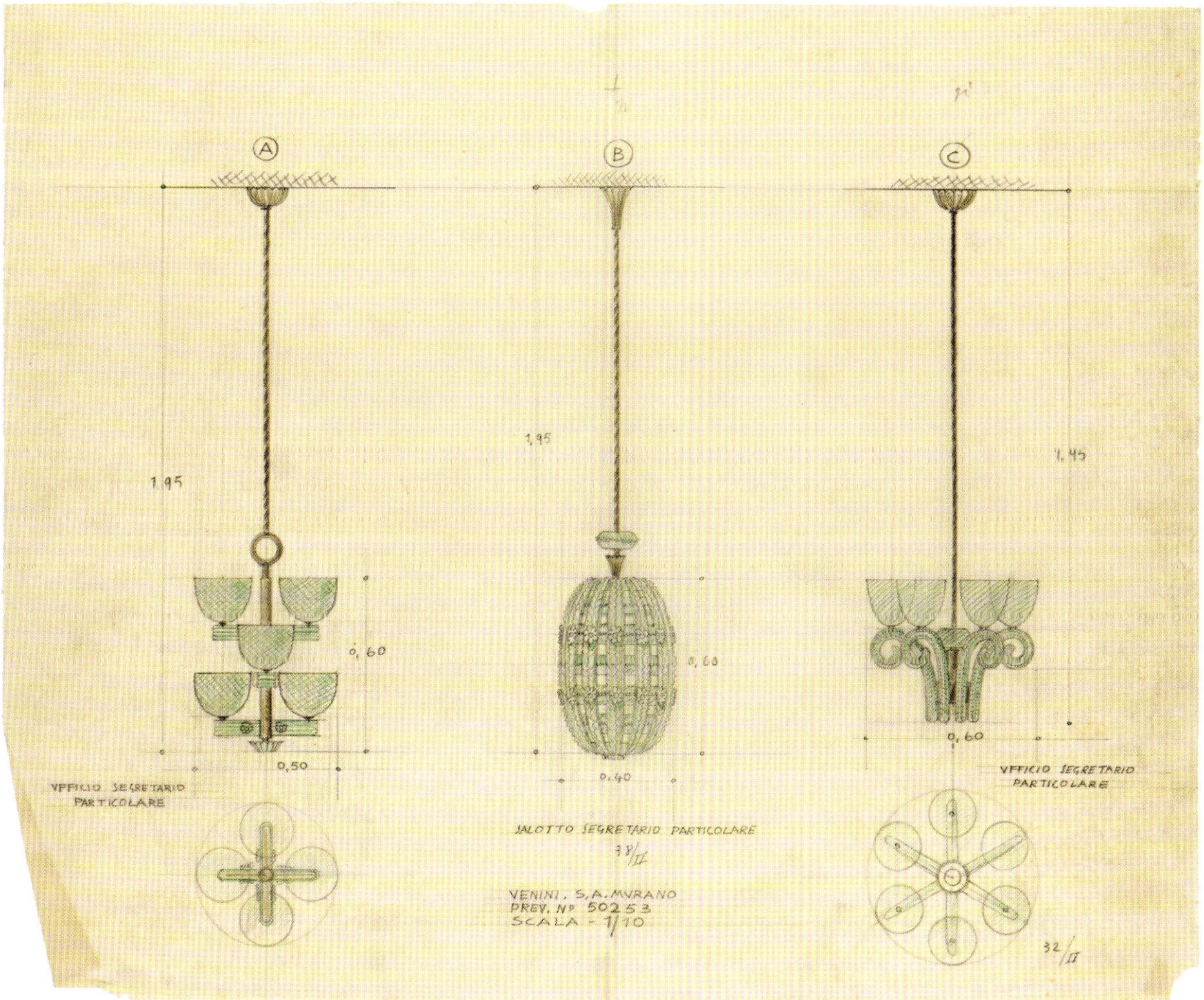
A
B
C
1,95
1,95
1,45
0,60
0,60
0,60
0,50
0,40
VFFICIO SEGRETARIO PARTICOLARE
SALOTTO SEGRETARIO PARTICOLARE
38/II
VENINI. S.A. MVRANO
PREV. Nº 50253
SCALA - 1/10
VFFICIO SEGRETARIO PARTICOLARE
32/II

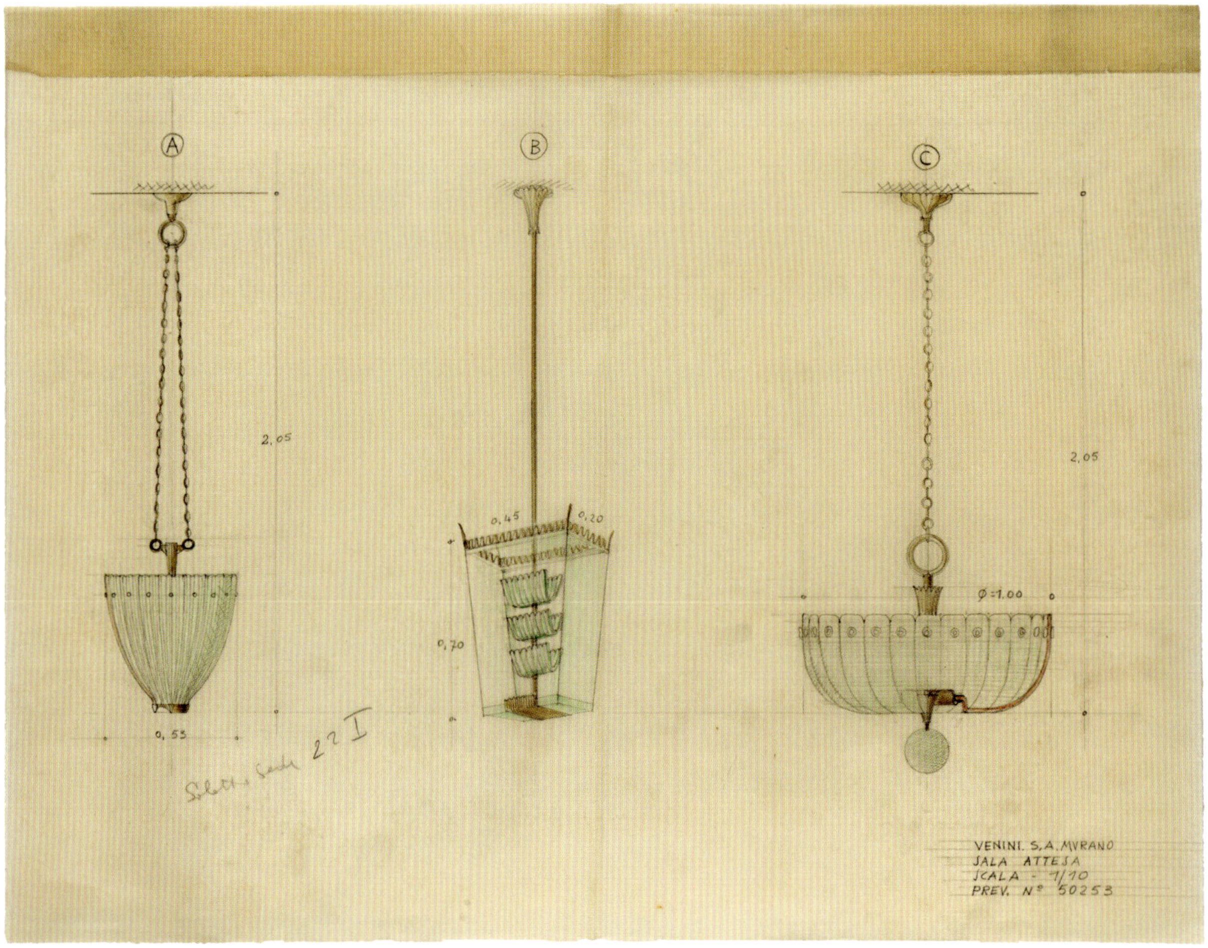
A
B
C
2,05
0,45
0,20
0,70
Ø=1.00
2,05
0,55
VENINI. S.A. MVRANO
SALA ATTESA
SCALA - 1/10
PREV. N° 50253

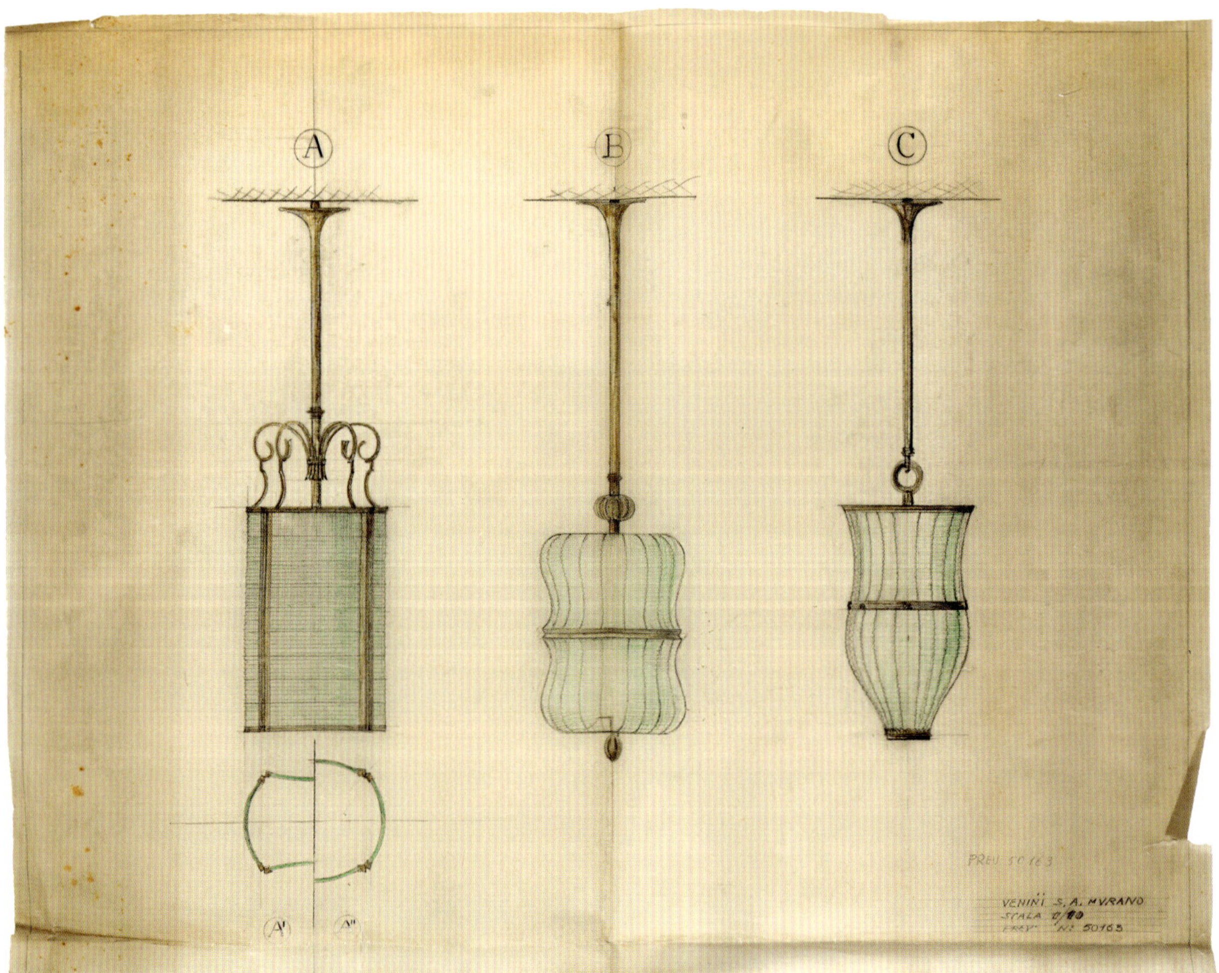
A
B
C
PREV 50163
VENINI S.A. MVRANO
N° 50163

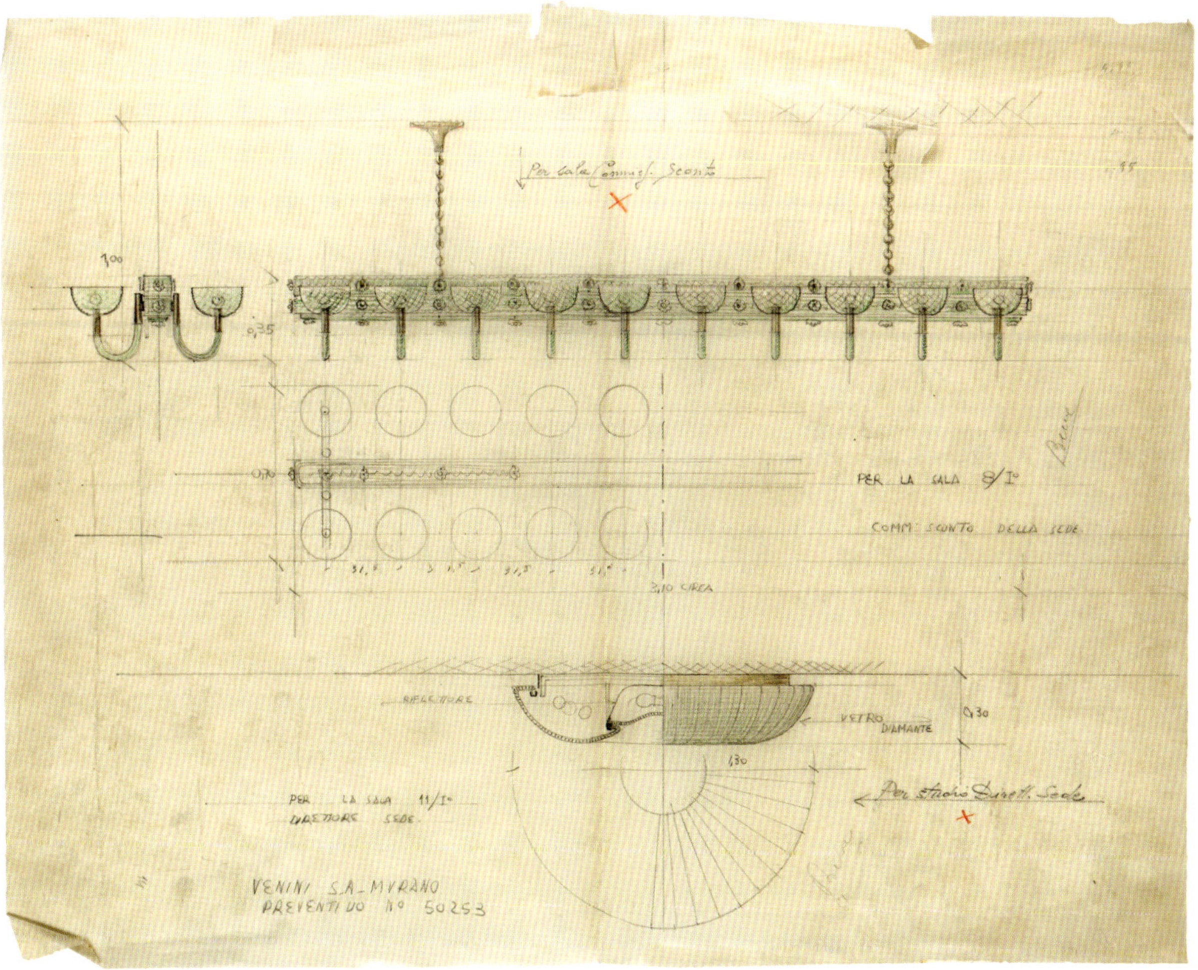
PER LA SALA 8/I°
COMM. SCONTO DELLA SEDE
3,10 CIRCA
VETRO DIAMANTE
0,30
PER LA SALA 11/I°
DIRETTORE SEDE
VENINI S.A. MURANO
PREVENTIVO N° 50253

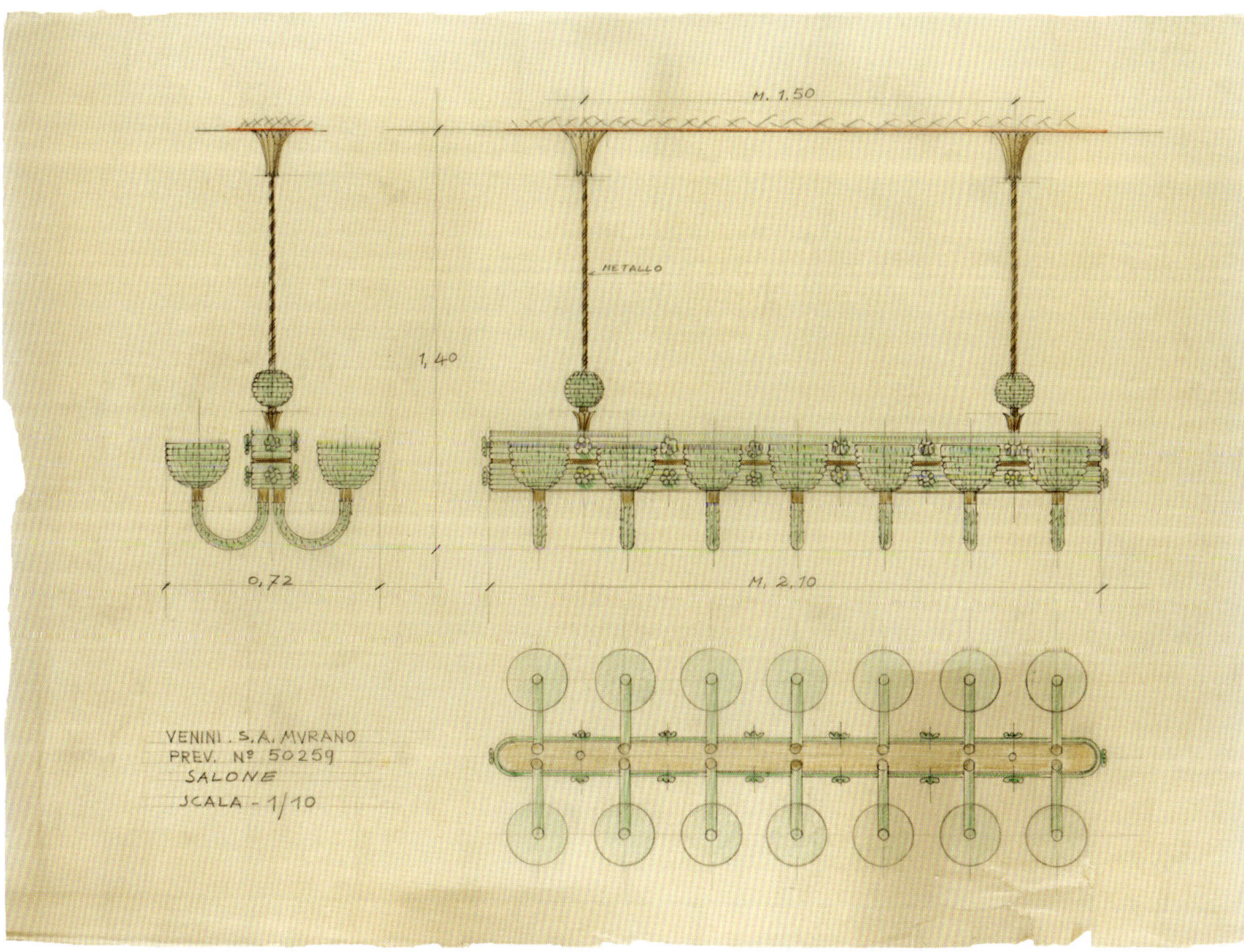
M. 1.50
METALLO
1,40
0,72
M. 2,10
VENINI. S.A. MURANO
PREV. N° 50259
SALONE
SCALA - 1/10

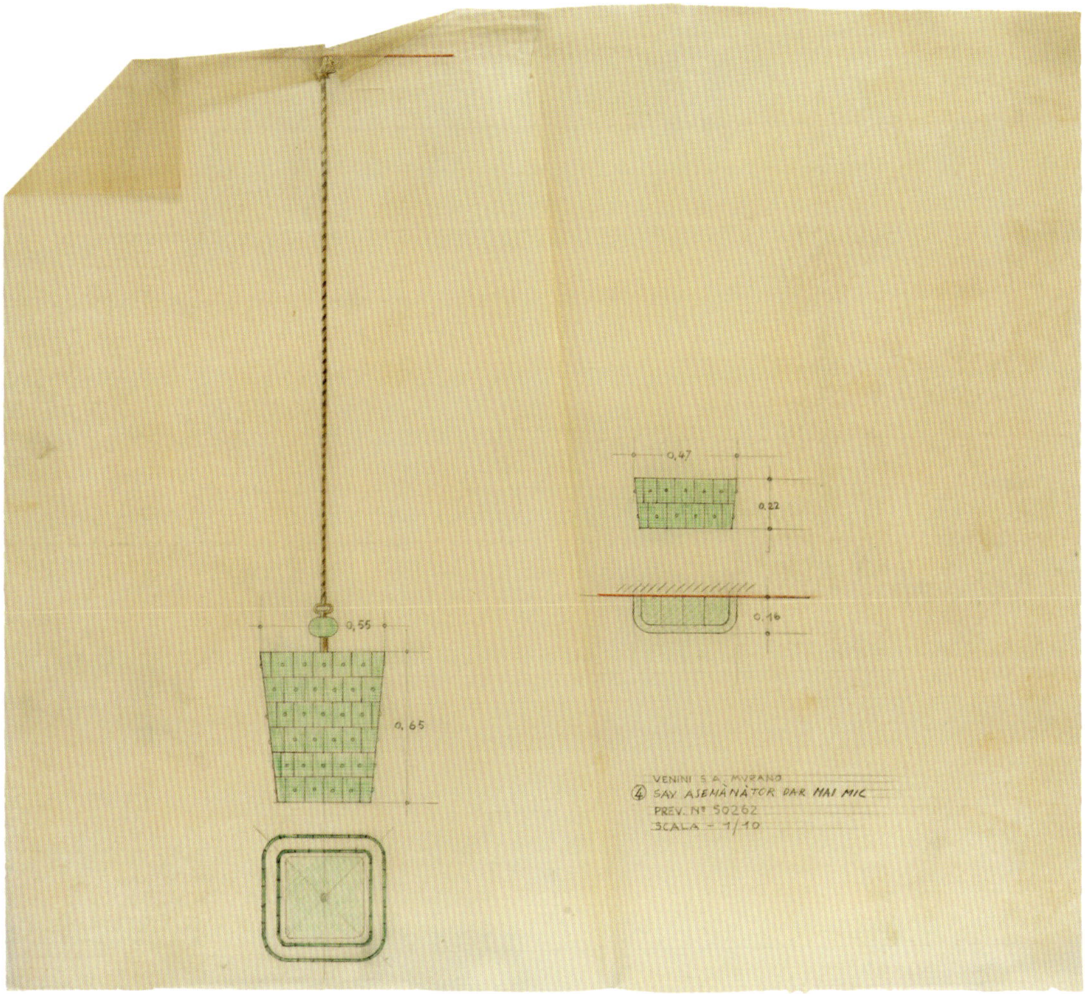
0,47
0,22
0,16
0,55
0,65
VENINI S.A. MURANO
④ SAV ASEMĂNĂTOR DAR MAI MIC
PREV. Nº 50262
SCALA - 1/10

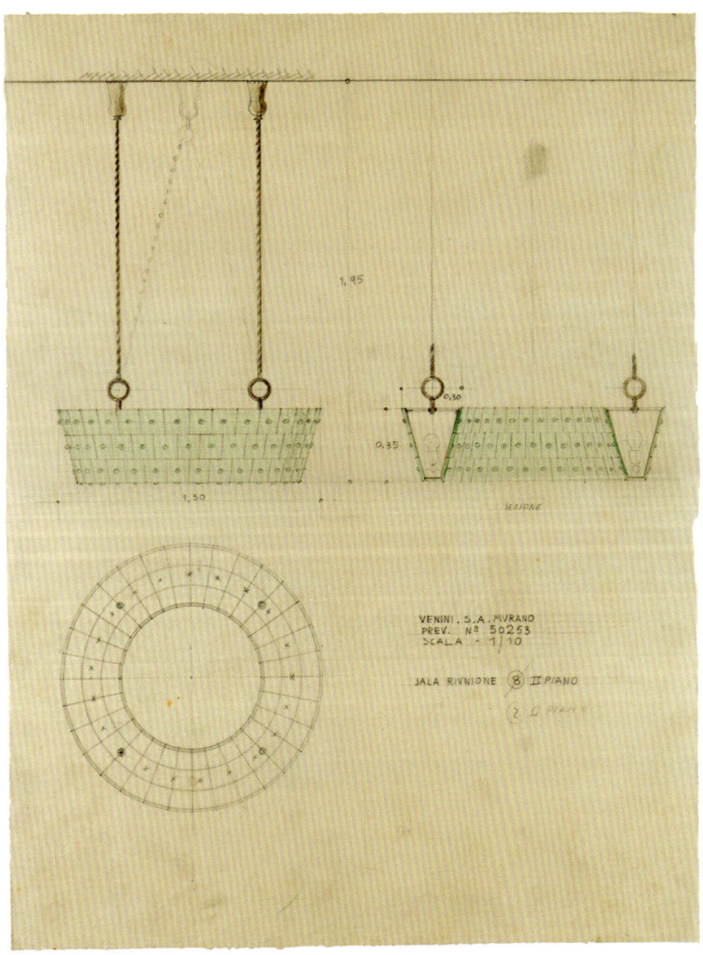
1,95
0,30
0,35
1,50
SEZIONE
VENINI. S.A. MURANO
PREV. Nº 50253
SCALA - 1/10
SALA RIUNIONE ⑧ II PIANO

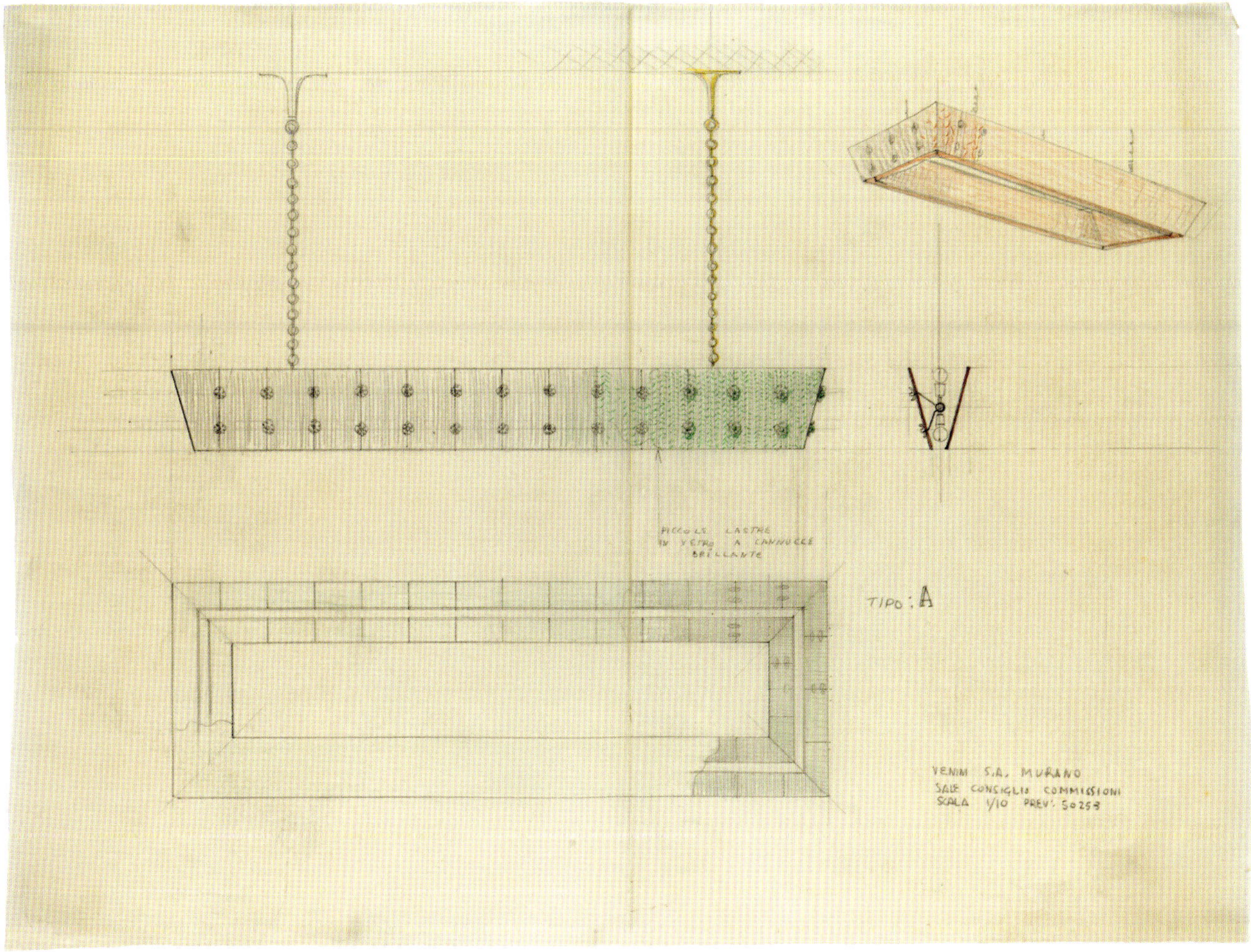
PICCOLE LASTRE
IN VETRO A CANNUCCE
BRILLANTE
TIPO: A
VENINI S.A. MURANO
SALE CONSIGLIO COMMISSIONI
SCALA 1/10 PREV: 50258

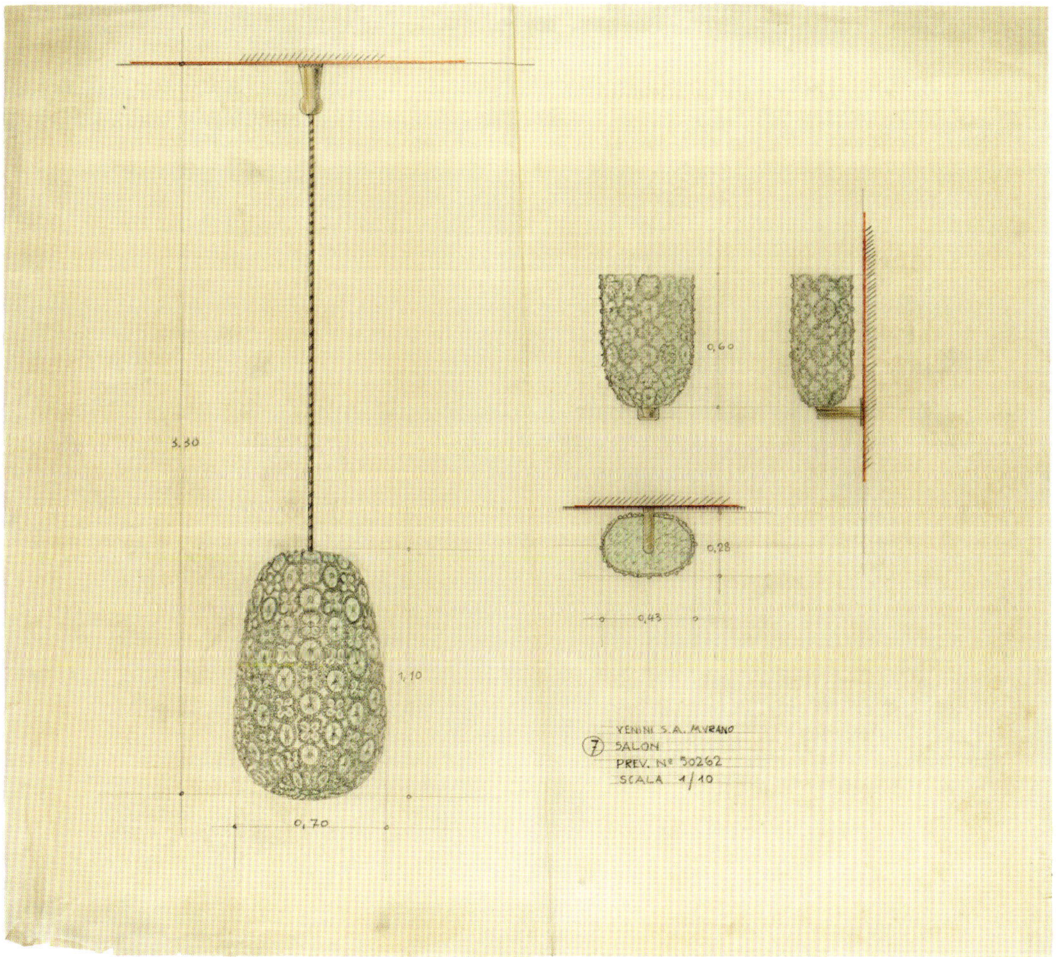
3,30
0,60
0,28
0,43
1,10
0,70
7
VENINI S.A. MURANO
SALON
PREV. Nº 50262
SCALA 1/10

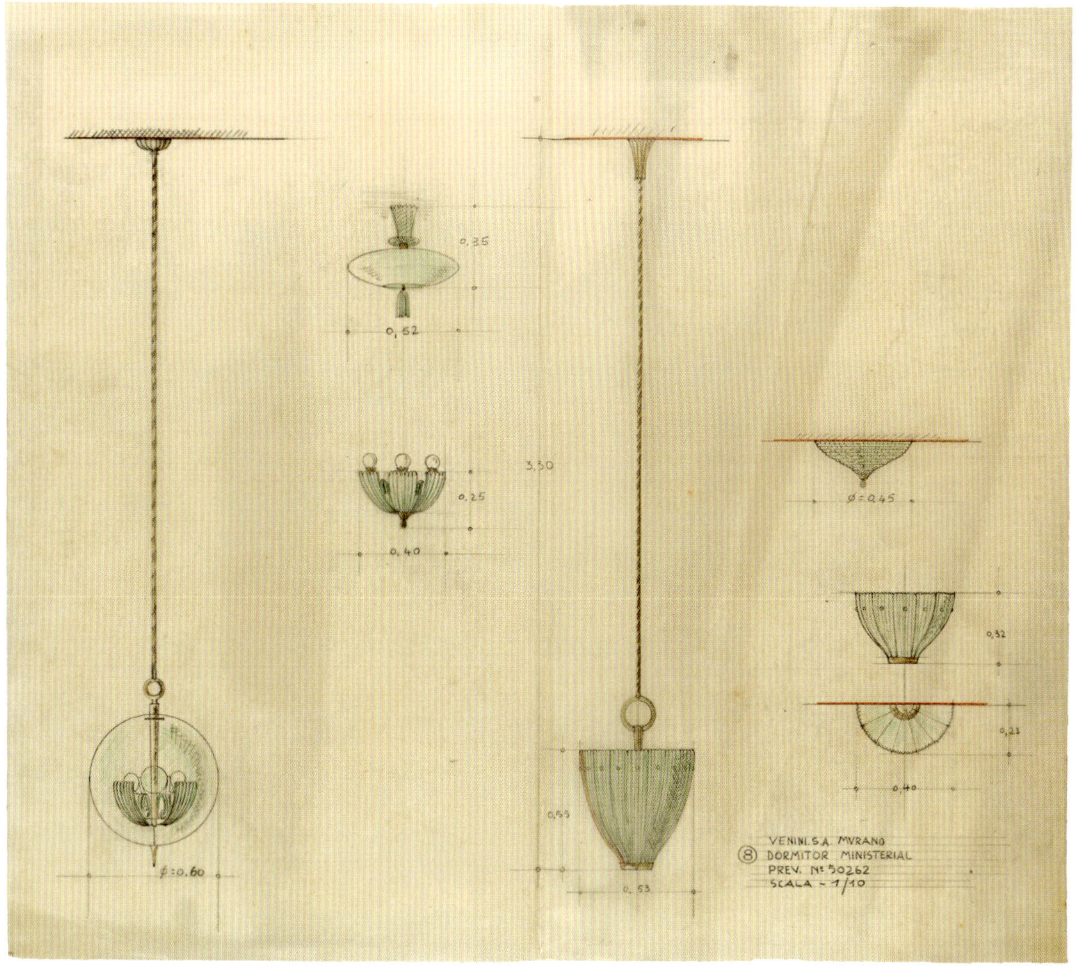
0,35
0,52
0,25
0,40
3,30
Ø=0,45
0,32
0,21
0,40
0,55
Ø=0,60
0,53
VENINI. S.A. MVRANO
8 DORMITOR MINISTERIAL
PREV. Nº 50262
SCALA - 1/10

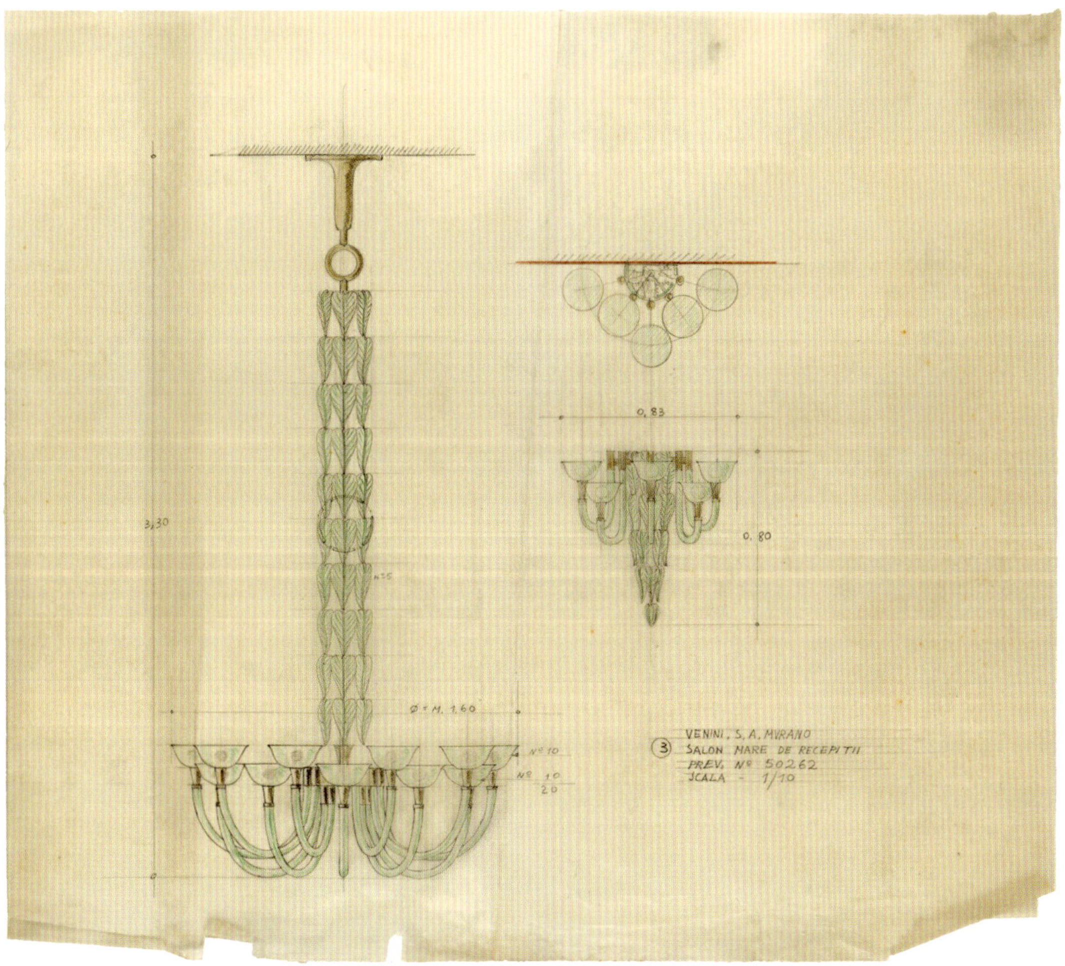
0,83
0,80
3,30
Ø=M. 1,60
VENINI. S. A. MVRANO
3 SALON MARE DE RECEPTII
PREV. Nº 50262
SCALA - 1/10

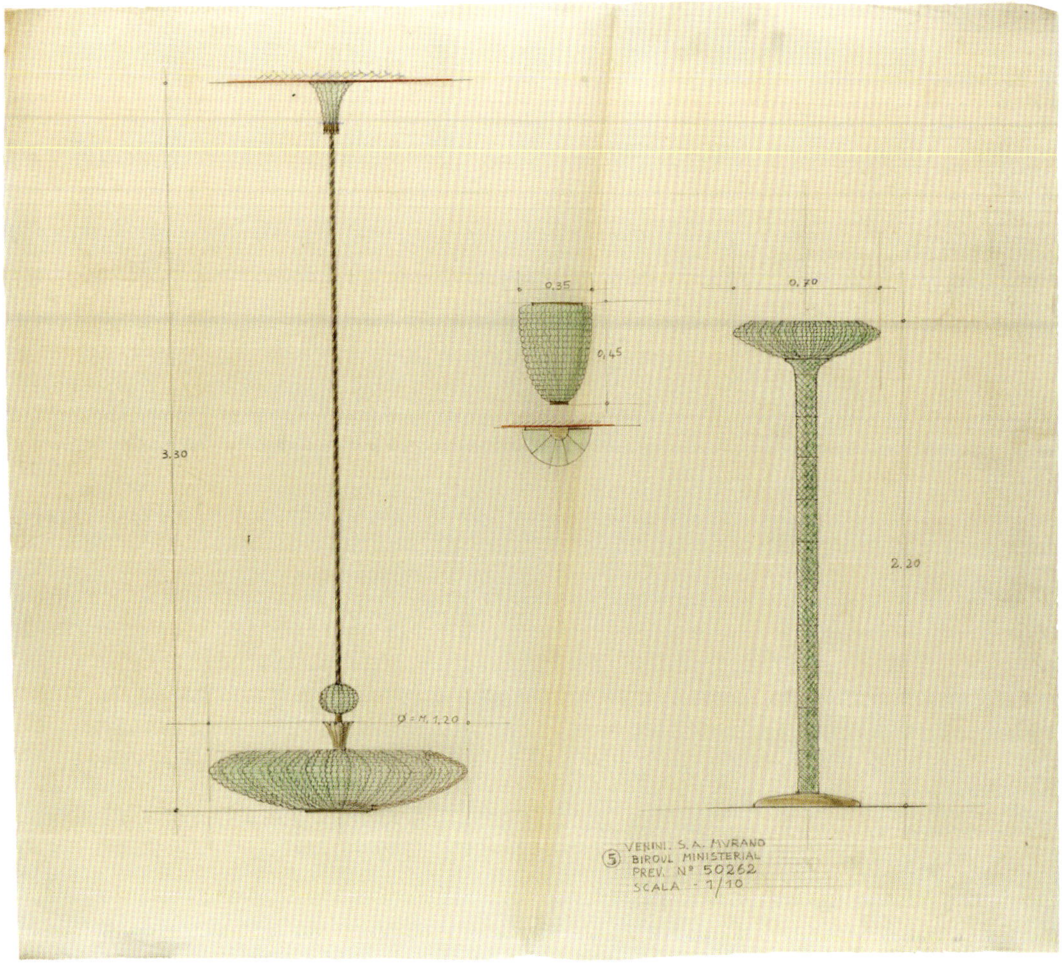
0.35
0.45
0.70
3.30
2.20
Ø = M. 2.20
VENINI. S.A. MURANO
5 BIROUL MINISTERIAL
PREV. Nº 50262
SCALA - 1/10

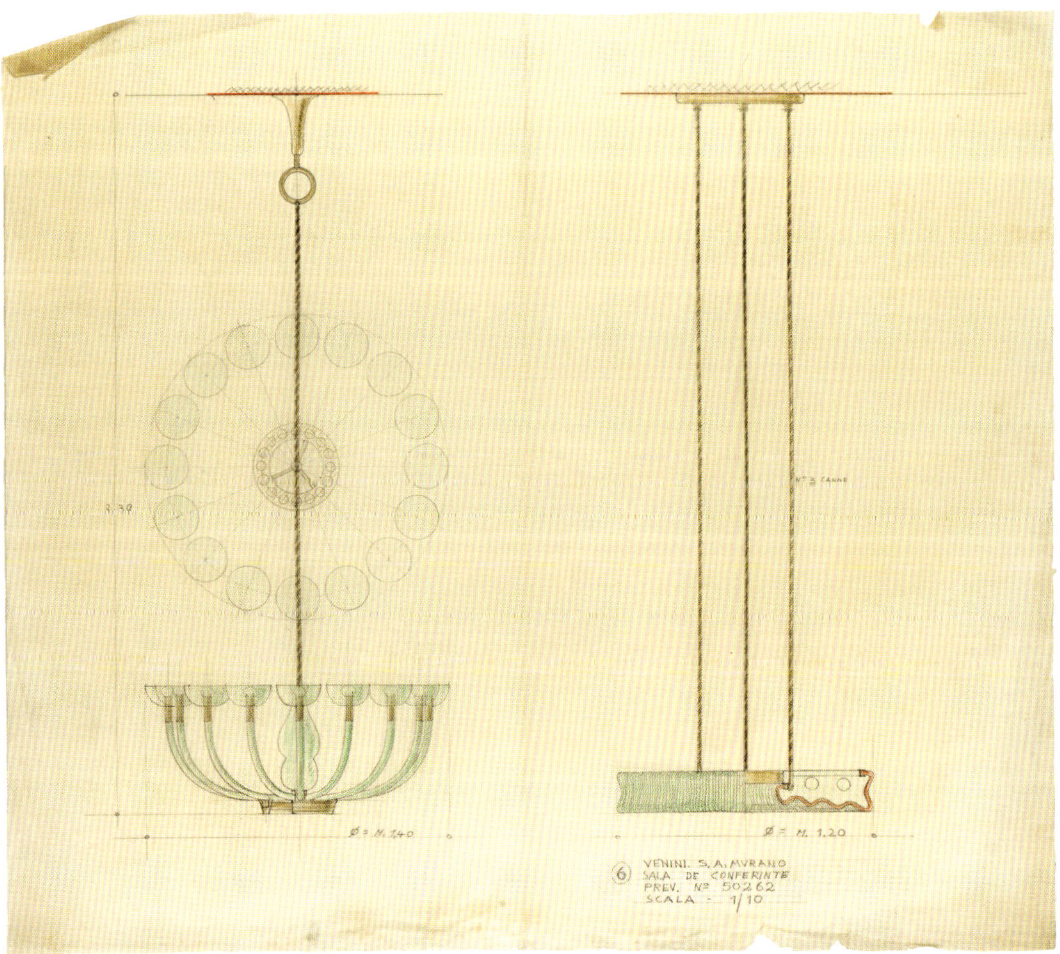
Ø = M. 2.40
Ø = M. 1.20
VENINI. S.A. MURANO
6 SALA DE CONFERINTE
PREV. Nº 50262
SCALA - 1/10

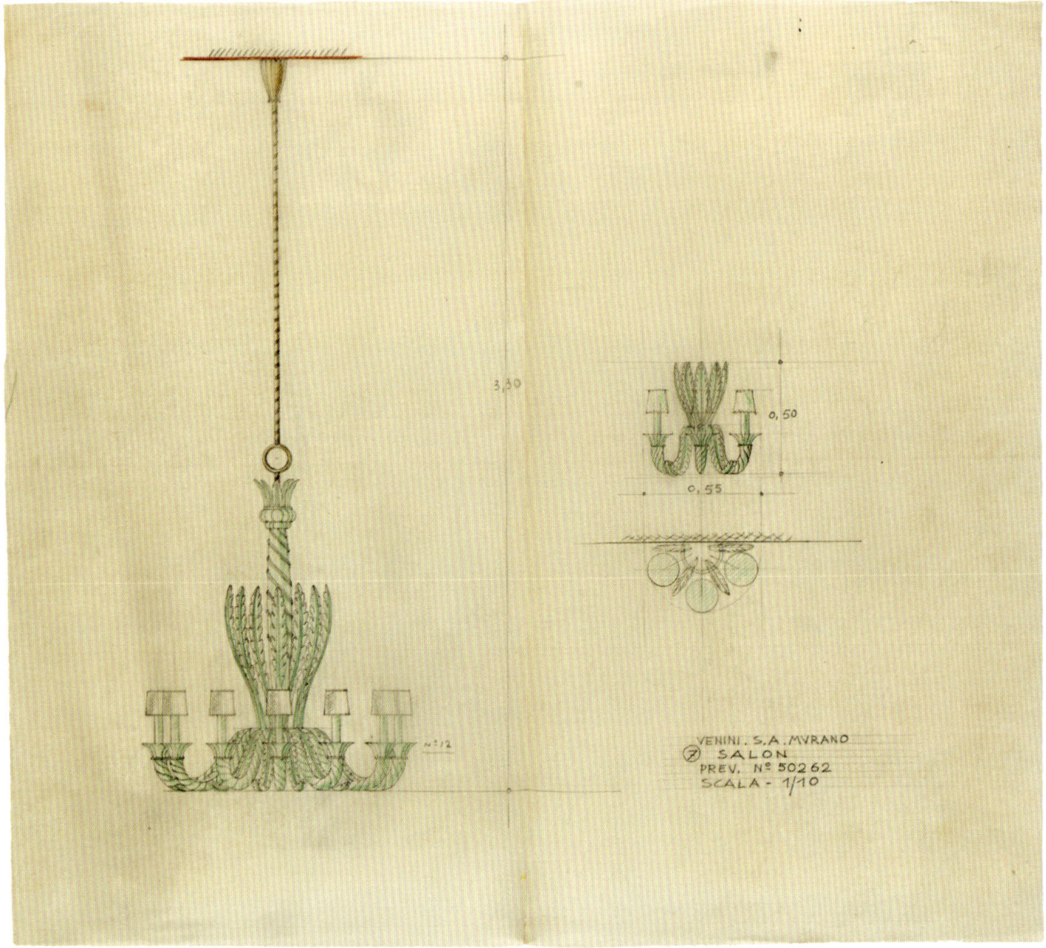
3,30
0,50
0,55
VENINI. S.A. MVRANO
7 SALON
PREV. Nº 50262
SCALA - 1/10

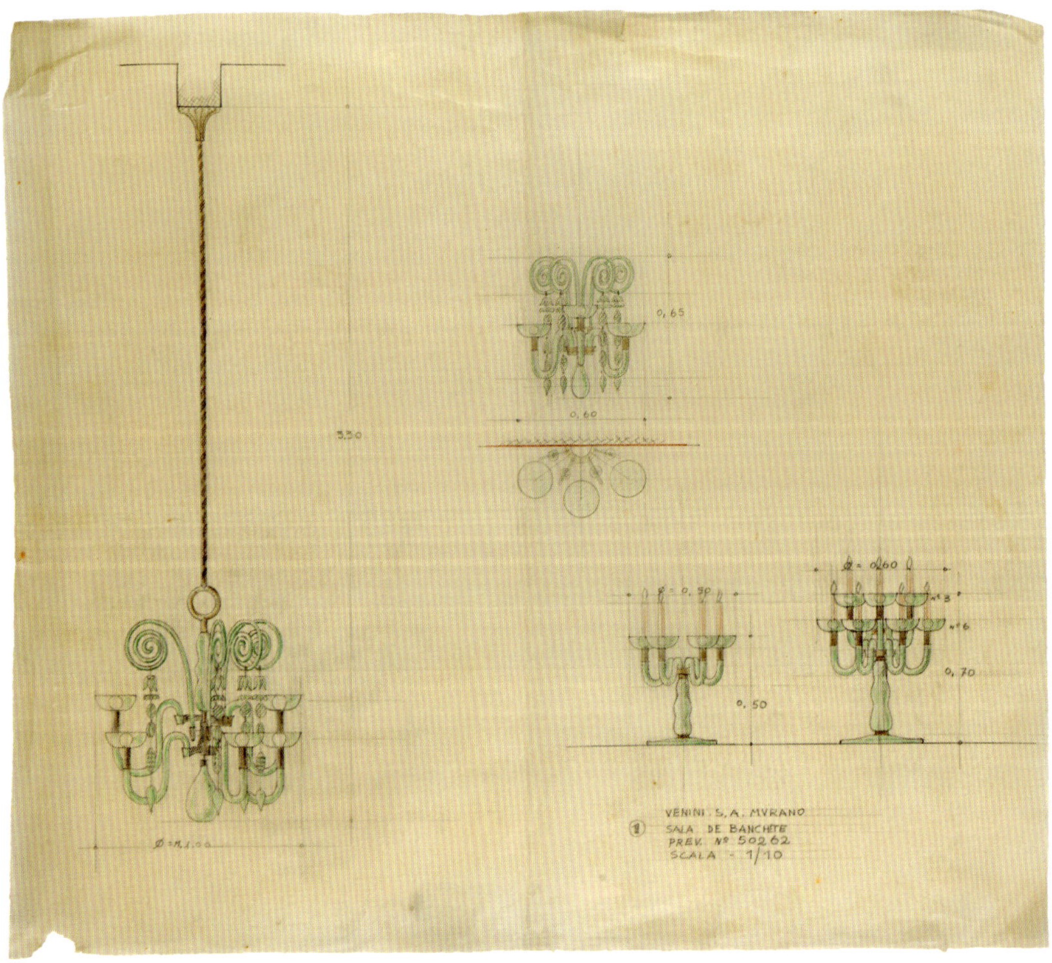
5,50
0,65
0,60
0,50
0,70
VENINI. S.A. MVRANO
1 SALA DE BANCHITE
PREV. Nº 50262
SCALA - 1/10

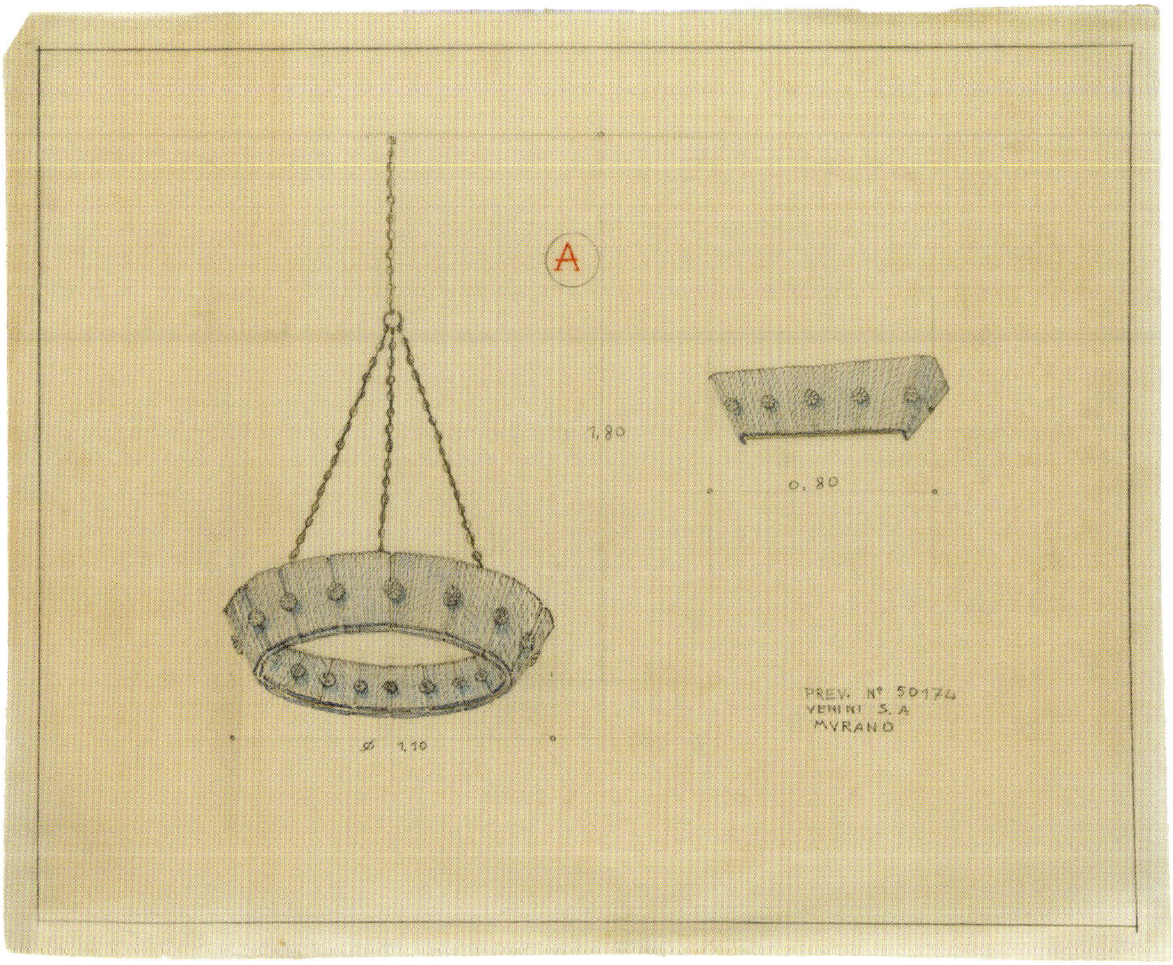
A
1,80
0,80
ø 1,10
PREV. N° 50174
VENINI S.A
MVRANO

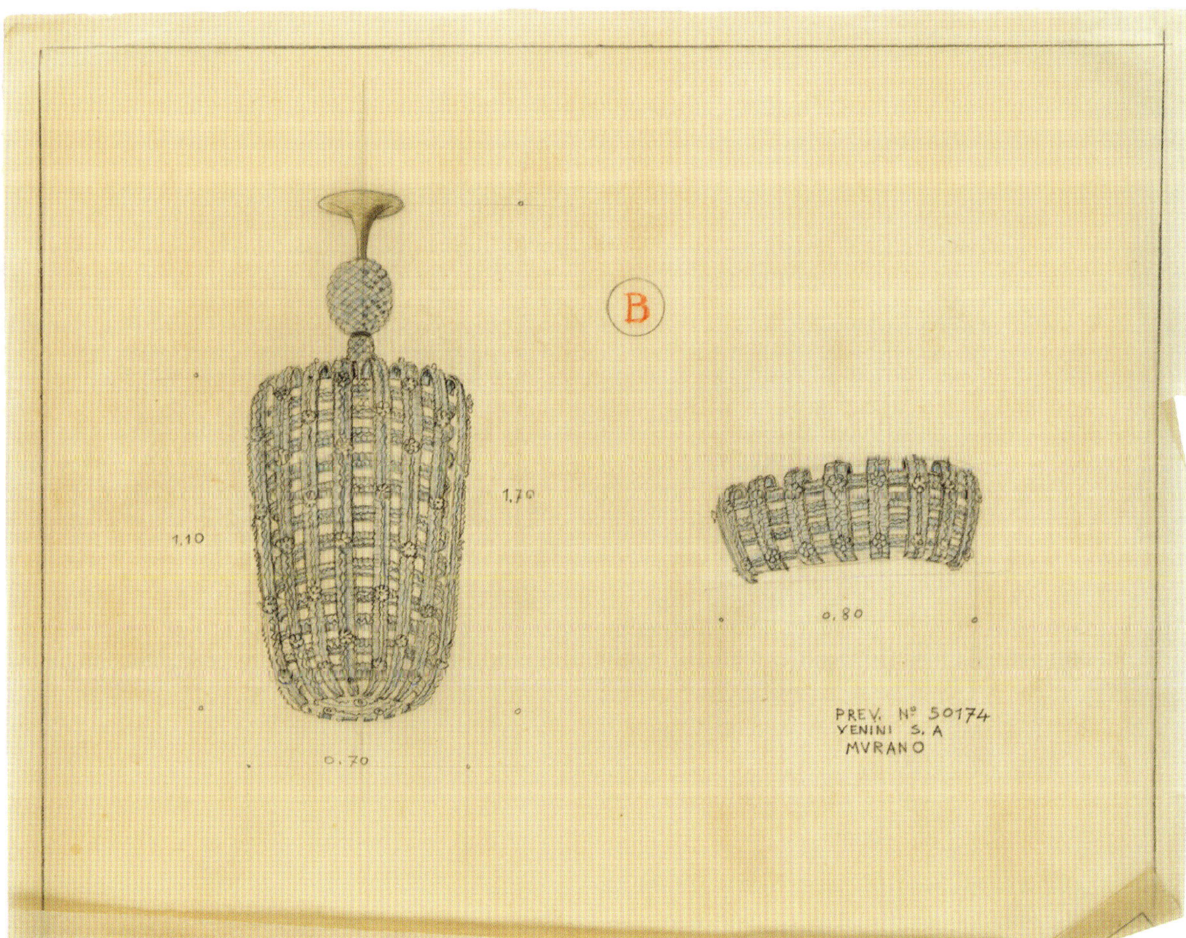
B
1,70
1,10
0,80
0,70
PREV. N° 50174
VENINI S.A
MVRANO

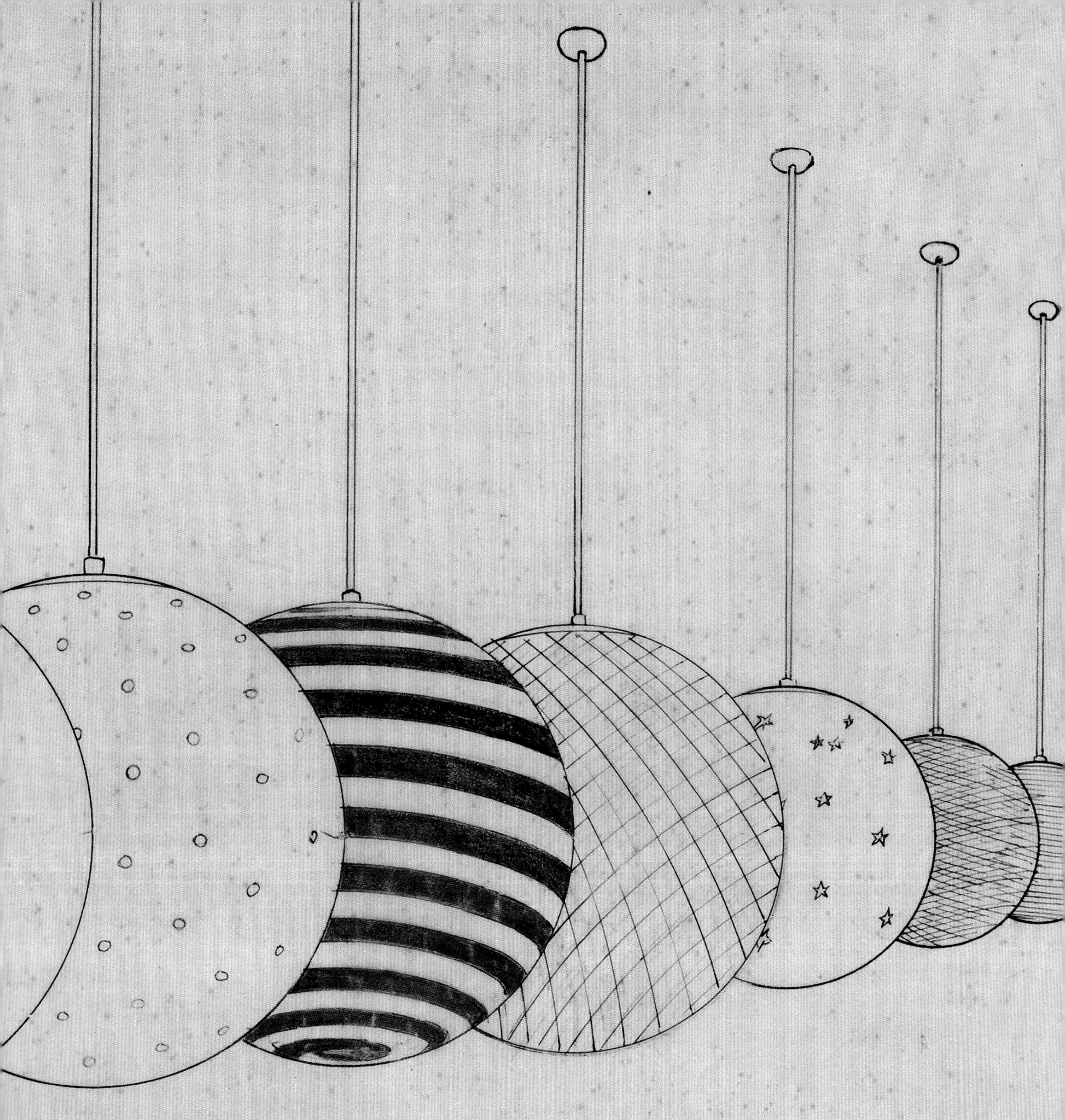

5258

BLUE CATALOGUE: DRAWINGS FOR LIGHTING

The tracing sheets are presented here with which the blueprint copies used for producing the famous Blue Catalogue were executed, in the section dedicated to lighting. Produced in the course of the 1930s and into the early 1940s, the catalogue illustrates a selection of models covering a period extending from 1921 to 1942.

1:10

2001

VENINI MVRANO

101

SOFFIATI 1926-1930

1:10

5074

VENINI MVRANO

102

SOFFIATI 1926-1930

1:10

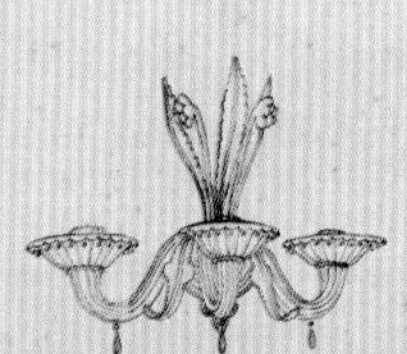

2183

5075

VENINI MVRANO

103

SOFFIATI 1926-1930

1:10

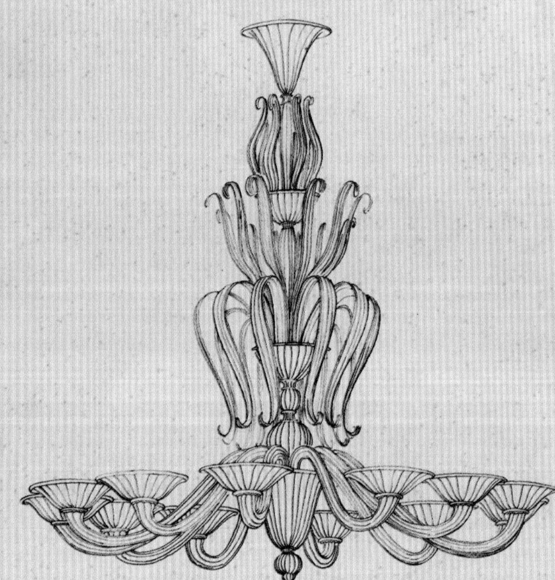

5001

VENINI MVRANO

104

SOFFIATI 1926-1930

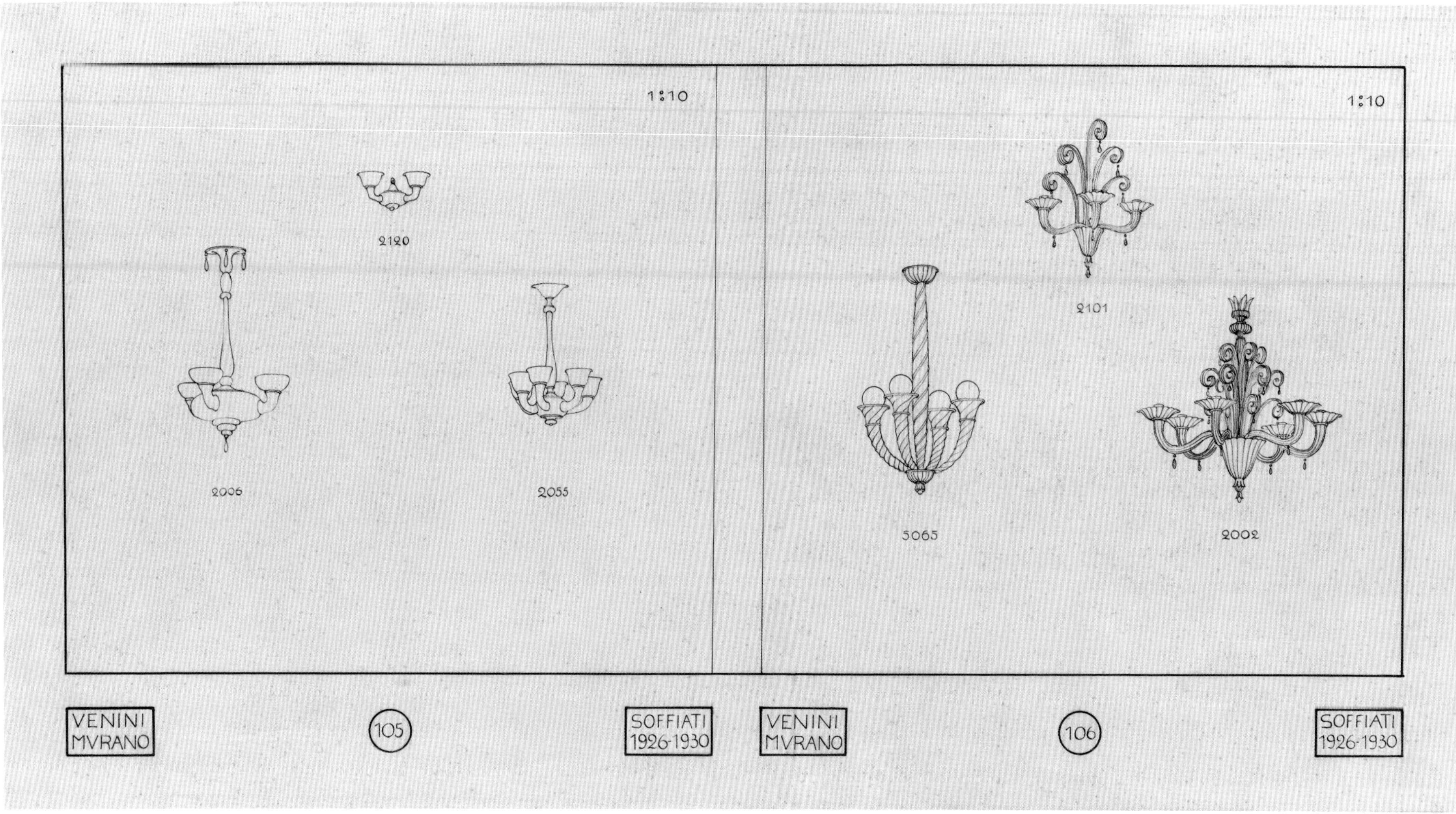
1:10
2120
2006
2055
VENINI MVRANO
105
SOFFIATI 1926-1930
1:10
2101
5065
2002
VENINI MVRANO
106
SOFFIATI 1926-1930

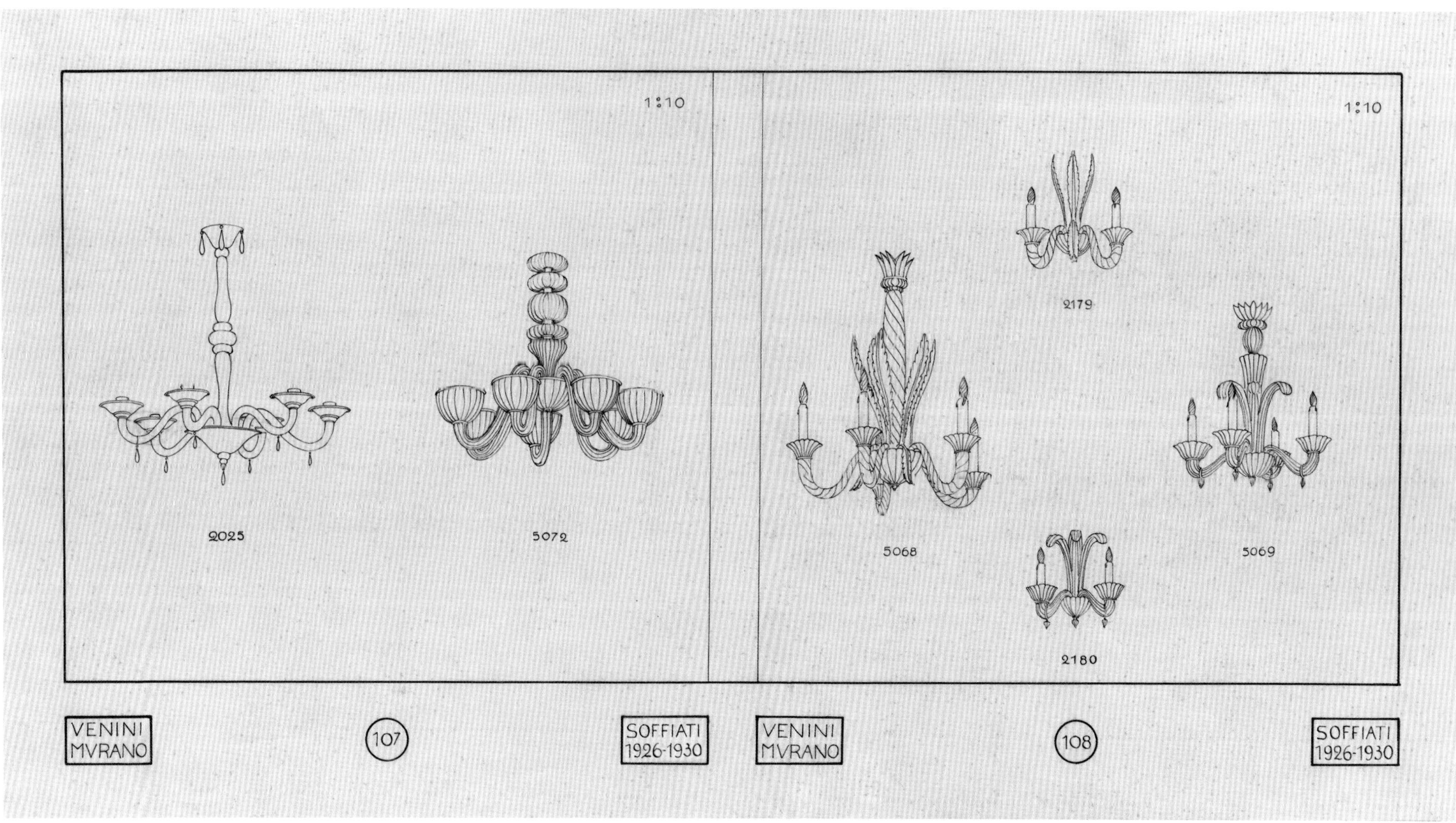
1:10
2025
5072
VENINI MVRANO
107
SOFFIATI 1926-1930
1:10
2179
5068
5069
2180
VENINI MVRANO
108
SOFFIATI 1926-1930

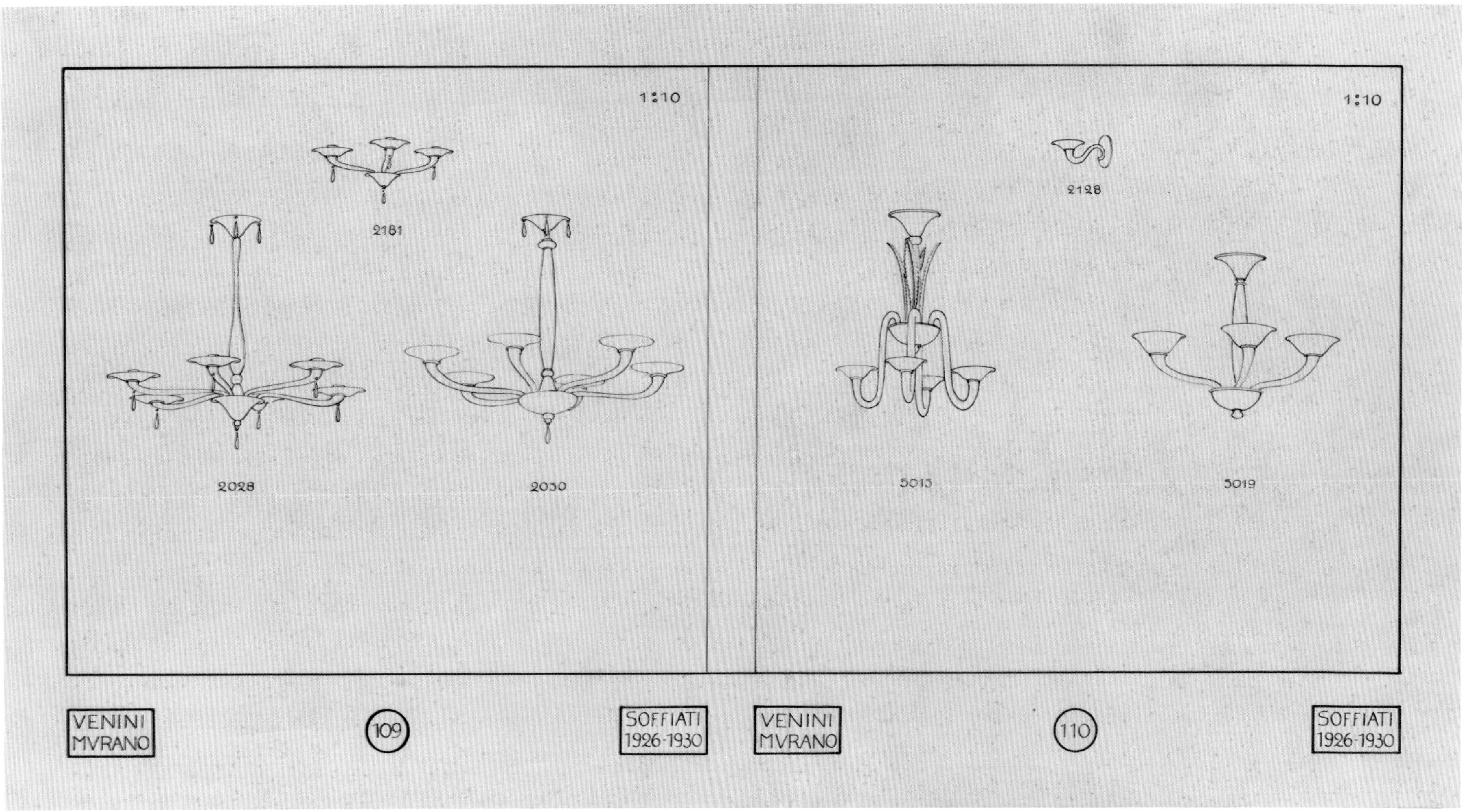
1:10
2181
2028
2030
VENINI
MVRANO
109
SOFFIATI
1926-1930
1:10
2128
5013
5019
VENINI
MVRANO
110
SOFFIATI
1926-1930

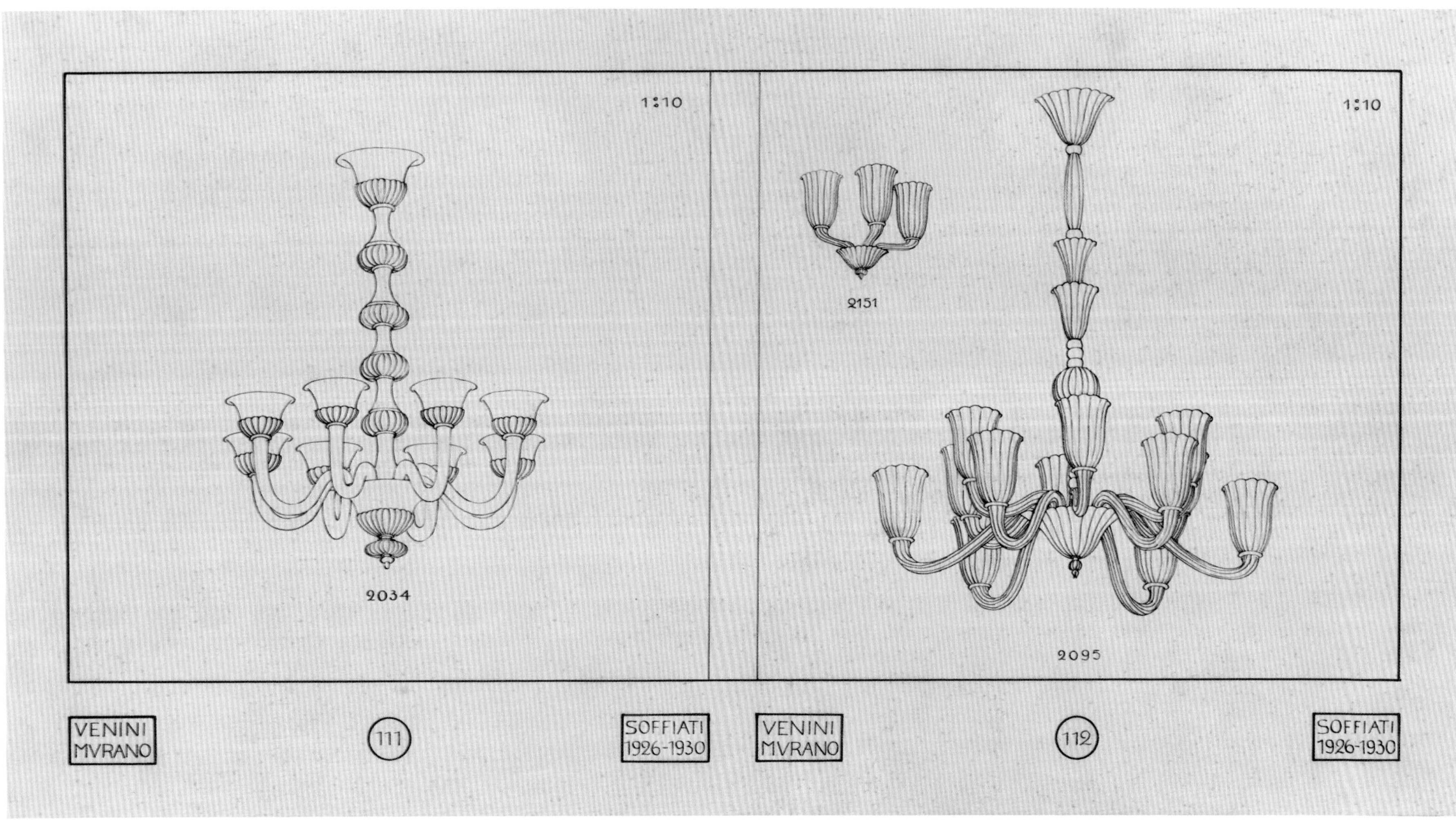
1:10
2034
VENINI
MVRANO
111
SOFFIATI
1926-1930
1:10
2151
2095
VENINI
MVRANO
112
SOFFIATI
1926-1930

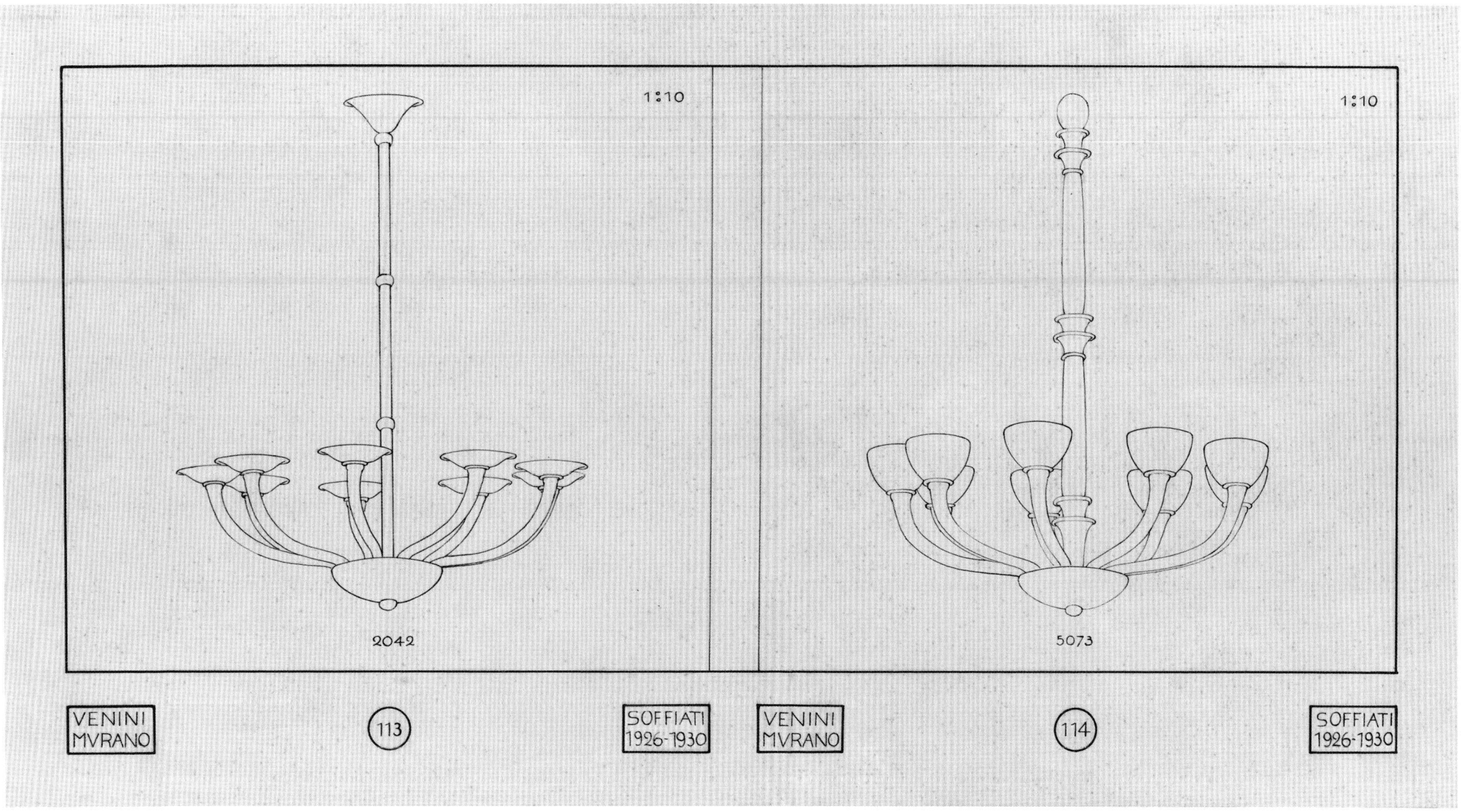
1:10
2042
VENINI
MVRANO
113
SOFFIATI
1926-1930
1:10
5073
VENINI
MVRANO
114
SOFFIATI
1926-1930

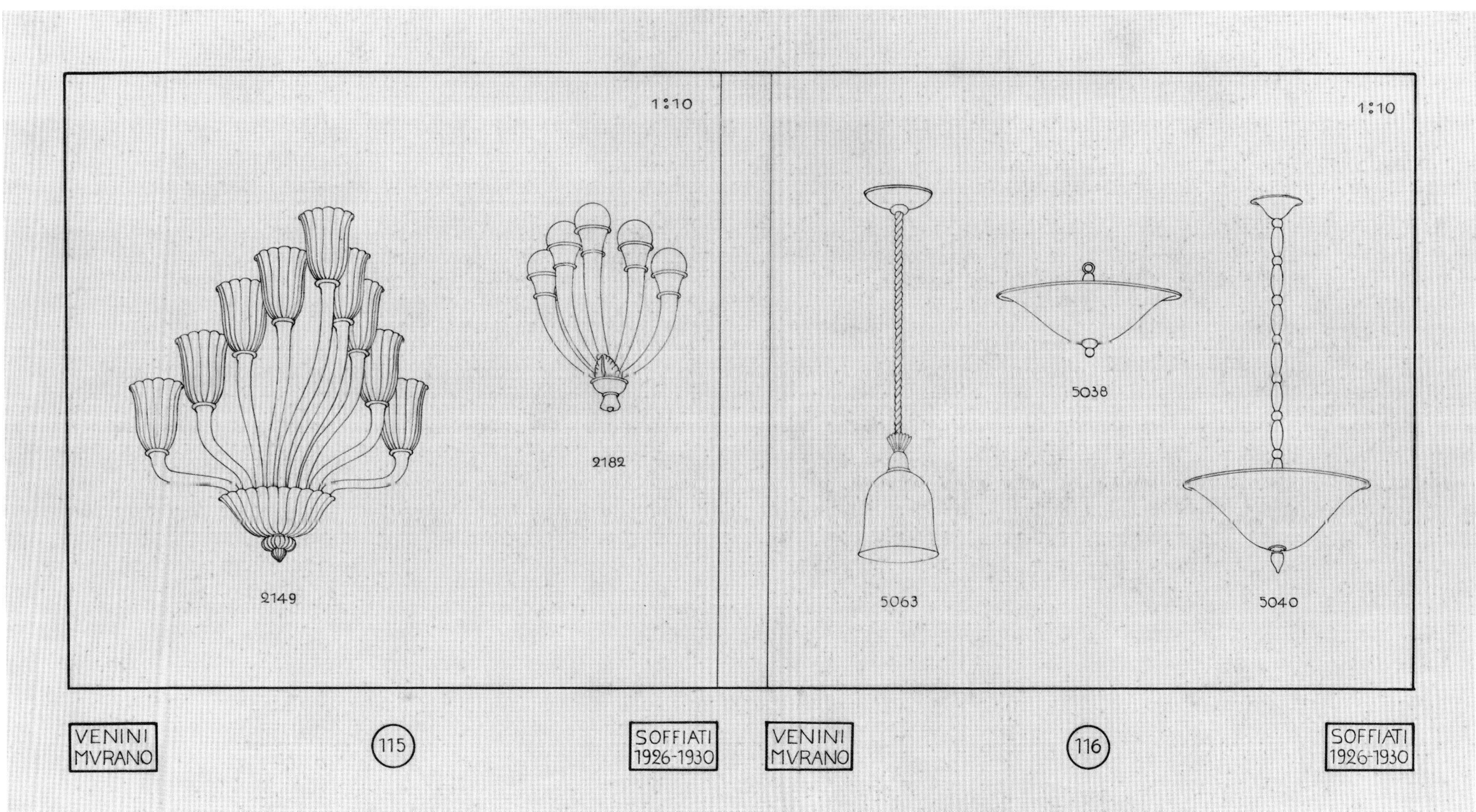
1:10
2149
2182
VENINI
MVRANO
115
SOFFIATI
1926-1930
1:10
5063
5038
5040
VENINI
MVRANO
116
SOFFIATI
1926-1930

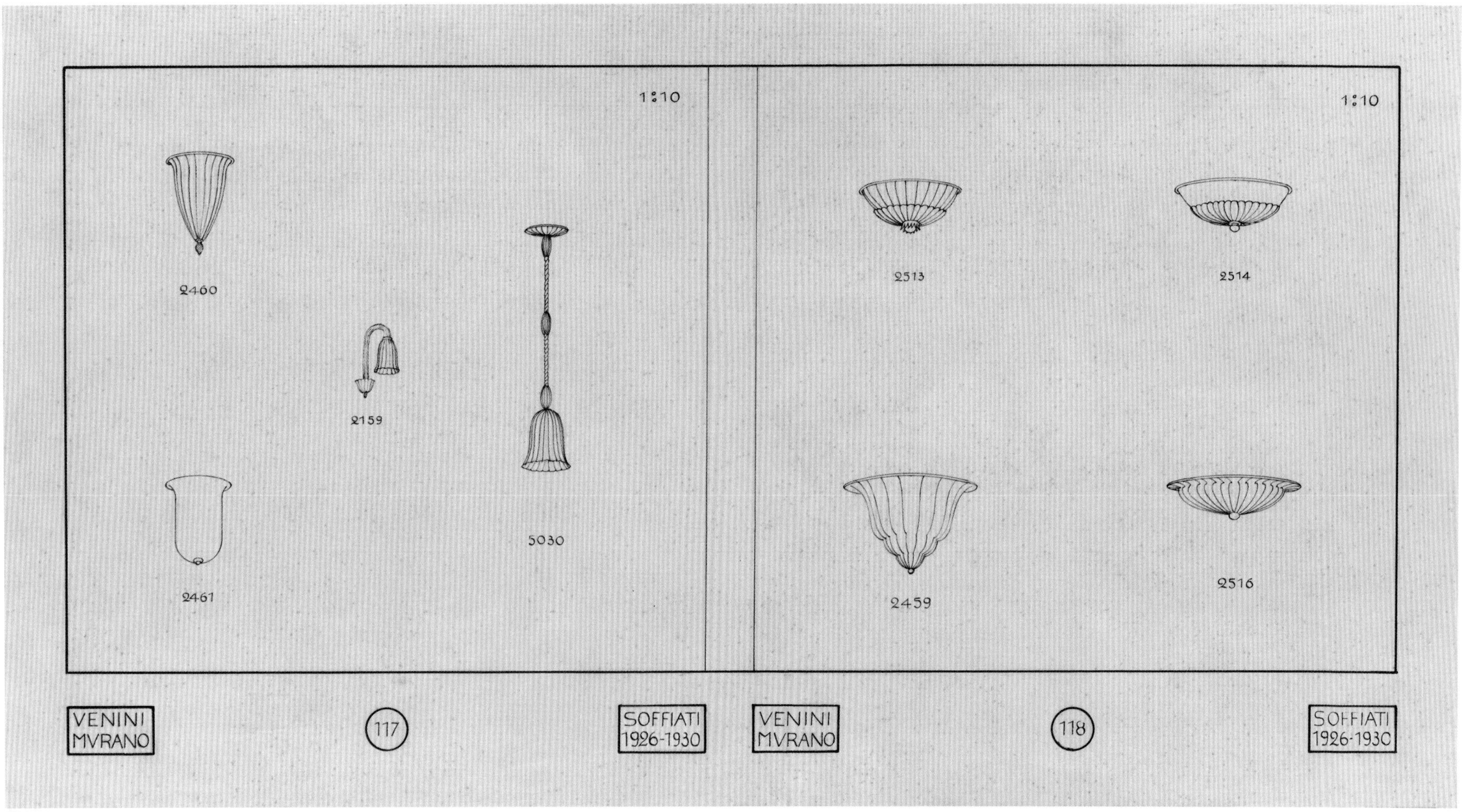
1:10
2460
2159
5030
2461
VENINI
MVRANO
117
SOFFIATI
1926-1930
1:10
2513
2514
2459
2516
VENINI
MVRANO
118
SOFFIATI
1926-1930

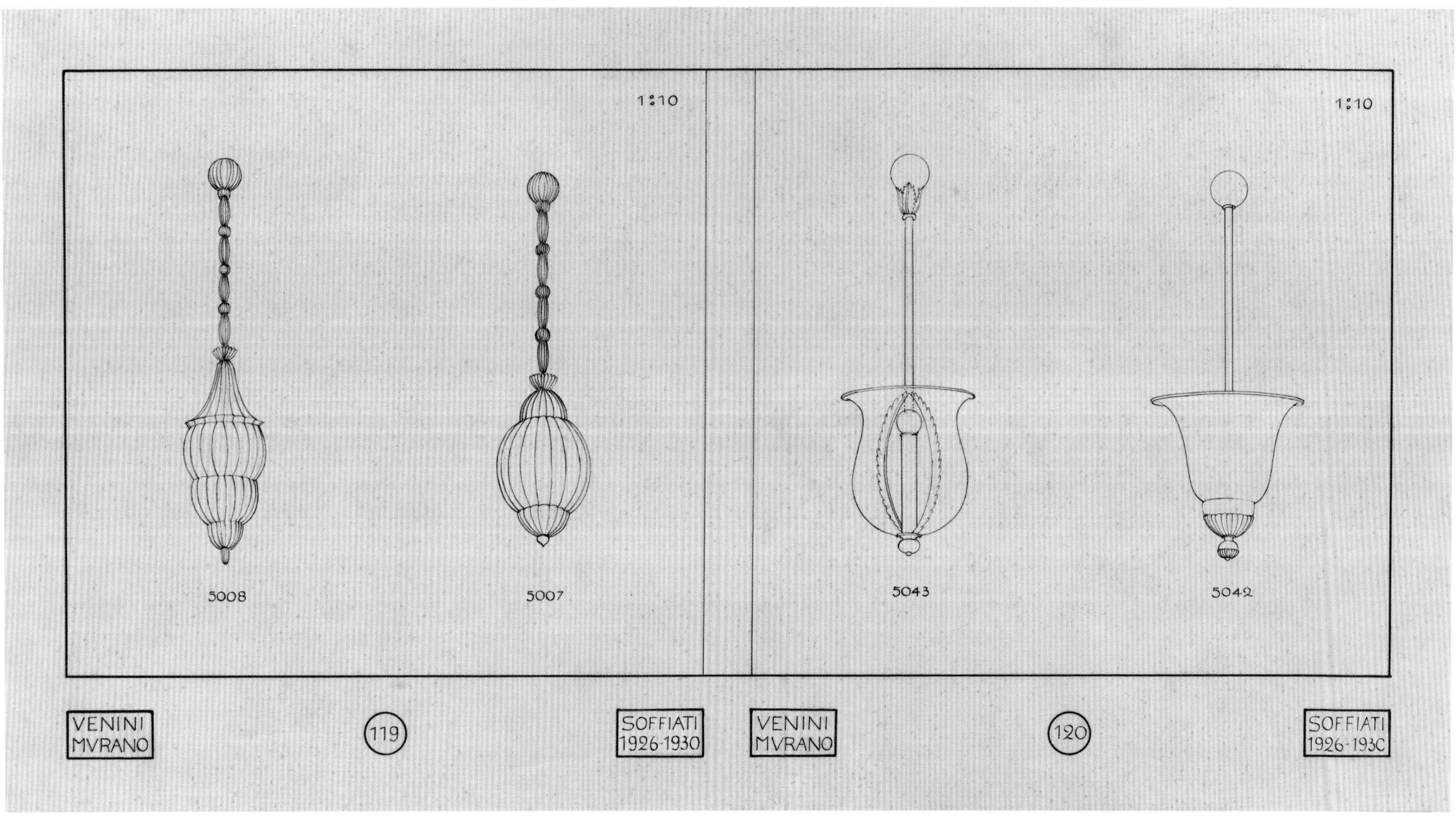
1:10
5008
5007
VENINI
MVRANO
119
SOFFIATI
1926-1930
1:10
5043
5042
VENINI
MVRANO
120
SOFFIATI
1926-1930

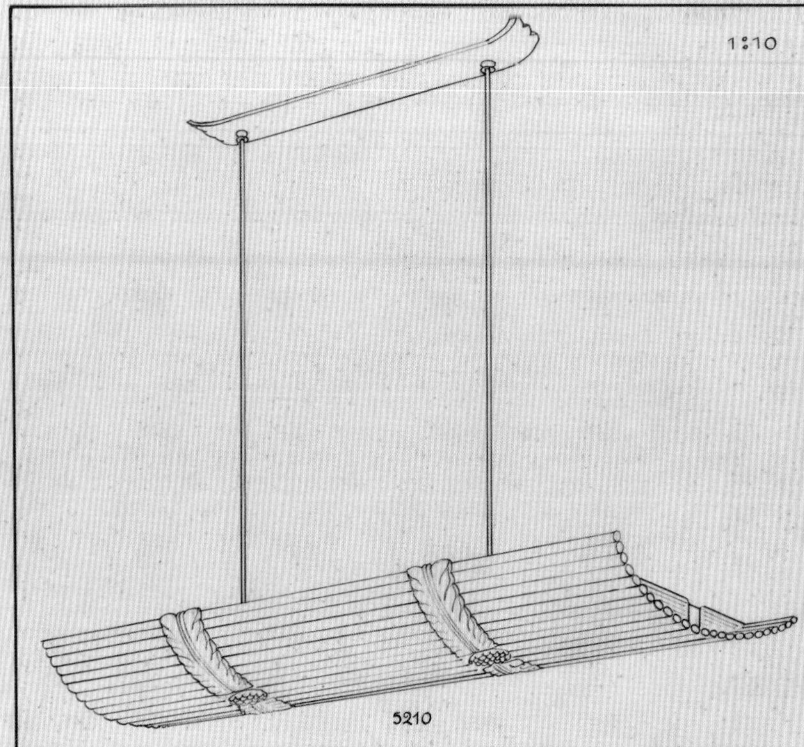

VENINI MVRANO

121

CANNE E FOGLIE 1931 - 1935

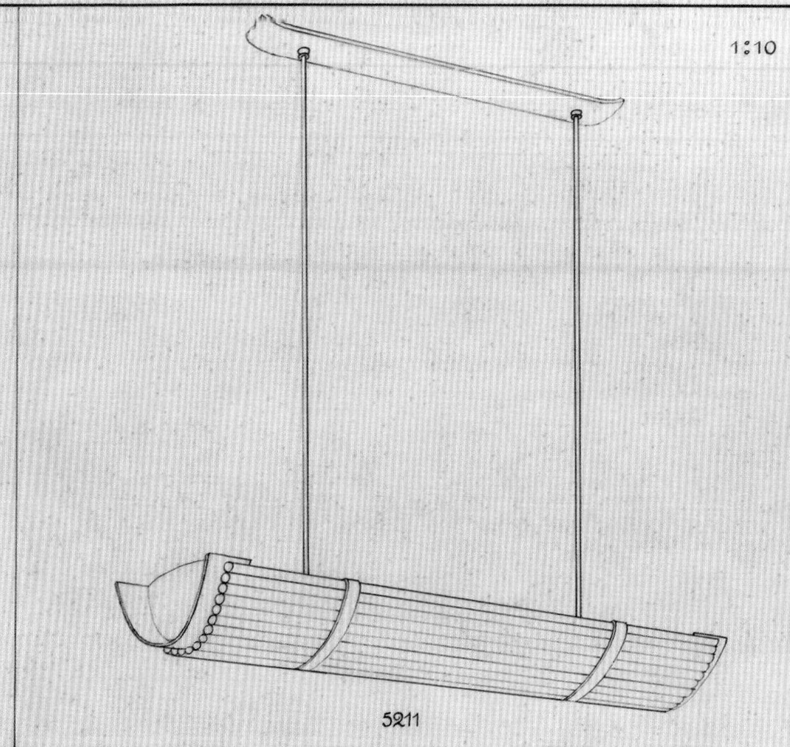

VENINI MVRANO

122

CANNE 1931-1935

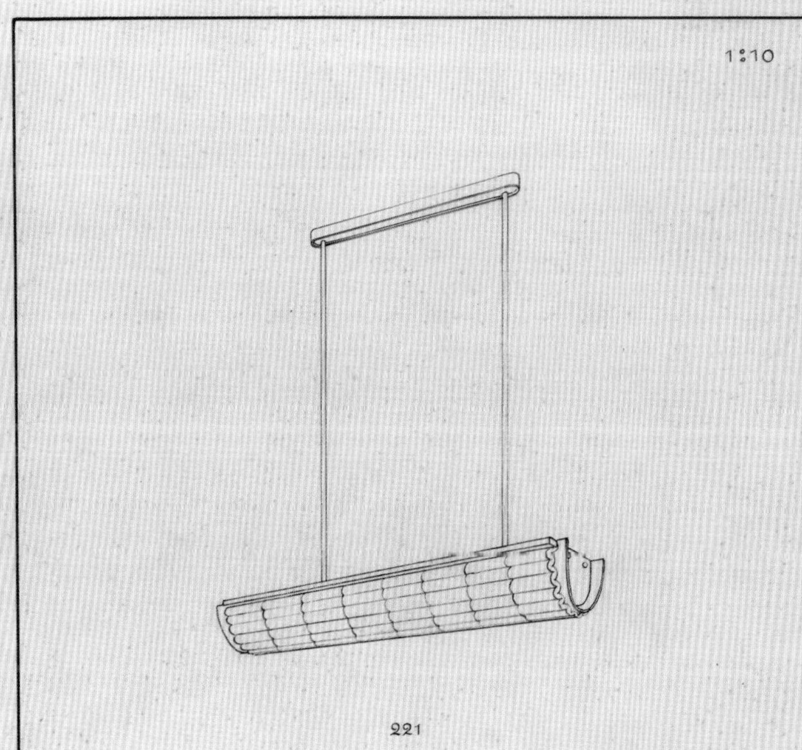

VENINI MVRANO

123

ONDVLATO 1931-1935

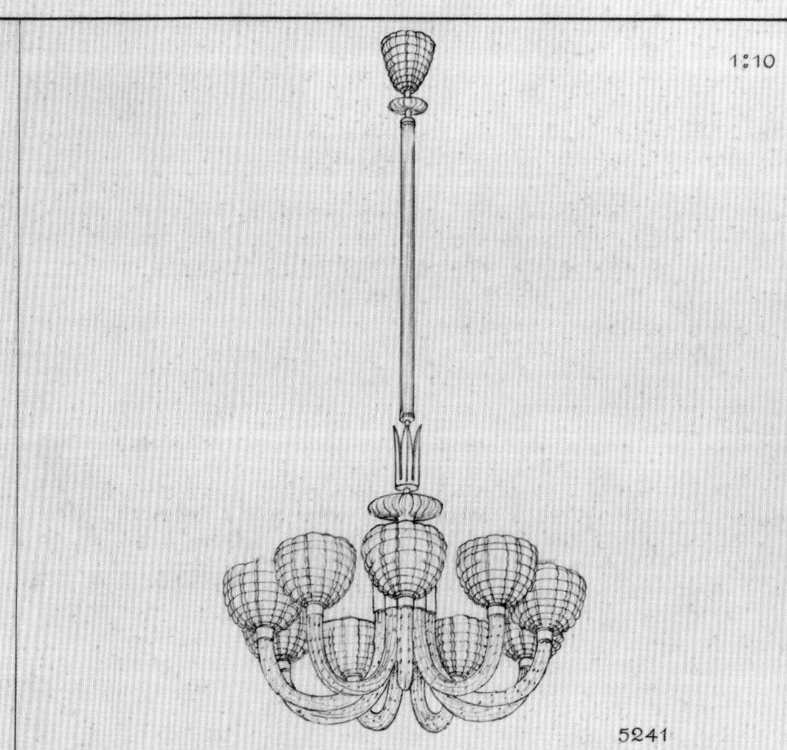

VENINI MVRANO

124

BUGNATO SPECCHIATO 1931 - 1935

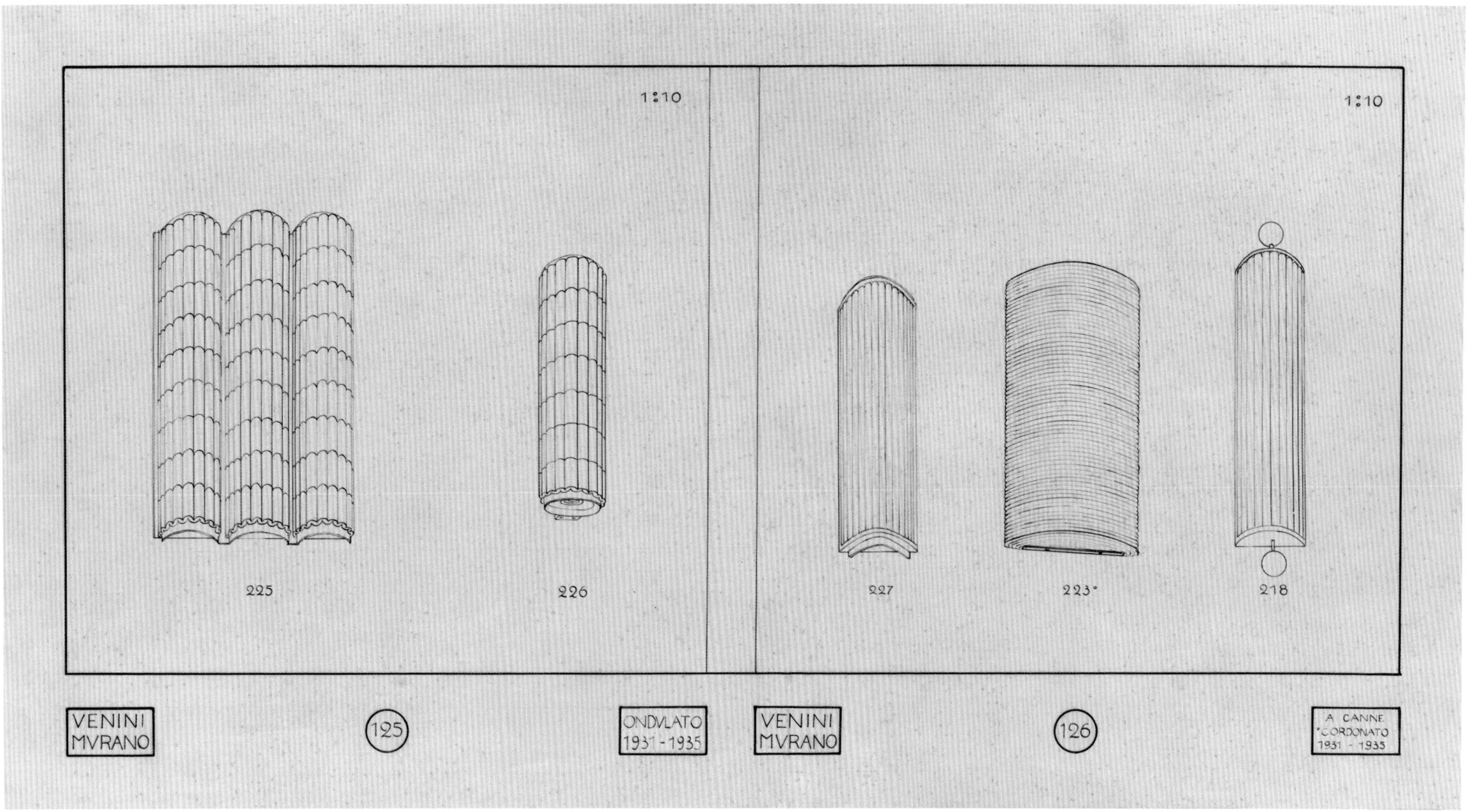
1:10
225
226
ONDVLATO
1931 - 1935
1:10
227
223°
218
A CANNE
°CORDONATO
1931 - 1935
VENINI
MVRANO
125
VENINI
MVRANO
126

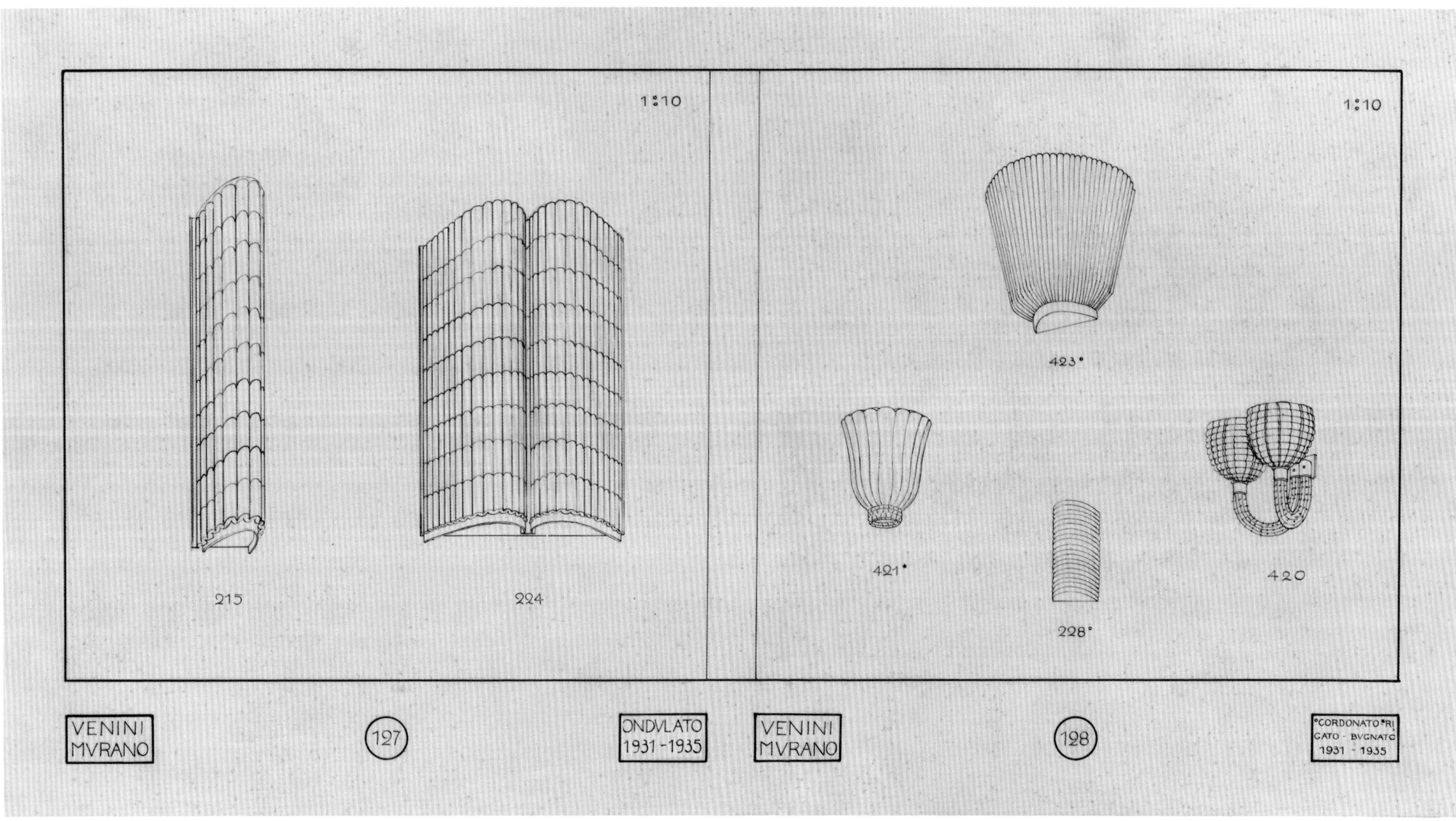
1:10
215
224
ONDVLATO
1931 - 1935
1:10
423°
421°
228°
420
°CORDONATO °RI
GATO - BVGNATO
1931 - 1935
VENINI
MVRANO
127
VENINI
MVRANO
128

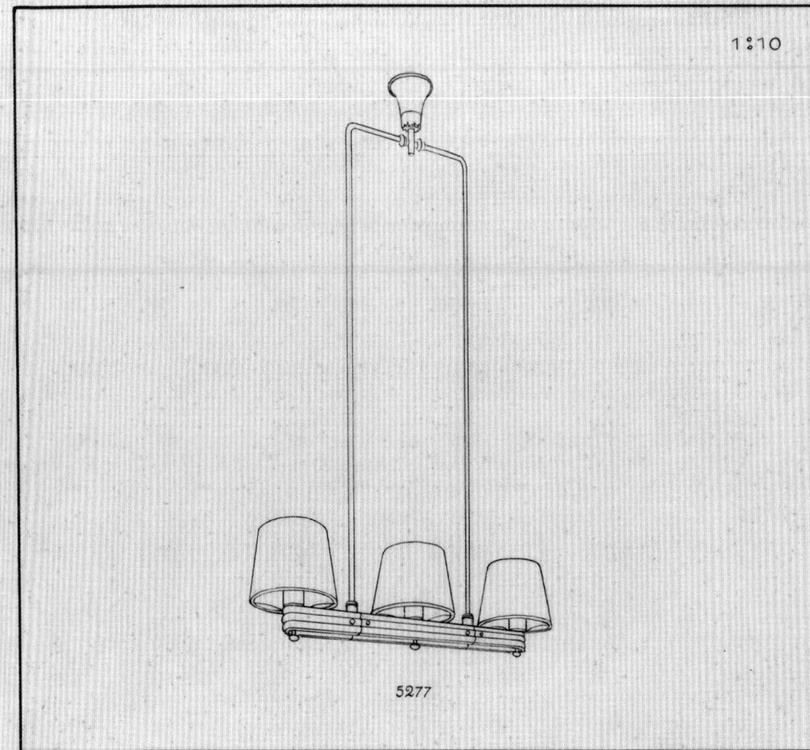

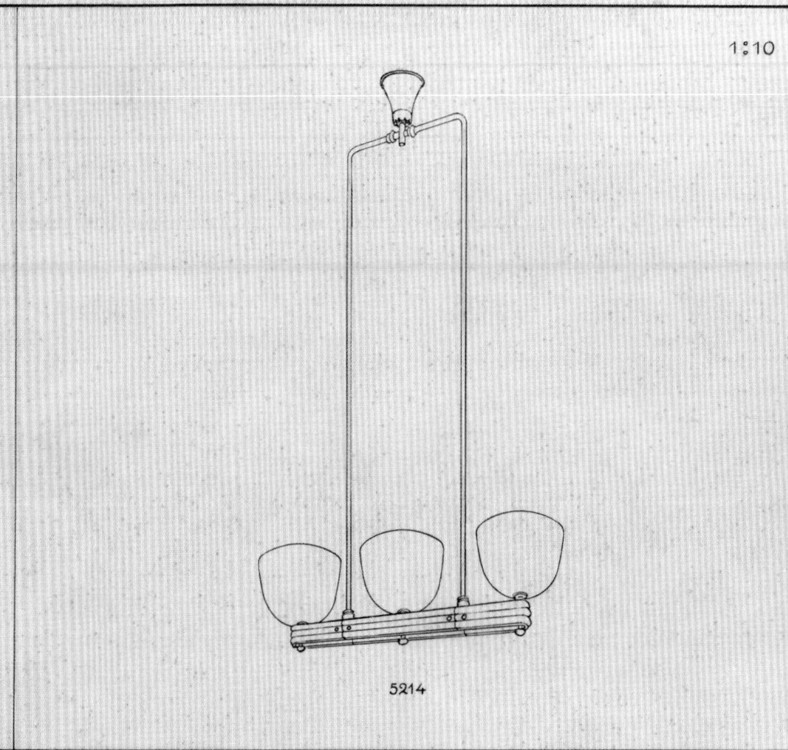

VENINI MVRANO | 129 | SOMMERSI 1931-1935

VENINI MVRANO | 130 | LATTIMO O FILIGRANA 1931-1935

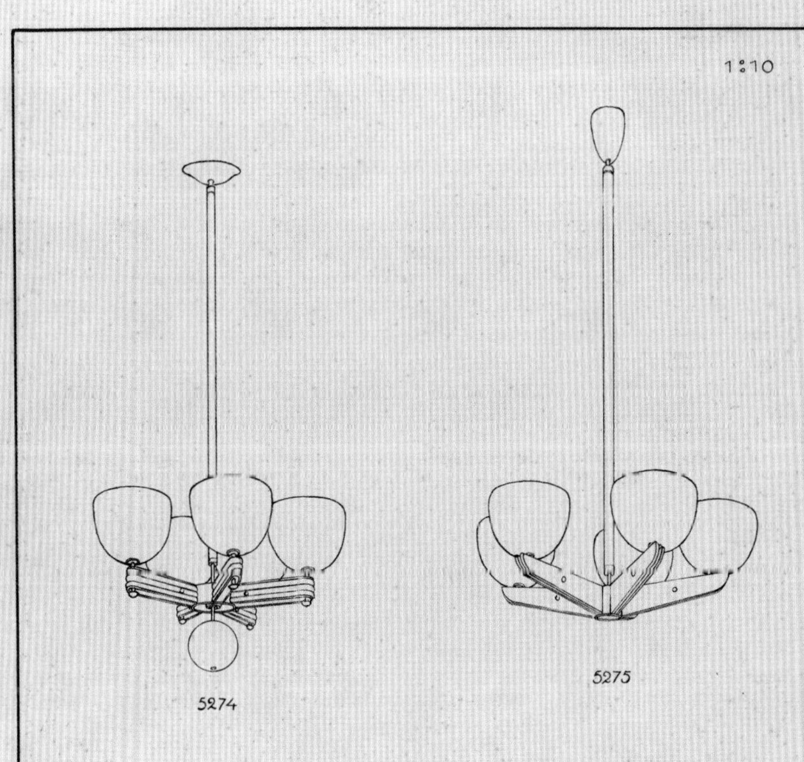

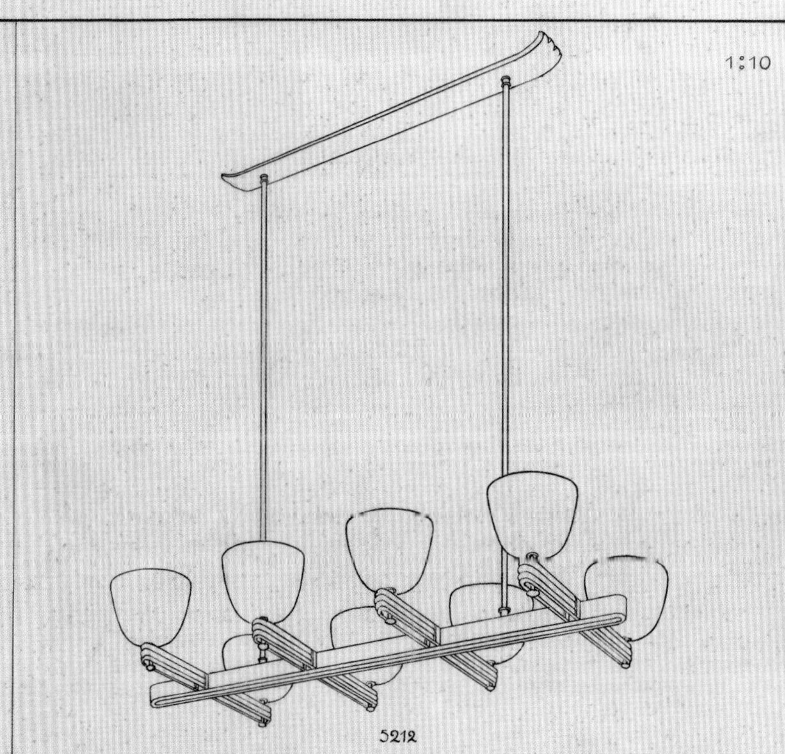

VENINI MVRANO | 131 | LATTIMI E SOMMERSI 1931-1935

VENINI MVRANO | 132 | LATTIMO O FILIGRANA 1931-1935

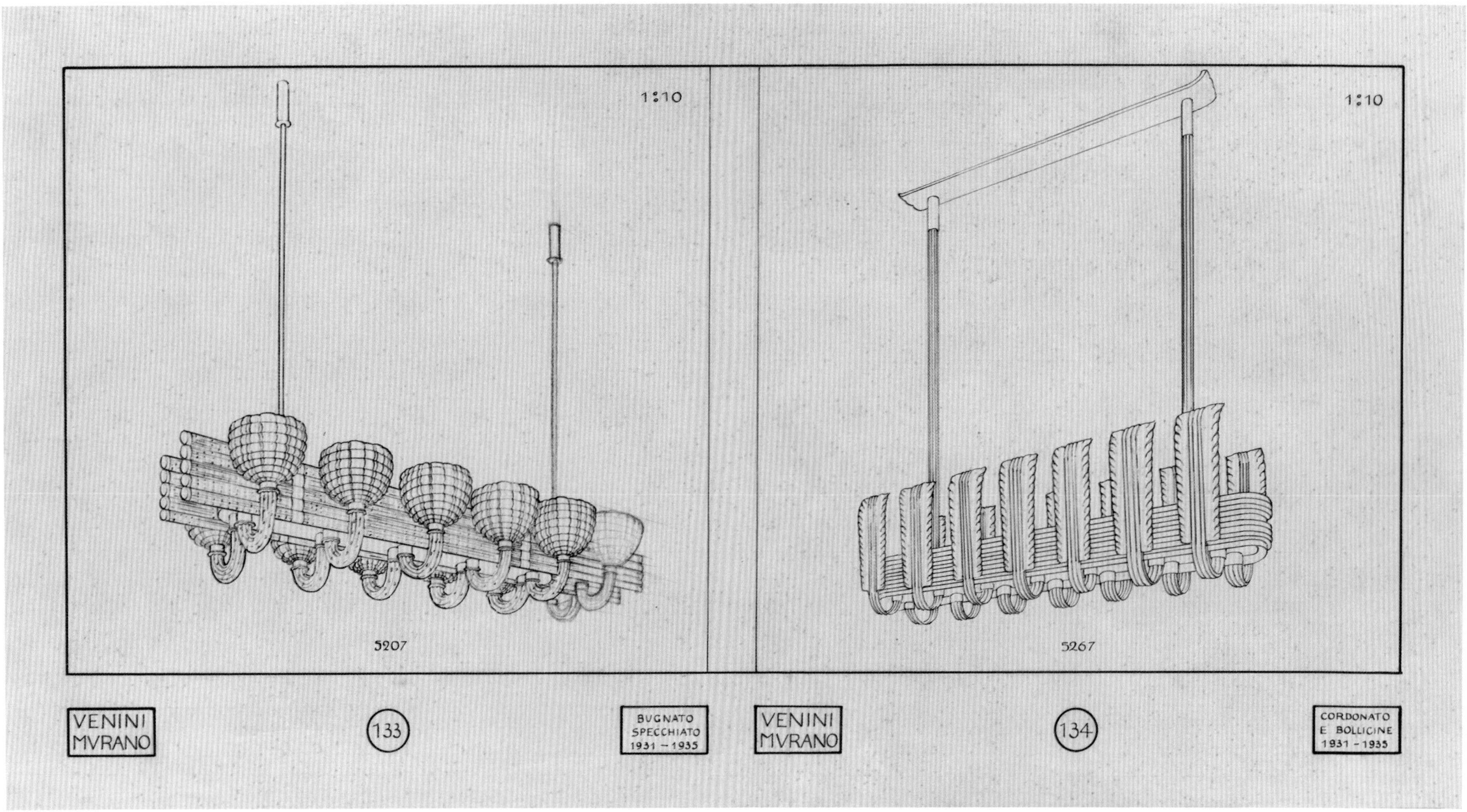
1:10
5207
VENINI
MVRANO
133
BUGNATO
SPECCHIATO
1931 – 1935
1:10
5267
VENINI
MVRANO
134
CORDONATO
E BOLLICINE
1931 - 1935

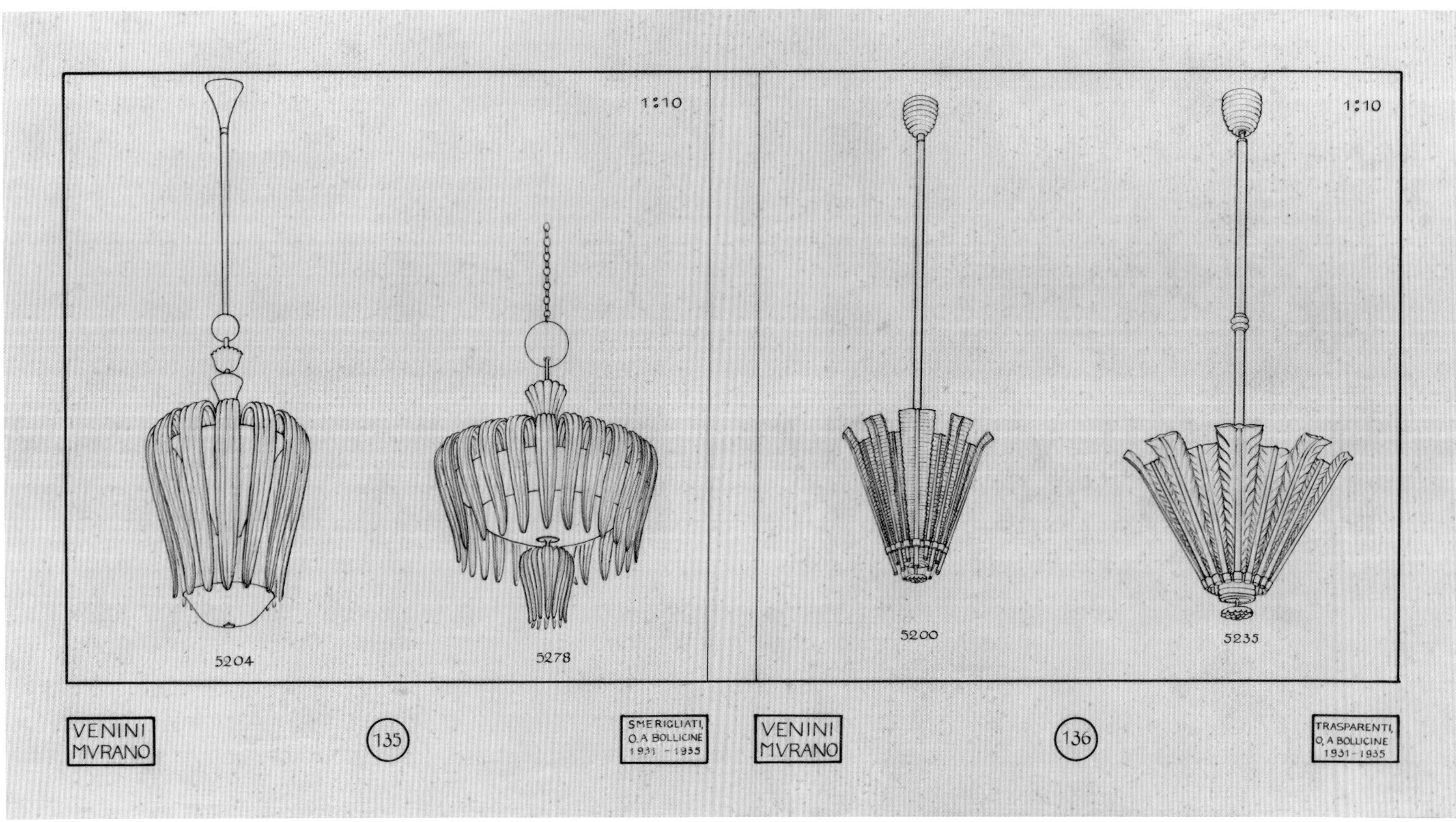
1:10
5204
5278
VENINI
MVRANO
135
SMERIGLIATI,
O. A BOLLICINE
1931 - 1935
1:10
5200
5235
VENINI
MVRANO
136
TRASPARENTI,
O. A BOLLICINE
1931-1935

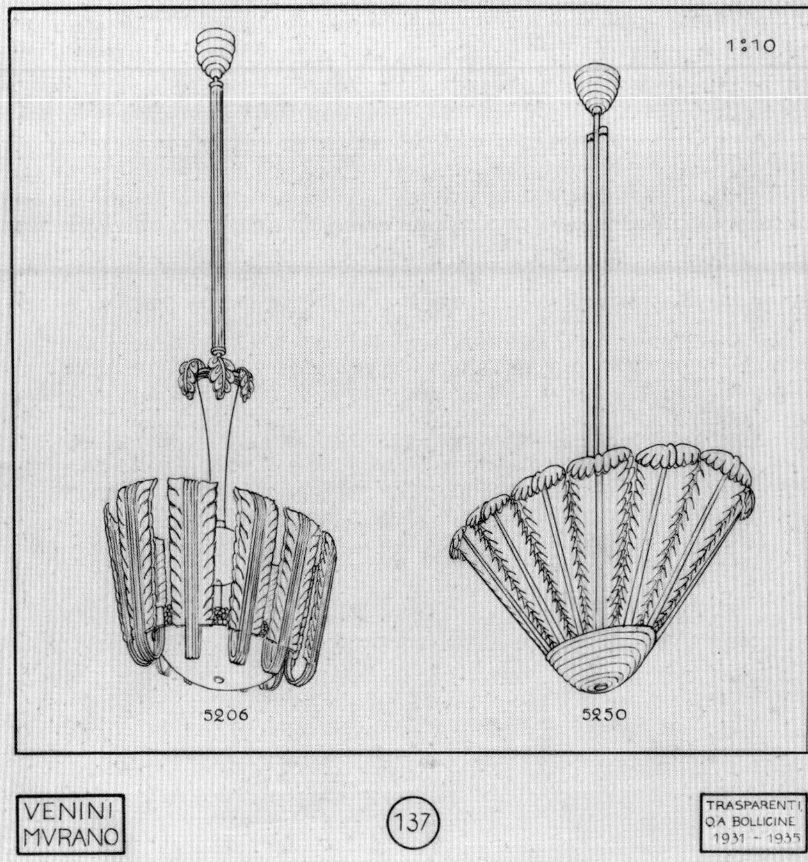
1:10
5206
5250
VENINI MVRANO
137
TRASPARENTI, O.A BOLLICINE 1931 - 1935

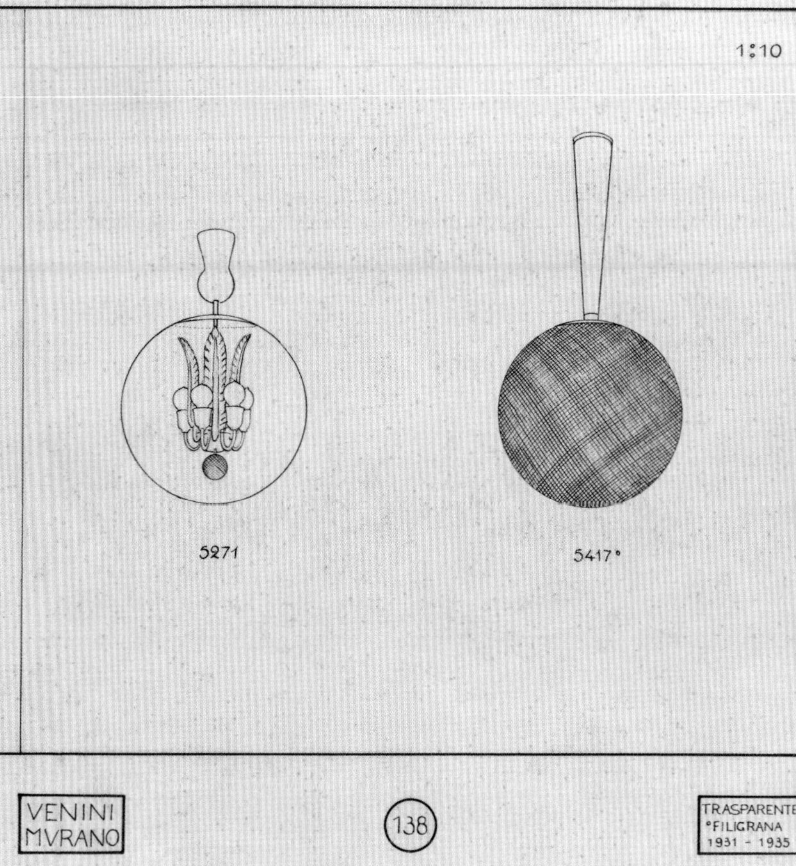
1:10
5271
5417*
VENINI MVRANO
138
TRASPARENTE *FILIGRANA 1931 - 1935

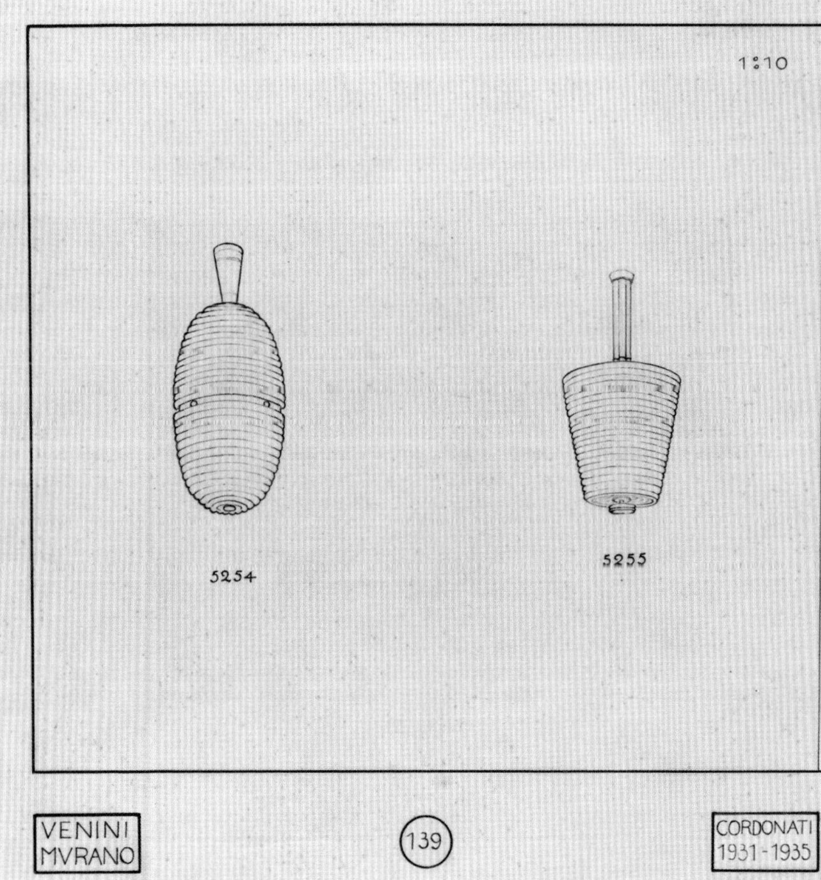
1:10
5254
5255
VENINI MVRANO
139
CORDONATI 1931-1935

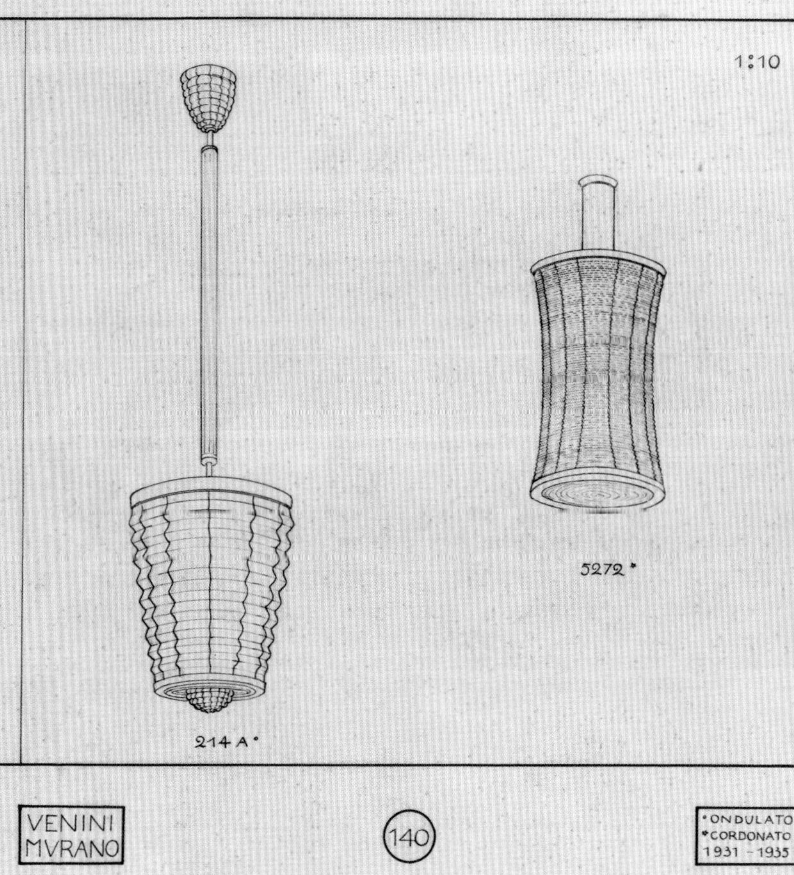
1:10
214 A*
5272*
VENINI MVRANO
140
*ONDULATO *CORDONATO 1931 - 1935

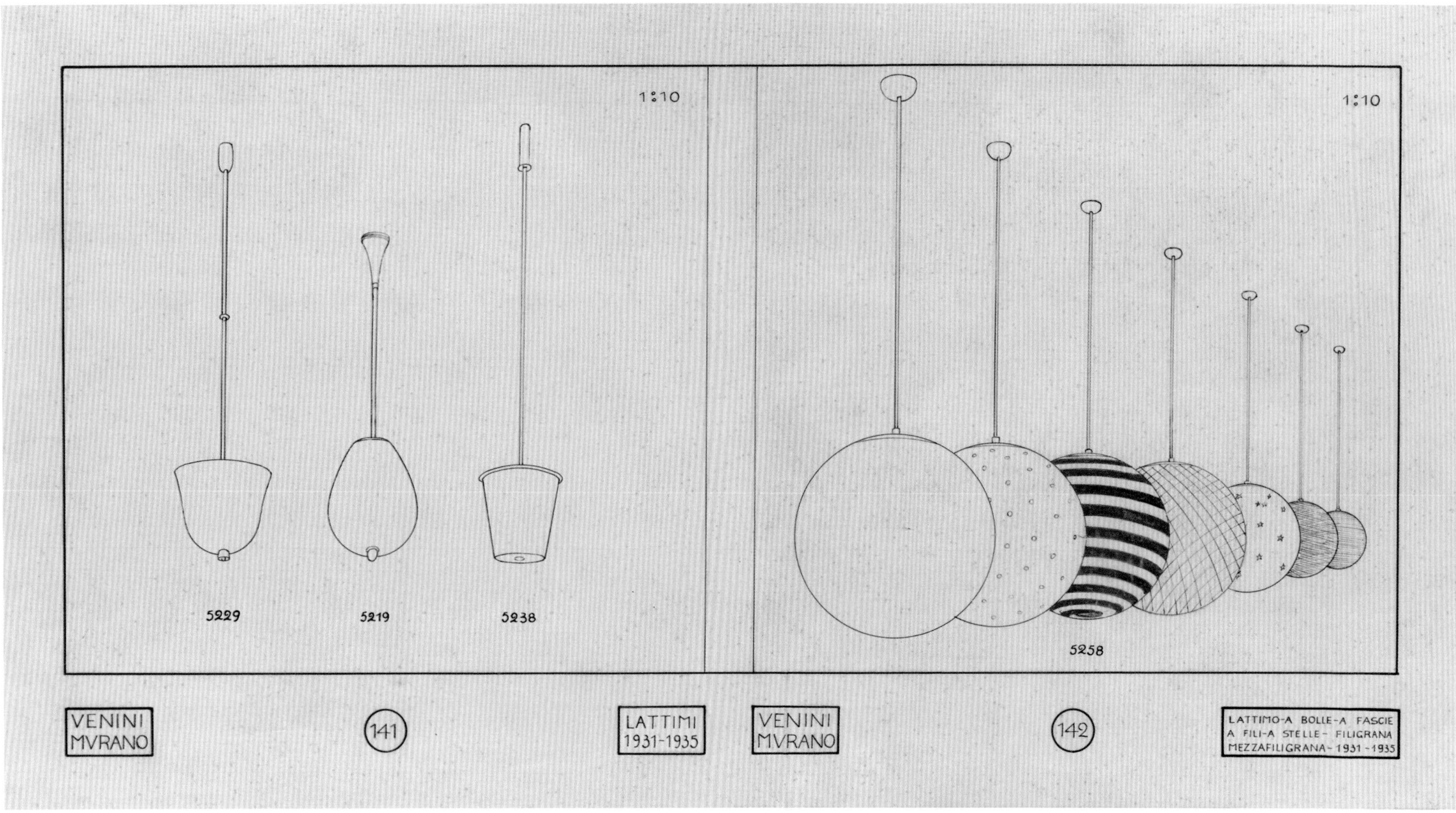
1:10
5229
5219
5238
VENINI
MVRANO
141
LATTIMI
1931-1935
1:10
5258
VENINI
MVRANO
142
LATTIMO-A BOLLE-A FASCIE
A FILI-A STELLE- FILIGRANA
MEZZAFILIGRANA-1931-1935

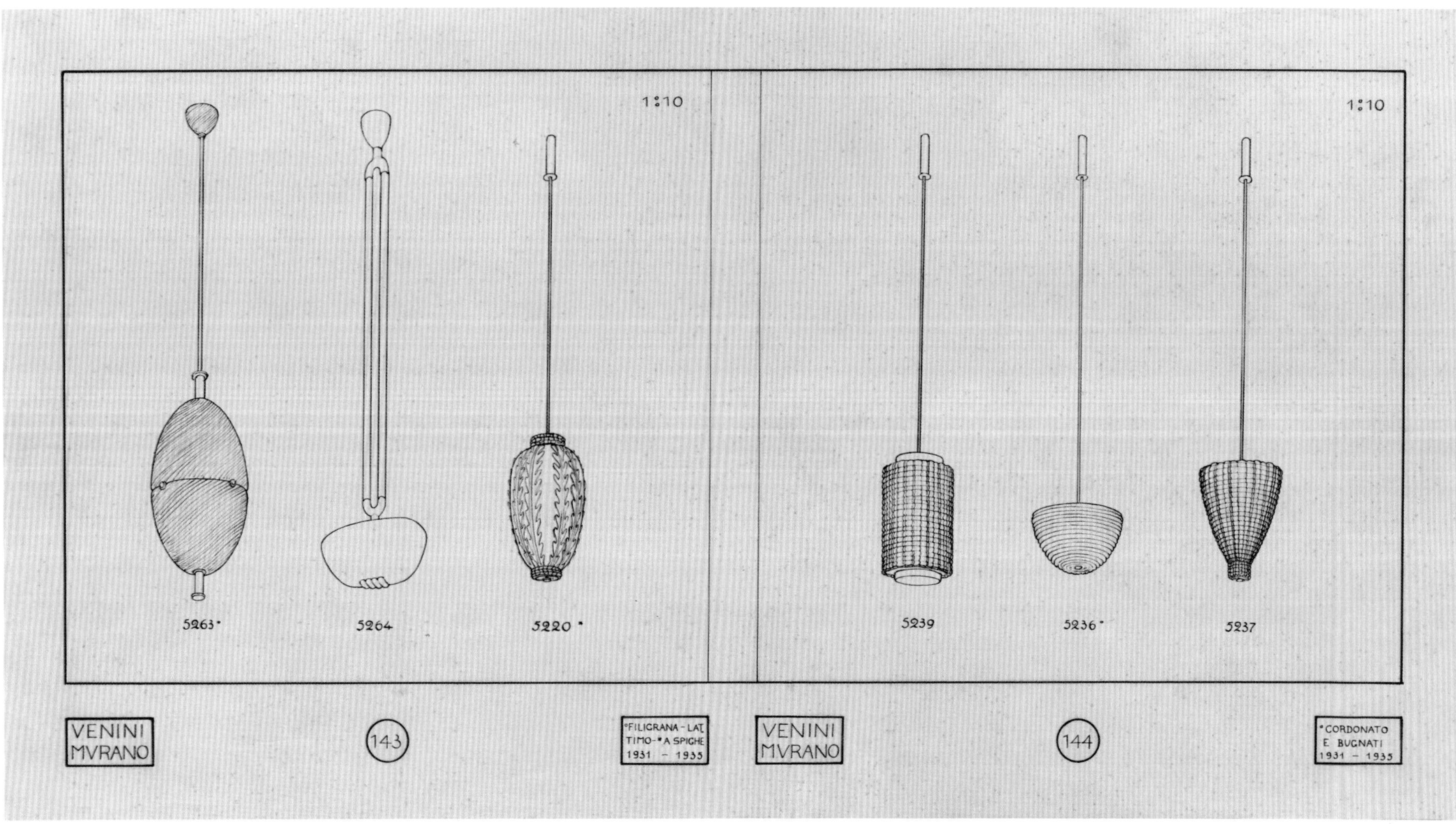
1:10
5263*
5264
5220*
VENINI
MVRANO
143
*FILIGRANA-LAT
TIMO-*A SPIGHE
1931 - 1935
1:10
5239
5236*
5237
VENINI
MVRANO
144
*CORDONATO
E BUGNATI
1931 - 1935

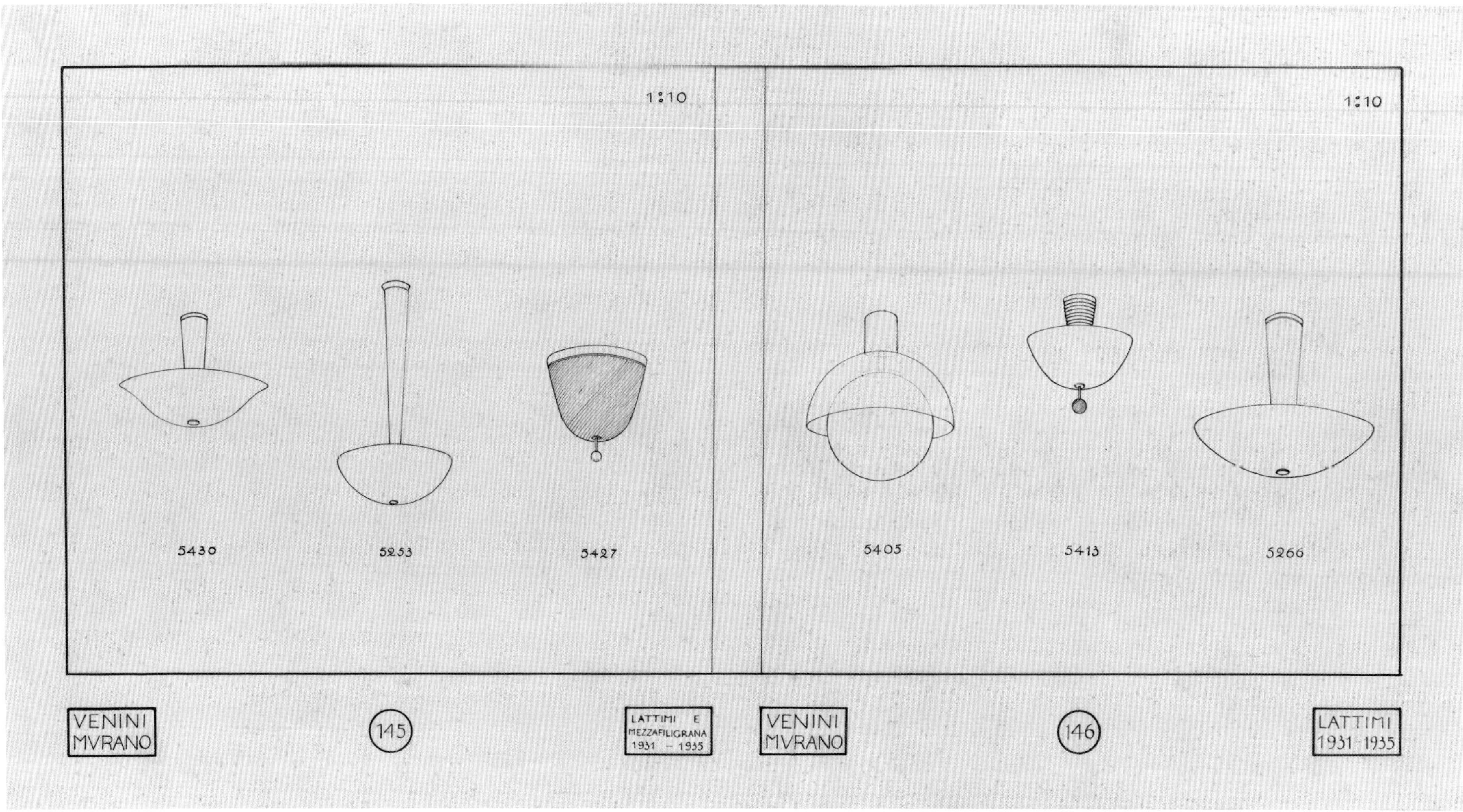
1:10
5430
5253
5427
VENINI
MVRANO
145
LATTIMI E
MEZZAFILIGRANA
1931 – 1935
1:10
5405
5413
5266
VENINI
MVRANO
146
LATTIMI
1931-1935

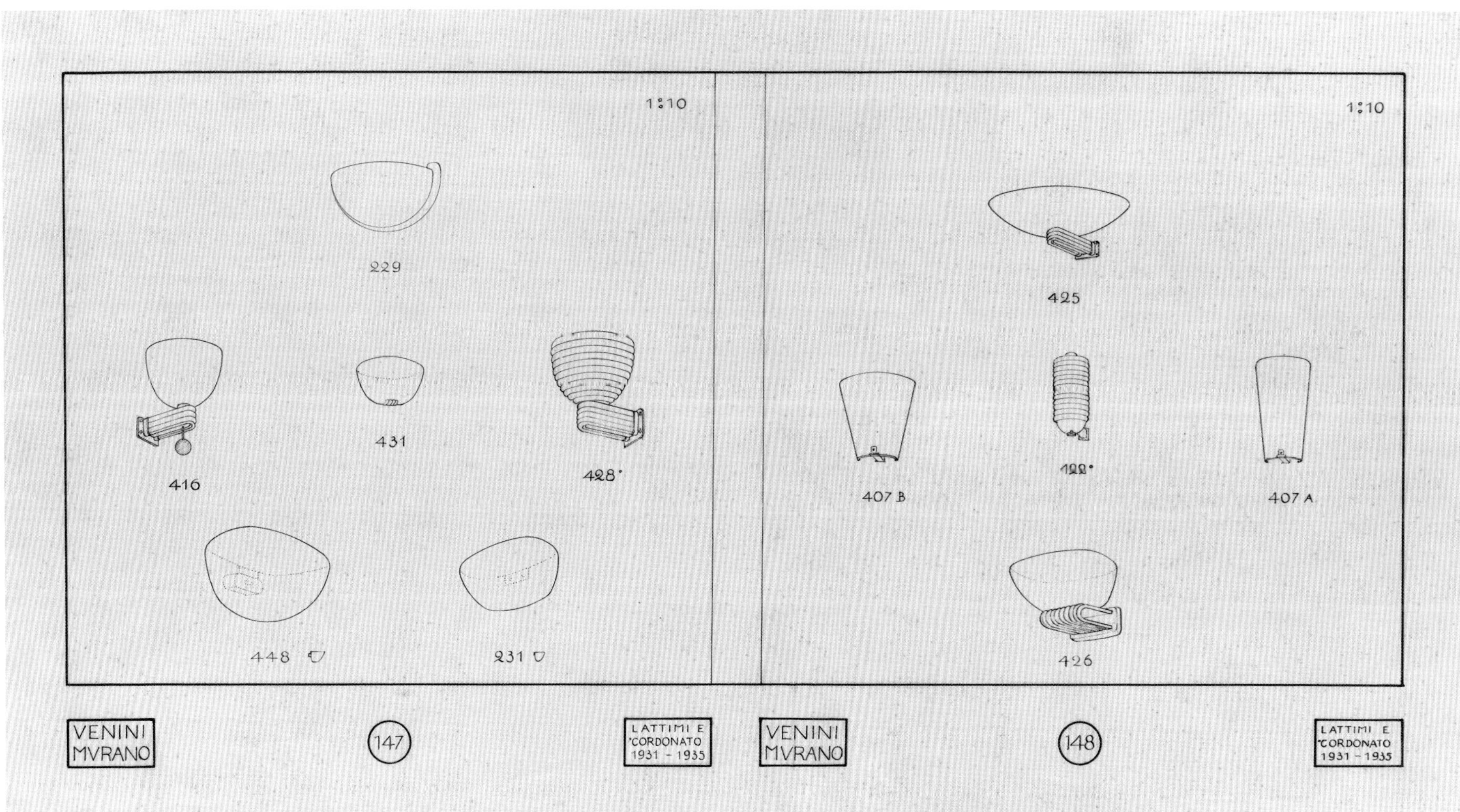
1:10
229
416
431
428°
448
231
VENINI
MVRANO
147
LATTIMI E
CORDONATO
1931 – 1935
1:10
425
407 B
422°
407 A
426
VENINI
MVRANO
148
LATTIMI E
CORDONATO
1931 – 1935

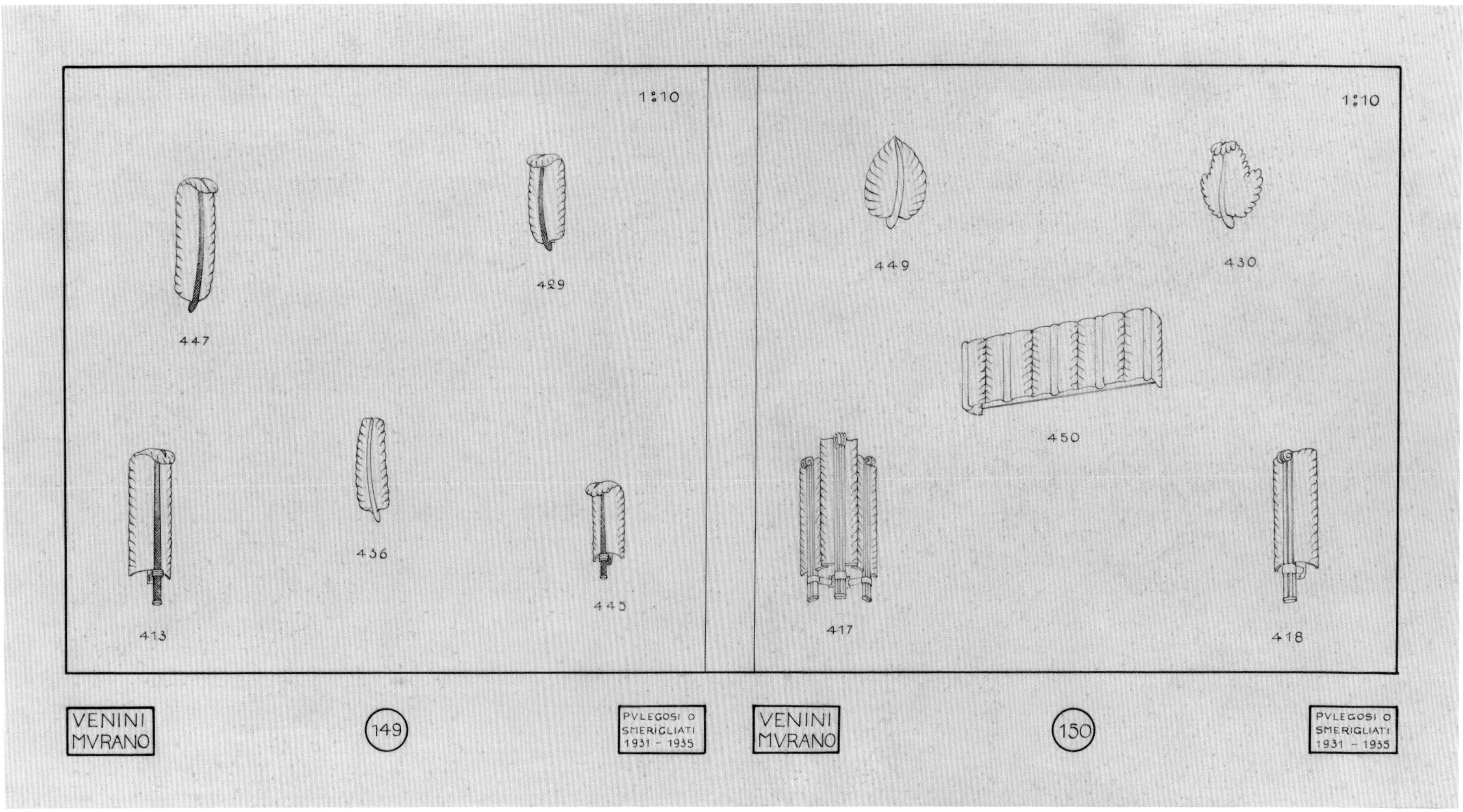
1:10
447
429
413
436
445
VENINI MVRANO
149
PVLEGOSI O SMERIGLIATI 1931 - 1935
1:10
449
430
450
417
418
VENINI MVRANO
150
PVLEGOSI O SMERIGLIATI 1931 - 1935

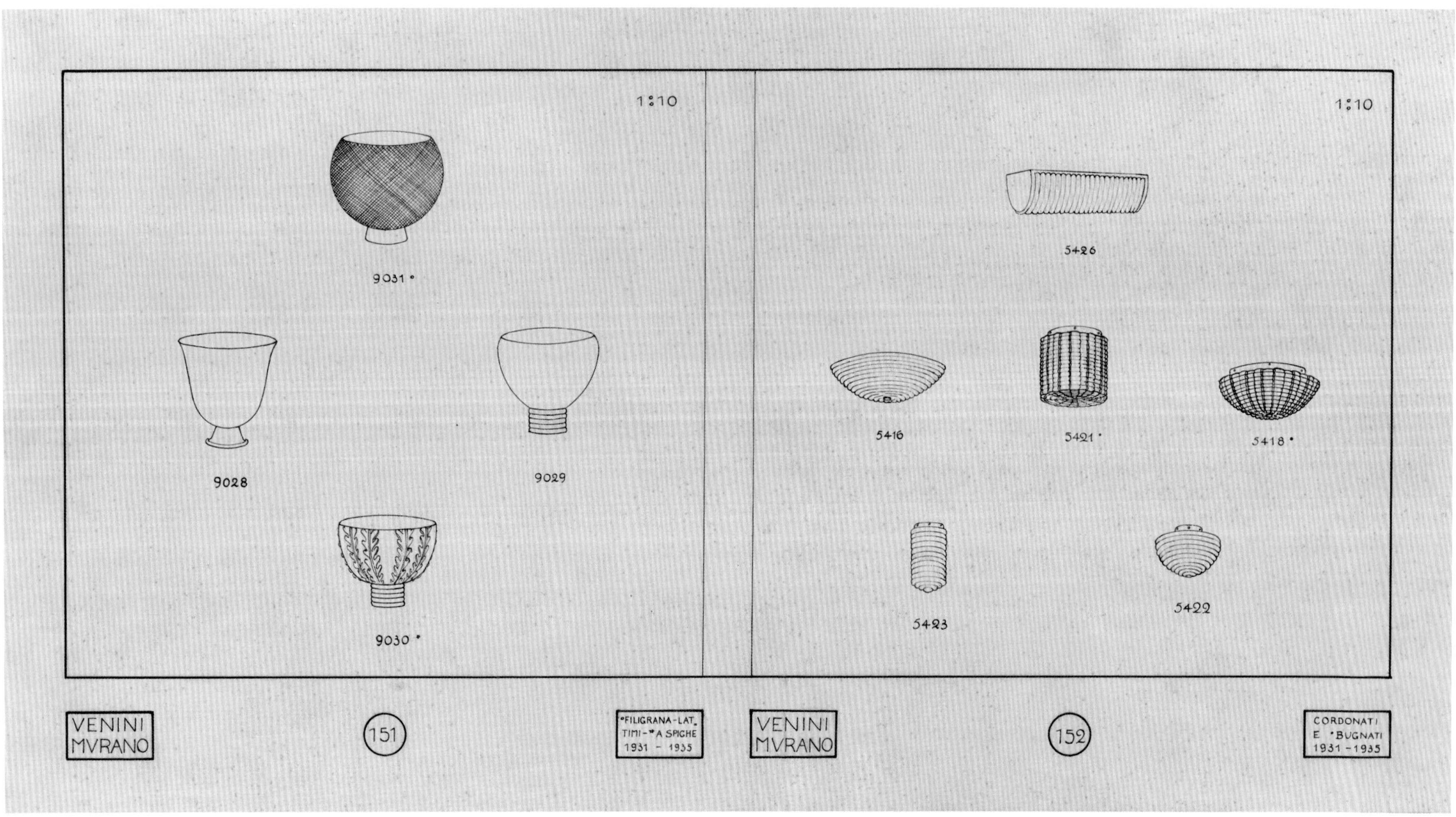
1:10
9031 *
9028
9029
9030 *
VENINI MVRANO
151
*FILIGRANA-LAT. TIMI-** A SPIGHE 1931 - 1935
1:10
5426
5416
5421 *
5418 *
5423
5422
VENINI MVRANO
152
CORDONATI E *BUGNATI 1931 - 1935

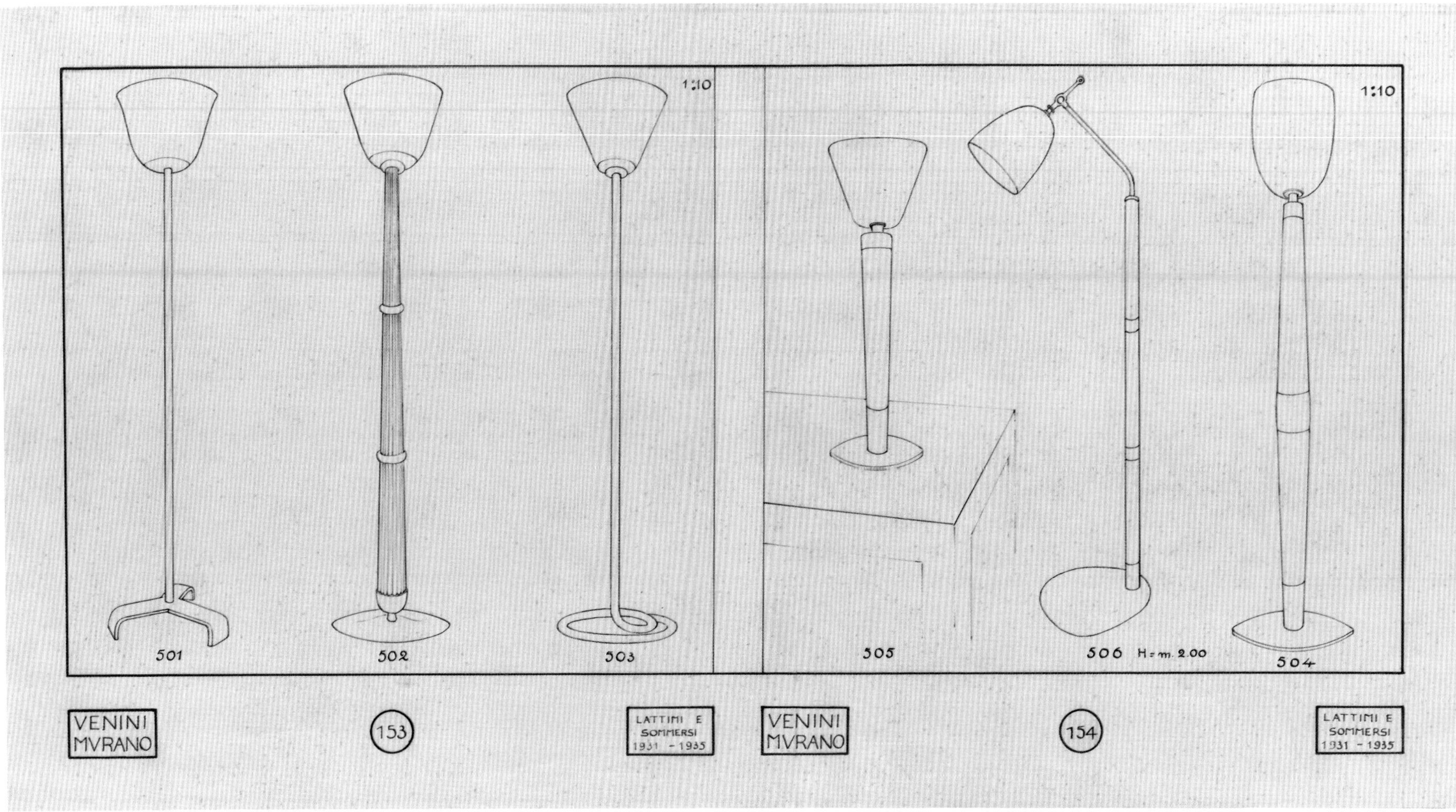
1:10
501
502
503
VENINI MVRANO
153
LATTIMI E SOMMERSI 1931 - 1935
1:10
505
506 H=m. 2.00
504
VENINI MVRANO
154
LATTIMI E SOMMERSI 1931 - 1935

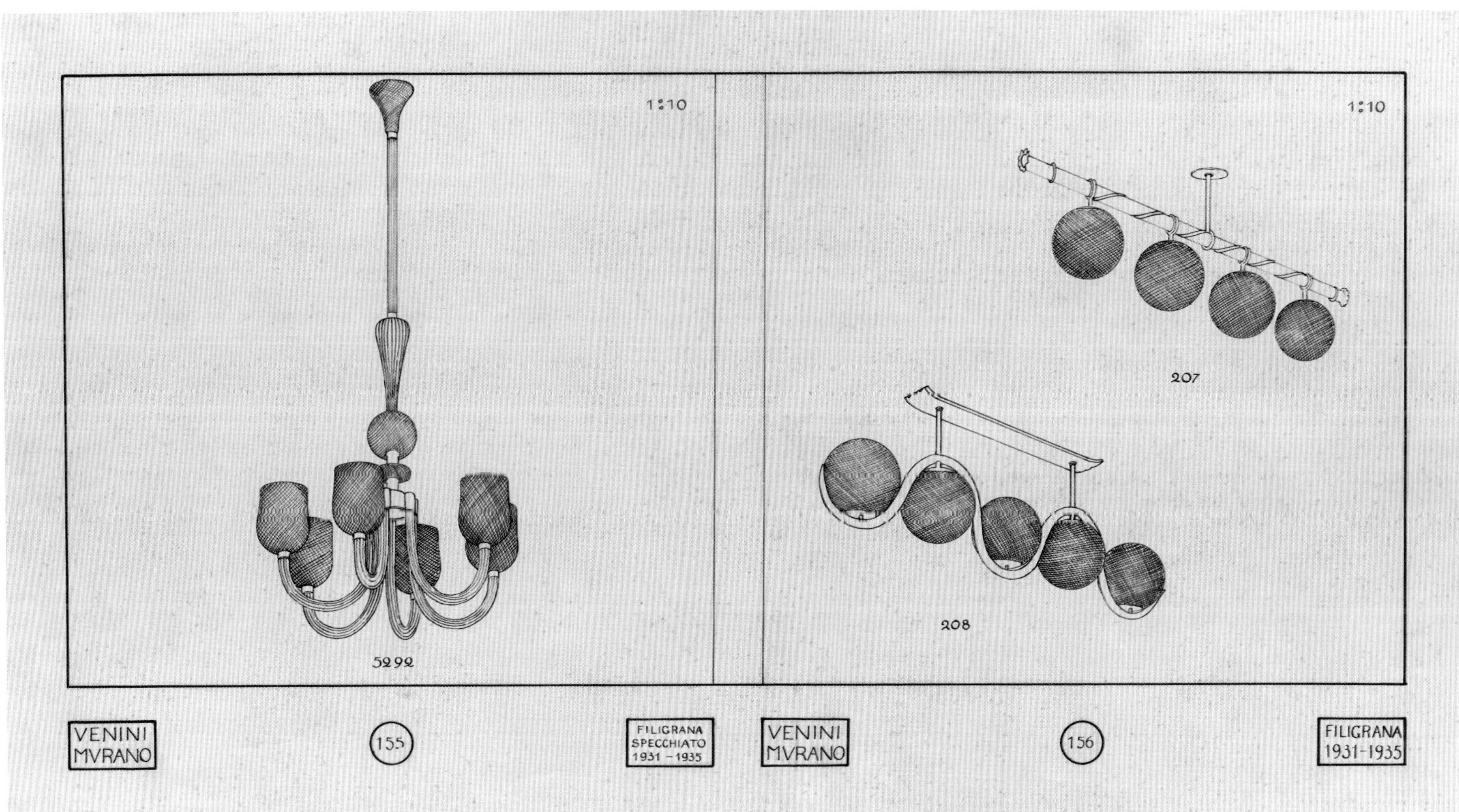
1:10
5292
VENINI MVRANO
155
FILIGRANA SPECCHIATO 1931 - 1935
1:10
207
208
VENINI MVRANO
156
FILIGRANA 1931-1935

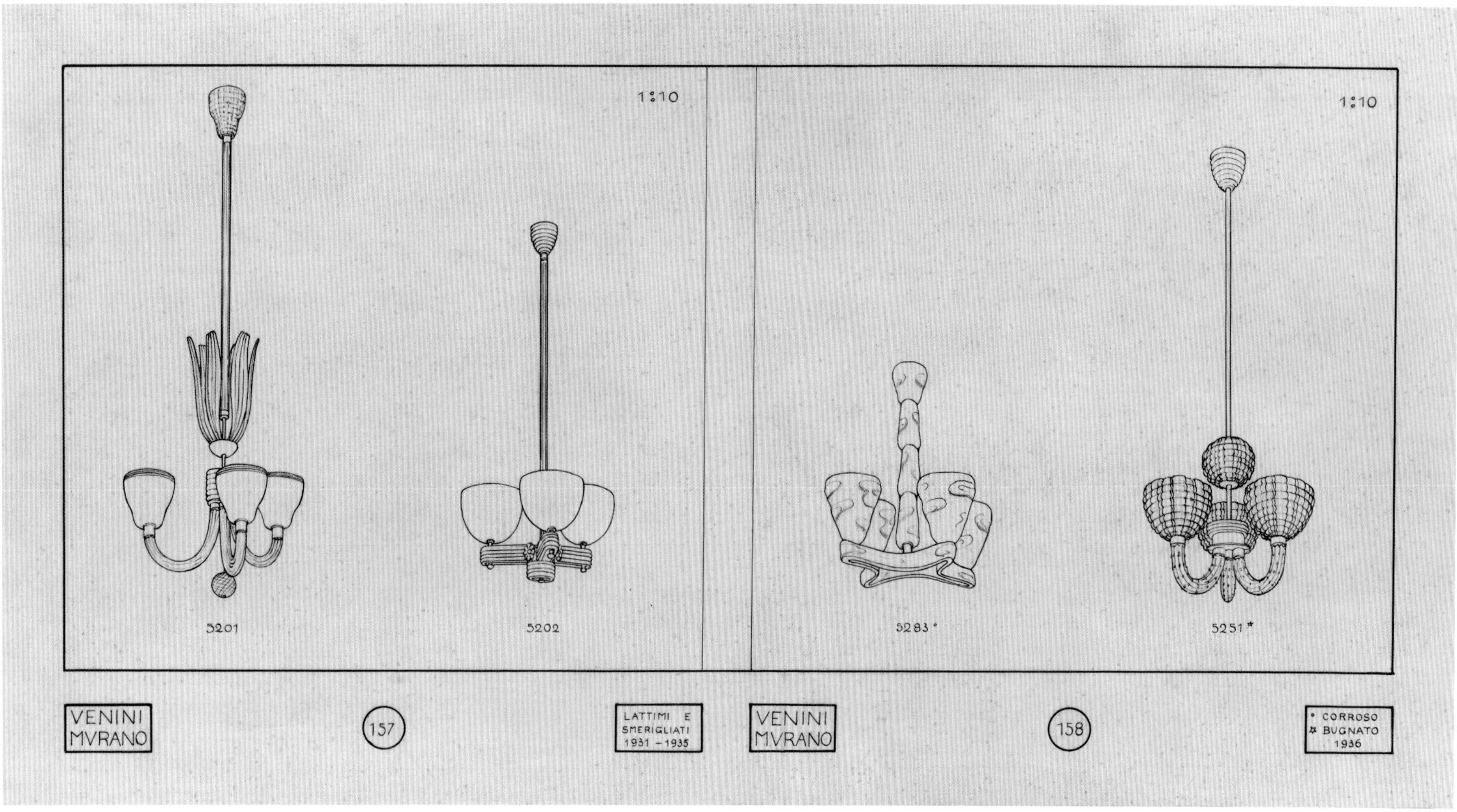
1:10
5201
5202
VENINI MVRANO
157
LATTIMI E SMERIGLIATI 1931 - 1935
1:10
5283°
5251*
VENINI MVRANO
158
° CORROSO
* BUGNATO
1936

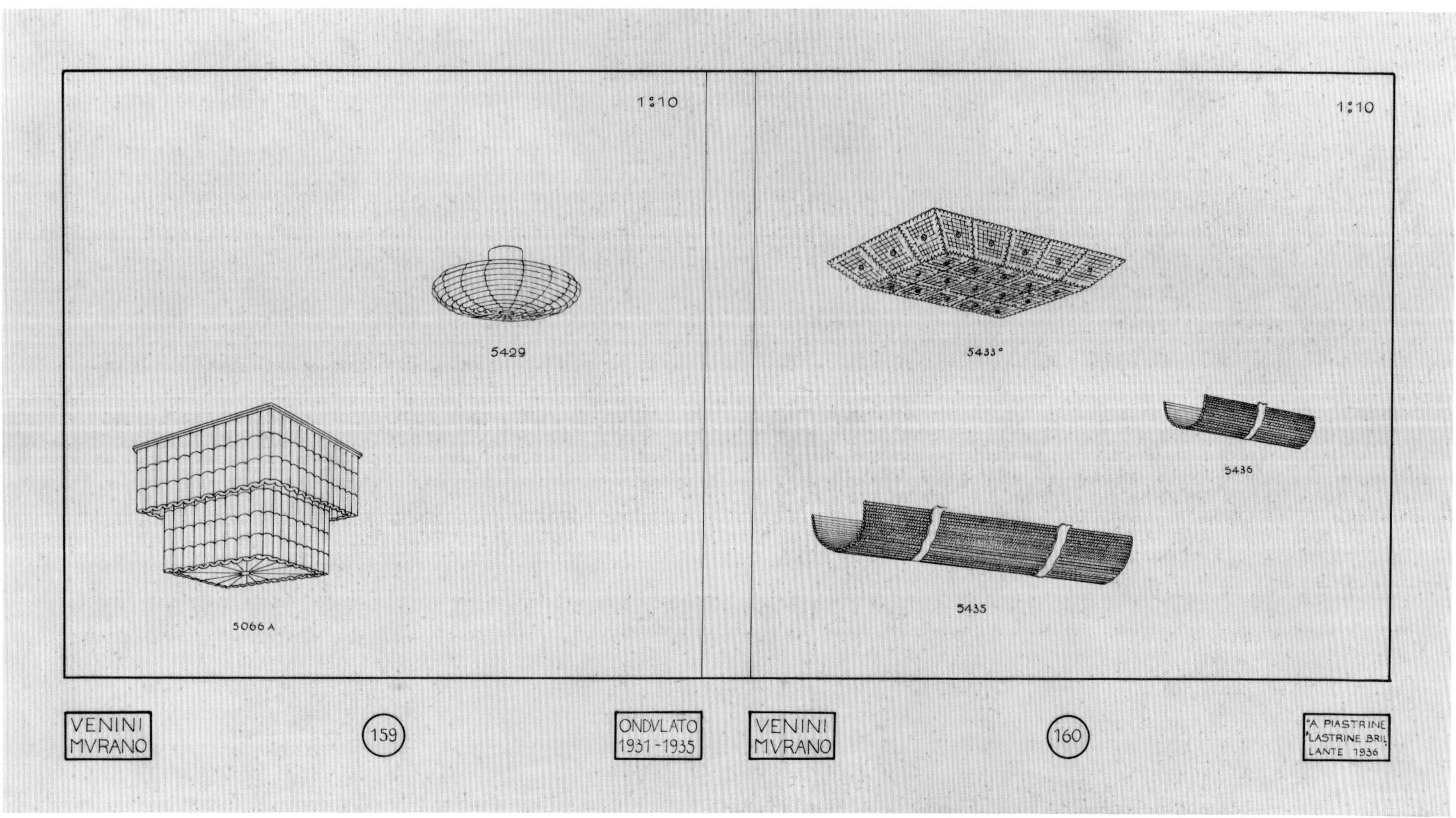
1:10
5429
5066 A
VENINI MVRANO
159
ONDVLATO 1931-1935
1:10
5433°
5436
5435
VENINI MVRANO
160
°A PIASTRINE
'LASTRINE BRIL LANTE 1936

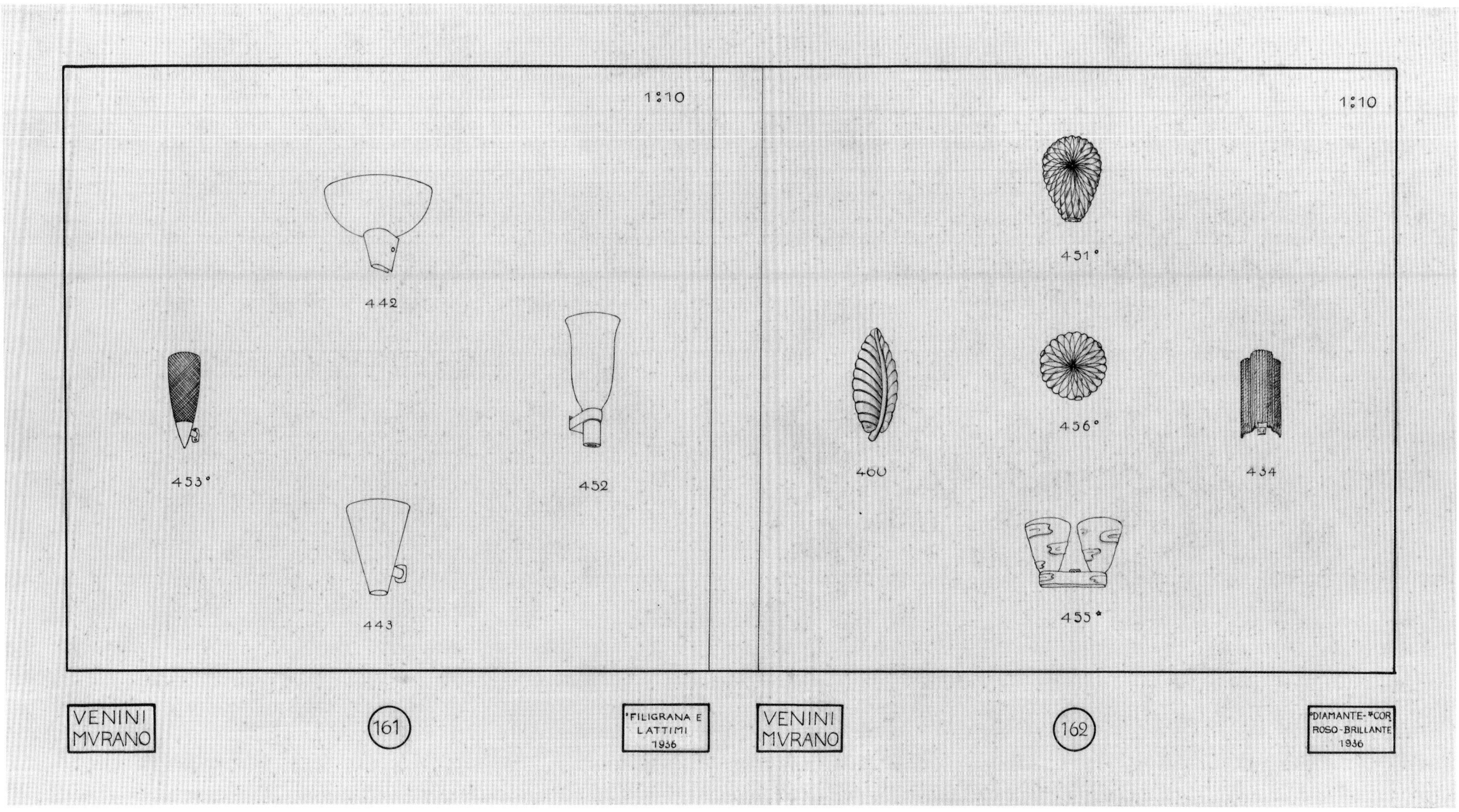
1:10
442
453°
452
443
VENINI MVRANO
161
°FILIGRANA E LATTIMI 1936
1:10
451°
460
456°
434
455°
VENINI MVRANO
162
°DIAMANTE-°COR ROSO-BRILLANTE 1936

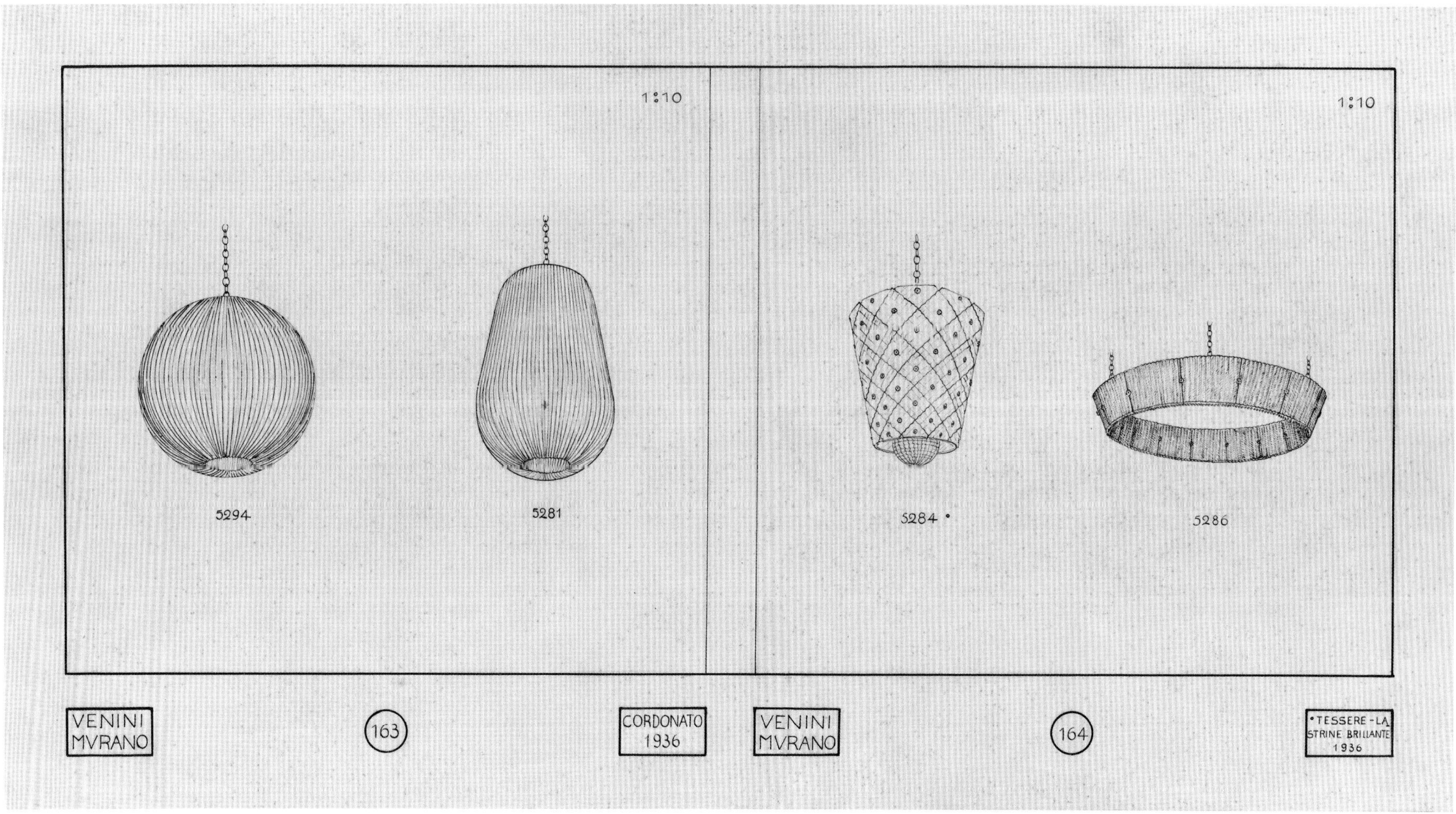
1:10
5294
5281
VENINI MVRANO
163
CORDONATO 1936
1:10
5284 °
5286
VENINI MVRANO
164
°TESSERE-LA STRINE BRILLANTE 1936

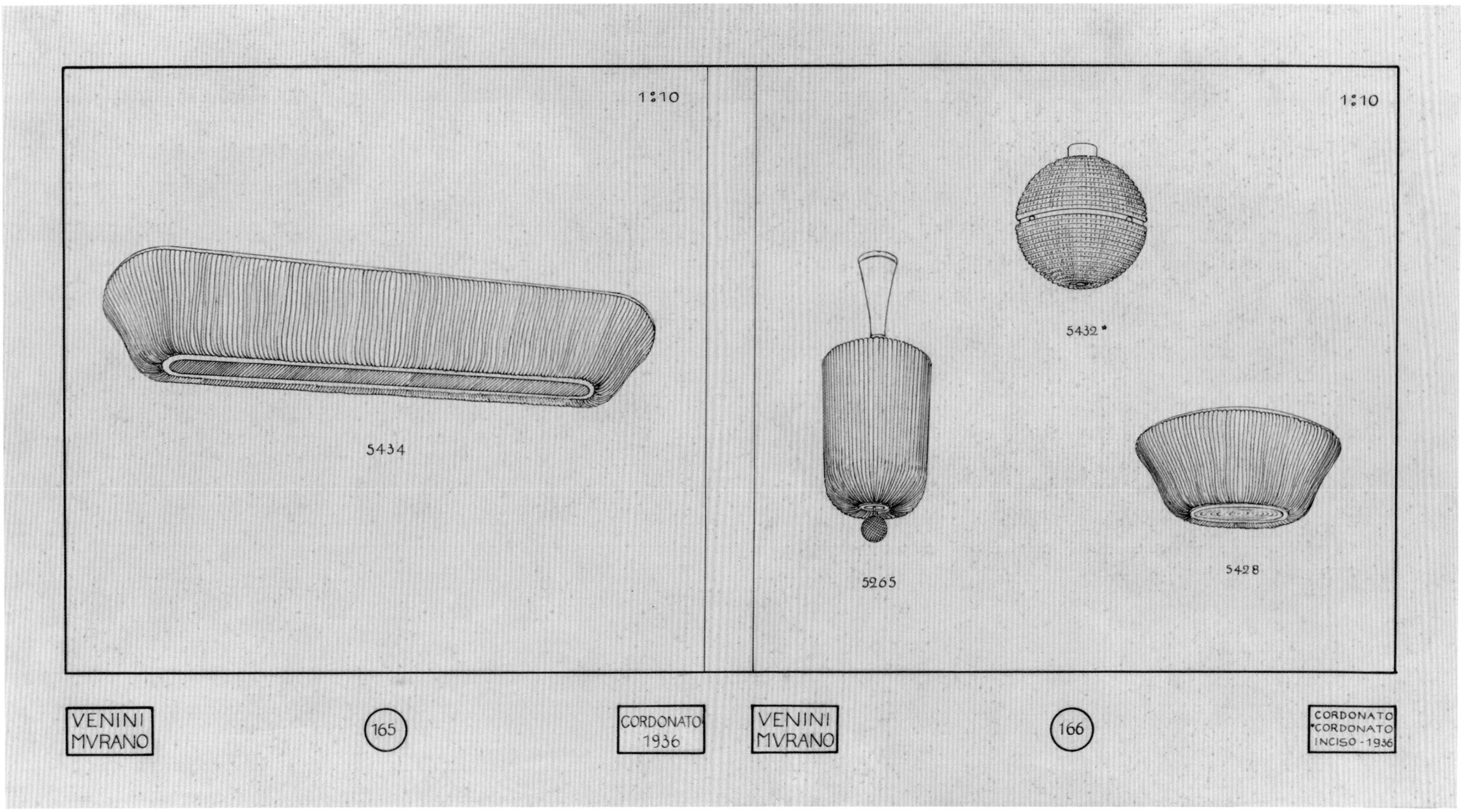
1:10
5434
VENINI
MVRANO
165
CORDONATO
1936
1:10
5432 *
5265
5428
VENINI
MVRANO
166
CORDONATO
*CORDONATO
INCISO - 1936

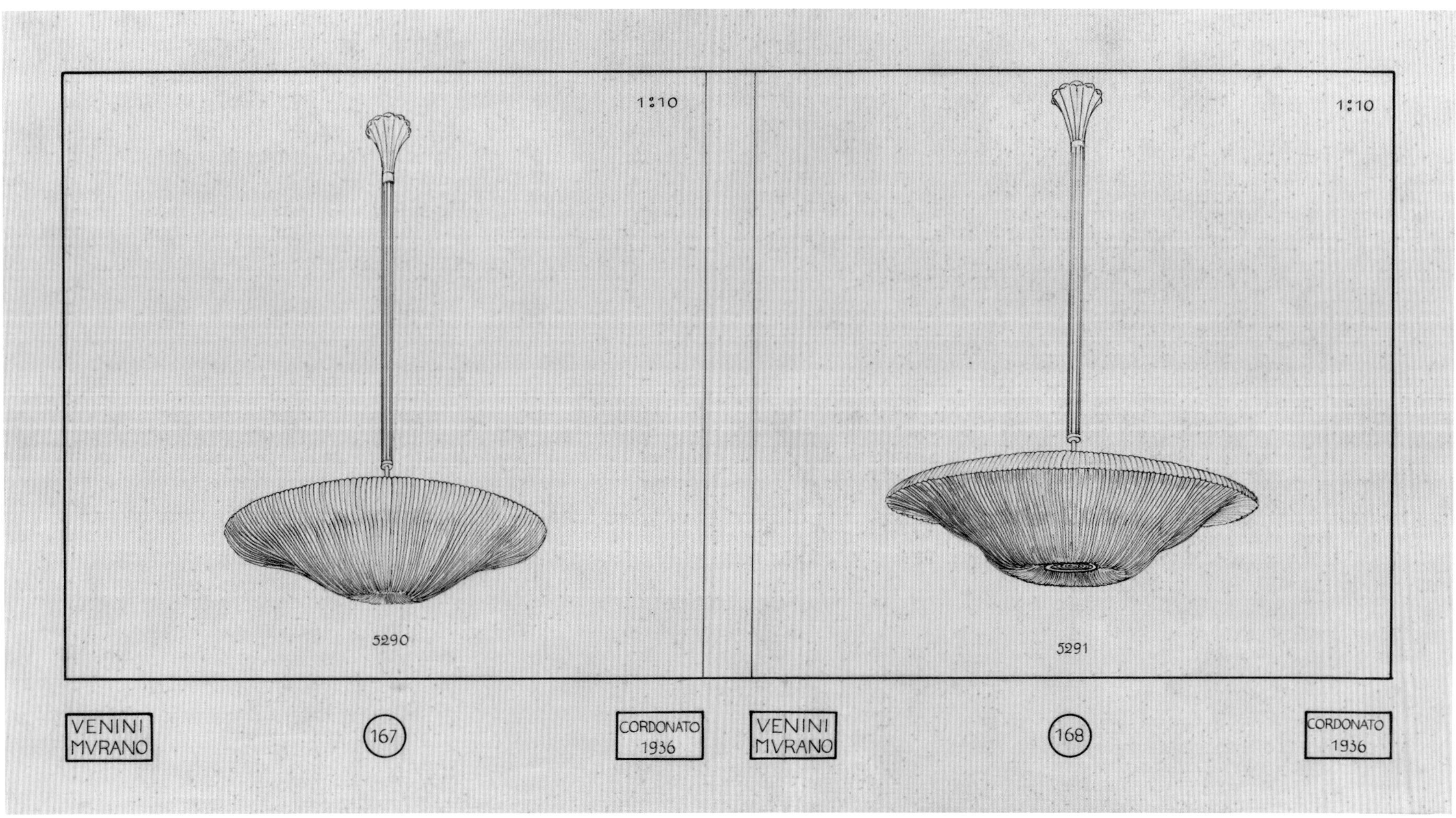
1:10
5290
VENINI
MVRANO
167
CORDONATO
1936
1:10
5291
VENINI
MVRANO
168
CORDONATO
1936

1:10

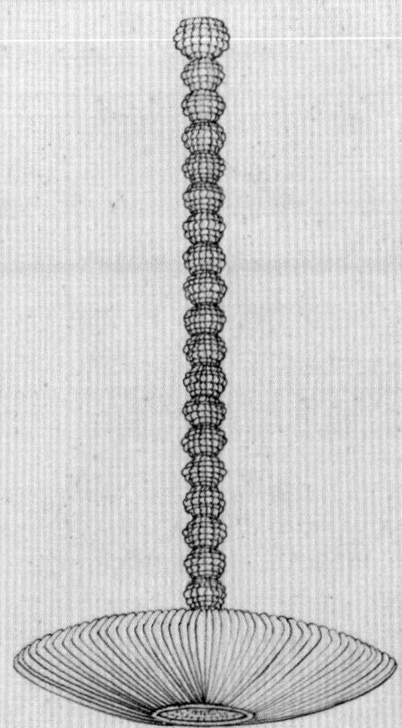

5296

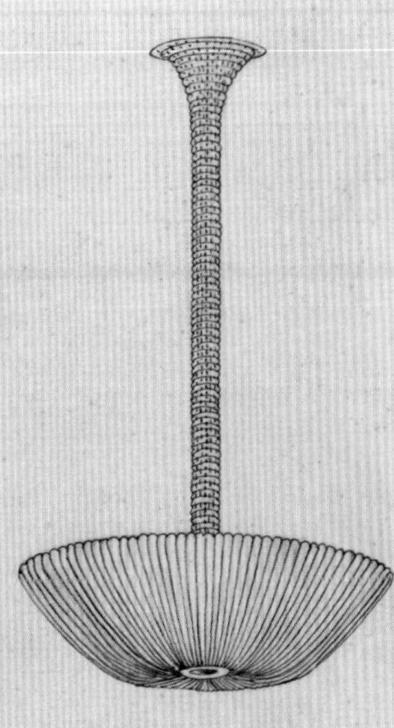

5302

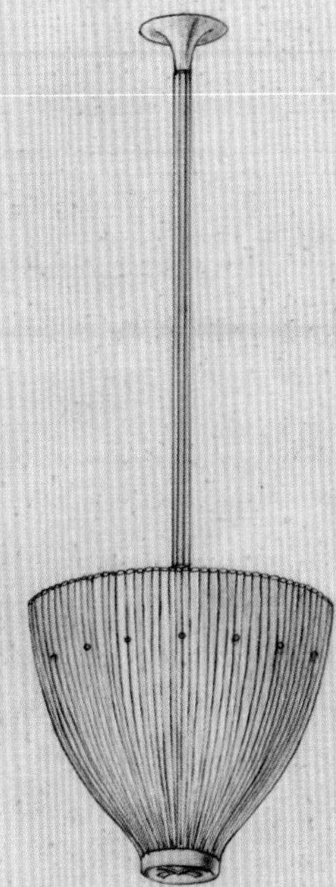

5301

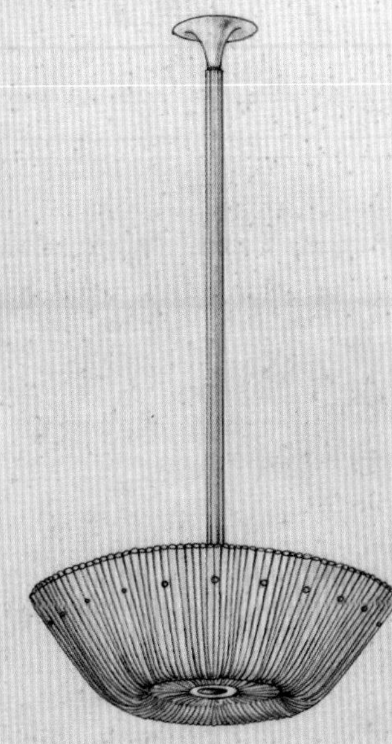

5303

VENINI MVRANO | 169 | CORDONATO E CORDONATO INCISO - 1938

VENINI MVRANO | 170 | CORDONATO E CORDONATO INCISO - 1939

1:10

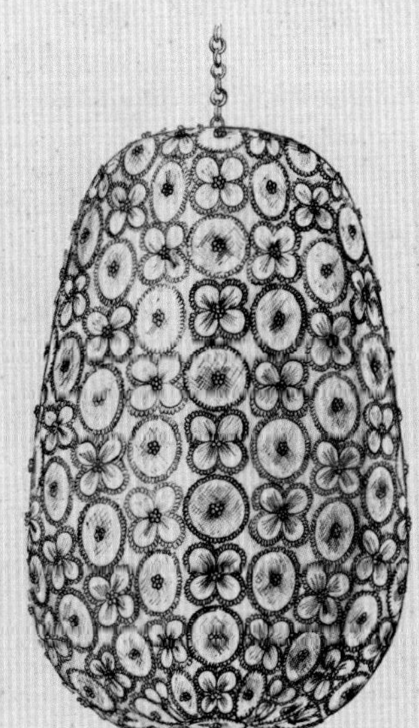

5282

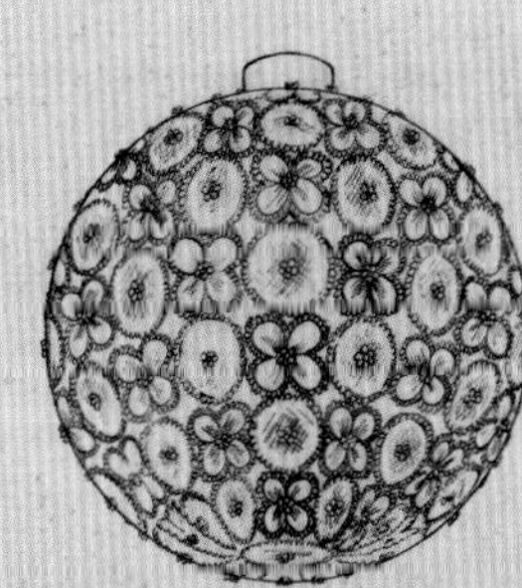

5293

VENINI MVRANO | 171 | A FIORI 1936

VENINI MVRANO | 172 | A FIORI 1936

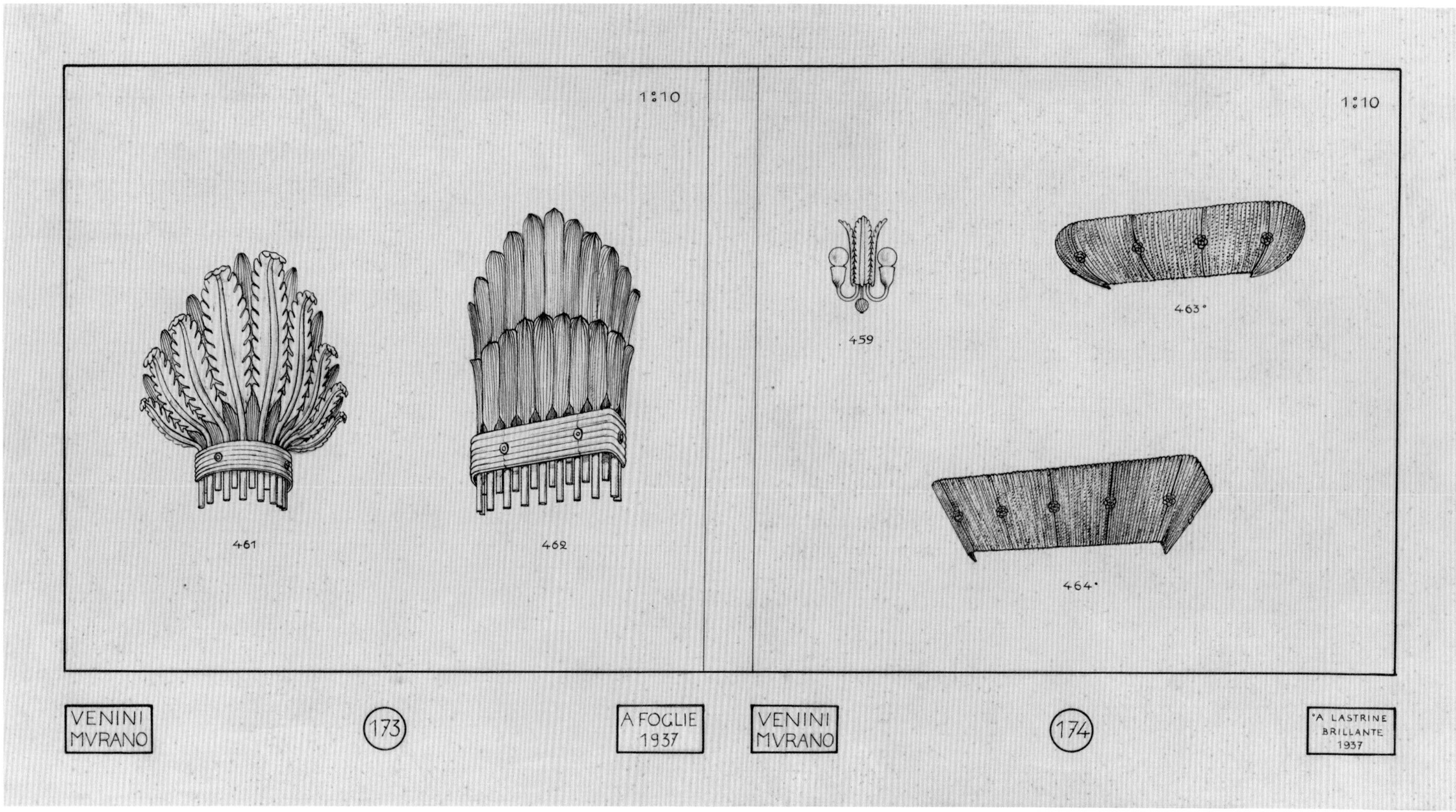
1:10
461
462
VENINI MVRANO
173
A FOGLIE 1937
1:10
459
463*
464*
VENINI MVRANO
174
*A LASTRINE BRILLANTE 1937

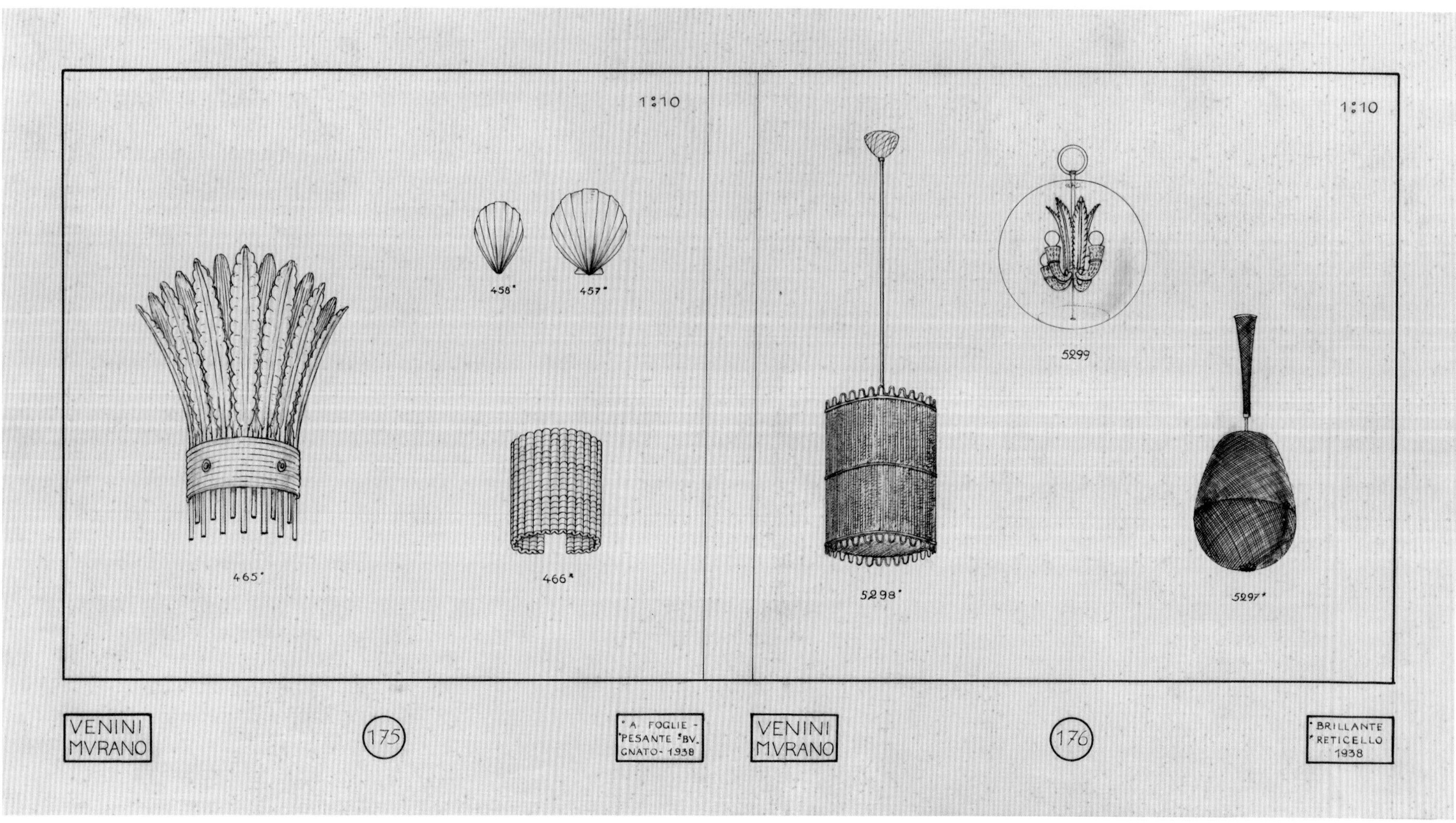
1:10
458*
457*
465*
466*
VENINI MVRANO
175
*A FOGLIE - *PESANTE *BV. GNATO - 1938
1:10
5299
5298*
5297*
VENINI MVRANO
176
*BRILLANTE *RETICELLO 1938

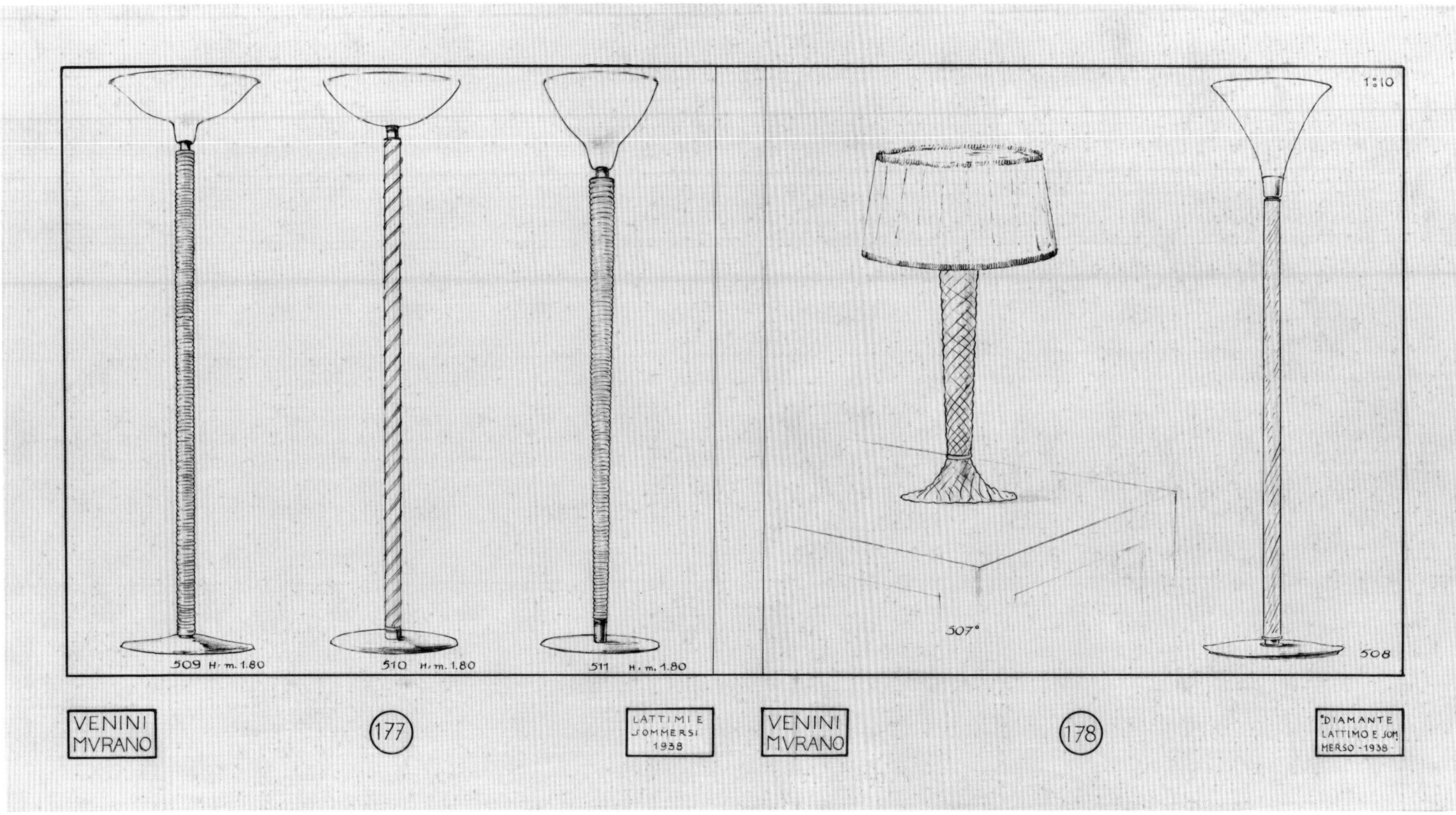
509 H. m. 1.80
510 H. m. 1.80
511 H. m. 1.80
VENINI MVRANO
177
LATTIMI E SOMMERSI 1938
1:10
507°
508
VENINI MVRANO
178
"DIAMANTE LATTIMO E SOM- MERSO -1938-

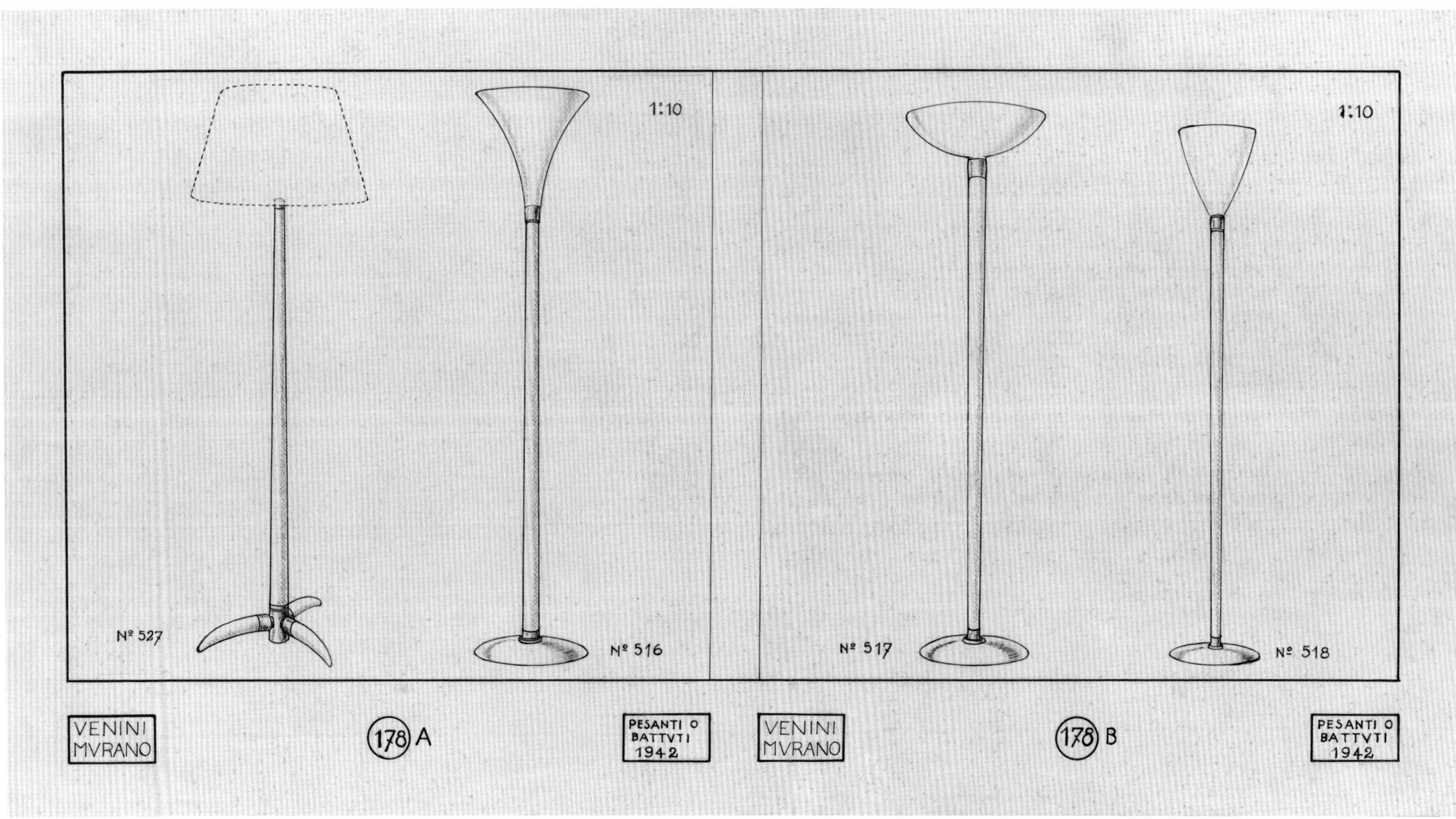
1:10
Nº 527
Nº 516
VENINI MVRANO
178 A
PESANTI O BATTVTI 1942
1:10
Nº 517
Nº 518
VENINI MVRANO
178 B
PESANTI O BATTVTI 1942

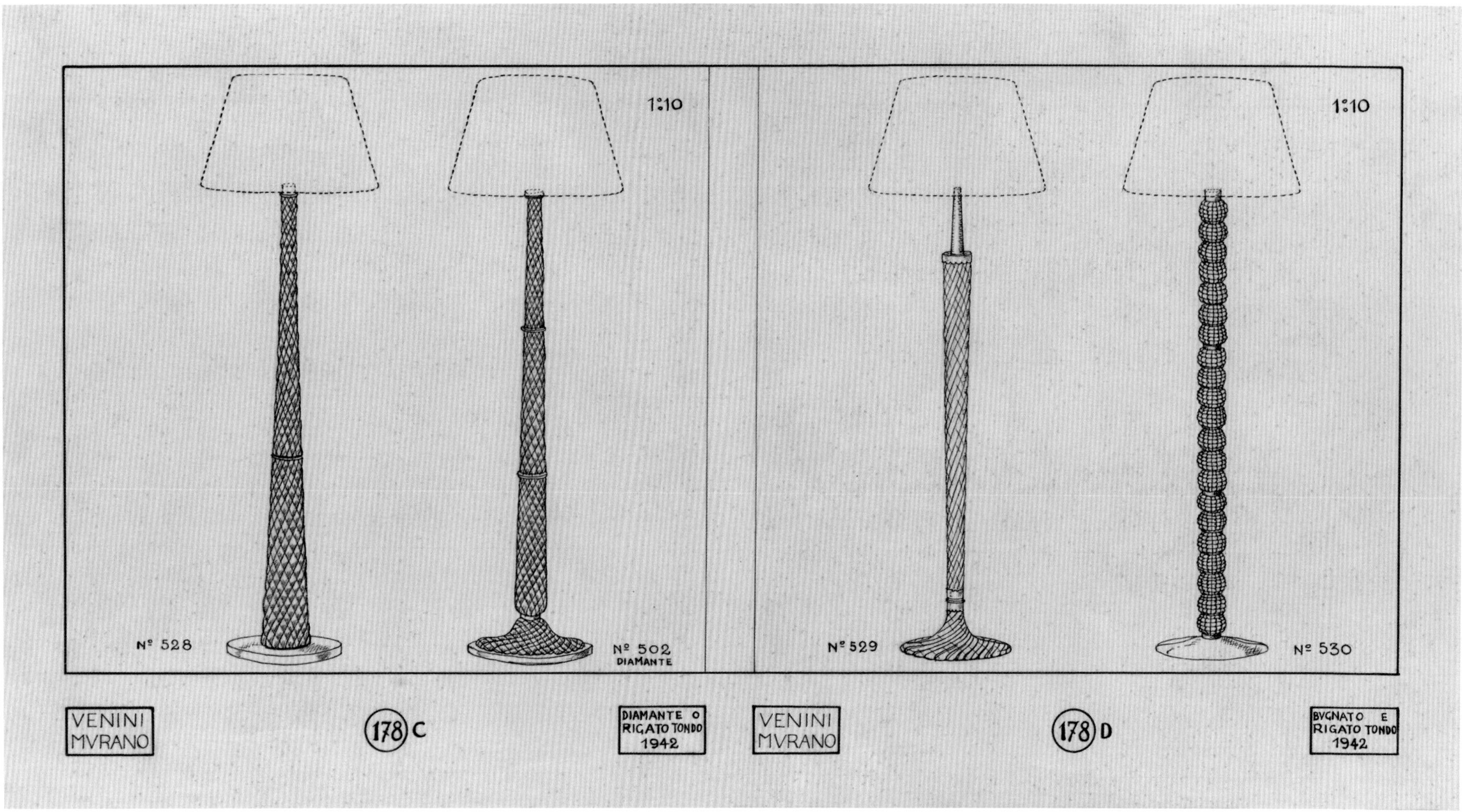
1:10
Nº 528
Nº 502
DIAMANTE
VENINI
MVRANO
178 C
DIAMANTE O
RIGATO TONDO
1942
1:10
Nº 529
Nº 530
VENINI
MVRANO
178 D
BVGNATO E
RIGATO TONDO
1942

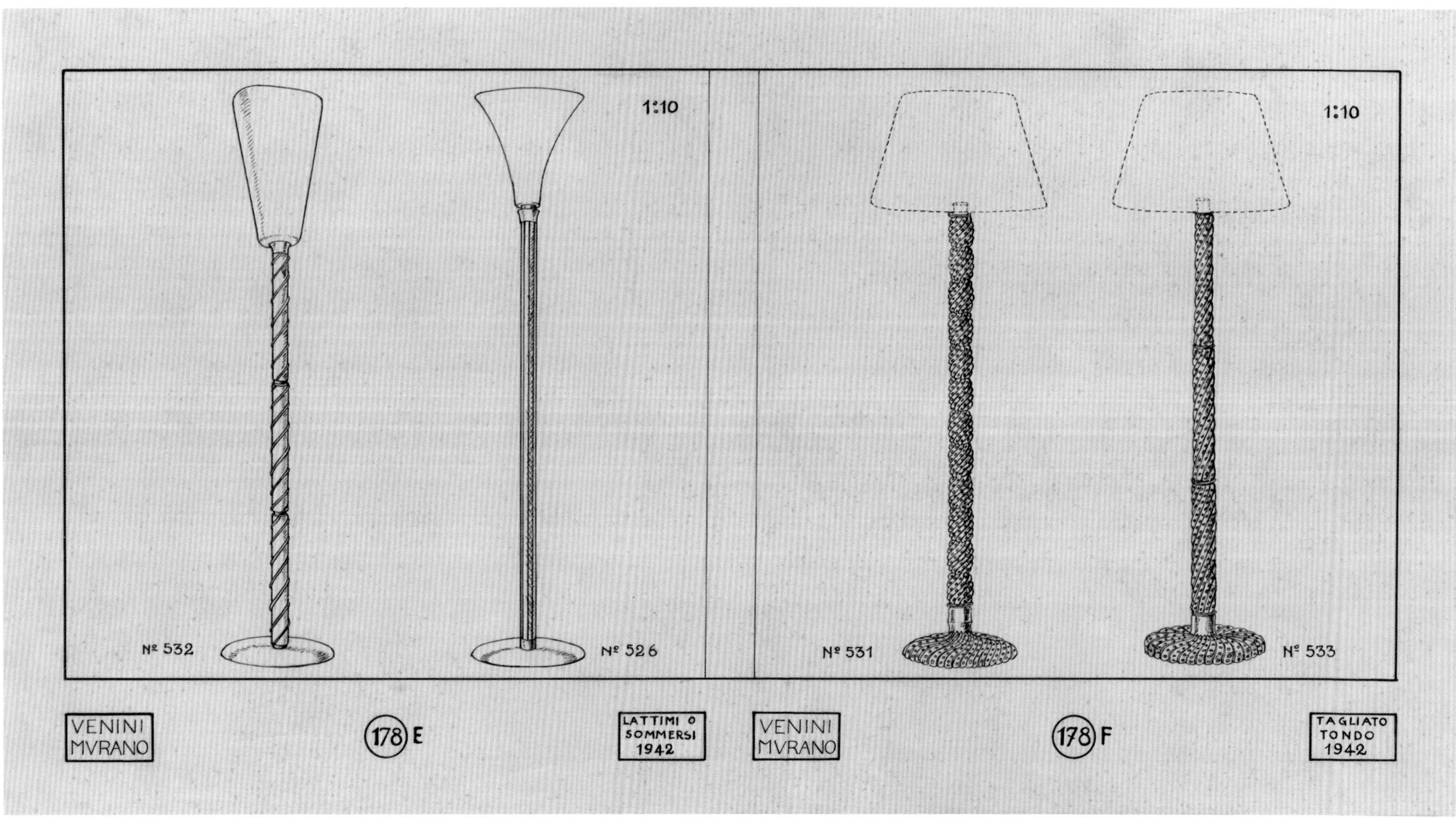
1:10
Nº 532
Nº 526
VENINI
MVRANO
178 E
LATTIMI O
SOMMERSI
1942
1:10
Nº 531
Nº 533
VENINI
MVRANO
178 F
TAGLIATO
TONDO
1942

1:10

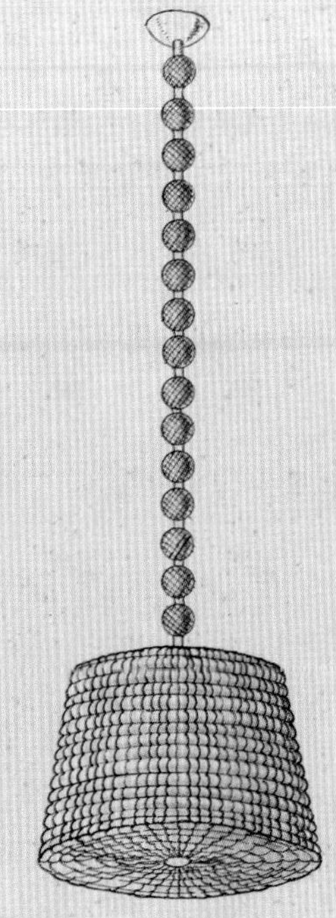

5310

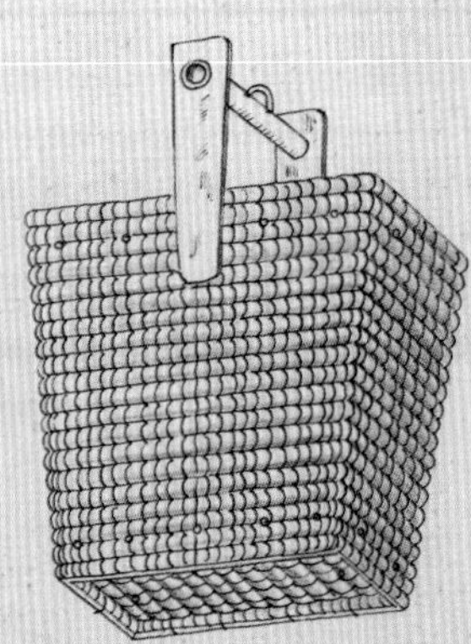

5300

VENINI MVRANO

179

BVGNATO 1939

1:10

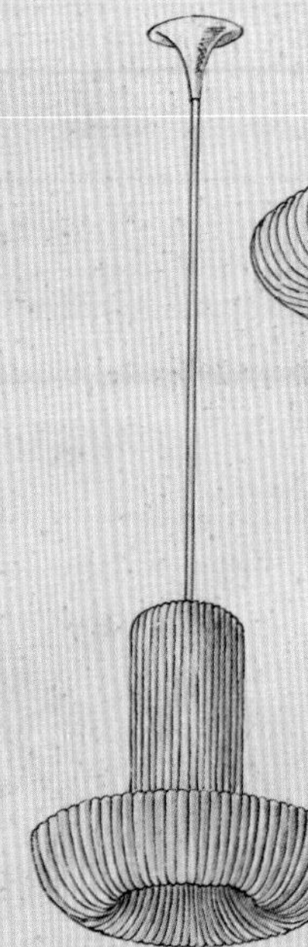

5309

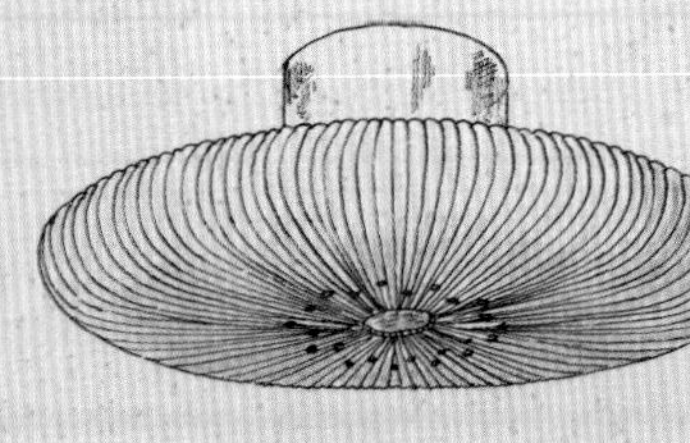

5306

5305

VENINI MVRANO

180

CORDONATO RIGATO 1939

1:10

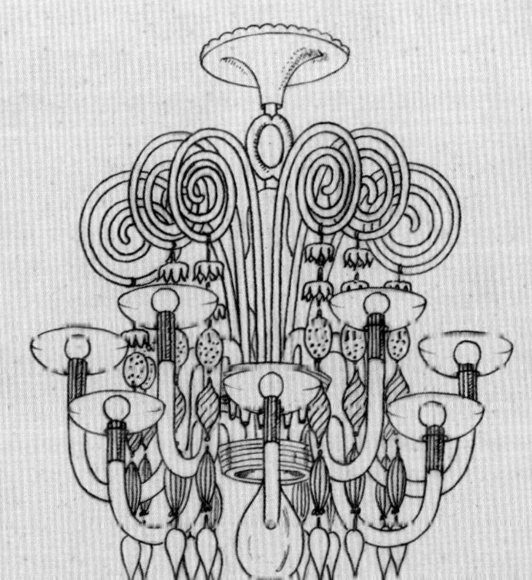

5315 A 12

VENINI MVRANO

181

SOFFIATI 1941

1:10

5330 A 5

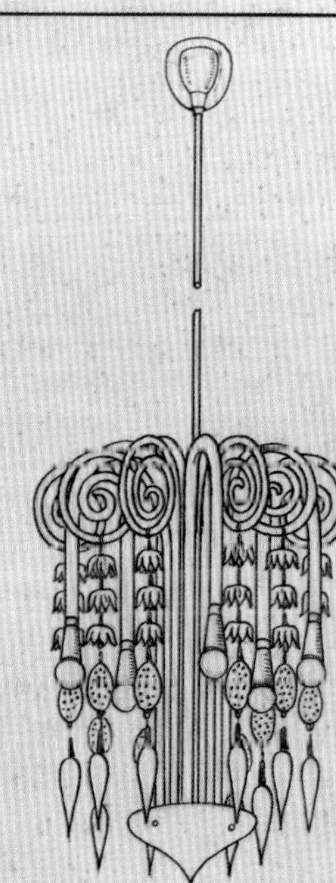

5333 A 5

VENINI MVRANO

182

SOFFIATI 1941

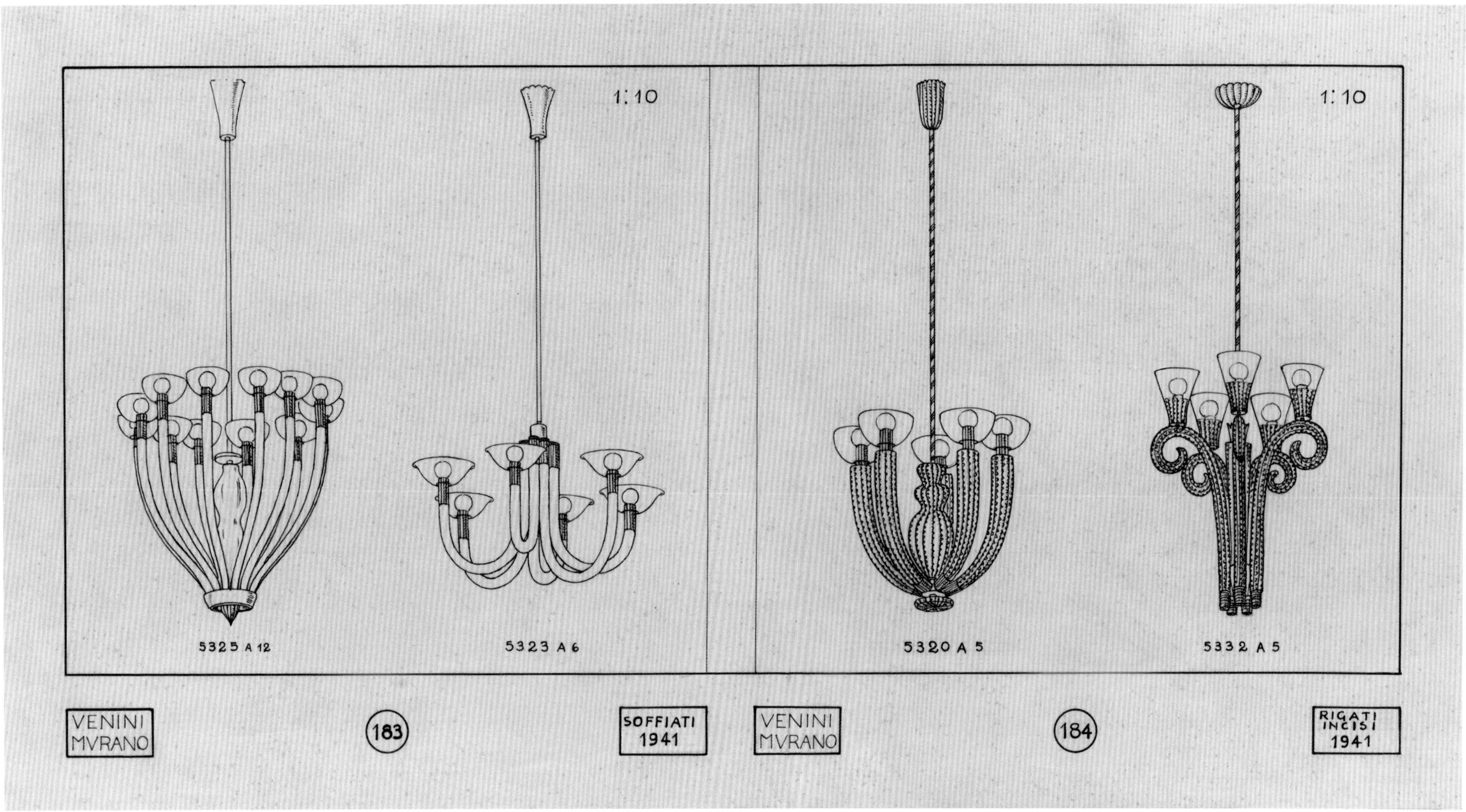
1:10
1:10
5325 A 12
5323 A 6
5320 A 5
5332 A 5
VENINI MVRANO
183
SOFFIATI 1941
VENINI MVRANO
184
RIGATI INCISI 1941

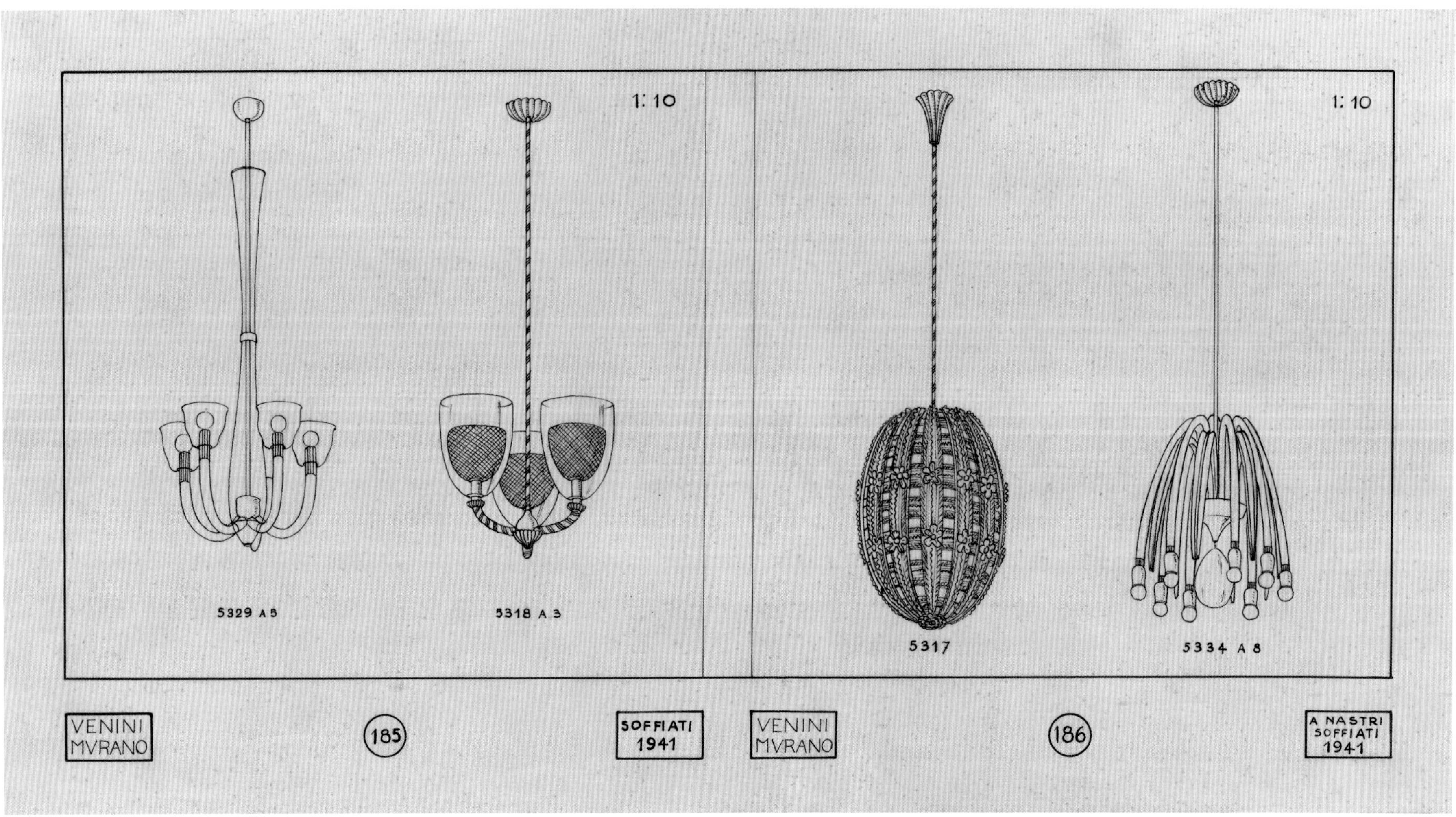
1:10
1:10
5329 A 5
5318 A 3
5317
5334 A 8
VENINI MVRANO
185
SOFFIATI 1941
VENINI MVRANO
186
A NASTRI SOFFIATI 1941

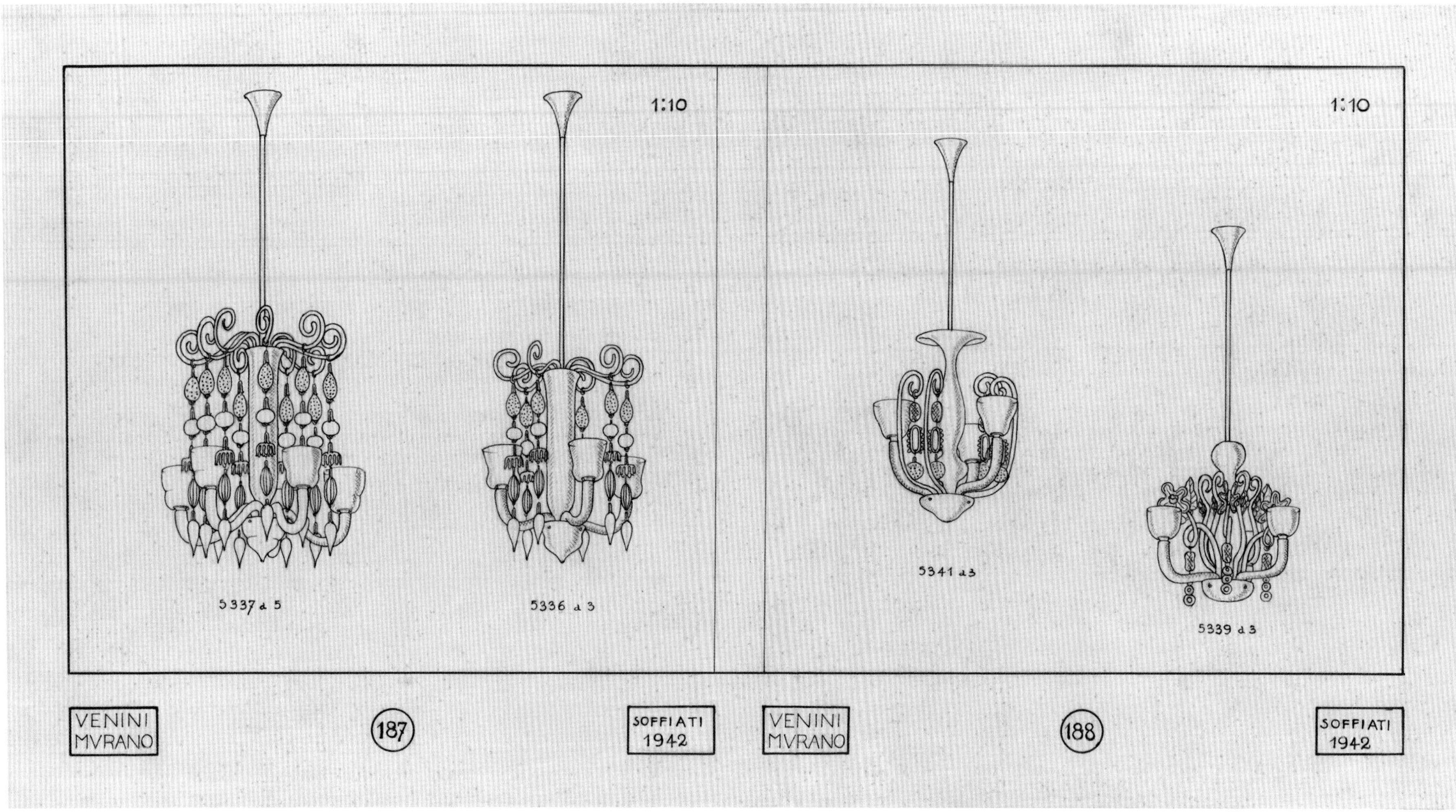
1:10
5337 a 5
5336 a 3
VENINI
MVRANO
187
SOFFIATI
1942
1:10
5341 a 3
5339 a 3
VENINI
MVRANO
188
SOFFIATI
1942

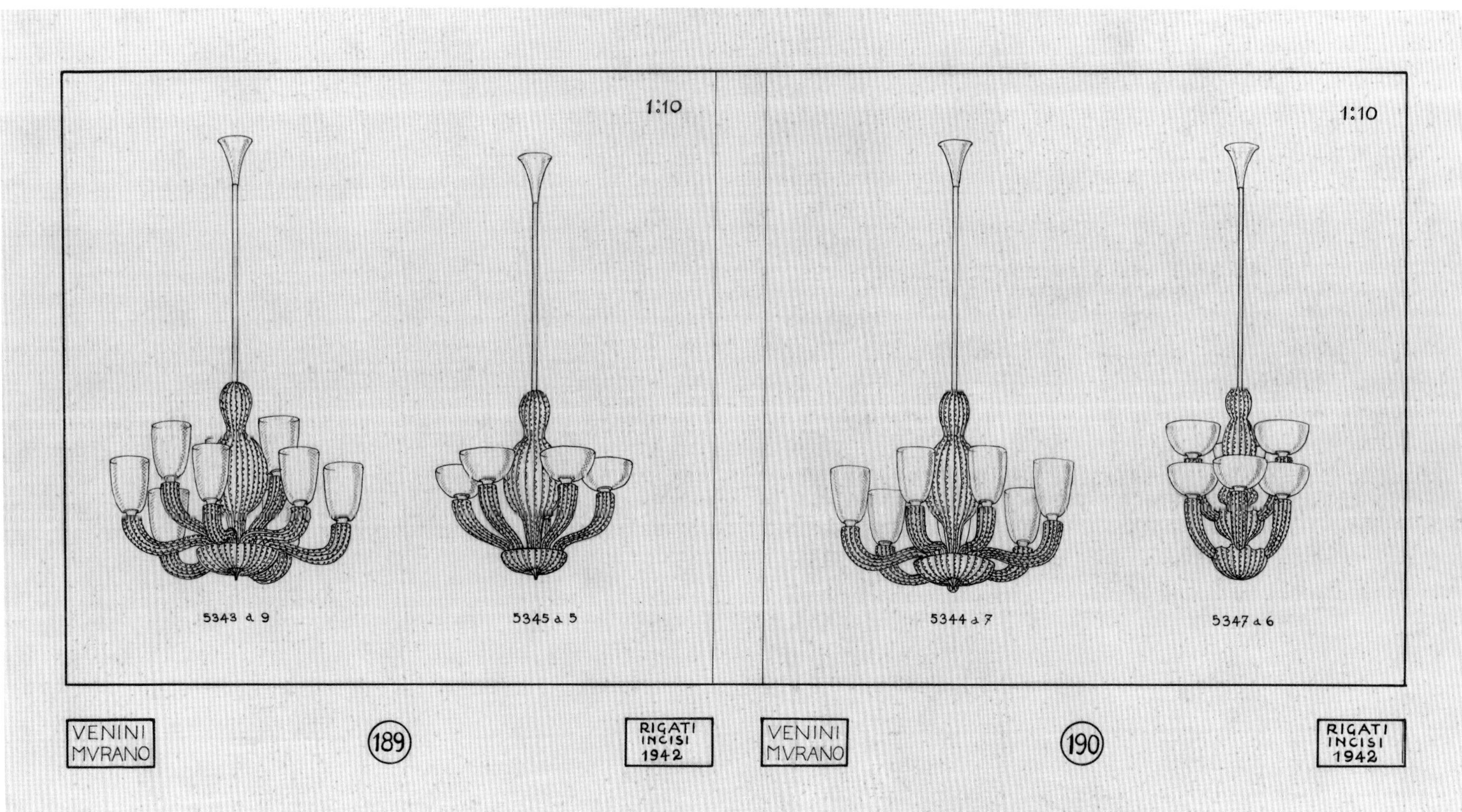
1:10
5343 a 9
5345 a 5
VENINI
MVRANO
189
RIGATI
INCISI
1942
1:10
5344 a 7
5347 a 6
VENINI
MVRANO
190
RIGATI
INCISI
1942

1:10

5340 a 10

VENINI MVRANO

191

SOFFIATI 1942

1:10

5342 a 5

5338 a 9

VENINI MVRANO

192

SOFFIATI 1942

1:10

ONDVLATO
BREV. Nº 29778

1

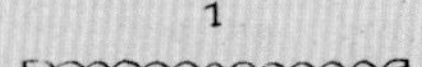

←---- LVCE NETTA ---→
←--- LVNGHEZZA TOTALE --→

ONDE		
7	m/m 245	m/m 285
8	„ 280	„ 320
9	„ 315	„ 355
10	„ 350	„ 390
11	„ 385	„ 425
12	„ 420	„ 460
13	„ 455	„ 495
14	„ 490	„ 530
15	„ 525	„ 565
16	„ 560	„ 600
17	„ 595	„ 635
18	„ 630	„ 670
19	„ 665	„ 705
20	„ 700	„ 740

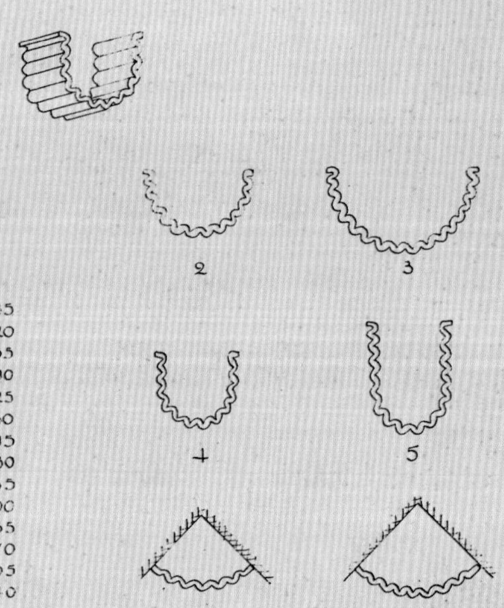

VENINI MVRANO

C

TVTTI I LISTELLI SONO DELLA LARGHEZZA DI cm. 10

1:10

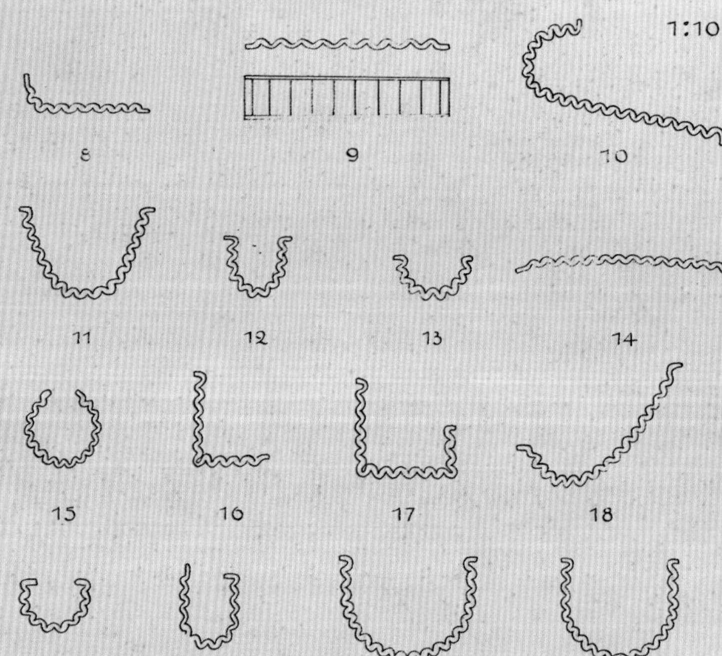

VENINI MVRANO

C1

TVTTI I LISTELLI SONO DELLA LARGHEZZA DI cm. 10

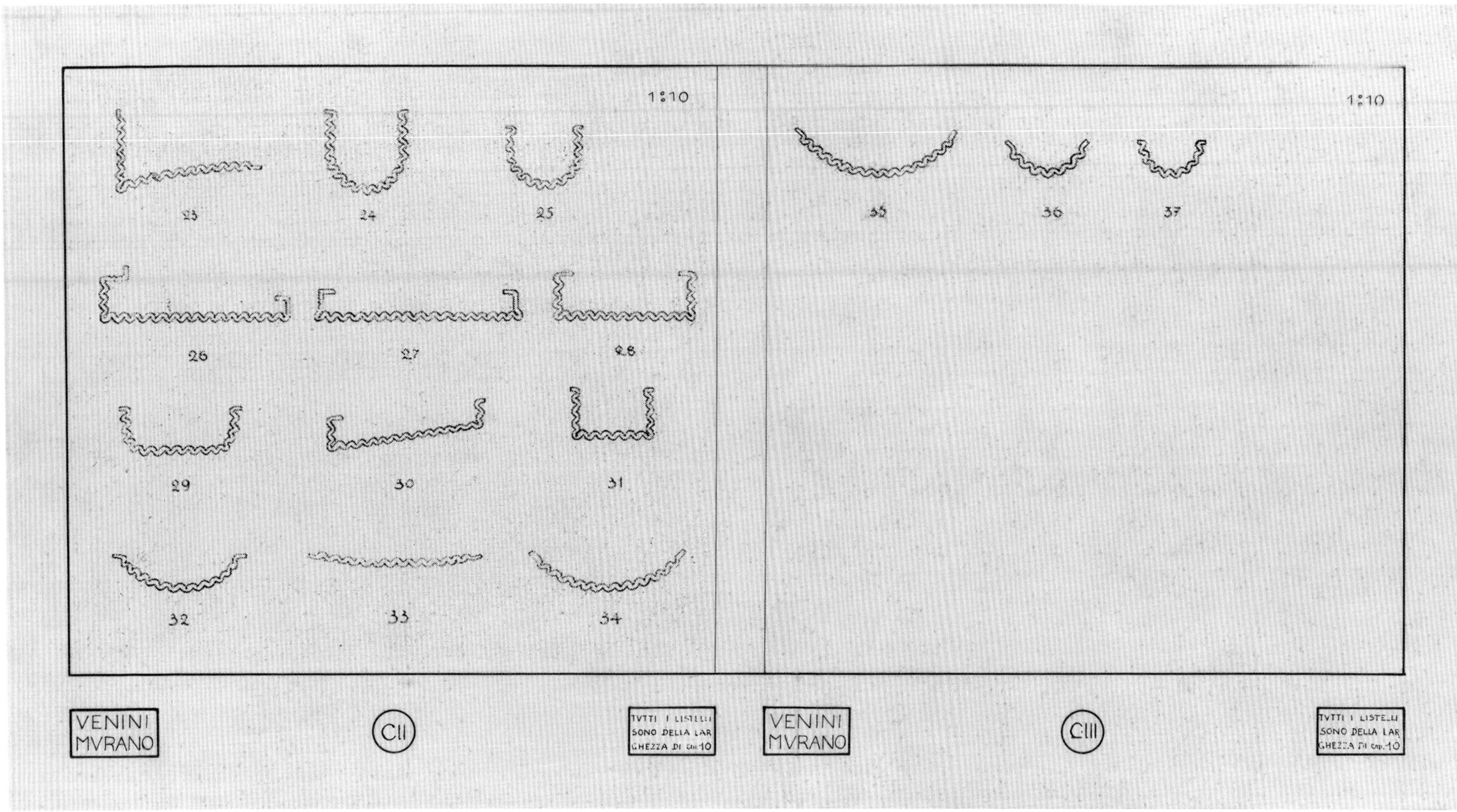
1:10
23
24
25
26
27
28
29
30
31
32
33
34
1:10
35
36
37
VENINI MVRANO
CII
TVTTI I LISTELLI SONO DELLA LARGHEZZA DI cm.10
VENINI MVRANO
CIII
TVTTI I LISTELLI SONO DELLA LARGHEZZA DI cm.10

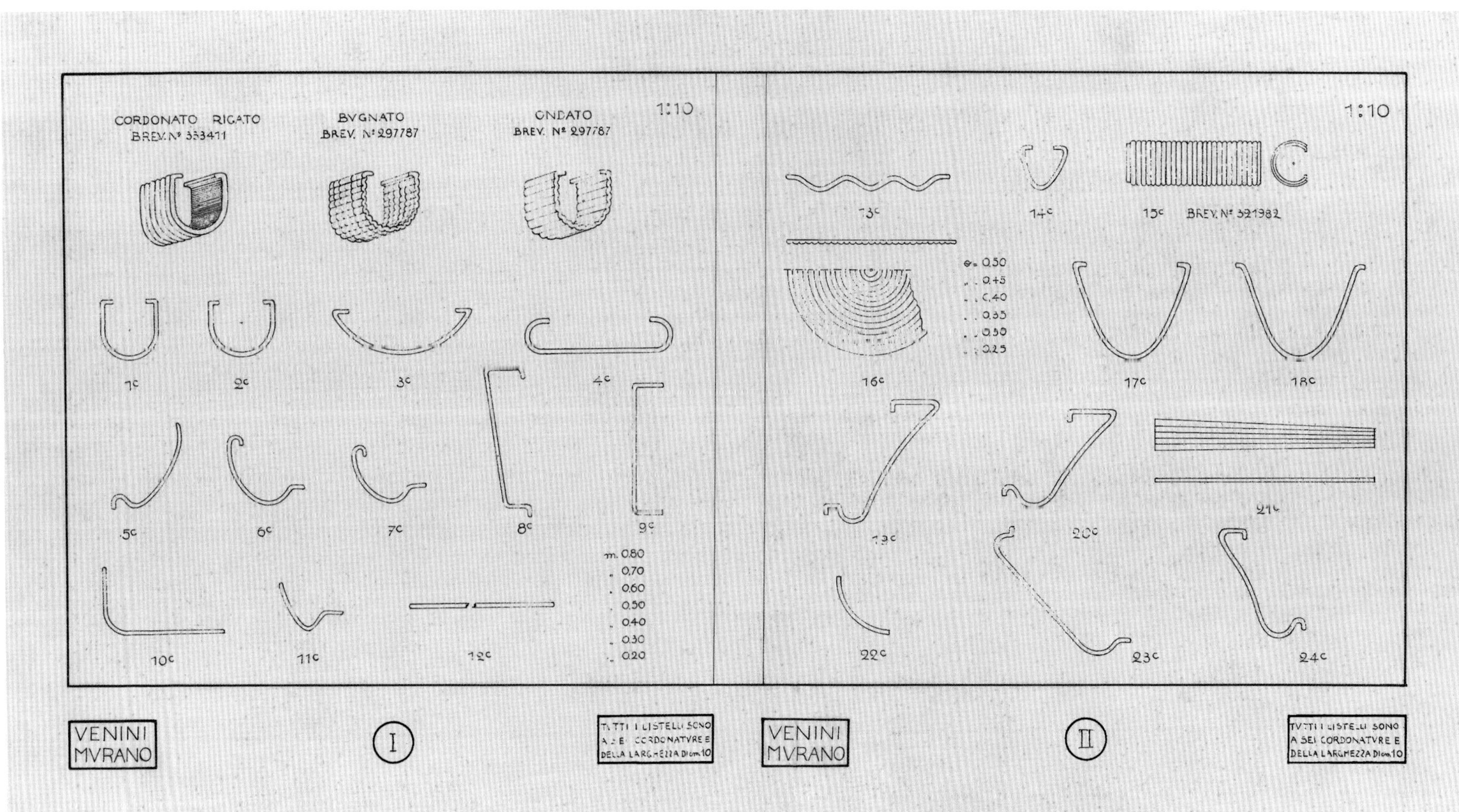
CORDONATO RIGATO
BREV. N° 333471
BVGNATO
BREV. N° 297787
ONDATO
BREV. N° 297787
1:10
1c
2c
3c
4c
5c
6c
7c
8c
9c
10c
11c
12c
m. 0.80
0.70
0.60
0.50
0.40
0.30
0.20
1:10
13c
14c
15c
BREV. N° 321982
16c
17c
18c
19c
20c
21c
22c
23c
24c
VENINI MVRANO
I
TVTTI I LISTELLI SONO A SEI CORDONATVRE E DELLA LARGHEZZA DI cm.10
VENINI MVRANO
II
TVTTI I LISTELLI SONO A SEI CORDONATVRE E DELLA LARGHEZZA DI cm.10

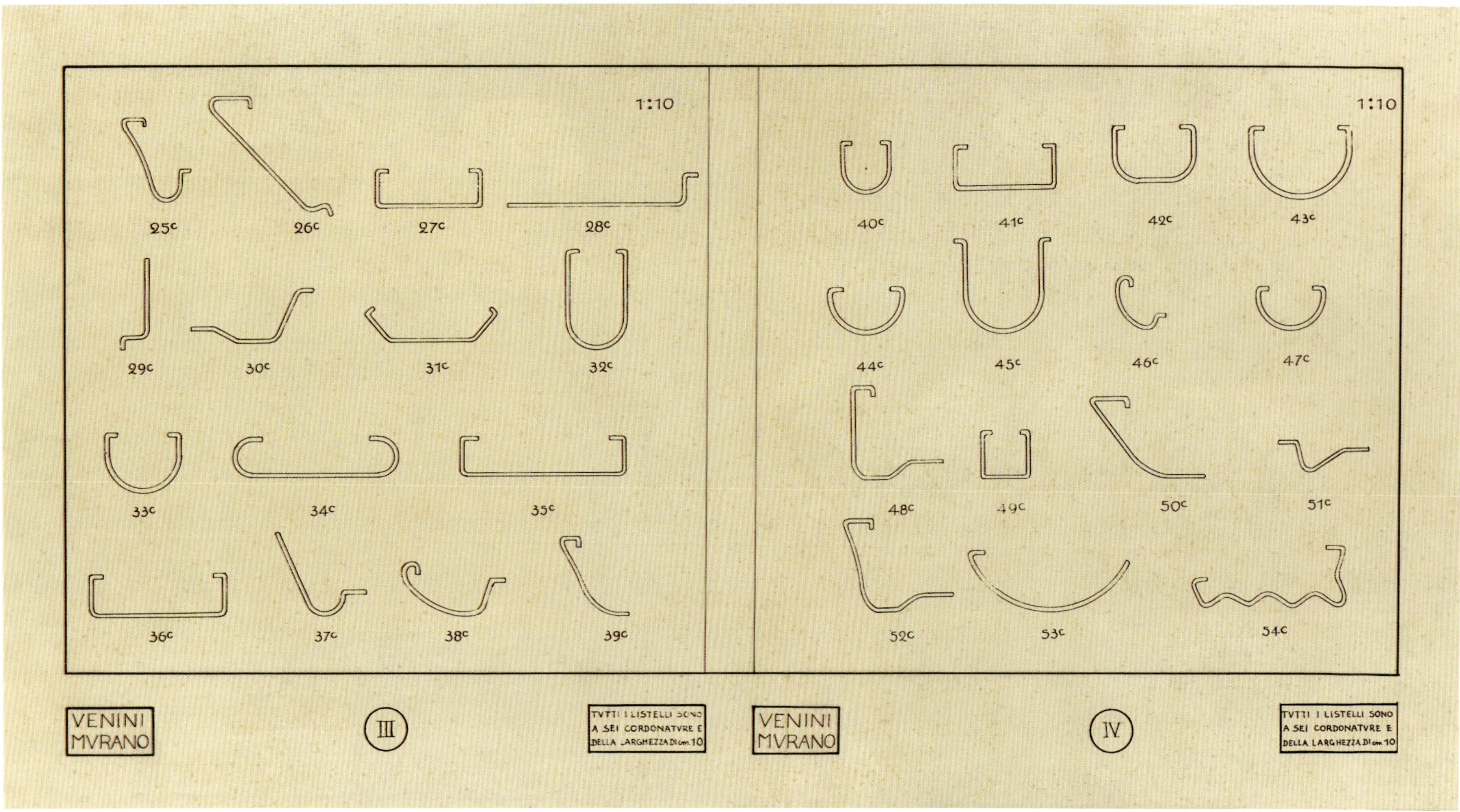
1:10
25c
26c
27c
28c
29c
30c
31c
32c
33c
34c
35c
36c
37c
38c
39c
1:10
40c
41c
42c
43c
44c
45c
46c
47c
48c
49c
50c
51c
52c
53c
54c
VENINI MVRANO
III
TVTTI I LISTELLI SONO A SEI CORDONATVRE E DELLA LARGHEZZA DI cm 10
VENINI MVRANO
IV
TVTTI I LISTELLI SONO A SEI CORDONATVRE E DELLA LARGHEZZA DI cm 10

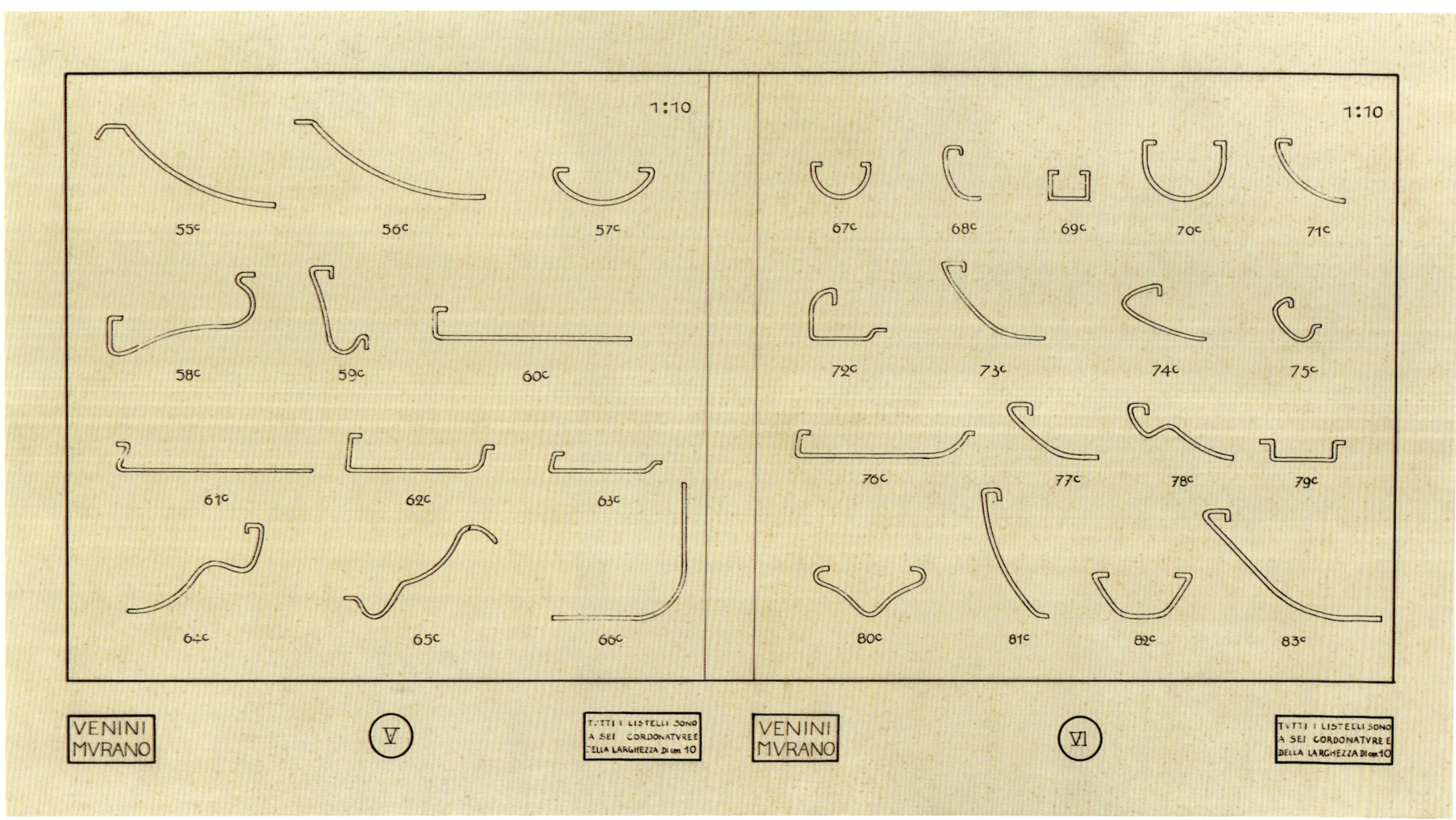
1:10
55c
56c
57c
58c
59c
60c
61c
62c
63c
64c
65c
66c
1:10
67c
68c
69c
70c
71c
72c
73c
74c
75c
76c
77c
78c
79c
80c
81c
82c
83c
VENINI MVRANO
V
TVTTI I LISTELLI SONO A SEI CORDONATVRE E DELLA LARGHEZZA DI cm 10
VENINI MVRANO
VI
TVTTI I LISTELLI SONO A SEI CORDONATVRE E DELLA LARGHEZZA DI cm 10

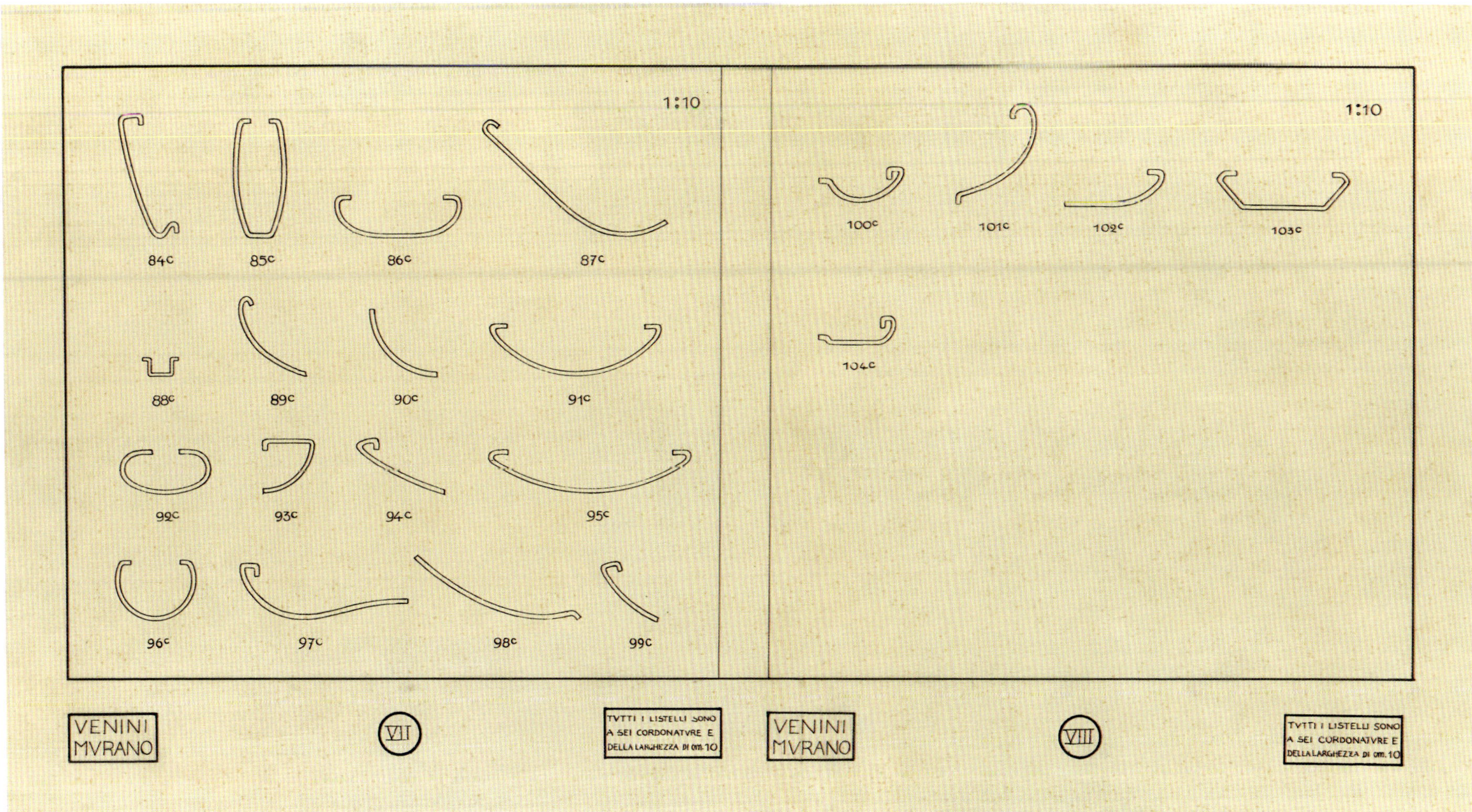
1:10
84c
85c
86c
87c
88c
89c
90c
91c
92c
93c
94c
95c
96c
97c
98c
99c
VENINI MVRANO
VII
TVTTI I LISTELLI SONO A SEI CORDONATVRE E DELLA LARGHEZZA DI cm. 10
1:10
100c
101c
102c
103c
104c
VENINI MVRANO
VIII
TVTTI I LISTELLI SONO A SEI CORDONATVRE E DELLA LARGHEZZA DI cm. 10

RED CATALOGUE: MODELS FOR LIGHTING

Published below are the pages of the Red Catalogue concerning lighting, a reference point for the production of the 1950s. The catalogue includes a selection of models of the 1920s, 1930s and 1940s presented with a new numbering, as well as models designed in the post-War period. Forming a sort of appendix to the catalogue and presumably produced in the second half of the 1950s are ten pages with the series no. 960 and no. 961, which include a selection of models of chandeliers and sconces with arms, drawn from the original body of the said Red Catalogue and renumbered.

Lampade da pavimento

2224	200	Trasparente coppa opaca
	250	Sommersa coppa opaca dorata
	160	Trasparente senza coppa
	200	Sommerso senza coppa
2225	250	Ritorto tondo senza coppa
2226	700	Cordonato
	750	Bugnato
2227	160	Trasparente senza coppa
	185	Corroso " "
	240	B attuta " "
2228	120	Ritorto tondo senza coppa
2229	240	Ritorto tondo senza coppa
	340	Tagliato tondo " "
2230	225	Retorto tondo senza coppa
	325	Tagliato tondo " "
2231	130	Ritorto tondo senza coppa resse 138
	230	B attuta senza coppa
2232	250	Trasparente dorato - seza oro 220
2233	315	Zanfirico
2234	325	Zanfirico
2235	250	Trasparente dorato
2236	350	Zanfirico
2237	250	Trasparente dorato
2238	250	Trasparénte dorato
2241	180	Striscie colorate (senza paralume)
2242	200	Elementi " " "
2243	180	Pezzata " "

Lampadari — Lampade a parete

5I0I/24		900	Soffiato	570I/3	150
/12		550	"	/2	110
/ 6		325	"		
/ 4		225	"		
5I02/ 5		300	Soffiato	5702/2	100
		360	" bracci e rivestimento lattimo		120
5I03/ 4		200	Soffiato	5703/2	90
5I04/12		1.200	Soffiato	5704/3	190
6		500	"	/2	150
5I05/12		900	Soffiato	5705/3	190
6		450	"	/2	150
5I07		500	Bollicine		
		625	Dorato		
5I08		300	B ollicine bacinelle velate	5708	60
		350	Dorato		70
		400	Sommerso bacinella filigrana		80
5I09		350	Coppe lattimo foglie smerigliate		
		500	Dorato		
5II0		100	Smerigliato od opaco		
5III		600	Bollicine		
		800	Foglie dorate rivestimento lattimo oro		
5II2	Ø 40	100	Cordonato o bugnato		
		150	Cordonato inciso		
	Ø 35	70	Cordonato o bugnato		
		105	Cordonato inciso		
5II3		120	Cordonato o bugnato		
5II4		120	Cordonato o bugnato	57I4	60
5II5		550	Bracci rigadin coppe cordonato o bugnato	57I5/2	80
5II6		225	B racci rigadin coppe cordonato o bugnato		
5II7		90	Smerigliato,opaco o bollicine		
		110	Dorato		
5II8		150	Cordonato,bugnato o bollicine	57I8	35
		225	Cordonato inciso		50

Lampadari — Lampade a parete

5II9	Ø 45	80	Trasparente,opaco o bollicine		
		100	A stelle o spira		
		130	Filigrana		
		180	Reticello		
	Ø 32	45	Trasparente,opaco o bollicine		
		55	A stelle o spira		
		65	Filigrana		
		85	Reticello		
	Ø 22	32	Tras parente,opaco o bollici ne		
		40	A stelle o spira		
		45	Filigrana		
		57	Ret icello		
5I20		320	Cordonato		
		330	Cordonato rivestimento dorato		
		350	Cordonato " lattimo oro		
		350	B ugnato		
		360	B ugnato rivestimento dorato		
		380	Bugnato " lattimo oro		
5I2I		1.200	Bollicine o smerigliato	572I/3	180
		1.450	Dorato		220
			Bollici ne o smerigliato	572I/1	70
			Dorato		85
5I22		260	Trasparente o bollicine	5722	100
		280	Dorato		110
5I23		350	Trasparente o bollici ne ,coppe opache		
		500	Sommerso,bacinelle filigrana		
5I24		400	Cordonato		
		440	B ugnato		
5I25		900	A tessere		
5I26	Ø 100	720	Cordonato		
		800	B ugnato		
	Ø 90	640	Cordonato		
		700	Bugnato		
	Ø 80	500	Cordonato		
		540	B ugnato		
	Ø 70	420	Cordonato		
		450	Bugnato		

Lampadari — Lampade a parete

5I27	Ø 110	920	Cordonato		
		1.000	Bugnato		
	Ø 100	800	Cordonato		
		875	B ugnato		
	0/ 90	660	Cordonato		
		720	Bugnato		
	Ø 80	580	Cordonato		
		620	B ugnato		
	Ø 70	500	Cordonato		
		535	B ugnato		
5I28		390	Rigato,bacinelle e palla rigadin ritorto		
		700	Filigrana		
5I29		800	A fiori e patere		
		1.000	Decorazione oro		
5I30		425	Cordonato	5730	110
		500	B ugnato		120
5I3I		520	Cordonato		
		550	B ugnato		
5I32		150	Opaco o bollicine	5732	50
		230	Filigrana		70
		165	Dorato		55
5I33		350	Trasparente	5733	120
		380	Interno dorato		140
		420	" lattimo		160
		450	" " oro		180
5I34		400	Cordonato	5734	I30
		440	B ugnato		145
	Ø 42	320	Cordonato		
		350	B ugnato		
5I35		520	Cordonato		
		570	B ugnato		
5I36		475	Cordonato		
		525	B ugnato		
5I37/12		1.300	Trasparente bracci e pastorali anima lattimo.		
		1.500	Idem bacinelle filigrana		
5I37/6		700	Trasaparente bracci e pastorali anima lattimo		
		800	Idem bacinel le filigrana		

Lampadari			Lampade a parete	
5I38	200	Ritorto tondo	5738	100
5I39	440	Trasparente bracci anima lattimo	5739/3	115
5I40 Ø 50	120	Opaco		
" 40	100	"		
" 32	90	"		
5I4I	320	Trasparente	5741 92	
5I42	380	Trasparente	5742	125
	435	Dorato		150
5I43	425	Trasparente	5743/3	185
	460	Decorazione oro		200
	550	Dorato		235
		Trasparente	5743/2	145
		Decorazione oro		160
		Dorato		180
5I44	650	Trasparente	5744/2	150
	700	Decorazione oro		165
5I45	650	Trasparente	5745	170
	725	Decorazione oro		185
5I46	450	Trasparente	5746	140
5I47/6	350	Trasparente		
5I47/4	250	Trasparente	5747	125
	270	Decorazione oro		135
	340	Dorato		165
5I48/6	450	Trasparente	5748	150
	490	Decorazione oro		160
5I48/4	350	Trasparente		
	380	Decorazione oro		
	430	Dorato		
5I49	220	Trasparente	5749	85
5I50/6	475	Trasparente	5750	170
	500	Decorazione oro		100
5I50/4	350	Trasparente		
	370	Decorazione oro		

Lampadari			Lampade a parete	
5I5I/6	575	Trasparente	575I	185
	630	Decorazione oro		200
5I5I/4	425	Trasparente		
	450	Decorazione oro		
5I52/10	700	Trasparente	5752/3	195
5I54 Ø40	350	Cordonato		
	375	B ugnato		
	500	Ondulato		
Ø30	275	Cordonato		
	300	Bugnato		
	350	Ondulato		
5I55	260	Ondulato	5755	225
		Trasparente od opaco	5756/5	280
		Dorato		350
		A canne	5758	225
		Smerigliato, opaco o bollicine	5759	80
		Smerigliato o bollicine	5760	65
		Dorato		75
		Smerigliato o bollicine	576I	50
		Dorato		60
		Opaco cm.19	5762	30
		Dorato		35
		Opaco cm.22		40
		Dorato		50
		Opaco cm.25		50
		Dorato		60
		Pesante o bollicine	5763	110
		Corroso		125
		Bollicine	5764	110
		Cordonato	5765	140
		B ugnato		155
		Cordonato o bugnato	5766	65
		B ollicine o smerigliato	5767	60
		Dorato		70

Lampadari			Lampade da parete	
		B ollicine o smerigliato	5768	40
		Dorato		48
		Pesante o bollicine	5769	55
		Dorato		65
		Pesante o bollicine	5770	50
		Dorato		60
		Pesante, opaco o bollicine	577I	65
		Dorato o ritorto tondo		75
		Trasparente	5772	35
		Corroso		40
		Trasparente	5773	45
		Corroso		55
		Trasparente o bollicine	5774	290
		N astro sommerso foglie oro		400
		Ritorto tondo	5775	65
		Ritorto tondo	5776	80
		B ollicine	5777	35
		B ollicine	5779	50
		Bollicine gambo filigrana decorazione oro	5780	110
		Opaco dorato	578I/9	580
		Trasparente	5782	80
5I83/6	480	Trasparente		
5I84/6	6I0	"		
5I85/8	580	"		

Lampadari			Lampade a parete	
		Filigrana	5786	100
		Zanfirico		110
		Bambù cm. 70	5787	100
		cm.130		140
600	5188	Bianco e lattimo dec. oro	5788	240
		Nastro lattimo nero dec.oro	5789	60
1.500	5190	a 12 bracci soffiato		
		zanfirico	5791	65
		Bambù cm. 70 x 15	5792	90
		50 x 13		70
		a 2 vetri		180
		Bambù stretto a 2 cm. 70	5793	200
		" "	5794	90
			5795	100
		a prismi	5796	200
		"	5797	425
350	5198/5	Soffiato	5798/2	95
450		Opaco		120
315	5199/5	Soffiato		
330		" catene dec. oro		
435	5500	"		
455		" dorate		
280	5501/4	Lanterna soffiata senza vetri esterni		
300		" " dec.oro		
600	5502	Soffiato		
415	5503	"	5803/3	200
110	5504/3	"	5804/2	55
140	/4	"	/3	80
170	/5	"		
200	/6	"		
		Foglia bambù	5805	35
		Zanfirico	5806	55
		"	5807	55
		Bambù	5808	30
240	5509/4	zanfirico e pizzo	5809/1	50
			/2	110
			/3	170

Lampadari			Lampade a parete	
700	5511	a fiori e foglie	5811	200
		soffiato	5812/2	95
275	5513/6	dec.acquamare e ciclamino	5813/2	135
275	5514/6	soffiato dec.oro	5814/2	145
275	5515/5	soffiato palla argentata	5815/2	120
		" palla velata e smerigliata		115
330	5516/6	soffiato bacinelle smer.		
400		opaco		
330	5517/5	soffiato bacinelle smer.		
400		opaco		
150	5518	coppa velata		
900	5520	soffiato dec. in colore		
120	5521/3	soffiato		
130		iride		
225	5522/6	soffiato		
340	5523/8	"		
575	5524/6	"		
		zanfirico	5825	55
		"	5826	55
		"	5827	75
		bambù cm. 30	5828	30
		35		35
		40		40
		50		50
		bambù cm. 70	5829	100
		coppa zanfirico	5830	250
		bambù	5831	45
		"	5832	40
		" cm.130	5833	150
		" "	5834	55
720	5535/20	soffiato		
660	5536/18	"		
440	5537/8	"		
135	5538	zanfirico		
125	5539	"		
125	5540	"		

Lampade a soffitto			
5405		180	Coppa opaca globo filigrana
54I3		80	Opaco
		100	Dorato
54I6	Ø 45	90	Cordonato o bugnato
		150	Cordonato inciso
	Ø 40	70	Cordonato o bugnato
		120	Cordonato inciso
	Ø 35	55	Cordonato o bugnato
		95	Cordonato inciso
	Ø 30	45	Cordonato o bugnato
		75	Cordonato inciso
	Ø 25	35	Cordonato o bugnato
		60	Cordonato inciso
54I7	Ø 45	150	Filigrana cono lattimo oro
	32	110	idem
	22	70	idem
54I8		90	Cordonato o bugnato
542I		60	Cordonato o bugnato
5422		40	Cordonato o bugnato
5423		40	Cordonato o bugnato
5427		120	Filigrana
5428	Ø 60	430	Cordonato
		480	Bugnato
	Ø 80	620	Cordonato
		680	B ugnato
	Ø 96	750	Cordonato
		820	Bugnato
5429		350	Ondulato
		300	Bugnato
		280	Cordonato
5430		110	Opaco
		135	Dorato
5432	Ø 40	180	Cordonato o bugnato
	Ø 35	140	Cordonato o bugnato

Lampade a soffitto			
5434		1.100	Cordonato
		1.200	B ugnato
5438		60	Cordonato o bugnato
5440	Ø30	36	cordonato
		56	cordonato inciso
	Ø35	45	cordonato
		70	cordonato inciso
	Ø40	55	cordonato
		90	cordonato inciso
544I	Ø30	35	bambù
	Ø35	40	bambù
5442		90	Coppa velata decorazione opaca
5443	Ø 25	50	Cordonato con rosone di finale
	Ø 30	60	cordonato " " " "
5444	Ø 60	450	Cordonato
5445		150	Zanfirico
5446		140	Zanfirico
5447		120	Zanfirico
5448		140	Zanfirico

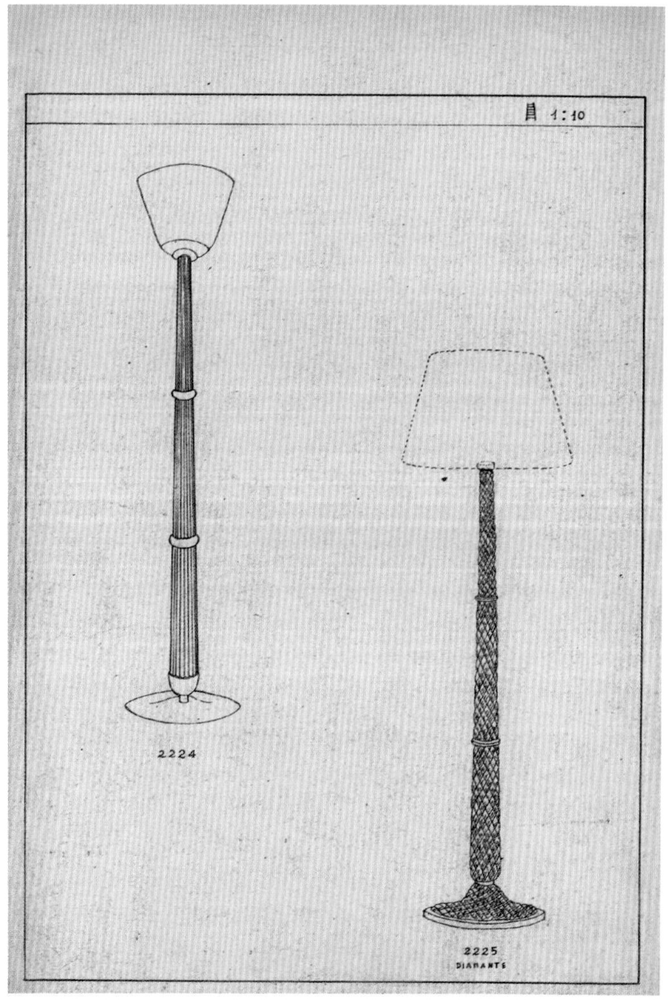

1:10
2227
2226

1:10
2228
2229

1:10
2230
2231

1:10
2232
2233

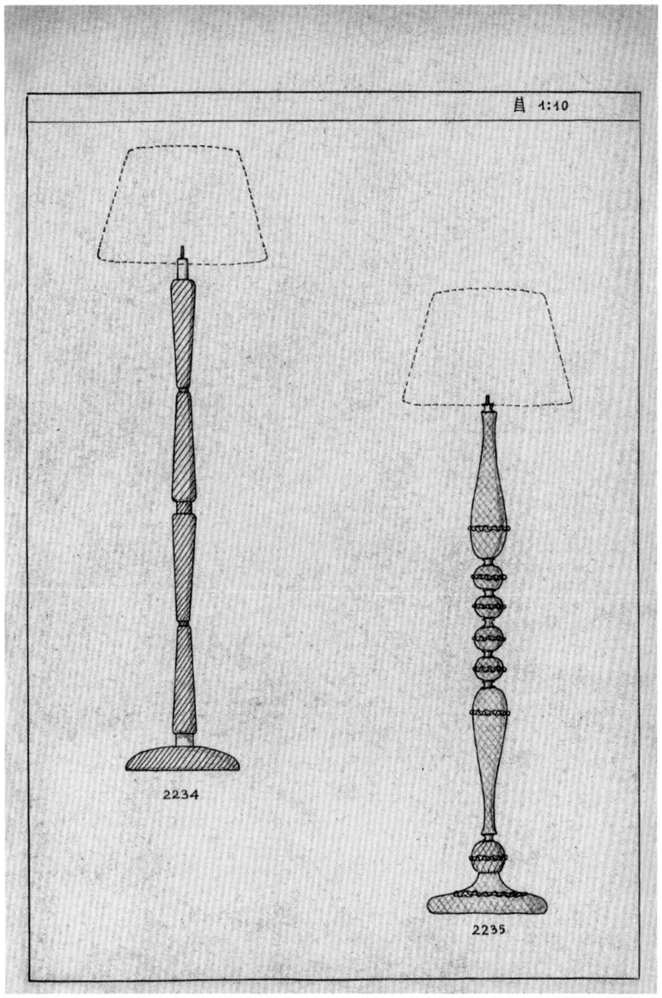
1:10
2234
2235

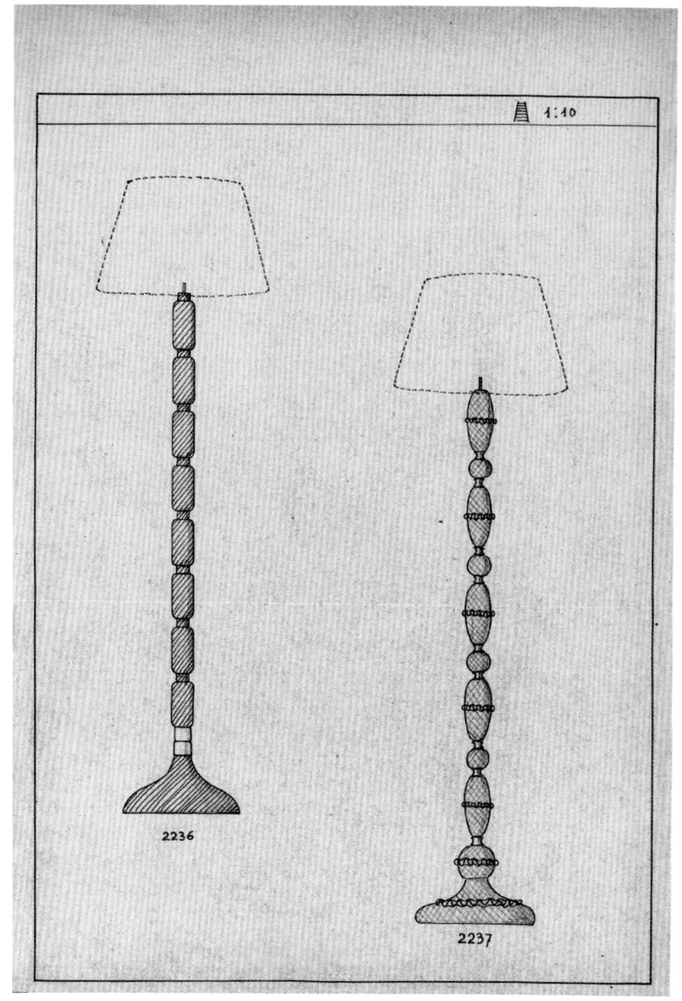
1:10
2236
2237

1:10
2238

1:10
2241
2242

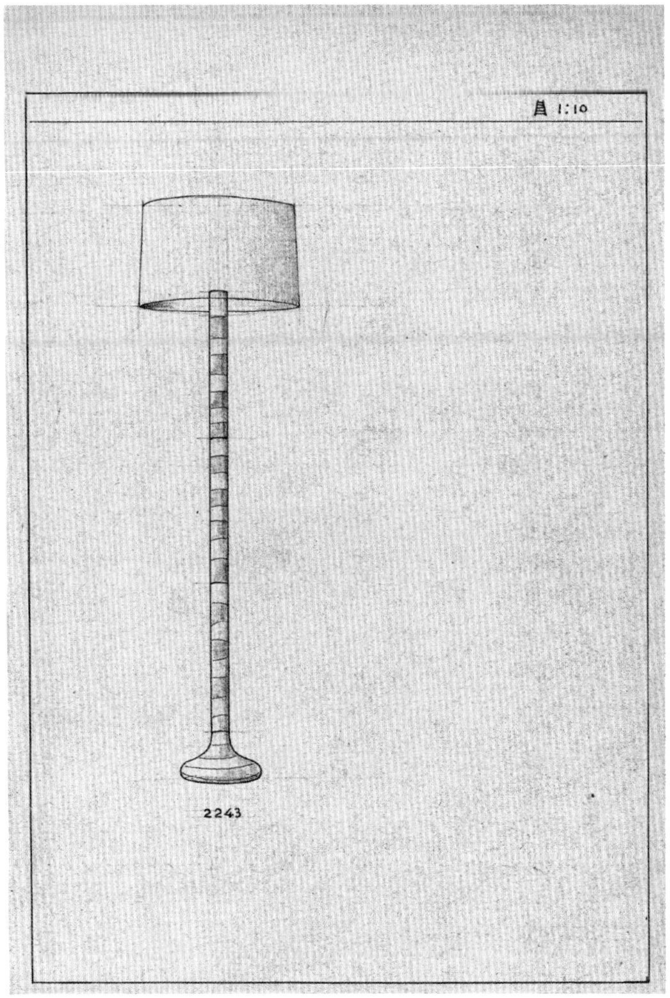
1:10
2243

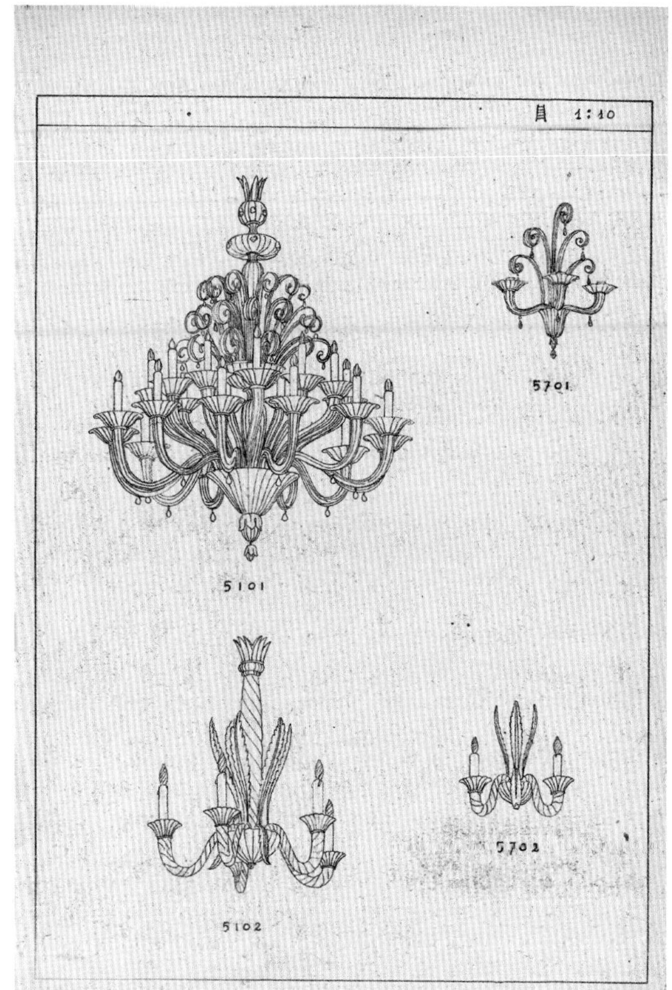
1:10
5101
5701
5102
5702

1:10
5103
5703
5104
5704

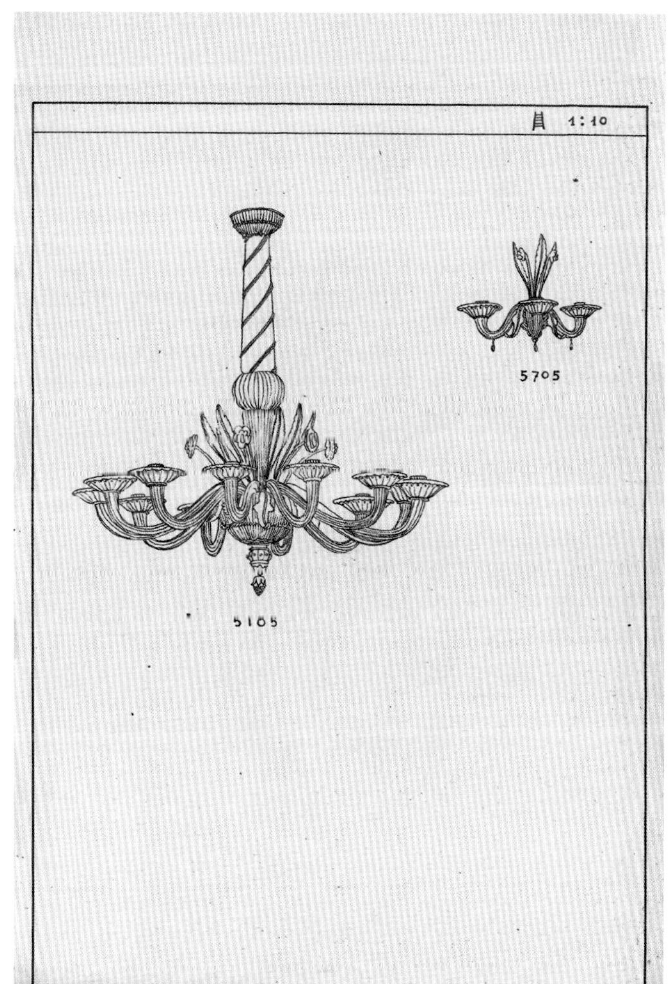
1:10
5705
5105

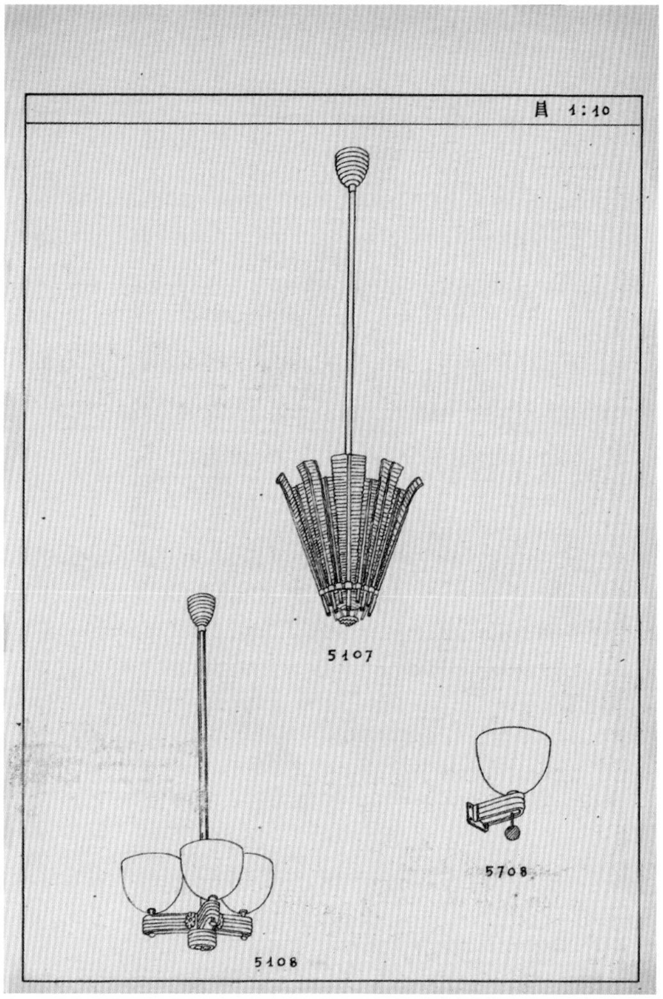
1:10
5107
5108
5708.

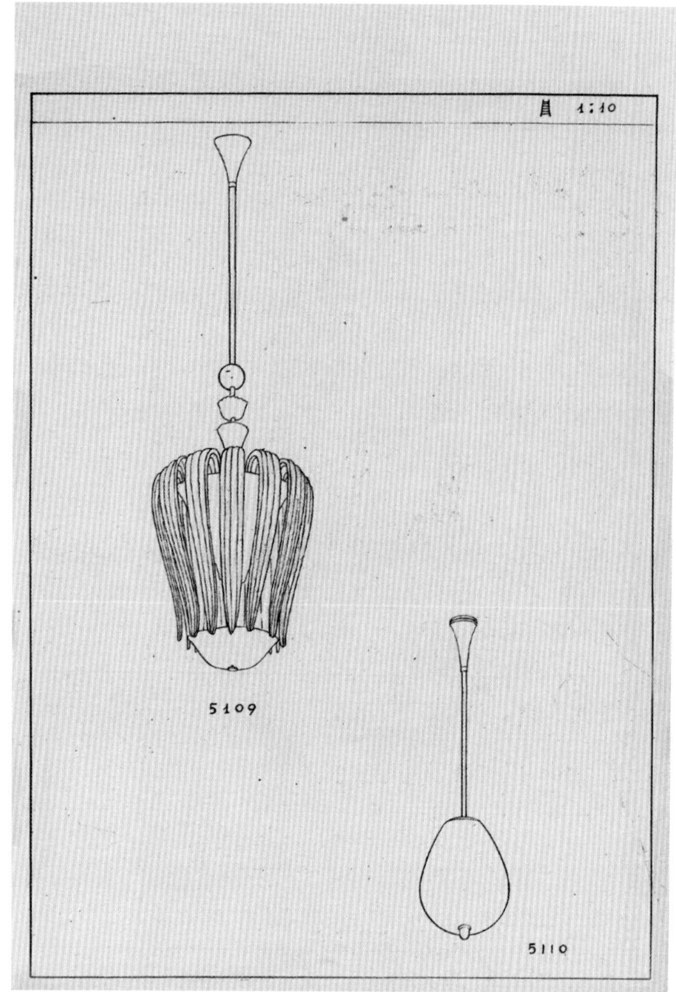
1:10
5109
5110

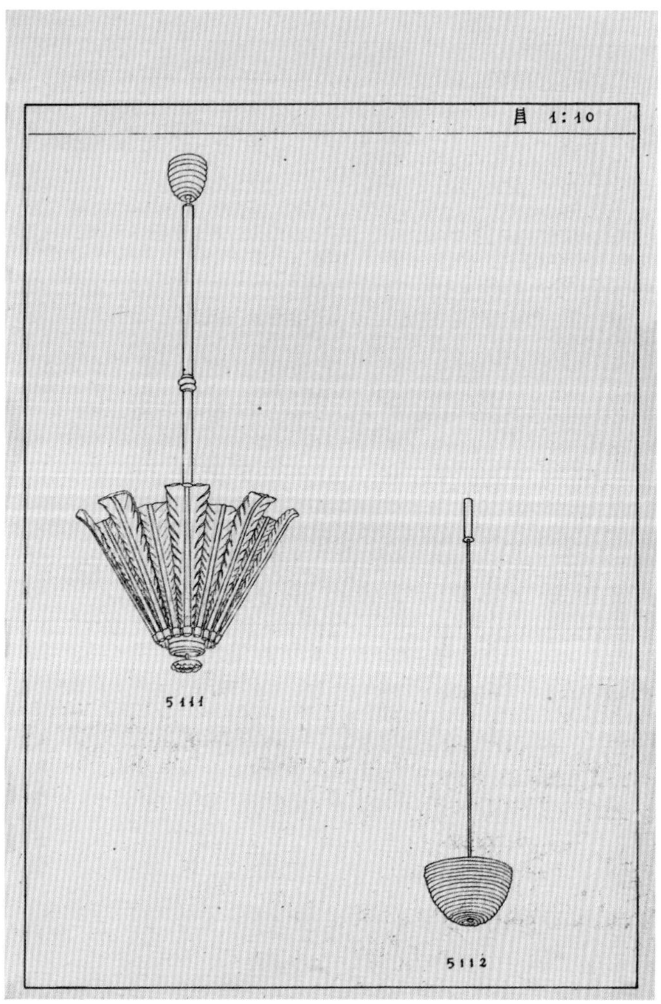
1:10
5111
5112

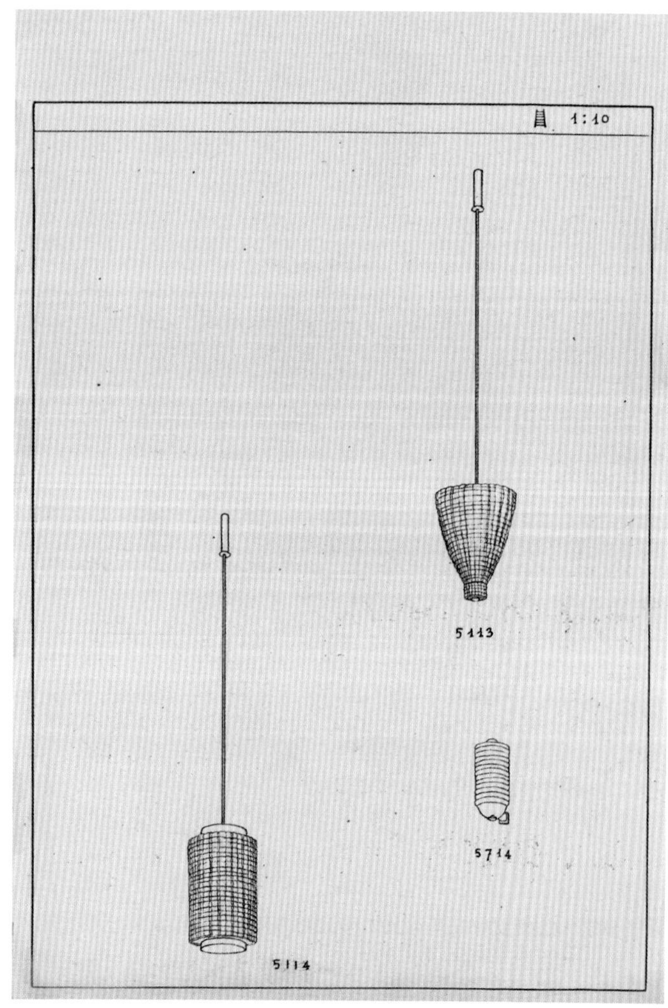
1:10
5113
5714
5114

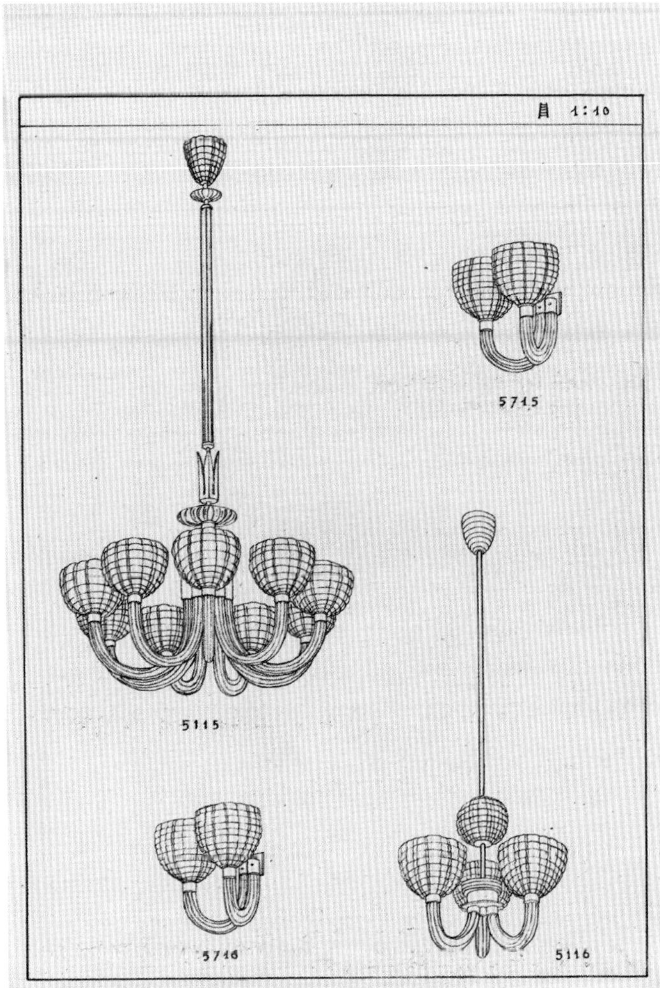
1:10
5715
5115
5716
5116

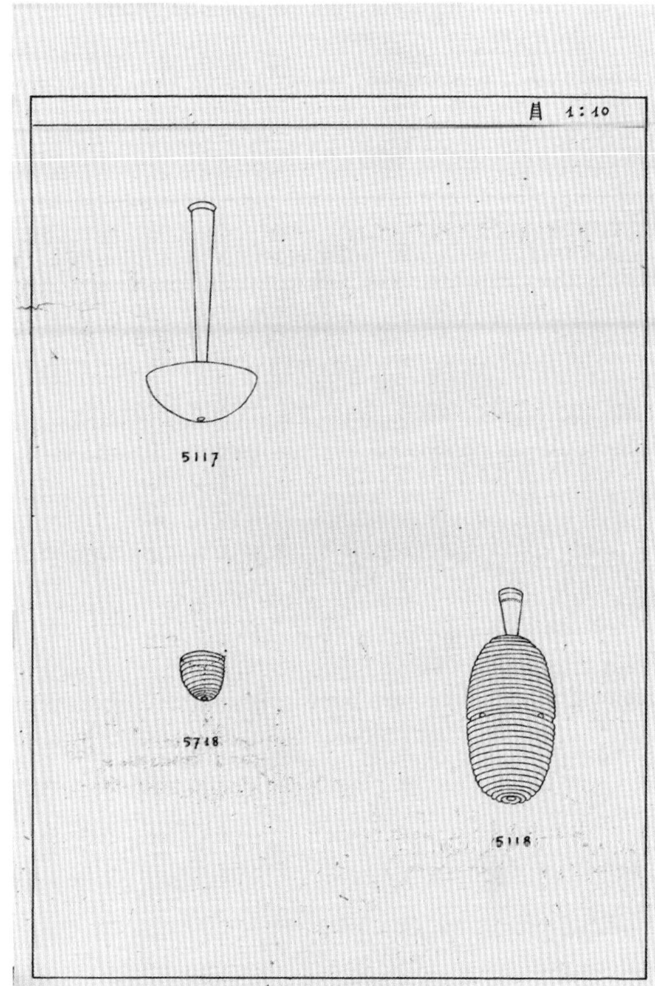
1:10
5117
5718
5118

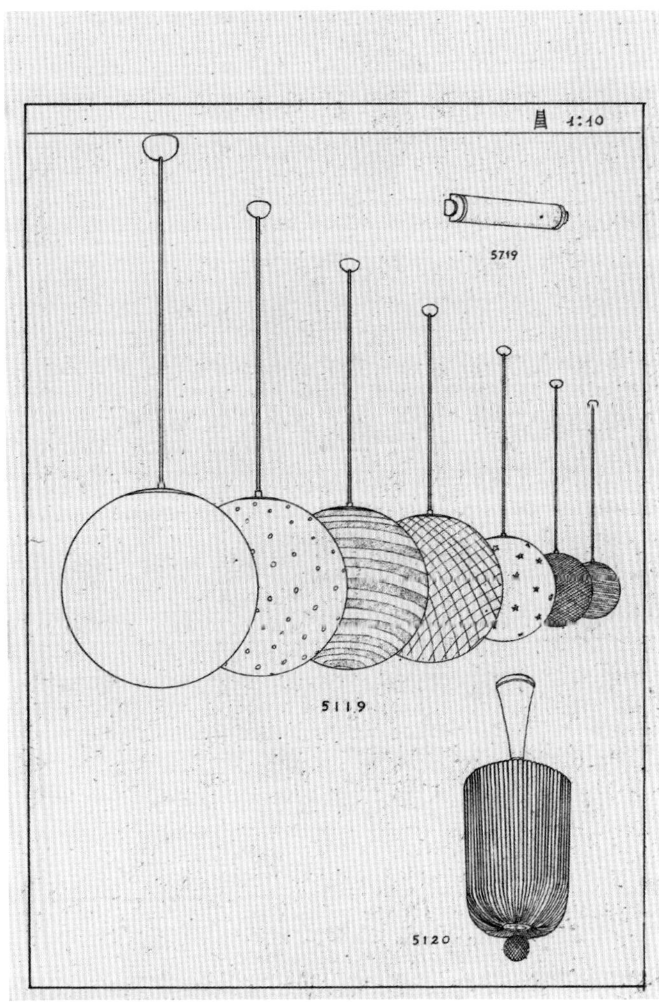
1:10
5719
5119
5120

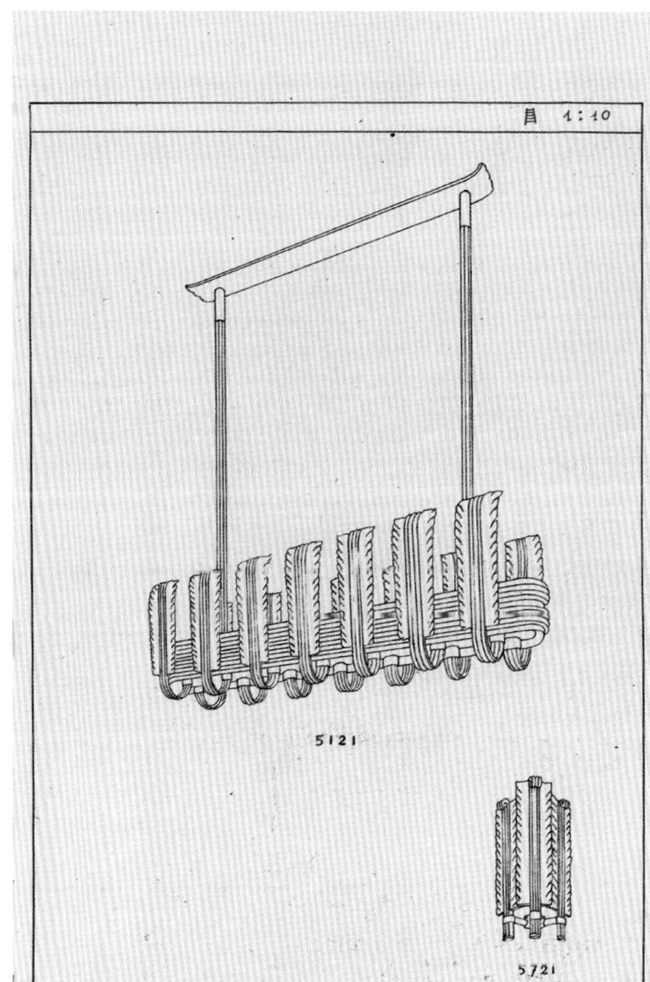
1:10
5121
5721

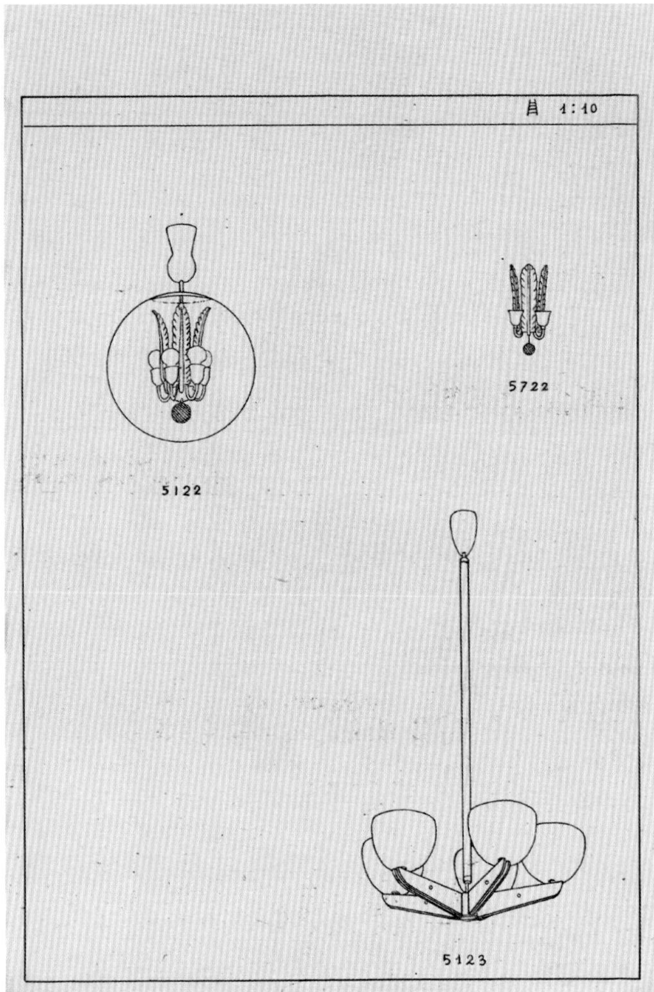
1:10
5122
5722
5123

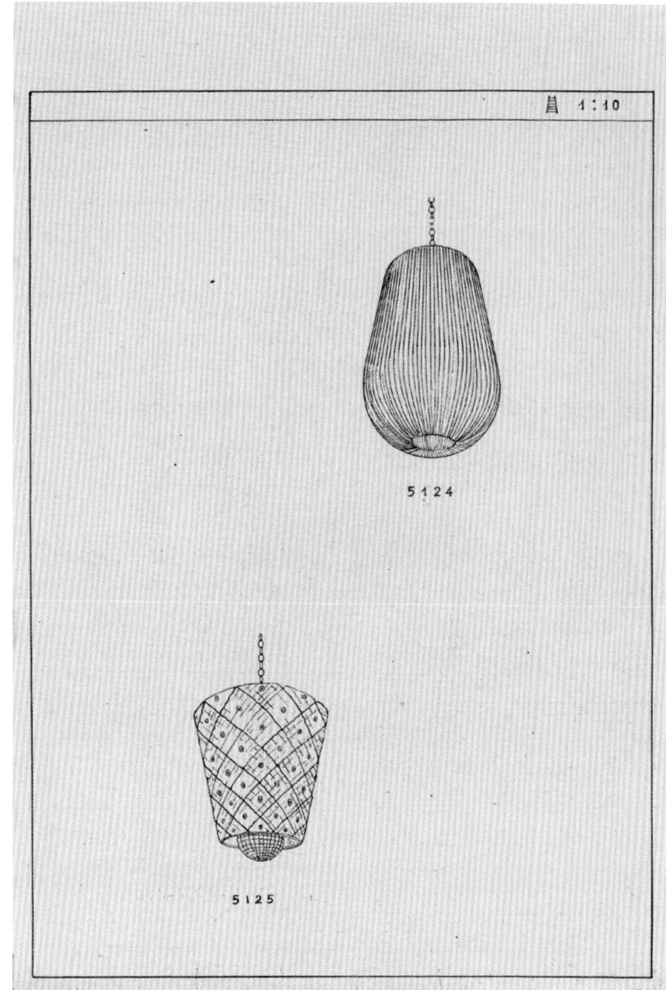
1:10
5124
5125

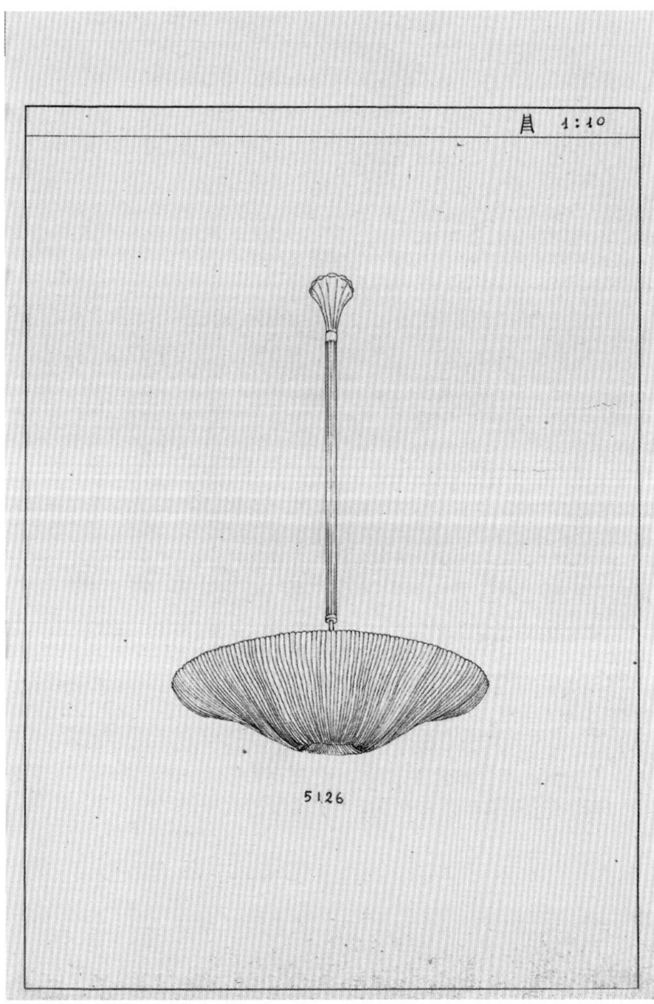
1:10
5126

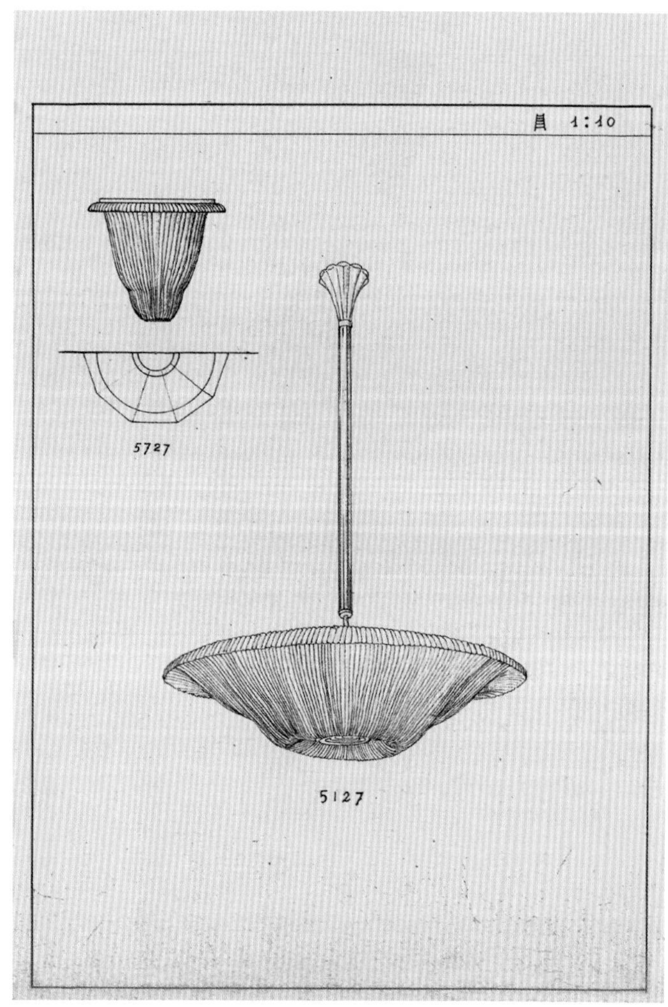
1:10
5727
5127

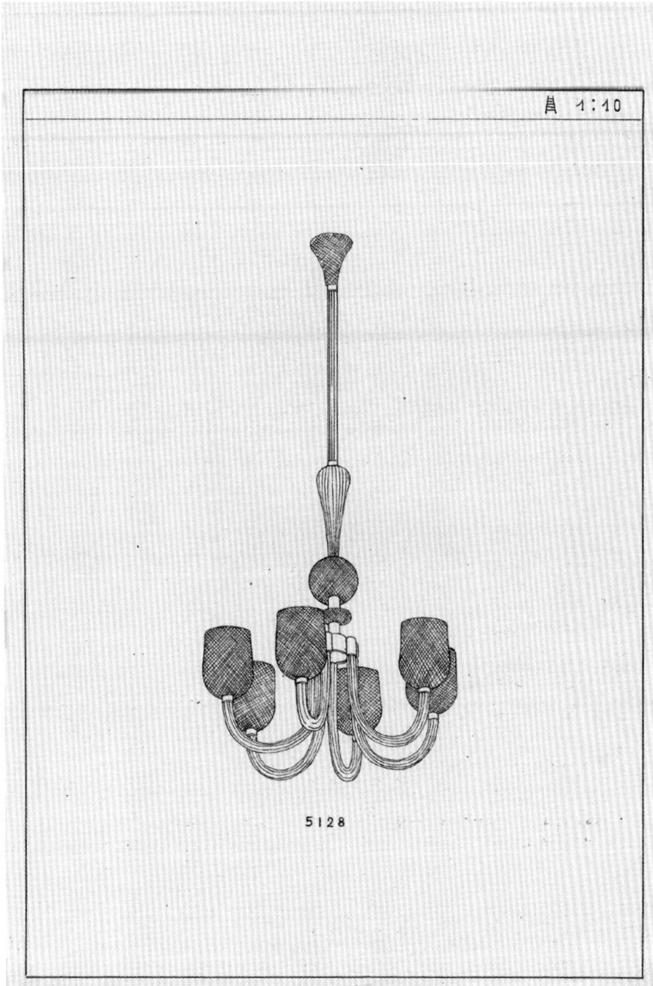
1:10
5128

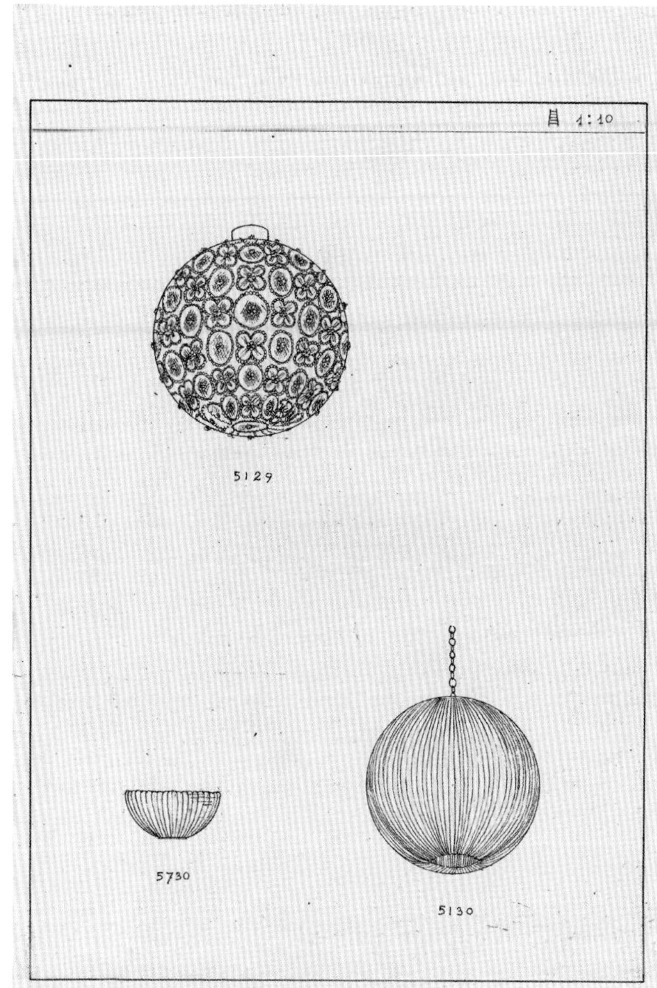
1:10
5129
5730
5130

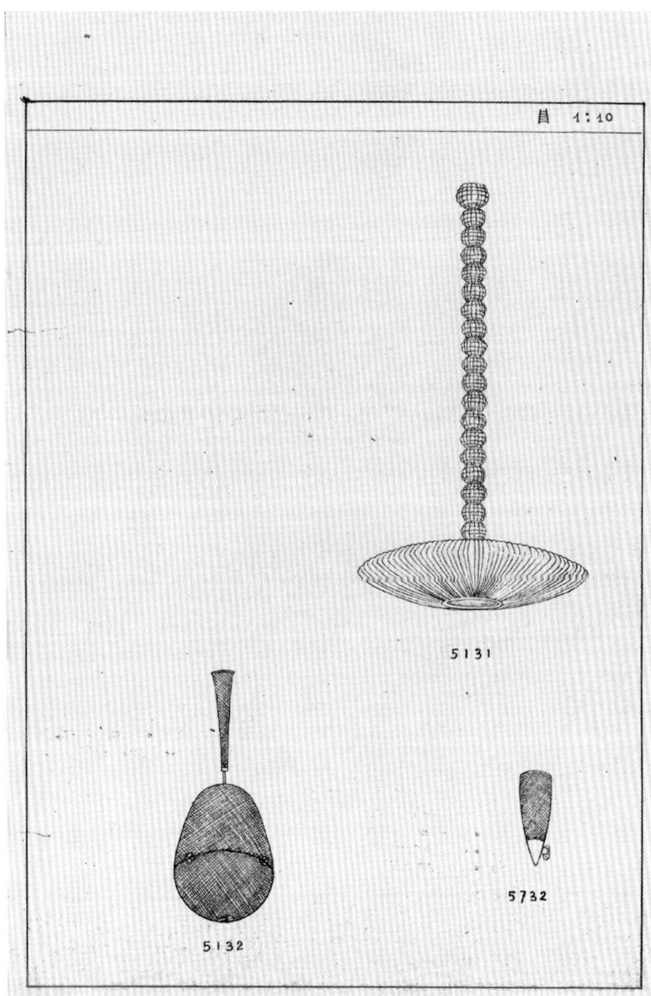
1:10
5131
5132
5732

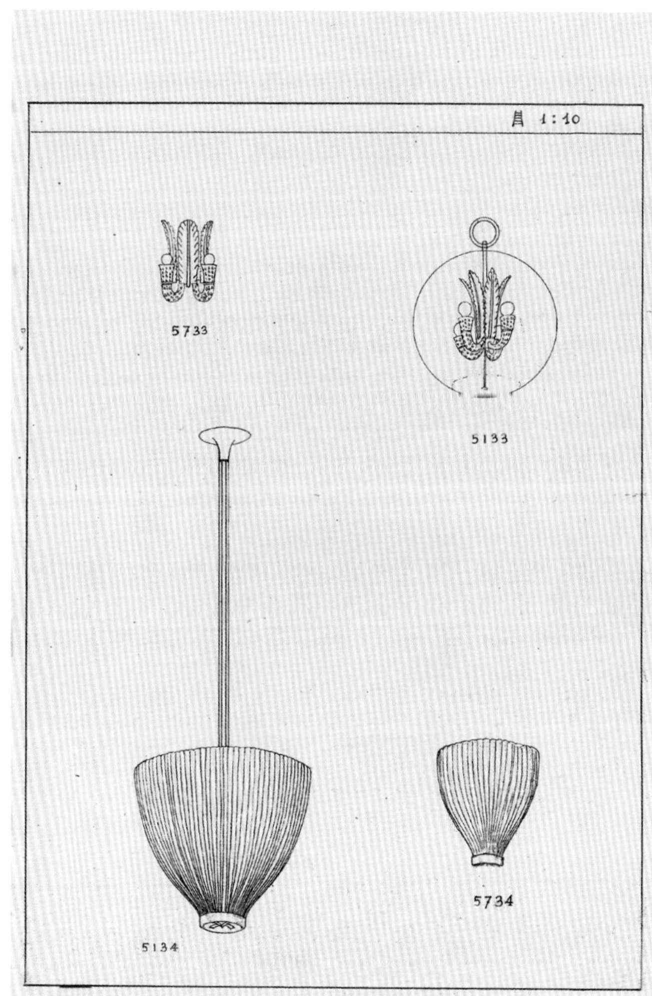
1:10
5733
5133
5134
5734

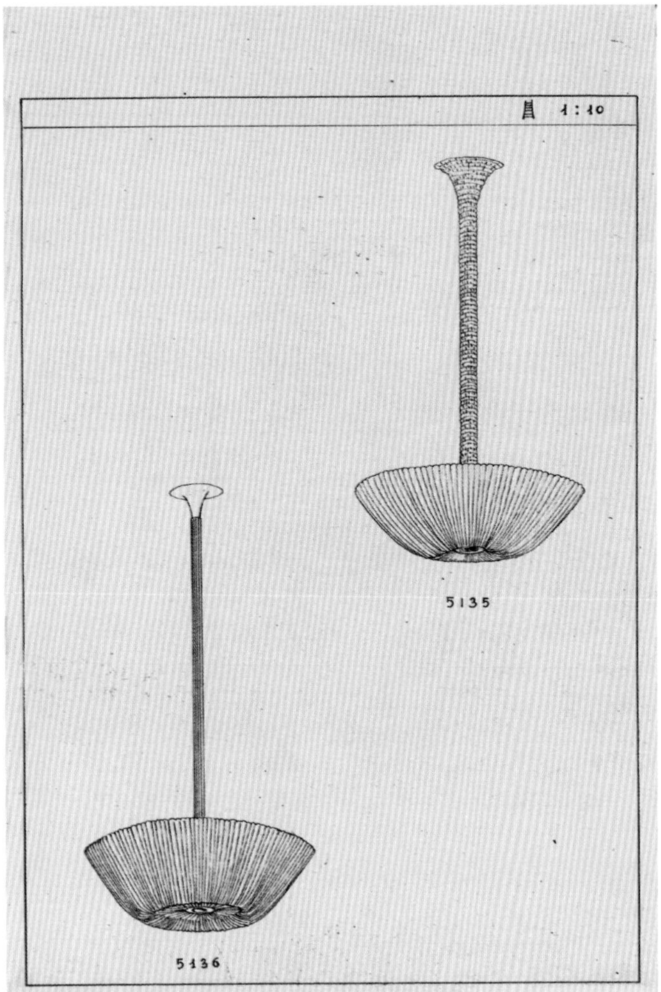
1:10
5135
5136

1:10
5137
5738
5138

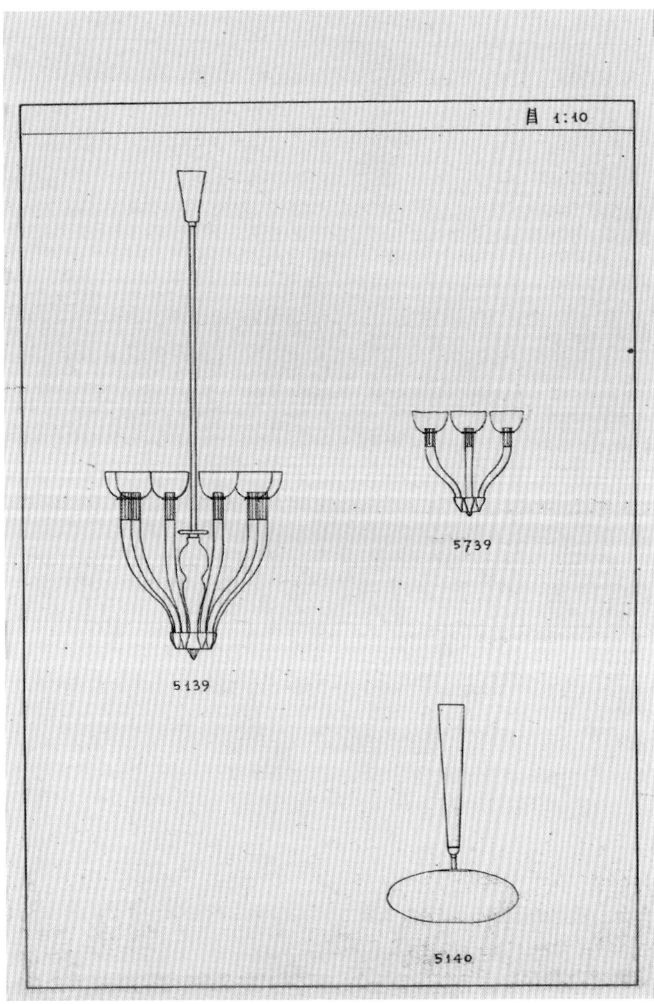
1:10
5739
5139
5140

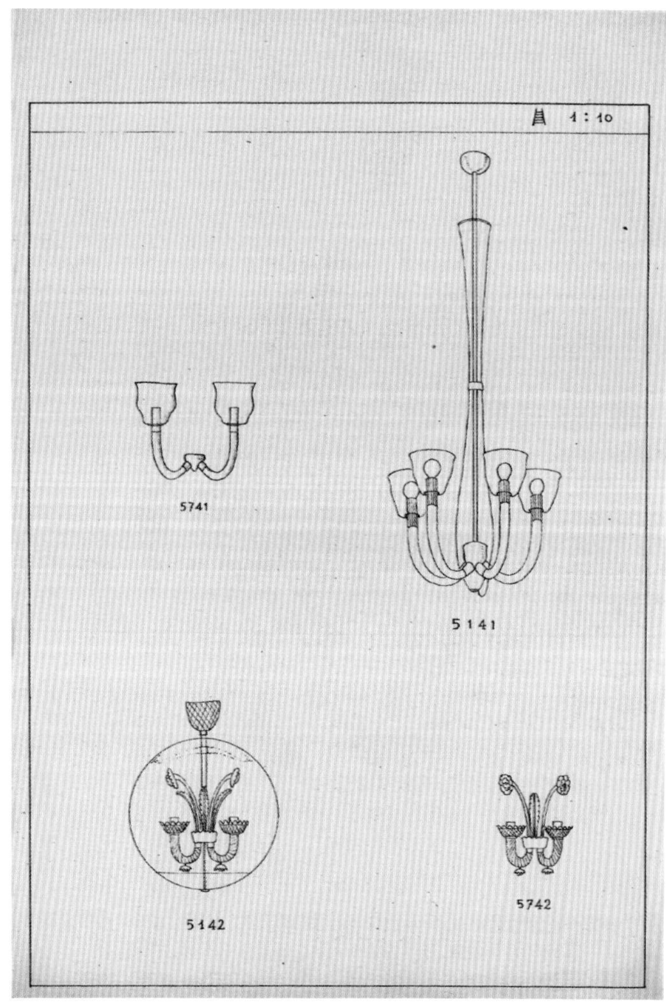
1:10
5741
5141
5142
5742

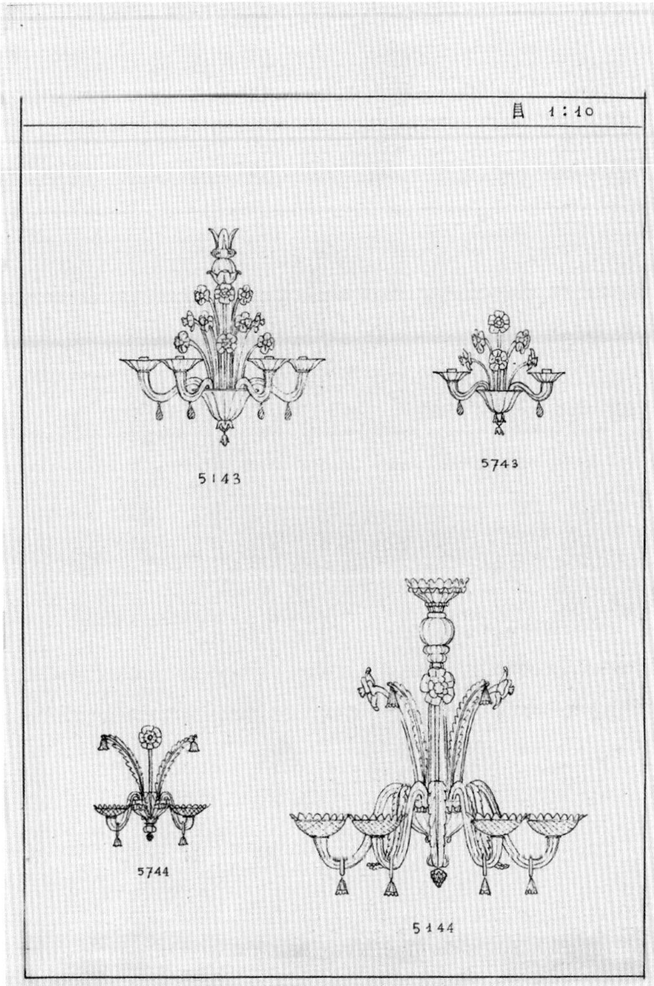
1:10
5143
5743
5744
5144

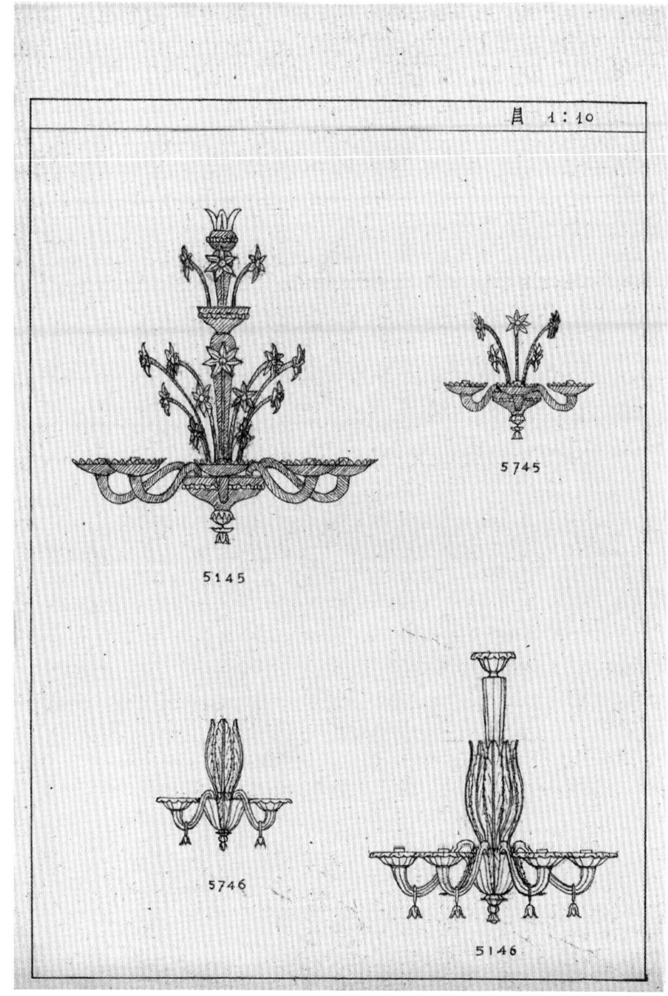
1:10
5145
5745
5746
5146

1:10
5147
5747
5748
5148

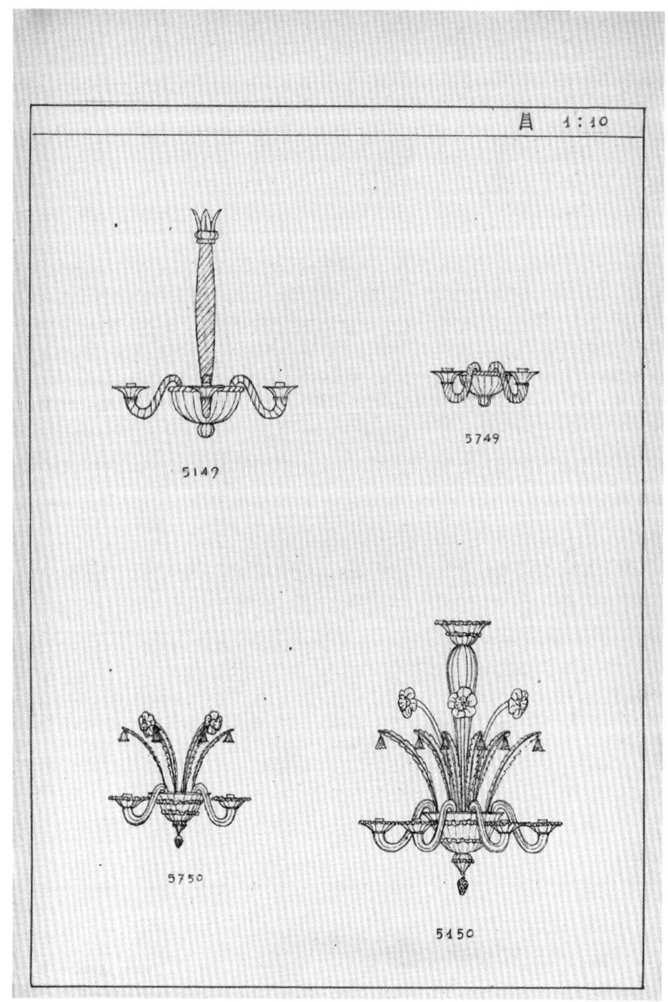
1:10
5149
5749
5750
5150

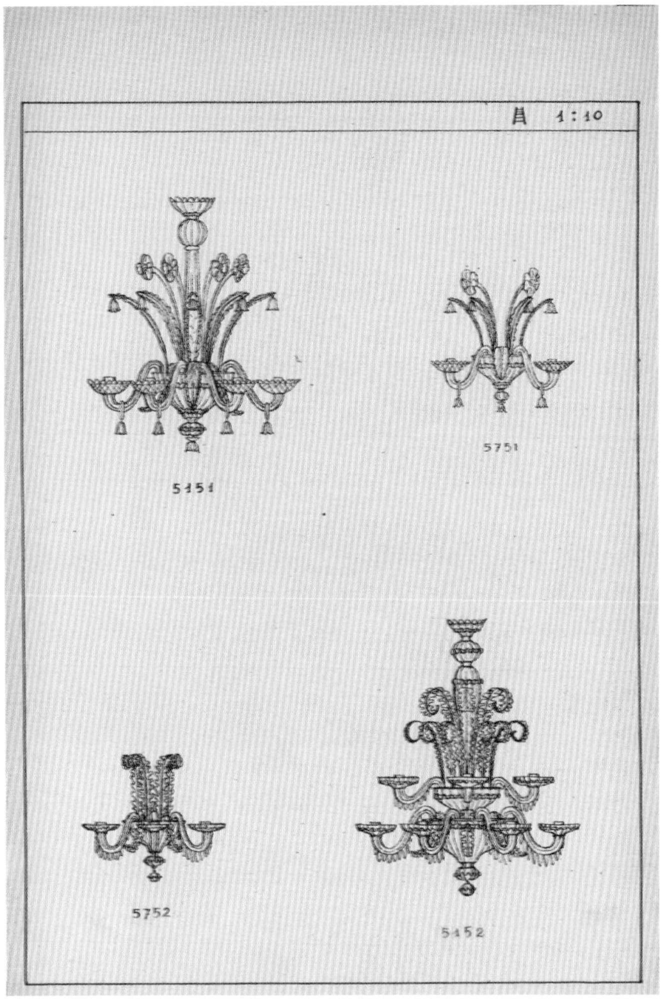
1:10
5151
5751
5752
5152

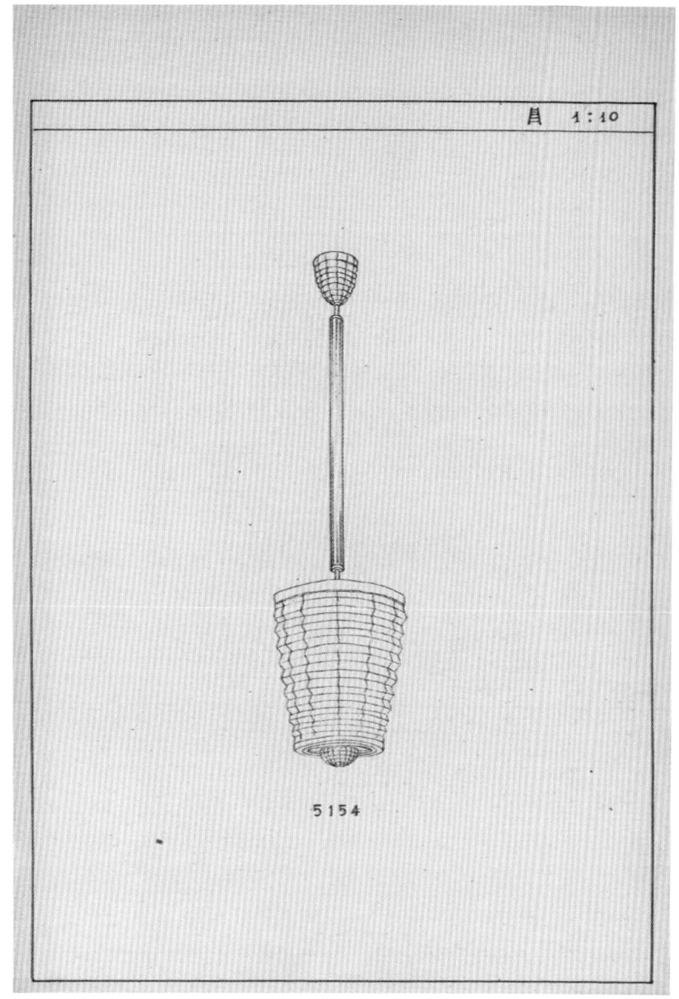
1:10
5154

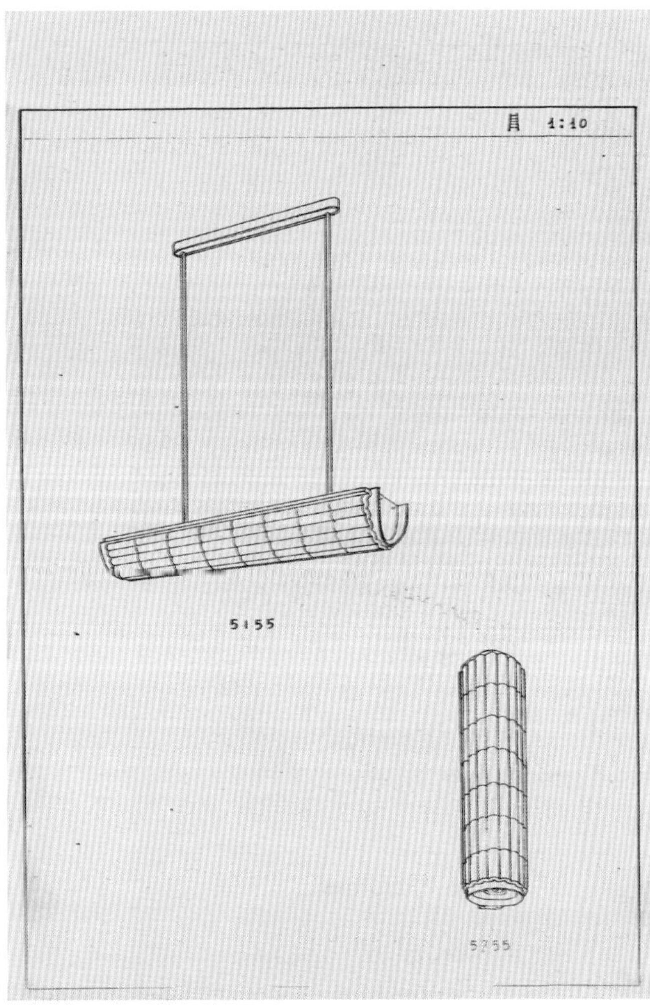
1:10
5155
5755

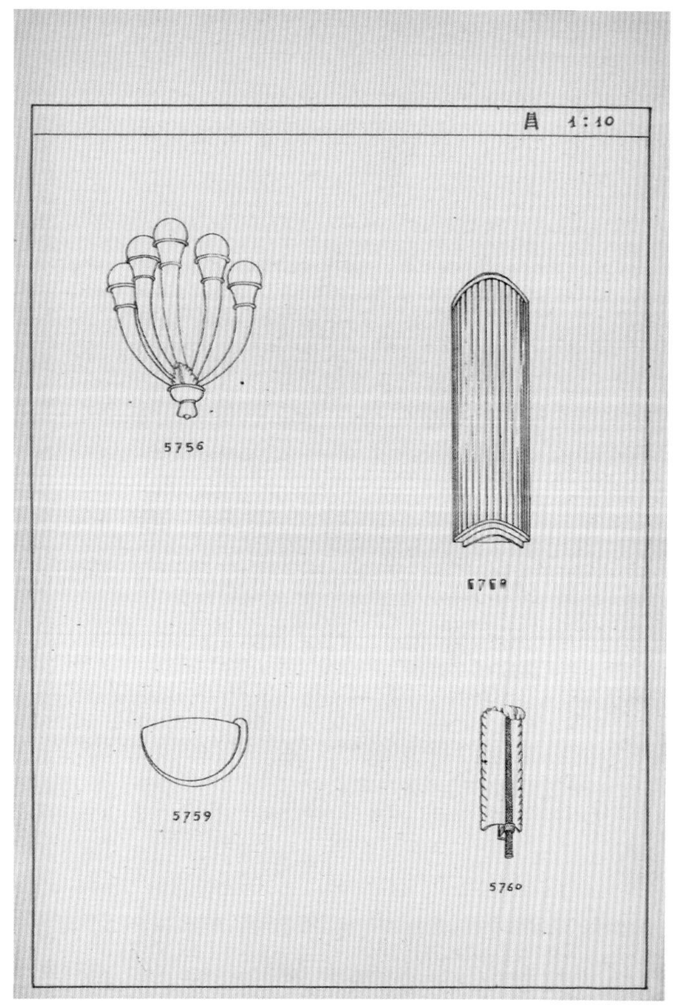
1:10
5756
5758
5759
5760

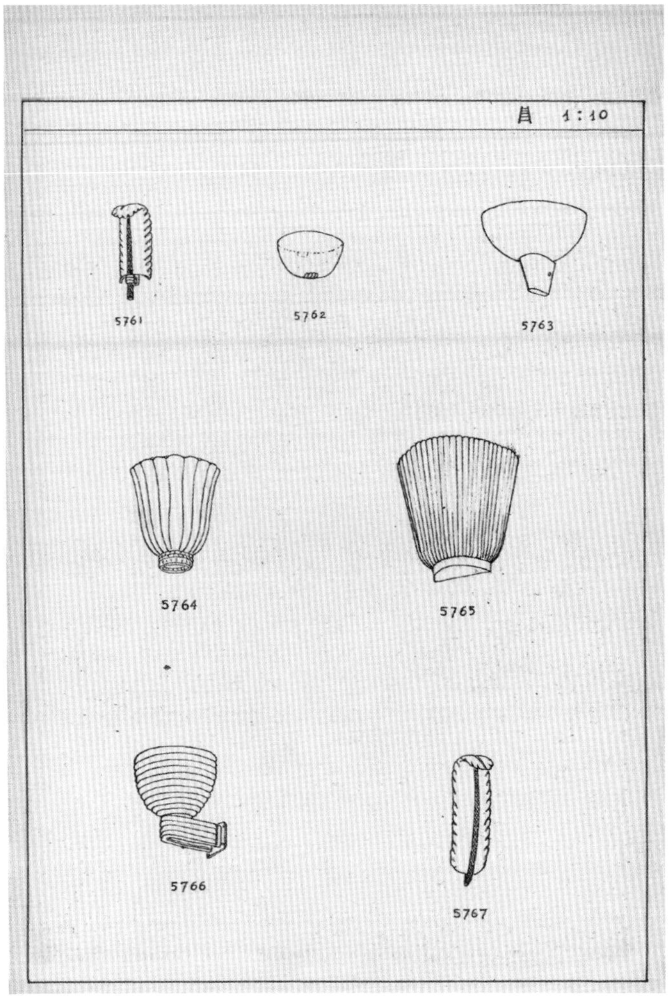
1:10
5761
5762
5763
5764
5765
5766
5767

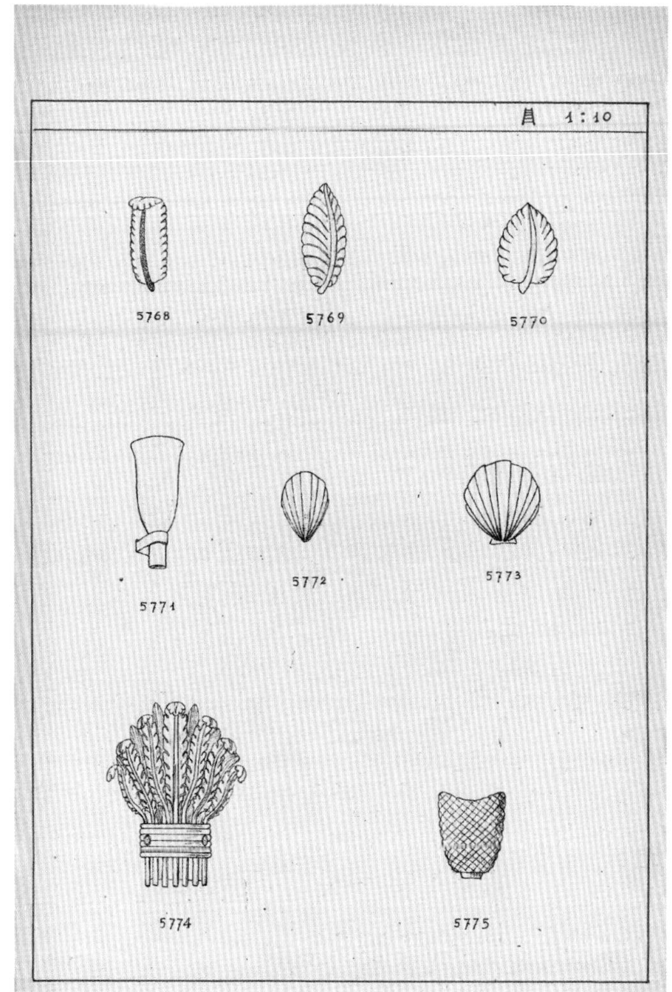
1:10
5768
5769
5770
5771
5772
5773
5774
5775

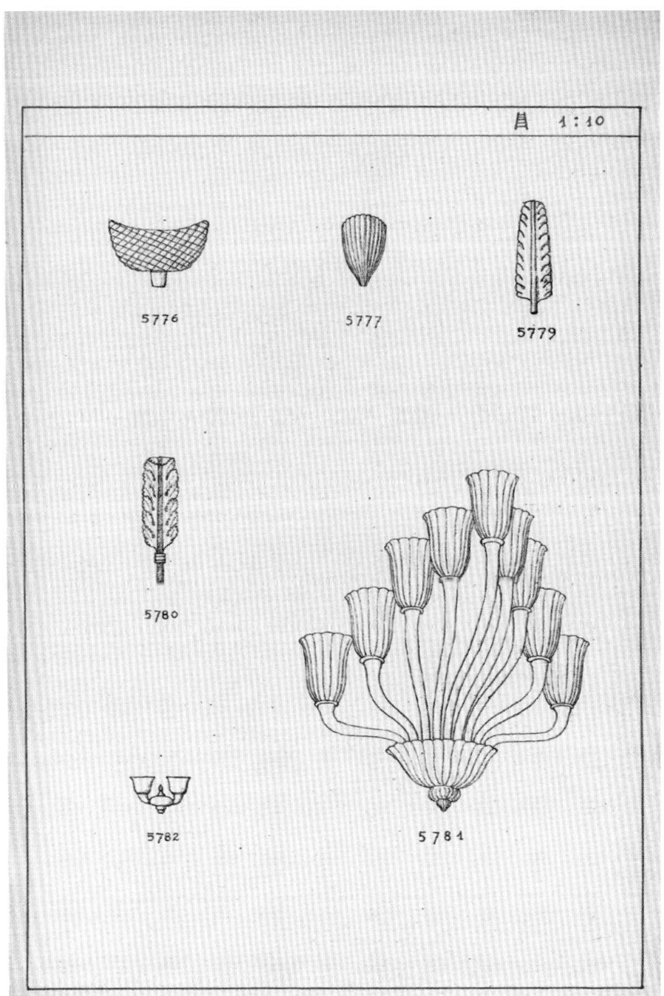
1:10
5776
5777
5779
5780
5782
5781

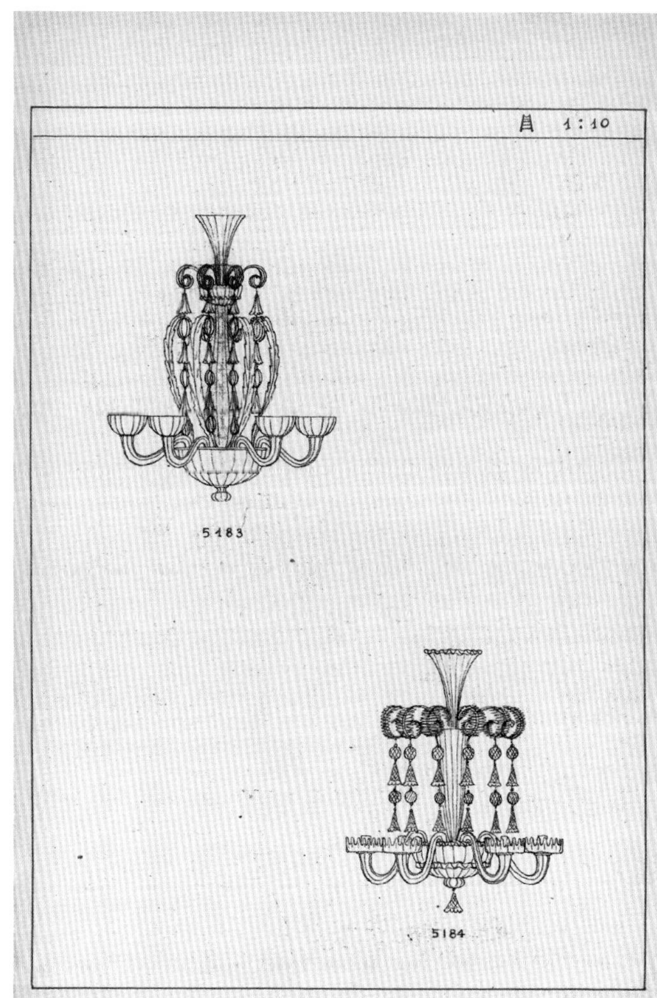
1:10
5183
5184

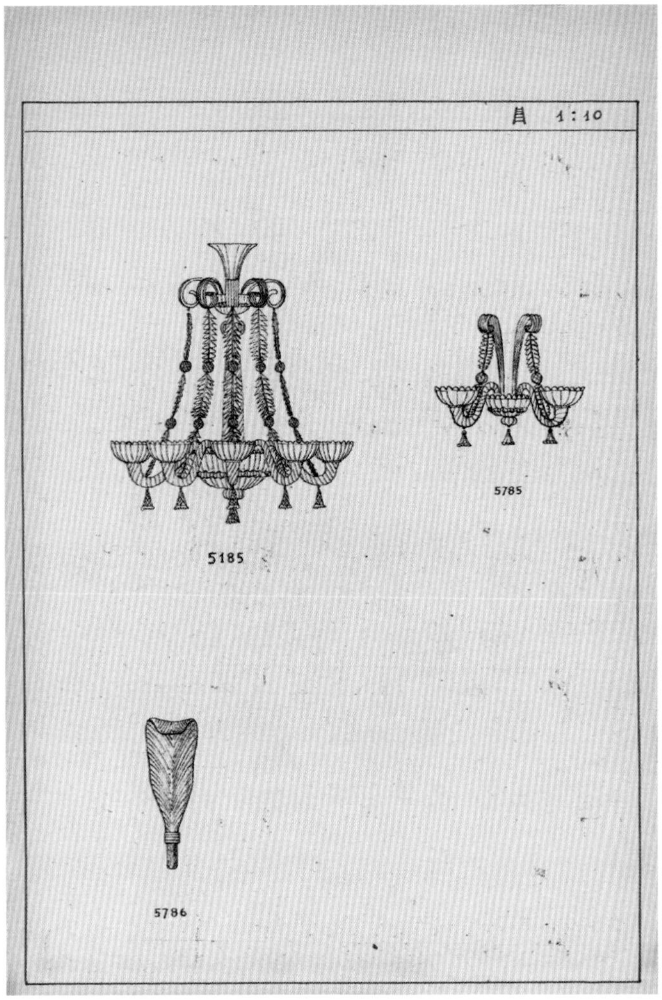
1:10
5185
5785
5786

1:10
5188
5788

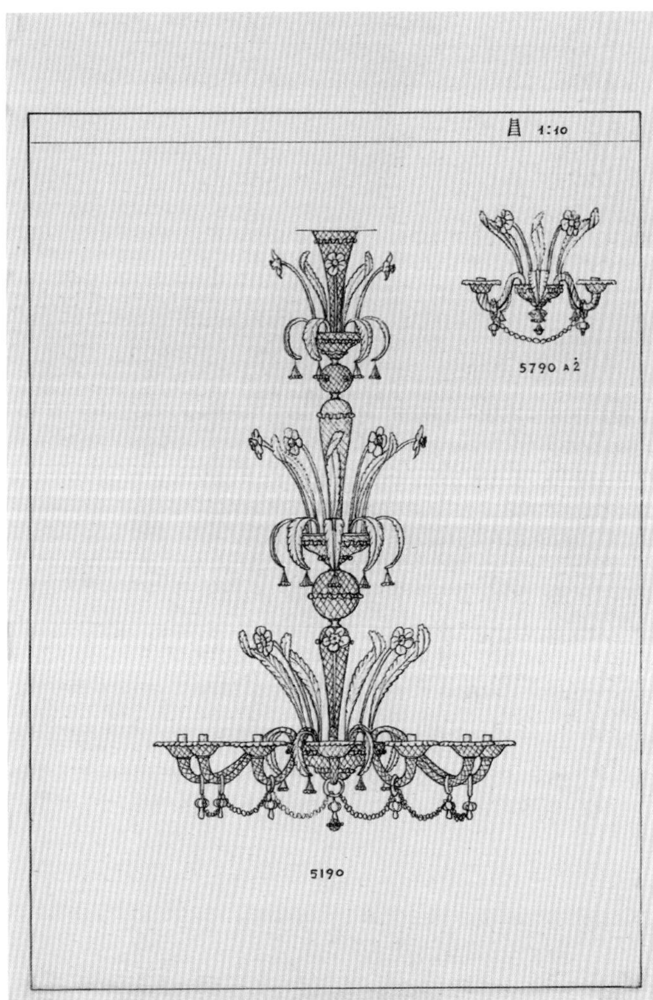
1:10
5190
5790 A 2

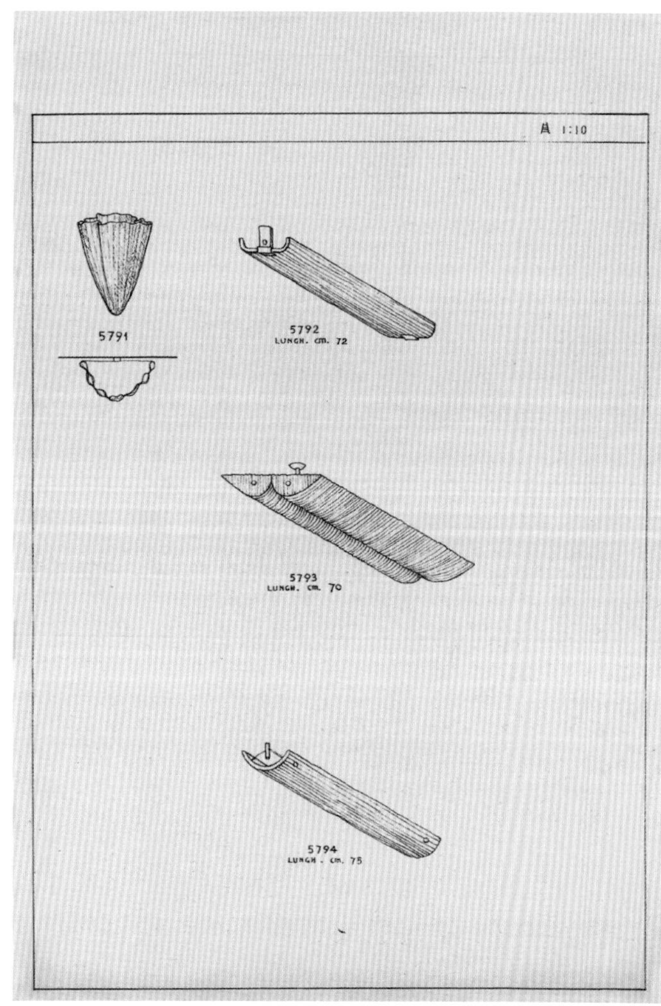
1:10
5791
5792
LUNGH. CM. 72
5793
LUNGH. CM. 70
5794
LUNGH. CM. 75

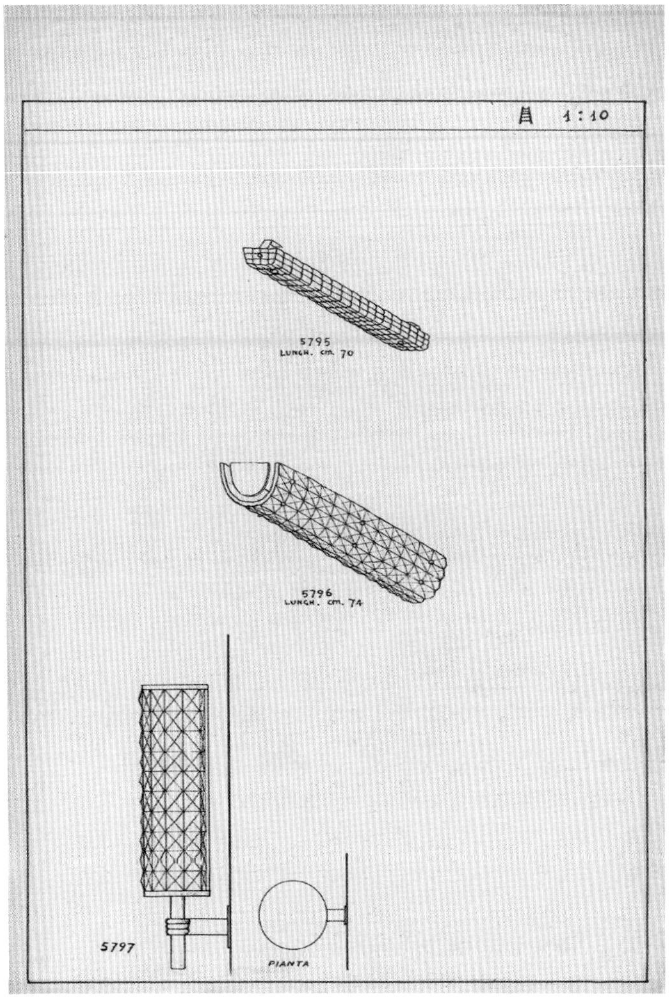
1:10
5795
LUNGH. cm. 70
5796
LUNGH. cm. 74
5797
PIANTA

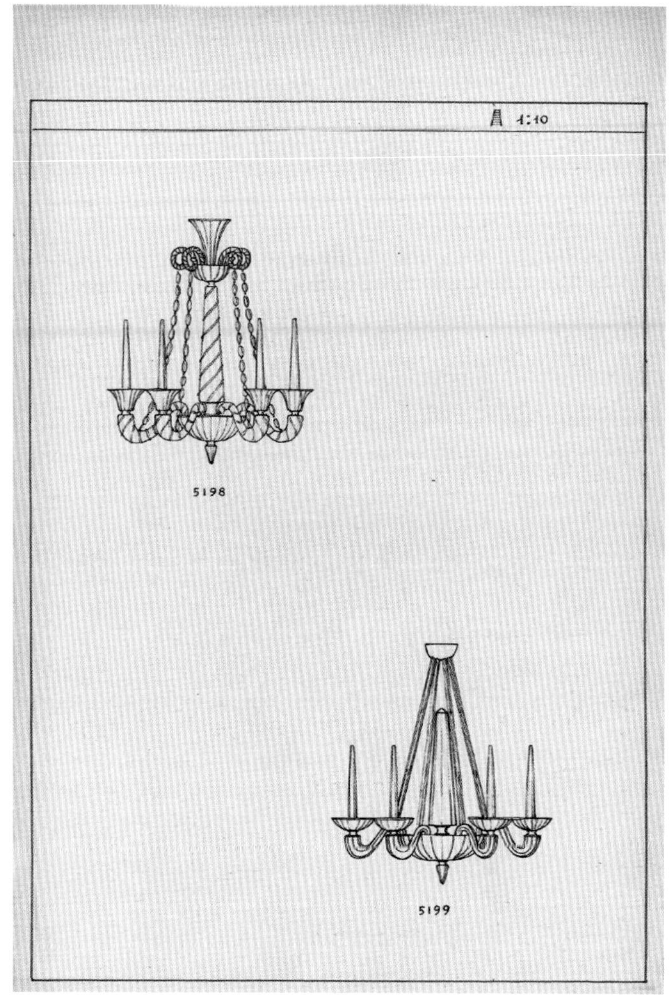
1:10
5198
5199

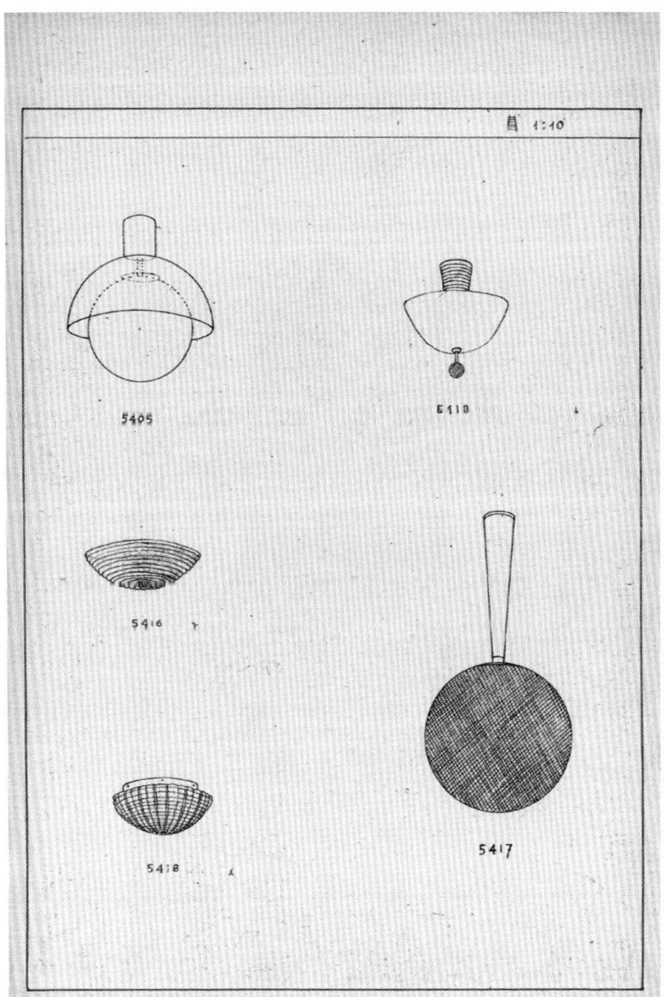
1:10
5405
5416
5418
5417

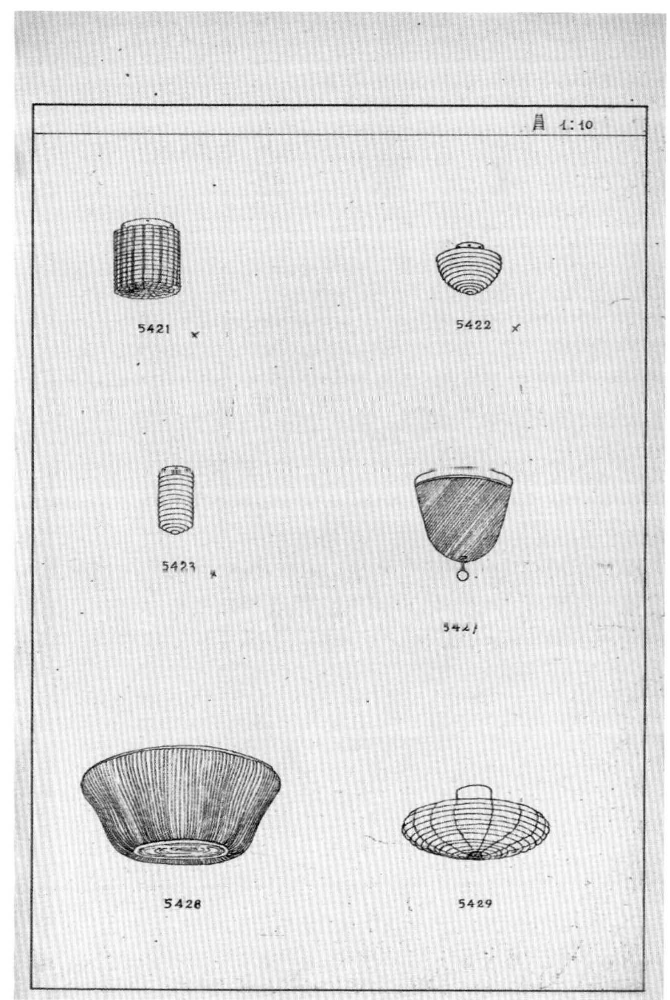
1:10
5421
5422
5423
5428
5429

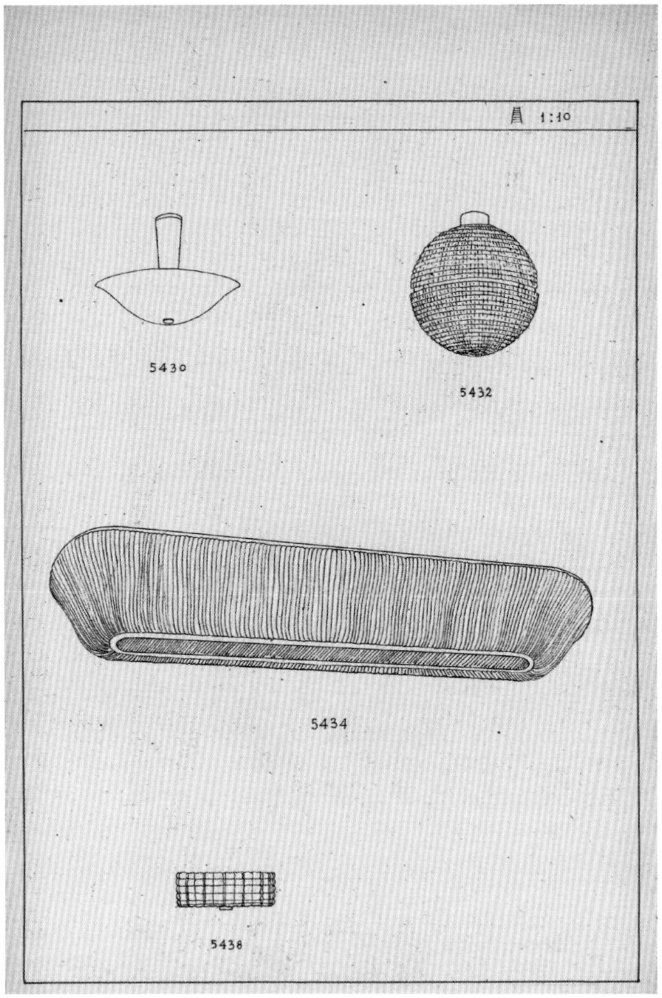
1:10
5430
5432
5434
5438

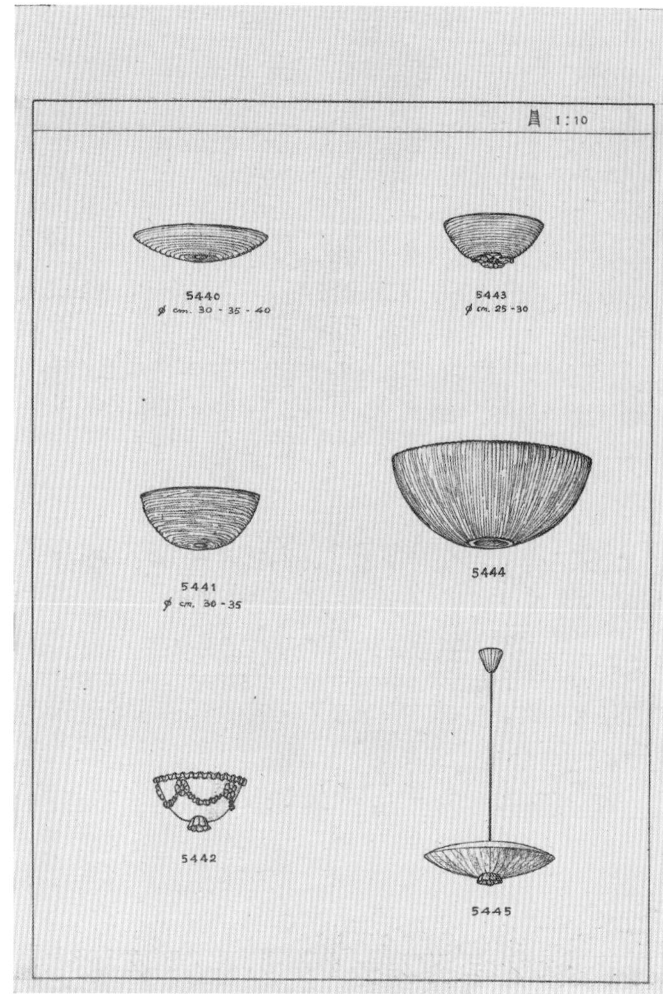
1:10
5440
ø cm. 30 - 35 - 40
5443
ø cm. 25 - 30
5441
ø cm. 30 - 35
5444
5442
5445

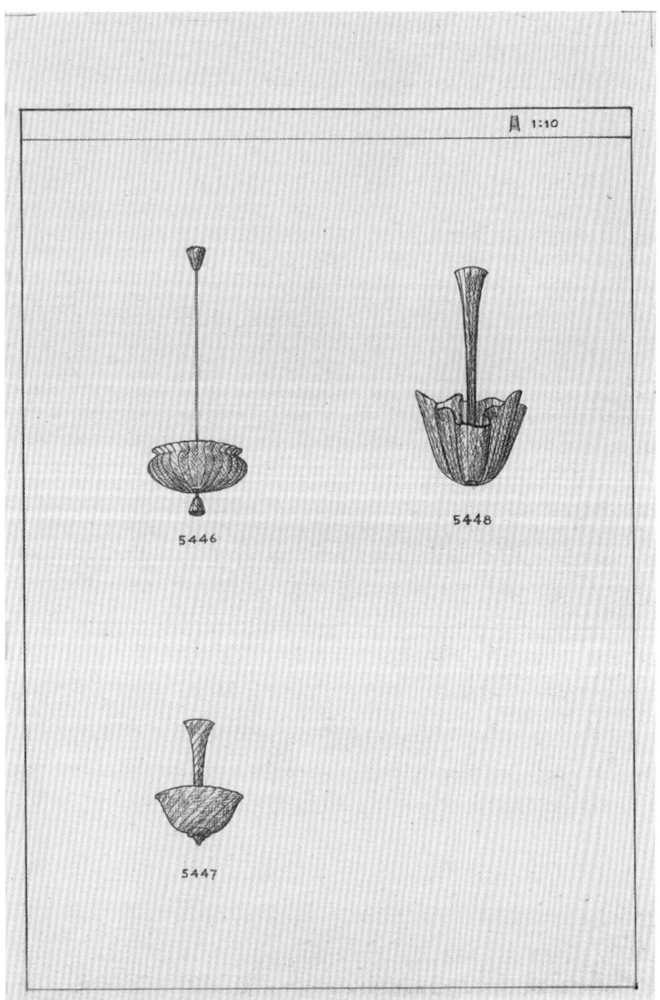
1:10
5446
5448
5447

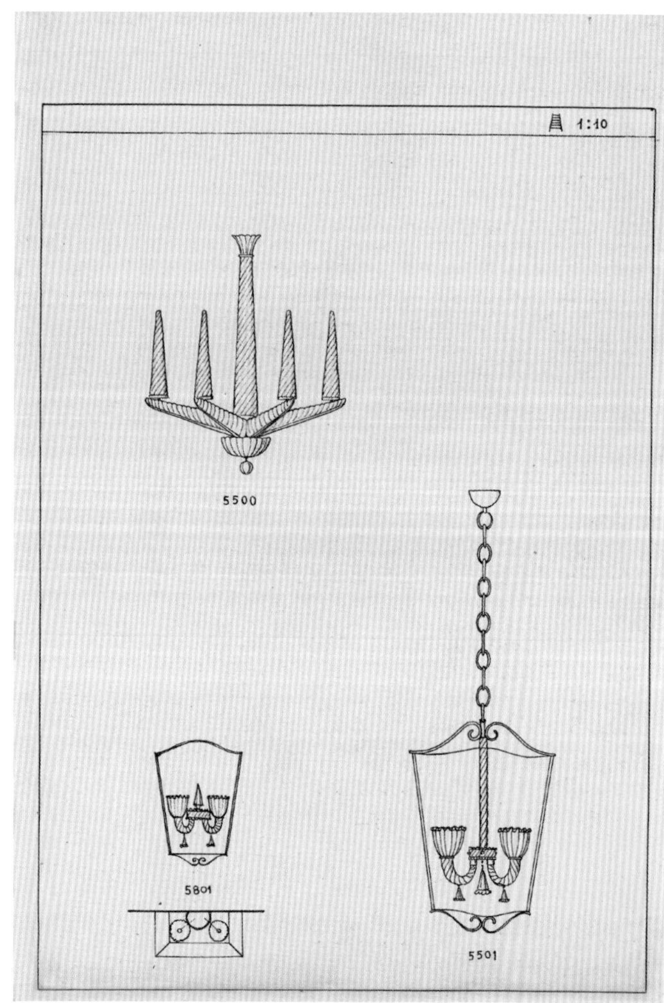
1:10
5500
5801
5501

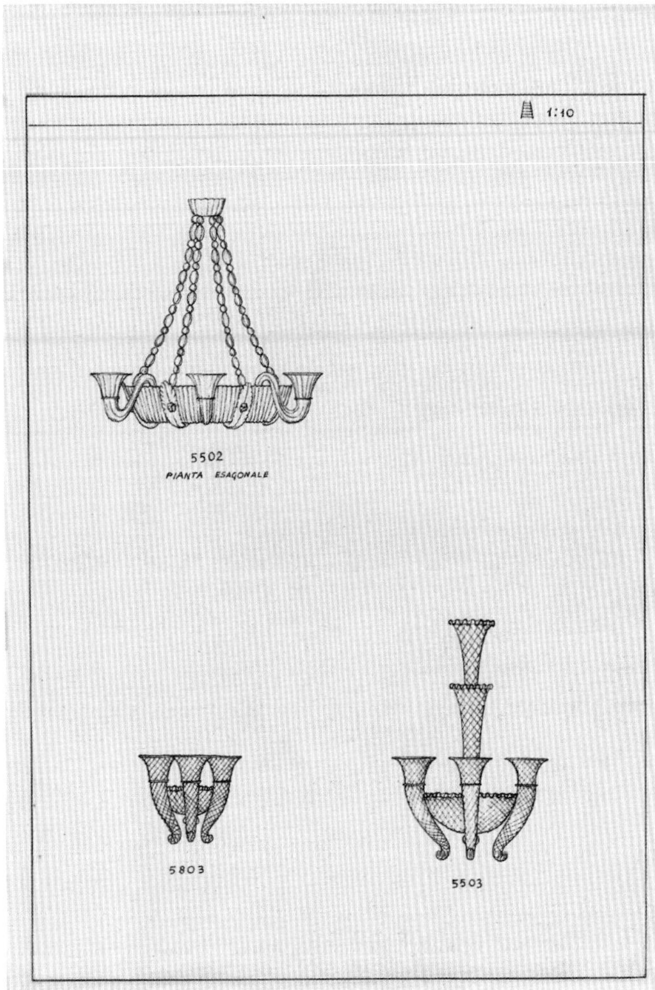
1:10
5502
PIANTA ESAGONALE
5803
5503

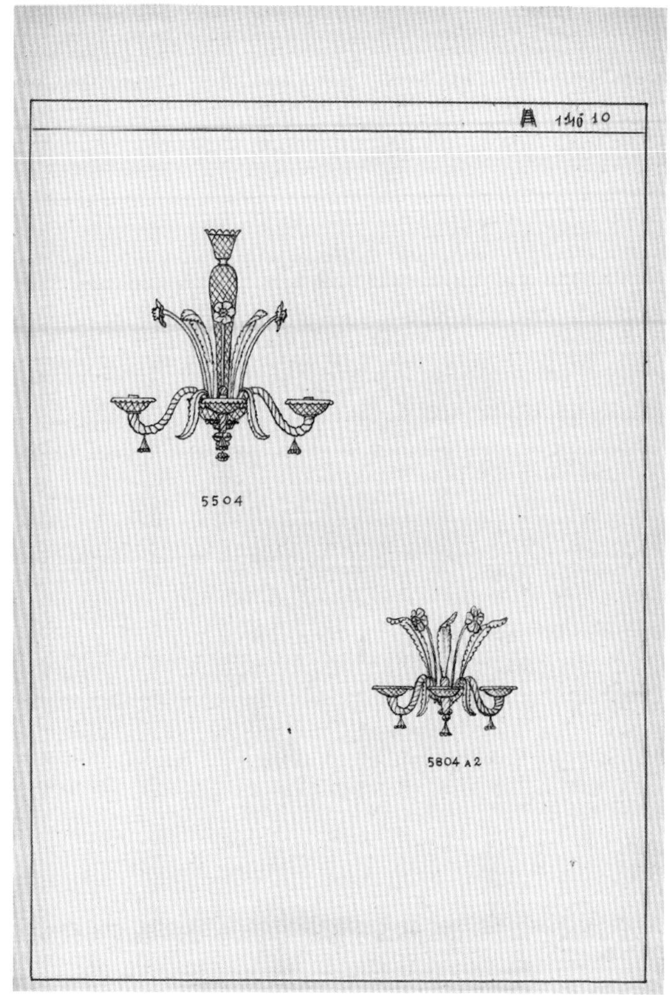
1:10
5504
5804 A 2

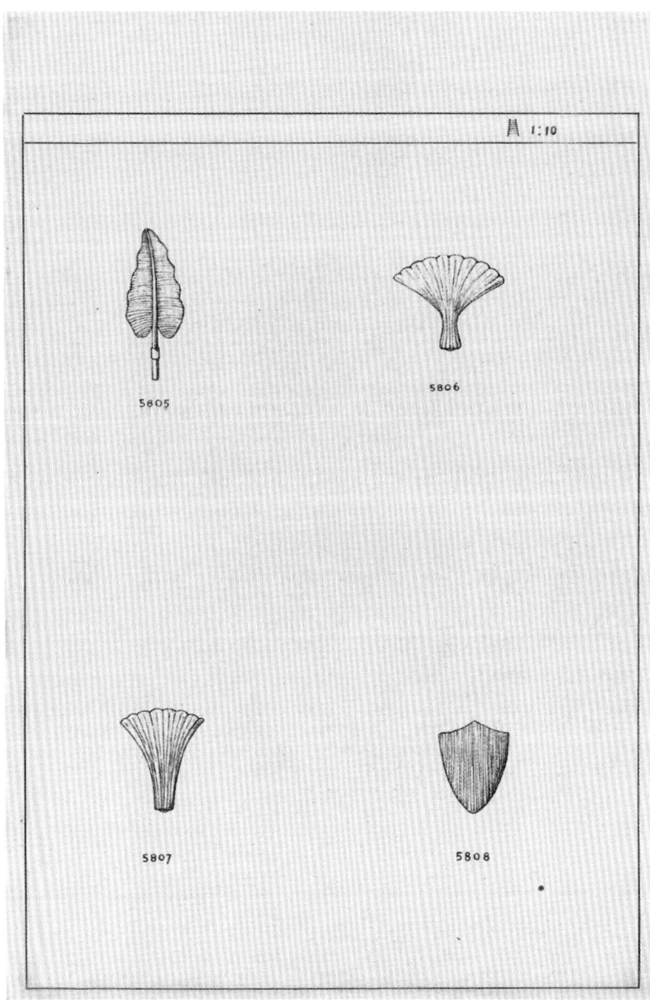
1:10
5805
5806
5807
5808

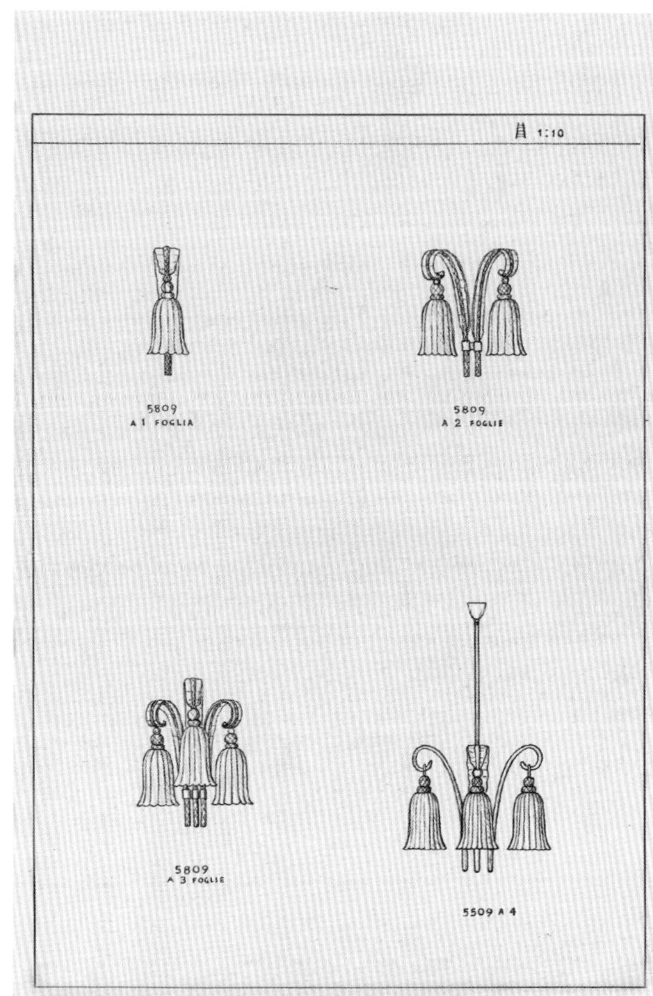
1:10
5809
A 1 FOGLIA
5809
A 2 FOGLIE
5809
A 3 FOGLIE
5509 A 4

1:10
5513 A 6
5813 A 2
5814 A 2
5514 A 6

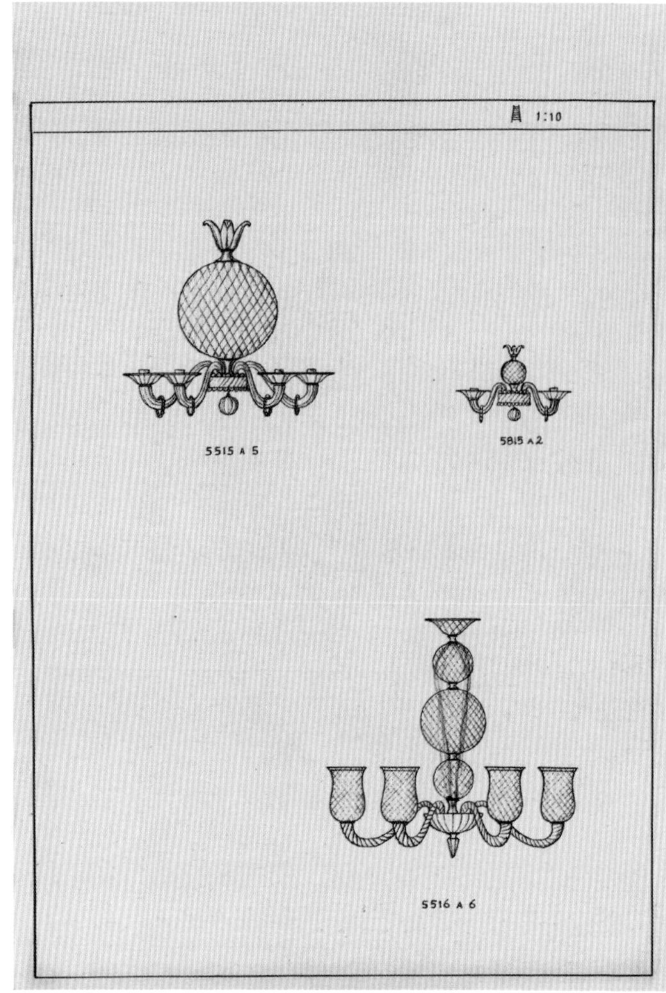
1:10
5515 A 5
5815 A 2
5516 A 6

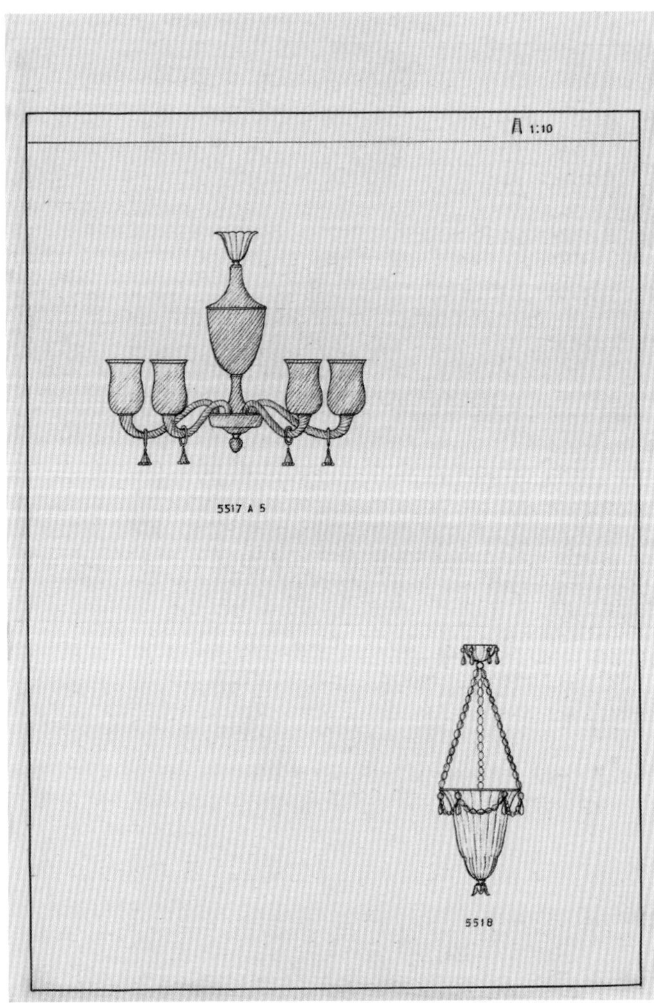
1:10
5517 A 5
5518

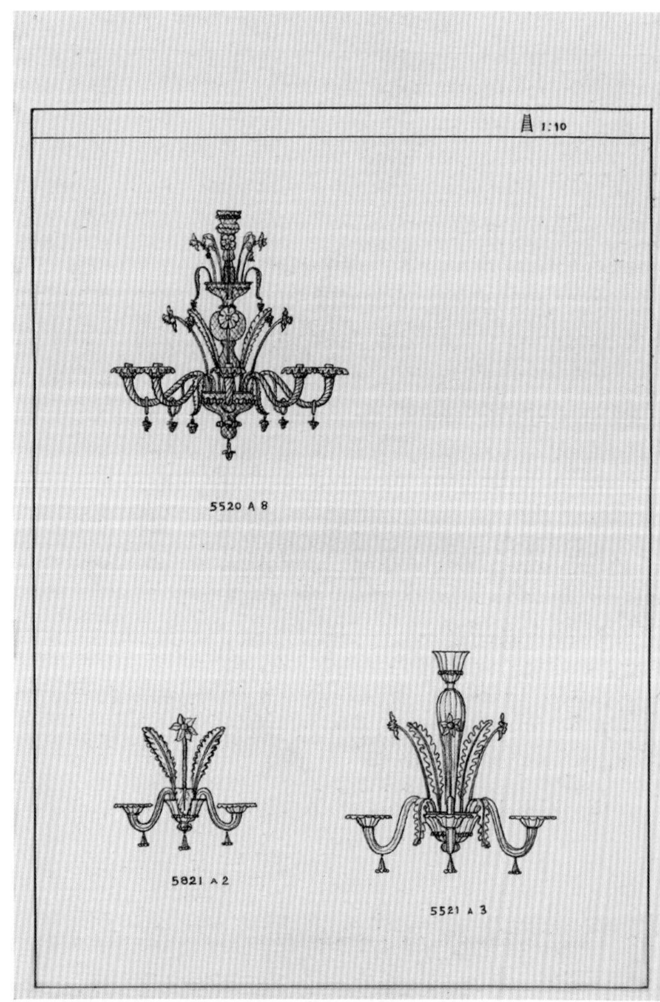
1:10
5520 A 8
5821 A 2
5521 A 3

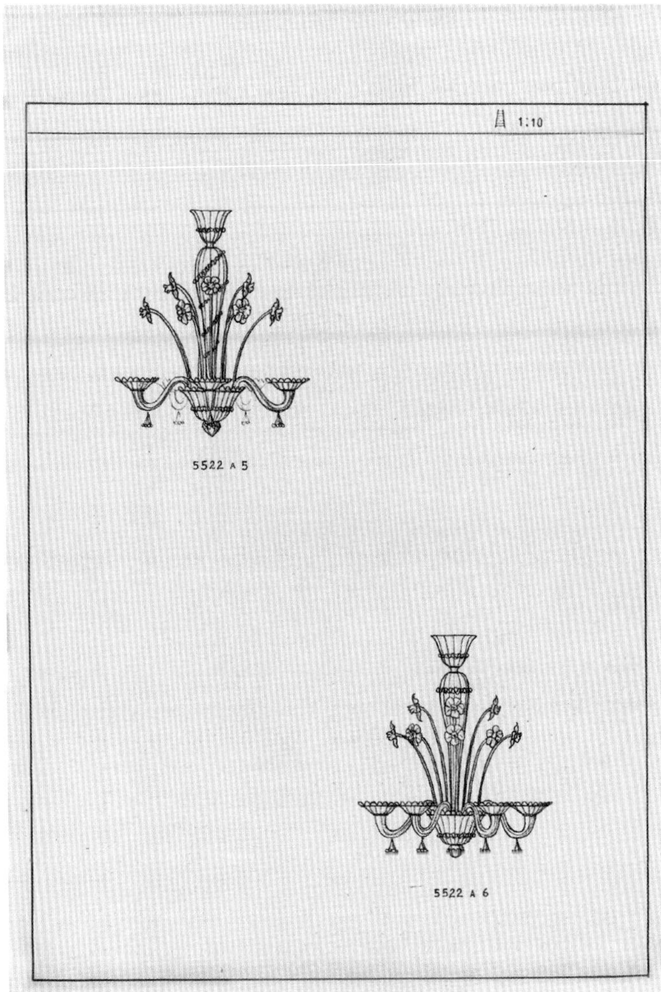

1:10
5522 A 5
5522 A 6

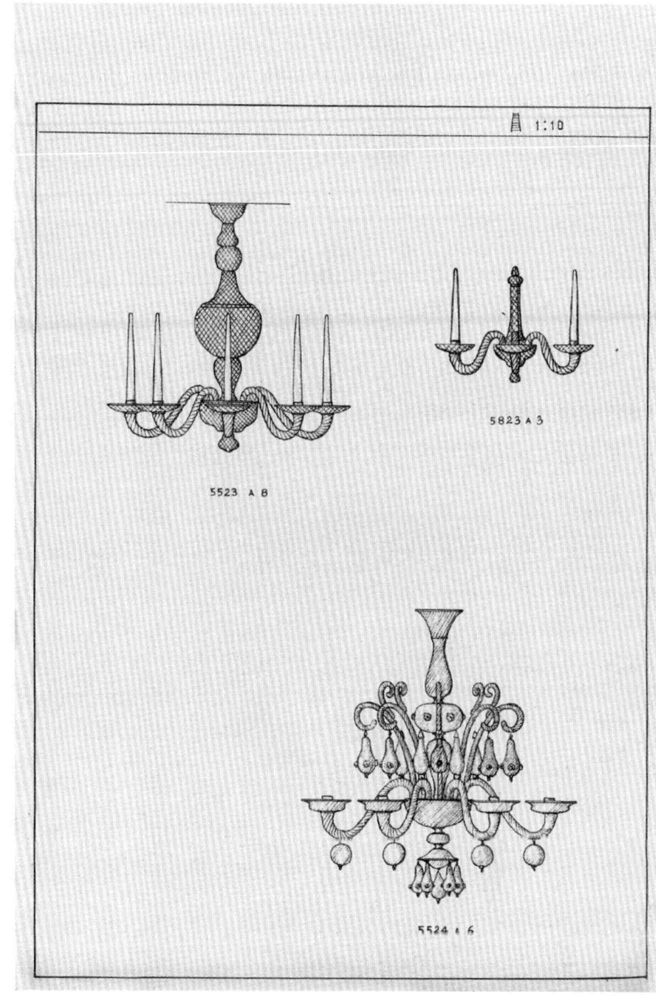

1:10
5523 A 8
5823 A 3
5524 A 6

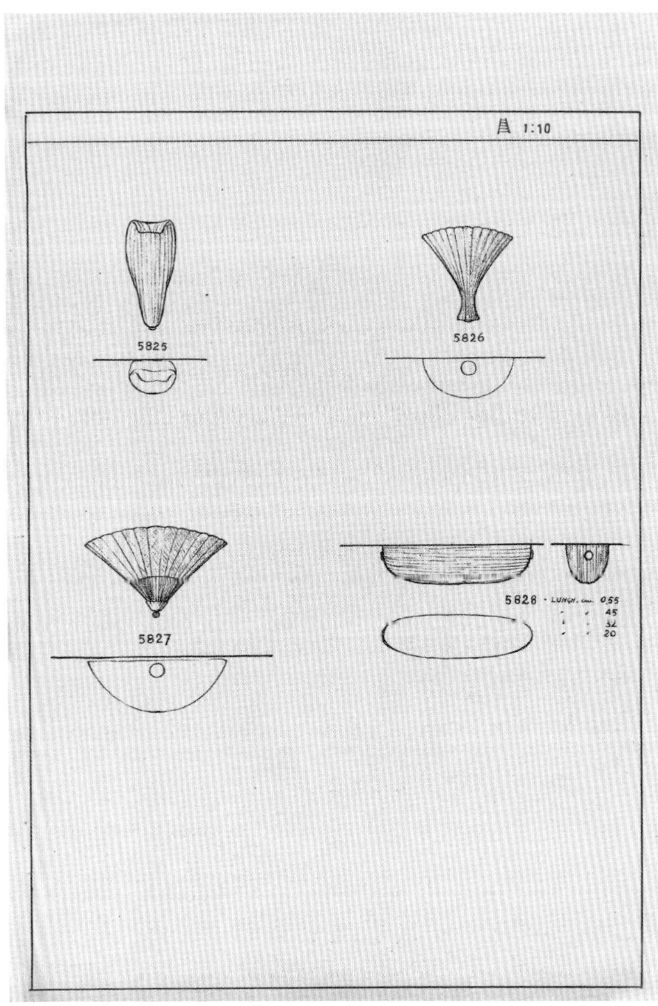

1:10
5825
5826
5827
5828 - LUNGH. cm. 0,55
45
32
20

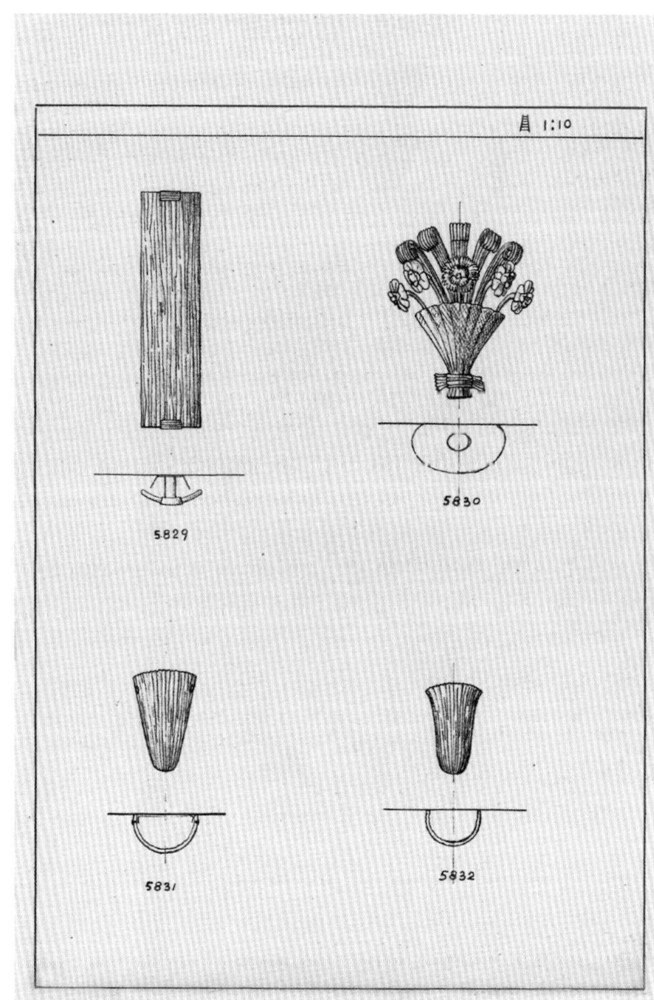

1:10
5829
5830
5831
5832

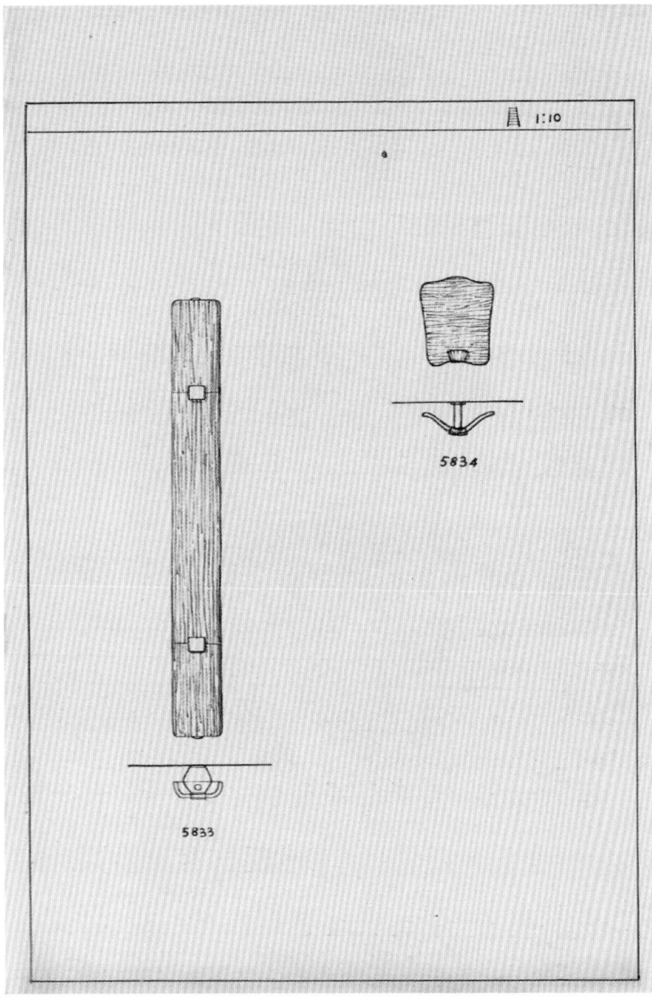
1:10
5834
5833

1:10
5535 A 20

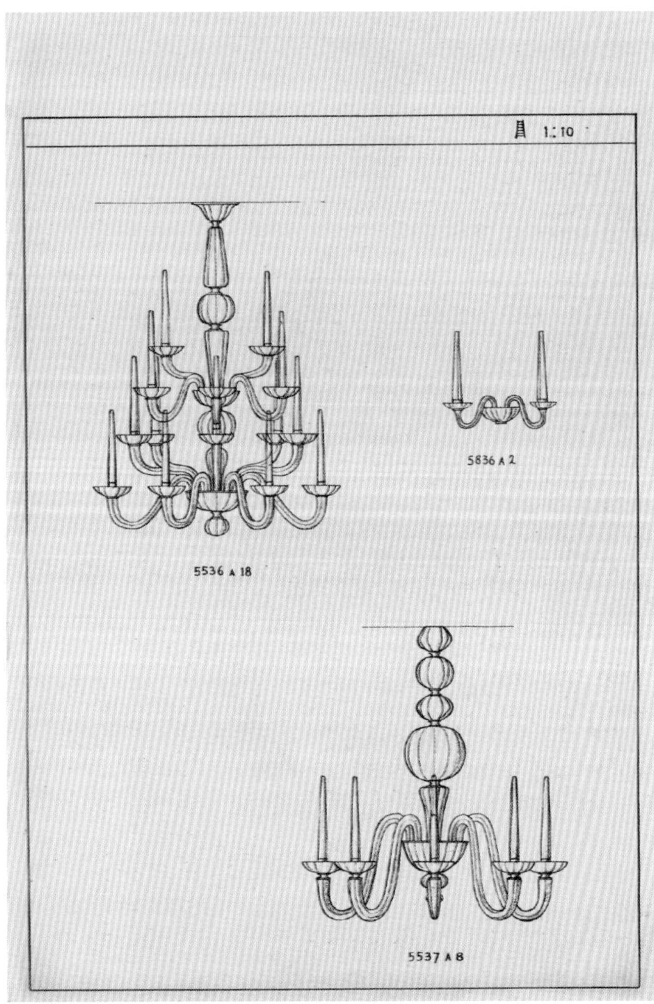
1:10
5836 A 2
5536 A 18
5537 A 8

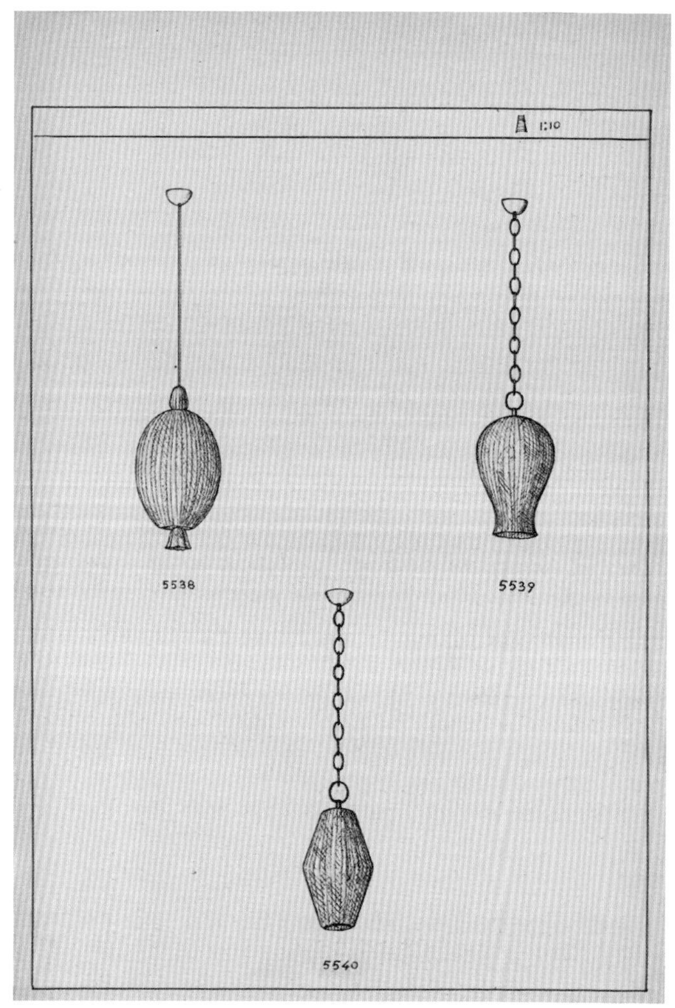
1:10
5538
5539
5540

1:10
5550 A 3
5850 A 1

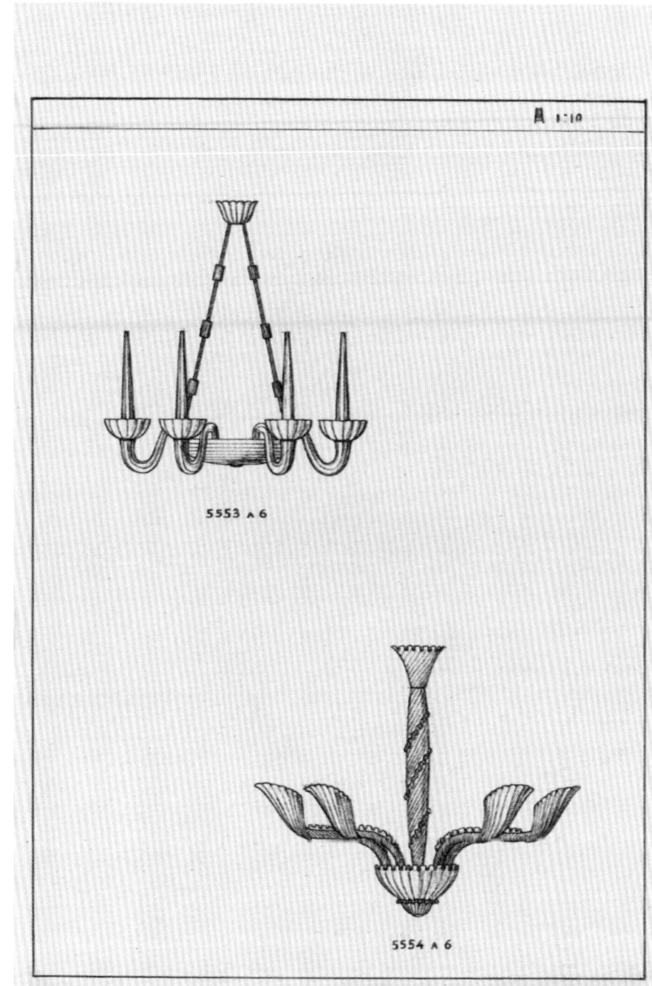
1:10
5553 A 6
5554 A 6

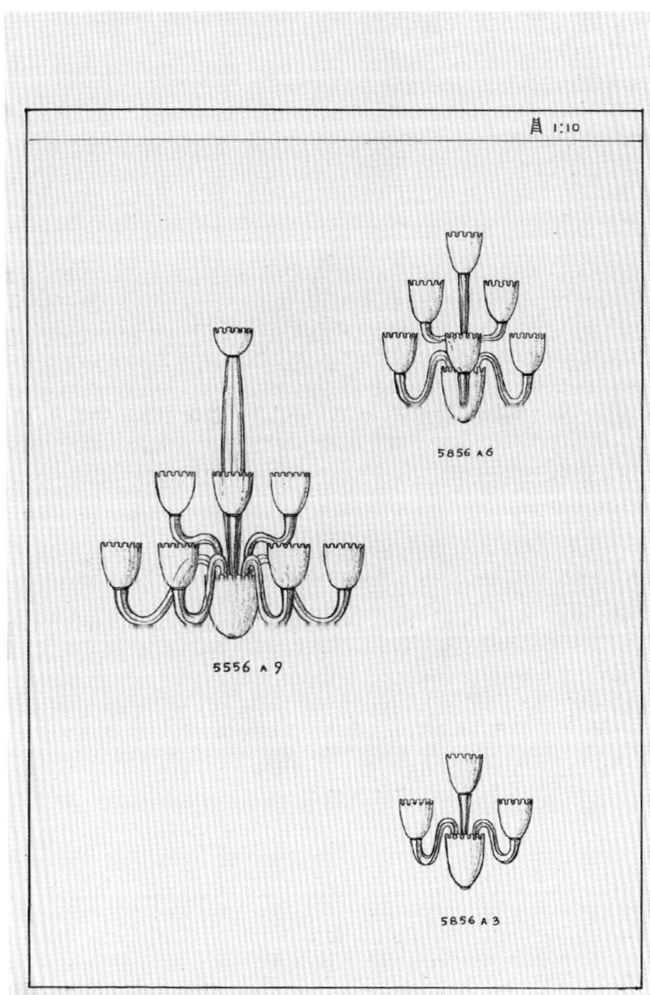
1:10
5856 A 6
5556 A 9
5856 A 3

1
1:10
960/0-6
961/0-2
960/1-8
961/1-3

2
1:10
960/2-6
961/2-2
960/3-8

5
1:10
960/5-8
961/5-2
961/6-2
960/6-6

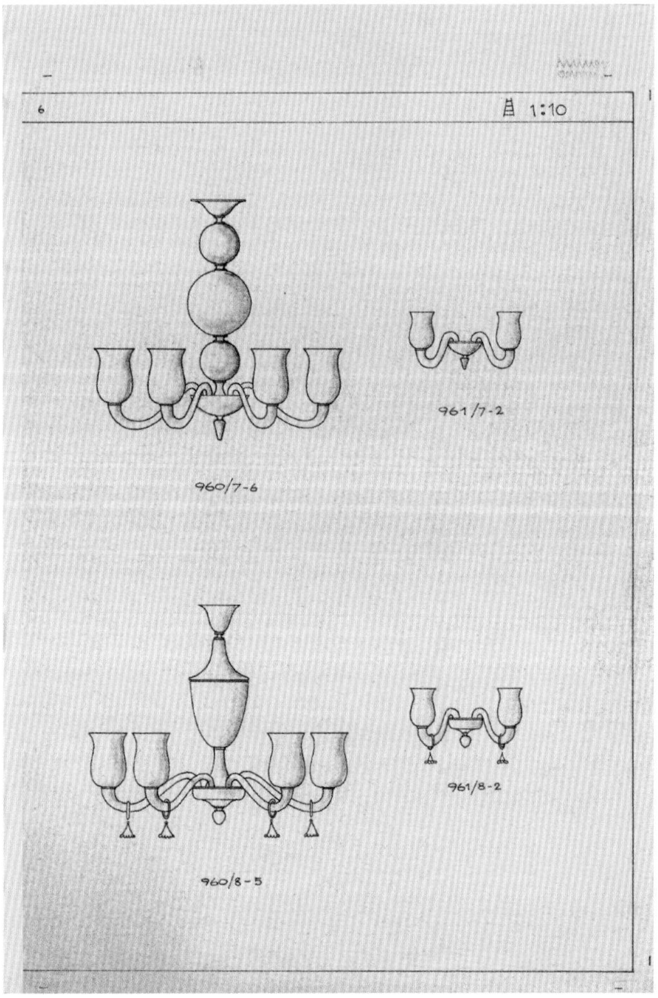
6
1:10
960/7-6
961/7-2
961/8-2
960/8-5

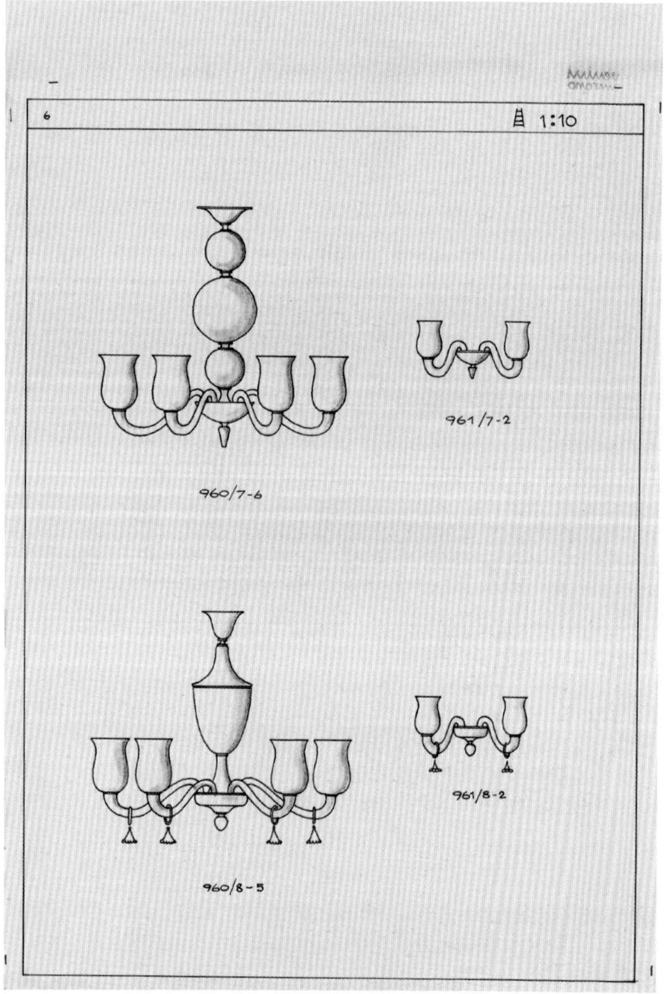
6
1:10
960/7-6
961/7-2
961/8-2
960/8-5

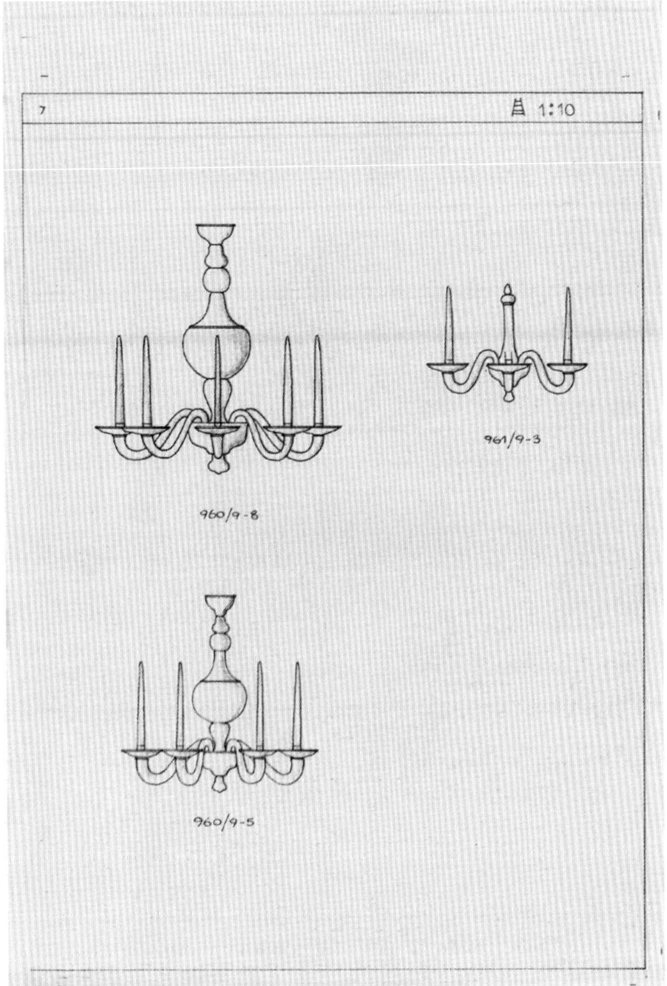
7
1:10
960/9-8
961/9-3
960/9-5

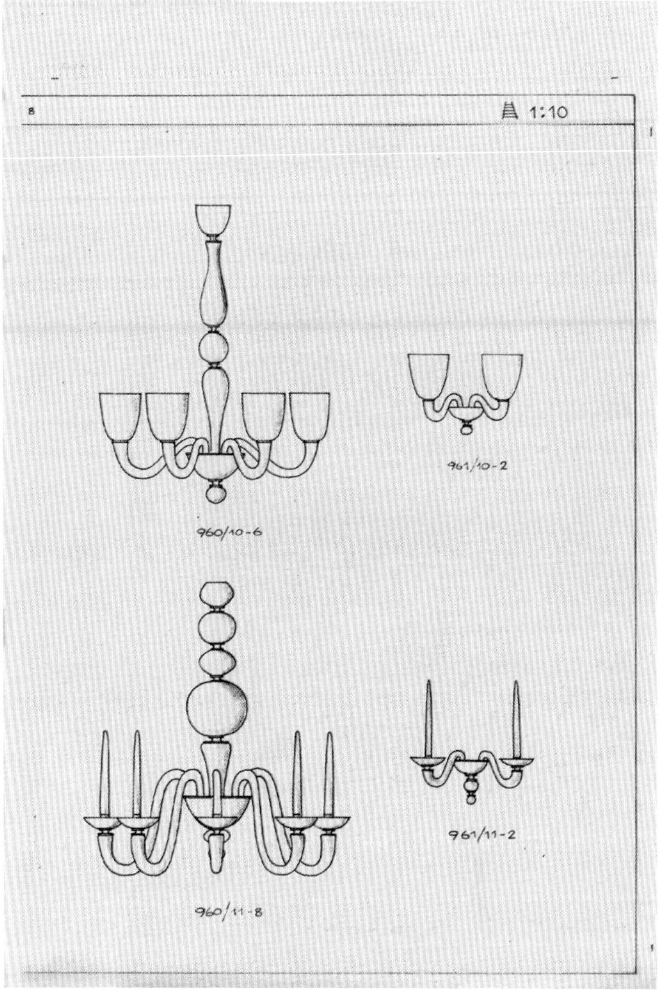
8
1:10
960/10-6
961/10-2
960/11-8
961/11-2

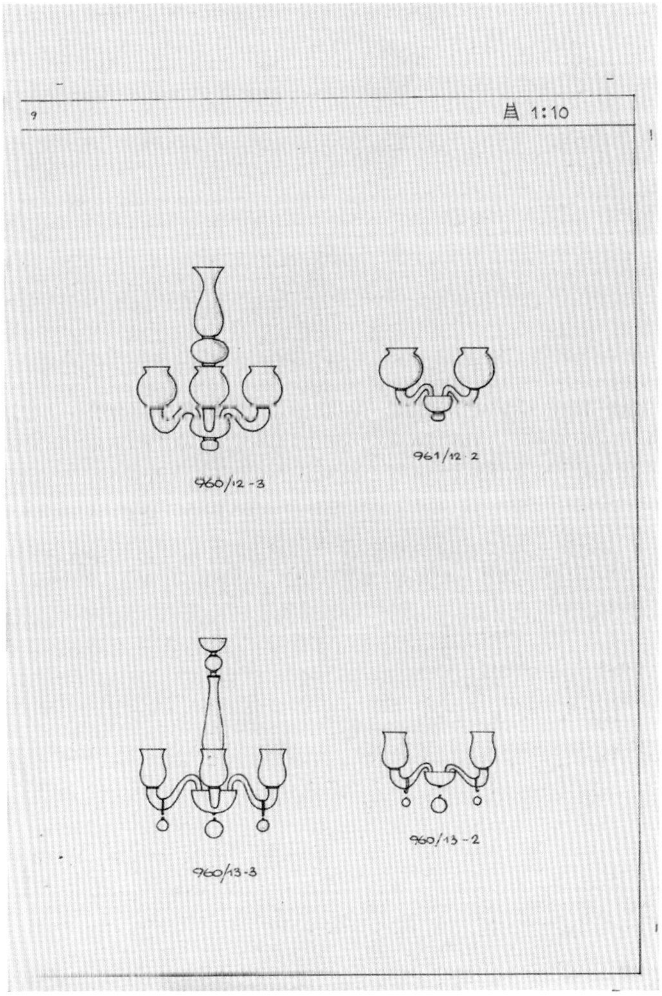
9
1:10
960/12-3
961/12-2
960/13-3
960/13-2

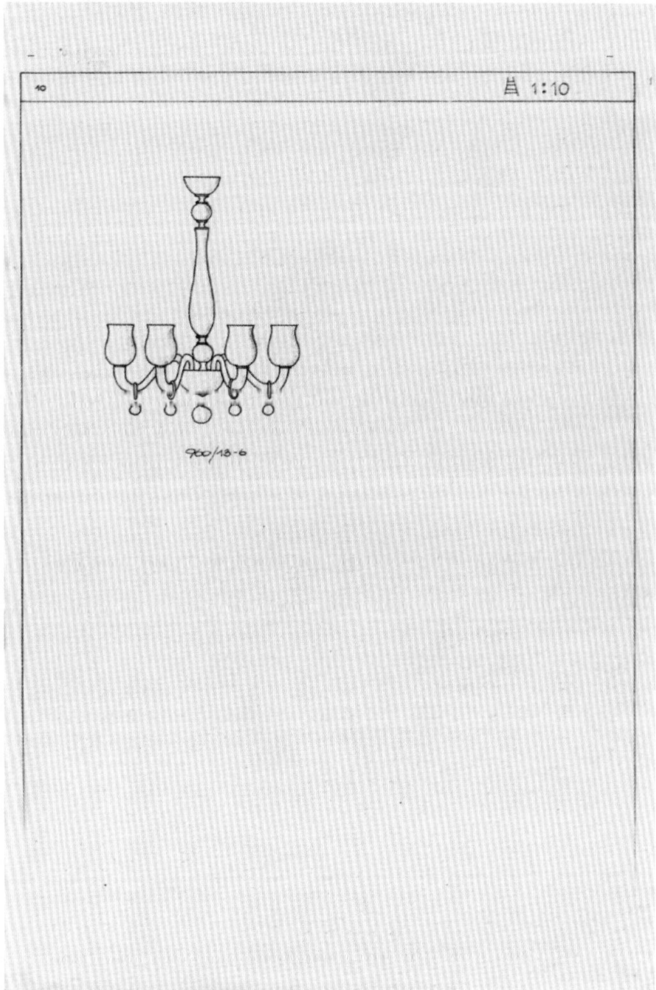
10
1:10
960/13-6

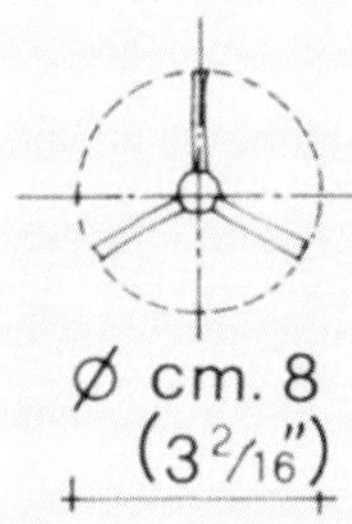
Ø cm. 8
(3 2/16")

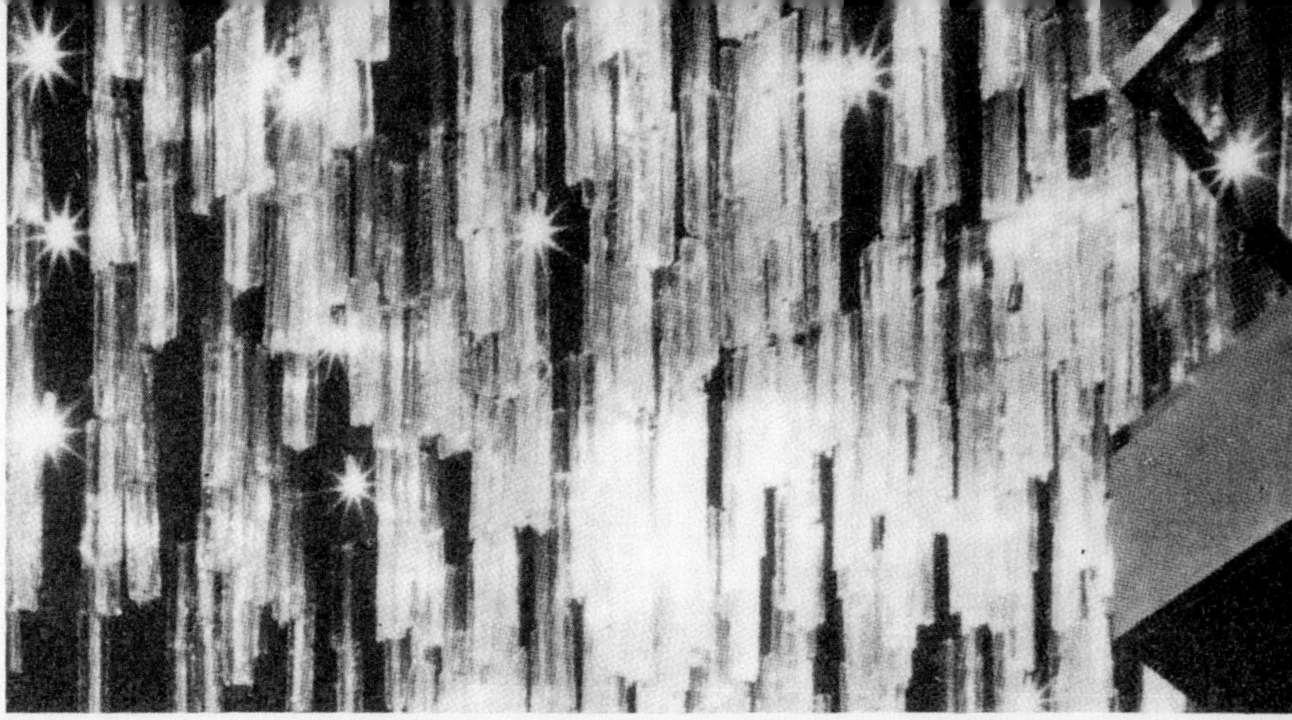

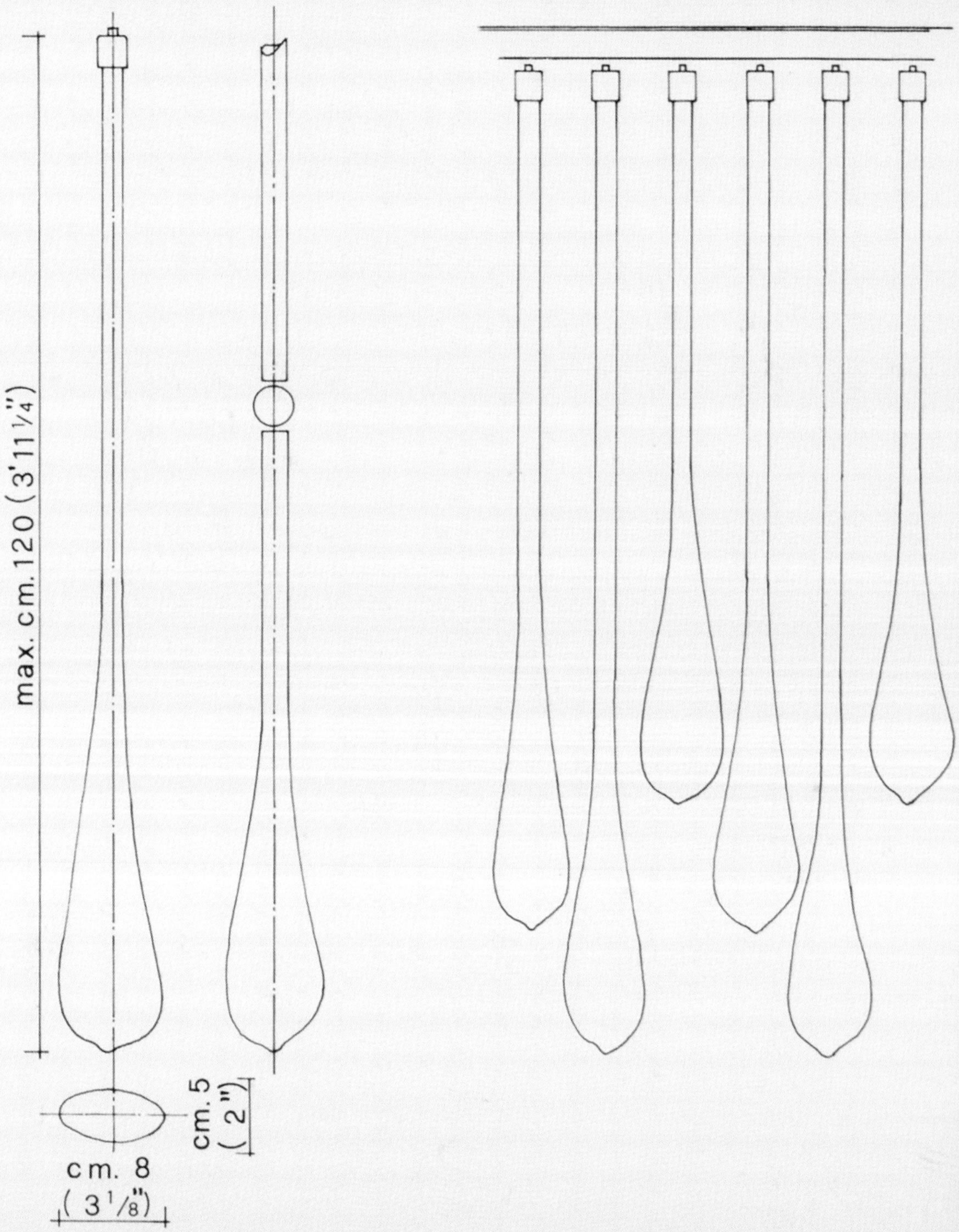
max. cm. 120 (3'11 1/4")
cm. 5
(2")
cm. 8
(3 1/8")

VENINI 75 CATALOGUE: SISTEMI PER FORNITURE

There are many catalogues presenting modular items extending over a time period from 1966 to 1985. As an example, we decided to publish an extract from the catalogue *Venini 75: Catalogo di illuminazione* (1975) where the different types of modular elements are summarised (*Sistemi per forniture*).

pannelli

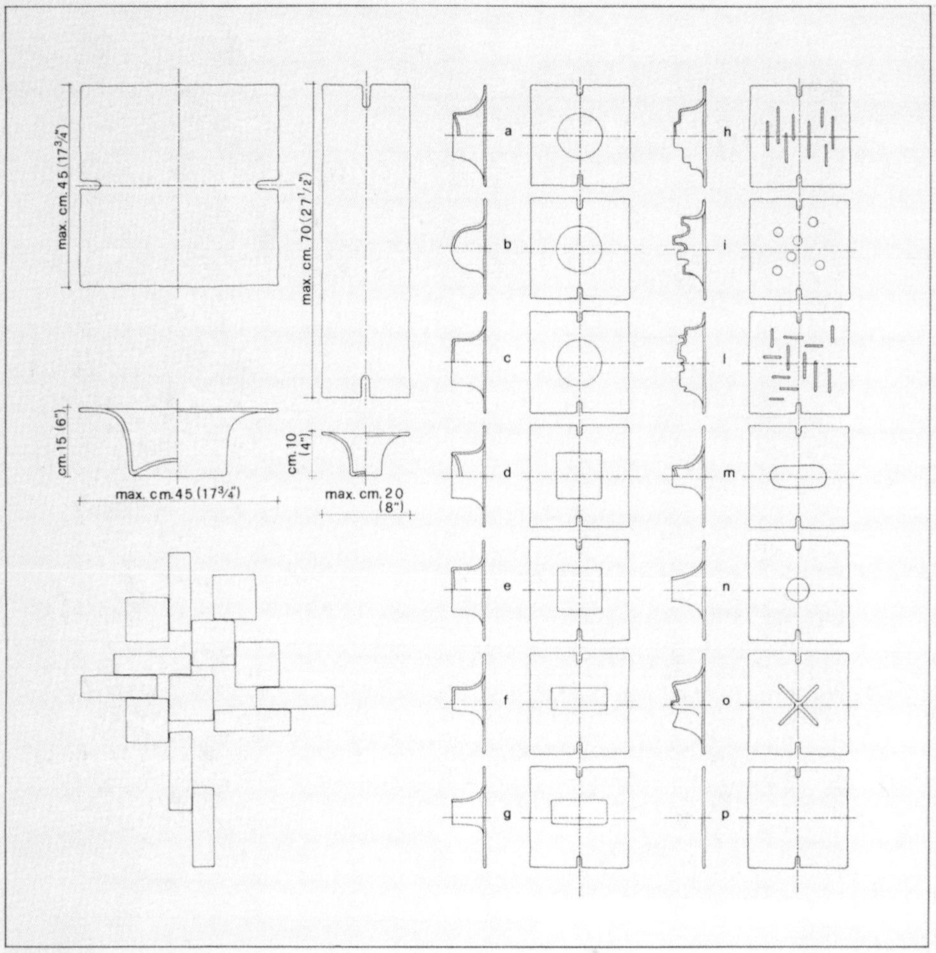

Abbiamo in produzione dei pannelli in vetro stampato e tirato. Possono essere realizzati nelle massime misure indicate e nelle misure intermedie.
Possiamo fornirli in cristallo, in colore leggero oppure con macchia o fascia di colore.
Abbiamo indicato quattordici sagomature possibili che si possono realizzare in diverso modo a seconda della forma e della misura scelta di pannello.
Il fissaggio avviene mediante due borchie bronzate avvitate su telai o correnti in ferro.

We produce panels in hand-pressed and shaped glass. They can be made in the maximum sizes specified and obviously in any intermediate size.
We can make them in clear or light coloured glass and with a darker coloured spot or band.
We suggest fourteen different sculptured shapes which can be used differently depending on the size and shape of the panel.
Each panel is fixed by two bronzed screws to a metal frame or bar.

Nous avons en production des panneaux en verre imprimé et tiré. Is peuvent être réalisés dans les dimensions maximum indiquées ou dans les dimensions intermédiaires.
Nous pouvons les faire en verre clair ou légèrement coloré ou avec une bande ou une tâche de couleur plus foncée.
Nous avons indiqué quatorze moulages différents que nous pouvons réaliser avec des variations selon la forme et la dimension du panneau choisi.
Chaque panneau est fixé par deux boutons à vis bronzés sur des châssis ou des barres métalliques.

Wir erzeugen gedruckte und gezogene Glaspaneele.
Sie können in den Grösst-und Zwischenausmassen geliefert werden.
Wir können sie in Kristall, leicht gefärbt oder gefleckt oder gestreift liefern.
Wir haben 14 mögliche Formen, welche in verschiedener Art je nach Ausmass und des Form des gewählten Paneels ausgeführt werden.
Die Befestigung wird mit zwei verschraubten Ringen an einen Rahmen oder einer Stange ausgeführt.

Tenemos en producciòn retablos en vidrio estampado y traido. Pueden ser realizados en las màximas medidas indicadas y en las medidas intermedias.
Podemos proveerles en cristal, ligeramente colorado o con mancha o faja de color.
Habemos indicado catorce formas posibles las cuales se pueden realizar de varia maneva segùn la forma y la medida del retablo escogido.
La fijaciòn se hace por medio de dos bullones bronceados atornillados sobre bastidores o barras de hierro.

tubo

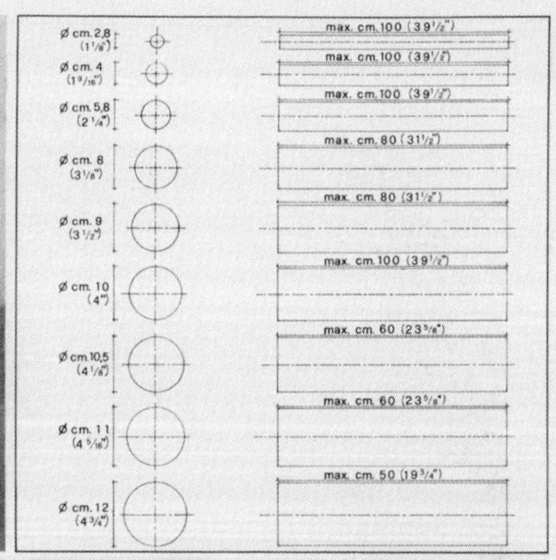

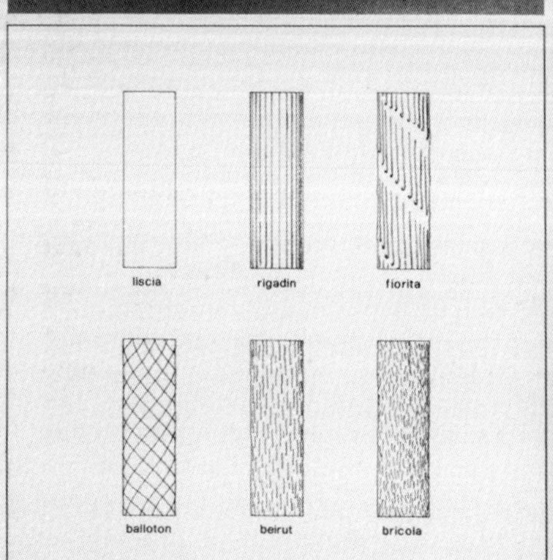

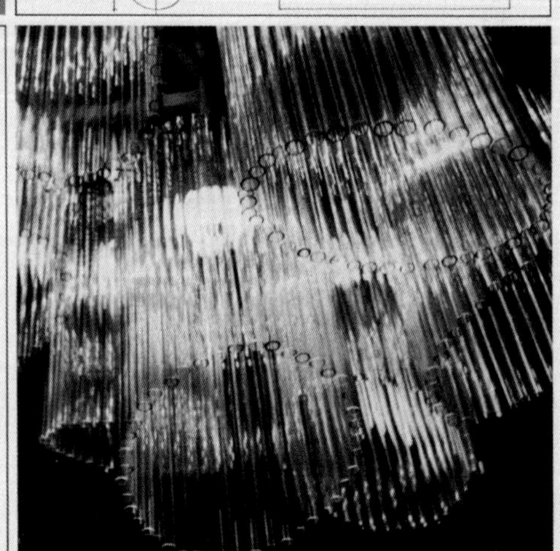

Sono disponibili dieci diversi diametri di canna a sezione tonda.
La tabella accanto indica queste sezioni e, per ognuna, la massima lunghezza realizzabile.
Inoltre per ogni tipo viene indicata, ove esista, la possibilità di realizzare una decorazione superficiale (stampatura).
Le canne possono terminare con un taglio a 90° oppure a 45° (con aumento di costo)

We have ten different diameters of round tubes available. The drawing shows for each diameter the maximum available length.
For each type we also specify the possibility to have a surface pattern.
The tubes can be cut at 90° or at 45° (with an extra cost).

Nous avons dix différents diamètres de cannes à section ronde disponibles. Le dessin indique ces diamètres et aussi pour chaque diamètre la longueur maximum qui peut être réalisée.
Pour chaque type nous indiquons aussi la possibilité de réaliser des décorations de surface (imprimées).
Les cannes peuvent être coupées à 90° ou à 45° (avec augmemtation de prix).

Wir koennen 10 verschiedene Durchmesser bei runden Roehren anbieten. Die Zeichnung zeigt fuer jeden Durchmesser die maximal zur Verfuegung stehende Laenge.
Fuer jede Type geben wir auch die Moeglichkeit einer bedruckten Oberflaechendekoration an.
Die Roehren koennen mit 90° oder 45° geschnitten werden (Mit Preisaufschlag)

Tenemos disponibles diez diametros diferentes de tubos redondos. El dibujo enseña el largo máximo disponible para cada diametro. Para cada tipo también especificamos la posibilidad de obtener una decoración imprimida en la superficie. Los tubos se pueden cortar en 90° o 45° (con aumento de precio).

quadro

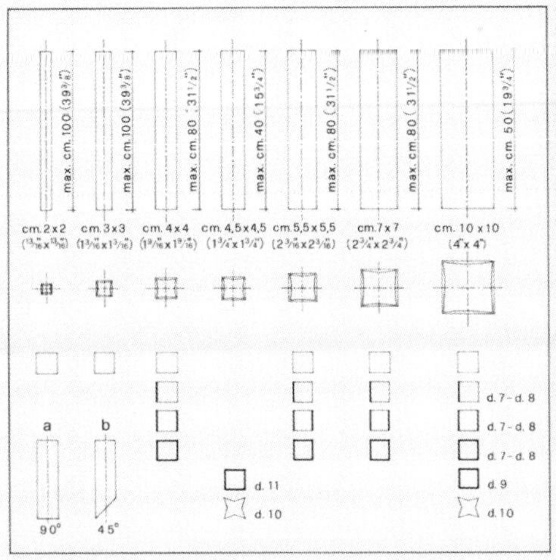

Sono disponibili sette diverse misure di canne a sezione quadrata.
La tabella accanto indica queste sezioni, le massime lunghezze realizzabili.
Inoltre per ogni tipo viene indicata, ove esista, la possibilità di realizzare, su una, due o quattro facce, una decorazione superficiale (stampatura).
Le canne possono terminare con un taglio a 90° oppure a 45° (con aumento di costo).

We have seven different sizes of square tubes available. The drawing shows the different sections and the maximum lengths which can be blown.
For each type we also specify the availability of a surface pattern on one, two of four faces The tubes can be cut at the bottom at 90° or 45° (with an extra cost).

Nous avons sept différentes mesures de cannes à séction carrée.
Le dessin indique ces mesures et aussi les longueurs maximum qui peuvent être réalisées. Pour chaque type nous indiquons aussi la possibilité de réaliser des décorations de surface sur une, deux ou quatre faces.
Les cannes peuvent être coupées à 90° ou à 45° (avec augmentation de prix).

Wir haben 7 verschiedene Groessen in viereckigen Rohren zu Ihrer Verfuegung. Die Zeichnung zeigt die verschiedenen Gruppen und die maximal zu erzielenden Laengen.
Fuer jeden Typ geben wir auch die Moeglichkeit einer Oberflaechendekoration fuer 1, 2 oder 4 Seiten an. Die Rohre koennen an der Unterseite mit 90° oder 45° geschnitten werden. (Mit Preisaufschlag).

Tenemos 7 tamaños diferentes de tubos cuadrados. El dibujo enseña las secciones diferentes y los largos máximos que se puede obtener. Para cada tipo tambien especificamos la posibilidad de una decoración en un, [illegible] lados.
Los tubos pueden ser cortados en la parte de abajo en 90° o 45° (con aumento de precio).

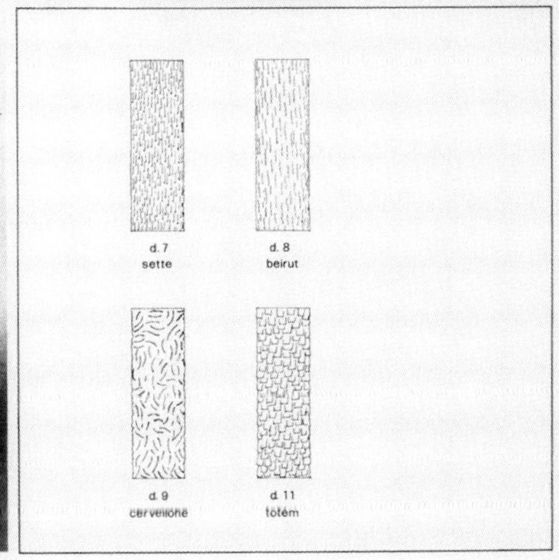

stellare

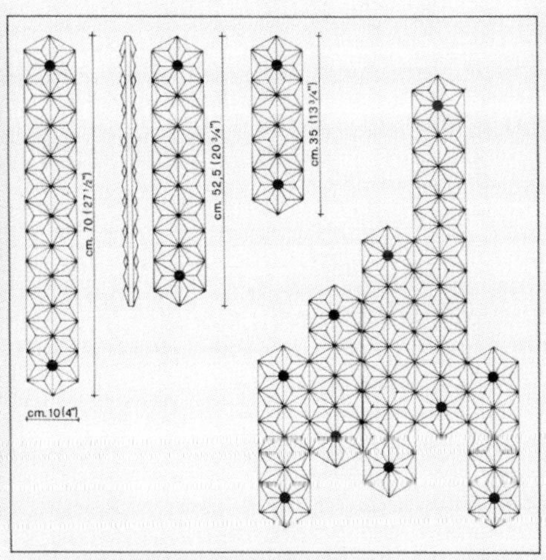

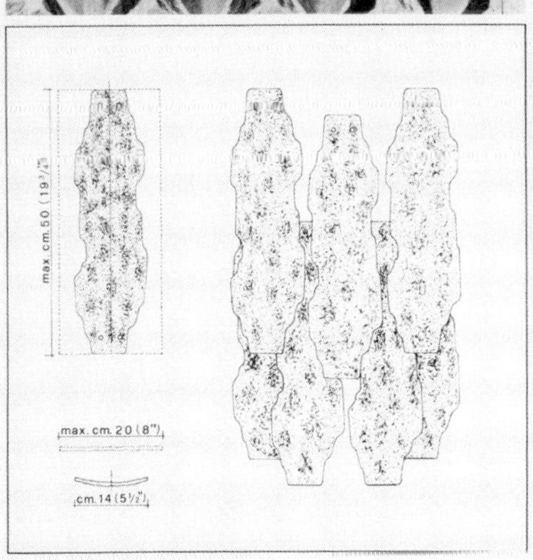

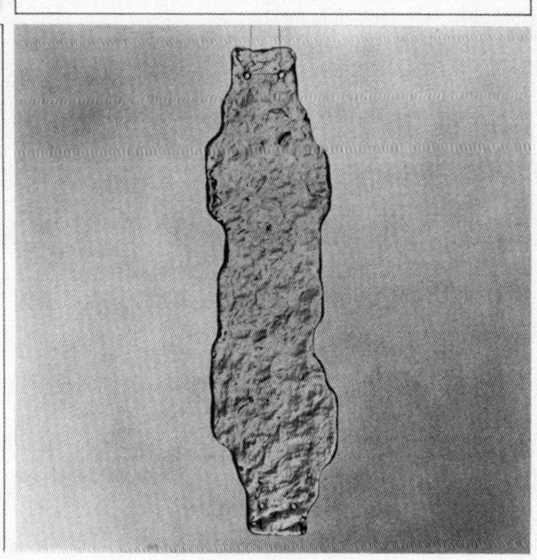

grezzo

Abbiamo in produzione delle piastre colate con stampatura « stone » di forma e misure massime come da disegno.
Si assemblano in catene mediante appositi accessori metallici.

We manufacture this type of cast glass with a « stone » print panels of the shape and maximum sizes shown in drawing. They can be assembled in chains by using a special metal accessory.

Nous produisons ce type de panneau en verre coulé avec impression « stone » de la forme et des dimension maximum indiquées sur le dessin.
Ils peuvent être assemblés en chaines par un accessoire métallique spécial.

Wir erzeugen gegossene Platten in « Stone ». Druck deren Form und Grösstausmasse auf der Zeichnung dargestellt sind.
Sie werden im Band zusammengestellt mit Hilfe der dazu vorgesehenen Metallzubehöre.

Tenemos en producción chapas fundidas con impresiòn « stone » de forma y medida màximas indicadas en el dibujo. Estan montadas en cadenas por medio de especiales accesorios metàlicos.

sfere

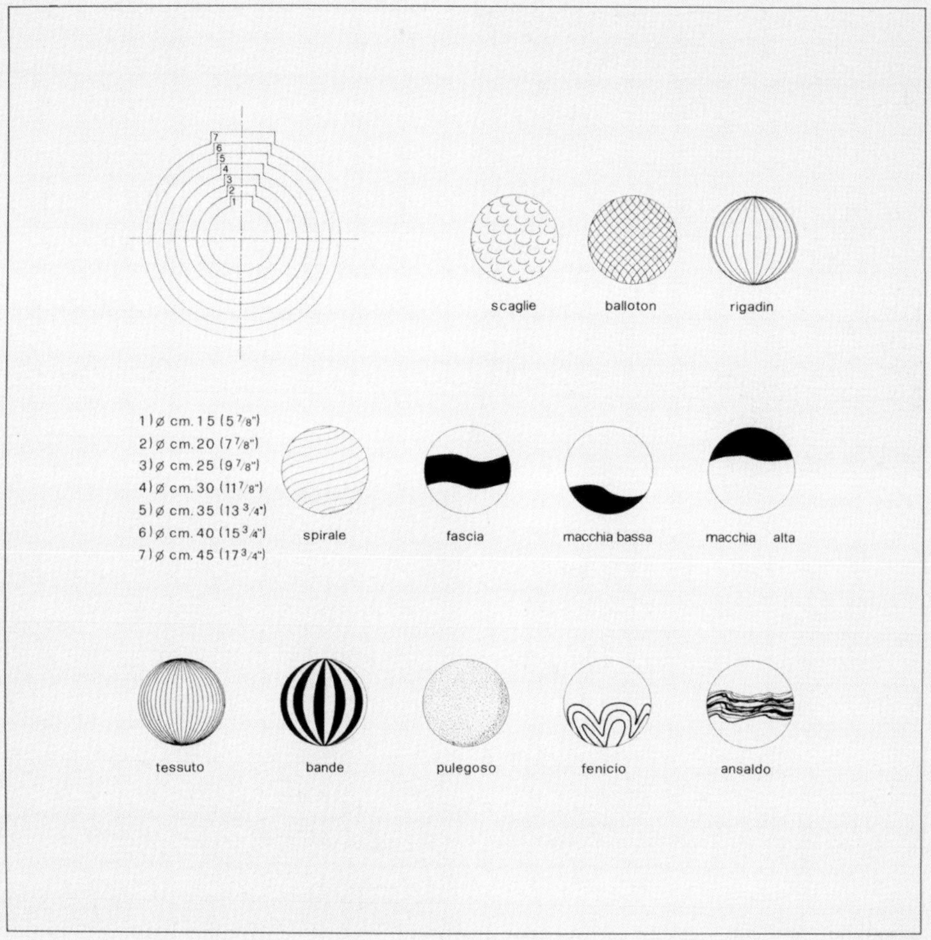

Abbiamo in produzione sfere di 7 diversi diametri da cm. 15 a cm. 45.
Possono essere in vetro trasparente o opalino colorato oppure decorate in vari modi come è esemplificato in questo disegno.
Prezzi, particolari di esecuzione ed accessori di metallo da precisare su richiesta.

We manufacture spheres in 7 different diameters 15 cm. (5 7/8") to 45 cm. (17 3/4").
They can be in clear, transparent or opaline colour or decorated in differen ways as per examples shown in this drawing.
Prices, details of construction and metal accessories to be confirmed on request.

Nous fabriquons des sphères de 7 diamètres différents de 15 cm. à 45 cm.
Elles peuvent être en verre clair, transparent ou opaline, coloré ou décoré de différentes manières, comme les examples de ce dessin montrent.
Les prix, les détails de construction et les accessoires métalliques seront confirmés sur demande.

Wir erzeugen Kugeln von 7 verschiedenen Durchmessern, u. zw. von 15 bis 45 cm.
Diese können in durchsichtigem oder gefärbten opalinglas verschieden dekoriert, wie auf diesem Plan aufgeführt, hergestellt werden.
Preise, Ausführungsdetails sowie Metallzubehöre werden auf Anfrage präzisiert.

Producimos globos de 7 diferentes diàmetros desde 15 hasta 45 cm.
Pueden ser in vidrio transparente o opalino colorado o decorados en varias maneras como està demostrado en este dibujo.
Precios, detalles de ejecuciòn y accesorios metàlicos segùn pedido.

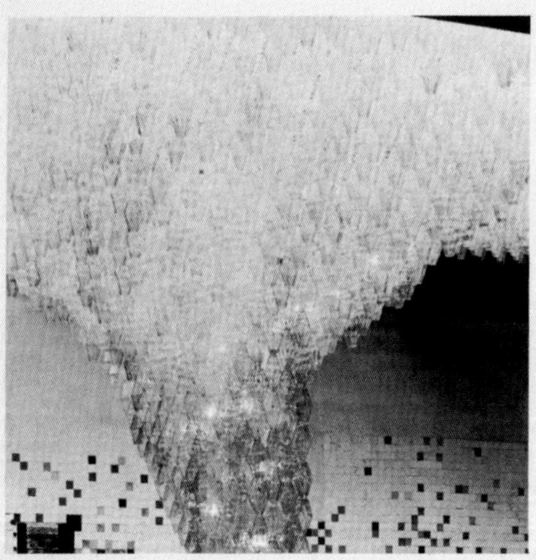

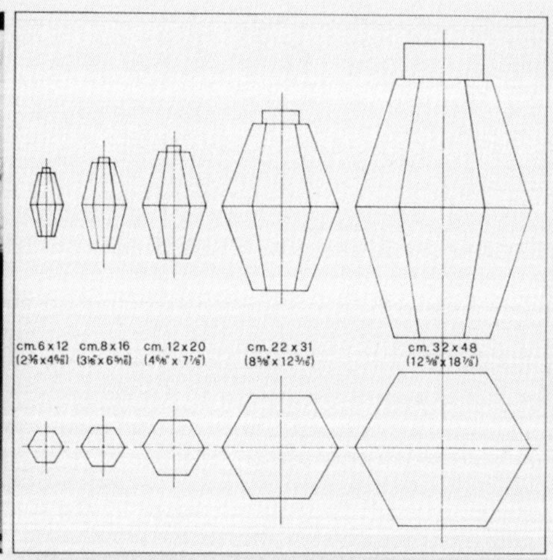

poliedro

Sono disponibili componenti in vetro soffiato a forma poliedrica di cinque misure.
Le quattro misure minori possono essere montate a catena mediante appositi accessori metallici.

We have five different blown-glass components in the shape of a polyhedron. The four smaller sizes can be assembled in chains by using special metal accessories.

Nous avons cinq différentes mèsures de verres soufflés en forme de polyhèdre. Les quatre mésures plus petites peuvent être assemblées en chaines avec des accessoires métalliques spéciaux.

Es stehen geblasene Glaskomponenten in Polyederform in fünf Ausmassen zur Verfügung.
Die vier kleineren können mit entsprechendem Metallzubehör zu Ketten vereint werden.

Tenemos disponibles componentes en vidrio soplado en forma poliédrica de cinco medidas. Las cuatro medidas menores pueden ser montadas en cadena por medio de especiales accesorios metàlicos.

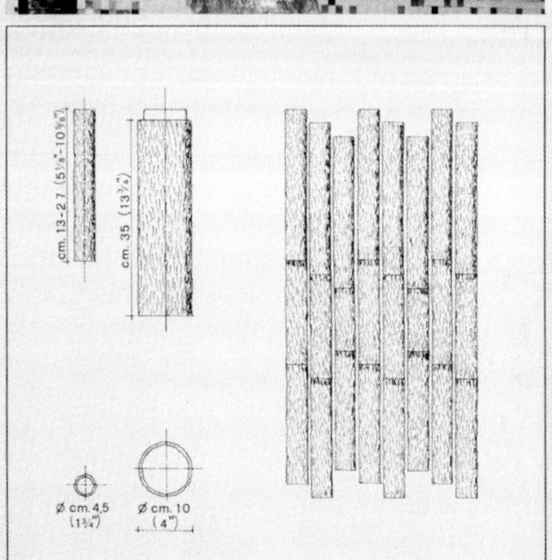

bricola

Sono disponibili due diversi diametri di vetri soffiati con stampature profonde a « bricola » in diverse misure.
Possono essere assemblati in catena con appositi accessori metallici.

We have two different diameters of blown glasses with a deep « bricola » print, in different lengths.
They can be assembled in chains using special metal accessories.

Nous avons en production deux diamètres diffèrents de verrerie soufflée avec impression profonde « bricola » en différentes longueures Ces éléments peuvent être assemblés par chaines avec des accessoires métalliques spéciaux.

Es stehen zwei verschiedene Durchmesser von geblasenem mit tiefem Bricola-Druck versehenen Glas in verschiedenen Ausmassen zur Verfügung.
Es kann mit entsprechendem Metallzubehör vershen, zu Ketten vereint werden.

Tenemos disponibles dos diferentes diàmetros de vidrios soplados con impresiones profundas a « bricola » en diferentes medidas.
Pueden ser montados en cadena con especiales accessorios metàlicos.

iceberg

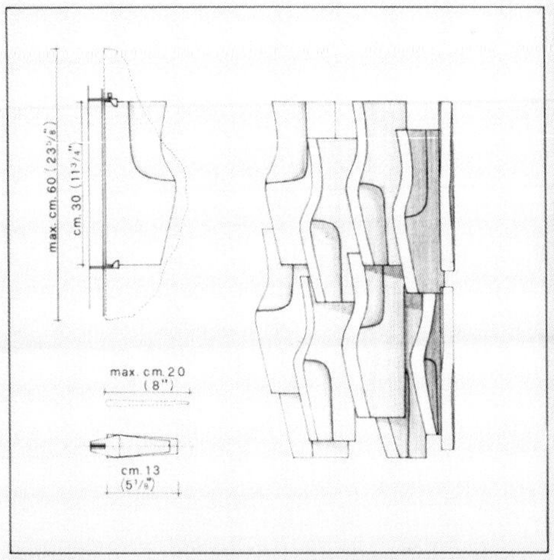

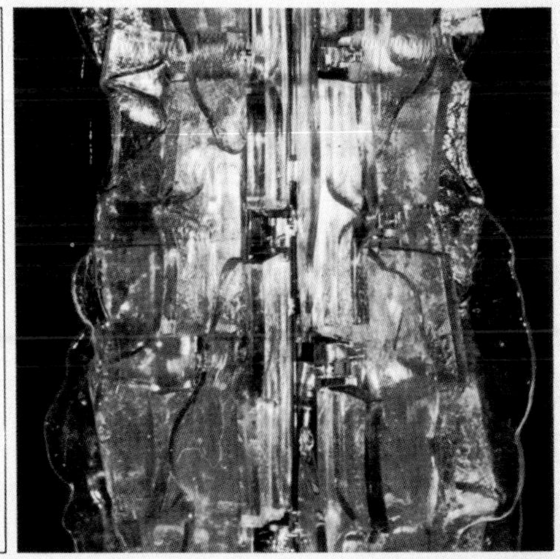

Elemento in vetro colato sagomato utilizzabile per sculture luminose montato su telai metallici. Il vetro può essere in cristallo o colore molto leggero e può essere corroso all'acido.

Cast glass component to be used in lighting sculptures assembled on metal frames. The component can be in clear glass or in very light colours. It can be deeply acid-etched.

L'élément est en verre coulé et peut être utilisé pour des sculptures lumineuses sur châssis métallique. Le verre peut être transparent clair ou très légèrement coloré. Il peut être creusé à l'acide.

Gegossenes Glaselement das benutzt werden kann in Lichtskulpturen, montiert auf Metallrahmen. Das Element kann in klarem Glas geliefert werden oder in sehr hellen Farben. Es kann auch geaetzt werden.

Elemento de vidrio fundido para utilizar en esculturas de iluminación montadas en marcos de metal. El elemento puede ser en vidrio claro o en colores muy claros. Puede ser grabado al agua fuerte.

mandarin

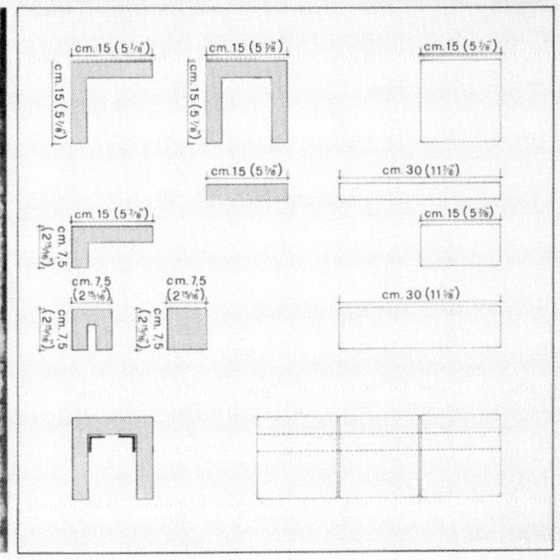

Vetri colati profilati in sagome geometriche. Cristallo o colore leggero corroso. Da assemblare su telai metallici o con parziale incollaggio epossidico.

Cast glass geometrical profiles. Crystal or very light colours, deeply acid-etched. To be assembled on metal frames of partly glued with epoxy.
Verres coulés à profiles géometriques.

Verre clair ou couleur très légère, creusés à l'acide. Assemblés sur châssis métallique ou partiellement collés avec rèsines épossydiques.

Gegossenes Glas - geometrische Profile Kristall oder sehr helle Farben, geaetzt. Montiert auf Metallrahmen oder teilwaise mit Epoxi geklebt.

Vidrio fundido - perfiles geometricos. Colores cristal o muy claros, grabado al agua fuerte. Montados en marcos de metal o parcialmente pegados con resina epoxi.

volumi

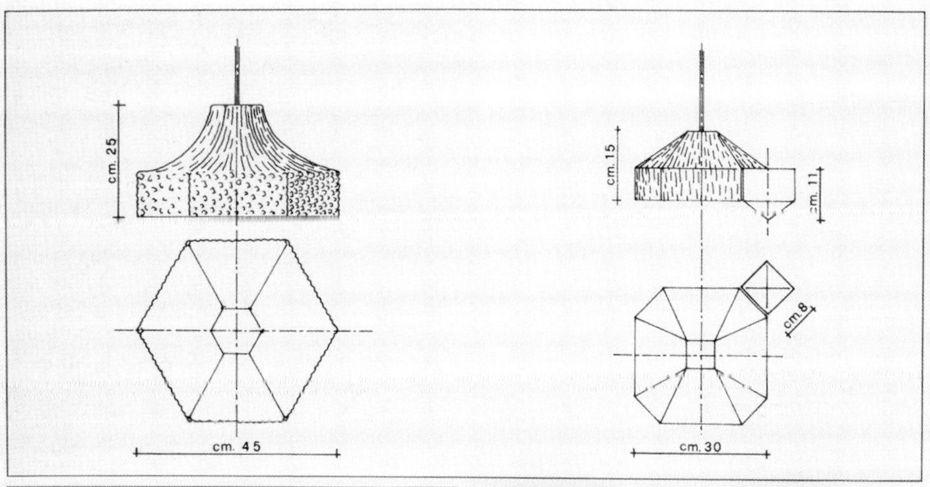

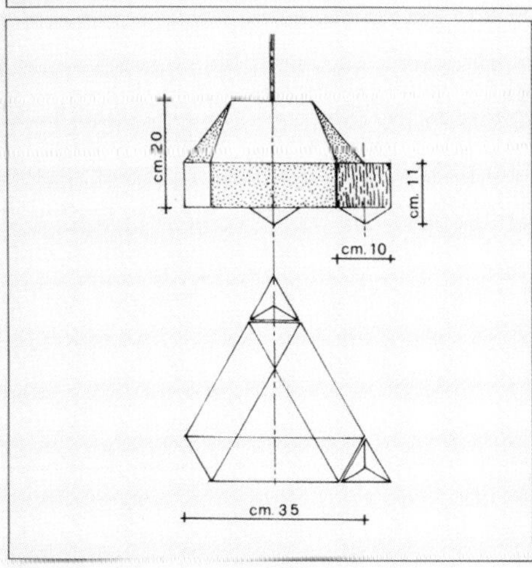

Produciamo alcuni tipi di volumi geometrici in vetro soffiato che possono essere sospesi con appositi accessori metallici. Incastrando queste forme si possono realizzare delle soffittature di grandi dimensioni.

We manufacture some types of geometrical blown-glass volumes which hang by special metal fittings. By combining these shapes we can cover large areas of ceiling surfaces.

Nous produisons des types de volumes géometriques en verre soufflé qui peuvent être suspendus par des accessoires métalliques spéciaux. En encastrant ces formes nous pouvons réaliser des plafonnages de grandes surfaces.

Wir Erzeugen einige Arten von geometrischen Figuren in geblasenen Glas welche mit entsprechenden Metallzubehören aufgehängt werden können. Durch die Vereinigung zweier dieser Figuren, Können riesige Plafondfiguren erzielt werden.

Producimos algunos tipos de volùmenes geomètricos en vidrio soplado que pueden ser colgados con apropiados accesorios metàlicos. Ensamblando estas formas se pueden cubrir largas superficies de techo.

elica

Componibile in vetro soffiato e lavorato a mano. Due sezioni e varie misure disponibili come da disegno. Assemblaggio a mezzo di tiges metalliche con gancio.
Colori: cristallo o cristallo con anima di colore.

Blown and hand-shaped glass component. Two sections and different sizes as per drawing. Hanging by steel rods with a hook.
Colours: clear or clear with coloured core.

Elément en verre soufflé et formé à la main. Deux sections et différentes longueurs disponibles. voir le dessin. Suspension par tige métallique et crochet.
Couleurs: verre clair ou avec âme de couleur.

Geblasene und handgefertigte Glaselemente. 2 Teile und verschiedene Groessen wie aus der Zeichnung ersichtlich. An Stahlstangen mit Haken haengend.
Farben: Hell oder hell mit farbigem Mittelpunkt.

Componentes de vidrio soplados y elaborados a mano. 2 partes y varios tamaños disponibles, como pueden ver en el dibujo. Colgando de tubos de acero con un gancho.
Colores: claro o claro con centro en color.

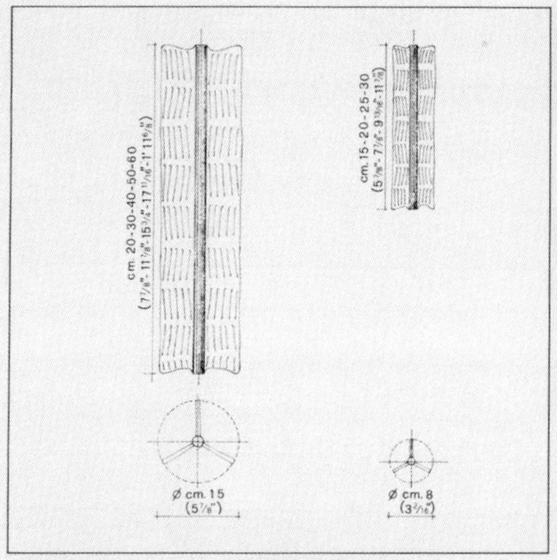

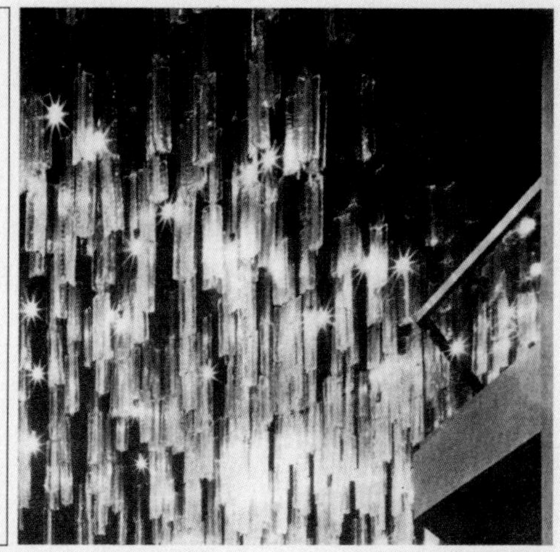

goccia

Elementi in vetro soffiato utilizzabili per creare volumi luminosi di forma libera. Sospensione con cavi metallici. Massime dimensioni dei vetri indicate nei disegni. Le singole gocce possono essere prolungate con canne vuote con interposta pallina in vetro.
Colori: cristallo oppure cristallo con macchia di colore leggero.

Blown glass components that can be used to assemble free-shaped lighting volumes. Hanging by steel cables. Maximum available sizes as per drawing. Single drops can be prolonged by using blown round tubes with small glass spheres in between. It is better to insert the top of the volume in a recess in the ceiling.
Colour: clear or clear with a light coloured spot.

Eléments en verre soufflés avec lesquels on peut créer des volumes lumineux à forme libre. Accrochage par câbles métalliques. Dimensions maximum des éléments indiquées sur le dessin. Les gouttes peuvent être prolongées par des cannes rondes avec sphères en verre interposées.
Couleurs: verre clair ou avec une tâche de couleur légère.

Geblasene Glaselemente mit denen frei geformte Lichtvolumen geschaffen werden konnen. An Stahlkabeln haengend. Die maximal zur Verfuegung stehende Laenge gemaess Zeichnung. Einzelne Tropfen koennen durch rund, geblasene Rohre mit kleinen Kugeln dazwischen verlaengert werden.
Farbe: Hell oder hell mit einem hellen Farbfleck.

Elementos de vidrio soplados con los cuales se puede crear volumnes de iluminación en forma libre. Colgando por cables de acero. Los tamaños máximos disponibles según dibujos. Las gotas pueden ser alargadas utilizando tubos redondos aoplados con pequeñas esferas de vidrio entre medio.
Color: claro o claro con una mancha de color claro.

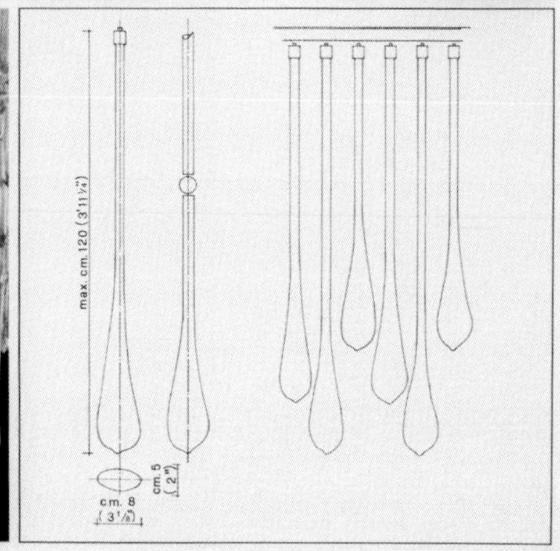

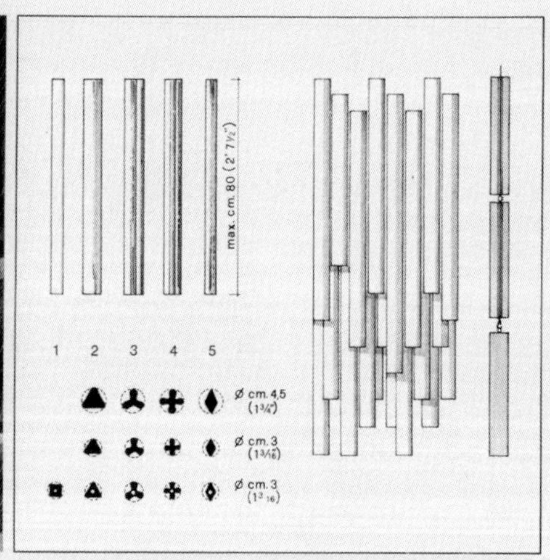

canna

Produciamo cinque diverse sezioni di canna piena tirata a mano, di due diametri diversi (45 mm. e 30 mm.) e nella massima lunghezza di cm. 80. Possono essere forate per assemblaggi di lampadari di grande altezza. Sono montate con accessori metallici: ganci, cavi, catenelle.

We manufacture five different shapes of solid hand-drawn rod, of two different diameters (1 3/4'' and 1/16'') and in the maximum length of 2'7½''. There can be a central hole to assemble long chandeliers. They are assembled with metal accessories: hooks, cables and chains.

Nous produisons cinq diffèrentes sections de canne pleine de deux diamètres différents (45 mm. et 30 mm.). Elles peuvent être trouées pour les assemblages de lustres de grande hauteur. Elles sont montées avec des accessoires métalliques: chochets, câbles, et chainettes.

Wir erzeugen fünf verschiedene Querschnitte von handgezofienen, Glasstangen mit zwei verschiedenen Durchmessern (45 und 30 mm) von max. 80 cm Länge.
Sie können gebohrt werden um zur Zusammenstellung von sehr grossen Lampen zu dienen. Sie sind mit Metallzubehör wie Haken, Drähten versehen.

Producimos cinco diferentes secciones de caña llena de dos diàmetros diferentes (45 mm. y 30 mm.) y en la màxima largueza de 80 cm., las cuales pueden ser horadadas para el montaje de arañas de grande altura. Estan montados con accesorios metàlicos: ganchos, cables, cadenillas.

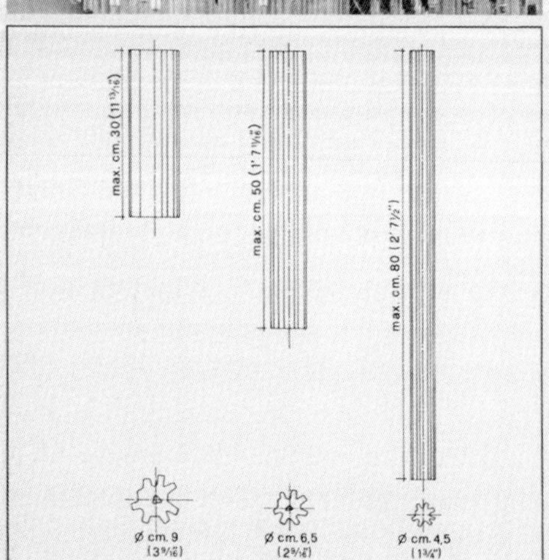

fiocco di neve

Vetri di tre diverse sezioni irregolari con foro centrale per l'assemblaggio.
Le massime lunghezze disponibili sono indicate nel disegno.
Possono essere in cristallo o con una anima colorata.

Glass components of three different irregular sections with central hole for assembling. Maximum available sizes specified on the drawing.
They can be either in clear or with a central coloured core.

Eléments en verre de trois sections irrégulières avec trou d'assemblage au centre. Les longueurs maximum réalisables sont indiquées sur le dessin.
Ils peuvent être en verre clair ou avec un centre de couleur.

Glaselemente aus 3 unregelmaessigen verschiedenen Gruppen mit einem Loch in der Mitte fuer die Montage. Die máximal zur Verfuegung stehende Laenge ist auf der Zeichnung angegeben. Die Elemente koennen entweder in hell oder mit einem farbigen Mittelpunkt geliefert werden.

Elementos de vidrio de tres secciones irregulares diferentes con agujero central para el montaje. Tamaños máximos disponibles estan especificados en el dibujo.
Pueden ser claro o con centro de color.

ballotton

Usando sfere stampate a « ballotton » di diversi diametri, in cristallo o in colori chiari, si possono realizzare soffittature, cortine o anche forme luminose volumetriche.
Assemblaggio a mezzo di cavi d'acciaio su telaio centrale e/o periferico in metallo.

Using blown glass spheres printed « a ballotton » of different diameters, in clear or very lightly coloured glass, we can build up tent-like ceilings, screens or even lighting volumes.
Assembling of the spheres is done with steel cables fixed to a central and/or peripherical metal frame.

En utilisant des boules en verre soufflé imprimées « à ballotton » de différents diamétres, en verre clair ou légèrement coloré, nous pouvons réaliser des plafonds, des rideaux ou des volumes lumineux.
L'assemblage des sphères est faite par des câbles d'acier fixés sur une structure centrale et/ou périphérique.

Unter Benutzung von geblasenen Glaskugeln bedruckt « á balloton » mit verschiedenen Durchmessern, in klarem oder sehr leicht gefaerbtem Glas, koennen wir Decken, « Gardinen » oder sogar Beleuchtungsvolumen herstellen. Die Montage der Kugeln wird mit Stahlkabeln durchgefuerhrt die an einer Zentrale besfestigt sind und/oder an einem Metallhaken der Peripherie.

Utilizando esferas de vidrio sopladas estampadas « à balloton » de diferentes diametros, en vidrio claro o muy poco colorido, podemos obtener techos, cortinas o volumenes de iluminación. El montaje de las esferas se efectua con cables de acero fijados en una central y/o un marco de metal periferico.

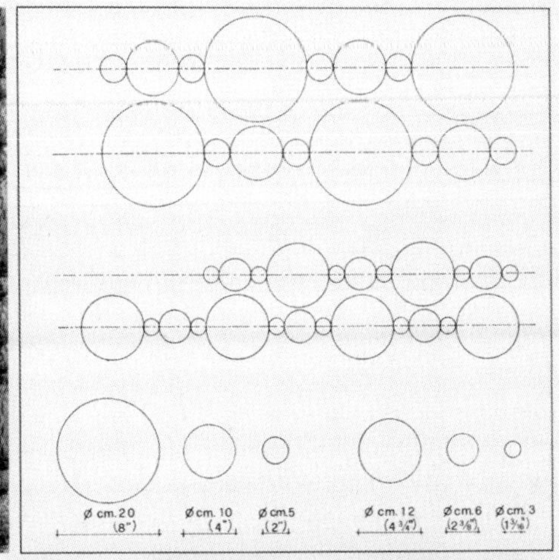

cubo

Cubi in vetro di quattro misure con vetro stampato su due facce oppure lisci. Colori leggeri oppure cristallo.
Assemblaggio con catene di uno o più cubi, giustapponibili, dotate di gancio superiore di attacco.
Per i modelli da cm. 20 e cm. 15 si possono inserire dei portalampade dentro i cubi.

Glass cubes of four sizes, plain or with two patterned faces. Light colours or clear glass. Assembling by chains of cubes which can be situated next to each other. Top hook. 8'' and 6'' models can have sockets inside the cubes.

Cubes en verre de quatre diménsions, lisses ou avec deux faces imprimées.
Couleurs très légères ou verre clair.
Assemblage par chaines de un ou plusieurs cubes, juxtaposées, avec crochet supérieur. Pour les modèles de 20 cm. et 15 cm. une douille peut être montée à l'intérieur des verres.

Glaswuerfel in 4 Groessen, einfach oder mit 2 bedruckten Seiten. Klare Farben oder klares Glas.
Montiert mit Ketten von Wuerfeln, die nebeneinander angebracht werden koennen. Oberhaken. Bei den Modellen von 20 und 15 cm kann die Gluehbirnenfassung in den Wuerfeln angebracht werden.

Cubos de vidrio en cuatro tamaños, lisos o con dos lados estampados. Colores claro o vidrio claro.
Montaje por cadenas de cubos que se puede colocar juntos los unos a los otros. Gancho superior. En los modelos de 20 y 15 cm se puede colocar el portalámparas dentro del cubo.

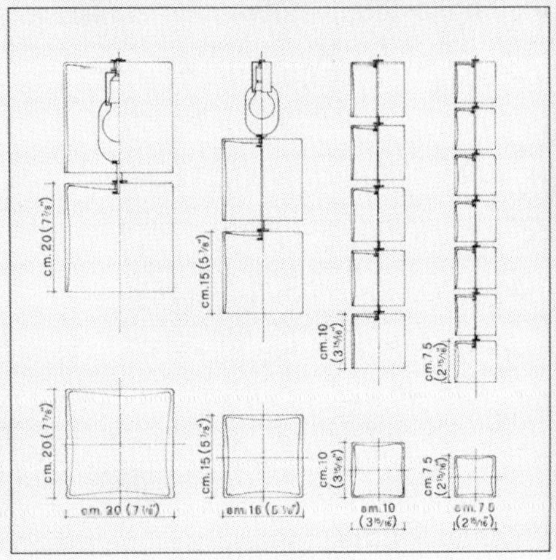

APPENDIX

MODULAR ELEMENTS 1951-1985

Following is the complete list of the modules put into production from c. 1951 to 1985 and here presented in their order of appearance. The time sequence was deduced from cross-checking the information found in the period catalogues and the chronology of the lighting projects completed by the firm.

1951
Sfere
Palazzo Grassi, Venice

1957
Canne (with light source at the extremity)
XI Triennale di Milano, Milan

1958
Poliedri
XXIX Esposizione Biennale Internazionale d'Arte, Venice; Italian pavilion, *Exposition Universelle et Internationale de Bruxelles*, Brussels

1959
Canne (with light source hidden)
Offices of the Provincial Tourist Board, Naples

1960
Gocce (also called ***mazze***)
Chez Vous, Excelsior Hotel, Venice

1960-61
Canne quadre
Olivetti shop, Düsseldorf;
Municipal Opera House, Florence

Cubi
Municipal Opera House, Florence

1962
Triangolo
23rd Mostra Internazionale d'Arte Cinematografica di Venezia, Venice

1963-65
Globi stampati
Michelangelo Transatlantic Liner

1964
Elementi esagonali
Plaza Hotel, Abano; Olivetti Office Building, Ivrea

Elementi ottagonali
Plaza Hotel, Abano

Esprit
Plaza Hotel, Abano

1966
Bricole
Fiat, Pescara; *Venini lighting catalogue*, 1966

Cheerio
RAI Management, via Cernaia, Torino;
Bertha Hotel, Montegrotto

Ghiaccioli (from 1975 ***Eliche***)
Venini lighting catalogue, 1966

Totem
Bertha Hotel, Montegrotto

1969
Fiorito
Venini lighting catalogue, 1969

Trilobi
Venini lighting catalogue, 1969

1970
Patchwork
XXV Esposizione Biennale Internazionale d'Arte, Venice;
Cassa di Risparmio di Cento, Cento

Pannelli
Cassa di Risparmio di Cento, Cento

Piastra Quilt
Mediocredito delle Venezie, Venice

1971
Elementi profilati
The Mandarin Singapore Hotel, Singapore

1972
Calza
Airport, Frankfurt

Pastorale
Nuovo catalogo di illuminazione 1973, 1972

1973
Iceberg
Banca Depositi e Gestioni di Credito, Lugano

1974
Lago
Sofitel Vieux-Port Hotel, Marseille

Rombo
Venini, 1974, poster

1975
Alga
Venini 75: Catalogo di illuminazione, 1975

Cervelloni
Hess's Restaurant, Lancaster;
Venini 75: Catalogo di illuminazione, 1975

Fiocco di neve
Venini 75: Catalogo di illuminazione, 1975

1976
Dorica
Mandarin Oriental Manila Hotel, Makati

1978
Betulla
Venini illuminazione d'architettura, [1978]

Fiore
Moulin Rouge, Paris

Savoy
Venini illuminazione d'architettura, [1978]

Piastre Taif
Sheraton-Al Hada Hotel, Taif

1980
Canne-sfere
Royal Saudi Military Academy, Jubail

Nastri
Euroluce, 1980

1983
Piastra Nuvola
Casinò de la Vallée, Saint-Vincent

1985
Asta Esalobo, Ipsilon, Penta, Quadrilobo, Tonda Fili, Tortiglione, Triedro
Barra Taif
Canna 007, d'Organo, Rigadin
Croce Miami
Listello Brunei, Bustan, Palude
Poliedro Riyadh
Stella Esprit
Tegoloni Bor
Trapezio Riyadh
Tubo Corteccia, Ottagonale, Ottolobo, Stella, Tronco
Venini, 1985

OTHER LIGHTING PROJECTS FROM THE VENINI CATALOGUES

In the following pages the list of the projects indicated in the appendices of the glassworks' catalogues, in particular in *Venini lavori di illuminazione 1973* (1972) and in *Venini* (1985). The list has been supplemented with the list supplied by the Caliari company archive, the Venini dealer in Turin. It has been decided to reproduce the subdivision by continent and building type (e.g. hotels, restaurant and clubs, banks etc.) already used in the said catalogues. Each entry (names, places, architects) faithfully follows that present in the original lists, therefore the document is presented in Italian.

ALBERGHI, RISTORANTI, CLUB

ITALIA

Albergo Capranica, Roma
Albergo Monaco, Venezia
Carimate Country Club, Carimate
Casina Valadier, Roma, arch. Chellini, Cittadini
City Hotel, Torino, arch. Ternetti
Dancing Le Roi, Torino, arch. Molino
Grand Hotel Delfino, Taranto, arch. Accolti-Gil
Grand Hotel, Sestriere, arch. Albertini
Gritti Palace, Venezia, arch. Gardella, Menghi
Harry's Bar, Venezia
Hotel Al Cason, Padova
Hotel Alaska, Cortina d' Ampezzo
Hotel Ambasciatori, Chianciano Terme, arch. Angelucci
Hotel Astoria, Bormio
Hotel Astoria, Sestriere, arch. Cracci
Hotel Astoria, Stresa, arch. Cracci
Hotel Beatrice d'Este, Padova
Hotel Byron, Roma
Hotel Carlton-Senato, Milano
Hotel Cipriani, Venezia, arch. Gallet
Hotel Commodoro, Roma
Hotel Continental, Abano Terme
Hotel de la Poste, Cortina d'Ampezzo
Hotel de la Ville, Roma, arch. Loreti
Hotel De Rose, Castrovillari
Hotel des Palmes, Palermo
Hotel Duca d'Aosta, Trieste, arch. Pianon
Hotel Duchi D'Aosta, Sestriere, arch. Albertini
Hotel Eliseo, Abano Terme
Hotel Europa, Abano Terme, arch. Trevisan
Hotel Excelsior, Cesenatico
Hotel Excelsior, Lido di Venezia, arch. Menghi
Hotel Flamingo, Santa Margherita di Pula
Hotel Fons Salera, Casale Monferrato
Hotel Garden, Garda
Hotel Imperiale, Roma
Hotel Majestic, Galzignano
Hotel Mar del Plata, Grado, arch. Camporese
Hotel Miramare, Castiglione della Pescaia, arch. Chellini
Hotel Mondial, Roma, arch. Dall'Olio
Hotel Monte Bianco, Pré-Saint-Didier, arch. Dina
Hotel Palace, Bari, arch. Braghirdi
Hotel Palace, Catania, arch. Braghirdi
Hotel Palace, Sauze d'Oulx, arch. Cracci
Hotel Palace, Torino, arch. Chabloz
Hotel Paradiso, Asiago
Hotel Pila, Aosta
Hotel Principe, Avezzano
Hotel Principi di Piemonte, Sestriere
Hotel Rosa Pineta, Pollina, arch. Foscari, Flé
Hotel Royal, Torino
Hotel Savoia, Cortina d' Ampezzo
Hotel Sitea, Torino
Hotel Tritone, Abano Terme, arch. Genta
Lloyd's Baia Hotel, Vietri sul Mare
Park Hotel, Ravenna
R.E.S.O. Tourist Village, Baia Domizia, arch. Chellini
R.E.S.O. Tourist Village, Castiglione della Pescaia, arch. Chellini
Residence Hotel Villa Sassi, Torino, arch. Cuzzi
Ristorante Arc-en-Ciel, Casteggio
Ristorante Arc-en-Ciel, Milano
Ristorante Frascati, Roma
Ristorante Tropicana, Torino, arch. Colli
Terme di Chianciano, Chianciano Terme, arch. Lugli, Loreti

EUROPA

Albany Hotel, Glasgow
Barracuda Restaurant, Londra
Bristol Hotel, Bonn
Café de la Paix, Poitiers
Carlton Gardens, Londra
Casino, Evian
Cumberland Hotel, Londra, arch. Lennon
Dragonara Hotel, Leeds
Duke's Head Hotel, King's Lynn
Esso Motor Hotel, Wembley, arch. Garnett, Cloughley, Blakemore
Golden Sands Hotel, Nicosia, arch. Garnett, Cloughley, Blakemore
Grand Hotel, Stoccolma
Hannafore Point Hotel, Hannafore
Hilton Hotel, Amsterdam
Hilton Hotel, Monaco
Hotel Baur-au-Lac, Zurigo, arch. Samuel
Hotel Concorde La Fayette, Angers
Hotel de l'Ours, Huez
Hotel du Printemps, Parigi
Hotel Eden, Lugano
Hotel Europa, Londra
Hotel Frantel, Rungis
Hotel Friedland, Parigi
Hotel Imperial Playa, Las Palmas de Gran Canaria
Hotel Le Grand Monarque, Chartres
Hotel Le Zenith, Saint-Bon-Tarentaise
Hotel Palace, Lesina
Hotel Vendôme, Parigi
Hotel Wellington, Ostenda
Hyatt Regency Hotel, Bruxelles
Intercontinental Hotel, Ginevra
Intercontinental Hotel, Vienna
Kursaal Hotel, Bad-Ragaz
Kursaal, Ostendea
L'Hostaria, Bruxelles
Le Grand Hotel, Parigi
Leefe Robinson Restaurant, Uxbridge
Metropole Hotel, Brighton
Night Club Le Nouveau Lido, Parigi, arch. Bartoccini
Night Club Paradis Latin, Parigi, arch. Simonin
Res Hotel, Lucerna
Ringbaren Restaurant, Gävle
Royal Kensington Garden Hotel, Londra, arch. Bayes
Sheraton Heathrow Hotel, Londra
Sheraton Hotel, Lisbona
Sheraton Malta, Malta

Transat Hotel, Bastia
Villa Backer, Oslo
White House, Londra

AMERICA

Americana Hotel, Hartford
Americana Hotel, Miami Beach
Bonnie Bar Country Club, New York City
Brione Restaurant, New York City
Briors Country Club, Westport
Caribe Hilton Hotel, San Juan, arch. Branston
Carlton Towers Bistro, Ottawa
Four Season Restaurant, New York
Happy Bar Hotel, Kingston
Hendrick Hudson Hotel, Troy
Hilton Hotel, Caracas, arch. Branston
Horn & Hardard, New York City
La Scala Restaurant, New York City
Lone Palm Golf Club, Lakeland
Marbley & Carew Snack Bar, Forestville
Marriott Hotel, Los Angeles
New York Plaza Club, New York City
Ocean Dune Hotel, Myrtle Beach
Pinnacle Club, New York City
Pine Hollow Country Club, Long Island
Plaza One Restaurant, New York City
Ristorante Castle Fleur des Lilles, Atlanta
Ruc Restaurant, New York City
Sheraton Motor Inn, Fayetteville
The Conrad Hilton Hotel, Chicago
Restaurant, Pan-Am Building, New York City

ASIA

Apollo Hotel, Singapore
Borobudur Intercontinental Hotel, Giacarta, arch. Keller, Marsteller
Chosun Hotel, Seul
Club degli Ufficiali, Marina Imperiale, Teheran
Yogyakarta Hotel, Giacarta, arch. Ti Seow
Phoenix Hotel, Singapore
Royal Ramada Hotel, Singapore

MEDIO ORIENTE

Abu Dhabi Sheraton Hotel, Abu Dhabi
Bustan Hotel, Mascate
Conference & Guest Center, Taif
Dubai Intercontinental Hotel, Dubai
Hotel Carlton, Nahariya, arch. Akady
Hotel Le Meridien, Sharjah
Hotel Park, Natanya
Intercontinental Hotel, Mekkah
Le Méridien Hotel, Al-Khobar
Muscat Intercontinental, Mascate
Red Sea Hotel, Jeddah

AFRICA

Eko Hotel, Lagos
Hotel Bel-Azur, Hammamet
Hotel Cairo Concorde, Cairo
Hotel de la Ville, Yaoundé, arch. Salomon
Hotel Le Président, Yamoussoukro, arch. Del Sasso
Khartum Hilton Hotel, Khartum, arch. Keller
Sheraton Hotel, Lagos

BANCHE

ITALIA

Associazione delle Casse di Risparmio, Roma
Banca Cattolica del Veneto, Torri di Quartesolo, arch. Dellavilis
Banca d'Italia, Alessandria
Banca d'Italia, Aosta
Banca d'Italia, Ascoli Piceno
Banca d'Italia, Avellino
Banca d'Italia, Bologna
Banca d'Italia, Centro Sportivo, Roma
Banca d'Italia, Chieti
Banca d'Italia, Cosenza
Banca d'Italia, Cremona
Banca d'Italia, Direzione Generale, Roma
Banca d'Italia, Gorizia
Banca d'Italia, L'Aquila
Banca d'Italia, Macerata
Banca d'Italia, Messina
Banca d'Italia, Milano
Banca d'Italia, Pavia
Banca d'Italia, Perugia, arch. Pascoletti
Banca d'Italia, Pescara
Banca d'Italia, Piacenza
Banca d'Italia, Pisa
Banca d'Italia, Ravenna
Banca d'Italia, Siracusa
Banca d'Italia, Taranto
Banca d'Italia, Torino
Banca d'Italia, Treviso
Banca d'Italia, Udine
Banca d'Italia, Ufficio Fondo Monetario, Roma
Banca d'Italia, Ufficio Normativa Interventi, Roma
Banca d'Italia, Viterbo
Banca del Monte dei Crediti, Pavia, arch. Aschieri
Banca Federale di Amatrice, Roma, arch. Mazzocca
Banca Morgan-Vonwiller, Milano
Banca Nazionale del Lavoro, Roma
Banca Nazionale del Lavoro, Torino, arch. Bordogna
Banca Popolare di Lodi, Lodi, arch. Rozza
Banca Popolare di Padova Treviso, Padova
Banca Popolare di Vicenza, Vicenza
Banca Privata Finanziaria, Milano
Banca Tiburtina e Servizi, Tivoli, arch. Mannu
Banco di Napoli, Milano, arch. Borsani
Banco di Napoli, Udine, arch. Avon
Banco di Roma, Campobasso
Banco di Roma, Cuneo
Banco di Roma, Firenze
Banco di Roma, Perugia
Banco di Roma, Torino
Cassa di Risparmio di Asti, Asti, arch. Ercole
Cassa di Risparmio, Alba, arch. Barberis
Cassa di Risparmio, Ascoli Piceno
Cassa di Risparmio, Civitavecchia, arch. Antonini
Cassa di Risparmio, Cuneo, arch. Morelli
Cassa di Risparmio, L'Aquila
Cassa di Risparmio, Roma, arch. Coltellacci
Cassa di Risparmio, San Benedetto del Tronto, arch. Teodori
Cassa di Risparmio, Teramo
Cassa di Risparmio, Viterbo
Credito Agrario Bresciano, Milano, arch. Salotti
Credito Italiano, Torino, arch. Burs
Istituto Bancario San Paolo, Genova
Istituto Centrale delle Banche Popolari Italiane, Roma
Istituto Credito Agrario Italia Centrale, Roma, arch. Pozzi
Monte dei Paschi di Siena, Arezzo
Monte dei Paschi di Siena, Bari

EUROPA

Amsterdamsche Bank, Amsterdam
Banca d'Italia, Bruxelles
Banca Cornhill, Londra
Banco di Roma France, Grenoble
Banco di Roma France, Montecarlo
Banco di Roma France, Nizza
Banco di Roma France, Rungis
Bank Melli Iran, Londra
Bank of London and South America, Londra
Bank of Scotland, Londra
Banque Industrie et Commerce, Parigi
Barclay's Bank, Londra
Childs Bank, Londra
Crédit General, Parigi
Kreditbank, Lussemburgo, arch. De Capitani
Marine Midland Bank, Londra
New York Trust Co., Parigi
Société Générale, Parigi
Standard Bank, Londra

AMERICA

Arlington Federal Savings and Loan Association, Baltimora
Chase Manhattan Mortgage & Trust Co., New York City
Citizens' National Bank, Waco
Clarendon Bank & Trust Co., Arlington
F.M. Bank, Tulsa
Farmer's Bank, Wilmington, arch. Stonorov
First Federal Savings & Loan, Statesmen Club, Rapid City
First National Bank, Clovis
Franklin National Bank, New York City
Irving Trust Co., New York City
Manufacturers' Bank, Detroit
Mercantile Trust Co., St. Louis
Philadelphia National Bank, Philadelphia
Provident Tradesmen Bank & Trust Co., Philadelphia

Sterling National Bank, New York City
Swiss Bank, World Trade Center, New York City
Texas State Bank, Austin
The Cornelian Bank, Cornelia

ASIA

Chase Manhattan Bank S.A., Seul

COMMERCIO

ITALIA

Anonima Castelli, Milano
Atelier Borsato, Padova, arch. Paparotto
Caflish, Palermo
Calzature Barilla, Roma, arch. De Marinis
Centro Frau, Bari
Centro Ortofrutticolo Ente Delta Padano, Ferrara, arch. Giordani
City Club, Milano
Cusi Jewellery, Milano
De Montis, Fiumicino, Roma, arch. Chellini, Cittadini
Elle Altamoda, Reggio Calabria
Ferragamo, Genova
Ferragamo, Milano
FIAT Showroom, Alessandria
FIAT Showroom, Bologna
FIAT Showroom, Novara
FIAT Showroom, Varese, arch. Alzona
Gioielleria Parodi, Genova
Gioielleria Spallanzani, Milano, arch. De Bartolo
Giuliani, Roma, arch. Giuliani
La Boutique, Abano Terme, arch. Genta
La Calza, Roma
Magli, Bologna
Omega, Milano
Orologeria Hausmann, Roma
Ottica La Barbera, Roma, arch. Micozzi
Parigiotto Scarpe, Bologna
Pellicceria Bresciani, Milano, arch. Canozzi
Pellicceria Fratelli Trione, Bari
Pellicceria Passi, Roma, arch. De Marinis
Sartoria Palazzi, Roma
Varese Scarpe, Messina
Varese Scarpe, Milano, arch. Fiocchi
Varese Scarpe, Nuoro
Varese Scarpe, Sassari
Vasari Ottica, Roma

EUROPA

Bradleys, Londra
Burberry, Parigi
Burton of London, Lione
Burton of London, Parigi
Burton of London, Roissy-en-France
Burton of London, Bruxelles
Castelli, Londra
Debenham & Freebody, Londra
Drugstore Ponthien, Parigi
Drugwest, Parly II, Parigi
Elizabeth Arden, Bruxelles
Galerie de Peinture David, Parigi
Harrods, Hairdressing Saloon, Londra
Harvey Nichols, Londra
Jaeger Shop, Birmingham, arch. Lennon
L'Arlequin, Parigi
L'Atrium, Parigi
L'Oréal, Parigi, arch. Merlotti
Le Grand Zinc, Parigi
Le Massiglia, Parigi
Magli Shoes, Londra, arch. Ellis
Max Factor, Londra
Negozio Arcet, Parigi
Ralli, Londra

AMERICA

Avon Products Inc., New York City
Avon Products, Atlanta
Barrett Towers, Northbrook
Benton & Bowles Inc., New York City
Capri's Jewellery, New York City
Caribe Times, Little Switzerland, St. Thomas, Virgin Islands
Christie's of London, New York City
Daitchy Shopwell, Bronx
Daitchy Shopwell, Norwalk
Design One Studio Inc., New York City
Eaton's Department Store, Toronto
F.S. Smithers & Co, New York City
Fabergé Inc., New York City
Filene's, New York City
Foley's Shopping Center, Houston
Hudson Department Stores, Detroit
Jordan Marsh Co., Rhode Island
Jordan Marsh Gift Shop, South Portland
Kettering Industries, Englewood Cliffs
Lobby, 16 West 61st Street, New York City
Magnin's, Century City
Magnin's, Torrance
Mayor's Jewellers, Miami
Nazareno Gabrielli, Beverly Hills, arch. Massoni
Neiman-Marcus, Dallas
Neiman-Marcus, Houston
Neiman-Marcus, New York City
Perl Organization, Florham Park
Potter Materials Services, Indianapolis
Southland Shopping Centre, Minneapolis
Tordan Marsh, Providence
Wellington Jewels, Atlanta
Zancopè, San Paolo del Brasile

ASIA

Djaya Pura Pte.Ltd., Singapore
Pontiac Trading Co., Singapore

EDIFICI CULTURALI

ITALIA

Centro Internazionale di Perfezionamento Professionale e Tecnico, Torino
Facoltà di Architettura, Messina
Facoltà di Legge, Catania, arch. Leone
Istituto di Chimica Biologica, Torino, arch. Colli
Università, Padova, arch. Brunetta
Università, Venezia, arch. Venturini

EUROPA

Académie d'Architecture, Parigi
Centro Culturale, Chelles
Conservatorio musicale, Rouen
Maison de la Culture, Reims
Musée de l'Orangerie, Parigi
University College, Londra

AMERICA

Convention Hall, New Orleans
Dag Hammarskjöld Library, New York City
Dickinson Library, Harrison
New York University, New York City
Ringling Museum of Art, Sarasota
Scuola pubblica, Wilton
State University of New York, Albany

MEDIO ORIENTE

Beit Greza Cultural Center, Mascate
Royal High School, Ryadh

EDIFICI RELIGIOSI

ITALIA

Cappella del Presepe, Roma
Casa della Missione, Sassari, arch. Figari
Cattedrale, Catania, arch. Leone
Chiesa delle Suore del Sacro Cuore, Roma, arch. Costa
Chiesa delle Suore di Nevers, Roma, arch. Sterbini
Chiesa di San Giorgio, Torino, arch. Nori
Chiesa di San Maurizio, Ivrea, arch. Radic
Chiesa di Santa Maria Goretti, Sant'Ambrogio, arch. Figari
Chiesa Madonna del Rosario, Torino, arch. Merlotti
Chiesa, Castiglione Olona, arch. Fiocchi
Collegium Seraphicum, Roma, arch. Sterbini
Convento Suore della Consolata, Torino, arch. Aloisio
Istituto Figlie di Maria Ausiliatrice, Torino, arch. Nori
Istituto Suore Adoratrici di Gesù, Rivolta d'Adda, arch. Galli
Istituto Suore del Sacro Cuore, L'Aquila, arch. Sterbini
Monastero della Visitazione, Moncalieri, arch. Aloisio
Seminario Vescovile, Camerino, arch. Lenti

EUROPA

Sinagoga Whitefilds, Manchester

AMERICA

Tempio Beth Abraham, Tarrytoren
Tempio Sinai, Bergen County, Tenafly

ASIA

Moschea, Singapore

MEDIO ORIENTE

Moschea, Makkah

AFRICA

Cattedrale, Meru, arch. Aloisio
Moschea, Kairouan

RESIDENZE

ITALIA

Casa degli Architetti, Torino
Casa Monti, Milano
Case Popolari, interno del tipo 7, Roma
Condominio Buonarroti, Milano, arch. Nardini
Condominio d' Azeglio, Torino, arch. Silvestrini
Condominio Gabriella, Como, arch. Cagnardi
Condominio Via Bronzetti, Milano, arch. Pedroni
Costruzioni Grieco, Roma
Palazzina Musolino, Taranto
Residence Casa Fiorita, Roma, arch. Leoni
Residenza Bertone, Rivoli, arch. Davico
Residenza Faccenda, Vernante, arch. Mandraci
Residenza Melani, Pontedera, arch. Fasana
Residenza Perlini, Verona, arch. Nordio
Residenza Stoppani, Padova
S.C.I. Villa Bonelli, Roma
Società Immobiliare Bandello, Milano, arch. Baldizzone
Società Immobiliare Imperia, Biella, arch. Bastianello
Società Immobiliare Toro, Torino, arch. Silvestrini
Società Luset Palazzine, Roma, arch. Di Giulio
Villa Alamia, Palermo
Villa Arman, Coazze, arch. Merlotti
Villa Badino, Albissola, arch. Rossigno
Villa Baggi, Inverigo, arch. Invernizzi
Villa Baldi, Roma, arch. Portoghesi
Villa Barcella, Bagnatico, arch. Colleoni
Villa Bardelli, Milano, arch. Belloni
Villa Bona, Torino, arch. D'Imperio
Villa Bonotti, Roma, arch. Frisardi
Villa Botto, Biella, arch. Graziosi
Villa Bruneri, Torino, arch. Barello
Villa Buzzetti, Varese
Villa Campion, Coazze, arch. Merlotto
Villa Cavaretta, Torino, arch. Torino
Villa Cogolo, Trieste
Villa Corbucci, Roma, arch. Frisardi
Villa Efrati, Roma, arch. Protopapa
Villa Filiberti, Gallarate
Villa Frey, Como, arch. Parigi
Villa Galardi, Milano, arch. Colma
Villa Galliani, Milano, arch. Crotti
Villa Genoso, Settimo Torinese, arch. Sorra, Bottinelli
Villa Ghione, Torino, arch. D'Imperio
Villa Gorla, Milano
Villa Graziotti, Grosseto, arch. Chellini, Cittadini
Villa Maggiora, Rivoli, arch. Cucchi
Villa Manca, Como
Villa Mancini, Roma, arch. De Santis
Villa Mandelli, Torino, arch. Cuzzi
Villa Manfredi, Anzio
Villa Marenzi, Lesa, arch. Cracchi
Villa Marsetti, Bergamo, arch. Pierpaoli
Villa Marxer-Olivetti, Ivrea, arch. Cucchi
Villa Massaglia, Asti, arch. Vernero
Villa Maumary, Milano, arch. Farina, Morez
Villa Mazzini, Novara, arch. Cazzola
Villa Migliasso, Torino, arch. Clemente
Villa Milanaccio, Inverigo, arch. Arcelli
Villa Momigliano, Pinamare Andoro, arch. Caliari
Villa Montalboldi, Viterbo, arch. D'Imperio
Villa Moraglione, Valenza Po, arch. Mandracci, Stano
Villa Nava, Erba, arch. Chiodi
Villa Necchi, Nervi, arch. Buzzi, Marelli
Villa Nesti, Varese
Villa Oddera, Garma, arch. Bonatti
Villa Oldani, Milano, arch. Capra
Villa Papasergio, Belvedere Marittima, arch. De Vita
Villa Pianelli, Bardonecchia, arch. Caliari
Villa Pianelli, Finale Ligure, arch. Barello
Villa Pianelli, Rivoli, arch. Pellegrino
Villa Pianelli, Torino
Villa Pizzicanella, Rocca di Papa
Villa Pofferi, Roma, arch. Padovano
Villa Prini, Genova, arch. Cracchi
Villa Redaelli, Milano, arch. Capra
Villa Rindone, Catania
Villa Riva, Varese, arch. Pavesi
Villa Rossi, Cunardo, arch. Bonatti
Villa Schanzer, Roma
Villa Sterzi, Milano, arch. Albini
Villa Toffoloni, Santa Margherita Ligure
Villa Traversa, Rivalta, arch. Caliari
Villa Viberti, Rivoli, arch. Aloisio
Villa Villata, Pino Torinese, arch. Del Mastro
Villa Vittoria, Firenze, arch. Buzzi
Villa Zampogna, Gioia Tauro

EUROPA

Casa Stenman, Londra
H.M. the Queen's Library, Copenaghen
H.R.H. the Princess Shams Pahlavi, Parigi
Immobile, rue de l'Assomption, Parigi
Immobile, rue de la Faisanderie, Parigi
Immobile, rue de Longchamp, Parigi
Immobile, rue de Montevideo, Parigi
Immobile, rue des Belles-Feuilles, Parigi
Résidence de l'Aube, Collonge-Bellerive
Résidence Grenelle, Parigi
S.C.I. Maurice Barres, Parigi
The White House Mansions, Londra
Villa Fenyo, Lugano, arch. Monesi
Villa Mondadori, Saint-Jean-Cap-Ferrat, arch. Ridolfi
Villa Vornoro, Montecarlo

AMERICA

12200 Lake Shore Apartments, Oakland
16 West 61st Street, New York City
185 East 85th Street, New York City
201 East 19th Street, New York City
400 Madison, New York City
Aron Birmann's Residence, San Paolo del Brasile, arch. Libeskind
Century 21th, Century City, Miami
Clermont South, New York City
Clermont Tower North, New York City
Concord Homes, Bethesda
Crystal House, Teaneck
Flamingo Residences Club, Miami Beach
Fox Plaza, San Francisco
Gateway Towers, Pittsburgh
Harmonis Residence, New York City
Henry Kaiser's House, Honolulu
Minoru Yamasaki's Residence, Troy, arch. Yamasaki
North Park Towers, Detroit
Oscar Stonorov's House, Philadelphia
Oyster Bay Estates, New York City
Park Grand Apartments, New York City
Paul Rudolph's House, Sarasota Fl., arch. Rudolph
Playboy Mansion, Chicago
Plaza 800, Miami
Plaza Buildings, New York City
Regency Tower, Las Vegas
Riverside Presbyterian Apartments, Jacksonville
Seacoast Tower, Miami Beach
The Montclair, New York City
The Mountains, Lake Lure
The Versailles Apartments, New York City
The Watergate Apartments, Washington D.C.
Thornton Ladd's House, Los Angeles
Tower Apartment House, 888 Eighth Ave., New York City
Tsai Residence, Byram
Villa Cabouli, Buenos Aires, arch. Cavallari

ASIA

Ang. E.J. Residence, Singapore, arch. Lee Sian Teck
Chuang Residence, Singapore
E.G. Tan Residence, Singapore
H. Kwee Residence, Singapore, arch. Seow Lee, Heah
H.H. the Raja Muda of Selangor Residence, Kumpulan Senireka

H.H. the Sultan of Selangor Residence, Selangor, arch. B.E.P.
H.H. the Sultan Tengku Mahkota of Johore Residence, Johor
H.R.H the Princess Shams Pahlavi Residence, Mar Caspio, arch. Borsani
L.K. Kwee Residence, Singapore, arch. Seor Lee, Heah
Pereira Residence, Singapore, arch. Woo

MEDIO ORIENTE

Al-Futtaim Residence, Dubai, arch. Casati, Ponzio
H.H. the Princess Shams Pahlavi Residence, Teheran
H.R.H. the Prince Reza Pahlavi, Teheran
H.R.H. the Prince Sultan ben-Fahd ben-Abdul Aziz Residences, Riyadh
H.R.H. the Princess Shams Pahlavi Residence, Teheran, arch. Borsani
Nemazee's Residence, Teheran, arch. Ponti
Private Villa, Makkah
Sheikh Abdul-el-Aziz Al Saleh Residence, Riyadh
Sheikh Alid-al-Ammad Ben Sabah Residence, Kuwait
Villa a Baghdad, arch. Gima
Villa a Obhor, Riyadh
Villa Al-Humeid, Riyadh, arch. Design 2000
Villa in Saudi Arabia, arch. Turzi
Villa in Saudi Arabia, arch. Bersane
Villa in Saudi Arabia, arch. Centrodom
Villa Kater, Riyadh, arch. Design 2000
Villa Kurdy, Riyadh, arch. Design 2000

AFRICA

Sayedh Abdallah's Residence, Benghazi
Villa privata, Tangeri

AUSTRALIA

Russel Slade's House, Camperdown

SALE DI SPETTACOLO

ITALIA

Auditorium Vaticano, Città del Vaticano, arch. Piacentini
Cinema Alexander, Milano
Cinema Arlecchino, Torino
Cinema Astra, Monza
Cinema Corallo, Milano, arch. Signorelli
Cinema Dante, Sesto San Giovanni
Cinema Doria, Torino
Cinema Embassy, Treviso
Cinema Fiamma, Torino
Cinema Olimpico, Roma
Cinema Teatro Ariston, Sanremo
Cinema Teatro San Marco, Venezia
Conservatorio Giuseppe Verdi, Torino, arch. Ricci
Politeama Genovese, Genova
Teatro Gobetti, Roma
Teatro Goldoni, Foyer, Venezia
Teatro La Fenice, Venezia
Teatro La Pergola, Firenze

EUROPA

Cinema Le Français, Parigi
Cinema Le Gaumont, Parigi
Cinema Le Paris, Chambéry
Cinema Le Select, Fontainebleau
Kammerspiel Theater, Linz, arch. Holzmeister
Landestheater, Linz
Salzburger Groß Festspiel Haus, Salisburgo, arch. Holzmeister
Teatro, Montpellier
Teatro, Troyes
Teatro, Villeneuve-Saint-Georges

AMERICA

Center for the Performing Arts, Houston
Cinema II, Framingham
Civic Auditorium, San Francisco
Fox Theater, Columbia
Honolulu Theater, Honolulu
Mann Theater, Minneapolis, arch. Gingold
Opera House, New Orleans
Rogers Theater, Chattanooga
Woodbridge Theater, Lodi

MEDIO ORIENTE

Teatro, Gorgan

TRASPORTI

ITALIA

M/N Italia, Genova, arch. Pulitzer
Pakistani Airlines, Biglietteria, Roma, arch. Teodori
Stazione F.S. Termini, Sale Presidenziali, Roma

EUROPA

Aeroporto, Marignane, arch. Salmon
S/S Queen Elizabeth II, Liverpool

AMERICA

Alitalia, New York City
American Airlines, Biglietteria, New York City
Japan Airlines, San Francisco
Pakistani Airlines, Biglietteria, Washington D.C.
Pan-American Airlines, Ufficio, New York City

UFFICI

ITALIA

Acque Sangemini, Direzione, Roma
Ala Assicurazioni, Roma, arch. Carino
Alta Italia Assicurazioni, Roma
Assicurazioni Generali, Foresteria, Trieste, arch. Armeri, Bolco
Associazione Calcio Torino, Torino, arch. Bordogna
Cartiere Burgo, Milano, arch. Martinengo
Cassa Nazionale del Notariato, Roma, arch. Bruno
Cassa Nazionale Dottori Commercialisti, Roma, arch. Mazzi, Cantatore
CEAT, Torino, arch. Dezzuti
Centro Legale Internazionale, Torino, arch. Cefalù
CONI, Roma, arch. Del Debbio
ENAOLI, Roma, arch. Ginosa
ENEL, Sede, Roma, arch. La Padula
ENPAS, Roma
FIAT, Palazzo Uffici, Torino, arch. Stupanengo
Herno spa, Lesa, arch. Cracchi
Impresa Costanzo, Direzione, Catania, arch. Leone
INA, Trapani
INPS, Sede, Terni
IRI, Direzione Centrale, Roma
RAI, Direzione Generale, Roma
RAI, Sede, Genova, arch. Beverasco
Riunione Adriatica di Sicurtà, Roma, arch. Pascoletti
SIPRA, Torino, arch. Aloisio
Società Danubio, Roma, arch. Ginosa
Società First, Milano, arch. Ulrich
Società Giustina, Settimo Torinese, arch. Biscaretti
Società Grassetto, Padova, arch. Trevisan
Società Le Petit, Roma, arch. Indirizzi
Società Reale Mutua di Assicurazioni, Torino, arch. Decker
Società Valstura, Torino, arch. Panié
Toro Assicurazioni, via Arcivescovado, Torino
Unione Italiana di Riassicurazioni, Roma

EUROPA

Automobile Club, Parigi
Brooke, Bond, Liebig Ltd., Londra
Champagne Veuve-Clicquot, Parigi
Cofica, Parigi
Cogifrance, Parigi
Commercial Union, Londra
Cook International, Parigi
Électricité de France, Melun
Elvinger, Parigi
Établissement Coutant, Parigi
Europe-Secrétariat, Parigi
Fédération Mutualiste de la Seine, Parigi
Hall d'Information U.A.P., Parigi
Hazelmere Estates Ltd., Londra
Independent Broadcasting Authority, Winchester
La Belle Jardinière, Parigi
La Préservatrice Foncière, Parigi
La Préservatrice, Parigi
Lefort-Franchetean, Parigi
Maisons des Centraux, Parigi
Ozalid Ltd., Birmingham
Radio Luxembourg, Parigi
Vauxhall Motor Works Ltd., Luton
Waddington Ltd., Leeds

AMERICA

Allied News, New York City
Bacon, Stevenson & Reeves Lare Offices, New York City
Caribe Time, Little Switzerland, St. Thomas
Correctional Associates of New York, New York City
Eli Power Equipment Co., Columbus
F.T.D. Enterprises, Edison
Hygiene Industries, New York City
Johns-Manville Corp., Denver
Johns-Manville Corp., Jefferson
Kettering Industries, Englewood Cliffs
Lincoln National Life Insurance Co. of New York, New York City
Louis Dreyfus Corp., New York City
Maritime Overseas Corp., New York City
Minerals & Chemicals Philipp Corp., New York City
Montgomery-Ward, Chicago
Omega, New York City
Standard Oil Co., New York City
The New York Telephone Co., New York City
Warner-Lambert Pharmaceutical C., New York City
Ford Motor Co., Chassis Division, Sterling Heights

ASIA

Herno Japan, Tokyo
Jardine-Matheson, Hong Kong, arch. Ashton
Saint George's Building, Hong Kong, arch. Marmorek, Womersley

AFRICA

Bureau B.E.A.C., Bafoussan

UFFICI STATALI ED ENTI LOCALI

ITALIA

Ambasciata d'Italia presso la Santa Sede, Roma
Ambasciata della Costa d'Avorio, Roma
Ambasciata di Gran Bretagna, Roma, arch. Spence, Bloc
Camera di Commercio Italo-Germanica, Milano
Camera di Commercio, Brescia
Camera di Commercio, Carrara, arch. Chiarini
Camera di Commercio, Messina, arch. Puglisi, Allegra
Camera di Commercio, Padova
Camera di Commercio, Ravenna, arch. Manzone
Camera di Commercio, Torino, arch. Mosso
Camera di Commercio, Vercelli
Consolato del Canada, Milano
Consolato del Giappone, Milano
Consolato di Spagna, Milano
Ente Regione Emilia Romagna, Bologna
Ente Regione Friuli-Venezia Giulia, Trieste, arch. Bellavitis
Ente Regione Piemonte, Torino
Ente Turismo, Aosta, arch. Piccato
Ministero del Tesoro, Roma
Ministero della Difesa, Stato Maggiore Esercito, Roma
Ministero delle Poste e dei Telegrafi, Roma, arch. Foderà
Municipio, Como, arch. Sossnowsky
Municipio, Saint-Vincent, arch. Caliari
Municipio, Torino, arch. Burzio
Municipio, Vittorio Veneto
Palazzo del Comune, Roma
Palazzo della Provincia, Viterbo, arch. Ridolfi
Prefettura, Viterbo, arch. Ridolfi
Provveditorato per le Opere Pubbliche, L'Aquila, arch. Cortelli
Provveditorato per le Opere Pubbliche, Roma, arch. Cortelli

EUROPA

Accademia di architettura, Parigi
Ambasciata del Canada, Bonn
Ambasciata del Congo, Parigi
Ambasciata del Kuwait, Londra
Ambasciata del Madagascar, Parigi
Ambasciata del Sudafrica, Parigi
Ambasciata della Malesia, Parigi
Associazione Sauvegarde de l'Art Français, Parigi
Camera di Commercio, Châteauroux
Camera di Commercio, Le Mans, arch. Legrand
Chambre Syndicale des Agents Immobiliers de l'Île-de-France, Parigi
Derbyshire County Council, Derby
Hotel de Ville, Angers
Hotel de Ville, Yvetot, arch. Chauveau
Hotel Högland, Nässjö
Ministero delle Finanze, Parigi
Municipio, Fontainebleau
Municipio, La Garenne-Colombes
Municipio, Neuilly-sur-Marne
Municipio, Sainte-Geneviève-des-Bois
Municipio, Villeneuve-Saint-Georges
Official Residence, Canadian Permanent Mission to the Europeans Communities, Bruxelles
Palazzo Reale, Amsterdam
Prefettura Loiret, Orléans
Prefettura Meurthe-et-Moselle, Nancy
Prefettura Nord, Lille
Prefettura Seine-Maritime, Rouen, arch. Dussault-Leroy
Prefettura, Nanterre, arch. Charpentier
Royal Air Force, High Wycombe
Uffici 18th Cent. Building, Londra

AMERICA

Alberta Government House, Edmonton
Government of Qatar Residence, New York City
Lobby 888 Avenue, New York City

ASIA

Casa del Parlamento, Kuala Lumpur
New Istana Palace, Brunei, arch. Locsin, Keller

MEDIO ORIENTE

City Hall, Dubai, arch. Riva
Guest Palace & Government Center, Abha
Palazzo del Governo, Bahrein
Palazzo Reale, Agadir
Palazzo Reale, Dammam
Palazzo Reale, Jeddah
Palazzo Reale, Makkah
Palazzo Reale, Medina
Palazzo Reale, Riyadh
Royal Kuran Printing Shop, Medina

AFRICA

Ambasciata dell'Arabia Saudita, Tunisi
Circolo Militare, Hotel du B.R.A.S., Orano
Palazzo presidenziale, Libreville, Gabon
Palazzo Reale, Casablanca
Palazzo Reale, Fez
Palazzo Reale, Ifrane
Palazzo Reale, Marrakech
Palazzo Reale, Meknes
Palazzo Reale, Rabat

VARIE

ITALIA

Cantieri Baglietto, Genova, arch. Caliari
Cantieri Baglietto, Varazze
Cantieri Riva, Sarnico, arch. Pagani
Casa di Cura Quattro Marie, Milano, arch. Ventura
Casa di Cura San Michele, Bra, arch. Caliari
Clinica Villa Gina, Roma
Esposizione delle Piccole Industrie e dell'Artigianato, Firenze
Esposizione Eurodomus, Torino
Esposizione Nazionale e Internazionale Artigianato e Piccole Industrie, Torino
Esposizione Opera Bevilacqua La Masa, Venezia
Fiera di Milano, Milano
Mostra Nazionale d'Arte Marinara, Roma
Naval Meccanica, Castellamare di Stabia
Sede Ordine dei Medici, Torino, arch. Caliari

EUROPA

Centre Médical Moderne, Parigi
Clinique de l'Archer, Orléans
Stadtliches Berner Waisenhaus, Berna

AMERICA

International Exhibition, Italian Pavilion, Montreal, arch. Scarpa
New York World Fair, Gas Pavilion, New York City
Northern Shore Hospital, Manhasset

BIBLIOGRAPHY

1922
13. Esposizione internazionale d'arte della città di Venezia, 1922: catalogo, exhibition catalogue, 2nd ed., Florence
Catalogo ufficiale Fiera di Milano, exhibition catalogue, Milan

1923
Catalogo della prima mostra internazionale di arti decorative, exhibition catalogue, Milan-Rome

1924
14. Esposizione internazionale d'arte della città di Venezia, 1924: catalogo, exhibition catalogue, 2nd ed., Venice

1925
Catalogo seconda mostra internazionale delle arti decorative, exhibition catalogue, Milan
Exposition internationale des arts décoratifs et industriels modernes 1925 Paris, exhibition catalogue, Paris
U. Nebbia, 'L'Italia all'Esposizione Internazionale di Parigi di Arti Decorative ed Industriali Moderne', in *Emporium*, 367, pp. 17-36

1926
15. Esposizione Internazionale d'Arte della città di Venezia, exhibition catalogue, Venice
'Il monumento alla Madre italiana in Santa Croce', in *L'illustrazione italiana*, 7 November

1927
II Mostra d'Arte Marinara: I Mostra d'Arte Fiumana, exhibition catalogue, Rome
Catalogo ufficiale della III Mostra Internazionale delle Arti Decorative, exhibition catalogue, Milan

1928
'Alla Penna d'Oca', advertising insert, in *Domus*, January, p. 44
C. Clerici, 'Architetture moderne ed illuminazione', in *Domus*, May, pp. 32-33, 46-47
Domus [G. Ponti], 'Orientamenti del gusto nell'arredare la casa', in *Domus*, March, p. 41
G. Marangoni, 'L'illuminazione e la sua nuova estetica', in *La Casa bella*, June, pp. 11-14
U. Nebbia, *La Casa Madre dei Mutilati in Roma: 4 novembre 1928*, Milan-Rome

1929
Catàlogo Històrico y Bibliograàfico de la Exposición Internacional de Barcelona, exhibition catalogue, 2 vols., Madrid
Le XIX salon des artistes decorateurs, in *'Art et décoration'*, January, p. 25
'La Casa madre dei mutilati in Roma dell'Architetto Marcello Piacentini', in *Architettura e Arti Decorative*, June, pp. 433-458
'Le mobilier et les arts decoratif au salon d'automne', in *Art et décoration*, November, pp. 177-179
'Nuovi lampadari di Murano', in *La Casa bella*, December, pp. 30-32
G. Canesi, 'Tendenze moderne nell'illuminazione', in *Rassegna di Architettura*, May, pp. 176-185
Dir. [G. Ponti], 'Nuovi vetri muranesi', in *Domus*, February, pp. 31-33
G. Jellinek, 'Luce e architettura', in *Architettura e arti decorative*, October-November, pp. 61-72
E. L. [Lancia], 'Apparecchi moderni di illuminazione', in *Domus*, December, pp. 42-43

1930
'Ambienti d'oggi', in *Domus*, November, pp. 62-63
Catalogo Ufficiale della IV Esposizione Triennale Internazionale delle arti decorative ed industriali moderne, exhibition catalogue, Milan
Cover, *Domus*, November
A. Cassi Ramelli, 'L'illuminazione alla Triennale di Monza', in *L'illuminazione razionale*, June-July, pp. 43-47
A. Cassi Ramelli, 'Si cerca un lampadario', in *La Casa bella*, February, pp. 45-49
C.A. Felice, *Arte decorativa 1930 all'esposizione di Monza*, Milan
F. Reggiori, 'La Triennale di Monza. IV mostra internazionale delle arti decorative', in *Architettura e arti decorative*, July, pp. 505-507

1931
Mostra di vetri, ceramiche e merletti d'arte moderna italiana. Tentoonstelling van glas, aardewerk en kant, van moderne italiaansche kunstnijverheid, exhibition catalogue, Milan
Prima Quadriennale d'arte nazionale, exhibition catalogue, Rome
F. Businari, *L'architettura nei palazzi per le poste e telegrafi costruiti e da costruirsi a cura dell'amministrazione delle ferrovie dello stato - II congresso nazionale degli ingegneri italiani Roma 1931*, Milan-Rome

1932
'Il luna park del lido di Venezia, arch. Antonio Cassi-Ramelli', in *Rassegna di Architettura*, October, pp. 405-418
A. Cassi Ramelli, 'Apparecchi di illuminazione muranesi', in *L'illuminazione razionale*, December, pp. 269-272
A. Cassi Ramelli, 'Il "Luna Park" del Lido di Venezia', in *L'illuminazione razionale*, October, pp. 205-212
A. Fallica, 'Alcuni interni in Catania dell'arch. Francesco Fiducia', in *Architettura*, November, p. 623
'P. Ma. [Marconi], Il Padiglione per il porto industriale di Venezia-Marghera alla Fiera campionaria di Padova', in *Architettura*, July, pp. 365-368
R. Pacini, 'La sistemazione del centro di Brescia dell'architetto Marcello Piacentini', in *Architettura*, December, pp. 649-673
G. Vaccaro, 'Edifici postali e stazioni ferroviarie dell'arch. Angiolo Mazzoni', in *Architettura*, May, pp. 223-235

1933
I mostra nazionale della moda, exhibition catalogue, Turin
L'illuminazione alla V Triennale, in *L'illuminazione razionale*, May, pp. 125-127
L'illuminazione alla V Triennale, in *L'illuminazione razionale*, June, pp. 157-160
La mostra della moda italiana di Torino, in *L'illuminazione razionale*, April, pp. 100-101
'Il Palazzo delle Poste e dei Telegrafi di Massa-Carrara dell'architetto Angiolo Mazzoni', in *Sant'Elia*, December, p. 3
'Lo stadio Mussolini a Torino', in *Casabella*, December, pp. 26-29
Triennale di Milano: catalogo ufficiale, exhibition catalogue, Milan
[A. Cassi Ramelli], *Nuovi aspetti e nuove applicazioni del vetro muranese di Venini*, in *Architettura*, May, no page number
L. Lenzi, 'Lo stadio Mussolini in Torino', in *Architettura*, July, pp. 403-416

G. Marussig, 'Le arti decorative nel nuovo palazzo delle borse', in *Rassegna di Architettura*, March, pp. 119-121
R. Pacini, 'La mostra della Moda italiana a Torino', in *Architettura*, June, pp. 377-386
[G. Ponti], 'I vetri d'arte italiani alla Triennale', in *Domus*, July, pp. 379-381
[G. Ponti], 'I vetri d'arte italiani alla Triennale', in *Domus*, May, p. 236

1934
'Alcuni particolari dell'arredamento nelle sale da tè Motta di Milano', in *Domus*, March, pp. 34- 38
'La fontana luminosa a ricordo degli operai caduti nella costruzione della Direttissima Bologna-Firenze', in *L'illuminazione razionale*, February, pp. 82-83
'Un negozio d'eccezione, negozio Motta a Milano di M. Bega', in *Domus*, February, pp. 28-31
'Il nuovo negozio di Motta-panettoni in piazza del Duomo a Milano', in *L'illuminazione razionale*, March, pp. 51-57
'Palazzi delle poste e telegrafi a Bari e a Savona, architetto Roberto Narducci', in *Architettura*, October, pp. 679-688
'Per la vostra casa moderna', in *Domus*, January, p. 31
Sant'Elia, 15 March, p. 3
Ga. Mi. [Minnucci], 'La torre di Maratona, il campo di atletica leggera e la piscina allo stadio Mussolini di Torino', in *Architettura*, January, pp. 31-34

1935
'La nuova stazione passeggeri dell'aeroporto di Lido', in *Rivista di Venezia*, January-February, p. 57
'Realizzazioni dell'Italia nuova, edilizia delle comunicazioni', in *Le vie d'Italia*, November, p. 813

1936
'Casa P. a Milano', in *Domus*, April, pp. 25-33
'Colonia marina femminile dei fasci italiani all'estero a Tirrenia. Architetti Mario Paniconi e Giulio Pediconi', in *Architettura*, December, pp. 577-589
Guida della Sesta Triennale, exhibition catalogue, Milan
'Ricostruzione di un vecchio isolato nel secondo tratto della via Roma a Torino', in *L'architettura italiana*, September, pp. 195-215
R. Pacini, 'La stazione di Firenze Santa Maria Novella', in *Architettura*, April, pp. 145-165

1937
Exposition Internationale des arts et des techniques dans la vie moderne - Paris 1937, exhibition catalogue, Paris
'Il ministro Thaon di Revel inaugura il grande albergo "Principi di Piemonte"', in *La Stampa*, 24 December
'Le nuove stazioni ferroviarie di Siena e Reggio Emilia. Ing. Angiolo Mazzoni', in *Architettura*, March, pp. 125-144
'Il padiglione italiano all'Esposizione di Parigi', in *Casabella*, July, pp. 14-21
C.A. Felice, *Arti industriali d'oggi, Quaderni della Triennale*, Milan

1938
'Ricchezza di Murano', in *Domus*, June, p. 56
R. Fagnoni, 'La scuola di applicazione per la R. Aeronautica a Firenze', in *Architettura*, June, pp. 329-369
A. Melis, 'La ricostruzione del secondo tratto di via Roma a Torino', in *L'architettura italiana*, December, pp. 347-420

1939
III Quadriennale d'Arte Nazionale. Catalogo generale, exhibition catalogue, Rome
'Novità nel paese dei lampadari', in *Il vetro*, May, pp. 191-193
'La ricostruzione del secondo tratto di via Roma a Torino', in *Architettura*, June, pp. 339-362
E. Miozzi, 'Il nuovo Casino di Venezia', in *L'ingegnere*, June, pp. 493-500
E. Miozzi, 'Il vetro nel nuovo Casino di Venezia', in *Il vetro*, November, pp. 404-409
E. Zorzi, 'Una importante iniziativa veneziana nel campo dell'arredamento: il "Gruppo Arti Decorative"', in *Le Tre Venezie*, July-August, pp. 237-248

1940
22. Esposizione biennale internazionale d'arte, exhibition catalogue, Venice
VII Triennale di Milano. Guida, exhibition catalogue, Milan
G. Canesi, A. Cassi Ramelli, *Architetture luminose e apparecchi per illuminazione*, 2nd ed., Milan
R. Papini, 'Le arti a Milano nell'anno XVIII', in *Emporium*, May, p. 217
G. Ponti, 'Venini o della castigatezza', in *Domus*, June, pp. 57-61

1942
'Impianto idroelettrico nel bellunese, ingegnere Carlo Semenza e architetto Duilio Torres', in *Architettura*, April, pp. 110-116
'L'Istituto Svedese in Roma', in *Architettura*, January-February, pp. 49-51
R. Calzini, 'Il palazzo di Giustizia di Milano', in *Architettura*, January-February, monographic number

1950
M. Piacentini, 'Cinema-Teatro Palazzo Sistina di Roma', in *Edilizia Moderna*, June, pp. 47-50

1951
'A Palazzo Grassi. Il costume ritratto nel tempo', in *Il Gazzettino*, 24 August
'Apparecchi per l'illuminazione', in *Domus*, September, pp. 30-33
Centro Internazionale delle Arti e del Costume. Palazzo Grassi, Venice-Milan
Nona Triennale di Milano: catalogo, exhibition catalogue, Milan
'"Vernice" di due eccezionali rassegne. La moda e i suoi libri nel tempo da domani in vetrina a Palazzo Grassi', in *Il Gazzettino*, 22 August

1952
R. Aloi, *L'arredamento moderno*, Milan

1954
Decima Triennale: Milano 1954, exhibition catalogue, Milan
'Fifth Ave. Showroom', in *Architectural Forum*, August, pp. 98-103
'Italia a New York: un nuovo negozio Olivetti', in *Domus*, September, pp. 3-10
'Venini / Murano', in *Revue Internationale d'Eclairage*, June, pp. 200-205

1955
R. Aloi, *Vetri d'oggi. Esempi di decorazione moderna di tutto il mondo*, Milan

1956
La Biennale di Venezia: 28. esposizione biennale internazionale d'arte, exhibition catalogue, Venice
'Note sull'illuminazione in Italia', in *Rivista Internazionale d'Illuminazione*, January, p. 96
'Turboliner "Cristoforo Colombo"', in *International Lighting Review*, May, pp. 153-158

1957
Forme nuove in Italia: stile, forma, colore nell'artigianato e nell'industria, Rome
'Piccoli lampadari decorativi Venini / Murano', in *Rivista Internazionale d'Illuminazione*, January, pp. 172-173
Premio La Rinascente compasso d'oro 1956 per l'estetica del prodotto, Milan
Undicesima Triennale, exhibition catalogue, Milan
G. Mariacher, *Antichi lampadari vitrei veneziani*, Venice

1958
La Biennale di Venezia: 29. biennale internazionale d'arte, exhibition catalogue, Venice
Bruxelles 1958 Exposition Universelle, exhibition catalogue, Brussels
'Padiglioni nazionali: Italia', in *Rivista Internazionale d'Illuminazione*, March-April, pp. 110-111
'L'Italia all'Expo di Bruxelles', in *Edilizia Moderna*, August, pp. 65-74
'Lustre italien de Venini', in *Revue Internationale d'Eclairage*, June, pp. 194-195
Venedig Zeigt Glas aus Murano, exhibition catalogue, Vienna
F. Martinengo, 'La sede di una cartiera a Torino', in *Edilizia Moderna*, December, pp. 15-24
E.N. Rogers, 'A l'Expo '58 il futuro (dell'architettura) non è cominciato', in *Casabella-continuità*, September, pp. 2-21

1959
Glass 1959: A Special Exhibition of International Contemporary Glass, exhibition catalogue, Corning
'Lampadario di Venini', in *Rivista Internazionale d'Illuminazione*, June, pp. 194-195
'Venini', in *Domus*, December, pp. 31-46

1960
P. Tynell, 'Produzione di oggetti artistici', in *Rivista Internazionale d'Illuminazione*, June, p. 2

1961
'Dalla babele dei dialetti nasce sul Po la più spettacolare sintesi dell'Italia', in *La Stampa*, 26-27 April
'Italia '61 a Torino. Alla Mostra delle regioni, Il Veneto', in *Domus*, August, pp. 14-16
'L'Italia '61 a Torino. La mostra delle regioni', in *Casabella-continuità*, June, pp. 12-13

'La Mostra delle Regioni', in *L'architettura. Cronache e Storia*, August, pp. 262-272
'Nei diciannove padiglioni delle Regioni le belle tradizioni e le nuove conquiste', in *La Stampa*, 4-5 May
'Ristoranti', in *Rivista Internazionale d'Illuminazione*, June, pp. 203-204
C. Bassi, 'La giornata del Veneto', in *Il Gazzettino*, 26 June, pp.
R. Pedio, 'Negozio Olivetti a Düsseldorf', in *L'architettura. Cronache e storia*, December, pp. 524-527
P. Santini *'Italia 61'. La mostra delle regioni*, in *'Comunità'*, 90, pp. 10-19
L. Sollazzo, 'Acqua e colore del Veneto alla mostra delle regioni', in *Il Gazzettino*, 19 October

1962
'Places des Arts Montreal', in *The Canadian architect*, November, pp. 47-65
N. Graziani, *Castrocaro Terme: terra del sole*, Bologna
R. Musatti, 'Il negozio Olivetti di Düsseldorf', in *Domus*, September, pp. 9-14
C. Santini, 'Un'opera distrutta di Carlo Scarpa', in *Zodiac*, 9, pp. 146-161

1963
'Venini Murano - Manchester Airport - arch. Buzas', advertising insert, in *Domus*, July, no page number
'Venini Murano per il Teatro comunale dell'opera - Firenze', advertising insert, in *Domus*, October, no page number
'Vetreria Venini', in *Rivista Internazionale d'Illuminazione*, February, pp. 48-51
M. Cerruti, 'Il negozio Olivetti a Parigi', in *L'architettura. Cronache e storia*, January, p. 593

1964
'IHC - Hotel Intercontinental, Frankfurt/ Main' in *Deutsche Bauzeitung*, April, pp. 257-280
R. Aloi, *L'arredamento moderno*, Milan
D. Phillips, *Lighting in Architectural Design*, New York

1966
'Hotel mandarino, Hong-Kong', in *Rivista Internazionale d'Illuminazione*, February, pp. 57-60
R. Pedio, 'Palazzo della direzione Olivetti ad Ivrea', in *L'architettura. Cronache e storia*, August, pp. 220-233

1967
G. Mariacher, *I vetri di Murano*, Milan

1969
'Révillon, Parigi', in *Rivista Internazionale d'Illuminazione*, February, pp. 50-52

1970
Catalogo della XXXV Biennale Internazionale d'Arte Venezia, exhibition catalogue, 1st ed., Venice

1971
H. Schubert, *The Modern Theater: Architecture, Stage Design, Lighting*, New York

1978
Catalogue Foire Paris, exhibition catalogue, Paris
Schlosstheater Fulda, Fulda

1979
J. Tognell (edited by), *Cinquant'anni del Teatro dell'Opera: Roma 1928-1978*, Rome

1981
Vetri Murano Oggi, exhibition catalogue, Milan

1984
Venini: The Spirit of the Moment, exhibition catalogue, New York
F. Dal Co, G. Mazzariol (edited by), *Carlo Scarpa. Opera Completa*, Milan
J. Donahue, *The Finest in the Land: the Story of the Petroleum Club of Houston*, Houston
A. Forti (edited by), *Angiolo Mazzoni (1894-1979): architetto nell'Italia tra le due guerre*, Casalecchio di Reno

1985
Lumières: je pense à vous, exhibition catalogue, Paris
M. Porta (edited by), *L'architettura di Ignazio Gardella*, Segrate
D. Riccesi (edited by), *Gustavo Pulitzer Finali: il disegno della nave. Allestimenti interni (1925-1967)*, Venice

1988
S. Barizza (edited by), *Il Casino municipale di Venezia: una storia degli anni '30*, exhibition catalogue, Venice
A. Mazza, *Vittoriale: casa del sogno di Gabriele d'Annunzio*, Brescia
V. Savi, *Teatro della Compagnia, Firenze*, in *Domus*, January, pp. 42-51

1989
E. Bassi, *Palazzo Ferro Fini: la storia, l'architettura, il restauro*, Venice
S. Tagliapietra, 'Ludovico Diaz de Santillana', in *Giornale Economico*, March, pp. 36-37
M. Urzì, *Palazzo ducale di Bolzano. Villa Reale "Roma"*, Calliano

1991
M. Lupano, *Marcello Piacentini*, Rome

1992
M. Barovier (edited by), *Napoleone Martinuzzi vetraio del Novecento*, Venice
F. Buzzi Ceriani (edited by), *Ignazio Gardella: progetti e architetture 1933-1990*, exhibition catalogue, Milan

1993
P. Alberti, C. Salomoni (edited by), *Il Grand Hotel et de Milan. Storia e restauro di un albergo ottocentesco*, Venice
R. Barbiellini Amidei, *La Casa madre dei mutilati di guerra*, Rome
C. De Sessa, *Luigi Piccinato architetto*, Bari
F. Gurrieri, L. Macci, U. Tramonti, *Italo Gamberini. L'architettura dal razionalismo all'internazionalismo*, Florence

1994
S. Maffioletti (edited by), *BBPR*, Bologna

1995
A.S. De Rose, *Marcello Piacentini: opere 1903-1926*, Modena

1996
A. Bettagno (edited by), *Gli artisti Venini. Per una storia del vetro d'arte veneziano*, exhibition catalogue, Milan

1997
M.R. Intrieri (edited by), *Le sale cinematografiche tra ricordo e attualità*, Rome
A.S. Massaia, 'Giovanni Chevalley architetto (1868-1954) dall'Eclettismo allo Stile Novecento', in *Studi piemontesi*, March, pp. 19-46
C. Olmo (edited by), *Mirafiori*, Turin

1998
R. Barovier Mentasti, *Tra creatività e progettazione: il vetro italiano a Milano 1906-1968*, exhibition catalogue, Milan

1999
Guida di Torino Architettura, Turin
C. Semenzato, *L'Università di Padova. Il Palazzo del Bo: arte e storia*, Padua

2000
Venetian Glass: the Nancy Olnick and Giorgio Spanu Collection, exhibition catalogue, New York
R. Astarita, *Gli architetti di Olivetti. Una storia di committenza industriale*, Milan
E. Garbero Zorzi, L. Zangheri (edited by), *I teatri storici della Toscana. VIII. Firenze*, Venice
A. Venini Diaz de Santillana, *Venini. Catalogo ragionato 1921-1986*, Milan

2001
C. Bordogna Neirotti (edited by), *Carlo Alberto Bordogna: 65 anni di architettura*, Turin

2002
F. Canali, *Architettura nell'Istria italiana (1922-1942),* in *'Quaderni'*, vol. 14, pp. 345-411

2003
M. Cozzi, E. Godoli, P. Pettenella (edited by), *Angiolo Mazzoni (1894-1979) Architetto Ingegnere del Ministero delle Comunicazioni*, Milan

2004
E. Godoli, A.I. Lima (edited by), *Architettura ferroviaria in Italia - Novecento*, Palermo
G. Penzo, *Vaporetti: un secolo di trasporto pubblico nella laguna di Venezia*, Chioggia
M. Pisani, *Architetture di Marcello Piacentini: le opere maestre*, Rome
M. Schwarz, 'Wiederkehr des Interieurs', in *Bauwelt*, 5, pp. 24-25

A. Simonato, P. Verardo, *La Cassa di Risparmio: immagini di una storia*, Venice

2005
A. Magnaghi, M. Monge, L. Re (edited by), *Guida all'architettura moderna di Torino*, 2nd ed., Turin
G.M. Pilo, L. De Rossi, D. Alessandri, F. Zuanier (edited by), *Ca' Foscari: storia e restauro del palazzo dell'Università di Venezia*, Venice

2006
J. Cha, 'La Construction et le Mythe de la Place des Arts: Genèse de la Place Montréalaise', in *JSSAC/JSEAC*, 2, pp. 37-64
C. Conforti, R. Dulio, M. Marandola, *Giovanni Michelucci: 1891-1990*, Milan
F. Gay, *Le stazioni di Angiolo Mazzoni 1931-43: anatomia di un'architettura moderna*, doctorate thesis

2007
P. Ciorra, A. d'Onofrio, L. Molinari, *Studio Valle 1957-2007. Cinquant'anni di architettura*, Milan
L. Creti, T. Dore, *Attilio Lapadula: architetture a Roma*, Rome
F. Deboni, *I vetri Venini*, 2 vols, Turin
L. Gibello, P. M. Sudano, *Annibale Fiocchi architetto*, Florence
A. Giuntini (edited by), *Le Poste in Italia tra le due guerre 1919-1945*, Bari
E. Neudecker, *Gli edifici postali in Italia durante il Fascismo (1922-1944)*, Latina
P. Piccione, *Gio Ponti: le navi: il progetto degli interni navali 1948-1953*, Viareggio
S. Polano, *Carlo Scarpa a Palazzo Grassi. Allestimento della mostra 'Giuseppe Samonà 1923-1975. Cinquant'anni di architetture', Venezia 1975*, in *Casabella*, February, pp. 10-13
G. Potestà (edited by), *Istituto di Scienze Militari Aeronautiche: l'architettura di Raffaello Fagnoni per la Scuola di Applicazione Aeronautica, Scuola di Guerra Aerea*, Florence

2008
A. Barbieri, *A regola d'arte. Pittori, scultori, architetti, fotografi, scenografi, ceramisti, galleristi, critici e storici d'arte nel modenese dell'Ottocento e nel Novecento*, Modena
A.G. Cassani, *Tomaso Buzzi. Il principe degli architetti 1900-1981*, Milan
M.A. Giusti, R. Tamborrino, *Guida del Piemonte. Architettura del Novecento*, Turin

2009
M. Barovier, C. Sonego, 'Cappellin Venini & C. Progetti di illuminazione in vetro di Murano 1921-1932', in *Forme Moderne*, 2, pp. 88-91
C. Biagini, M. Fabbrini, 'Verso un'architettura della luce: la "lucicultura" in Italia negli anni '20', in *Bollettino ingegneri*, 8/9, pp. 14-20
E. Procida (edited by), *La Sede storica dell'INAIL a Roma. Il palazzo in via IV Novembre*, Rome
M. Scimemi, *Architettura del Novecento a Venezia: il palazzo Rio Nuovo*, Venice

2010
G. Ciucci, S. Lux, F. Purini (edited by), *Marcello Piacentini architetto 1881-1960*, Rome
L. Quattrocchi (edited by), *Architettura nelle terre di Siena. La prima metà del Novecento*, Milan
V. Sassoon, *Vidal: The Autobiography*, London

2011
R. Martellacci, *Italo Gamberini architetto (1907-1990)*, Florence

2012
M. Barovier (edited by), *Carlo Scarpa. Venini 1932-1947*, exhibition catalogue, Milan

2013
M. Barovier (edited by), *Napoleone Martinuzzi. Venini 1925-1931*, exhibition catalogue, Milan
M. Giacomelli, E. Godoli, A. Pelosi (edited by), *Angiolo Mazzoni in Toscana*, exhibition catalogue, Florence
J.L. Olivié, 'Un lustre pour le Pavillon italien à Paris en 1925', in *Glasklar.Festschrift für Helmut Ricke*, Petersberg, pp. 118-129
S. Zagnoni, *I negozi di Adriano Olivetti. Coerenza di stile e immagine non-coordinata*, in '*LUK. Studi e attività della Fondazione Ragghianti*', 23, pp. 155-165

2014
A. Anselmi, *Tomaso Buzzi e Venini: clienti e committenti*, in '*Saggi e Memorie di storia dell'arte*', XXXVIII, pp. 179-183
M. Barovier, C. Sonego (edited by), *Tomaso Buzzi alla Venini*, exhibition catalogue, Milan
C. Massi, *Architettura e paesaggio a Montecatini. Itinerari metropolitani nella città termale*, Florence

2015
M. Barovier, C. Sonego (edited by), *Fulvio Bianconi alla Venini*, exhibition catalogue, Milan
L. Greco, S. Mornati, *La Torre Galfa di Melchiorre Bega: architettura e costruzione*, Rome
D. Lacagnina (edited by), *Alle origini dell'Unione Europea. Architettura e arte italiana per il Palazzo della Farnesina*, Milan

2016
M. Barovier, C. Sonego (edited by), *Paolo Venini e la sua fornace*, exhibition catalogue, Milan
C. Beese, *Marcello Piacentini: Moderner Städtebau in Italien*, Berlin
S. Maffioletti (edited by), *La concezione sperimentale. L'opera di Nani Valle*, Venice

2017
S. Bandini, M. Eliseo, *Michelangelo e Raffaello. La fine di un'epoca*, Milan
M. Barovier, C. Sonego (edited by), *Vittorio Zecchin. I vetri trasparenti per Cappellin e Venini*, exhibition catalogue, Milan
C. Colin, *Il viaggio di Francesco Binfaré attraverso il design dagli anni 60 a oggi*, Milan
M. Savorra, 'Il lusso borghese negli anni '30. I negozi di Melchiorre Bega', in *Casabella*, October, pp. 26-34

2018
M. Barovier, C. Sonego (edited by), *La vetreria M.V.M. Cappellin e il giovane Carlo Scarpa 1925-1931*, exhibition catalogue, Milan
F. Nodari (edited by), *Boico / Cervi / Frandoli / Nordio, Interni navali tra arte e design 1949-1967*, exhibition catalogue, Monfalcone

2019
M. Barovier, C. Sonego (edited by), *Thomas Stearns alla Venini*, exhibition catalogue, Milan
D. Lacagnina, *La Farnesina. Il palazzo, gli artisti, le opere*, I , Rome

2021
M. Fochessati, *Anselmo Bucci, tre navi. Arte e allestimento navale di un pittore del Novecento*, in *Ceramica e Arti Decorative*, VII (edited by P. Piccione), pp. 37-54
E. Marantz, 'La villa Arson (1967-1970, arch. Michel Marot)', in *In Situ: Revue des patrimoines*, 43, pp. 1-31

2022
G. Cosentino, *Paesaggi interni. I negozi Olivetti a New York, Parigi e Düsseldorf*, Parma

INDEX OF PROJECTS 1921-1985

1940s

1950s

1960s

1970s

1980s